CONCORDIA UNIVERSITY
T58.R62   C001 V
MANAGEMENT AND THE WORKER CAMBRIDG

3 4211 000097671

WITHDRAWN

MANAGEMENT AND THE WORKER

MANAGEMENT AND THE WORKER

An Account of a Research Program Conducted by
the Western Electric Company, Hawthorne Works, Chicago

BY

F. J. ROETHLISBERGER

PROFESSOR OF HUMAN RELATIONS
HARVARD GRADUATE SCHOOL OF BUSINESS ADMINISTRATION

AND

WILLIAM J. DICKSON

CHIEF OF EMPLOYEE RELATIONS RESEARCH DEPARTMENT
WESTERN ELECTRIC COMPANY, HAWTHORNE WORKS

with the assistance and collaboration of
HAROLD A. WRIGHT
CHIEF OF PERSONNEL RESEARCH AND TRAINING DIVISION
WESTERN ELECTRIC COMPANY, HAWTHORNE WORKS

KLINCK MEMORIAL LIBRARY
Concordia Teachers College
River Forest, Illinois

HARVARD UNIVERSITY PRESS
CAMBRIDGE, MASSACHUSETTS
1961

COPYRIGHT, 1939
BY THE PRESIDENT AND FELLOWS OF HARVARD COLLEGE

Twelfth Printing

DISTRIBUTED IN GREAT BRITAIN
BY OXFORD UNIVERSITY PRESS
LONDON

PRINTED IN THE UNITED STATES OF AMERICA

CONTENTS

PART IV — SOCIAL ORGANIZATION OF EMPLOYEES

PART V — APPLICATIONS TO PRACTICE OF
RESEARCH RESULTS

LIST OF TABLES

from hand to mouth, is committed to the futility of endless repetition of some former discovery. The interesting *aperçu*, the long chance, may not be followed: both alike must be denied in order that the group may "land another job." This confusion of research with commercial huckstering can never prosper: the only effect is to disgust the intelligent youngster who is thus forced to abandon his quest for human enlightenment. But for an endowment from the Rockefeller Foundation, Harvard University would have been unable to permit so many men to participate in an inquiry that has developed, at a varying pace, over a period of twelve years.

Can anyone doubt the need for inquiries of this type? The spectacle of Europe, erstwhile mother of cultures, torn from end to end by strife that she can by no means resolve, should give pause to the most "practically-minded," should make such persons ask what type of research is likely to be most practically useful at the moment. The art of human collaboration seems to have disappeared during two centuries of quite remarkable material progress. The various nations seem to have lost all capacity for international co-operation in the necessary tasks of civilization. The internal condition of each nation is not greatly better: it seems that only a threat from without, an unmistakable emergency, can momentarily quiet the struggle of rival groups. In this general situation it would seem that inquiries such as those undertaken by officers of the Western Electric Company have an urgent practical importance that is second to no other human undertaking. How can humanity's capacity for spontaneous co-operation be restored? It is in this area that leadership is most required, a leadership that has nothing to do with political "isms" or eloquent speeches. What is wanted is knowledge, a type of knowledge that has escaped us in two hundred years of prosperous development. How to substitute human responsibility for futile strife and hatreds — this is one of the most important researches of our time. It is our hope that the inquiries described in this book are the beginning of a small contribution to such knowledge.

ELTON MAYO

July 15, 1939

the need for more effective human collaboration in industry we ourselves have learned something of the art.

Of none of us is this more true than of the authors of this book. Both have been continuously and intimately associated with the work — Roethlisberger for Harvard University, Dickson for the Company; both are still so associated. Everyone concerned was content that they should assume the task of revision for report and publication, and we believe that they have done it well. The work that they report is the work of many hands — their own and others — but the selection, development, and presentation of topics are their own. Where intelligent elaboration has been needed, they have provided it. In this they have had the support and aid of the Company and of Harvard University.

And this last should be acknowledged also: Collaboration in work of this kind presumes not only an active relation between workers of the university and of the industry, it presumes also a relation between institutions. The aid given by Harvard University has been as admirable in its way as the freedom to inquire and the support given by the Company. Over a period of twelve years the investigation has benefited by the collaboration where required of the Fatigue Laboratory, the Graduate School of Business Administration, the Medical School, the Department of Anthropology in Harvard College. Dean Wallace B. Donham and Dr. Lawrence J. Henderson, both of the Committee on Industrial Physiology, must be considered to have been actively participant in the research from the beginning. Their role in the University group is comparable with that of Mr. C. G. Stoll and Mr. W. F. Hosford of the New York office and Mr. C. L. Rice of Hawthorne in support of Mr. G. A. Pennock, Mr. G. S. Rutherford, Mr. M. L. Putnam, and the Company group. There can be no question that Dean Donham and Dr. Henderson have fulfilled an important function in the general development of the study.

The authors ask me to acknowledge the invaluable aid in preparation of this book for publication given by Mrs. Hilda Richardson Carter, secretary of the Industrial Research Department. Mrs. Carter has revised and edited the manuscript, has prepared the index, and read the proof sheets as they came off the presses. Miss Helen M. Mitchell prepared the figures.

One other comment must be made. Researches of this type are usually impossible because of a foolish convention that institutions engaging in industrial research are expected to "pay their way" or "earn their keep." This means, in effect, that any such institution, living eral effect that rest periods (of a certain length and periodicity) lead, of themselves, to improvement in production and morale. But Mr. Pennock and his colleagues were not satisfied that the continuous improvement could be so directly related to rest periods, and the "return to original conditions" (see page 69) was instituted as Period XII. This critical change proved fruitful for the whole course of the inquiry; it led indeed to a clear realization of the need for other and supplementary investigations. From this point on, a constant shift to inquiries not anticipated in the original plan became characteristic.

The authors nevertheless succeed in demonstrating that, in spite of this constant shift, the relationship between the original and the supplementary inquiries was always maintained. In the end a considerable enlightenment was gained that applied to every item in the series. In using the phrase "considerable enlightenment" I must not be understood to claim that it was either very extensive or very profound; the authors of this book and those who participated in the work would alike repudiate such claim. The fact remains, however, that those who took part feel that they have learned something of the facts of human association in work, something about techniques of human investigation; they know also that what they have learned was, to them at least, novel and unexpected. But they regard this as a beginning rather than an end.

What there is of achievement must be credited in large measure to G. A. Pennock, to M. L. Putnam, who succeeded him in control of the experiments, and to the officers of the Western Electric Company generally. It took courage and determination to persist with inquiries that often seemed doomed to inconclusiveness. The recurring need to find a way around obstacles that seemed insuperable demanded insight and ingenuity. It is also to the credit of the Company itself that there were no prohibitions: every participant in the investigation was free to find what he could find, provided always that such observation would stand up against the immediate critical inspection of his colleagues and would reveal itself unshakeably as fact. For this reason the work has been extraordinarily interesting to all those who have shared it. They have been many, and for all of us, whether our participation has been continuous and intimate or episodic and remote, there are pleasant memories of occasions when our colleagues have said to a diffident suggestion, "Why — of course." I cannot name all who have thus participated, who can thus think with satisfaction of the experience: an attempt to name everyone would read, a colleague suggests, like a telephone book. But it can at least be claimed that in studying

PREFACE

ABOUT TWELVE years ago the Western Electric Company, at its Hawthorne plant, began the series of inquiries into the human effect of work and working conditions described in this book. In the last six or seven of these years many papers, monographs, books, have been published describing the investigation or analyzing some aspect of it. My own Lowell Lectures in published form (*The Human Problems of an Industrial Civilization*, The Macmillan Company, 1933) gave three short chapters to "the Hawthorne experiment." North Whitehead's *The Industrial Worker* (Harvard University Press, 2 volumes, 1938) is a careful analysis, partly statistical, of the original "test room" records. A monograph by the authors of this book, Roethlisberger and Dickson, "Management and the Worker" (Harvard Business School, Division of Research, Business Research Studies, No. 9, 1934), attracted much interest in the United States and in Europe: it was even quoted in an industrial case in the Chancery Division in London. The general effect of these and many other publications has been to give industrial audiences an illusion of familiarity when the Hawthorne experiment is mentioned. But this is illusion: many of us have long been aware that there is no sufficiently general understanding in industry, or elsewhere, of the course that the inquiry ran, of the difficulties it encountered, and of the constant need to revise and renew the attack upon the diverse problems presented. This book offers for the first time a continuous history of the entire series of experiments; it also relates together the many different inquiries.

It is too often assumed that almost any young university graduate of sufficient intelligence can charge out of university and into industry and, armed with some rags and tatters of scientific method borrowed mainly from physics or chemistry, can proceed to make interesting findings. This belief ignores completely the mutual dependence and complexity of the facts of human association. If Mr. G. A. Pennock, who began and developed this series of experiments, had not been intimately acquainted with this human complexity, if he had not been thus inspired to critical inspection of the first apparent findings, then this history would not have been written. It would have been easy, for example, to shut down the "test room" at the conclusion of Period XI and to announce to the world another observation to the gen-

participated in this work. The members of the research staff were constantly inspired by the spirit of helpfulness of the many hundreds of employees who expressed themselves so fully to the interviewers and by the wholehearted co-operation and interest of the group of employees who through a considerable period participated in the various test room experiments. The willingness of employees to collaborate in the studies and the co-operation which they gave the people conducting this research contributed in a large measure to its success.

C. G. STOLL

Western Electric Company
New York, N. Y.
July 15, 1939

One may well ask what success our management has had in applying these developments to the human problems of the business, since this is a phase of the work not directly discussed by the authors. Throughout the course of these studies, the points of view which were emerging were frequently lifted out for application to current situations. At the Hawthorne Works, where the studies were made, there was continuous use of the better understanding of human reactions which was developing, not only in dealing with specific situations but in training supervisors in more human and effective methods of dealing with their workers. Much experience has been had in trying out and testing the findings of this research in real work situations and it seems clear that the knowledge acquired has been increasingly helpful in our efforts to create a better relationship between supervisors and workers, the kind of relationship which contributes naturally to proficiency and a high state of morale.

The nature of these studies was such as to require the collaboration of many individuals, both within and without the Company. In such a comprehensive project, mention can be made of only a few of the many who have contributed to the progress of the work.

The advice and assistance given by Professor Elton Mayo of the Industrial Research Department of the Harvard Graduate School of Business Administration were of the highest character and deserve special commendation. He and his staff actively participated in these studies almost from their inception, and the results obtained are due in large part to their enthusiastic interest in the work and to their valuable contributions to it.

Professors F. J. Roethlisberger and W. Lloyd Warner made particularly helpful and enlightening contributions at many critical stages. Professor T. N. Whitehead made an exhaustive and valuable analysis of the records of the Relay Assembly Test Room, which he has summarized in his book *The Industrial Worker*. Professor Clair E. Turner of the Massachusetts Institute of Technology did much helpful work in connection with the relay assembly studies.

Within the Company much credit is due to those who were in active direction of this research: to Mr. G. A. Pennock, who was in general charge from its beginning; to Messrs. M. L. Putnam, H. A. Wright, and W. J. Dickson, who were associated with him in planning and supervising the work; and to Messrs. H. Hibarger and A. C. Moore, who made outstanding contributions in conducting particular experiments.

Perhaps the greatest credit should go to the many employees who

FOREWORD

THE WORK described in this volume grew out of our experience in other investigations which revealed a considerable deficiency in our knowledge of the intangible factors in the work situation that affect the morale and productive efficiency of shopworkers. These previous studies had indicated that the human reactions of people engaged in productive work have a much more important effect on their morale and efficiency than had previously been realized. The investigations reported in this book were undertaken in the hope that the light which they would throw on this little-understood subject would be of real value in improving our methods of dealing with employees.

The first organized effort to expand our understanding of the human reactions of employees, which began in 1927, was necessarily crude, but the work progressively took on a research character as it advanced from one development to another, each step pointing the way to the next. This process of evolution is still under way and, as the knowledge acquired is far from complete, the research is continuing very largely in directions which are self-determining.

Originally we were asking ourselves a few rather simple but fundamental questions, the answers to which required knowledge not then available — the natural beginning of a research effort. As the studies progressed, simple and specific answers to the questions we had in mind were not forthcoming, but rather the studies unfolded a much broader understanding of worker attitudes and reactions than had been anticipated. This knowledge resulted not only in a better understanding of the effect on employees of various types of action taken by management and by supervisors but also in a more adequate method of evaluating and dealing with the human problems arising in the business. It became clear that what really was most significant was not conclusive answers to specific questions, but a development in the understanding of human situations which would help to improve employee relations and aid in resolving the problems arising in them when and where they occur. This is the principal contribution of the research, and Messrs. Roethlisberger and Dickson are deserving of much credit for the fine work which they have done in analyzing the results of these studies and recording them in a clear and comprehensive manner.

58626

To the

EMPLOYEES, SUPERVISORS, AND OFFICERS

OF THE

WESTERN ELECTRIC COMPANY

WHOSE CO-OPERATION MADE POSSIBLE THIS BOOK

LIST OF FIGURES

PART I

WORKING CONDITIONS AND
EMPLOYEE EFFICIENCY

CHAPTER I

INTRODUCTION

The Scope and Duration of the Inquiry

THE experimental studies of human relations to be reported in this book were conducted at the Hawthorne Works of the Western Electric Company in Chicago. They were begun in the spring of 1927, when five employees were segregated from a regular operating department for special study. At the beginning of the inquiry the general interest was primarily in the relation between conditions of work and the incidence of fatigue and monotony among employees. It was anticipated that exact knowledge could be obtained about this relation by establishing an experimental situation in which the effect of variables like temperature, humidity, and hours of sleep could be measured separately from the effect of an experimentally imposed condition of work.

Little was it doubted that within a year, or perhaps less, definite answers to these questions could be obtained. But the inquiry developed in an unexpected fashion. In most cases the results obtained, instead of giving definite answers to the original questions, demanded a restatement of them. More adequate working hypotheses had to be formulated. Old methods had to be modified, and quite frequently new methods had to be introduced. As a result, the inquiry continued for five years, from 1927 to 1932, when for reasons unconnected with the experiment it was suspended. From the original observation of five workers, the investigation during one phase of its development had expanded until it included studies of about 20,000 individual employees.

Problems of Presentation and Selection

In reporting an inquiry of such magnitude the authors were faced with many problems. There were problems of presentation: How was the material to be presented so as to give a clear account which would involve the least possible distortion of the way in which things actually took place? How could the studies be presented without placing those people or groups of people with whom they dealt in an unfavorable or ambiguous position? There were problems of selection and emphasis: What weight was to be given to the theories which the investigators separately or collectively held? Where and when were the practical implications of the findings for industry to be discussed? To help them in solving these problems, the authors adopted certain guiding principles.

(1) In an experiment which ran over such a long period of time, and in which there was a considerable time interval between the conclusion of the experiment and the publication of the results, two alternative methods of presentation were possible. Either the authors could take the standpoint of the investigators at each stage of the inquiry, describing in chronological order the things they did, the discriminations they made, the leads they followed, and the conclusions they drew; or the authors could take the standpoint of the investigators at the end of the inquiry, presenting in a more systematic and logical order the results obtained and interpreting them in terms of the final conceptual scheme. Either approach had its advantages and disadvantages.

The authors finally decided to follow the chronological form of presentation for the following reasons. Although a narrative account of what was done step by step would bear the stamp of human imperfection, nevertheless it would describe what actually took place. It would picture the trials and tribulations of a research investigator at his work, and thus allow future investigators to see and to profit from the mistakes which were made. In turn, the authors would be spared the task of having to strengthen weak places and make their façades more imposing.

The authors realized that among the readers of the book there might be a substantial number of the Western Electric supervisory force and many of the workers themselves. They recognized their obligation to these people and to the company, which at all stages of the inquiry had done everything possible to protect these individuals or groups of individuals whose situations were being studied. It was important that no one employee or group of employees should feel that the company, of which they were justly proud, had not protected their interests in allowing certain material to be published. The authors felt that they could best fulfill their obligation to all parties concerned by maintaining a spirit of scientific objectivity, by being faithful to the data before them, and by presenting them, in so far as they were humanly capable of doing so, free from bias. In no other way could the authors represent better to the employees who might read the book the purpose of the inquiry and the attitude of management toward it, which can be described as a sincere desire on management's part to understand better the facts of human behavior, their own as well as that of their employees.

(2) In presenting the material, it was decided to keep separate the facts observed, as well as the uniformities among them, from the methods, working hypotheses, theories, or conceptual schemes employed by the investigators. The original facts of observation, as well as the final facts of verification, were to be granted primary importance. Theories were conceived of as only part of the working equipment of the investigators and never as ends in themselves. Therefore, it was decided to include for discussion only those theories or ways of looking at facts which assisted the research investigators to find more facts or to make more adequate discriminations in fact.

(3) During the inquiry many studies developed as offshoots from the main line of the experiment and ran their own course as more or less separate and independent phases. Although such studies have not been entirely omitted from this book, as in many cases they were of great interest, preference has been given to those studies which contributed more directly to the development of the inquiry and to the understanding of the investigators.

(4) The narrative form of presentation made it difficult at times to elaborate certain findings of the research with reference to industrial problems without, at the same time, losing the trend of the inquiry. Therefore, it was decided to leave such a discussion until the last part (Part V) of the book, where it would also be possible to discuss some of the practical problems of industry in terms of the final conceptual scheme which the investigators achieved.

(5) Chronologically, the inquiry divided itself naturally into four stages, each stage representing a major change in working hypothesis and method. The first four parts into which the book is divided correspond to these four stages of the inquiry. Part I is concerned with an experiment on working conditions and employee efficiency. During this phase of the inquiry the "test room method" was developed. Part II is concerned with an experiment in interviewing some 20,000 employees from all parts of the Hawthorne plant with a view to determining those aspects of their working environment which they either favored or disliked. In Part III the comments obtained in the interviews are analyzed and a general theory is presented to explain the nature of employee satisfaction and dissatisfaction. In Part IV a study of fourteen male operators is reported; in this study the interviewing method elaborated in the second phase was supplemented and reinforced by direct and simultaneous observation.

The Western Electric Company Organization

It may be helpful to describe briefly the setting of the Hawthorne plant, in which the tests were conducted. This description applies only to the company at the beginning of the inquiry. Many changes have occurred since then which, although not altering the general picture conveyed in this material, nevertheless would make the following description inaccurate at the present time in specific details.[1]

The Hawthorne Works of the Western Electric Company is situated partly in the city of Chicago at its western border and partly in the town of Cicero, Illinois. This plant is the largest unit of the Western Electric Company, which, in turn, is the supply organization for the telephone companies of the Bell System. Hawthorne covers many acres of floor space and gives employment to thousands of men and women engaged in the manufacture of telephones, central office equipment, loading coils, telephone wire, lead-covered cable, toll cable, and other forms of telephone apparatus. A wide range of type and grade of occupation is to be found, from iron worker to diamond cutter, from toolmaker to accountant, from apparatus assembler to engineer, from wire-drawer to textile dyer, from office boy to superintendent. By imagining the kind and amount of equipment necessary to serve millions of telephone subscribers, some impression of the exacting quality and tremendous quantity of small piece parts which are manufactured and assembled can be obtained.

In 1927, when the studies commenced, the company employed approximately 29,000 workers, representing some 60 nationalities. About 75 per cent of the employees were American born. The Poles and Czechoslovakians were by far the largest foreign groups; there was a fair sprinkling of Germans and Italians.

Eight Functional Organizations

The primary manufacturing activities of the plant were divided among eight functional organizations which the company called branches. These branches were Accounting, Operating, Production, Inspection, Technical, Specialty Products, Public Relations, and Industrial Relations. Except in the case of the Industrial Relations Branch, it will not be necessary to give detailed accounts of the functions of these respective branches. In passing, it can be said that the Technical Branch

---

[1] In presenting this material, the past tense has been frequently used, even though at times awkward, in order to remind the reader constantly of the fact that this description is of the years 1927 to 1929.

set piece rates, maintained the plant, and serviced machinery. The Production Branch provided material, scheduled work, followed production, maintained stocks, and handled and stored materials. The Operating Branch made the products. The Specialty Products Branch planned the manufacture of and made special products and articles of small demand. The Inspection Branch controlled the quality of output. The Accounting Branch paid employees, figured costs, prepared local budgets, and issued financial reports. The Public Relations Branch maintained local publicity and civic contacts and promoted safety and health.

Inasmuch as the company's terminology differed slightly from that in use in other industries, it is well to distinguish the functions of the Operating Branch from those of the Production Branch. It was the Operating and not the Production Branch which made the products. The Operating Branch was that part of the company which carried out the actual shop operations necessary to convert raw material into finished telephone equipment. The Production Branch, on the other hand, controlled all direct manufacturing work performed by the company: It gave the shop information concerning what, how much, and when to manufacture and assumed responsibility for meeting delivery dates. It was the duty of this branch to issue and trace all orders through the shop and to maintain stocks of raw material, piece parts, and apparatus sufficient to meet the manufacturing requirements. In terms of the number of people employed, the Operating Branch was by far the largest of the eight branches.

The Industrial Relations Branch

The Industrial Relations Branch was on a co-ordinate basis with the other branches and had as its function all those activities which have to do with employee relations. A prominent part of the Industrial Relations activities were discharged by a personnel organization working within each one of the eight branches. The major responsibility of these organizations was to supervise the carrying out of the company's employee relations policies [1] within the respective branches. To see that

---

[1] In a statement issued by the company to employees responsible for directing the work of others, the company's Employee Relations Policies (referred to frequently as the "Ten Commandments") are stated as follows:

It is the policy —

I. *To pay all employees adequately for services rendered.*
When the individual records of all employees are reviewed periodically, it is your duty to see that their rates of pay are adjusted fairly. Compensation should be based upon ability, responsibility, length of service and capacity for growth.

the employees were properly placed in work best suited to them, to arrange the transfer of employees for training, advancement, or vocational adjustment purposes, to keep adequate records of each employee's service, to advise with employees about personal problems, education, health, advancement, thrift, vocational opportunities, and individual welfare, to assist worker and supervisor alike in carrying on their daily

giving due consideration to cost of living, general business conditions and wages paid by other concerns in the same territory for comparable work.

II. To maintain reasonable hours of work and safe working conditions.
Special attention must be paid to conserving the well-being of employees in equipping and maintaining shops, warehouses, offices, restaurants and rest rooms and other facilities for comfort and convenience. Careful consideration must be given to hours of work, vacations, medical service and payment in case of absence.

III. To provide continuous employment consistent with business conditions.
In the management of the business a continuous effort must be made to provide steady work and permanent employment. When reduction in force is unavoidable, consideration should be given to retaining long-service employees. When additions are made to the force, preference should be given to former employees. Continuity of employees' service records should be guarded.

IV. To place employees in the kind of work best suited to their abilities.
Consideration must be given to placing each employee in the kind of work which offers opportunity for his maximum growth and usefulness. Great care should be used in assigning employees to work when they are first employed, and trial should be given on different types of work when necessary.

V. To help each individual to progress in the Company's service.
When vacancies occur, those already in the Company are entitled to first consideration. Every employee should understand the relation of his work to that of the Company as a whole, and there should be provision for training on the job, variety and progression of experience. Information and advice should be made available for those wishing to take advantage of outside educational opportunities.

VI. To aid employees in times of need.
It is necessary for you to understand fully the purpose and scope of the Employees' Benefit Fund for giving aid in times of disability due to sickness or accident, and for granting retiring allowances. You should keep informed regarding loan funds available for meeting other emergencies.

VII. To encourage thrift.
You are responsible for keeping your people informed and interested in the Stock Purchase Plan and other means available for encouraging thrift. Employees desiring information and counsel should be put in touch with those best qualified to advise on matters of home buying or building, use of banking facilities, insurance programs and other personal financial problems.

VIII. To cooperate in social, athletic and other recreational activities.
Encouragement may be given by supplying facilities, by sharing in the operating expenses of organized activities of this character, and by making better use of opportunities existing in the community.

IX. To accord to each employee the right to discuss freely with executives any matters concerning his or her welfare or the Company's interest.
It is your duty to establish the conviction among those whom you direct or with whom you come in contact that sympathetic and unprejudiced consideration will

work; these were some of the many duties of the branch personnel units. Meanwhile the tasks of running a restaurant that served some seven thousand meals a day, a fully equipped and modern hospital, an employment division to hire and place people, an organization to administer accident, sickness, and pension benefits, and an organization to conduct job training in various lines were assumed by a group of functionalized units within the Industrial Relations Branch.

Agencies for Carrying out Employee Relations Policies

There were a number of agencies for carrying out the company's employee relations policies. It will suffice to mention some of them briefly:

(1) There were plans designed to encourage the practice of thrift. Among these was a stock participation plan which made it possible for the employees to subscribe to American Telephone & Telegraph Company stock.

(2) In order to help the worker protect his dependents, arrangements were made with one of the large and sound insurance companies by which the insurance company set up within the plant a local office and maintained a sufficient staff to act as insurance advisers and counselors to all employees who desired this assistance. Careful consideration was given to the individual requirements of each employee seeking this service, and all of the standard forms of insurance were made available to him and could be paid for through weekly deductions from his pay.

(3) There was a building and loan association operated by and for employees only, which was used by them for saving and investment as well as for home building.

(4) There was a ready money plan to assist employees in carrying out a systematic program of personal finance. Under this plan the company would withhold at the employee's bidding any stipulated amount from the employee's pay and deposit such amount periodically with well-selected savings banks at current interest rates.

(5) There were also benefit plans to provide relief for sickness, accident, and death of employees while working at the company.

---

be given to any employee who wishes to discuss with you and with Company executives matters of his or her welfare or the Company's interest.

X. *To carry on the daily work in a spirit of friendliness.*

As the Company grows it must be more human — not less so. Discipline, standards and precedents become more necessary with size, but the spirit in which they are administered must be friendly as well as just. Courtesy is as important within the organization as in dealing with outsiders. Inefficiency and indifference cannot be tolerated, but the effort of supervisors must be increasingly directed at building up in every department a loyal and enthusiastic interest in the Company's work.

MAY, 1924.

(6) There was a pension plan on a noncontributory basis whereby employees became eligible for pension after a certain age and period of service.

(7) Another activity of the company was safety and health promotion. Health bulletins, pamphlets, and lectures were placed constantly before the employees; health classes were maintained; Red Cross first aid courses were given; and mechanical safeguards or devices were installed wherever practical. Furthermore, a modern hospital, completely staffed and equipped, was maintained for the emergency treatment of sickness or accidents, for the physical examination of applicants for employment and of employees returning from sick leave.

(8) Closely allied with this health program was a program of recreational, social, and athletic activities. All these activities were conducted by an employees' organization known as the Hawthorne Club. All employees belonged to this organization. They elected their own officers and promoted a wide variety of activities ranging from motion picture productions to track meets, and from target practice to checker tournaments. Gymnastics and athletic sports were conducted in a gymnasium and on an athletic field. Entertainments of all sorts — bands, orchestra, glee club, prominent speakers, dancing — were on the calendar during the noon and evening programs. An evening school, with over 3,000 students in attendance, receiving instruction in 45 different subjects, was conducted by this club.

The Supervisory Organization

Generally speaking, the type of company organization was a combination of function and line. The units into which the organization was divided were functional, that is, each branch performed a group of logically related and interdependent activities. Within each functional unit, however, the general method by which authority was exercised and delegated was "line control."

According to the supervisory structure of the company, a superintendent was in charge of a branch; an assistant superintendent was in charge of a subbranch; a general foreman was in charge of a division; a foreman was in charge of a department; an assistant foreman assisted the foreman in the supervision of the department and sometimes was in charge of several sections of that department; a section chief was in charge of one section composed of several groups; and a group chief was in charge of one group of operators.

The name "supervisor" was often given in a general sense to all ranks of supervision above the worker. In most cases, however, any supervisor in a shop organization whose rank was above that of section chief was given his more specific title of foreman, general foreman, superintendent, and so on. The first-line supervisor, that is, the man who was in direct charge of and in contact with the workers, was in

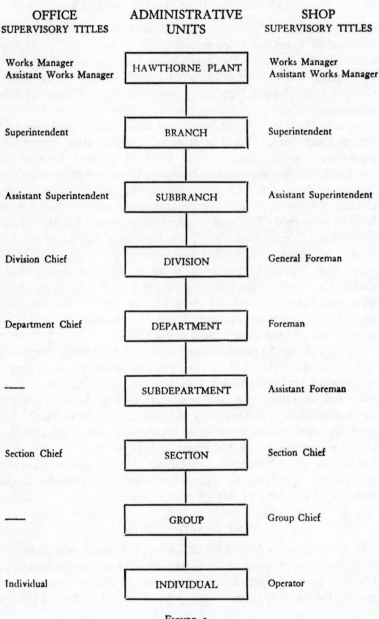

OFFICE SUPERVISORY TITLES	ADMINISTRATIVE UNITS	SHOP SUPERVISORY TITLES
Works Manager Assistant Works Manager	HAWTHORNE PLANT	Works Manager Assistant Works Manager
Superintendent	BRANCH	Superintendent
Assistant Superintendent	SUBBRANCH	Assistant Superintendent
Division Chief	DIVISION	General Foreman
Department Chief	DEPARTMENT	Foreman
——	SUBDEPARTMENT	Assistant Foreman
Section Chief	SECTION	Section Chief
——	GROUP	Group Chief
Individual	INDIVIDUAL	Operator

FIGURE I

OFFICE AND SHOP SUPERVISORY ORGANIZATIONS

HAWTHORNE PLANT

this organization a "group chief." In other industrial organizations this kind of supervisor is sometimes called a "gang boss" or a "straw boss." At the company the benchworker or employee of nonsupervisory status was referred to as an "operator." This word was used in preference to the term "operative," which is common in many other industries.

Some of the titles differed, depending upon whether one was referring to a member of a shop or of an office organization. In an office organization ranks comparable to those of assistant foreman and group chief in the shop were not common. Usually, there were only the department head, one or more section chiefs, and the individual employees. Therefore, in an office organization a section chief was the first-line supervisor. The head of a department in an office organization was called a "department chief"; the head of a division, a "division chief." Moreover, in an office organization the term "individual," rather than "operator," was given to an employee of nonsupervisory status. The word "employee" in its limited sense referred to persons who were not supervisors, but in a broader sense it was sometimes applied to both workers and supervisors. In this book the word "employee" will be used in its limited sense.

Figure 1 shows the major divisions into which a branch was divided and the corresponding rank of the supervisor in charge, depending on whether the organization was a shop or an office. According to the office and shop distinction, the functional units of the company were divided as follows: The activities of Industrial Relations, Public Relations, and Accounting, for example, were strictly office; the Operating unit was identified with the shop; in between were the Technical, Production, and Inspection organizations. Most of the supervisors in these latter units, however, regarded themselves as office rather than shop people and were usually given office space.

WAGE INCENTIVE SYSTEMS [1]

In no sense is this description of the wage incentive systems in operation at the company to be taken as a detailed and complete account. It will be merely a brief outline for purposes of general orientation. In general, the forms of incentive compensation could be divided into two

---

[1] Two articles have been used freely in preparing this section: Holmes, Stanley S., "Extra Incentive Wage Plans Used by the Hawthorne Works of the Western Electric Company, Inc.," *The American Management Association*, Production Executives' Series, No. 17, 1925; and Hosford, William F., "Wage Incentive Applications in the Western Electric Company," *N. A. C. A. Bulletin*, Vol. XII, No. 21, 1931.

kinds: individual payment and group payment. In both cases, however, the company operated on the so-called "straight-line" principle of compensation, according to which the remuneration was directly proportional to individual or group output. Under both plans the day rate, or base wage, was guaranteed.

Basic Labor Grades and Hourly Rate Ranges within Each Labor Grade

The foundation upon which the wage incentive plans were laid was the labor grading system. This consisted of a series of labor grades covering all hourly rated operations performed in the plant. The lowest grade covered the simplest types of operations; the highest grade covered those operations involving the greatest amount of skill or responsibility; all other operations were placed in intermediate grades according to the skill or responsibility involved. Ranges of pay for these basic labor grades were so established that they would be comparable to the rates of pay prevailing throughout the Chicago district for similar classes of work. New employees were hired, and assigned an hourly rate, at the minimum rate of pay for the labor grade into which their work fell, and they were advanced within the rate range, or progressed to higher grade classifications, as they became more skilled and proficient. These labor grades supplied the base rates for the determination of incentive or piece rates.

Straight Piecework

The straight piecework system involved the establishment of a money rate per unit of output and was applied to operations completely performed by one employee, and to classes of work in which each employee's production was easily distinguished. The employee received the rate per unit multiplied by the number of units completed regardless of the time involved, except when the total piecework value was less than the total daywork value of his time, in which case he received his guaranteed day rate. The total daywork value for each employee was his hourly rate multiplied by the number of hours he worked.

Group Piecework

Under group piecework a money rate was assigned to a given amount of work or unit of production for those jobs which required the cooperative services of two or more employees. This system was confined largely to those departments where the multiplicity of the operations performed made it difficult to employ straight piecework. The earnings of the group were determined by the number of good pieces it completed, multiplied by the rate per piece. The amount thus earned by the group each week constituted the fund out of which all wages were paid. The allocation of the weekly group earnings to the individuals in the group was based upon their hourly rates. The hourly rate of each employee multiplied by the number of hours he had worked during the week constituted the daywork value of the work he had done. At the end of each week, the total piecework earnings of all work produced by the group and the total daywork value of all time charged by the group were determined. The excess of total piecework earnings over total daywork value was expressed as a percentage of the total daywork value. Each employee's earnings were determined by multiplying his hourly rate by this percentage. The resulting hourly earnings figure multiplied by the number of hours he had worked during the week constituted a person's weekly earnings. Therefore, variation in individual earnings in a group depended entirely on differences in hourly rates. As under the straight piecework system, the operator's day rate was guaranteed.

The "Bogey" System

One feature of the group incentive system needs more explanation. Under straight piecework the maintenance of individual performance records was practically automatic, since comparative earnings were a direct measurement of relative performance of operators in the same labor class. The group payment system, however, did not provide a means of measuring the performance of individuals. In order to fill this need under group piecework, the company used what is called a "bogey" system of individual rating. The bogey, which was set up for each operation, represented a level of performance which could be sustained by a skilled and efficient operator. Records were kept of each individual's performance, and efficiency was figured weekly, using the bogey as a basis for comparison. The supervisor used the bogey in this manner to keep records of individual progress and ability and to detect irregularities of performance.

EXPERIMENTS ON ILLUMINATION

In November, 1924, the Western Electric Company, in connection with the National Research Council of the National Academy of Sciences, planned to study the "relation of quality and quantity of illumination to efficiency in industry." These experiments lasted until April, 1927, a period of two and one-half years. Since the results from these experiments played an important part in the future research of the company on employee effectiveness, they will be briefly described. In the absence of any final formal report of this work it is impossible to give a complete, detailed statement, and therefore only a summary of the first tentative conclusions drawn by the Council's representative in charge of the work at Hawthorne will be reported.[1]

The First Illumination Experiment

The first experiment on illumination was conducted in three different departments carefully selected for the purposes of the test. In the first department the employees were inspecting small piece parts; in the second department the employees were assembling relays; the third department employed coil winders.

The general test procedure for each department was the same. First, there was a preliminary period during which the operatives worked under the existing lighting installation supplemented by daylight. The average production rates obtained during this preliminary period furnished base lines for calculating any future production changes.

The level of artificial illumination intensity was then increased at stated intervals. Mr. Snow reports the results as follows:

The various levels of average illumination intensity [for the first department] were 3, 6, 14, and 23 foot-candles. The corresponding production efficiencies by no means followed the magnitude or trend of the lighting intensities. The output bobbed up and down without direct relation to the amount of illumination.

The illumination intensities [in the second department] were 5, 12, 25, and 44 foot-candles. The efficiency of this department increased more or less continuously during the test, but not as a sole function of illumination.

The various levels of average illumination intensity [in the third department] were 10, 16, 27, and 46 foot-candles. The production efficiencies corresponding to these periods of different lighting intensities were always higher than the starting level and did not always fall off with a decrease in illumination.

Mr. Snow concludes by saying:

The results of this first winter's test . . . brought out very forcibly the necessity of controlling or eliminating the various additional factors which affected production output in either the same or opposing directions to that which we can ascribe to illumination.

[1] Snow, C. E., "A Discussion of the Relation of Illumination Intensity to Productive Efficiency," *The Tech Engineering News*, November, 1927.

The Second Illumination Experiment

The second experiment was designed to eliminate some of the difficulties of the first. Only one of the above three departments was chosen for study. In this department the operators were engaged in winding small induction coils on wooden spools. It was decided to divide the workers into two groups, each group composed of an equal number of operators of about the same experience. These groups were so selected that at the beginning of the test each had about the same average output. One group, called the "test group," was to work under variable illumination intensities; the other group, called the "control group," was to work under an intensity of illumination as nearly constant as possible. The groups were located in different buildings in order to reduce the influence of any spirit of competition. The test group worked under three different intensities of light, 24, 46, and 70 foot-candles, while the control group worked under a more or less constant level of 16 to 28 foot-candles.[1] It was thought that by this method the differences in production efficiency could be related directly to differences in illumination intensity. Again, let us quote from Mr. Snow's report:

This test resulted in very appreciable production increases in both groups and of almost identical magnitude. The difference in efficiency of the two groups was so small as to be less than the probable error of the values. Consequently, we were again unable to determine what definite part of the improvement in performance should be ascribed to improved illumination.

The Third Illumination Experiment

Because it was thought that the combination of artificial with natural illumination during the previous test had resulted in a lack of definite control of the illumination intensities, a third test was conducted. In this third test only artificial lighting was used. The test group and the control group were used as outlined in the previous test. The control group was provided with a constant level of 10 foot-candles, while the test group was provided with intensity levels from 10 to 3 foot-candles in steps decreasing 1 foot-candle at a time. Mr. Snow says of this experiment:

After the level of illumination in the test group enclosure changed to a lower value, the efficiencies of both the test and control groups increased

---

[1] The increase in daylight accompanying the advancing season was responsible for the amount of variation in illumination.

slowly but steadily. When the level of the illumination for the test group finally reached 3 foot-candles, the operatives protested, saying that they were hardly able to see what they were doing, and the production rate decreased. The operatives could and did maintain their efficiency to this point in spite of the discomfort and handicap of insufficient illumination.

Further Informal Experimentation

Shortly after the completion of these three tests, the representative of the company who had collaborated with Mr. Snow in the research received permission to submit two operators to still further experimentation. Two capable and willing operators were selected. They were provided with working facilities in a locker room which could be made completely dark. The illumination at the bench in this room was cut down from the original amount of light to which the girls had been accustomed to 0.06 of a foot-candle, an amount of light approximately equal to that on an ordinary moonlight night. Even with this very low intensity of light, the girls maintained their efficiency. They said that they suffered no eyestrain and that they became less tired than when working under bright lights.

The experimenter was not yet completely satisfied that it had been clearly demonstrated that the effects of the illumination secured in the previous studies were more "psychological" than real. He therefore decided to try further tests on the girls in the coil winding group. First, the amount of light was increased regularly day by day, and the girls were asked each day how they liked the change. As the light was increased, the girls told the investigator that they liked the brighter lights. Then for a day or two the investigator allowed the girls to see the electrician come and change the light bulbs. In reality, the electrician merely took out bulbs of a given size and inserted bulbs of the same size, without in any way changing the amount of light. The girls, thinking that the light was still being "stepped up" day by day, commented favorably about the increase of light. After a few days of this, the experimenter started to decrease the intensity of light, keeping the girls informed of the change and soliciting their reaction. After a period of this day-by-day decrease in illumination, he again allowed the girls to see the electrician change the bulbs without really changing the intensity of illumination. Again the girls gave answers that were to be expected, in that they said the "lesser" light was not so pleasant to work under as the brighter light. Their production did not materially change at any stage of the experiment.

Conclusion

Although the results from these experiments on illumination fell short of the expectations of the company in the sense that they failed to answer the specific question of the relation between illumination and efficiency, nevertheless they provided a great stimulus for more research in the field of human relations. They contributed to the steadily growing realization that more knowledge concerning problems involving human factors was essential. As a result of the illumination experiments, the experiment to be described in the next chapter was started.

CHAPTER II

PLANNING THE RELAY ASSEMBLY TEST ROOM

THE TEST ROOM METHOD

FROM the illumination experiments those in charge of the work for the company drew two conclusions:[1]

(1) that light is only one, and apparently a minor, factor among many which affect employee output;

(2) that the attempt to measure the effect of one variable had not been successful because (a) the various factors affecting the performance of the operators had not been controlled, and hence the results could have been influenced by any one of several variables; (b) in studies conducted in regular shop departments or on fairly large groups of people there were so many factors affecting the reactions of the workers that it was hopeless to expect to evaluate the effect of any single one of them.

From the point of view of the company, then, the illumination experiments had not been unsuccessful, for the investigators felt that they had gained valuable experience in the technique of conducting tests involving human behavior. They were eager to make use of their new insight in a study of the various factors which contributed to employee effectiveness. As a result, they began the Relay Assembly Test Room, an experiment which, although planned for a much shorter period, continued for five years.

It was decided to isolate a small group of workers in a separate room somewhat removed from the regular working force, where their behavior could be studied carefully and systematically. Although there was no idea of a complete control of all the factors affecting work performance, it was thought that by selecting a small group of employees the number of variables which inevitably creep into a large group situation could be somewhat diminished. Such influences as the amount of work ahead of the operators, changes in type of work, the introduction of inexperienced operators, the shifting of personnel because of fluctuation in work schedules could be largely eliminated. In a small group it would be possible to keep certain variables roughly

[1] Pennock, G. A., "Industrial Research at Hawthorne," *The Personnel Journal*, Vol. VIII, 1930, p. 296.

constant; experimental conditions could be imposed with less chance of having them disrupted by departmental routines. It would also be easier to observe and record the changes which took place both without and within the individual. And lastly, in a small group there was the possibility of establishing a feeling of mutual confidence between investigators and operators, so that the reactions of the operators would not be distorted by general mistrust.

The Kind of Job Selected

The major considerations in the selection of the kind of job suitable for the test were as follows: First, because of the increasing tendency in industry toward mechanized and repetitive tasks and because of the growing interest in the effect of such processes upon those engaged in them, a task representative of this kind of situation should be chosen. Secondly, all the members of the group should be engaged in the same operation, as only in this way could accurate comparisons between individuals be made. Thirdly, since the output records would furnish the chief basis for statistical studies, a kind of work should be chosen in which a complete operation could be performed in a relatively short time, preferably in not more than one minute. Such a task would allow the building up of a larger statistical population than could be obtained in working with jobs requiring a longer interval for completion. Hence a more adequate analysis would be possible. Fourthly, that the job selected should be one on which employment would continue for a considerable length of time, and that it should not entail the costly movement of material or machines, were practical considerations that had to be taken into account. Lastly, because it was thought best to have the speed of the operation wholly controlled by the operator, machine work was excluded as a possibility.

The job finally chosen as best fulfilling these requirements was the assembly of telephone relays, an operation performed by women, which consisted of putting together approximately 35 small parts in an "assembly fixture" and securing them by four machine screws. The various parts entering into the assembly were placed in front of the operator in small bins. The selection of the parts was done by the operator, using both hands, and considerable skill was required in picking them up and placing them in the "pile-up" in front of her. The complete operation required about one minute; consequently, the task might be said to be highly repetitive, as each operator assembled approximately 500 relays each day. Figure 2 illustrates the number and comparative size of the parts and also the completed relay.

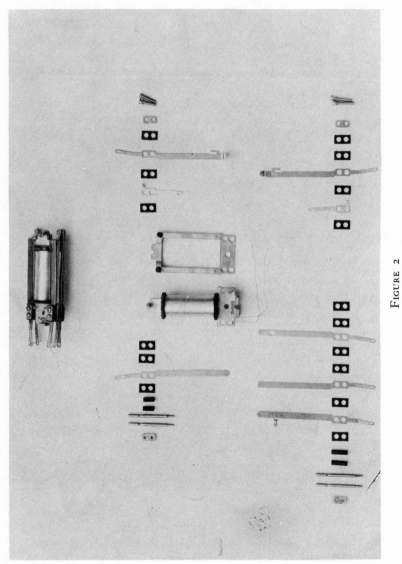

FIGURE 2

PHOTOGRAPH OF RELAY PIECE PARTS AND COMPLETED RELAY

The one requirement which the relay assembly job did not wholly satisfy was the second mentioned above, namely, that of having the girls engaged in exactly the same operation. There were several hundred different types of relays which the company manufactured for telephone apparatus, some varying considerably in respect to the assembly operation, and others varying only slightly. No one type was manufactured in sufficient quantity to occupy fully the time of all the test room operators. However, it was possible in the experimental room to have the girls assemble only those types which were similar in all essential characteristics, their differences being mainly in the number of parts entering into the assembly. Even with this reduction in the number of types, however, there remained the problem of transposing the output data to some comparable basis.

The Operators Chosen for the Test Room

Certain problems arose in selecting the girls for the test. First, in order to avoid the influence of the element of "learning" upon the results, only operators who were thoroughly experienced in relay assembly work were selected. Secondly, it was desirable that the girls selected should be willing and co-operative, in order that their reactions to the changing conditions of the test would be normal and genuine. The illumination experiments had demonstrated that an employee's response to an experimental change could not be ascribed solely to a simple physiological reaction. Some girls were on the defensive or suspicious and held back their output, while others, overly anxious to co-operate, increased their output by "spurting" when illumination was increased. In planning this test, the investigators wished to secure a kind of relationship with the participants which would insure their working at a natural pace and "as they felt."

The method adopted for selecting such a group was to invite two experienced operators who were known to be friendly with each other to participate in the test and ask them to choose the remaining members of the group. The group thus selected consisted of six girls: five to do the actual assembly operation, which has already been explained, and the sixth to act as layout operator. The latter's duties were of a minor supervisory character and consisted of assigning work and procuring parts for each assembler. This arrangement of having a layout operator serve the assemblers was identical with that in the regular relay assembly department, with the exception that quite frequently in the regular department one layout operator served six or seven girls instead of five as in the test room.

In order to facilitate reference and to protect the identity of the operators, each assembler was assigned a number from 1 to 5 corresponding to her particular position at the bench in the test room. This number will be used instead of a name in referring to a particular assembler. The term "layout operator" will be used in designating the sixth girl, whose duties are explained above.

Table I gives the age, nationality, education, and experience of each of the girls chosen.

The Test Room Observer

Besides the girls who composed the group under study, there was a person in the experimental room who was immediately in charge of the test. This position of test room observer was given to the man who more than anyone else had been responsible for initiating and planning these new experimental studies. Not only had he participated in the illumination experiments previously mentioned, but also he was thoroughly familiar with shop practices and had had considerable experience in setting piece rates. As test room observer, his function was twofold: (1) to keep accurate records of all that happened, and (2) to create and maintain a friendly atmosphere in the test room.

The Location, Size, and Equipment of the Test Room

The test room occupied approximately 562 square feet of floor space in a corner of one of the regular shop rooms and was enclosed by a board partition which extended part way to the ceiling. It was located on the fifth, or top, floor, far enough removed from the regular relay assembly department so that the test operators did not come in constant and direct contact with the main group, yet close enough to permit easy trucking of parts and completed relays. This same room had been used for the illumination experiments previously mentioned and was already equipped with lighting fixtures which allowed for slightly more uniform distribution of light than in the regular department. These lighting fixtures and some electric fans, which had also been used previously, were retained in the experimental room. Daylight was admitted through skylights and large windows on one side of the room; this arrangement, however, was about the same as in the regular department.

The room was large enough to accommodate one regular-sized workbench, which was moved from the relay assembly department. So far as possible, the work equipment was not altered. Chairs, fixtures, and work layouts were identical with those in the regular department.

TABLE I

COMPOSITION OF THE GROUP
RELAY ASSEMBLY TEST ROOM

Operator	Year of Birth	Birthplace	Birthplaces of Parents		Education	Date of Employment	Work Experience before April, 1927	
			Father	Mother			Other Companies	Western Electric Company
1A *	1908	Chicago, Ill.	Poland	Poland	Grade school	Sept., 1925	Clerk in mail order house, 2½ yrs.	Relay assembler 1 yr., 8 mos.
2A *	1907	Chicago, Ill.	Poland	Poland	7th grade	July, 1923	None	Relay assembler 3 yrs., 10 mos.
3	1908	Pennsylvania	Poland	Poland	Grade school	June, 1925	None	Paper insulating machine operator 3 mos. Relay assembler 1 yr., 8 mos.
4	1907	Cicero, Ill.	Poland	Poland	2 yrs. high school	Oct., 1923	Shop work, filing gaskets 10 mos.	Relay assembler 3 yrs. Layout operator 6 mos.
5	1898	Norway	Norway	Norway	7th grade (Norway)	March, 1926	Sardine canner (Norway)	Relay assembler 1 yr., 1 mo.
Layout operator	1903	Chicago, Ill.	Czecho-slovakia	Czecho-slovakia	Grade school	Dec., 1920	None	Relay assembler 2 yrs., 5 mos. Layout operator 3 yrs., 11 mos.

* These operators were replaced by two others later in the text (see Chapter IV and Table IA, p. 61).

The only exception to this was a hole in the bench at the right of each girl's position through which the completed relays were dropped and which formed part of the production recording apparatus, to be described shortly. Besides the standard workbench, along which the five girls sat, there were other smaller benches for accommodating the recording apparatus, a desk for the test room observer, space for storing parts, and clothes lockers (see Figure 3).

The Measurement of Output

Considerable attention was given to the problem of determining the exact time taken by each girl to assemble each relay. This was accomplished by adapting an old-type printing telegraph which functioned by perforating holes in a moving paper tape. These holes were punched in five separate rows. Each row of holes represented one girl's production, and each hole signified a completed relay. The tape moved through the mechanism at a constant rate of one-quarter inch per minute; thus the space between perforations represented the time taken to assemble a relay. In order to eliminate the necessity of counting the holes, except when careful analysis was desired, a numerical register or counter was included in the circuit for each row on the tape, and by reading these counters at specified intervals it was possible to secure directly a record of the number of relays completed.

The other part of the recording device was attached to the workbench. The hole in the bench to the right of each girl's position, through which the completed relays were dropped, was the entrance to a chute in which there was a flapper gate actuated by the relay in its passage. The opening of the gate closed an electric circuit which sent an impulse to the corresponding arm of the perforating device and thus registered the completion of the relay in two ways: (1) by perforating a hole in the tape, and (2) by advancing the counter (see Figure 4).

The record of each day's output was thus recorded on a tape of approximately 120 inches in length. Since the mechanism was used continuously throughout the studies, the records thus accumulated are probably unique, both in their accuracy and, more particularly, in the length of time over which they extend.

Recording of Data: the Log Sheet

Most of the problems met in the beginning of the study were related to the general question of determining what data were to be collected and the manner in which they were to be recorded. One record, sup-

FIGURE 3

PHOTOGRAPH OF RELAY ASSEMBLY TEST ROOM

FIGURE 4

PHOTOGRAPH OF RECORDING DEVICE
RELAY ASSEMBLY TEST ROOM

plementary to the automatic recording device, was developed by the observer for checking both the productive and nonproductive activities of each operator. This record, known as the log sheet, gave a daily chronological account of each operator's activities, and on it were entered the particular type of relay worked upon, the exact time work began on that type, the time at which changes from one type to another were made, and all intervals of nonproductive time such as time out for personal reasons, repairs, and so forth.

Operators' Performance Record

The operators' performance record was a regular company departmental form which had to be filled out daily for purposes of pay roll routine. In the regular department this record was kept by the layout operator for each of the six or seven workers she normally served. It contained information as to the type of relay worked upon, the number of relays completed, and the time taken to complete units of 50 relays. Other items, such as breaks in the working day and repair time, were included. The layout operator in the test room kept these records for the departmental files. They were later returned to the test room, where they were filed for future use. These company records provided daily output data which were independent of those obtained from the recording device or the log sheet.

Half-Hourly Readings

As a part of the regular test room routine, readings were taken from the automatic recorder each half-hour during the day. It was thought that such data would be useful in studying and comparing variations in output rates. These half-hourly readings were totaled each day, and the figures thus obtained were checked against those recorded in the operators' performance record.

Quality of Output Records

Some method had to be devised to take account of variations in the quality of output. The errors or defects occurring in the assembly operation may be roughly divided into two classes: (1) those errors for which the operator was responsible, and (2) those errors which arose because of faulty parts which could not be detected by the assembly operator. In assembling relays, the operator was charged with the responsibility of selecting good parts. She had to be sure, for instance, that the contact springs had suitable contact points, and that the insulators were not broken and were of the proper thickness. This meant that the operator had to be constantly on the alert to select those parts which were suitable and to reject those which were not. The rejected parts she threw into a special bin or receptacle placed in front of her for that purpose. If she failed to detect a defect which she should have noticed and allowed the part to enter the assembly, the entire relay, of course, was found defective during inspection. There were, however, some defects occurring in parts which the operator could not detect. Chief among these were defects in the resistance of the coil winding, short circuits, and so forth. These errors were not charged to the operator. The quality of output, therefore, was reflected in two ways: (1) by the number of defective relays assembled, and (2) by the number of parts rejected by the operator. Suitable forms were designed to record these two measures of quality.

In planning the test room experiment, it was desired to have each operator's output inspected as soon as possible after completion so that the various errors could be related to the time at which they occurred. Each operator was responsible for repairing her defective relays and the matter of quality was, therefore, partly compensated for in the output records, as the more errors made, the greater the length of repair time, which was included as regular working time in computing her rate of output.

Converted Output

The difficulty which arose because the operators did not always assemble the same type of relay has already been mentioned. It was possible, however, to confine the number of different types assigned to the test room group to a relatively small number. Moreover, only those types were selected which were essentially similar, their differences being mainly variations in the number of piece parts. Exception to this rule was made only in the case of Operator 5, who continued to assemble a large number of types, making on some days as many as seven or eight changes.

In addition to controlling so far as possible the number of different types assigned to the test room, a method was worked out for reducing the original output data to a common denominator. This was accomplished by selecting a base type relay, technically known as type E901, and comparing the piecework rate of each relay type to the piecework rate of the base type relay. This yielded what was called a "conversion factor" for each relay type, by which any output figure for a particular relay type was multiplied. The results thus gave an output figure in terms of the E901, or base type, relay. For example, an operator assembled three different types of relays during the day. Her output was tabulated as illustrated in Table II.

This method had certain limitations. In the first place, its accuracy depended upon the accuracy with which the piecework rates were established, that is, the degree of accuracy with which the piecework rates expressed the comparative difficulty of assembling each type. However, it should be noted that the piecework rates used in determining these conversion factors had been derived from rates in use prior to the beginning of the test room experiment and had been established by people responsible for computing piece rates throughout the plant.

TABLE II

METHOD OF CONVERTING RELAY TYPES TO COMMON BASIS
RELAY ASSEMBLY TEST ROOM

1 Relay Type	2 Hours	3 Output	4 Conversion Factor	5 E901 Equivalent (3 × 4)
B412	2:51	188	.798	150
B1	5:34	354	.77	273
B16	:10	9	.77	7
		551		430

This, at least, eliminated the possibility of any bias resulting from a desire for a favorable showing in the test room. The other limitation in the use of such conversion factors was the underlying assumption that the relative difficulties of assembling the different types of relays were the same for the different operators. This obviously might not be true.

Daily History Record

Another important account kept was the daily history record. This was designed to give a complete account of the daily happenings in the test room: what changes were introduced, the remarks made by the operators (both spontaneous and in reply to questions), the daily problems with which the investigators were concerned, and all other observations that might be of value in interpreting the output curves of each operator or of the group. This record was invaluable in reconstructing the history of the test room. It not only contained the dates of various events but it also indicated the kinds of questions the investigators were asking themselves at various stages of the experiment.

Temperature and Humidity Record

Early in the study, the investigators decided to record the temperature and the humidity in the test room. On May 24, 1927, they began taking hourly readings of room temperature, as well as hourly readings of both a wet-bulb and dry-bulb thermometer to determine humidity. These readings were taken each day for several years and were posted on appropriate forms.

Physical Examinations

One important question which inevitably arises in studying a worker's efficiency is whether or not increases in output are obtained at the expense of the general health and well-being of the operator. In the test room experiment it was planned to take health into account as one of the important variables. Even though rest periods and other innovations might not result in increased output, they might be associated with marked gains in the health of the workers and, on that account, could be demonstrated to be of value. While it is true that no definite criteria exist by which the physiological condition of a person can be quantitatively stated, nevertheless frequent observations by a physician are likely to disclose any major changes in health, especially those changes which can be considered detrimental. A definite part of the test room procedure, therefore, included a periodic physical examination of each operator at intervals of about six weeks. Since company physicians and complete laboratory equipment were already available, the physical examinations were easily arranged.

Organization of the Test into Periods

At the beginning of the inquiry, the investigators had certain specific questions to which they hoped to find answers. All the factors which influence the reactions of the worker could not be studied at the same time; certain factors had to be studied before others. The original inquiry started with six questions, all of which were related, more or less, to the problem of fatigue:

1. *Do employees actually get tired out?*
2. *Are rest pauses desirable?*
3. *Is a shorter working day desirable?*
4. *What are the attitudes of employees toward their work and toward the company?*
5. *What is the effect of changing the type of working equipment?*
6. *Why does production fall off in the afternoon?*

These questions were originally chosen because they were typical of the questions being asked at the time. Rest pauses and fatigue were controversial topics in industrial circles. Furthermore, the illumination experiments had cast serious doubt on the method by means of which most conclusions on such topics had been reached.

The test was organized into periods, each period representing the number of weeks during which a specific condition of work was in force. The exact nature of the experimental conditions for all periods was not determined at the beginning of the experiment. It was thought best to plan only one step at a time and to let the results obtained in one period determine the conditions of the next period. The original questions with which the investigators started dictated the first set of experimental conditions imposed.

For convenience, the schedule of test conditions for the first thirteen periods is presented in Table III. The periods were numbered consecutively. Periods I–III constituted an introductory phase, the purpose of which was preparation for experimentation. During Period I the operators were still in the regular department. Period II, which covered the first few weeks the operators were in the test room, was planned to permit the girls to become familiar with their new surroundings. In Period III a change in wage payment was introduced, a necessary step before the experiment proper could begin. Periods IV–VII were concerned entirely with rest periods and constituted the second phase of the test. In Periods VIII–XIII the investigators experimented with a shorter working day and week.[1]

---

[1] It is well to keep in mind the fact that the Relay Assembly Test Room actually continued for five years (1927–1932), although only the first thirteen periods (1927–1929) will be reported in this book. The reason for this partial treatment will become clear to the reader as the inquiry is more fully developed. The first tentative conclusions from the test room were reached in June, 1929, after the completion of thirteen test periods. These findings so completely altered the direction of the inquiry that although the test room continued for three years longer, the data accumulated during this period were never organized and systematically studied until 1932. Since then, Mr. T. N. Whitehead, Associate Professor, Harvard Graduate School of Business Administration, has made an exhaustive statistical analysis of the entire body of data collected during the five years, a study which has been published under the title *The Industrial Worker* (Harvard University Press, 1938).

Inasmuch as the first rough approximations reached in 1929 were the basis of the later, more detailed studies, the authors decided, in line with their policy of chronological exposition, to report the findings of the test room as they were obtained by the original investigators. From the point of view of methods in human research, these first thirteen periods, in the authors' opinion, are of sufficient importance to warrant separate treatment. Moreover, they constitute the first step in the development of the inquiry, leading directly to the interviewing program, to be reported in Part II.

Following the same chain of reasoning, the authors also decided to omit from their

TABLE III
SCHEDULE OF TEST PERIODS
RELAY ASSEMBLY TEST ROOM

Period Number	Special Feature	Dates Included	Duration in Weeks	Times of Rest Pauses A.M.	Times of Rest Pauses P.M.
I	In regular department	4-25-27 to 5-10-27	Approx. 2	None	None
II	Introduction to test room	5-10-27 to 6-11-27	5	None	None
III	Special group rate	6-13-27 to 8-6-27	8	None	None
IV	Two 5-min. rests	8-8-27 to 9-10-27	5	10:00	2:00
V	Two 10-min. rests	9-12-27 to 10-8-27	4	10:00	2:00
VI	Six 5-min. rests	10-10-27 to 11-5-27	4	8:45, 10:00, 11:20	2:00, 3:15, 4:30
VII	15-min. A.M. lunch and 10-min. P.M. rest	11-7-27 to 1-21-28	11	9:30	2:30
VIII	Same as VII but 4:30 stop	1-23-28 to 3-10-28	7	9:30	2:30
IX	Same as VII but 4:00 stop	3-12-28 to 4-7-28	4	9:30	2:30
X	Same as VII	4-9-28 to 6-30-28	12	9:30	2:30
XI	Same as VII but Sat. A.M. off	7-2-28 to 9-1-28	9	9:30	2:30
XII	Same as III (no lunch or rests)	9-3-28 to 11-24-28	12	None	None
XIII	Same as VII but operators furnish own lunch, company furnishes beverage	11-26-28 to 6-29-29	31	9:30	2:30

Period Account of Test Room

In the remainder of this chapter and in the two chapters that follow, a detailed description of the major events that took place during the first thirteen periods of the test will be given. This method of presentation has been chosen in order to set forth a kind of evidence which does not lend itself easily to summary treatment. For, at every stage of the inquiry, the attitudes of the investigators as well as those of the operators toward the test, and their interactions, were important determinants of the results obtained. In order to describe these attitudes as concretely as possible, it has been necessary at times to give rather lengthy accounts of certain happenings which may appear somewhat irrelevant to the test proper. Only in this way, however, is it possible to present certain data of which important use will be made later in the interpretation.

Period I
(April 25, 1927–May 10, 1927)

During this two-week interval the operators selected for the test remained in the main relay assembly department, having not yet been transferred to the test room. The purpose of this period was to obtain certain records which could be used as a base against which the effects of any subsequent changes could be checked. Two factors in particular were important for future comparisons: (1) the output of each girl before entering the test room, and (2) her physical condition.

How Output Was Measured in Period I

Because of the fact that whenever a new plan of recording employees' output is instituted there is very likely to be an immediate reaction on the part of the employees in the direction of either increasing or decreasing their output, it was necessary to obtain base period records while the operators were still in the regular department. The output records obtained for this period were taken, therefore, from the regular departmental records used for pay roll purposes (operators' performance record).

---

treatment of the first thirteen periods of the Relay Assembly Test Room all problems and questions which were either irrelevant to the major discriminations reached by the investigators in 1929 or which could be handled more effectively and systematically by considering the five years' data as a whole.

The First Physical Examinations

The first physical examinations were given during the second week of Period I, just before the operators were transferred to the test room. These first examinations were more thorough than subsequent ones in order that any abnormalities or incipient conditions present prior to the beginning of the test might be disclosed. The findings of the first examinations were, for the most part, negative. Three of the girls, Operators 2A, 3, and 4, were reported as having slightly enlarged thyroid glands, and Operator 2A's blood count showed a slightly anaemic condition. Otherwise, the physician's reports indicated five normally functioning organisms.

Informing the Operators of Plans for the Studies

While the five girls were still in the regular department they were informed of the nature and purpose of the studies. A meeting was held at the office of the then superintendent of the Inspection Branch, who was at that time personally supervising the experiment. In this meeting great care was taken to convince the girls that the purpose of the test was not to "boost" production but rather to study different types of working conditions so that the most suitable environment for work could be found. They were urged not to hurry or "drive," but to work at a natural pace, as only in this way would the results have any significance. The following quotation is an excerpt from the superintendent's notes of this meeting:

First, we told them briefly about the illumination test, and how we had found employees generally hesitant about answering questions frankly. Although we could appreciate their reticence and timidity, nevertheless we felt that there ought to be some means whereby management and employees could discuss their problems frankly. Therefore, we decided to set up a small test group and see if after a reasonable period such a condition could not be established. We outlined briefly the questions that we had in mind but told the operators that we had no very clear notion of just what might come out of the test but were willing to get started and await developments.

We told them that we had in mind trying out several changes in working conditions, such as rest periods, lunches, the various lengths of working days and weeks, and that any changes of this sort would be discussed with the operators with the idea of getting their thoughts and comments before making the change. We assured them that we would tell them all we ourselves knew about the results as we went along,—in other words, put all our cards on the table — and the employees were requested to be equally frank with us.

We told them that there might be changes made in working conditions which would be beneficial or desirable from the employees' point of view, and in such cases if they were practical there was no reason why the company should not be willing to make them, as it was our feeling that any change resulting in greater satisfaction of employees would benefit both the employees and the company, regardless of any change in production rate.

The group were assured that the test was not being set up to determine the maximum output, and they were asked to work along at a comfortable pace and particularly not to attempt to see how much they could possibly do. If increased output resulted from better or more satisfactory working conditions, both parties would be the gainers, but we assured them that no attempt would be made to force up production.

We told them that we had no idea how long the test might run — perhaps six months or longer — but the length of the test would be determined by the results. Finally, we assured each girl that it was not necessary for her to join the test group if she had any hesitation about it. Each girl was asked to express her feelings, and all of them decided to try it out.

Period II
(May 10, 1927–June 11, 1927)

On the afternoon of May 10, 1927, the operators moved from the regular department to the test room, which had been previously prepared and equipped. In the test room the operators normally worked a 48-hour week consisting of five 8¾-hour days, from Monday to Friday inclusive, and one-half day on Saturday. The hours of work were from 7:30 to 12:00 and from 12:45 to 5:00. On Saturdays they worked from 7:30 to 12:00. They were paid time and a half for overtime in excess of eight hours; that is to say, on weekdays they received time and a half for the 45 minutes they worked in excess of eight hours.

Period II was designed to allow some time for the operators to become accustomed to the test room environment and also to give the investigators time to establish a routine for recording data and to make the final adjustments of the recording device. Care was taken not to make any changes in the method of work, and only one exception, the use of the chute mechanism into which the completed relays were dropped, was necessary. In the regular relay assembly department the operators had been required to place the completed relays in a small compartment or box in front of them, an operation demanding a little more care and time. From the beginning, the operators expressed a preference for the chute mechanism because it made the work slightly easier.

The Second Physical Examinations

One event occurred in these early weeks which is of interest because it illustrates the attitudes of the operators toward a certain feature of the test, as well as the way in which the situation was handled by the investigators. When it was time for the second physical examinations the girls, with Operator 1 as spokesman, expressed a dread of the examinations and objected to submitting to them so frequently. In order to dispel some of their qualms, the investigators again explained the purpose of the examinations and made arrangements for the operators to go to the hospital together instead of separately, as before. After the examinations, the physician and other members of the hospital staff met with the girls for a friendly talk, the purpose of which was to break down the formality of the occasion. During this meeting it was suggested that ice cream be served on these occasions. This suggestion met with the immediate approval of the operators, who offered to furnish a cake. Plans were made for a "party" at the next meeting. This method of treating the situation seemed to satisfy the girls, for when the next examinations came around, they made no complaints.

Period III
(June 13, 1927–August 6, 1927)

Change in Piece Rates

On June 13, 1927, the test room operators were formed into a separate group for the purpose of computing piecework earnings. Previously, in the regular department, the girls had been paid as members of a group of about one hundred operators. Now they were to be paid as members of a group of five. Since it was expected that this change might have a noticeable effect upon output, Period III was allowed to continue for about eight weeks so that the effect of the new pay incentive would work itself out before any additional changes were introduced.

This change in method of payment necessitated a change in piece rates, the purpose of which is best described in the test room progress report of February 25, 1928:

It was desirable that some method of payment should be introduced which would pay the operators in direct proportion to their efforts while on the test. It was felt that unless this was done the operators would not respond with the full co-operation essential to a test of this nature.

Also, it was necessary that the operators should feel assured that they would not suffer financially in any way as a result of their participation in the test. They were told, then, that a method of payment would be introduced after the test was well under way which would assure them of earnings equal to what they had been getting in the past, with the possibility that these earnings would actually be increased should their output in the test room increase over what it had been in the regular department.

The chief consideration in setting the new piece rates was to determine a rate for each relay type which would pay the operators the same amount of money they had received in the regular department for an equivalent amount of work. The average hourly earnings of these five girls in the regular department were determined by the following procedure:

(a) The average earnings of the five test room assemblers were computed for the months of March, April, and May, 1927. It was found that during this period they had received an average of $.553 per hour.

(b) The average earnings of the layout operator were figured for the same three months. These earnings averaged $.659 per hour.

(c) The average earnings of the layout operator were 23.8% of the total earnings of the five girls:

$$\frac{.659}{5 \times .553} \times 100 = 23.8\%$$

(d) To cover the amount paid to the layout operator, who shared in the earnings but did not assemble relays, it was necessary to increase the average hourly earnings figure of $.553 by 23.8%, giving a figure of $.686. This was the amount of money that each new piece rate had to return to the group per assembler for one hour's work, providing, of course, output remained the same as in the regular department.

The average hourly output for each relay type during Period I was next determined. Then, from the average hourly earnings, on one hand, and the average hourly output, on the other, the new piece rates could be figured as follows:

(e) The total output during Period I was expressed in terms of the number of piece parts handled. (It will be remembered that the distinguishing factor between types was a difference in the number of small piece parts entering into the assembly.)

(f) The average time for handling one piece part was determined by dividing the hours worked during Period I by the total number of piece parts handled.

(g) The time required to assemble one relay of any particular type was then figured by multiplying the number of piece parts in that type by the average time for handling each piece part.

(h) The rate per hour for assembling each type of relay was computed by dividing 60 by the number of minutes required to assemble each type.

(i) The new piece rate for each type was then determined by dividing $.686 (under (d)) by this rate per hour as computed above (under (h)).

Repairing Defective Relays

In Period III two minor changes in the method of work were introduced. The first of these was a change in the time at which each operator repaired the defective relays she had assembled. The usual procedure had been for the inspector to return defective relays to the operator some time during the afternoon. Repairs were made at once so that the completed relays could be shipped out of the test room without delay. This meant that each day there was a break in the output records which, although it amounted to only a few minutes, interfered with the continuity of the record. (Of course, repaired relays were not put down the chute of the recording mechanism.) To overcome this difficulty, it was decided that defective relays should be repaired only on Wednesday and Friday afternoons. On these two afternoons each operator repaired all the defective relays she had assembled since the last repair time. The time required varied from 3 to 25 minutes and averaged about 15 minutes.

Method Used to Check Irregularities in Working Procedure

The other change in the method of work was a temporary one, lasting for a period of five weeks, beginning July 11, 1927. It was introduced for the purpose of studying irregularities and interruptions in working procedure. The system adopted was for each operator to call out whenever she encountered a difficulty in the assembly operation, naming the kind of difficulty it was, e.g., defective clamp plate, bushing, screw, or coil. The test room observer then marked these interruptions on the perforated tape in accordance with a code. Such interruptions as taking time out for eating, drinking, combing hair, talking, and visiting were noted by observation and were also recorded on the tape by code.

Supervision in the Test Room

Several interesting observations relating to the general topic of supervision in the test room were recorded in the daily history record for these eight weeks. In planning the studies, no definite arrangements for supervision had been made. The girls had been previously under the direct supervision of a group chief, who in turn reported to a section chief, whose superiors were the assistant foreman and foreman of the department. Inasmuch as the test room observer could assume responsibility for most of the day-to-day supervision, it was unnecessary to transfer the group chief to the test room. But some supervisory connection for the purposes of accounting, rate revision, promotion, etc., had to be maintained between the test group and the regular department, and in these matters the foreman exercised certain of his supervisory responsibilities. Consequently, the supervision of the test room came to be divided between the test room observer and the foreman.

The test room observer was chiefly concerned with creating a friendly relation with the operators which would ensure their co-operation. He was anxious to dispel any apprehensions they might have about the test and, in order to do this, he began to converse informally with them each day. Sometimes the topics he brought up pertained to their work, sometimes to personal matters, and occasionally they took the form of a general inquiry as to the attitude of the operators toward the test. The following excerpts from the daily history record, in which he entered information and observations, illustrate the way in which the supervisory functions were being performed:

Monday, June 13, 1927

    Operator 1A: Said she was tired today.

    Operator 2A: Tired also and said her head ached.

    Operator 3:   Was asked if she thought she did more, less, or about the same amount of work.

                Ans.: "More, I'm almost up to Operator 4 and I have a bigger relay."

    Operator 4:   "I feel fine today, not tired or anything."

    Operator 5:   "I'm tired today and sleepy."

Tuesday, June 21, 1927

The foreman informed the group of their low activity for the past week. The weather was more favorable for work, cloudy and raining.

    Operator 1A: "I feel fine today. Just right for work."

    Operator 2A: "Today is fine for work."

    Operator 3:   "I went to bed at 9 o'clock last night and feel O. K. today."

    Operator 4:   "I feel great today."

    Operator 5:   "A day like this is much better for work than yesterday."

Tuesday, July 5, 1927

The operators were notified of their visit to the hospital tomorrow. They were told of the plans for a "party" following the examination. They were also shown how to figure earnings.

Operator 1A: "We like it better in here because some of the girls didn't get along with us so well."

Operator 2A: "We'll not have any ice cream or party at the hospital. I don't believe we'll have a party at all."

Operator 3: "I'll not believe we'll have a party until Mr. —— [the foreman] comes in and tells us."

Operator 4: "I like to work in here better than in the department because one don't have so many changes of layouts. It's nicer when we run along on one kind of relay."

Operator 5: Absent today.

Wednesday, July 6, 1927

The group visited the hospital for an examination today.

Dr. —— [the physician in charge] informed us that the general condition of the group had improved considerably and that two of the tendencies to enlarged thyroid glands were much improved.

Operator 2A: "The next time they ask us to tell them what we want, Operator 1A and I are going to tell them we want to eat our lunch about 11 o'clock. You get so hungry by then."

Operator 3: "When do we go to the hospital again?"

Operator 4: "If I had known for sure you wanted to have cake with the ice cream, I would have baked it."

Operator 5: "The next time we go to the hospital, I'll bake a cake."

Tuesday, August 2, 1927

Operators 1A, 2A, 3, and 4 laughed and talked about 75 per cent of the day, more than ever before. These four girls were called into the office by the foreman and given a talk regarding their behavior.

Wednesday, August 3, 1927

Operators were asked if they had to think about the work or if they could think about something else. This was brought about by their being "called" for talking yesterday.

Operator 1A: "Oh, I can think about other things, but it's better when you can talk."

Operator 5: "Sure, I can think about anything and work too."

A marked difference in attitudes was noticeable today after yesterday's reprimand for talking. Operator 1A seemed to resent the reprimand more than any of the other girls.

SUMMARY OF CHANGES INTRODUCED IN PERIODS I–III

For convenience, it may be well to summarize the various changes in working conditions which had taken place in preparation for experimentation during Periods I–III. Most of these changes were essential to the test and had to be made before the subsequent experiment on rest pauses could be undertaken. They were changes from the conditions existing in the regular department which should be kept in mind, for later the performance of the operators in the test room will be compared with that of the operators in the regular department.

(1) The girls were moved into a smaller room, i.e., the test room.

(2) The test room, as compared with the regular department, was equipped with better lighting fixtures which allowed a slightly more uniform distribution of light.

(3) The test room was equipped with fans; the regular department was not. These fans were, of course, only in use on certain days in the summer.

(4) In the test room there was one layout operator for the five girls. This arrangement was slightly different from that in the regular department, where one operator frequently served six or seven girls.

(5) The chute mechanism attached to each girl's bench was new and involved a procedure for handling relays which made the work slightly easier than in the regular department.

(6) The girls, with the exception of Operator 5, had to assemble fewer types of relays.

(7) The rates by which the operators were paid were altered. These rates did not at the beginning change their customary weekly earnings. They did, however, allow each girl to earn an amount more nearly in proportion to her individual effort, since she was paid with a group of five instead of with a group of one hundred. In this sense the change constituted a slight increase in pay incentive.

(8) The procedure for handling repairs was altered.

(9) A new method of calling out defects and interruptions in work was instituted. This method continued for only five weeks.

(10) Not only as a wage payment group, but also sociologically speaking, the girls were members of a small group rather than of a large one.

(11) The test room observer took over some of the supervisory functions.

(12) The girls were given periodic physical examinations. They had been invited to the office of the superintendent, who had talked to them, and in various other ways they had been made the object of considerable attention.

(13) The girls were allowed to talk more freely in the test room than in the regular department.

Most of these changes were clearly recognized by the investigators. The significance of certain changes, however, such as those cited in items 10, 11, 12, and even 13, was not fully understood at the time.

CHAPTER III

EXPERIMENT WITH REST PAUSES

The second phase of the Relay Assembly Test Room experiment, covering an interval of approximately seven months, was concerned with the effects of various kinds of rest pauses. There were four distinct periods, each of which had a different arrangement of rest period time. In this chapter there will be reported for each period separately: (1) the experimental conditions introduced, (2) the major events which took place, and (3) the operators' attitudes. At the end of the chapter the concomitant changes in output will be summarized, and the conclusions which the investigators drew will be presented.

Period IV
(August 8, 1927–September 10, 1927)

Experimental Conditions

The investigators thought it best to start with rather short rest periods and to lengthen them later after the operators had become accustomed to them. For the first experiment, therefore, two rests of five minutes each were chosen, one to be placed some time during the morning, and the other in the afternoon.

The question regarding the time of day at which the rests should be placed was considered carefully. Inasmuch as the rest pauses were looked upon as a means of reducing fatigue, it was decided to place them at those intervals in the day when output began to decline. To determine these critical points the variations in the rate of output for each operator during the day were studied. From these records there was some slight evidence in favor of placing the morning rest some time between 9:30 and 10:00 o'clock, but there was no clear indication of when the afternoon rest should be introduced. Finally, in accordance with the general test room policy, it was decided to consult the girls themselves before the times for the rests were definitely fixed.

A meeting was called for August 5, 1927, at the superintendent's office. The girls were shown their output curves, and the low and high points in the day were pointed out. When asked at what times they would like to have their rests, they unanimously voted in favor of 10 o'clock in the morning and 2 o'clock in the afternoon. Accordingly, the investigators agreed to institute the rest pauses at these times. The net working hours were thus reduced to 47:05 hours per week, a decrease of 1.9 per cent from the standard 48-hour week.

During this meeting the girls explained their decrease in output occurring immediately after lunch by the fact that at this time they became sleepy and found it difficult to work fast. They also told the investigators that they ate very little for breakfast. To the question of what they ate for breakfast, they gave the following replies:

Operator 1A: "Sometimes I haven't time for any. When I do have time, I eat toast and coffee, sometimes a piece of cake."
Operator 2A: "Coffee only."
Operator 3: "Coffee and two cookies."
Operator 4: "One-half cup of coffee and sometimes cake."
Operator 5: "Toast and coffee."

At this point one of the investigators suggested that it might be advisable to serve a lunch during the morning rest period in order to alleviate the hunger which he thought occurred because of such light breakfasts, but it was decided to postpone this feature for a later experiment. As a preliminary step, however, the girls agreed to report to the test room observer what their meals consisted of for a period of one week, beginning the evening of August 7. By this means the investigators hoped to test their "hunch" that the early afternoon slump was primarily due to a large lunch, which in turn was the result of an insufficient breakfast. Although these records of meals eaten did indicate that most of the operators ate very little for breakfast, they offered no suggestion of abnormally large lunches.

Operators' Attitude toward Rest Periods

A review of the daily history record leaves little doubt that the operators' reactions to the rest periods were favorable. The following comments were typical:

Operator 1A: "Gee, that five minutes was like a dream it went so quickly."

At another time:

Operator 1A: "Gee, that's the berries! It rests you to have five minutes like that. [To Operator 3] Don't you like it?"
Operator 3: "Yes, I do."
Operator 4: "I like the rest period, but I think one every hour would be better."
Operator 5: "It rests you a little bit."

In spite of this favorable reaction, there was indication that "feelings of drowsiness" still persisted at certain times in the day. The following comments were recorded just prior to 2 o'clock, the time for the afternoon rest period:

Operator 1A: "I can't keep my eyes open."

Operator 3:   "I'm sleepy too." (Was sleepy all afternoon, working with her eyes closed at times.)

Operator 5:   "I don't think I'll move because I'm so tired."

It is interesting, also, to see how the girls tried to impress upon the test room observer the fact that they were working as hard as possible and resented any hint on his part that they could increase their output. One day, after he had informed them of their earnings for the previous week and they in turn had expressed their dissatisfaction with how "small" these earnings were, he asked them why they did not try to increase the percentage by 10 per cent. To this, two of the operators replied:

Operator 1A: "Gee, you're dead tired now when you get home at night. When Wednesday night comes I'm too tired to go out. Before we had the rest periods it was even worse. Then I'd get so sleepy I'd almost fall off of the chair and I was more tired when I got home at night."

Operator 2A: "We can't always make a big percentage; some days you feel more like working than others. Out in the other room they'd come around and tell you when you didn't make your rate and they'd bawl you out too. But in here with the rests you don't feel so tired and can work better."

The other operators agreed that the rests were beneficial but were of the opinion that the five-minute period was not long enough. The observer then told them that longer rests would no doubt be tried at some time in the future. Operators 1A and 2A expressed doubt as to whether or not they could make up for the time lost. Their comments follow:

Operator 1A: "Then we will have to make up for that lost time."

Operator 2A: "We can't work any faster than we are. If we make our rate,[1] that's good enough."

Operator 1A: "Why make a lot of money and ruin your health? You can always get money, but you can't get your health."

[1] The "rate" refers to the "bogey," which had been the method of measuring their efficiency in the department but had not been used in the test room. Apparently the idea was still present in their minds and, no doubt, operated as the fixed goal with which they compared their performance.

The observer then explained to them that one of the purposes of the rest pauses was to see if they could not accomplish as much work with less effort. He added that it was unlikely that they would notice the increased activity after the rests, "simply because they were rested." With this explanation both Operators 1A and 2A seemed to be satisfied and agreed that the rests were helpful and that they would be glad when they were lengthened.

The Use Made by Operators of Rest Periods

In the department it had been a matter of policy not to specify the time an operator could spend in attending to personal needs. When rest pauses were introduced in the experimental room, this policy was not altered. No suggestions were made to the operators as to how they should spend the time during rest pauses. Beginning with the first rest period, the girls voluntarily established the practice of going immediately to the rest room and of returning about one minute before time for resuming work. This practice was continued throughout the rest period experiments.

Questionnaire about Home and Social Environment

Because it was thought that the home and social life of each girl might have an important influence upon her capacity to work, especially if conditions were present which might be fatiguing or productive of worry, a list of thirteen questions, covering as much of the field as seemed necessary, was made up and presented on August 24, 1927, to each operator:

1. *What responsibility rests on you at home?*
2. *Do you contribute your entire earnings to the family budget?*
3. *Approximately how much do you have for yourself?*
4. *Are there any factors in your home situation which might react unfavorably on you?*
5. *What routine duties around the house do you have?*
6. *If you have any duties, on which days do you perform them?*
7. *How is your time usually occupied between supper and bedtime?*
8. *Do you have your own room, or do you sleep in a room with someone else?*
9. *Is your bedroom removed from any street noises which might affect your rest?*
10. *Have you gained or lost weight since being in the test room?*
11. *What are you most interested in doing outside of work?*
12. *Are your parents exacting in discipline?*
13. *If you were given a wish, what would it be?*

The impression received from this material can be stated only in general terms. Operator 1A, while she assumed no great financial responsibilities, did turn all her earnings in at home. Because of her mother's poor health, she did all the housework, which kept her occupied until 8 or 9 o'clock every evening. Wednesday and occasional week-end evenings were reserved for recreation, and her parents were not very exacting in discipline. In short, the answers Operator 1A made to the questionnaire gave the impression that her days were overcrowded with work, that she was a little tired of it all and would be glad when her coming marriage was consummated, "so that all the trouble and worry will be over."

Things seemed to run fairly smoothly for Operator 2A. Most of her weekly earnings were given to her parents, who allowed her $2.00 a week for spending money. At home there seemed to be little friction; her parents were not watchful of the hours she kept, and her household duties consisted of washing the supper dishes and helping clean house on Saturdays. The general impression she conveyed was that of being rather listless and tired.

Operator 3 and her father had together supported the family until her brother had started working shortly before this time. Her father seemed to be unusually reserved and scarcely ever talked to the children. To his daughter this did not seem unnatural. She did not have a great deal to do at home because a younger sister who went to school did most of the chores. Her parents maintained a rigid discipline and allowed her spending money only when she asked for it. She liked to visit and go auto riding. Although she said she did not worry, the test room observers felt that she had anxieties.

Operator 4 apparently did not demand very much for herself. Her mother allowed her $2.50 a week, which in the daughter's opinion was "too much to spend." She enjoyed her family relationships and liked "to take it easy around the house." She did say, however, that she did not understand her parents: "They want to know why I don't go out more. They want me to go out and they never bother me about the time I come in. My girl friend's folks are different; they are always bawling her out for being out late."

Unlike the others, Operator 5 was older and was not living with her family. Her parents, brother, and sister lived in Norway. She had no financial worries and had most of her evenings free, since she roomed out. She liked "the way things are going" and was thinking of marriage.

The Significance of the Change in Supervision

Although the significance of the difference between supervision in the test room and that in the regular department had not as yet come to the explicit notice of the investigators, nevertheless several entries in the daily history record reveal the gradual way in which supervision was being altered. As has been already mentioned, some of the functions of supervision in the test room had been taken over by the observer. It was likely that a certain amount of friction with the foreman would result. For instance, any noticeable increase of output in the test room might be interpreted by the foreman as an adverse reflection upon his main department. Likewise, any overt manifestation of authority on the part of the foreman might be interpreted by the test room observer as interference or meddling.

The following comment, taken from the daily history record of September 7, suggests this situation:

The earnings for the test room group for week ending September 3, 1927, were figured by the test room investigators as 70 per cent, whereas the department figured their earnings as 64 per cent. In checking up on this discrepancy, it was found that the departmental records had failed to include Saturday's work, which when added brought the test room earnings to 68.1 per cent as compared to 70 per cent, which are the correct earnings for week ending September 3.

Although this excerpt does not go on to explain the discrepancy still remaining between 68.1 per cent and 70 per cent, its very presence in the record seems to suggest an uneasy feeling on the part of the test room observer that the departmental authorities were trying to "pull down" the performance in the experimental room.

Such comments as this are significant in that they show how, even in the early stages of the experiment, a factor which at the time was beyond the explicit understanding of the investigators began to creep into and upset what was regarded as a "controlled experiment." The significance of the change in supervision was difficult to detect at the time because it was a change in human relations, and not in those physical circumstances to which attention was being directed. To criticize anyone for this failure to achieve a "controlled experiment" would be unfair. The foreman, since he was responsible for output and general discipline, had to be alert to detect conditions which warranted his attention. The test room observer himself was not disinterested in the girls' output. On August 9 we find the following entry:

The observer called the attention of Operator 3 to the fact that her output was low yesterday. Operator 3 replied, "What of it? That's nothing, but watch me tomorrow. I'll make up for it."

(The manner of her retort indicates a rather free and easy relation with the test room authority.) On August 12 we find this comment in the record:

Operator 1A said, "I wonder if this study will be a success." We told Operator 1A that success was expected inasmuch as the operators would benefit by having rests and improved working conditions.

PERIOD V

(September 12, 1927–October 8, 1927)

Experimental Conditions

As soon as it became apparent that the five-minute rests tended to increase, rather than to decrease, output, two ten-minute rests were introduced. That this was satisfactory to the operators was clearly shown by the following comments given in response to a direct question put to them by the observer on September 8:

Operator 1A: "I would like ten minutes."
Operator 2A: · "I would like ten minutes, too."
Operator 3:   "Oh, ten or fifteen minutes is all right."
Operator 4:   "Say, fifteen minutes would be swell."

Before the introduction of the ten-minute rests the operators were warned that the "lost time" might affect their earnings. In spite of this, they did not hesitate to accept the increase in nonproductive time, apparently having lost the "fear" they had expressed previously.

The two ten-minute rests were introduced on September 12, 1927, and for a period of four weeks no other changes were made. The times for the rests were the same, namely 10:00 A.M. and 2:00 P.M. This increase in nonproductive time reduced the weekly hours of work to 46:10, a reduction of 3.82 per cent when compared with the standard 48 hours.

Attitude of Operators toward Rests, Increased Output, and Increased Earnings

The introduction of the longer rests was accompanied by an immediate and definite rise in the average output rate. This increase, which became evident on the first day of the period, aroused considerable interest and enthusiasm, not only among those in charge of the experiment but also among the girls themselves. Output and its corollary, increased earnings, became the topics of the day. When the operators were notified on September 13 of their earnings for the day before (80.6 per cent), they were highly elated. Their comments were as follows:

Operator 1A: "Eighty per cent! No! Hurrah for our side! And on a Monday too. Isn't that nice?"

Operator 2A: "Gee! We made 80 per cent yesterday — today we ought to make 90 per cent. We all feel better now with ten-minute rest periods."

In explaining the immediate rise in output, the test room observer commented as follows: "This speeding up was, no doubt, due to an effort to compensate for the additional time off occasioned by the lengthened rests." However, the girls gave varied opinions when asked on September 14 to what they attributed the increased output. Operator 5, for instance, said, "Maybe it's the heat," while Operator 4 said, "Maybe it's the rests — that's the only thing I can think of for going so high when it's so hot." Operator 2A was more definite. Her answer was, "Sure, the rest period does it. You feel better, and then you know you are making a little more money and that makes some difference." Operator 1A did not agree that the increased earnings were of importance. She remarked, "I think the rest periods are what cause it. I don't think the earnings have much to do with it." And Operator 4, in agreeing with Operator 1A, said, "Yes, we earn 80 per cent, but we'll only get 60 per cent." These comments, while they appear to be somewhat conflicting, indicate the favorable attitude of the operators toward the ten-minute pauses.

Attitude of Girls toward Authority

In this period an interesting incident occurred which threw much light on the girls' attitudes toward their weekly earnings and, more particularly, toward authority. It is also illustrative of the test room method of supervision. On September 20, 1927, the test room investigators decided to pay the girls the same "percentage" [1] as was paid the operators in the department, and once each month to pay the difference between the departmental percentage and their actual earnings in the

---

[1] In group piecework the "percentage" is the amount by which the piecework value of the group's effort exceeds the daywork value of the time spent by the group (see p. 14).

form of a bonus. It was thought that this method would have a better "psychological effect," as it would tend to demonstrate to the operators the difference between their earnings and those of the department. When two girls were told of this possible move, they immediately volunteered the following opinions (September 21, 1927):

Operator 1A: "Why do you want to pay us like in the department? Just so you can ball us up, I bet, and then we can't keep a record."

Operator 2A: "It's better to get it each week, I think."

In short, the anticipated "psychological effect" was not realized, for the investigators had not taken into account the girls' attitudes. Their plans did not consider the latent suspicion, or apprehension of authority, in the minds of the girls, although echoes of such a preoccupation had been heard (for example, Operator 4's comment of September 14, previously mentioned, "Yes, we earn 80 per cent, but we'll only get 60 per cent"). No sooner had the girls' output increased than the "company" (in the form of the test room authorities) proposed a plan whereby their reward in increased weekly earnings would be postponed for a month. This proposition "lit up" their latent fears and anxieties. They were afraid that in some way or other the company would deprive them of their increased earnings. Operator 4 made the following comment on September 21, after she had been notified of her actual earnings for the previous day, "We'll never get all that money." When she was assured that there was no one else who would get it and as a joke was asked, "Who else could get it?," she replied quickly, "The bosses, I guess."

It is needless to say, of course, that these fears were not justified and that the girls were being "irrational" in having such anxieties. But because there was no justification in fact for the girls' suspicion of management, it did not follow that such fears were not present. The investigators sensed this intuitively; as soon as they became aware of the operators' reaction they quickly decided to drop the proposed alteration in method of payment. The next day the operators asked how they were going to be paid, and when they were told they would be paid each week just what they earned they were all highly pleased. Operator 1A said the following day: "Now we can work better when we are going to get what we make. Gee, that makes you feel swell."

From the standpoint of supervisory method, this incident reveals two facts of interest. In the first place, the operators felt free to express their attitudes toward the changes which were being introduced. In the second place, it shows that the investigators took these attitudes into account. In the incident mentioned, they abandoned a plan which from a strictly logical viewpoint should have been acceptable to the girls and re-established the plan the operators preferred. There was no attempt to "sell" the new plan to the operators. Their disapproval of it was taken as sufficient evidence of its unsuitability. Here the investigators sensed the latent apprehensions of the operators and, without explicitly saying so, addressed themselves to those fears. This was typical of the supervisory technique employed throughout the course of the experiment. It proved to be a factor of the utmost importance in interpreting the results of the study.

Period VI
(October 10, 1927–November 5, 1927)

Experimental Conditions

On October 3, 1927, a conference of investigators was held to decide on the kind of rest pauses to be introduced in the next period. Two proposals were made. One was to have two fifteen-minute rest pauses; the other was to have six five-minute pauses, three in the morning and three in the afternoon. The general opinion seemed to be in favor of the six five-minute rests on the ground that at a later date, when mid-morning lunches were to be served, the rest would have to be a single period of fifteen minutes anyway. Hence it would be better to experiment with the six five-minute rests first, before the lunch feature was introduced. On October 7 a meeting was held in the superintendent's office to discuss these proposals with the girls. At this meeting the girls were asked if they did not think fifteen minutes would be too long when compared with the present ten minutes. The girls' replies were illuminating:

Operator 1A: "It passes fast; it isn't too long."
Operator 2A: "I don't think fifteen minutes would be too long."
Operator 3: "I feel the same."

Some of the girls expressed the opinion that five-minute pauses would be too short and said, "You hardly get to the rest room and have to come back." In spite of the unanimity of opinion among the girls in favor of the single period of fifteen minutes, the investigators decided to try the six five-minute rests first and explained to the girls their reasons for doing so. They told them that following this experiment a fifteen-minute rest in the morning with a lunch and a ten-minute rest in the afternoon would be tried. The girls agreed to try the six five-minute rests.

Period VI was begun October 10, 1927, and terminated November 5, 1927, an interval of four weeks. The six five-minute rests were introduced at 8:45, 10:00, and 11:20 in the morning, and at 2:00, 3:15, and 4:30 in the afternoon. The net weekly working hours were 45:15, representing a reduction of 5.73 per cent from the standard 48-hour week.

Operators' Attitude toward Six Five-Minute Rests

The operators did not favor the six five-minute rests. Their dislike was apparent on the first day of this period and found expression chiefly through direct criticism, of which the following comments, recorded on October 11, 1927, were typical:

Operator 1A: "I don't like these rest periods. I just get started to work, then have to stop. When I come back, I don't feel like working."

Operator 2A: "I don't like it either."

Operator 3: "I feel the same as Operator 2A does about it."

At this point the observer suggested that perhaps the shorter and more frequent rests would be better liked after they had been given a longer trial.

Operator 4: "I didn't like it yesterday or today, so why should I like it tomorrow?"

The following comments, recorded on October 26, 1927, show that this attitude did not improve:

Operator 1A: "I don't feel like working this afternoon, although I feel some better now after taking a walk with Operator 2A."

Operator 2A: "I'm getting 'nuts' on this job. I don't know what I'm doing. When the whistle blows tonight, I won't have anything done. Everything slips out of my fingers. If I get any more repairs, I'm going on strike."

Operator 3: "I feel 'goofy' today."

The record covering these weeks suggests that in addition to direct criticism the operators were expressing their disapproval in more subtle and indirect ways. There are, for instance, such entries as "the operators returned late from the rest periods" and "the operators did a lot of talking and laughing today." Operator 2A seemed to be particularly troublesome and rebellious. She was the chief participant in excessive talking and laughing, and Operator 1A was almost always involved with her. Besides this, however, comments in the record such as the following indicate that Operator 2A was becoming especially difficult. We find this entry on October 25, 1927:

Operator 2A seemed angry. She said, "I don't like these straight-backed chairs." Later when asked by the layout operator if she would bake a cake for the hospital party on Thursday she replied, "Do you see any holes in my head?"

And again the same attitude is indicated in the following entry on November 2, 1927:

Operator 2A was three minutes late at the 8:45 rest period. She registered displeasure because she wished her layout [relay type] changed and this could not be done.

Period VII
(November 7, 1927–January 21, 1928)

Experimental Conditions

The particular kind of rest pauses for the next experiment had been determined prior to the introduction of the six five-minute rests. They were to be a fifteen-minute rest in the morning, during which a lunch was to be served, and a ten-minute rest in the afternoon.

In determining what should be served for these lunches, the company doctors were consulted and also the girls themselves. Arrangements were made with the organization in charge of the company restaurant to prepare and serve the food. When the final plans were made, the girls were called again into a meeting in the superintendent's office, and this next feature was discussed with them. At this meeting (November 4, 1927), the operators unanimously agreed that the six five-minute rests were objectionable because they caused "too much breaking up" of the working day. They further agreed that the two ten-minute rests had been the best feature tried thus far. It was decided to place the midmorning rest period at 9:30, as this was "nearer the halfway mark between breakfast and lunch" and to serve the lunch during the last five minutes of the period. The time for the afternoon rest was changed from 2:00 to 2:30.

Period VII continued for eleven weeks. The weekly working hours were 45:40, 4.86 per cent below the standard 48-hour week, but slightly more than the hours in Period VI. In Table IV the menus for the lunches during the first two weeks of Period VII are given.

TABLE IV

Lunches Served during First Two Weeks of Period VII
RELAY ASSEMBLY TEST ROOM

	First Week	Second Week
Monday	Postum, tomato sandwich (whole wheat bread) Apple (raw)	Coffee, tongue sandwich (rye bread) Sliced pineapple
Tuesday	Coffee, tongue sandwich (rye bread) Orange	Postum, tomato sandwich (whole wheat bread) Rice pudding
Wednesday	Tea, peanut butter and jelly sandwich (whole wheat bread) Sliced pineapple	Vegetable soup Apple (raw)
Thursday	Vegetable soup Stewed prunes	Orange juice, peanut butter and jelly sandwich (whole wheat bread) Banana
Friday	Orange juice, marmalade sandwich (whole wheat bread) Banana	Tea, egg salad sandwich (whole wheat bread) Orange
Saturday	Oatmeal with cream Apple (raw)	Oatmeal with cream Stewed prunes

Operators' Attitude toward Combined Lunch and Rests

There was no doubt that the girls favored the midmorning lunch and longer rest periods. From the first day their comments were favorable and remained so throughout this experiment. The following comments, recorded on November 8, 1927, were typical:

Operator 1A: "I can work better."
Operator 2A: "Gee, wasn't that a fine sandwich!"
Operator 3: "How long are they going to feed us?"
Operator 4: "They'll have to keep it up now or we won't work here."
Layout Operator: "Sure, we're spoiled already and only two days of it."

Study of Noon Lunches Eaten Before and After Introduction of Midmorning Lunch

It will be recalled that for a one-week period some time before this feature a record had been kept of the food eaten by each of the operators.[1] In order to discover what effect the midmorning lunches

[1] See p. 41.

would have on the noon lunches, a study was made comparing the noon lunches eaten by each operator prior to Period VII with those eaten during the first two weeks of this period.

These data did not support the expectation that the noon lunches would be less hearty after the midmorning lunches had been put into effect. Obviously, in order to make a valid comparison, the material would have to be reduced to some common basis, such as the number of calories consumed. But unfortunately, since no record was kept of the quantity of food eaten, no accurate comparisons could be made. Nevertheless, in spite of the fact that all the operators said during these weeks that "they ate less lunch at noon time," the records showed no appreciable tendency in this direction. Moreover, the early afternoon slump in output immediately following the noon lunch still continued.

Attitudes of Operators 1A and 2A

In Period VII a "personnel problem" involving Operators 1A and 2A, which had been smoldering for some time, began to flare up. It had been apparent for quite a while that these operators were not displaying that "wholehearted co-operation" desired by the investigators. (The antagonism between these two girls and the test room authorities is apparent in comments previously quoted.) Up to this time the chief symptom had been the "talking problem," which involved a lack of attention to work and a preference for conversing together for considerable periods of time. The amount of talking indulged in by all the operators had been one of the developments noted soon after the group was segregated in a small room. No attempt had been made to do away with this privilege, although several attempts had been made by the foreman to diminish what seemed to him to be an excessive amount of talking. Periodically the amount of talking in the room would increase. Operators 1A and 2A were nearly always the leaders in this movement, especially immediately before and after the marriage of Operator 1A, which took place during her vacation in Period VII. Any effort to reprimand them would bring the reply, "We thought you wanted us to work as we feel."

So much concern on the part of the experimenters over the problem of talking is, in itself, interesting. The apparent reason, it might seem, was that too much talking interfered with output; hence the results of the studies were being threatened. Now, although there was some evidence that in the wishful thinking of the experimenters the success of the experiment was identified with high output, nevertheless there was also another set of more logical considerations which prompted their concern. It will be recalled that in planning the studies a small group was selected for two reasons: first, because the number of variables which inevitably creep into a large group situation could be reduced, thus establishing a better control; and secondly, because with a small group a friendly relation leading to a "spirit of co-operation" could be established which would guarantee a "normal" and "natural" response to the various experimental conditions. Just what the experimenters meant by a "spirit of co-operation" or "natural" response was never very clearly stated. Judging from the events that followed, however, it seems very likely that a co-operative spirit meant an attitude on the part of the girls toward one another and the experimenters which, from the point of view of the variable conditions of the experiment, could be treated as constant. They wanted to treat the girls' attitude toward the test as a constant factor; therefore the "right" mental attitude was essential. In short, the girls were to be "pure laboratory specimens," responding only to this and that arrangement of their working situation, uninfluenced by any factor which they could "willfully" control. To the investigators their attitude toward the test was something the girls themselves could and should control. For any failure in this respect the girls were held responsible.

With this viewpoint, it was to be expected that the presence of what appeared to the experimenters to be behavior approaching gross insubordination on the part of two operators was viewed with apprehension. Their "controlled" experiment was being jeopardized, and something had to be done. Had the investigators possessed at that time the technique developed later, their interest would have been directed toward inquiring into the causes of this problem. Such an inquiry would have given interesting results, especially in the case of Operator 2A, as later investigation disclosed. But it was, as yet, too early for improved techniques, and the consequent result was to label the talking and antagonism "poor co-operation" and to try to remedy the situation.

The first attempt at correcting the situation was to reinstate, on November 17, the practice of having the operators call out their assembling difficulties. This time it was a direct effort to renew the operators' attention to their work.[1] The results were interesting. Notations like the following began to appear: "Operators 1A and 2A were so busy talking between 7:30 and 8:15 that they forgot to call out their defects." In other words, rather than eliminating the difficulty, this practice brought about an open defiance on the part of these two

[1] See p. 36 for the first time this practice was introduced and the reasons for doing so.

operators. The effect on the other girls was interesting. Operators 3 and 4 refused to talk with the offenders. The layout operator and Operator 4 began to ask that either they or Operators 1A and 2A be removed from the test room, and matters reached a point where direct action was necessary.

The first step was to call Operator 2A into a conference with the test room authorities. She was told of her offenses, of being moody, inattentive, and not co-operative. In this conference she was apologetic and promised to improve. But upon going back to the test room her old attitude returned immediately. She was later interviewed by the superintendent, with no better results. Her output continued downward, and her attitude became more hostile than ever. Operator 1A was clearly her ally, and her output was likewise affected, although both girls improved slightly during the last two weeks of the period.

It was finally agreed, however, that for the best interests of the test these two girls should be returned to the department and replaced by two new girls. The actual transfer was not effected until early in the first week of Period VIII. Therefore, the discussion of how the new operators were chosen will be taken up in the report of that period.

The Operators' Performance: Results and Conclusions

Apart from the varied problems, already described, which confronted the investigators in these early periods, there were those connected with the assessment and interpretation of the records. Many of the records, such as the record of temperature and humidity, for instance, did not warrant analysis at the time either because they had not extended over a sufficiently long period or they were not intimately enough connected with the experimental conditions under consideration. With output records it was a different matter. They were to provide the chief objective criteria of what transpired during each period and the means by which the effects of experimental changes could be compared.

Throughout the entire study the most common arrangement of output data used by the investigators to portray the general trend in efficiency of each operator and of the group was "average hourly output by weeks." This was derived by dividing the total number of relays assembled each week by the total number of hours worked that week. The total number of hours worked per week included both repair time and personal time, but excluded rest period time and all absences from work ordered by the investigators, such as hospital visits and conferences.

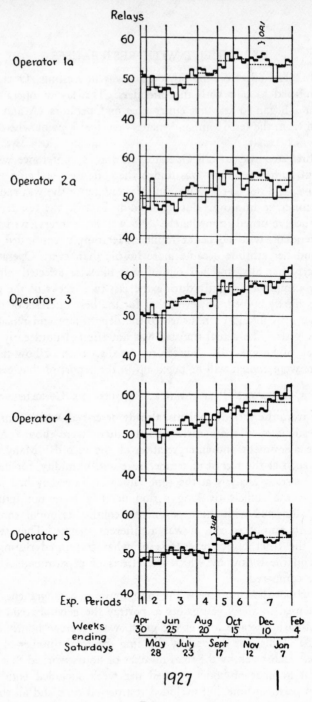

FIGURE 5

AVERAGE HOURLY OUTPUT PER WEEK, EXPERIMENTAL PERIODS I–VII

RELAY ASSEMBLY TEST ROOM

Of course, the output data were arranged in other ways for more specific purposes, particularly with regard to questions of fatigue and monotony. These other arrangements, such as (1) morning and afternoon average hourly output, (2) average hourly output for consecutive days of the week, and (3) the output rate for each 30-minute interval during the day, will be considered in Chapter V. In the present chapter, only the average hourly output by weeks will be considered, as it was this arrangement of the output data which provided the early tentative "leads" and conclusions.

In Figure 5 is shown the average hourly output by weeks for each operator during the first seven periods. To facilitate comparison of the general trend of one period with that of another, the average hourly output for each period has been computed and is indicated on the chart by dotted horizontal lines. From this figure it can be observed that:

(1) The trend seems to be most consistently upward throughout the test for Operators 3 and 4.

(2) The curve of Operator 5 differs from all the others in that it remains practically level through Period IV. Then, following her vacation, it jumps up approximately 5.4 per cent, retains the rise, and continues on that level for the following three periods.

(3) The trends of the curves for Operators 1A and 2A are quite similar to each other. For these operators the trend is downward until the third week in Period III. It then rises, with jumps during Periods IV and V, and finally drops off in Period VII to a level lower than in either of the two preceding periods.

Some of the tentative conclusions drawn by the investigators in these early periods can be summarized as follows:

(1) It was thought that the general improvement in rate of output had been due to the introduction of rest pauses. Relief from cumulative fatigue

LEGEND TO FIGURE 5

Period	Length in Weeks	Experimental Conditions of Work	Experimental Working Hours per Week *	% Decrease from Standard Working Hours
I	2	Standard	48	. .
II	5	Standard	48	
III	8	Standard	48	.
IV	5	Two 5-min. rests	47:05	1.9
V	4	Two 10-min. rests	46:10	3.8
VI	4	Six 5-min. rests	45:15	5.7
VII	11	15-min. A.M. rest and lunch 10-min. P.M. rest	45:40	4.8

* By "experimental working hours" is meant the total time lapse between official starting and stopping time for the day (standard working hours), from which only those time decreases due to the experimental conditions of work listed above have been deducted.

was the first hypothesis advanced to explain this improvement. A number of studies, to be reported in Chapter V, were made to test this hypothesis.

(2) It was thought that the newness of the whole test room situation accounted for the downward tendency in Period II. In passing, it may be interesting to comment on the fact that this same tendency has occurred in every similar study the company has undertaken.

(3) The fact that there was an increase in the output rate when the test room operators were put on a special group pay basis (Period III) suggested a possible relation between the operation of a wage incentive and the improvement. This hypothesis was made the subject of a special study to be reported in Chapter VI.

A number of observations of the girls' attitudes toward one another and toward the group were recorded. In most cases these attitudes seemed to be reflected in the output data. Although the full significance of these observations was not realized at the time, it may be well to mention some of them here, since later in the inquiry they contributed to the formation of an extremely fruitful hypothesis.

(1) There was a tendency for the output of Operators 1A and 2A, on the one hand, and Operators 3 and 4, on the other, to vary similarly. This was to be found not only in the general trend of the weekly average hourly output but also in the week-to-week variations. Although this tendency was not particularly noticeable until after Period IV, it showed up very clearly from that time onward.

(2) At the time no explanation was available for the antagonistic and un-co-operative attitude of both Operators 1A and 2A. It was not until much later in the investigation that an interpretation was made. Nevertheless, their attitude seemed to be reflected in the output of both girls. Their ouput rates began to decline in Period VI.

(3) Operator 5's output curve, which was different from that of the other girls, seemed to reflect her position in the test room. She was older than the rest of the girls and perhaps for this reason participated less in the social activities of the test room. Moreover, in her conditions of work she was differentiated from the rest of the girls: she was the only one who assembled a wider variety of relays.

In looking back it is clear that two essentially different sorts of changes occurred in the first seven periods of the experiment. There were those changes introduced by the investigators in the form of experimental conditions; these were well noted and recorded. There was another type of change, however, of which the investigators were not so consciously aware. This was manifested in two ways: first, in a gradual change in social interrelations among the operators themselves, which displayed itself in the form of new group loyalties and solidarities; secondly, in a change in the relation between the operators and their supervisors. The test room authorities had taken steps to obtain the girls' co-operation and loyalty and to relieve them of anxieties and apprehensions. From this attempt to set the proper conditions for the experiment, there arose indirectly a change in human relations which came to be of great significance in the next stage of the experiment, when it became necessary to seek a new hypothesis to explain certain unexpected results of the inquiry.

CHAPTER IV

EXPERIMENT WITH SHORTER WORKING DAYS AND WEEKS

FOLLOWING the studies of rest periods, a new series of experiments was started for the purpose of studying the effect of shortening the working day and week. This third phase of the test room studies was composed of three distinct experimental periods (Periods VIII, IX, and XI) interspersed with three "check" periods (Periods X, XII, and XIII) in which conditions of work similar to those of earlier periods were reinstated. As in the preceding chapter, a description of the major happenings in each period will be given before the results in terms of output are discussed.

PERIOD VIII
(January 23, 1928–March 10, 1928)

Experimental Conditions

At a meeting of investigators and operators before beginning this period, the operators were given the opportunity of choosing between either starting work one-half hour later in the morning or stopping work one-half hour earlier in the afternoon. They unanimously chose the latter alternative. Consequently, the working day was shortened by stopping work at 4:30 P.M., instead of at 5:00 P.M., during Period VIII. Rest periods as in Period VII (a fifteen-minute morning rest with lunch and a ten-minute afternoon rest) were continued. This arrangement of the rest period time became standard for all the remaining experimental periods with the single exception of Period XII, during which rest periods were removed entirely. The combined effect of the shorter day and rest period time was to reduce the weekly hours of work to 43:10, which was 10 per cent less than the original 48-hour week and 5.5 per cent less than the weekly hours in Period VII.

New Operators in Positions 1 and 2

Probably the most important change in this period was the replacement of those operators occupying positions 1 and 2 in the test room. This took place on January 25, 1928. The foreman, who chose the new girls, was asked to select girls who were experienced relay assemblers and desirous of participating in the test (these were the requirements used in selecting the original operators), and, moreover, whose hourly rates and weekly output performance were comparable to those of the operators to be replaced. These additional requirements were necessary in order to avoid altering the distribution of earnings among different members of the group and also to avoid too great an interference in the output data.

The new operators will be identified as Operators 1 and 2, while the reference numbers 1A and 2A will be used to indicate the original operators occupying these bench positions. Table IA gives the personnel data for the new operators.

TABLE IA
PERSONNEL DATA FOR OPERATORS 1 AND 2 *
RELAY ASSEMBLY TEST ROOM

	Operator 1	Operator 2
Year of Birth	1909	1907
Birthplace	Illinois	Illinois
Father's Birthplace	Poland	Italy
Mother's Birthplace	Poland	Italy
Education	Grade school	2 yrs. high school
Date of Employment	July, 1926	January, 1924
Work Experience in Other Companies	Miscellaneous shop work, 6 mos.	Light shop work, 5 mos. Packer, 2 yrs.
Previous Experience in Western Electric Company	Relay assembler, 1 yr., 6 mos.	Relay assembler, 1 yr., 11 mos. Adjustor, 10 mos.

* See Table I, p. 23, for comparable data about the other operators.

Operator 1 was not a stranger to the test room group, having acted as a substitute during the vacation of Operator 1A in Period VII. It was a standard practice to bring into the test room an assembler from the regular relay assembly department during the absence of any of the test room operators. The output records for these substitute operators are not used in this report, although their output while in the test room was recorded on the perforated tape.

Not much was known about Operator 2 except that her supervisors had recommended her for the test room experiment because she was upset over the recent death of her sister and they thought the change would do her good. Shortly after she entered the test room, she suffered an even greater shock when her mother died suddenly on March 5, 1928.

Attitude of Operators toward Shorter Working Day

All the operators with the exception of Operator 4 enjoyed the shorter day. The following responses in answer to the observer's question, "How do you like going home at 4:30?," showed their attitude:

Operator 1:   "It's fine, and we still make our rate too."

Operator 2:   "It's too good to be true. When I get home now I can help my mother with the supper and as long as we can make as much money it is fine."

Operator 3:   "I'll never get tired of it. Last night I had a whole streetcar all to myself."

Operator 4:   "I don't like it. It makes the evening too long, and all I can do is sit around the house. After this I'm going to wait for my girl friend, then I'll have somebody to walk home with."

Operator 5:   "I like it."

The reaction of Operator 4 furnished an interesting illustration of how her attitude was perhaps influenced by occurrences outside of the work situation. The following comment, recorded on the day before the above remark, threw some light on why she did not like the thought of long evenings at home: "I have to write a letter to my boy friend and tell him I can't go out with him any more because my mother doesn't approve of a fellow who isn't Polish."

PERIOD IX
(March 12, 1928–April 7, 1928)

Experimental Conditions

It had been the intention of the investigators to follow the experiment in Period VIII with a return to the original conditions of a full 48-hour week with no rests. But this plan was postponed when it was seen that output did not diminish during Period VIII (see Figures 6 and 7). The investigators decided to find out what would happen to output if the working day was shortened still further, and at what point in this process the total weekly output would begin to fall off. The daily working hours were therefore reduced by an additional half-hour.

Before these plans were introduced, following the customary test room practice, they were presented to the operators for their approval. The operators expressed themselves in favor of shortening the day still further, apparently having confidence that their earnings would not be affected. At this meeting they were also given the choice of taking the additional time off by either starting work one hour later in the morning or stopping one hour earlier in the afternoon. Again they chose the latter alternative. The experimental conditions for Period IX, therefore, consisted of a working day of 7¾ hours with rest pauses arranged as in Periods VII and VIII. This meant that the net weekly working hours of 40:40 were 15.3 per cent lower than the original 48-hour week and 5.8 per cent less than in Period VIII.

Operators' Attitude toward Shorter Hours

Even though at the beginning of the period the test room observer had suggested to the operators that they should not try to hurry, but on the contrary should try to work at a natural pace, there was some evidence that they did attempt to speed up in an effort to maintain earnings. This was especially noticeable in the case of Operator 2, who began to urge the other girls to increase their pace.

The following comments demonstrate the way in which Operator 2 exerted this influence and also illustrate the antagonisms which were aroused. For instance, on March 31, 1928, the record has this entry: "Operator 2 admonished Operators 3 and 4 for not working hard enough." And again, on April 3, 1928, Operator 2 said: "We have to make a high percentage today to make up for yesterday," to which Operator 3 replied, "I'm going to make more than you today." A few days later, April 6, 1928, Operators 1, 3, and 4 agreed to do no talking for an entire afternoon. On the following day, when told of the high earnings for the day before, Operator 2 again asserted herself by ordering the other girls to refrain fom talking. Her commands were immediately resented by Operators 3 and 4, who replied, "Oh, shut up yourself."

The above incidents are exceedingly interesting in the light of later developments, for they indicate that the position of leader finally attained by Operator 2 with respect to both output and personality was not secured without some struggle and conflict with the previous leaders, Operators 3 and 4.

Although the girls were in favor of a shorter working day, Period IX proved to be too drastic a cut. Total weekly output was lowered, and consequently earnings were affected (Figure 7). Nevertheless, the rate of output did not diminish in this period (Figure 6).

Period X
(April 9, 1928–June 30, 1928)

Experimental Conditions

The idea of returning to the full working week without rests in order to check the results of the study had been in the minds of the investigators for some time. When it became apparent in Period IX that total weekly output and earnings were definitely reduced, plans were made to return to the full working day. Contrary to the initial plans, however, the original conditions of work without rests, as in Period III, were not put into effect immediately. It seemed wiser to reinstate the original conditions gradually, and therefore the rest pauses were retained in this first "check" period. These plans, of course, were discussed with the test group at one of the regular meetings, and at this time the operators were told that later a period of full working hours without rests would be tried.

Period X, which lasted 12 weeks, was identical with Period VII, a full 48-hour week with a morning rest of 15 minutes, during which a lunch furnished by the company was served, and an afternoon rest of 10 minutes.

Operators' Attitude toward Conditions of Work in Period X

With the increase in the length of the working day, the test room observer watched the operators' comments carefully for evidence of an increased feeling of tiredness. In the first few weeks such comments were quite prevalent, but as the period progressed they became less frequent. The following comments in the early weeks were typical:

April 9, 1928
All operators with the exception of Operator 4 complained about the length of the day.

April 10, 1928
Operator 2: "My arms hurt. I can hardly move them."

April 13, 1928
Operator 2: "I'm not going to work as hard as I did yesterday."
Operator 3: "My back hurts today."
Operator 5: "I'm so tired today."

April 17, 1928
Layout Operator: "When we stopped work at 4 o'clock and I went out in the evening I felt all right the next day, but when I work until 5 o'clock I'm pretty tired the next day."
Operator 4: "Me, too."

On May 2, 1928, the observer asked each of the operators the following questions: "How do you like working until five o'clock? Do you think the increased earnings have anything to do with the way you feel about it?" Their answers showed a decided preference for the shorter day and tended to minimize the importance of the pay incentive. In the observer's notes they were indicated as follows:

Operator 1: Liked going home at 4 o'clock because it gave her a longer evening and more chance to get acquainted with the family. She also said she didn't mind the longer hours, but when pressed stated a preference for the 4 o'clock stop.

Operator 2: Would rather go home at 4 or 4:30 in preference to 5 o'clock, even though she needs the additional money which the longer day affords her. Said she is exhausted when 5 o'clock comes and wanted to know when the 5-day week would be tried.

Operator 3: Said she would do anything as long as she didn't have to work until 5 o'clock. Thought she made a lot of money when she stopped work at 4:30 anyway. Is more tired now than when she stopped work at 4 o'clock.

Operator 4: Would rather go home at 5 o'clock, as then she can walk home with her girl friend. Doesn't care about the increased earnings except that when she gives her mother a "big check" she is praised, and that makes her feel good.

Operator 5: Does not like working until 5 o'clock and wishes she could go home at 4 o'clock every day. Does not admit any incentive in the increased pay. Said, "Even if we only make 70 per cent, I don't care."

Layout Operator: Would rather go home at 4 than at 5 o'clock. Does not care about the increased earnings.

Obviously, it is difficult to interpret the comments of the operators apart from the context in which they were expressed. Taken from their background, individual comments such as those just quoted can be used to illustrate anything or nothing. It is well, for this reason, to be cautious about interpreting at their face value the feelings of fatigue and the comments about earnings expressed by the operators in this period. Granted that, apart from their historical setting (that is, the development of the situation with time), Periods X and VII with respect to conditions of work were identical, nevertheless Period X followed an eleven-week trial of a shorter working day. It might be expected that the girls would resent this abrupt return to "reality" and would express this resentment in terms of fatigue — a fatigue which they had not expressed in Period VII.

*Questionnaires regarding Changes in Health Habits and
Mental Attitudes*

The investigators thought that the frequent physical examinations
to which the girls were submitted, through bringing health to their
attention, might have resulted in some improvement in health practices. In a search for this kind of information, the following questions
were asked each of the five operators and the layout operator on
May 8, 1928:

1. In general health do you feel the same, better, or worse?
2. How about the amount of vegetables you now eat?
3. How about the amount of fruit you now eat?
4. Do you drink the same amount of water?
5. Do you drink the same amount of milk?
6. Do you sleep the same number of hours?
7. Have there been any changes in the way you spend your evenings?
*8. What do you think has made it possible for you to increase your earnings
   since you have been on the test?*

From the answers there was no evidence of any important changes
in health practices. Nevertheless, all the operators said that they felt
"better" in the test room, this for varied reasons. In answer to Question 8, the operators gave the following reasons for their increased
earnings: "greater freedom," "the absence of bosses," "more personal
attention," "the opportunity to set one's own pace and to earn what
one makes without being held back by a big group." Here was the
first attempt to evaluate the situation in terms other than fatigue and
wages; curiously enough, it came from the girls themselves.

Another questionnaire was given the operators on May 10, 1928.
This questionnaire was more closely related to specific items in the
test room situation and included 21 questions:

*1. Which place do you like to work in better, the regular department or
   the test room?*
2. Why?
3. What do you dislike about the test room?
4. Do you like being questioned?
5. Do you get any comments from the girls in the regular department?
6. Are the test girls all friendly?
7. Do you like freedom to talk?
8. Do you like additional money?
9. Do you like to have people come into the room where you are working?
10. Is noise objectionable?

11. *Do you like the small group?*
12. *Did you like the group chief [in the regular department]?*
13. *Did you like the foreman [in the regular department]?*
14. *Do you like a large room?*
15. *Have you ever worked for any other company?*
16. *How do conditions here compare with those under which you worked?*
17. *Why does output fluctuate on different days?*
18. *Why is Monday's output low?*
19. *Why is Saturday's output low?*
20. *What caused output to go up in the test room?*
21. *Which do you like better, a man or a woman supervisor?*

The answers to some of the questions were significant. All the operators agreed that they preferred working in the test room to working in the regular department. The explanations for this preference brought out some of the same reasons as were given in answer to Question 8 of the previous questionnaire: "smaller group," "no bosses," "less supervision," "freedom," "the way we are treated," etc. Questions 6 and 7 the girls answered unanimously in the affirmative. On Question 8 they were divided, although only one operator felt that the additional money earned in the test room was a "big factor." There was unanimous agreement in the affirmative on Question 11. Question 16 brought out the same reasons as Question 2, "less supervision" and "more freedom." Questions 17, 18, and 19 brought forth a large number of "I don't know" responses. In answer to Question 21 all, with the exception of the layout operator, who did not care, claimed to prefer a man to a woman supervisor.

The impression which the investigators received from the answers to this questionnaire was that freedom from rigid and excessive supervision was an important factor in determining the girls' attitude toward their work in the experimental room. "I like to come to work in the test room" was a common expression.

Outside Social Activities

In Period X the observer detected a growing amount of social activity among the test room girls outside of working hours and outside of the plant. The first occasion was a party which Operator 3 held at her home in honor of Operator 2 and which was attended also by Operators 1 and 4. This was followed in a short time by another party given by Operator 4, to which Operators 1, 2, and 3 were invited. This custom of meeting together at one another's homes came to be a common occurrence in the years that followed. Sometimes a theatre party was substituted for the usual home gathering. Operator 5 was rarely included, probably because of the fact that she was older, shortly to be married, and had different interests.

This movement, which began spontaneously, had a marked effect upon the operators' working relations within the test room. A spirit of friendliness, a willingness to help one another, and other manifestations of a group solidarity developed. The conversations among the girls grew more social and less personal. Confidential chats between particular operators still continued, but there was a marked increase in good-humored joking and raillery in which all participated. Curiously enough, this new attitude on the part of the girls extended to the test room observer and authorities, who were included in the joking and banter and even in the confidences on occasions. There was no question that the girls were enjoying their new freedom and the release from constraint which they had mentioned in the questionnaire answers. But this group solidarity displayed itself not only at the verbal but also at the work level. On June 22, 1928, we find that when Operator 2 was excused for the day Operators 1 and 3 immediately assigned themselves the task of keeping up the group earnings while she was away.

Period XI
(July 2, 1928–September 1, 1928)

Experimental Conditions

Quite obviously, the next step in the experiment would have been to return to the full 48-hour week without rest periods, as originally planned. But the investigators had promised the operators an experiment with a five-day week at some time during the summer months. As it was already the end of June, it seemed desirable to again postpone the return to the original conditions of work in favor of the five-day week experiment.

This period covered an interval of nine weeks, two of which were vacation weeks for the entire group. The girls worked only five days, with Saturday mornings off. Rest periods as in Period VII were continued. Weekly working hours were reduced to 41:40, or 13.2 per cent of the full 48-hour week. The experimental value of Period XI was lessened by the fact that the operators were paid their basic hourly rate for Saturday mornings, the time not worked. Just why this arrangement was made was never stated explicitly by the investigators. As far as can be determined, their action was guided by the feeling that the operators should not suffer a loss in earning capacity as a result of the particular experimental conditions imposed. Essentially the girls were in industry with the purpose of earning a living; they were not merely laboratory specimens. Nevertheless, whatever the reason, this change added a new factor to the situation which cannot be disregarded and which has to be taken into account in comparing this period with any other.

Operators' Attitude toward Five-Day Week

The operators had looked forward to this experiment with considerable interest. Shortly before the period was begun, each of the girls was asked how she would spend Saturday morning. The replies were as follows:

Operator 2: "I'll do my housework in the morning, and then I can help my married sister in the evening."
Operator 3: "I don't know."
Operator 4: "I'll do my housework in the morning."
Operator 5: "Oh, I don't know. I have so much to do I'll be busy every Saturday morning."

During the weeks that followed, practically no comments were recorded indicating what the operators' attitudes toward these new conditions were. Whether this was due to an actual absence of comments or to the fact that the observer was too occupied with other problems to record any comments is not clear, but the latter case is probable since a progress report of the studies was in process of completion during this time and several new studies were being planned. One event of interest in this period was the marriage of Operator 5, which took place during the vacation.

PERIOD XII
(September 3, 1928–November 24, 1928)

Experimental Conditions

The return to the original hours of work, 48 hours per week with no rest pauses, commenced September 3, 1928, and lasted for a period of 12 weeks. In order to prepare the operators for this change, they were told that this return to the original conditions was just another experimental feature which would continue for approximately three months and in no way was it to be regarded as completing the experiment. They were again advised to work at a natural pace.

Operators' Attitude toward the Conditions of Work in Period XII

The operators did not like the return to the full 48-hour week without rests, even though they understood from the beginning that these conditions would terminate after approximately three months. The following comments, recorded on August 27 and August 31, 1928, after they had been told about the plans for this period, illustrate their qualms about the approaching change:

August 27, 1928

Operator 2: "Why do we have to do that one so long? Three months! Gee, we didn't have Saturday mornings off for three months. It isn't so much the working on Saturdays as it is the loss of the rest periods. I dread that."

Operator 3: "Gee, you take them away just when we are getting used to them."

Operator 5: "I'll not miss the lunch so much, but the rest periods."

August 31, 1928

Operator 1: "I'll have to eat a bigger breakfast every morning, too."

Operator 2: "Next week we haven't much to look forward to, no eats, no rest, and no Saturday morning off."

Operator 3: "I'll sure miss those eats every morning at 9:30. I'll be getting up and walking around at that time."

After September 3 there was a period of gradual adjustment to the new conditions of work. At first the operators were hungry at noon and found the working day quite long. On Tuesday, September 4, the second day of the new period, the operators expressed themselves as follows:

Operator 2: (in the morning) "I can't work. I didn't have my rest period." (in the afternoon) "Oh, did I eat this noon! It cost me too much money."

Operator 3: "I'm not used to sitting so long. I never worked such a long day in my life. If I get home, it will be a miracle."

Within a day or two, however, new modes of behavior began to appear which seemed to indicate that some sort of adjustment to the new conditions was taking place. The daily history record reads:

Operators 1 and 2 were reading a newspaper between 8:45 and 9:00 A.M. In the afternoon these same operators passed candy around between

1:40 and 2:05. This made them thirsty, so a number of trips to the drinking fountain were taken. An unusual amount of inattention was evident, especially during the afternoon.

Symptoms of restlessness continued for some time, but gradually an informal organization of time developed to take the place of the former rest pauses. The operators frequently ate something at about 9:30 in the morning. In the afternoon, shortly after lunch, it became customary to slack off work and chat. During this interval there was a great deal of laughing and joking, which at times became quite boisterous.

The Relation between the Test Room Operators and the Observer

Period XII offers several illustrations of the attitude of the test room observer toward the girls, on the one hand, and the attitude of the girls toward the observer, on the other.

Toward the end of the period, on November 7, 1928, the observer again tried to stop the excessive talking among the girls. On this occasion he told them that unless the talking became more moderate it would be quite impossible to relate the output changes to the experimental changes. He wound up his argument by saying that unless excessive talking ceased it might become necessary to continue the experiment without rest pauses for a longer period, perhaps a month or two. The reaction of the girls to this reprimand and threat was interesting.

The following conversation took place the next day between the girls and the observer when they were attending the "party" which followed one of the regular physical examinations. The operators asked how long the test room experiment would last. They hoped it would continue for a long time, as they did not wish to return to the regular department. The observer replied that the conditions at present in the department were about the same as in the test room. To this statement the girls replied:

Operator 2: "Yes, but you can't scream and have the good times out there that we do in the test room, and the *fun* in the test room is what makes it worth while."

Operator 3: "Yes, there are too many bosses in the department."

Operator 1: "Yes, Mr. —— [the observer] is the only boss we have."

Operator 2: "Say, he's no boss. We don't have any boss."

Observer: (starting to speak) "But you know . . ."

Operator 3: "Shut up."

Operator 2: "Look at that. Look at the way she tells her boss to shut up."

These comments cannot be interpreted too literally, as they were made in a spirit of fun and on an occasion when the formal rules of conduct were in abeyance. Nevertheless, they indicate not only the high value the girls placed on the freedom from ordinary supervision in the test room but also their attitude toward the test room observer himself, whom they did not regard as a "boss" and whose verbal threats were not taken very seriously.

In a countless number of ways the test room observer had shown his personal interest in the girls and their problems. He had always been sympathetically aware of their hopes and fears. He had granted them more and more privileges. In Period XI it was he who had seen that they should be granted their hourly rates for the Saturday mornings on which they did not work. It was to be expected that the girls should regard him as a friend rather than as a boss and as one who took their side. He was ever alert to detect any apprehensions on their part and to dispel them as quickly as possible. For example, on September 24, 1928, the observer discovered that the girls were attempting to keep the output rate low during Period XII so as to make sure that rest pauses would be reinstated. Although they had been told that the experimental period without rests was only temporary, apparently their fears had not been entirely dispelled and they were making doubly sure that rest pauses would be reinstated by trying to decrease output. The observer met this situation with frankness. He promptly told them that no matter what happened to output, rest periods would be included in the next feature. Definite promises such as this were not the rule in supervisor-employee relations. Nor, it might be added, were they strictly in conformance with the logic of the original experiment. But it should be clear by now that the experiment which actually was being performed was quite different from the one originally intended.

Although the output rate for all operators except Operator 5 decreased in Period XII (Figure 6), total weekly output reached a new high level (Figure 7). In this connection the case of Operator 3 is of some interest. This operator in particular began to show a marked downward trend in her output rate, a result not unexpected with the removal of rest pauses. Operator 3 herself said, "Give me back the rests and see how my output goes up." However, one noon this girl had a talk with the layout operator, who later reported the conversation to the test room observer. Operator 3 was experiencing friction in her home life. Her brother in a moment of spite had told her mother that she was not bringing home all her money, and the outcome was that she had to give her pay check to her mother before cashing it. Besides this, the mother had borrowed $35 from her daughter's savings and as yet had not paid anything back.

Period XIII
(November 26, 1928–June 29, 1929)
Experimental Conditions

The rest periods were reinstated during this period in accordance with the agreement made with the operators during Period XII. The rests were arranged as in Periods VII and X with the exception that the operators were asked to furnish their own lunch for the morning rest period. The company continued to furnish hot tea.

Period XIII lasted for seven months, the longest interval for any of the experimental periods. The fact that this period continued for so long a time reflected a radical turning point in the direction of the inquiry. The experimental features which had identified each period, and which had been considered the important changes in working conditions for each period, grew insignificant in comparison with other factors.

Attitude of Operators during Period XIII

The operators welcomed the return of the rest pauses. "We never want to work without rest periods again" was the way they expressed themselves. During Period XIII the group reached one of its highest peaks in morale. This was demonstrated in a number of ways: by pride in their work, trying to beat their former output records, helping one another to maintain a high standard. Each girl was conscious of how much work she was doing. Frequent attempts were made by certain operators to break the record for a day's work. But there was no pressure exerted by any girl to increase output all along the line. The mere fact that one girl in particular performed well one day allowed another girl to take it more easily. If one girl wished to slack off, another girl, generally her neighbor alongside, would agree to speed up. Instead of antagonistic competition, there was concerted effort toward a common goal. The following recorded conversations illustrate this new development:

February 27, 1929

> *Operator 2:* "I'd rather work here any time, because in the other department we were working hard and others would be laying low on the job. In here, when some girl is sick we speed up and when I am sick the other girls speed up."

April 4, 1929

Operator 4 left at noon today in order to buy a new coat. Operator 2 remarked, "Did you ask anybody if you could go home?"

Operator 4: "I don't have to. You girls will work for me."

On April 19, 1929, at about 4:30 P.M., after the observer told the operators what their percentage for the previous day had been, the following conversation took place:

Operator 5: "I made it." (Referring to the percentage.)

Operator 4: "Say, Operator 1 and I made your percentage for you yesterday."

Operator 2: "I guess we all made it for Operator 5 yesterday. I can't understand, I'm working so hard today and I can't make as much as yesterday."

Operator 3: "I'm about 15 relays behind yesterday."

Operator 2: "Oh, don't say that! Don't you work according to the way you feel?"

Operator 3: "Do you?"

Operator 2: "I always do! Do you feel like working?"

Operator 3: "Sure, and how!"

Operator 2: "Well, go ahead, because I don't."

Operator 4: (to Operator 2) "Don't worry about your percentage. Operator 1 and I will make it for you."

Operator 5: "I made 421 yesterday and I'm going to make better today."

Operator 2: "That's fine."

This co-operative effort did not develop without some friction. Operator 2 quite frequently admonished one of the slower girls. Especially in the early part of the period she exerted pressure on Operator 3, with the result that these two girls did not talk to each other for several days. Gradually, however, the antagonism diminished. Instead of being "picked on" by Operator 2, Operator 3 became the butt of considerable joking from the whole group, which she took good-humoredly. This friendly, joking attitude is illustrated in the comments recorded on April 30, 1929:

Operator 1: "We had better stop razzing Operator 3 and we will always have a high percentage."

Operator 2: "What happened with her that she put out so many relays? Gee! That's the first time she was working so hard."

Operator 4: "I know why. Because we didn't razz her all day."

Operator 3: "Don't bother me because I won't make any percentage if you do."

The Effects upon the Operators of Experimental Changes in Working Conditions during Periods I–XIII

Thus far only a chronological account of the changes made in working conditions and of the operators' observable reactions to them has been given. Of necessity, this account has been rambling and unsystematic, as it has been intended not only to give an account of the changes introduced and the ideas which dictated these changes, but also to show how on occasions the planning and thinking of the investigators were influenced by sentiments and feelings which are very likely to crop up when experimenting with human beings and particularly under industrial conditions. From the point of view of a scientific experiment, a much more rigid control of variables might have been desirable. But, as it happened, many of the formal changes introduced brought in their train a number of new factors. Had it not been for the fact that the investigators kept a detailed record of the happenings in the test room, the technical difficulties of evaluating the results might have been more considerable. These minute and detailed observations, however, have made it possible to reconstruct the original situation and detect variables which had escaped notice at the time.

Let us now return to the point of view of the experimenters and ask the questions that they were raising at the time. Different working conditions had been introduced. What were their observable effects at the work level among the operators (1) in quantity and quality of output, (2) in bodily health, and (3) in mental attitude?

Experimental Periods and Output Rate

In Figure 6 is shown the average hourly output by weeks for each operator during the first thirteen periods. Average hourly outputs for each period are indicated by dotted horizontal lines. Examination of this chart reveals at once no simple correlations between the experimentally imposed changes in working conditions and rate of work.

(1) With the exception of Periods X, XI, and XII, the output rate for all the girls except Operator 1A and Operator 2A steadily rises from Period II onward. The output rate of Operator 4 in Period XIII had increased about 20 relays per hour, or approximately 40 per cent, over Period I, the base period.

(2) In Periods VII, X, and XIII identical conditions of work prevailed — a fifteen-minute rest in the morning with lunch and a ten-minute rest in the afternoon. Although the hourly rate of output declines slightly in the beginning of Period X, the average remains well above that of Period VII

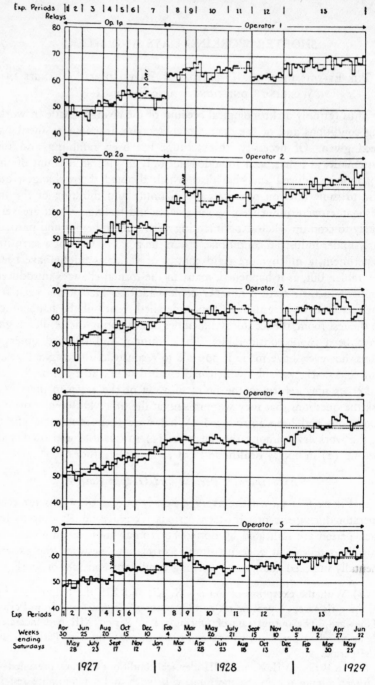

FIGURE 6

AVERAGE HOURLY OUTPUT PER WEEK, EXPERIMENTAL PERIODS I–XIII

RELAY ASSEMBLY TEST ROOM

for Operators 3, 4, and 5. In Period XIII there is an unexpected and sharp rise in hourly rate for all girls, with an average much higher than in either Periods VII or X.

(3) Periods X, XI, and XII also fail to reveal what might have been expected. These three periods varied widely in conditions of work, ranging from a 5-day week with rests, on one hand, to a full 48-hour week with no rests, on the other. Nevertheless during these three periods there is no appreciable change in the rate of output except for Operators 1, 2, and 3 in Period XII.

(4) In one case only (Period XII) does the hourly rate behave in the way it might have been expected to. But although the hourly rate for all operators starts to decline when the operators return to a full 48-hour week with no rests, it never reaches the level of Period III, when similar working conditions were in effect.

Experimental Periods and Total Weekly Output

Inasmuch as the industrial manager is interested not only in the rate of output but also in the total output, the total weekly outputs for each operator, together with the number of hours worked per week, are shown in Figure 7. Weekly hours of work include repair and personal time, but exclude rest periods, as well as time required for physical examinations, conferences, and other things done in conjunction with the experiment which were not normally required in the performance of the job. Average total weekly outputs for each period are indicated by dotted horizontal lines.

From this chart it can be seen that all the major dips in the output

LEGEND TO FIGURES 6 AND 7

Period	Length in Weeks	Experimental Conditions of Work	Experimental Working Hours per Week *	% Decrease from Standard Working Hour
I	2	Standard	48	
II	5	Standard	48	. .
III	8	Standard	48	. .
IV	5	Two 5-min. rests	47:05	1.9
V	4	Two 10-min. rests	46:10	3.8
VI	4	Six 5-min. rests	45:15	5.7
VII	11	15-min. A.M. rest and lunch 10-min. P.M. rest	45:40	4.8
VIII	7	Same as VII, but 4:30 stop	43:10	10.0
IX	4	Same as VII, but 4:00 stop	40:40	15.3
X	12	Same as VII	45:40	4.8
XI	9	Same as VII, but Sat. A.M. off	41:40	13.2
XII	12	Standard	48	
XIII	31	Same as VII	45:40	4.8

* By "experimental working hours" is meant the total time lapse between official starting and stopping time for the day (standard working hours), from which those time decreases due to the experimental conditions of work listed above have been deducted.

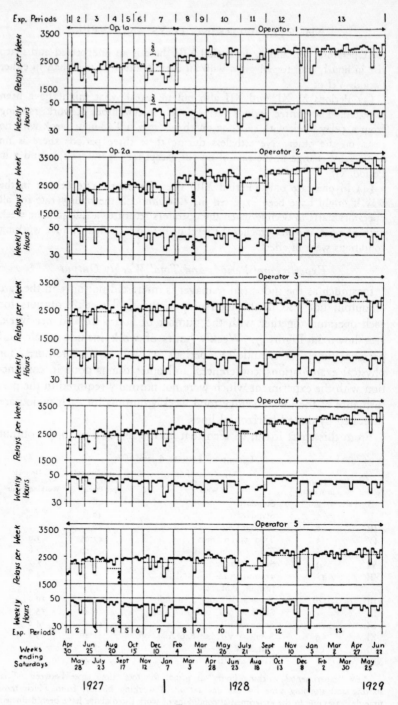

FIGURE 7

TOTAL WEEKLY OUTPUT, EXPERIMENTAL PERIODS I–XIII

RELAY ASSEMBLY TEST ROOM

curves correspond to large decreases in time worked which were not due primarily to the experimental changes.[1] Because these dips occur so frequently it is difficult for the eye to catch the weekly output changes corresponding to the experimental changes in working time. Nevertheless, the curves are sufficiently clear to answer the question for which they were specifically compiled: What happened to total weekly output when rest pauses were introduced and the length of the day was shortened? From Figure 7 it is apparent that:

(1) Total weekly output does not decline when rest pauses are introduced, but remains practically the same during all the rest period experiments. Although the average for Period VII shows a drop for every operator as compared with Periods V and VI, this decline, it can be seen, is brought about by a decrease in the number of hours worked due to factors other than rest pauses (holidays).

(2) The increase in the rate of production, as seen in Figure 6, compensates for the time lost because of shorter working hours in every period except IX and XI.

(3) In Period XII total weekly output reaches a new high level for every operator in spite of the fact that rate of output, as seen in Figure 6, decreases in this period.

Experimental Periods and Quality of Output

With rest pauses and shorter working hours, did the quality of output improve or diminish? In Table V is shown the average weekly repair time in minutes spent by each operator for each period.

Before drawing any conclusions from this table, it is well to keep certain facts in mind. Since it might be thought that the increase in rate of output was gained at the expense of the quality of the work, it should be remembered that the output data previously shown are in terms of perfect E901 relays assembled. That is to say, each girl repaired her imperfect relays during regular working time, and this repair time was included as regular working time in computing the rate of output. The output data, therefore, are free from complications because of variation in the quality of the product.

It is also well to remember that the repair time shown in Table V includes the time spent twice each week in repairing defective relays, and that these defects were due (1) to faulty piece parts which the operator allowed to enter the assembly even though on casual inspection she should have detected the defect, and (2) to other defective

---

[1] These large decreases in weekly hours of work are primarily due to holidays, absences or hospital visits.

piece parts which could not be detected on ordinary visual inspection by the operator and hence for which the operator was not responsible. For this reason, the difference in the amount of repair time required for each period might have been due, not only to the feature of that period, but also to the quality of the piece parts which were received for assembly during that period. It is obvious, therefore, that Table V

TABLE V

REPAIR TIME: AVERAGE NUMBER OF MINUTES PER WEEK TAKEN BY EACH OPERATOR IN PERIODS III–XIII

RELAY ASSEMBLY TEST ROOM

Periods	Op. 1A	Op. 1	Op. 2A	Op. 2	Op. 3	Op. 4	Op. 5	Group
III	19.0		13.5		12.3	10.6	19.0	14.9
IV	19.7		16.3		13.4	9.4	32.8	18.5
V	34.6		37.4		17.4	11.4	31.5	26.4
VI	38.0		36.3		21.2	12.5	50.3	31.7
VII	23.5		23.0		14.2	6.2	27.0	18.8
VIII		39.0		25.2	19.0	6.3	26.4	23.2
IX		30.5		16.8	16.3	6.0	16.3	17.2
X		24.1		20.0	12.5	3.5	18.7	15.8
XI		33.6		27.6	13.1	9.6	13.2	19.4
XII		23.7		22.9	11.0	3.8	5.6	13.4
XIII		22.3		19.0	13.8	7.8	8.9	14.4
Average	27.0	28.9	25.3	21.9	14.9	7.9	22.7	19.4

offers little evidence about whether or not the workers showed an improvement in the quality of their work. To determine this, it would be necessary to know whether or not the operators improved in their inspection of piece parts, and this improvement would have to be expressed as a ratio between the number of faulty piece parts given to the worker and the number of piece parts which the worker rejected as faulty, that is to say, in terms of an inspection efficiency.[1]

Rest Pauses and Personal Time

A question frequently asked about rest pauses is: Do they actually result in shortening the working hours or in most cases do they only decrease proportionally the workers' personal time out? Or, to put the question in a slightly different way: Do rest periods function as rest periods or are they merely a disguised form of personal time out? In "personal time" is included all the time away from work not ordered

[1] See *The Industrial Worker*, by Prof. T. N. Whitehead, Harvard University Press, 1938, Vol. I, pp. 86–87.

by those in charge of the work, as, for example, leaving work to obtain a drink of water, to go to the washroom, or for any other personal reason. It is conceivable that by introducing rest pauses the experimenters were merely substituting a method of organizing the time which the girls would spend away from work anyhow.

Table VI shows the average number of minutes per day taken by

TABLE VI

PERSONAL TIME: AVERAGE NUMBER OF MINUTES PER DAY TAKEN BY
EACH OPERATOR IN PERIODS II–XIII
RELAY ASSEMBLY TEST ROOM

Periods	Op. 1A	Op. 1	Op. 2A	Op. 2	Op. 3	Op. 4	Op. 5	Group	Rest Period Time	Time Cut Off Working Day
II	10.0		12.6		12.0	12.7	5.3	10.5	0	0
III	13.7		17.0		13.0	16.5	8.3	13.7	0	0
IV	8.8		4.8		11.0	13.9	6.5	9.0	10	0
V	9.8		9.3		9.3	12.8	6.5	9.5	20	0
VI	0.3		1.1		0.2	0.5	0.6	0.5	30	0
VII	11.4		6.1		10.3	9.0	5.1	8.4	25	0
VIII		0.5		5.3	1.3	4.5	2.2	2.8	25	30
IX		0.0		4.6	0.5	5.0	1.6	2.3	25	60
X		0.2		7.6	3.6	11.2	4.9	5.5	25	0
XI		0.0		8.9	4.3	13.8	4.8	6.4	25	0
XII		15.0		20.6	11.2	15.8	8.9	14.3	0	0
XIII		5.0		10.0	5.4	9.2	5.6	7.0	25	0
Average	9.0	3.5	8.5	9.5	6.8	10.4	5.0	7.5		

each operator in personal time for each period. Although personal time was appreciably decreased by rest pauses, the reduction was not in proportion to the time taken out by rest periods. This can be seen by noting first that Periods III and XII, representing full working hours with no rests, had almost the same amount of personal time, about 14 minutes. On the assumption that approximately 14 minutes per day was the average amount of time these assemblers took from their work under regular conditions without rest pauses, the probable reduction in the length of the working time can be roughly estimated. For example, Periods VII, X, and XIII had rest periods of 15 and 10 minutes, or a total of 25 minutes. The average personal time taken during these periods was about 7 minutes. Therefore it can be assumed (by subtracting 7 minutes from 14 minutes, the average personal time taken under regular conditions without rest pauses) that about 7 minutes of the rest period time was taken as personal time. Thus the actual working time per day was shortened by about 18 minutes, instead of by the entire 25 minutes allowed for rest periods. From these observations it seems probable that (1) rest periods in the test room did organize more effectively the personal time of the operators, (2) rest periods also actually shortened the working hours, that is to say, they did function as rest periods and not merely as a disguised form of personal time out.

Experimental Periods and Health of Operators

What effect did the new conditions of work have on the health of the operators? It had been agreed from the first that in the general interest of the experiment the operators should submit to periodic physical examinations. Although such general examinations could not measure precisely the minor organic changes, nevertheless it was thought that they would provide a rough estimate of the individual's general condition of health and at least would ensure the detection of any gross changes.

The first physical examination on May 5, 1927, was complete and thorough. It included the past medical history of the operator, her general health habits, a record of her height, weight, temperature, pulse, respiration, and blood pressure, an examination of the mouth, nose, eyes, ears, skin, nails, hair, glands, respiratory system, circulatory system and heart, and an analysis of the blood and urine. The subsequent examinations, of course, were not so complete as the first but they did include a record of the operator's weight, temperature, pulse, blood pressure, and an examination of the heart, chest, and throat.

In looking over 19 examinations given the operators during these first 13 periods the investigators found no indication of decline in the operators' health. Taking weight as a rough indication of the general health of an individual, they found that Operators 1A and 2A gained 3 and 3½ pounds respectively during their 8 months in the test room. Operator 1 was one pound lighter and Operator 2 was one pound heavier after 18 months in the test room. During 26 months Operator 3 gained 4 pounds, Operator 4, 16 pounds, and Operator 5, 5 pounds. Realizing that these fluctuations in weight are within the normal range of those found in any healthy adult, the investigators did not attach any great significance to them. Nevertheless, they could be reasonably sure that they were not in any serious way damaging the workers' health.

Attendance Irregularities among the Operators

An indication of the health of the operators was also looked for in their attendance records. In Table VII is given a record of attendance irregularities for the five assemblers and the layout operator while in the regular department and during the first 16 months of the test. Each item in this table represents any case in which the girl was either sick, excused, or late. From this table it can be seen that the group

TABLE VII

ATTENDANCE IRREGULARITIES OF THE OPERATORS BEFORE AND AFTER
ENTERING THE TEST ROOM
RELAY ASSEMBLY TEST ROOM
(May, 1927–September, 1928)

Operator	Before			After		
	No. of Months	No. of Times	Annual Basis	No. of Months	No. of Times	Annual Basis
1	18	10	6.6	8	1	1.50
2	28	71	30.4	8	6	9.00
3	23	29	15.1	16	3	2.25
4	43	7	1.9	16	1	0.75
5	14	6	5.1	16	10	7.50
Layout	32	85	31.9	16	0	0.00
Group	158	208	15.2	80	21	3.50

averaged 15.2 irregularities a year in the regular department and only 3.5 irregularities a year in the test room, or about one-fifth the former amount. The operators themselves had not been aware of this rather large reduction in the number of irregularities. The record was, therefore, all the more significant, since it indicated either an improvement in health or a change in their attitude toward work.

These findings prompted the investigators to compare the attendance irregularities of the test room operators with those of the girls in the regular relay assembly department. They therefore took a random sampling of 33 girls in the regular department. In Table VIII the attendance irregularities of this group for a 6 months' period, from November 1, 1928, to April 30, 1929, are compared with the attendance irregularities of the 6 girls in the test room for the same period. From this table it is apparent that the girls in the regular department had about 3½ times as many sick absences, a little less than 3 times as many personal absences, and about 3 times as many failures to regis-ter.[1] In tardiness, however, the two groups were about the same, with the rate in the test room slightly higher.

TABLE VIII

ATTENDANCE IRREGULARITIES OF TEST ROOM OPERATORS COMPARED WITH OPERATORS IN THE REGULAR RELAY ASSEMBLY DEPARTMENT

RELAY ASSEMBLY TEST ROOM

(November 1, 1928–April 30, 1929)

	Test Room (6 girls)			Regular Department (33 girls)		
	Total Days	Average per Individual	On Annual Basis for 100 Persons	Total Days	Average per Individual	On Annual Basis for 100 Persons
Sick Absences	12	2.00	400	231	7.00	1,400
Personal Absences ..	4	0.67	134	60.5	1.83	366
Late Absences	7	1.17	234	34	1.03	206
Failure to Register ..	2	0.33	66	30	0.91	182

Experimental Periods and Attitudes of Operators

Other changes, perhaps more difficult to evaluate but none the less real, had also taken place among the operators. These changes can best be summarized under three headings: (1) the girls' attitude toward the different experimental features, (2) their changing attitude toward those in charge of the experiment, and (3) the new attitude of the girls toward the working group of which they were members.

Attitude of Girls toward Different Experimental Features

The verbal reactions of the girls to the different conditions of work have already been mentioned. Only two periods, VI and IX, received unanimous disapproval: The girls did not like the six five-minute rests, which broke up their day; and they were not in favor of shortening the day by one hour, because of its appreciable effect in lowering their earnings. Although Period X was commented upon unfavorably by some of the girls, it is well to remember that Periods VII and XIII, with working conditions identical to those of Period X, did not arouse discontent. In the early part of Period XII, when the original 48-hour week with no rests was reinstated, there was considerable grumbling, but this disappeared as the period progressed and as the girls became adjusted to the new conditions. This rapid adjustment to more un-

[1] As part of the attendance routine it was necessary for the operators to punch a clock, registering the time they started and finished work.

favorable working conditions was interesting because it pointed to the formation of a new group spirit.

On October 10, 1928, in the middle of Period XII, a vote was taken in which each operator was asked to record the kind of working day she liked best and to number the other periods in order of preference. In Table IX the result of this vote is recorded. The five o'clock stop,

TABLE IX

TYPE OF WORKING DAY PREFERRED BY OPERATORS, ARRANGED IN
ORDER OF PREFERENCE
RELAY ASSEMBLY TEST ROOM

Type of Working Day	Choices					
	1st	2nd	3rd	4th	5th	6th
1. Sat. morning off, with rest and lunch ...	6	0	0	0	0	0
2. 4:30 stop, with rest and lunch	0	3	1	1	1	0
3. 5:00 stop, with rest and lunch	0	2	2	1	1	0
4. 4:00 stop, with rest and lunch	0	1	2	3	0	0
5. 5:00 stop, with rest but no lunch	0	0	1	1	4	0
6. 5:00 stop, with no rest and no lunch .	0	0	0	0	0	6

with no rest and no lunch, in other words the full 48-hour working week, was the least popular, any kind of rest period plan being preferable to it. Saturday morning off, with rests and midmorning lunch, was judged by every operator to be the best kind of working arrangement, but it is doubtful whether this preference would have been unanimous had the girls not been paid for Saturday morning off.

Operators' Attitude toward Test Room Authorities

More interesting, perhaps, than the girls' reaction to the different features was their changing attitude toward those in charge of the experiment. The girls came into the test with a somewhat suspicious and apprehensive attitude. At first they resented the periodic physical examinations. In Period IV they were worrying about how they would make up for the time they would lose when the two ten-minute rest pauses were introduced. When the introduction of these rests was accompanied by an immediate and definite rise in output, they began to worry about whether or not they would receive the increased earnings resulting from this rise. In other words, they were never sure that they were not going to be victimized in some fashion or other by the experimenters or by management. By Period XIII, however, this apprehension of authority was almost entirely dissipated. In this period

the girls expressed full confidence toward those in charge of the experiment. They were no longer afraid that they would be the losers from
the experimental changes. This increased confidence was expressed
not merely by the absence of obsessive doubts and qualms, but also by
verbal expressions of satisfaction with the test room situation. In
Period XII the one lingering fear was that the experiment might end
and that they would be sent back to the regular department. Over
and over again the girls expressed their contentment with the test
room and its pleasanter, freer, and happier working conditions. In
particular, they frequently commented on the freedom from constraint
and excessive supervision. In their eyes their first-line supervisor ceased
to be one who "bawled them out" in case things went wrong; instead
he came to be regarded as a friendly representative of management.
This was what Operator 2 meant when she said, referring to the
observer, "Say, he's no boss. We don't have any boss."

Attitude of Girls toward One Another and the Working Group

A change in morale had also been observed. No longer were the
girls isolated individuals, working together only in the sense of an
actual physical proximity. They had become participating members of
a working group with all the psychological and social implications
peculiar to such a group. In Period X a growing amount of social
activity developed among the test room girls outside of working hours
and outside of the plant. The conversation in the test room became
more socialized. In Period XIII the girls began to help one another
out for the common good of the group. They had become bound together by common sentiments and feelings of loyalty. They had their
leader in Operator 2.

Hypotheses to Explain Major Changes

In many respects these results were puzzling to the investigators,
for they were not what they had expected. The general upward trend
in output independent of any particular change in rest pauses or shorter
working hours was astonishing. The improvement in mental attitude
throughout the first two years of the experiment was also perplexing.
Neither one of these developments could be related to the kind of working day in any simple one-one correlation. The investigators thought
that the general rise in output could be related to the improved outlook of the girls toward their work and working environment; since
these two changes had gone hand in hand, it was reasonable to believe
that there was some connection. But still the question remained: To

what could this improved output, on the one hand, and improved mental attitude or morale, on the other, be related?

Five hypotheses or interpretations were suggested. The first hypothesis pointed to the improved material conditions and methods of work that had been introduced in planning the test room. The test room had slightly better lighting and equipment for ventilation. The chute mechanism attached to each girl's bench for the purpose of recording the output data involved a new procedure for the handling of assembled relays which was slightly easier than that in the regular department. The operators handled the repairing of defective relays differently, and with the exception of Operator 5 they assembled fewer different types of relays than in the regular department.

For many reasons this first interpretation was never very convincing to most of the investigators. In view of the previous illumination experiments, it seemed improbable that the slightly more uniform distribution of light in the test room could account for the improvement. Although the test room was equipped with fans, they were only in operation a small part of the year. Moreover, the test room girls were closeted in a rather small room, while the regular department was in a large open room, which allowed for a freer circulation of air. In lighting and ventilation, therefore, the investigators did not believe they could find the answer. The minor alterations in method of assembly operation seemed to be insignificant. The only improvement which seemed to be of any real importance was the difference in the number of types of relays assembled. The fact that most of the girls in the test room had to assemble fewer types of relays could not be entirely ignored. Operator 5's performance offered a convincing example. Of all the girls in the room she had had more different types of relays to assemble and of all the girls her output rate had shown the least improvement.

The second hypothesis was something as follows: Even though the major output change could not be attributed to this or that type of working day, nevertheless the rest pauses and shorter working hours had provided a relief from cumulative fatigue. According to this interpretation, the fact that the total volume of production did not drop during Period XII, when the original conditions of work were reinstated, suggested that the physical health of the operators had improved sufficiently to stand the strain of the full working hours without rests. Had Period XII continued long enough, it was argued, production might have decreased. In fact, there was rather convincing evidence in support of this argument. The rate of production for all operators, with the exception of Operator 5, was at a lower level during this period than in the previous period. Operator 3, in particular, was showing a steady decline in her hourly rate of output.

A third interpretation was that the introduction of rest pauses and shorter working hours had been effective not so much in reducing fatigue as in reducing the monotony of the work. There was every reason to believe that the assembling of relays was a type of work which required "enough attention to prevent mind-wandering but not enough for the complete absorption of mental activity."[1] According to Wyatt and Fraser, such a job is most conducive to boredom. By introducing suitable rest pauses during the working day, by allowing the operators to be paid more directly in accord with the output produced, by allowing them to work in a compact social group, rather than as isolated individuals, the monotony of their work had been dissipated; hence the steady improvement.

The fourth hypothesis was concerned with the increased wage incentive that had followed from the alteration in the method of payment in Period III. The distinct improvement in output, it was argued, could be said to begin with the introduction of this factor. According to this hypothesis, the girls were primarily motivated by economic factors. The girls came to the company not to enjoy congenial work surroundings but to earn as much money as they possibly could. In the test room an opportunity had been given them to earn wages more directly in proportion to the effort which they expended. Although they had been on group piecework in the regular department, the wage incentive had been very slight because the group was so large. In the test room, however, wage incentive had become an important factor. The girls were given an opportunity to earn more directly in proportion to effort expended, and hence production rose.

And finally there was this fifth suggested interpretation: The increased output and improved attitude in the test room could best be associated with the changes in the method of supervision that had gradually taken place. According to the proponents of this point of view, the experimental periods had been essentially carriers of social value. They had been most effective as a means of gaining the operators' confidence and of establishing effective working relations between operators and supervisors. Without ridding the operators of their apprehension of authority by better methods of supervision, and without

[1] Wyatt, S., and Fraser, J. A., assisted by Stock, F. G. L., "The Effects of Monotony in Work," *Great Britain Industrial Fatigue Research Board*, Report No. 56, London, 1929, p. 42.

the social changes which had accompanied this change in supervision, rest pauses and shorter working hours alone could not have produced the result. Social factors were the major circumstances limiting output.

These five hypotheses dictated the direction of the inquiry for many months to come. In the following chapters will be given the methods the investigators used and the results they obtained in attempting to check and verify these different formulations.[1] In Chapters V and VI, the factors of fatigue, monotony, and economic incentive will be considered. In Chapter VII, the fifth hypothesis will be examined, but this chapter will be only the beginning of a more extended inquiry with regard to supervisor-employee relations.

[1] The methods used by the investigators in order to test the first hypothesis, as well as all questions dealing with the relation between the physical circumstances of the operators and variations in output, will not be reported in this book. Although at the end of two years of experimentation the investigators made statistical studies of temperature, humidity, seasonal variation, and other physical circumstances in relation to variations in output, it is apparent that such questions can be answered best by considering the five years' data as a whole. These studies, therefore, are reported by Prof. T. N. Whitehead, who has analyzed the entire body of data collected during the five years of the experiment (see *The Industrial Worker*, Harvard University Press, 1938).

It can be said here that neither the preliminary studies made by the investigators nor the subsequent studies by Prof. Whitehead showed any conclusive evidence in favor of the first hypothesis. None of the studies on the relation between physical circumstances and variations in output showed any significant correlations. It was also concluded that the change from one type of relay to another familiar type did not sufficiently slow up output to explain the increased output of the relay test room assemblers as compared with the assemblers in the regular department.

CHAPTER V

TESTING THE FATIGUE AND MONOTONY HYPOTHESES

THE fatigue hypothesis was studied in relation to two sets of data. The first set was output data arranged to show variations in rate of work for consecutive days of the week, for morning and afternoon, and for a composite working day. The second set of data was composed primarily of organic indices and included such things as blood pressure readings and cardio-vascular skin reaction readings. Unlike the output studies, the latter were made intermittently and covered comparatively short periods of time.

It was recognized, of course, that fatigue and monotony are quite different phenomena. Yet the fact that the same arrangements of output data might yield evidence of one or the other made it advisable to keep both factors constantly in mind. For this reason the two subjects are combined in this chapter.

In examining the production data for signs of fatigue or monotony, the investigators were guided by certain current ideas as to the manner in which these phenomena, if present, would manifest themselves in output. For the sake of clarity, a simple statement of these ideas will be given.

The Fatigue Curve

It should be stated at the outset that the investigators were not concerned with the exact manner in which the expenditure of energy brought about the condition called fatigue. Such a problem could be handled better by specialized laboratory techniques. Fatigue was accepted as a fact of common experience and was defined simply as a diminished capacity for work resulting from previous work done. Statements corroborating this definition could be cited from various sources. For example, E. P. Cathcart, in discussing industrial fatigue, said, "Probably the best general definition, which does not commit us to any explanation of its nature, is that it is a reduced capacity for doing work."[1] Similarly, Morris S. Viteles has said, "Fatigue may be described as decreased capacity for work which results from work."[2]

From this definition of fatigue it follows that the effect of fatigue in

[1] *The Human Factor in Industry*, Oxford University Press, London, 1928, p. 20.
[2] *Industrial Psychology*, W. W. Norton & Co., New York, 1932, p. 441.

retarding the output rate becomes more noticeable as the work spell progresses, resulting, when outputs for short consecutive time intervals are plotted, in a curve similar to that in Figure 8.[1] According to H. M. Vernon,[2] the shape of such a curve is largely determined by the interplay of practice and fatigue, which are mutually antagonistic factors. The relatively low output at the beginning of a work spell is attributed to the fact that the worker is not "warmed up" to his job. As the

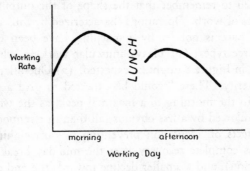

FIGURE 8
"TYPICAL" DAILY WORK CURVE

worker warms up to his task, his output rate rises. It continues to rise in the morning, until the cumulative fatigue effects of the work done balance with the gains due to practice. From that point on, fatigue effects outweigh practice gains, and the output rate tends progressively downward until the end of the morning work spell. Following the lunch period, during which the worker has had some opportunity to recuperate but at the same time has lost some of his gains due to practice, the curve starts at a point somewhat lower than in the morning, reaches a maximum more quickly, and again drops off, this time more rapidly than in the morning spell, until quitting time. There are variations from this general pattern, but in all of them fatigue causes the work rate to diminish progressively during the latter part of each work spell.

Caution should be exercised in reasoning about fatigue from production curves. Eric Farmer, in 1923, wrote:

Curves of output are regarded by some as directly comparable to fatigue curves obtained under laboratory conditions, and sometimes such curves

---

[1] Burtt, H. E., *Psychology and Industrial Efficiency*, D. Appleton & Co., New York, 1929, p. 154.
[2] *Industrial Fatigue and Efficiency*, George Routledge & Sons, London, 1921, p. 13.

are treated simply as fatigue curves. There is a certain amount of justification for this, inasmuch as laboratory fatigue curves and output curves are both curves of performance, but the factors which differentiate them are more important than those which they have in common. . . .

The general principle I wish to suggest is, that at least in our present state of knowledge, we should make no attempt to treat output curves as pure fatigue curves and obtain from them coefficients of fatigue.[1]

It is also well to remember that the shape of the output curve will vary with types of work. Operations characterized by muscular fatigue, in which the pace is not set by a machine, have been classified by Myers into three types: (1) Heavy muscular work in which a curve similar to that in Figure 8 might be expected. (2) Operations requiring skill and dexterity. These "would be expected to give a work curve rising slowly in the morning to a maximal peak, as the worker settles to his work, followed by a less obvious fall than in strenuous muscular work (the effects of adaptation preventing or outweighing those of fatigue), a less complete recovery after the mid-day break (owing to loss of adaptation), and a smaller decline towards the end of the afternoon."[2] (3) Operations characterized by rhythmical movements. Such work curves "may be expected to show a considerable increase during the morning as the worker settles down to his rhythm, after which the output is relatively well-maintained throughout the rest of the day provided that the hours of work be not excessive."[3] The task of assembling relays is clearly of the second type.

The Monotony Curve

Inasmuch as the assembling of relays is a light and repetitive task, the possibility of boredom or monotony also had to be considered. In defining monotony, Cathcart said, "The word literally means one tone. It suggests uniformity, changelessness, lack of variety, drabness, absence of stimulus of any kind."[4] The subjective nature of monotony has been stressed by writers on the subject.[5] According to these writers, monotony is not inherent in the task itself but depends for the most part upon the individual's temperament and attitude, as well as on environmental factors. It will vary with individuals and with the same individual at different times.

[1] Farmer, Eric, "The Interpretation and Plotting of Output Curves," *The British Journal of Psychology*, Vol. 13, 1923, pp. 308–309.
[2] Myers, C. S., *Industrial Psychology*, The People's Institute Publishing Company, New York, 1925, p. 70.   [3] Ibid.   [4] Cathcart, op. cit., p. 31.
[5] Ibid.; also cf. Wyatt, Fraser, and Stock, op. cit., p. 5 et seq.

Work curves for individuals experiencing monotony in their work are described [1] as being characterized by (1) a drop in the rate of work in the middle of the spell, (2) an increased variability in the rate of work, and (3) a tendency for the rate of work to increase at the end of the work spell. This tendency is called "end spurt" and is said to be due to the relief experienced in realizing that the work is about over. A curve illustrating these characteristics is reproduced in Figure 9.

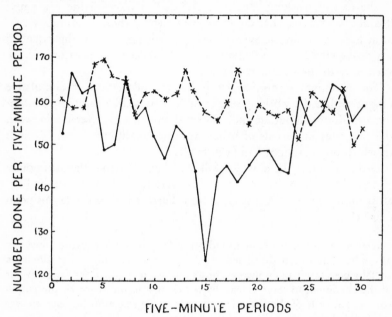

"Curves showing rate of working when (a) boredom was prominent and mind-wandering almost absent (continuous line), and (b) boredom was slight and mind-wandering prominent (broken line)." Reproduced with the permission of the Controller of His Britannic Majesty's Stationery Office, London, England, from Wyatt, Fraser, and Stock, op. cit., p. 37.

FIGURE 9
MONOTONY AND WORK RATE

Commenting on work curves having these characteristics, Viteles said, "The significant fact is that *such changes in the rate and variability of production, represented by a change in the shape of the work curve, appear only in the case of workers who express boredom and dissatisfaction with repetitive work*." [2]

[1] Wyatt, Fraser, and Stock, op. cit., p. 42; Viteles, op. cit., pp. 448, 521.
[2] Viteles, op. cit., p. 522.

*Alterations in the Shape of Work Curves due to Changes in
Working Conditions*

On the basis of these ideas, the investigators concluded that changes
in conditions of work designed to offset fatigue or monotony should
lead to certain predictable variations in the work curves. For example,
if rest pauses were introduced at the appropriate time,[1] the reduction
in the rate of working should be retarded. Following the rest pause
it could be expected that the work curve would show a secondary rise,
or at least maintain the average level for a longer time. The extent to
which the curve was leveled out would be reflected in measures of the
variability in the rate of working.

The investigators also believed that the alleviation of cumulative
fatigue within the working day could be detected by comparing morning and afternoon output rates. There should be less difference between
the two rates in periods of better working conditions than in periods
in which no alterations had been made.

Deductions like these, which followed logically from the assumption
of typical fatigue or monotony curves, were fairly common in the literature on the subject. A quotation from Farmer will illustrate this point
more clearly:

If an alteration is made in an industrial process and is unaccompanied by
any other innovation calculated to increase output, and if that alteration
actually does result in an increase of output, we may judge the fatigue value
of the alteration, to some extent, by the change in the shape of the output
curves. Any one of the following changes in the shape of the output curve
may take place.

(1) The output curve may remain the same shape but be on a higher
level. When this is the case, it seems to indicate that the new method of
doing the work is quicker (and possibly easier), so that the time per unit of
output can be reduced, whereas the increased number of operations which
this makes possible has the same fatiguing effect upon the worker as the
lesser number of more difficult operations. In other words, a greater output
has been obtained with the same amount of effort. The fatigue effect of the
day is the same, though presumably the effort required for each unit of
output is less.

(2) The output curve may be practically on the same level but of a far

---

[1] It is generally conceded that the rest pause should come somewhere between the
points just before and just after output begins to drop off. Preference is given to the time
just following maximum output by many investigators. Cf. Wyatt, S., "Rest-Pauses in
Industry," *Great Britain Industrial Fatigue Research Board*, Report No. 42, London, 1927.
pp. 2–3; Viteles, op. cit., p. 479.

better shape.[1] When this takes place we may assume that the operation has not been made easier to perform in the sense that it can be done more quickly, but that the cumulative effect of its constant repetition is less fatiguing than that of the original method.

(3) The output curve may be on a higher level but of a worse shape. If this takes place we may assume that the increase in output is due to a quicker method of working, but that this new method is more fatiguing to the worker than the original method. We should expect a result of this kind to follow where methods of 'speeding up' are introduced which pay little regard to the health of the worker.

(4) The output curve may be on a higher level and also of a better shape. If this takes place, we may assume that the increase in output is due to an easier and quicker method of working and that the new method is so much less fatiguing to the worker, that he suffers less fatigue during the day although he is repeating the operation an increased number of times.[2]

Such reasoning applied particularly to the detection of fatigue which accumulated within the working day. The investigators also assumed that if fatigue were cumulative from one day to the next, its presence or absence could be detected in two ways. First, it would show up in output for consecutive days of the week. It was well known that the output for Mondays and Saturdays is usually low and that the behavior of output on these days should not be seriously considered in a fatigue analysis. It was assumed, however, that if cumulative fatigue had been diminished, the difference between the output for the last days of the week and for the first ones would be less in periods with rest pauses and shorter working hours than in periods with standard working conditions. Secondly, if the week-end rest had not fully restored the individual to a state of organic equilibrium and if fatigue were accumulating from one week to the next, this condition would display itself in a diminishing weekly average hourly output. On the other hand, any alleviation of this condition would be accompanied by an improve-

---

[1] "A well-shaped work curve should not show too many irregularities throughout the day, for these indicate the excessive play of voluntary effort and effective influences and the inadequate help from habit and rhythm. Irregularities, initial rises and final falls there must always be; an absolutely flat curve is unobtainable. Short end spurts may or may not be present, but they are so variable in occurrence, that they cannot in general be considered as characteristic of a good or bad form of work curve. The curve should not decline too greatly near the end of the spell or day's work, for this indicates excessive fatigue. Nor should it show too prolonged or too high a rise towards the end, for this signifies either that the worker has been unduly 'saving himself' in the earlier hours of the spell or that the work is so monotonous and uncongenial that the increasing previous inhibition is only removed by awareness of the approaching end of the spell." Myers, op. cit., pp. 67–68.

[2] Farmer, op. cit., pp. 309–310.

ment in weekly average hourly output. The degree of improvement would be in direct relation to changes in working conditions.

That fatigue might accumulate in such a manner is indicated in the following quotation from Myers:

> Fatigue, in the sense of a diminution of efficiency owing to prolonged exercise, is of course a normal and healthy result of all work; it can only be considered serious and abnormal when, after the rest which follows any given spell of work, it is not, in general, wholly dissipated. For then, spell by spell, day by day, the fatigue effects accumulate, and sooner or later the time must arrive when healthy fatigue is replaced by pathological exhaustion.
>
> Taking the daily industrial work curve and comparing it throughout the week, sometimes we find evidence of such accumulation of fatigue, but in general it is dissipated by the week-end rest. The well-known 'Monday effect' is due to the loss of incitement and settlement [1] caused by the week-end rest.[2]

Should the effects of previous work result in mental fatigue as contrasted with physical fatigue, it was believed that they would not be cumulative. Variety and change in the hours away from work might be more effective than rest in overcoming this kind of fatigue.

In brief, the fatigue hypothesis stated that if fatigue were the major factor limiting production, it would be likely to manifest itself in characteristic work curves. Different but equally characteristic curves might be expected if operators were experiencing monotony in their work. Finally, improvements in conditions of work designed to offset fatigue or monotony should bring about certain predictable changes in the shape of the performance curve.

The foregoing discussion of fatigue and monotony is by no means complete. The purpose of it is to indicate the kind of logic the investigators used in examining output data for the influence of these two factors. According to this logic, if the upward trend in output were due to relief from fatigue or monotony, it had to be shown that there had been more fatigue or monotony in Periods I, II, and III, before rest pauses were introduced, than in any subsequent period except XII, when the original working conditions were re-established. Periods VII, X, and XIII, with identical working conditions, should have quite similar curves. Periods VIII and IX, with a shorter working day, and Period

---

[1] "Incitement" and "settlement" are defined by Myers as (a) "the warming up of the subject to his work after he has been withdrawn from it," and (b) "the recovery of lost rhythm and the neglect of distracting conditions," respectively. Op. cit., p. 44.

[2] Ibid., pp. 57–58.

XI, with a five-day week in addition to rest and lunch, should show less fatigue or monotony than any other period.

In terms of this logic, let us now examine the output data for evidence of an accumulation of fatigue (1) from day to day within the working week, and (2) within the working day.

VARIATIONS IN RATE OF OUTPUT FOR CONSECUTIVE DAYS OF THE WEEK

In Figure 10 A–E changes in the rate of working for consecutive days of the week are shown for each operator for Periods II to XIII inclusive. In constructing these graphs the total daily output, converted in all cases to E901 type relay, was divided by net working time,[1] from which repair time was deducted.[2] The average hourly output figures thus secured were then summed up and averaged for corresponding days in the weeks included in each period.[3] Finally, these averages were expressed as a percentage of their mean, i.e., of the mean average hourly output of the composite week. It is these percentages which are plotted in Figure 10 A–E.[4] The figures in parentheses show the average hourly output rate for each period.

In constructing these graphs, the investigators assumed: (1) that if there were an accumulation of fatigue from day to day, output would be lower during the last three days of the week than during the first three days of the week; (2) that if the rise in output rate common to all the operators during these experimental periods were due to relief from fatigue, Periods II and III, before rest pauses were introduced,

[1] Henceforward, the term "gross working time" will be used to designate the total time lapse between official starting and stopping time for the day. "Net working time" is gross working time from which all authorized stoppages, such as rest periods, hospital appointments, conferences, and fatigue readings have been deducted.

[2] Following the week ending July 9, 1927, all repair work was done on Wednesdays and Fridays. To include repair time in computing daily average hourly output would have unduly lowered the output rate on these two days. This difficulty does not arise in computing weekly average hourly output.

[3] Inasmuch as the reliability of a mean varies directly with the square root of the number of observations employed in its computation and inversely with their scatter, the composite daily means for Periods II, IV, V, VI, VIII, and IX are highly questionable because none of the periods includes more than seven weeks. Period I included only two weeks and had to be omitted. Periods III, VII, X, XI, and XII included from eight to twelve weeks. Period XIII extended over thirty-one weeks and is the only one with sufficient cases to enable the reliability of the mean to be determined with any accuracy.

[4] In constructing these graphs mean percentages and not mean outputs have been used. This was done because interest in this study lies in the degree of change from one specified time to another and not in the absolute change. Thus, if two operators, A and B, are assembling an average of 50 and 60 relays per hour respectively, an equal absolute increase of 10 relays per hour would represent a 20 per cent increase for A and a 16 2/3 per cent increase for B. Where it is wished to compare changes in output rate for different operators who are working at different output levels, percentages are preferable.

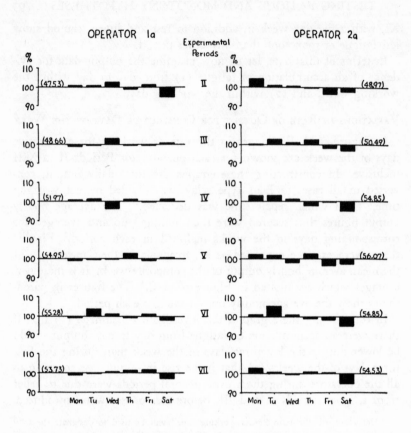

OPERATOR 1a   Experimental   OPERATOR 2a
                       Periods

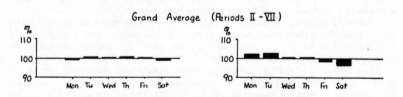

Grand Average (Periods II - VII)

FIGURE 10 A

AVERAGE HOURLY OUTPUT FOR CONSECUTIVE DAYS OF THE WEEK, EXPRESSED AS
A PERCENTAGE OF THE MEAN FOR EACH PERIOD

RELAY ASSEMBLY TEST ROOM

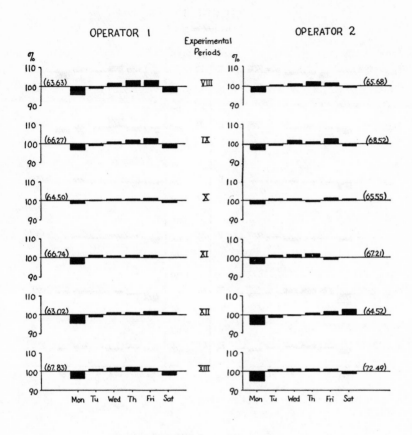

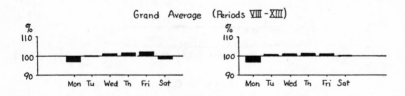

OPERATOR 1

OPERATOR 2

Experimental Periods

VIII IX X XI XII XIII

Grand Average (Periods VIII–XIII)

FIGURE 10 B

AVERAGE HOURLY OUTPUT FOR CONSECUTIVE DAYS OF THE WEEK, EXPRESSED AS A PERCENTAGE OF THE MEAN FOR EACH PERIOD

RELAY ASSEMBLY TEST ROOM

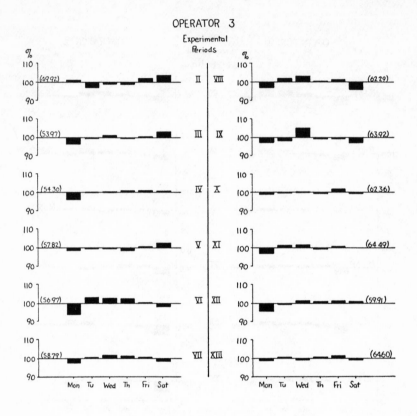

OPERATOR 3

Experimental Periods

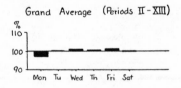

Grand Average (Periods II–XIII)

FIGURE 10 C

AVERAGE HOURLY OUTPUT FOR CONSECUTIVE DAYS OF THE WEEK, EXPRESSED AS A PERCENTAGE OF THE MEAN FOR EACH PERIOD

RELAY ASSEMBLY TEST ROOM

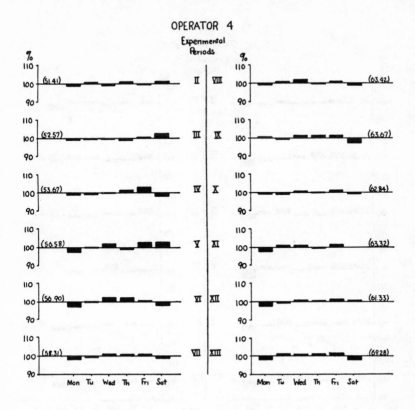

OPERATOR 4

Experimental
Periods

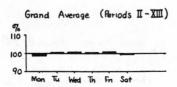

Grand Average (Periods II – XIII)

FIGURE 10 D

AVERAGE HOURLY OUTPUT FOR CONSECUTIVE DAYS OF THE WEEK, EXPRESSED AS
A PERCENTAGE OF THE MEAN FOR EACH PERIOD

RELAY ASSEMBLY TEST ROOM

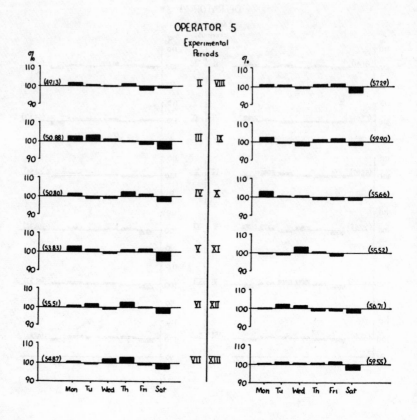

OPERATOR 5

Experimental
Periods

Grand Average (Periods II - XIII)

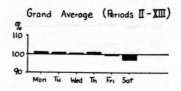

FIGURE 10 E

AVERAGE HOURLY OUTPUT FOR CONSECUTIVE DAYS OF THE WEEK, EXPRESSED AS
A PERCENTAGE OF THE MEAN FOR EACH PERIOD

RELAY ASSEMBLY TEST ROOM

would show the greatest decline in work rate as the week progressed. The results, as an inspection of the graphs in Figure 10 A–E will show, did not support either of these expectations. Saturday's output did tend to be low, but so did Monday's. As mentioned previously, a low output on Monday is usually explained as being due to "loss of incitement and settlement caused by the week-end rest."[1] While a low output on Saturday could hardly be attributed to loss of practice, it could be attributed to restlessness in anticipation of the week-end holiday or other interferences of a similar nature; hence little physiological significance can be attached to the lowered output on either of these two days. Between Mondays and Saturdays the output rates of these operators were practically constant. There were minor variations, but they were too small to be of any significance. Furthermore, they did not adhere to any general pattern; sometimes the highest output for the week occurred on Tuesday, sometimes on Friday, and so on. In short, the output data when plotted this way did not give any support to the fatigue hypothesis. What they did show was a relatively low output on Monday and Saturday, with a fairly constant rate on the intervening days. This conclusion was based upon the following observations of the graphs for each operator:

Operator 1A

The grand average curve for Periods II to VII has no significance because (1) the period averages upon which it is based vary widely, and (2) with the exception of Period II, the variations in work rate which occur are so small as to be insignificant. In Period II Saturday's output rate is 7.7 per cent, or about 3.5 relays per hour, lower than on Wednesday; but, for reasons indicated above, this drop can hardly be attributed to fatigue.

Operator 2A

The grand average curve for Periods II to VII resembles the period curves upon which it is based and may be regarded as reflecting quite faithfully the changes which took place in this operator's work rate throughout the week. This curve shows a fairly low Saturday output rate and a fairly constant rate on the other days of the week, with a slight tendency for the output rate to be higher in the first than in the last part of the week. This downward tendency between Monday and Friday, however, is too small to be of statistical significance.

Looking next at the curves for each period, it will be seen that those for Periods III, IV, V, and VII may be dismissed as not being indicative of fatigue. In Period II the output rate tends progressively downward and on Friday it is 8 per cent lower than on Monday. This curve by itself might

---

[1] See quotation from Myers, p. 96.

be construed as indicative of cumulative fatigue, but it should be noted that the curve for Period VI is even more suggestive of fatigue than this one. In Period VI there were six five-minute rests especially designed to offset muscular fatigue, and theoretically these rests should have resulted in a much more uniform output rate throughout the week. It might be argued, of course, that Operator 2A's output rate had risen in Period VI as compared to Period II and that she was achieving this higher output with about the same fatigue effects. But here again there is conflicting evidence. She was working faster in Period V than in Period VI, yet showed less fatigue in Period V in spite of the fact that during that period there were only two ten-minute rests as compared with six five-minute rests in Period VI. The evidence in this case is so conflicting that it is futile to attempt to base conclusions on it.

Operator 1

This operator tends to work somewhat slower on Mondays and Saturdays than on the intervening days of the week. On the other days her output rate is fairly uniform, particularly in Periods X, XI, XII, and XIII. In no period is there any indication of cumulative fatigue.

Operator 2

This operator works relatively slowly on Mondays. On the other days of the week her output rate is remarkably uniform. None of these graphs suggests cumulative fatigue.

Operator 3

Operator 3 also works more slowly on Mondays than on the other days of the week. For the most part, the variations represented in these graphs are within the range of chance fluctuations and have little significance.

Operator 4

The variations in this operator's work rate between different days of the week show no evidence of cumulative fatigue.

Operator 5

The above observation is equally true of the graphs for this operator. Here, as in the graphs for Operators 3 and 4, there is no indication· of cumulative fatigue or of any other major variable systematically affecting the day-to-day work rates.

VARIATIONS IN RATE OF OUTPUT FOR MORNING AND AFTERNOON

There remained the question of accumulation of fatigue within the working day. Was the major rise in output attributable to the alleviation of such fatigue by rest pauses, midmorning lunches, and shorter working hours?

That the operators experienced feelings of tiredness at the end of their day's work was scarcely questioned; people usually claim to be more tired in the evening than in the morning. Their comments, as recorded in the daily history record, frequently testified to this fact. It was curious, however, that often their comments were in the nature of "I feel tired today" or, on the contrary, "I feel like working today," suggesting not the effect of a slow accumulation of fatigue as a result of a day's work but rather an attitude especially characteristic of a given morning and persisting throughout the day.

To throw light upon the above question, studies were made (1) of the difference between morning and afternoon output rates in different periods, and (2) of composite daily work curves based on consecutive half-hourly readings.

Figure 11 shows the percentage differences between morning and afternoon average hourly output in selected periods for each operator and the group. The morning and afternoon average hourly output rates were derived from the study of consecutive half-hourly output rates. These will be reported in the next section, where the reasons for grouping certain periods together and the details of calculation will also be discussed. It is sufficient here to note that only those periods were combined in which working conditions were fairly similar, and that the morning and afternoon output rates used in this study represent the output rate during uninterrupted working time. In arriving at the percentages plotted in Figure 11, the afternoon rate was subtracted from the morning rate, and the difference, whether plus or minus, was divided by the morning rate. Anything above the zero line, therefore, indicates that the morning rate was higher than the afternoon rate by the percentage shown. Anything below the zero line indicates that the morning rate was lower than the afternoon rate by the percentage shown.

Here, too, the investigators reasoned that in order to prove relief from fatigue, it had to be demonstrated that there was more fatigue during periods of standard working conditions than in those periods in which changes in working conditions had been made. More specifically, it was thought (1) that the morning rate would be higher than the afternoon rate if fatigue were cumulative within the day, and (2) that if fatigue did depress the afternoon rate, any change designed to offset fatigue should result in lessening the difference between afternoon and morning rates. In terms of periods, this meant that morning average hourly output should exceed afternoon average hourly output to a greater degree in Periods II, III, and XII, when fatigue was more likely to occur, than in any other period. Likewise, the greatest im-

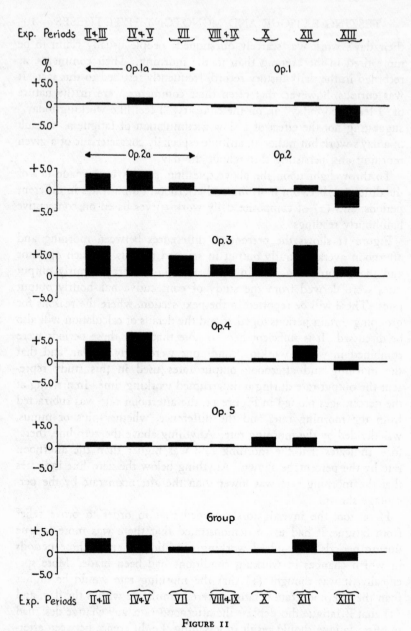

FIGURE 11

AMOUNT BY WHICH THE MORNING OUTPUT RATE EXCEEDS OR FALLS SHORT OF THE
AFTERNOON RATE, EXPRESSED AS A PERCENTAGE OF THE MORNING RATE

RELAY ASSEMBLY TEST ROOM

provement was to be expected in Periods VIII and IX, with Periods VII, X, and XIII tied for second place.

It is apparent, from examining the group curve in Figure 11, that the morning rate exceeds the afternoon rate in Periods II and III by an average of 3.3 per cent. In Periods VIII and IX this difference drops to an average of 0.3 per cent. In Period XII, when working conditions were relatively adverse, the average difference mounts to 2.9 per cent. Although all these percentage differences are very small, the variations which occur are strictly in accordance with the fatigue hypothesis. There are, however, certain contradictory changes.

First, in Periods IV and V the group average percentage difference between morning and afternoon rates is 3.9 per cent, whereas it is 3.3 per cent in Periods II and III. In other words, if any significance can be attached to these figures at all, there is as much indication of fatigue in Periods IV and V as in Periods II and III. Inasmuch as rest pauses were first introduced in Periods IV and V, a tendency in the opposite direction was expected. A common way of explaining this contradiction is to say that perhaps the rest pauses had not been in effect long enough for the operators to derive much benefit from them. In view of the fact that there was a general increase in average hourly output during Periods IV and V, this argument assumes that the operators were stimulated to work faster even though they may not have had time to adjust, physiologically, to the better conditions of work. Their increases in output, therefore, must have been accompanied by an increase in fatigue. This explanation is highly questionable.[1]

The second and most striking contradiction is the pronounced relative increase in the afternoon rate for all operators during Period XIII. During this period the group average afternoon rate exceeds the morning rate by an average of 1.6 per cent. Operator 3 is the only one whose morning rate is higher, but even for her the difference is less than in any preceding period. It is difficult to reconcile this contradiction with the fatigue hypothesis. At best, the fatigue hypothesis might

---

[1] It is frequently claimed in the literature on industrial fatigue (cf. Viteles, op. cit., Ch. XXII) that the organism adjusts slowly to changes in conditions of work. Where the change is such that a learning factor is involved, this seems plausible. It is questionable, however, when the change consists simply of a rest pause or shortened hours of work. The only experimental evidence of a physiological nature that has come to the authors' attention shows that the organism responds very quickly to a rest immediately after exercise. The facts usually cited in support of the opposite view consist of output data alone with no experimental evidence of corresponding organic changes to support them. The latter are inferred from the former and, strictly speaking, should be viewed not as fact but as hypothesis.

explain equal morning and afternoon rates, but it cannot account for a higher afternoon rate on this kind of work.

To summarize, although there is considerable evidence in the morning and afternoon output data to support the case for relief from accumulation of fatigue within the working day, there are several important observations which cannot be reconciled with this interpretation. Before drawing any conclusion, it might be well to examine the composite daily work curves. From them a more definite picture of the operators' performance throughout the morning and afternoon can be obtained.

Variations in Rate of Output during a Composite Working Day

The Construction of Composite Daily Work Curves

The composite daily work curves shown in Figure 12 A–C are based upon readings taken from the numerical counter.[1] These readings were taken for all operators every 30 minutes throughout the working day and covered the entire period of the test up until March 8, 1932. The perforated tapes provided a source from which data could be derived for shorter time intervals, but use of these data was limited by the practical difficulty of counting the perforations.

The records derived from the numerical counter contained two kinds of errors. The first arose from the fact that the counter recorded only completed relays. The reading for a particular interval might be off any fraction of a relay. If, however, the outputs for any interval were averaged for a large number of days (40 to 50), such errors would tend to cancel out. For the purposes of this study errors arising in this way were negligible.

The second source of error was in the routine task of recording the readings every half-hour. The clerk to whom this task was assigned had all his time fully occupied, and it was only reasonable to assume that occasionally a reading was taken a minute or so late. Unfortunately, there was no way of correcting for errors of this sort. Furthermore, the readings had to be recorded for five operators, and human limitations prevented taking these readings simultaneously. Errors of this kind were mitigated by the fact that the readings for the different operators were taken in the same sequence each time, and that approximately the same time lapse occurred between the first and last readings. The interval between readings for any one operator, therefore, would very closely approximate one half-hour, although the read-

[1] See p. 25.

ings for all five operators might not include exactly the same half-hour.

A different kind of limitation was that imposed by the length of the time interval chosen. Many investigators, in constructing work curves, prefer shorter intervals, ranging from five to fifteen minutes, on the ground that the shorter the time interval, the more sensitive the work curve is to variations in the output rate. Short-time variations will disclose the presence of factors which are not apparent when longer intervals are used.

On the other hand, there are certain arguments in favor of the longer interval. Inasmuch as in these studies the chief interest lay in detecting evidences of fatigue as a major factor limiting output, the use of a very short time interval might obliterate the more general tendencies of the daily work curve. If minor variations were wiped out, the presence or absence of fatigue might be brought out more strikingly. Another argument in favor of the longer interval is that

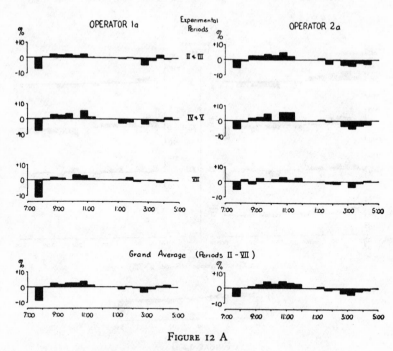

FIGURE 12 A

HALF-HOURLY OUTPUT RATIO, EXPRESSED AS A PERCENTAGE DEVIATION FROM THE OPERATOR'S MEAN RATE OVER THE PERIOD INVOLVED

RELAY ASSEMBLY TEST ROOM

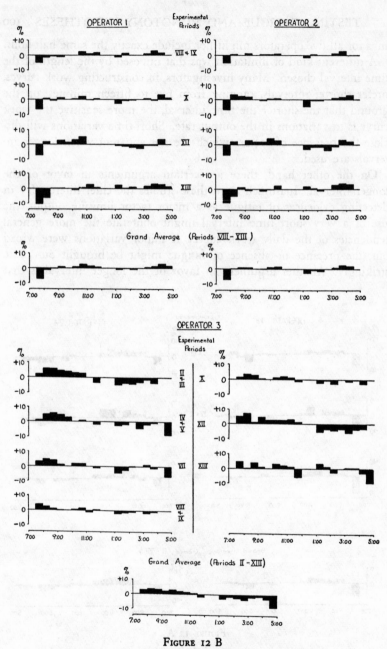

FIGURE 12 B

HALF-HOURLY OUTPUT RATIO, EXPRESSED AS A PERCENTAGE DEVIATION FROM THE
OPERATOR'S MEAN RATE OVER THE PERIOD INVOLVED

RELAY ASSEMBLY TEST ROOM

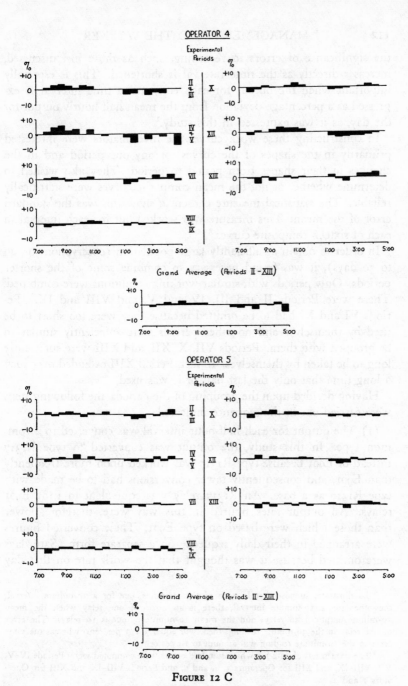

FIGURE 12 C

HALF-HOURLY OUTPUT RATIO, EXPRESSED AS A PERCENTAGE DEVIATION FROM THE
OPERATOR'S MEAN RATE OVER THE PERIOD INVOLVED

RELAY ASSEMBLY TEST ROOM

the significance of errors in recording, such as those just discussed, increases directly as the time interval is shortened. This is especially important when the output for each consecutive time interval is expressed as a percentage deviation from the mean half-hourly output for the day, as it was expressed in this study.[1]

In constructing these work curves the investigators were interested primarily in the shapes of the curves for any one period and in the changes in their shapes from period to period. They also wished to determine whether or not the mean composite curves were statistically reliable. The statistical measure chosen to show this was the standard error of the mean. This measure was worked out for each interval in each of sixteen composite curves.[2]

In order to obtain a sufficiently large population (observations on 40 to 50 days), it was found necessary to combine some of the shorter periods. Only periods with similar working conditions were combined. These were Periods II and III, IV and V, and VIII and IX.[3] Periods VI and XI had to be omitted because they were too short to be used by themselves and no other periods were sufficiently similar to be grouped with them. Periods VII, X, XII, and XIII were sufficiently long to be taken by themselves. In fact, Period XIII extended over such a long time that only the last half of it was used.

Having decided upon the grouping of the periods, the following steps were carried out in the sequence indicated:

(1) The output for each half-hour interval was converted to a common type. In this study, the output was converted to type R1317 instead of E901 because type R1317 was worked upon more frequently than E901, and consequently fewer conversions had to be made with type R1317 as a base. An R1317 relay was equivalent to 1.101 E901 relays. All output rates figured in this way were, therefore, lower than those which were based on type E901. These converted figures were arranged in their daily sequence on a separate form. Saturdays were omitted because it was thought that the work rate on that day

---

[1] To illustrate, suppose that in each of two readings, one for a 30-minute interval, the other for a 10-minute interval, there is an error of one relay when the mean 30-minute output is 30 relays and the mean 10-minute output is 10 relays. The error of one relay in the 30-minute reading, then, will equal 3 1/3 per cent, whereas the same error in the 10-minute reading will amount to 10 per cent.

[2] The sixteen sets of data for which standard errors were computed were: Periods IV–V, VII, VIII–IX, and XIII for Operators 3, 4, and 5, and Periods VIII–IX and XIII for Operators 1 and 2.

[3] These combined periods will be referred to as Period II–III, Period IV–V, and Period VIII–IX.

was affected by interferences of a personal or social nature to a much greater extent than on other days of the week.

(2) All intervals during the day in which an operator stopped assembling relays were canceled. It will be recalled that records were kept of personal and repair time and other interruptions. Inasmuch as the exact time of the interruption was always noted, it was possible to relate these stoppages to the intervals in which they occurred. It would have been possible to calculate the output rate for such intervals by correcting for the time out, but such a procedure involved the assumption that the output rate for the whole interval was the same as for a part of the interval, which was probably as frequently untrue as it was true.

It so happened that most of the operators, when they took personal time out, did so during the terminal intervals of each work spell. The net effect of this was to reduce the population from which the composite figure for any one half-hour would be calculated so much that the whole half-hour interval had to be omitted from the composite curve. It is unfortunate, especially from the standpoint of a fatigue analysis, that this situation frequently occurred in the terminal intervals; yet some investigators are agreed that a low output at the very end of the spell should not be construed too literally in terms of fatigue. In fact, because of the many interferences which usually occur just before quitting time, it is questionable whether the terminal intervals should be considered in a fatigue analysis. Moreover, if fatigue is depressing the output rate, its presence should be detected before the closing intervals.

If a change of relay type occurred within an interval, the whole interval was omitted instead of attempting to prorate the output in proportion to the time spent on each type. If a change of type occurred at the beginning of an interval, but was unaccompanied by a change in the operator's jig, which would necessitate a short stoppage, the interval was not canceled.

In Period II–III repair and personal time records for several days were missing. To supply this deficiency, the perforated tapes were resorted to. These were marked off into intervals corresponding to the numerical register readings, and all intervals were canceled in which there was no record of a completed relay for approximately two consecutive minutes. Since the average time to complete one relay is approximately one minute, a lapse of about two minutes was assumed to indicate a stoppage. A comparison of the number of intervals canceled in this way with the number canceled in accordance with the ordinary records showed that many more were deleted when the tapes were used. The data for Period II–III, accordingly, are not strictly comparable with those for subsequent periods; yet any marked characteristics of the curves for Period II–III should be fairly reliable.

(3) Having corrected the output data for changes in relay type and for stoppages, the next step was to compute the figures which, when plotted, make up the graphs in Figure 12 A–C. Two different methods were used in arriving at these figures, a long method and a short method. The long method was used in the sixteen periods for which standard errors were computed.[1] The short method was used in all the remaining periods.[2]

---

[1] The method used in computing standard deviations, from which standard errors are derived, varied from the standard formula $\sigma = \sqrt{\dfrac{\Sigma d^2}{N}}$ in that a constant multiplying factor was substituted for the process of squaring the deviations and extracting the square root. The formula used was $\sigma = \dfrac{\Sigma d}{N}$ (1.253). Standard errors of the averages were computed in the usual way $\sigma_M = \dfrac{\sigma}{\sqrt{N}}$.

The step-by-step process used to compute the standard error was as follows:

(a) The daily mean half-hourly output was computed for each day included in the period. These daily means were, of course, based on those intervals which were not canceled.

(b) The readings for each interval within a day were subtracted from the daily mean. These deviations were then expressed as a percentage of the mean. Percentage deviations were used instead of absolute deviations to correct for whatever upward trend or shifting might have occurred in the rate of working from day to day within the period.

(c) All the percentage deviations occurring in any one interval, e.g., 7:30 to 8:00, were then summed up with respect to sign, and their mean obtained. This figure represented the average of the percentage deviations of the readings in that half-hour interval from their respective daily mean half-hourly output. It is these figures which, when plotted, make up the composite work curves shown in Figure 12 A–C.

(d) Next, the day-to-day percentage deviations in each interval were subtracted from their mean, i.e., the mean computed in (c), preparatory to computing the standard deviation or scatter of such readings. These deviations were then summed up without respect to sign, divided by the number of observations in the interval, and the quotient thus obtained was multiplied by the constant 1.253.

(e) Finally, the standard deviations, computed in (d), were divided by the square root of the number of observations in each interval. This gave the standard errors of the means computed in (c).

[2] The short method was as follows: After the half-hour data had been converted and corrected as described in (1) and (2) in text above, the procedure was:

(a) The absolute half-hour outputs in each interval, e.g., 7:30 to 8:00, for all the days included in each period were added and their mean obtained. These

The accuracy of the short method was tested by employing it on the same data used in the long process, and comparing the results. The two sets of data obtained for each of the sixteen periods in which this was tried were plotted by superimposing one upon the other. In all cases the two sets of graphs very nearly coincided. In no case was the difference sufficiently large to be of any significance in this study.[1]

The Reliability of the Mean Composite Daily Work Curves

The figures which, when plotted, constitute the curves shown in Figure 12 A–C are averages and are affected by the value of every observation upon which they are based. The question therefore arises: How reliable are they? Given another set of output data secured under the same conditions of work, how much is the mean of the additional sample likely to differ from the known mean of the sample studied? To answer this question standard errors[2] of the mean were used. These measures were computed for the mean of each half-hourly interval in the sixteen sets of data upon which the long method of arriving at the mean daily composite work curves had been used.

In this study, variations in rate of working from one half-hour to another were not regarded as significant unless they differed by ± 3 standard errors. This test, applied to the sixteen sets of data under consideration, showed that most of the variations in half-hour work rates

---

half-hour means for the intervals in the morning and afternoon work spells were summed up and averaged to obtain the morning and afternoon work rates previously discussed.

(b) The means obtained in (a) were then added together (i.e., the means of each half-hour interval in the composite day), and their mean was obtained.

(c) Each mean obtained in (a) was expressed as a percentage deviation from the mean obtained in (b). These percentage deviations corresponded to those obtained under (c) (footnote, p. 114).

[1] The short process could not be used in computing standard errors because it did not correct for day-to-day fluctuations in the average rate of working. In some of the periods there was an appreciable upward trend in output rate. If this trend were left in, the percentage deviations of the readings taken in the first and last part of the period would be exaggerated, while those in the middle part of the period would be too small. A fairly accurate way of correcting for trend and for fluctuations in daily output rates is to express each reading as a percentage deviation from its daily mean, as was done in the long method.

[2] The meaning of the standard error may be briefly indicated. When a distance equal to one standard error is laid off above and below the known mean, the chances are 2 to 1 that the mean of an additional sample, chosen at random, will lie within that range. When two standard errors are laid off above and below the known mean, the chances are 21 to 1 that the mean of an additional sample will lie within that range. The chances that the mean of another sample will deviate from the known mean by more than 3 standard errors is 1 to 369. It is practically certain, in other words, that the true mean lies within the range of ± 3 standard errors.

represented by these graphs were well within the range of chance variation; hence no significance could be attached to them. Only those points which differed widely, by at least 5 per cent, had statistical significance. Most of the curves for Operators 1, 2, 4, and 5 were well within the range designated by ± 3 standard errors and could, for the purposes of this analysis, be regarded as straight lines. The question of fatigue, therefore, was practically disposed of at the outset. Yet it might be well to examine the curves for each operator, to note their similarities and differences, and to observe those upward or downward movements in rate of working which are of obvious significance or are likely to be of significance.

Analysis of Mean Composite Daily Work Curves for Evidence of Fatigue

Operator 1A

The curves for this operator show a consistently low output rate during the first half-hour of the day, after which the output rate rises rapidly and is sustained throughout the morning spell. During the afternoon spell her output rate is also fairly uniform. None of these curves suggests fatigue.

Operator 2A

The curves for this operator are characterized by a relatively high, well-sustained output rate throughout the morning spell and a consistently lower rate during the afternoon spell. The fact that the curves remain substantially the same in each period indicates that the output changes cannot be attributed to relief from fatigue. Either the changes in output were accompanied by approximately the same fatigue effects, or the shape of the curves resulted from other forces.

Operators 1 and 2

The curves for these two operators are remarkably similar. They are characterized by a relatively low output rate during the first half-hour of the day, followed by a relatively high and consistently maintained rate throughout the remainder of the day. There is no suggestion of fatigue in any of these curves.

Operator 3

This operator's work curves not only approximate one another in shape, but they are distinctly different from those of any other operator in the group. The output for the first half-hour tends to be well above the mean for the day. The highest output in each period is reached during the first ninety minutes, after which the general tendency is downward throughout the morning spell. There is a distinctly downward trend throughout the afternoon spell only in Period XIII. In all the other periods the afternoon rate, though lower than the morning rate, is sustained on a fairly even plane, with an occasional sharp drop at the end of the spell.

It is at once evident that the shapes of these curves do not alter in accordance with improvements in working conditions. Periods IV–V and VII do not result in curves appreciably different from that for Period II–III. In fact, the general characteristics of this operator's work curves remain the same regardless of the experimental conditions under which she was working. Inasmuch as there is no general improvement in the shape of the curves, there is no evidence of relief from fatigue. That the curves tend to resemble fatigue curves in spite of improvements both in working conditions and in the output rate suggests that the basic tendency in this operator's rate of working throughout the day might not be a fatigue resultant.

Operators 4 and 5

With the exception of the curve for Operator 4 in Period IV–V, the curves for both these operators tend to oscillate about their means in both the morning and afternoon spells. Pronounced upward or downward trend in rate of working is completely lacking. The presence of fatigue or any other single factor presumed to have a characteristic, predictable effect upon the shape of the performance curve cannot be found.

Analysis of Mean Composite Daily Work Curves for Evidence of Monotony

Operator 1A

In Period II–III there is a marked drop between 2:30 and 3:00, followed by a rapid rise. This midafternoon drop is less marked in Period IV–V, after rest pauses were introduced, and disappears in Period VII. Furthermore, there is an improvement in the afternoon rate in Period VII as compared with Period II–III. Most of the evidence for this operator tends to substantiate the hypothesis that rest pauses brought about the increase in output by diminishing the monotony of the task.

Operator 2A

During the afternoon spell her rate tends to decrease until about 3:30, after which, in Period VII at least, there is a substantial recovery. At first glance one might suppose the afternoon sections of these curves to be indicative of monotony. It was reasoned, however, that if the increase in output following Period II–III were due to relief from monotony, there should have been a fairly marked improvement in the afternoon curve in Period IV–V, after rest pauses had been introduced.

Summary

An analysis of the composite daily work curves for each operator failed to support the hypothesis that relief from fatigue or monotony accounted for the changes in output from period to period. The curves for Operators 1, 2, 4, and 5 failed to show the presence of these factors in the periods in which they would most likely occur. Neither were there any marked changes in the shape of the output curves during those periods in which better working conditions prevailed. The resemblance to a fatigue curve in the case of Operator 3 and to a monotony curve in the case of Operator 2A was not very conclusive. In both cases the curves retained their essential characteristics irrespective of changes in conditions of work or in the output rate. The curves for Operator 1A alone tended to confirm the monotony hypothesis. In the case of this operator the resemblance to a monotony curve in Period II–III disappeared with the introduction of rest pauses, and this change was accompanied by an increase in the output rate.

Blood Pressure Readings in Relation to Output, Fatigue, and Efficiency

Early in the studies the experimenters realized the need of obtaining some quantitative measure of the organic changes which occurred in each operator throughout the working day. Only in this way could they obtain some idea of each girl's efficiency, i.e., her output in terms of the energy which she was expending to achieve that output. In industry, efficiency is likely to be confused with the actual amount of production and to be identified with high output rather than with a high output per unit of energy expenditure or a capacity to maintain physiological equilibrium as exertion increases.

Moreover, it had been found that changes in production throughout the day were alone insufficient to detect the presence or absence of fatigue. Without a corresponding knowledge of the diurnal organic changes taking place, it was difficult to appraise depressions in the work curve correctly. Were they manifestations of fatigue or of slacking off for some other reason?

Naturally, an index of organic change had to be found which would be suitable for use in the factory, involving simple apparatus and disturbing the normal working environment as little as possible. Blood pressure readings seemed to offer the best possibility. Studies had shown that the pulse product [1] was a rough but sufficiently accurate measure of organic balance. It correlated with oxygen consumption, it increased with the amount of energy used in muscular work, and it also increased in emotion and in efforts of attention.[2]

Lovekin showed that ". . . the height and fluctuations of the pulse

---

[1] The difference between the systolic and diastolic pressures, multiplied by the pulse rate, and divided by 100.

[2] Lovekin, O. S., "The Quantitative Measurement of Human Efficiency under Factory Conditions," *Journal of Industrial Hygiene*, Vol. XII, 1930, pp. 99–120, 153–167.

product, combined with production records, can be used to distinguish variations in efficiency when comparing departments, workers, or different periods in the day."[1] Skilled and efficient work was associated in general with a high output and a low and regular pulse product. Lack of equilibrium in work could be detected by an unduly high and irregular pulse product. If, in turn, this irregularity of pulse product was accompanied by low output, fatigue was very likely to be present. To put it more exactly, an increasing pulse product accompanied by a decreasing output would offer a rough but fairly reliable indication of fatigue. A high output and a high pulse product would indicate strenuous but not necessarily efficient work. Low production with a low pulse product would indicate sluggish but not necessarily inefficient work.

In interpreting the blood pressure curves of individual workers, Lovekin pointed out the need for making certain corrections:

There are certain diurnal fluctuations . . . that appear in the average curves with considerable regularity. Perhaps the most pronounced of these is the rise in pulse product due to eating. This is most noticeable after lunch, but because of the fact that many workers come to the factory in the morning with little or no breakfast it may also appear after a morning rest period, when they have had a chance to visit the canteen. The usual causes of an increased pulse product after meals are a higher systolic pressure, an increased pulse rate, and a lower diastolic pressure. The increased pulse rate is almost always found; the other changes are not so uniform. . .

The average curve for pulse product tends to drop throughout the day, as a result of the wearing off of the effect of meals, and of the natural reaction to the day's work.[2]

A correction, therefore, must be made for the variations in blood pressure during the working day resulting from the taking of food.

In comparing the curves of individuals, Lovekin says, "the average height will vary not only according to the demands of the job, but also with the constitutional differences between workers."[3] These constitutional differences must also be taken into account when interpreting pulse product readings.

Blood pressure readings were taken on the five operators in the Relay Assembly Test Room each hour of three working days, April 25, 1928, April 26, 1928, and November 14, 1928. The first two days occurred in Period X, when there were two rest periods, fifteen minutes in the morning with lunch and ten minutes in the afternoon. The last

[1] Ibid., p. 167.   [2] Ibid., pp. 158–159.   [3] Ibid., p. 160.

day, November 14, 1928, occurred in Period XII, when there were no rests or lunch. Figure 13 shows the pulse product readings and the output for each operator throughout each of these three days. From this figure it is apparent that:

(1) The readings for April 25 show that the pulse products of Operators 2, 3, 4, and 5 are all fairly low throughout the day. The average of the afternoon readings for these operators tends to be lower than the average of the morning readings. Operator 1's pulse product tends to be higher than that of the other operators.

Although there are hour-to-hour variations in the pulse product of each operator, these changes do not consistently relate to changes in output in such a way as to suggest fatigue. In no case is a declining output rate accompanied by a high and rising pulse product. For two operators, 3 and 4, a fairly constant output rate throughout the afternoon is accompanied by a slowly rising pulse product; but the absolute level of their pulse product is lower than in the morning, and hence this does not suggest fatigue.

(2) The readings for April 26 do not differ appreciably from those for April 25. Those for Operators 2, 3, 4, and 5 continue to be low and for Operators 4 and 5, at least, quite uniform. Operator 1's pulse product is again higher than the others and mounts steadily from nine in the morning until two o'clock in the afternoon, when it begins to decrease in spite of the fact that output increases.

(3) In the readings for November 14, the day without rest periods, Operator 2 presents one of the best illustrations of efficient and skilled work, namely, a diminishing pulse product in the morning and in the afternoon, as output steadily advances through the day. Operator 1 has a steadier and lower pulse product on this day than on either of the two days when there were rest periods. The pulse product readings for this day, November 14, differ from the two days with rests chiefly in that the afternoon readings are on an average higher than the morning readings.

Any deductions from this evidence cannot be considered conclusive in view of the fact that the data included only the five operators on three days. Nevertheless, this limited evidence seemed to indicate that all the operators were working well within their physical capacities. Operators 2 and 4 both tended to have low pulse products which remained steady or decreased as their output increased. Operator 3 gave the appearance of being a more energetic and strenuous worker by the fact that her pulse product tended to rise when output increased. Operator 5's pulse product and output tended to be low, with slight variations, indicating slow and plodding but not necessarily inefficient work habits. Operator 1's pulse product was considerably higher than that of any of the operators, but this was a constitutional difference

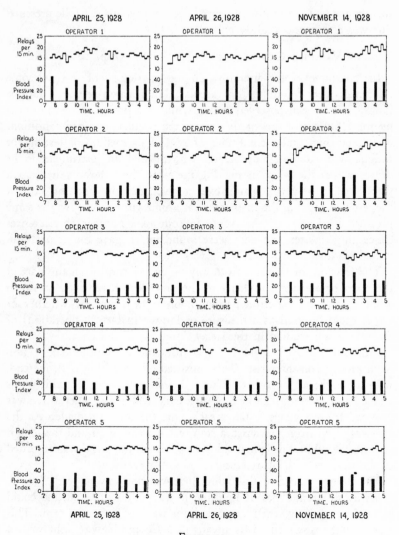

FIGURE 13

HOURLY VARIATIONS IN PULSE PRODUCT COMPARED WITH 15-MINUTE OUTPUT

RELAY ASSEMBLY TEST ROOM

mainly due to a high pulse pressure [1] because of a low diastolic pressure. She was a thin and slightly anaemic girl.

THE VASCULAR SKIN REACTION TEST IN RELATION TO FATIGUE

In looking over the literature on the physiology of fatigue, some references were found to the vascular skin reaction test as a fatigue index. It has been observed that a white line produced on the wrist by some blunt instrument disappears more quickly under conditions of fatigue than under conditions of rest. This method of testing for fatigue was elaborated by Ryan,[2] who devised an instrument to be drawn across the wrist in making the white line. Ryan relied upon the extension of a coil spring over a given distance and the skill of the tester in moving the instrument at a uniform rate to give the same pressure conditions on the wrist. In spite of a number of references concerning this test, no data were found which gave the actual individual readings.

The freedom of this test from any voluntary control on the part of the operator and the simplicity of the procedure made it seem worth while to attempt experimentation in order to determine whether or not it could be used as a measure of fatigue in factory operations of the type being studied in the Relay Assembly Test Room.

Professor Turner [3] devised a new instrument for producing a uniform pressure on the wrist. This consisted of a rod hinged at one end, with a weight at the other. This rod, the lower edge of which was formed into a round surface of necessary width and curvature, was dropped from a given distance each time the test was made. As the rod was lifted from the wrist, a stop watch was started and the length of time the white line remained discernible on the wrist was recorded to the nearest tenth of a second.

The disappearance of this white line was not easy to read, but, by studying different types of lighting, it was found that the line could be read most easily when a purple light was cast upon the arm. This type of light was secured by means of a Cooper-Hewitt light with a standard C-blue filter such as is used for photographic purposes. This modification of lighting made it easier to determine the end point at which the white line completely disappeared and gave somewhat

[1] The difference between the systolic and diastolic blood pressures.

[2] Ryan, A. H., "The Quantitative Measurement of General Fatigue," *American Journal of Physiology*, Vol. 45, 1918, p. 537.

[3] Dr. C. E. Turner, Professor of Biology and Public Health at the Massachusetts Institute of Technology, was one of the chief advisers of the test room investigators. It was under his direction that most of the early statistical studies were made.

longer readings than would have been obtained under ordinary light.

There are two types of readings which can be made from vascular skin reaction tests. When pressure is first applied to the skin, a sharp white line appears which lasts for less than three seconds. A few seconds after this white line disappears, another faint white line appears which lasts for several seconds. The figures given in this study show only the time taken for the first white line to disappear.

With these improvements in method, these tests were given to the five operators for the seven working weeks in Period XI (July 2 to September 1, 1928). Five readings were made for each operator 30 minutes after starting work in the morning and 30 minutes before closing time at night. Following the afternoon test, the operator fatigued the muscles of the hand and lower arm by closing the fingers of the hand tightly and then straightening them out several times. Following this local fatigue, a second series of five readings was made.

In spite of these improvements in the method of making vascular skin reaction tests, the successive individual readings varied widely. They commonly varied by 25 per cent, and occasionally the lowest reading would be not more than 50 per cent of the highest reading. It was at first thought that these variations in individual readings might be due to the subjective differences in determining when the end point was reached and in operating the stop watch, but further studies made by Professor Turner at the Massachusetts Institute of Technology, in which the disappearance of the white line was recorded by a motion picture camera, indicated the same variability and inconsistency with successive readings.

The averages of all morning readings and of both sets of afternoon readings over the period of seven weeks were figured for each operator and for the group. The probable error of the difference between the morning and afternoon averages was also computed. These figures are shown in Table X. It will be seen that the grand average of the morning readings was 1.71 seconds; that of the afternoon readings, 1.35 seconds; and that of the afternoon fatigue readings, 1.00 second. There was about as much difference between the afternoon fatigue test and the afternoon readings as between the morning and afternoon readings. In other words, the local fatigue produced by clenching the hand reduced the vascular skin reaction readings as much as the work of the whole day.

The investigators felt that these tests were not sufficiently exact to record slight differences in fatigue. Attempts to discover any relation between these readings and the daily variations in output were entirely unsuccessful. Furthermore, the variations in any particular set of readings made it clear that minor variations in the amount of fatigue could not be determined by this test. At the most, all that could be concluded from the readings was that some fatigue was developed during the day. How much fatigue was developed was problematical. In view of the

TABLE X

RESULTS OF VASCULAR SKIN REACTION TESTS
RELAY ASSEMBLY TEST ROOM
(July 2, 1928–September 1, 1928)

Operator	Average A.M. Reading	Average P.M. Reading	Average Fatigue Reading	Average Difference between A.M. and P.M.	Probable Error of Difference
	(sec.)	(sec.)	(sec.)	(sec.)	
1	1.68	1.33	.96	.35	.0211
2	1.79	1.36	1.14	.43	.0213
3	1.62	1.31	.91	.31	.0217
4	1.66	1.34	.94	.32	.0243
5	1.81	1.43	1.06	.38	.0275
Average	1.71	1.35	1.00	.36	.0104

fact that the local fatigue of the hand and wrist muscles following a brief period of exercise reduced the vascular skin reaction readings as much as they were reduced by the work of the day, it seemed reasonable to conclude that the amount was small, if not negligible.

SPEED TESTS IN RELATION TO FATIGUE

One of the routine procedures in the test room, lasting from July 9, 1929, to September 1, 1930, except for two short periods when it was discontinued, was timing with a stop watch the assembly cycle for one relay for each operator while working at her top speed. These timings took place at 10:30 in the morning and, until May 5, 1930, at 4:30 in the afternoon. On May 5, 1930, the stopping time of the operators was changed to 4:15, thereby necessitating a change in the time of the afternoon reading from 4.30 to 4:00 o'clock.

On September 1, 1930, the routine was slightly altered. The assembly cycles for three relays (not consecutive) for each operator were timed at 10:30 in the morning and at 4:00 in the afternoon, and the fastest of these three tests was recorded. This speed test procedure lasted until January 9, 1931.

From January 12 to November 20, 1931, the routine was again changed to timing the assembly of five consecutive relays. The assembly time for each of the five relays, as well as the total time elapsed during the assembly of the five relays, was recorded. These tests were also given at 10:30 in the morning and at 4:00 in the afternoon. An additional fact was recorded which subsequently proved to be of great value. Whenever an unexpected delay occurred in assembling any one relay, such as "wrong spring," "coil stuck," "pin fell," or ."bushing slipped," the cause of the delay was also recorded against the time taken to assemble that relay.[1] The results of these speed tests were intended to serve in two ways: (1) as an indication of fatigue, and (2) as a means of measuring the efficiency and improvement of the operators. In this section the tests will be discussed only in relation to fatigue.

It was the intention of the experimenters to place the morning test long enough after beginning work so that the operators would have gone through the "warming up" period, and to put the afternoon test early enough so that the operators would not be primarily concerned with quitting time. The assumption was that if fatigue were present, it would tend to slow up the speed in the afternoon.

The data in Table XI were collected after Period XIII and there-

TABLE XI

COMPARISON OF MORNING AND AFTERNOON SCORES IN SPEED TESTS
RELAY ASSEMBLY TEST ROOM
(August 19, 1929–January 6, 1931)

Operator	Number of Days Averaged	Average Speed in Minutes	
		Morning	Afternoon
1	229	.742	.736
2	239	.685	.683
3	234	.741	.751
4	238	.712	.713
5	125	.850	.861
5A	105	.830	.819

fore do not throw any light on the question of fatigue during the first two years of the test. They are included here chiefly because they illustrate another of the many methods the investigators used in testing for evidence of fatigue. Table XI gives a comparison between the

[1] These data were of great help to Prof. Whitehead in making some of his statistical studies on output rate and will be reported by him.

morning and afternoon speed tests. It is apparent that for Operators 1, 2, and 5A the average time required to assemble a relay was slightly less in the afternoon than in the morning. For the other three operators it was slightly more. In no case, however, was there an appreciable difference.

Figure 14 shows the averages of the speed tests for consecutive days of the week. The numbers next to each dot show the number of read-

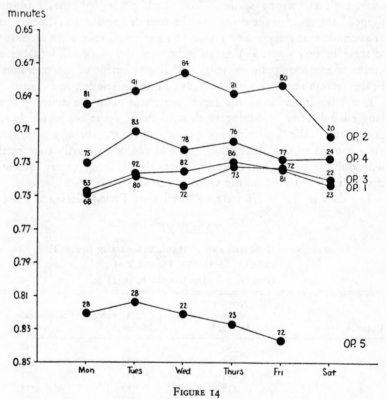

FIGURE 14

SPEED TESTS AVERAGED FOR CONSECUTIVE DAYS OF THE WEEK

RELAY ASSEMBLY TEST ROOM

ings upon which each average is based. These curves show wide differences in the speed of different operators. Operator 2 is well above and Operator 5 is well below the other operators. Slowest speeds tend to occur on Mondays and Saturdays. In this respect the speed tests substantiate the output studies, which showed less production on Mondays and Saturdays than on the intervening days. On the other days of the week, there is no pronounced trend in speed changes except for Operator 5. She achieves her greatest speed on Tuesday, with a continuous slowing up for the remainder of the week. This, by itself, is suggestive of cumulative fatigue during the week. However, in Operator 5's output curve for consecutive days of the week, production was so uniform during the first five days that no suggestion of fatigue could be found. The production data for this operator, in other words, do not imply increasing fatigue throughout the week, as the speed test data alone suggest.

CONCLUSION

On the basis of the studies reported in this chapter, the investigators concluded that these operators were at all times working well within their physical capacity. There is no evidence in support of the hypothesis that the increased output rate of all these operators during the first thirteen experimental periods was due to relief from fatigue. This hypothesis, which at first seemed most plausible, had to be abandoned.

With respect to the monotony hypothesis, no definite conclusion could be drawn. A curve resembling what is claimed to be a typical monotony curve was not encountered except in the case of Operator 1A. It was clearly understood, however, that monotony in work is primarily a state of mind and cannot be assessed on the basis of output data alone. Although the observer's records gave little evidence of boredom or apathy, it was believed that more exacting inquiries into the operators' attitudes should be made in order to warrant treating the available evidence as conclusive. Furthermore, monotony is subject to such a wide variety of interpretations that almost any improvement in mental attitude may be said to be due to relief from it. A careful statement of the kind of changes which had taken place in the attitudes of the operators, and of the relation of such changes to alterations in the work situation, seemed more urgent and more important than a decision as to whether or not monotony was being experienced in this or that degree. Inasmuch as the attitudes of the operators will be discussed fully in Chapter VIII, this whole subject may best be omitted here.

CHAPTER VI

TESTING THE EFFECTS OF WAGE INCENTIVE; THE SECOND RELAY ASSEMBLY GROUP AND THE MICA SPLITTING TEST ROOM

How much did the change in the method of payment introduced in the Relay Assembly Test Room during Period III contribute to the upward trend in output? The attempt to answer this question led to two separate studies known as the Second Relay Assembly Group and the Mica Splitting Test Room.

It will be remembered that while the test room operators were in the regular relay assembly department they participated in the earnings of a group of approximately one hundred employees. Obviously, since the group was so large, the output of any one worker was not directly reflected in her weekly wages. As an additional incentive, however, the group payment plan was supplemented by the "bogey" system, which rated each worker's performance in terms of an output standard. The individual's rating in terms of the bogey was used as a basis for determining her hourly rate of pay.

Each of these systems was altered in the Relay Assembly Test Room. The group payment plan was altered in Period III by forming the members of the test room into a separate group for the purpose of payment. The effect of the bogey was nullified by telling the operators to work at a comfortable and natural pace. It is very probable, of course, that the bogey continued to function in the sense that each operator had in mind some such standard of what constituted in the eyes of the company a "good day's work." But the change from a large group to a small one for the purpose of payment was a major change. It meant that each operator's earnings would fluctuate more directly in proportion to her output. Her monetary incentive was appreciably enhanced.

It is regrettable, perhaps, that the test room experiment, which had for its purpose the study of the influence of factors other than method of remuneration, had to be complicated by this extra variable. But this very same error, according to Farmer, is inevitable in many industrial investigations, especially in the field of time and motion study. A common difficulty encountered in such studies is the simultaneous introduction of a new system of work and of a new wage incentive "calculated to stimulate increased effort and to penalise any falling away from the [new] standard that has been set." [1] Obviously, when another variable is introduced, it is not valid to conclude that the resulting increase in output is due to the new system of work alone.

In two respects, however, the test room studies differed from those referred to by Farmer. In the first place, the change in the method of payment was the first change made and was not introduced simultaneously with any other factor. Not until the operators had worked under the new payment system for eight weeks were any other changes imposed. In the second place, the test room studies were not devised to increase production. Rather, they were designed to test the effects of changes in working conditions, the factor of wage incentive remaining constant. In other words, the inquiry was not concerned at first with comparing the test room with the regular department, but rather with studying the output changes occurring in the test room itself and relating them to the experimentally imposed conditions. It was only after output rose, irrespective of the particular experimental conditions, that the question of wage incentive had to be reopened and re-examined.

In order to study the effect of the change in payment, two experiments were conducted. The aim of the first experiment was to reproduce the test room situation only in respect to the one factor of method of payment, using another group of operators. Since method of payment was to be the only alteration from the usual situation, it was thought that any marked changes in output could be reasonably related to this factor. In the second experiment, the test room situation was to be duplicated in all respects except for the change in pay incentive. If, in this latter group, output showed a trend similar to that noted in the Relay Assembly Test Room, it would suggest that the change in wage incentive was not the dominant factor in the situation.

THE SECOND RELAY ASSEMBLY GROUP

The first experiment was performed on a group of operators known as the Second Relay Assembly Group. Five experienced relay assemblers were selected by the foreman of the regular department and formed into a special group to be paid separately from the rest of the department. This change in wage incentive, identical with that introduced in the test room at the beginning of Period III, was made on

[1] Farmer, Eric, "Time and Motion Study," *Great Britain Industrial Fatigue Research Board*, Report No. 14, London, 1923, p. 25.

November 26, 1928. Before the study began, these five operators had been scattered throughout the assembly group, but for purposes of the study and especially to facilitate record taking, they were moved to adjacent positions at a bench in the regular department. No other changes were made; supervision and general working environment remained the same.

This experiment continued for a period of nine weeks, at the end of which it became necessary to return the operators to the old method of payment. Output records were continued for a few weeks, however, until the operators included in the study were transferred to other work. There were three periods into which the study can be divided:

(1) A base period [1] consisting of five weeks between August 27 and September 29, 1928.

(2) The experimental period, during which the method of payment was altered, and which consisted of nine weeks between November 26, 1928, and January 26, 1929.

(3) A period of approximately seven weeks immediately following the return of the operators to the old system of payment.

Changes in Output

Figure 15 shows the average hourly output by weeks for each of the operators in the Second Relay Assembly Group during the entire time for which records were obtained. From the curves it can be seen that the output rate for each operator was higher during the experimental period than during the base period, although it is doubtful if much statistical significance can be attached to the changes in rates for Operators R_1 and R_2. When the old method of payment was restored, the hourly rates for Operators R_1, R_2, and R_3 fell quickly.

In Table XII the amounts of these changes are expressed as percentages of the average number of relay parts per hour assembled by each girl during the base period. The individual increases in output, as measured by comparing the experimental period with the base period, ranged from 8.3 per cent in the case of Operator R_1 to 17.4 per

[1] In planning the experiment it had been the intention of the investigators to take as a base, against which subsequent output changes could be measured, the output records for a period of one or two weeks immediately before the change in wage incentive. However, during the third week of the experimental period, it became necessary for the operators to work overtime: one extra hour on Mondays, Tuesdays, Thursdays, and Fridays, and three and one-half hours longer on Saturdays. For this reason, the base period record was selected from a period having similar overtime conditions; it covered five weeks from August 27 to September 29, 1928. In the case of Operator R_1 and Operator R_2, output records for only two weeks and one week respectively during this period were obtainable, as they were doing miscellaneous work at the time.

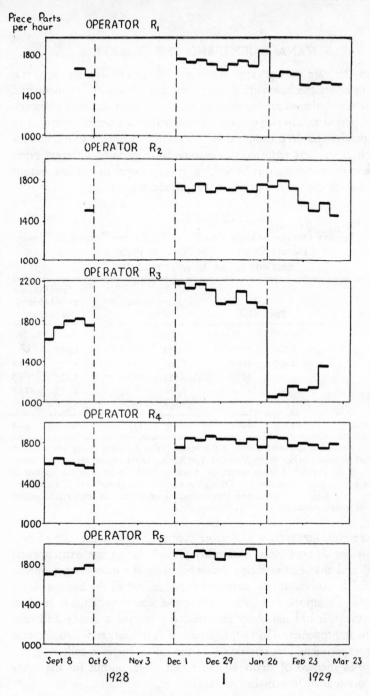

FIGURE 15

AVERAGE HOURLY OUTPUT PER WEEK

SECOND RELAY ASSEMBLY GROUP

131

cent in the case of Operator R_3, while the group average was 12.6 per cent above the base period. After the old method of payment had been restored, the output in all cases was lower than during the experimental period and in two cases it fell below the base period figure. The most precipitous drop occurred in the output of Operator R_3, but inasmuch as she was required to assemble from 50 to 60 different types of relays daily during this period,[1] a direct comparison of her output with that of the other operators was impossible.

TABLE XII

AVERAGE HOURLY OUTPUT IN EACH PERIOD AND PERCENTAGE CHANGE IN AVERAGE
HOURLY OUTPUT FROM PERIOD TO PERIOD *

SECOND RELAY ASSEMBLY GROUP

Operator		Base Period		Experimental Period		After Return to Old Method of Payment	
		A.H.O.	%	A.H.O.	%	A.H.O.	%
R_1	. . . . . .	1,605	100.0	1,739	108.3	1,580	98.4
R_2	. . . . . .	1,477	100.0	1,703	115.3	1,617	109.4
R_3	. . . . . .	1,749	100.0	2,053	117.4	1,133	64.7
R_4	. . . . . .	1,595	100.0	1,810	113.5	1,795	112.5
R_5	. . . . . .	1,745	100.0	1,894	108.5	. . . .	. . . .
Average	. . . . . .	1,634.2	100.0	1,839.8	112.6	1,531.3	96.2

* The method of recording output in the Second Relay Assembly Group was different from that employed in the Relay Assembly Test Room. Instead of expressing the output in terms of the number of relays assembled, it was expressed in terms of the number of relay parts assembled. This method, although not so accurate as the method used in the test room, eliminated the difficulties encountered in attempting to convert the output figures to a common basis.

There was, however, a noticeable contrast between the rate of output for the Second Relay Assembly Group during the experimental period and that of the Relay Assembly Test Room operators during Period III. Although the output of the members of the Second Relay Assembly Group showed an immediate rise after the change in method of payment, it did not show any tendency toward a steady and continuous improvement. In fact, Operator R_3's output tended to decrease as the experiment progressed. Once the initial increase following the change in method of payment had taken place, output for the other operators tended to remain constant.

[1] The daily number of changes of relay types per operator in the regular department was about 15.

There were, however, two important qualifications. In the first place, because of the short duration of the experiment it was difficult to say what changes might have taken place in the direction of the output curve had the experiment continued longer. In the second place, the absence of comparable data for the two months directly preceding the experimental period made it difficult to say just how immediate the increase in output was. Output rates extending over a period of months often tend to exhibit gradual swings either in an upward or downward direction. The base period curves for Operators R_3 and R_5 show a definite upward trend; the curve for R_4 is slightly downward, while the base period data for the other two operators were insufficient to show any direction. In view of these considerations, therefore, it is difficult to conclude whether the increase in output was an immediate response to the change in wage incentive or was merely representative of the top level of a more or less normal upward swing.

Further Results and Conclusions

In general, the findings from the Second Relay Assembly Group tended to substantiate the hypothesis that the formation of a small group for the purpose of determining piecework earnings was an important factor in the Relay Assembly Test Room performance. That the output remained on a rather constant level throughout this experiment, however, suggested that the subsequent increases in the test room throughout the course of the studies could not be explained in terms of this factor alone.

Further observations about the Second Relay Assembly Group, although they shed no additional light on the question of wage incentive, proved to be of significance in connection with subsequent experimental studies. After a few weeks of the experiment, the foreman began to report to the investigators that the presence of the special group in his department was causing considerable friction among the other employees, as they too wanted similar consideration. This difficulty continued to become more and more acute until finally it became necessary, in order to preserve the department's morale, to return the operators to the regular method of payment.

The way in which the operators in the Second Relay Assembly Group felt about this study could not, of course, be accurately observed and recorded, as the mere presence of an observer would have introduced a factor which the investigators wished to avoid. But one source of information, the comments of the test room operators, threw some light on the question. Even though the test room operators were isolated from the regular department, old friendships and the custom-ary gossip served to keep them informed of events in the regular depart-ment. Moreover, the duties of the layout operator required that she go to the regular department quite frequently, and thus she was able to keep in touch with current topics and report them to the girls in the test room. It was with reference to such an occasion that the following entry appeared in the daily history record on November 27, 1928, the second day after the small group method of payment had been started in the special group:

The layout operator reported that there was quite a lively interest being taken by members of Group 2 [the Second Relay Assembly Group] in the output of Group 3 [the Relay Assembly Test Room].[1]

The Mica Splitting Test Room

In the second experiment, called the Mica Splitting Test Room, the objective was to create a new test room situation wherein changes in working conditions similar to those imposed in the Relay Assembly Test Room could be introduced without changing the wage incentive method. This was accomplished by selecting a group of operators who were working on individual piecework and segregating them in a small room (see Figure 16).

Two secondary objectives were considered in planning the Mica Splitting Test Room. One of the factors which had rendered an in-terpretation of the results in the Relay Assembly Test Room difficult had been the short duration of each of the experimental periods. In this new test room the periods were to be lengthened so that sufficient time would elapse in each period to assure a complete adjustment to the experimental change before a new condition was imposed. Sec-ondly, it was desired to study the effects of overtime. The company had been operating for some time at full capacity, and many shop departments had had to resort to the use of overtime as a method of meeting schedules. The results of the Relay Assembly Test Room had shown that the operators almost invariably increased their effi-ciency when the weekly hours of work were shortened; consequently, there was some doubt concerning the value of overtime. The chief objective, then, of the Mica Splitting Test Room was to study the effects of the change in the wage incentive in the Relay Assembly Test

[1] While, at the time, such findings as these were considered to be of minor importance and external to the point in question, results of later studies tended to emphasize their significance. They will therefore be reconsidered after these subsequent studies have been reported (Chapter XXV).

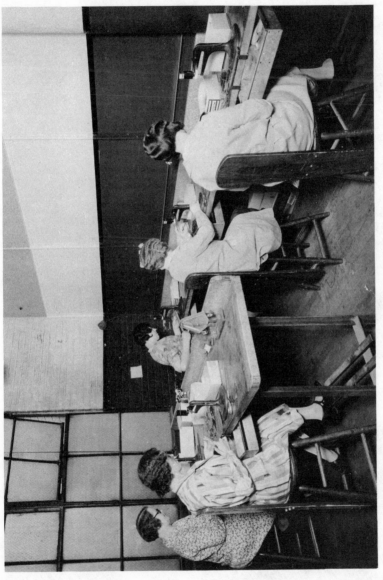

FIGURE 16

PHOTOGRAPH OF MICA SPLITTING TEST ROOM

Room; secondary objectives, however, were concerned with the effects of longer experimental periods and of overtime.

The Job of Mica Splitting

The job selected was performed by women employees who were paid on an individual piecework basis. It was highly repetitive in nature, but required considerable skill and consequently was well paid. Because it combined relatively high earnings with work which was rather easy from the standpoint of physical exertion, mica splitting was considered one of the most desirable shop jobs for women available in the Hawthorne plant. It afforded a steady flow of work, and the equipment employed was easily portable.

The mica came to the operators in blocks approximately two to four inches wide, three to five inches long, and 3/32 of an inch thick. From these blocks, the operators were required to split off thin layers or sheets, a few thousandths of an inch thick, to serve as insulating material in telephone apparatus. The first operation was to slide the block of mica against an adjustable triangular knife blade fastened to the bench in front of the worker. After this operation, a needle, a sharp-pointed instrument about ten inches long, was used to split the mica into thinner pieces. After the mica was split to an appropriate thickness, it was tested by inserting it into a lever-type indicating gauge. If the indicating needle on the gauge showed the mica sheet to be within the required dimensions (.0012 to .0016 of an inch), the rough edges were trimmed with scissors to prevent the sheet from cracking. The operation was then complete. This work required precise movements and close attention. Experience had shown that the learning process sometimes continued for two or three years.

Each day's output for each operator was inspected by a sampling method. An inspector selected a random sample of an operator's output and tested it. If five per cent or more of the split pieces of mica were found to be defective, the entire day's output was returned to the operator, who would then regauge the entire lot and repair any defective pieces. Pieces which were already too thin had to be thrown away. Following inspection, the output was hand-counted by a special counting group. The operator was paid on the basis of her output counted in this way. The test study was also made on the basis of these figures; no special measuring device similar to the one in the Relay Assembly Test Room was used.

Selection of Operators

At first a group of five experienced mica splitters were chosen at random, but when these operators were asked if they wished to participate in the study only two agreed to do so. These two were then asked to select three others. This was the same method employed in selecting the original Relay Assembly Test Room operators. When the group was thus chosen, meetings were held with the superintendent, similar to those held with the relay group, and detailed plans were discussed with the operators.

Table XIII gives the age, nationality, education, and work experience of each of these five operators.

EXPERIMENTAL CONDITIONS AND MAJOR HAPPENINGS FOR EACH PERIOD

In general, the situation in the Mica Splitting Test Room duplicated that in the Relay Assembly Test Room. The operators were isolated from their regular work group and placed in a small room provided for the purpose of the test. Supervisory duties, while nominally in charge of the regular foreman, were for the most part performed by the observer. The observer's duties were identical with those of the observer in the Relay Assembly Test Room. The records kept were also essentially the same, with some modification due to the fact that the output was not recorded mechanically. Periodic physical examinations were given these operators, but they were not so frequent as in the Relay Assembly Test Room.

The study was officially begun on October 22, 1928, when the operators were moved to the test room. Overtime hours, which had been in force for some time in the regular department, were continued in the test room. No changes were introduced in the first five weeks after moving to the test room, in order to allow the operators ample time to become accustomed to the new environment. Two ten-minute rest pauses were then instituted, one at 9:30 A.M. and the other at 2:30 P.M., and these rest pauses remained standard throughout the experiment. On June 17, 1929, another change was made: the overtime hours were discontinued and the operators were returned to the standard working week of 5½ days, 8¾ hours on 5 days, with 4½ hours on Saturday. On May 19, 1930, the final change in working conditions was made, not as an experiment but rather because of the general business depression. The length of the working day was reduced to 8 hours, and Saturday work was eliminated entirely. These conditions continued until the

TABLE XIII

COMPOSITION OF THE GROUP
MICA SPLITTING TEST ROOM

Operator	Age at Beginning of Test	Birthplace	Birthplaces of Parents		Education	Date of Employment	Work Experience before Oct., 1928	
			Father	Mother			Other Companies	Western Electric Company
M₁	39	Massachusetts	U.S.A.	Austria-Hungary	Grade school	Nov., 1919	Office work	Punch press op. Benchwork Mica spl., 5 yrs.
M₂	41	Illinois	Germany	U.S.A.	"	April, 1917	Factory, 18 mos.	Punch press op. Benchwork Mica spl., 2½ yrs.
M₃	28	Wisconsin	Germany	Germany	"	Aug., 1919	Factory, 4 mos.	Punch press op. Benchwork Mica spl., 4 yrs.
M₄	37	Germany	Germany	Germany	"	May, 1909 June, 1921	Factory and office work	Punch press op. Mica spl. and instruc. in mica spl., 12 yrs.
M₅	18	Austria-Hungary	Czecho-slovakia	Austria-Hungary	7th grade	Jan., 1927 Feb., 1928	Store and factory work	Punch press op. Mica spl., 1 yr.

study was terminated on September 13, 1930, when the mica splitting
job was discontinued. The study, therefore, covered approximately two
years and was divided into five periods. Table XIV summarizes these
periods and the working conditions in each.

PERIOD I

(August 27, 1928–October 20, 1928)

In order to furnish a base record against which subsequent changes
might be compared, output data for each of the test operators were
secured for an eight-week period while the operators were still in the
regular department.

TABLE XIV

SCHEDULE OF TEST PERIODS

MICA SPLITTING TEST ROOM

Period Number	Special Feature	Dates Included	Duration in Weeks
I	In regular department; overtime, no rests	8–27–28 to 10–20–28	8
II	Moved to test room; overtime, no rests	10–22–28 to 11–24–28	5
III	Overtime with two 10-min. rests	11–26–28 to 6–15–29	29
IV	No overtime, two 10-min. rests	6–17–29 to 5–17–30	48
V	8-hour day, 5-day week, two 10-min. rests	5–19–30 to 9–13–30	17

In the Mica Splitting Test Room study there was, with one exception, no problem of transposing the output figures to a common basis.
Some variations in the type of work did occur in the regular department, but throughout the major part of the test only one type of work
was encountered. A variation in the type of work was a difference in
the thickness to which the mica sheets were split. Naturally, it was
much quicker to turn out relatively thick pieces than very thin ones,
and consequently the piece rate per one hundred pieces was higher
when the finished pieces were thin than when they were thick. The
type which predominated throughout the study carried limits of .0012
to .0016 of an inch; that is to say, the operators were required to split
the block mica into sheets with a thickness falling between these limits.
Although during the base period some of the operators occasionally

had to split mica to different specifications, by far the greatest part of their time was spent on the type which became standard in the test room. Therefore, only the output and time spent on the standard type of work were used in computing the average hourly output for Period I. During the last 26 weeks of the study, however, the operators were required to work on mica of different specifications, and the output had to be converted to one standard type of mica.[1]

During the base period a meeting of the operators, superintendent, and representatives of the research group was held. As in the first meeting with the Relay Assembly Test Room group, care was taken to explain fully the nature of the study, to convince the operators that "boosting" production was not its purpose, and to give the reasons for having rather frequent physical examinations. When the operators were asked if they wished to work the same amount of overtime as in the regular department, they were unanimously in favor of doing so.

Period II
(October 22, 1928–November 24, 1928)

During Period II, which included the first five weeks in the test room, no changes in working conditions were made. Overtime was continued as in the regular department, which meant a working week of 55½ hours arranged by working 9¾ hours on Monday, Tuesday, Thursday, and Friday, 8¾ hours on Wednesday, and 7¾ hours on Saturday. The operators were paid 50 per cent extra for overtime.

In Period II the operators became acquainted with the observer and with one another. Fairly early in the period they began to express a liking for the test room. Two reasons were given more frequently than others: "We like it better in the test room because it is quiet and we can work better"; "We get things here as soon as we ask for them and don't have to wait as we used to." The latter comment probably referred to the fact that the test room observer made every effort to comply with any reasonable request.

As the test became established, a "freer" atmosphere became more noticeable. Frequently, one or another of the operators stopped work to talk, and at times, on their own admission, they talked so much that it interfered with their work. However, this was not considered a problem either by the girls or by the investigators.

[1] See footnote, p. 146, for a description of how this was done.

Period III
(November 26, 1928–June 15, 1929)

On November 26, 1928, the first change in working conditions was made when two ten-minute rest pauses were introduced, one at 10:00 A.M. and the other at 2:30 P.M. Overtime hours were continued throughout Period III, and on seven occasions Sunday work was added. The operators were paid 100 per cent extra for Sundays and 50 per cent extra for overtime.

As in the Relay Assembly Test Room, there was an immediate acceptance of the rest pauses by the operators. The following comments, taken from the daily history record, were typical:

November 27, 1928
    Operator M_4: "Even though we have only had the rest pauses for one day, I would miss them if we didn't have them any more."

November 28, 1928
    Operator M_1: "The rest pauses give me a chance to lunch between meals."

January 21, 1929
    Operator M_1: "With the rest pauses I feel free to get up and walk around, while in the regular department I felt self-conscious if I left my bench."

Their attitude in the beginning of the test toward overtime was reflected in the following comment made by Operator M_4 on October 16, 1928:

"I don't mind overtime. I once worked overtime for five months and felt no ill effects."

Probably the opportunity for increased earnings fostered this attitude. But as overtime continued over a period of months this comparatively favorable attitude began to change. In January, after approximately five months of overtime, remarks like the following began to become more frequent:

January 17, 1929
    Operator M_2: "Overtime is all right for a couple of months, but we have had it since last September and it's beginning to get monotonous."

January 17, 1929
    Operator M_4: "I'm getting fed up on overtime. It gets monotonous after several months."

February 11, 1929
    Operator M₁: "I want Saturday afternoon off. That is all I want."

On May 27, 1929, the observer informed the operators that the over-time would be continued in the test room until August, providing the regular department did likewise, but that after that time the test room would return to regular hours regardless of the practice followed in the regular department. To this, Operator M₄ replied:

"That won't be so bad. We'll have something to look forward to, and we'll know definitely that we don't have to work and we can make plans."

There was a strong dislike of working on Sunday, as is apparent from the following comments:

December 28, 1928
    Operator M₁: (After being told of plans for working Sunday, December 30, 1928) "I don't know when I'll get caught up on my rest. I was just thinking how long I would sleep Sunday morning."

January 11, 1929
    Operator M₂: "I'm glad we aren't going to work Sunday."

February 14, 1929
    Operator M₃: (After being told of plans to work Sunday, February 17, 1929) "No rest for the wicked. I can't work Sunday because in the morning I have to sleep and in the afternoon I have to go downtown."

February 18, 1929
    Operator M₄: (In discussing low output) "That is because we worked yesterday [Sunday]. If they want us to work on Sunday, they may as well tell us to stay home on Monday. We're not here, that's all."

March 1, 1929
    Operator M₄: "I suppose we'll be working on Palm Sunday and Easter Sunday. We won't call it Sunday any more, we'll call it Slave Day. Well, girls, with this Sunday's pay I can make the last payment on my Rolls Royce."

PERIOD IV
(June 17, 1929–May 17, 1930)

Overtime was discontinued in the Mica Splitting Test Room on June 17, 1929, when the entire department to which the operators were attached returned to standard hours. This elimination of overtime came somewhat sooner than expected because of a reduction in the amount of mica required in the manufacturing program. No change was made in the rest period time; consequently, the only difference between Periods III and IV was with respect to overtime. Period IV continued for 48 weeks, but during the last 9 weeks there was a change made in the type of work for all the operators which consisted of their shifting to mica blocks which were comparatively easier to split. This proved to be more significant than it was thought to be at first and resulted in limiting the value of the output data for the final weeks of the study. More will be said of this later in a discussion of the output curves.

During Period IV certain events took place in connection with transferring a part of the mica splitting job from the Hawthorne plant to the Kearny plant, located in New Jersey. Similar transfers of work to the new plant at Kearny had been rather frequent in the few years previous to the test room study. In such cases, adjustments had to be made among the employees, which at best meant learning a new job and at worst a layoff. It had been customary to spread the transfers of work over a period of months so that there would be sufficient time in which to make the necessary adjustments. It was natural, therefore, for the employees to be alert for signs of such transfers and to entertain fears for the future.

The first event of this character which affected the Mica Splitting Test Room occurred on August 16, 1929. Apparently, a rumor was current among the regular operators that the mica splitting job was to be transferred to another building at Hawthorne, one somewhat removed from the main shop buildings, and consequently there was considerable speculation as to the possible meaning of this move. The daily history record describes the event as follows:

Operators M_2, M_3, and M_4 were talking about the mica group moving to the Merchandise Building. Operator M_4 said: "I heard that it was to be temporary and for a period of seven months, after which they were going to send the job to Kearny. My brother asked me what I was going to do if the job went to Kearny and I told him I would stay in the test room."

It was easy to observe the feelings of insecurity which followed such rumors, especially when they were finally verified by definite action. On September 16 the first move took place, and all the mica splitting operators in the regular department were enrolled in another department. Although this change did not affect the test room operators, nevertheless they shared the general fears of the other operators. A few months later, the company began to reduce the size of the regular mica splitting group, which seemed to verify the previous rumors. On January 15, 1930, the following conversation was recorded:

The operators were talking about the reduction of the mica group in the regular department due to transfers and layoffs.

Operator M₄: (to the observer) "Pretty soon you won't have any mica girls."

Observer: "Why not?"

Operator M₃: "Some girl from the regular department said they are only going to keep those girls on mica who have 15 years' service."

Operator M₂: "Someone is always starting rumors like that."

Operator M₃: "I heard they have one hundred girls on mica at Kearny."

Operator M₆: "My brother thinks he might get laid off."

The observer sensed the gravity of the situation and attempted to reassure the operators:

Informed the operators that the mica splitting group would be cut down, as the biggest part of the mica job would be at Kearny; but that, according to the foreman, there would always be from 20 to 25 operators on mica splitting at Hawthorne.

The final event of this nature occurred on March 17, 1930, when all the test operators were required to change to a new type of mica. This was concrete evidence that mica splitting was becoming slack, as they had worked on the former type of mica for over 18 months without any interruption in the flow of work.

The effect of these occurrences cannot, of course, be accurately measured. Even though the test room offered some security beyond that offered the operators in the regular department, it is doubtful if it was sufficient to allay the qualms and fears of the mica test room girls. It will be seen later that during the months of these adjustments output tended to fall off.

The operators in the Mica Splitting Test Room were interviewed early in 1930. These interviews gave a good picture of the operators' attitude toward the test room situation. The following excerpts are given as typical expressions of their attitude:

Operator M₁:

"It was the funniest thing about me getting in here [the test room]. It was just by chance. I was so discouraged in the department at that time that I thought I would take a chance in the test room. The girls all tried to say they were just going to get us in there and time us and then cut the rates, but I thought the other girls who were going were all nice and then, too, it would be quiet in there. It was terribly hard for me to work in the department with all that noise, people walking up and down, and the girls weren't nice to one another either. Here in the test room, there are all different types but they are all nice quiet girls."

Operator M_2:

"Right now I couldn't ask for anything better than I have. I just can't explain what it is but I sure like it in the test room. . . . It couldn't be any better. It will be hard on us if they ever decide to put us back in the department and it is hard to say just why we like it so well. . . . I think we work for the most wonderful man in the Western Electric Company. We have no boss. Mr. —— simply waits on us. I heard one of the girls mention that she didn't get a *Microphone* [employee newspaper] and today I noticed he brought some in. We have privileges that a lot of the other girls don't have. We are allowed to go down and lie on the couch when we are tired or don't feel good, and the matron was told not to say anything to us. Of course, none of us have done that yet because we always feel pretty good and we have rest periods and can do anything we want to in those ten minutes."

Operator M_3:

"Right now I am very satisfied. I couldn't ask for anything better than I have now; in fact, I would be very unreasonable if I did. I hope I am kept in the test room as long as I am working at the Western. . . . I love this little test room. It seems to be just the turning point in my life because I was thinking that something would have to happen. I was so dissatisfied. I don't do anything different here than I did in the department. I just sit and work away and have more of a chance to think. In fact, I dream during the day."

Operator M_4:

"I never dreamed it was going to be as good as it is, but when I was asked I thought I would take a chance. . . . There were three others asked but they foolishly didn't take it. They thought they would rather stay down in the department with the crowd, but another girl and I said we would go on the test and, believe me, we have never been sorry. Now that the work is dropping off, every time the other girls meet us, they ask, 'Are you still on mica?' When we tell them we are, I can see they are sorry although they don't say it."

Operator M_5:

"I don't think I would be on mica now if I were in the regular department. Maybe I would be laid off. . . . Why, there are only 35 girls on the mica job now, and as I was one of the last ones to be put on mica I am sure they would take me off first. . . . Yes, I like it in the test room better than in the department. . . . I guess it is because it is something different. They are making an experiment on our health by giving us a rest period. I was lucky to get in, not having much service. We have nice girls and we get along fine together. Three of them are married and the other one, although single, is older than I am."

It is interesting to note that the operators in this second test room, like those in the Relay Assembly Test Room, regarded the observer not as a "boss" but as a friend who was always ready to help them and protect their interests. Perhaps even more significant, however, were their statements indicating that the apprehension with which they had entered the test room had been dispelled.

Period V
(May 19, 1930–September 13, 1930)

The final change in working conditions came on May 19, 1930, when the working day was shortened from 8¾ hours to 8 hours. Saturday work was eliminated entirely, thus reducing the total working hours per week from 48 hours to 40 hours. This change was a part of the general program of retrenchment being carried out throughout the company and was identical with the changes in hours in all the shop departments. Even though these new conditions of work were not imposed intentionally as an experiment, the change was so radical that it was considered the beginning of a new period.

Curiously enough, this reduction in the hours of work did not give rise to any definite expressions of favorable or unfavorable attitude. The change was accepted, and throughout the period no comments were recorded indicating either like or dislike of these new conditions of work.

On September 13, 1930, the work schedules on mica were so radically reduced that the test room could no longer be kept in operation. The operators faced the announcement of this news with the same attitude with which they had met the reduction in hours of work. In the course of making the necessary adjustments, the operators were kept in the test room for a few months longer on new work, technically known as armature·straightening. While output records were kept for this period, the presentation of this part of the study is being omitted, as its inclusion would necessitate a discussion of topics not related to the major object of the test. The Mica Splitting Test Room study was thus concluded after a period of two years.

RESULTS

Changes in Average Hourly Output by Weeks in the Mica Splitting Test Room

Figure 17 shows the average hourly output by weeks for each operator during the entire period of the test. In the curves of each of the five operators five levels of output can be distinguished:

(1) The base period.

(2) A slight decline in rate of output during Period II, when the girls were moved into the test room.

(3) A moderate but steady rise in rate of output when rest pauses were introduced in Period III, a rise which was sustained until the fall of 1929, i.e., running through the first four months of Period IV.

(4) A slight and moderate decline in output from the fall of 1929 until about February or March, 1930.

(5) A fairly constant rate of output, although at a much lower level, during the last six months of the test.[1]

In Table XV the performance of each mica operator during the base period is compared with her performance during the high peak in the fall of 1929, as well as with her output rate around March, 1930. From this table it is apparent that the increases in output ranged from 5.9 per cent in the case of Operator M_3 to 24.1 per cent in the case of Operator M_5. During the following months, as shown in the third column, this increase was considerably diminished. At the end of the decline the average output for all the operators was only 4.4 per cent above that of the base period.

Inasmuch as the Mica Splitting Test Room was supposed to duplicate the Relay Assembly Test Room in every respect except for the one factor of a change in wage incentive, the similarities and differ-

---

[1] During the last six months of the test, when the operators were working on mica of different specifications, the output had to be converted to one standard type of mica. This was done by multiplying the actual output by the numerical ratio existing between the piece rate of the new type and the piece rate of the standard type. The accuracy of this method depends wholly upon the assumption that the ratio between the two piece rates expresses adequately the relative difficulty of the two jobs. The precipitous drop in output, as shown by the converted figures which are used in Figure 17, makes this assumption questionable. It is very probable that this drop reflects to a considerable degree a discrepancy in the piece rates. Both the investigators and the operators were of the opinion that the rate on the new piece parts was not high enough in comparison with the rate on the old. For these reasons a direct comparison of the hourly rate for the last six months with the hourly rate during the previous period in the test room becomes hazardous. The main utility of the figures for the last six months lies only in their portrayal of the trend during that period.

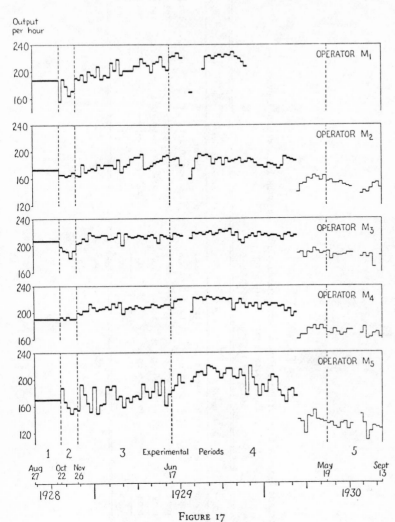

FIGURE 17

AVERAGE HOURLY OUTPUT PER WEEK

MICA SPLITTING TEST ROOM

TABLE XV

Changes in Average Hourly Output; Base Period Performance Compared with Highest and Lowest Performance during the Study

MICA SPLITTING TEST ROOM

Operator	Base Period A.H.O.	%	Peak Weeks Included	A.H.O.	%	End of Decline Weeks Included	A.H.O.	%
M₁	187.3	100.0	9-7-29 to 11-9-29	225.0	120.1	Absent	.....	.....
M₂	172.9	100.0	8-17-29 to 9-14-29	194.1	112.3	12-28-29 to 2-15-30	179.4	103.8
M₃	207.3	100.0	8-10-29 to 10-26-29	219.5	105.9	2-8-30 to 3-15-30	213.5	103.0
M₄	190.1	100.0	8-10-29 to 10-26-29	222.0	116.8	2-8-30 to 3-15-30	204.4	107.5
M₅	170.7	100.0	8-10-29 to 10-26-29	211.9	124.1	2-8-30 to 3-15-30	177.7	104.1
Average	185.7	100.0		214.5	115.6		193.8	104.4

ences in the results of the two studies attracted the most attention. In both test rooms, output tended to increase during the first year. Also in both cases the increases followed experimentally introduced changes in working conditions. With these two exceptions, however, no parallel developments in the two rooms could be detected. Even though output tended to increase during the first year in the Mica Splitting Test Room, there was a wide variation among individuals with respect to the extent of this increase. Only in the cases of Operators M_1 and M_5 was the increase in output in the first year in any sense comparable to the improvement shown by all the operators in the Relay Assembly Test Room. Probably even more striking was the decrease in output in the Mica Splitting Test Room after the first year; nothing like it had occurred in the Relay Assembly Test Room.

Rest Pauses, Overtime, and Fatigue

The Mica Splitting Test Room, like the Relay Assembly Test Room, was an experiment to study the effect of different conditions of work on employee effectiveness. From this point of view the relevant questions are: (1) Could the rise in output during the first year of the experiment be attributed to the improvement in working conditions? (2) Was elimination of fatigue the explanation of this rise? (3) If so, why did the output rate fail to rise during the second year?

In the Mica Splitting Test Room each period, compared to the period which preceded, was an improvement in working conditions. After being moved to the test room in Period II, the operators were given rest pauses in Period III. These were retained in Period IV, when overtime was also eliminated. Hours were further shortened, Saturday work was eliminated, and rest periods were continued in Period V. In view of these successive improvements, it might be expected that average hourly output would steadily rise. In Period IV, however, the rate of output began slowly to decline. Nevertheless, two increases in the hourly rate of output seemed to be related to the experimentally imposed conditions: (1) the rise during Period III, when rest pauses were introduced, and (2) the rise during the first few months of Period IV, when hours of work were reduced to the standard 8¾-hour day by the elimination of overtime and rest pauses were retained.

Of the first increase there was no question. The introduction of rest pauses in Period III was accompanied by an immediate and sustained rise in the weekly average hourly output for each operator, with Operator M_5 as a possible exception.[1] Furthermore, from Table XVI it is apparent that, although personal time tended to decrease under conditions of organized rest periods, the reduction was not sufficient to account for the full time of the rests. In other words, the rest periods here, as in the Relay Assembly Test Room, were functioning in part as such and not merely as a means of organizing personal time.

The increase in the early part of Period IV was not so clear. In the first place, it was somewhat clouded by a slump which began with

TABLE XVI

PERSONAL TIME: AVERAGE NUMBER OF MINUTES PER DAY TAKEN BY EACH
OPERATOR IN DIFFERENT PERIODS

MICA SPLITTING TEST ROOM

Period Number	Conditions of Work	Op. M1	Op. M2	Op. M3	Op. M4	Op. M5	Group	Rest Period Time
II	Overtime, no rests	8.0	8.0	13.3	6.8	14.1	10.0	0
III	Overtime, rests	8.4	2.4	8.3	4.8	12.3	7.2	20
IV	No overtime, rests	6.1	1.6	8.4	1.3	8.6	5.2	20
V	8-hour day, 5-day week, rests	7.9	1.0	8.8	1.1	5.8	4.9	20

the fifth week of this period, following a two weeks' vacation. In the second place, the increase was not sustained in this period. However, there still remained some evidence of an increase in average hourly output when overtime was first eliminated.

It might be expected that the elimination of fatigue accounted for the rises both in Period III and in Period IV. The following data give some evidence in favor of this interpretation:

(1) According to the fatigue hypothesis, curves representing the average hourly output for consecutive days of the week for each operator during Period II should show relatively more marked characteristics of fatigue than similar curves for Period III. Likewise, curves for Period III should show more marked fatigue effects than curves for Period IV. In Figure 18 this organization of the output data is given. If low Mondays and Saturdays be omitted as having no fatigue signifi-

---

[1] Operator M_5's weekly average hourly output fluctuated too much to determine any general trend over a short period. Her hourly rate did increase, however, in the latter half of Period III.

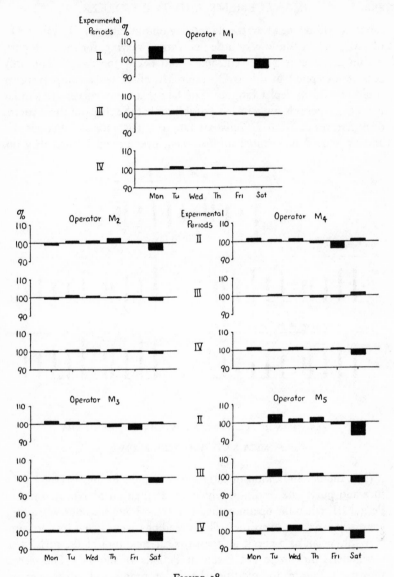

FIGURE 18

AVERAGE HOURLY OUTPUT FOR CONSECUTIVE DAYS OF THE WEEK, EXPRESSED AS
A PERCENTAGE OF THE MEAN FOR EACH PERIOD

MICA SPLITTING TEST ROOM

cance, it will be seen that the day-to-day output rates for Operators M_1, M_2, M_3, and M_4 show very little fluctuation, varying, for the most part, within a range of 2 per cent above and below the mean. The only possible exception to this is Operator M_5, all of whose output curves could be said to depict fatigue. The fact that these curves are similar in all three periods suggests the possibility that the shape of these curves does not result from cumulative fatigue. Theoretically, Periods III and IV should show more improvement over Period II than they do.

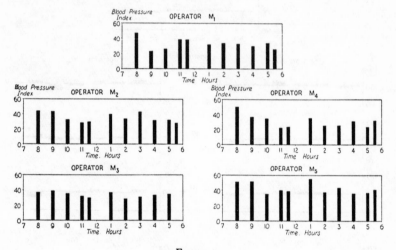

FIGURE 19

VARIATIONS IN PULSE PRODUCT WITHIN A WORKING DAY

MICA SPLITTING TEST ROOM

(2) Another indication of fatigue was sought in hourly blood pressure and pulse rate readings, which were taken on March 21, 1929, in Period III, when the operators had two ten-minute rests but when they were still working overtime. These readings were taken by the company physician as a check on the physical condition of the girls. Unfortunately, they were not taken in Periods II and IV. The curves shown in Figure 19, plotting the pulse product of each operator throughout the day, could not be compared with hourly output variations throughout the day, as such data were not available in the mica study. In themselves, however, they give no pronounced indication of fatigue. With the exception of Operator M_1, all the curves represent the normal diurnal variations, that is, the pulse products tend to decline or remain fairly steady throughout the day. Operator M_1's curve shows

a rapid rise after the morning rest period, which may have been due to eating. During the afternoon, however, her pulse product remains steady.

The Decline in Output during the Second Year

The cause of the decline in output during the second year was not difficult to locate. Everything pointed to its relation to the operators' anxieties over the uncertain future of the mica splitting job. The decline began shortly after the first rumors that the job might be transferred to Kearny appeared, and it progressed as the girls' fears about their future with the company became more acute. From August 16, 1929, when the first rumors were circulated, until September 13, 1930, when the test room was finally discontinued, the operators were under considerable tension. On September 16, 1929, all the mica operators in the regular department were transferred to a new location in the plant and assigned to a new department. In November, 1929, this department began to reduce its personnel. On March 17, 1930, the test room operators were shifted to a new type of mica after having worked for 18 months without interruption on one standard type. All these changes gave grounds for their fear that sooner or later the job would be discontinued at Hawthorne and that they themselves would be either transferred to other work or laid off. When on May 19, 1930, the hours of work were reduced and Saturday work was eliminated, they realized that the dreaded depression had at last begun to affect them. The daily history record, reporting the conversations which the operators had among themselves and with the observer, indicated the adverse effect which these various changes had on the girls.

In short, then, because these fears and anxieties so completely overshadowed the experimentally introduced changes, it was thought best to discount the last year of the experiment and to use only the first 14 months of the Mica Splitting Test Room data from which to draw conclusions and on which to base any comparisons with the Relay Assembly Test Room. Although this unexpected factor had interrupted the experiment proper, it brought out certain points which were of value in the general inquiry:

(1) It showed the effect of interfering preoccupations on the attitudes of the operators and, in turn, on their output.

(2) It showed that under certain conditions such preoccupations could become so acute as to nullify the effects of certain other factors influencing output and efficiency. This observation had also been

made in the Relay Assembly Test Room, where the "apprehension of authority" had nullified certain expected results.

(3) It provided a further warning against drawing hasty conclusions based on only a partial acquaintance with the human situation under investigation. Attitudes and preoccupations could not be ignored.

Supervision and Morale

The Mica Splitting Test Room can also be considered as an experiment in supervision and morale. According to one hypothesis, the altered type of supervision in the Relay Assembly Test Room had been the change which seemed to be more closely associated with the continual improvement in the output of the workers than any other. A new supervisor-employee relationship had developed in which there existed a spirit of co-operation with the experimenters and management. A situation had been created which was described by the operators as one in which there were no longer any "bosses." An improved group morale had been shown by (1) a decreased absenteeism, (2) an increased amount of social activity among the test room operators outside of working hours, (3) an increased amount of socialized conversation during the day, (4) a willingness to help one another for the common good of the group, (5) "pacing" each other in output. Were these effects duplicated in the Mica Splitting Test Room? Obviously, if the above effects were the result of the test room situation and its altered methods of supervision, similar effects should be apparent in the Mica Splitting Test Room.

The apprehension of the operators at the beginning of the mica study has already been mentioned. It was so great that of the five operators originally selected only two were willing to join the test group. These two were therefore delegated to select three other operators who would be willing to participate in the experiment. Eighteen months later, when the test room operators were interviewed, their fears seemed to be entirely relieved. All unhesitatingly expressed their complete satisfaction with the test room. In these interviews it was also quite clear that they did not regard the observer as a "boss." The evidence, both from recorded conversations and interviews, left little doubt that the change in attitude toward supervision previously noted among the relay assembly operators had been duplicated in the Mica Splitting Test Room.

The evidence of a change in attitude of the operators toward one another, however, was not so convincing. In fact, in this respect there seemed to be a decided difference between the relay assembly and the mica splitting operators.

(1) An examination of the attendance records of the mica operators before and after entering the test room showed no improvement common to all the operators such as occurred in the Relay Assembly Test Room. Table XVII shows that Operator M_1 improved in attendance during the first year but because of illness was much worse the second

TABLE XVII

ATTENDANCE IRREGULARITIES * OF OPERATORS BEFORE AND AFTER ENTERING
THE TEST ROOM

MICA SPLITTING TEST ROOM

| Operator | Number of Irregularities | | |
	One Year Before (10–22–27 to 10–20–28)	First Year After (10–22–28 to 10–19–29) **	Second Year After (10–21–29 to 10–18–30)
M_1	120.5	51.5	202.0
M_2	32.0	6.5	2.5
M_3	12.0	14.5	24.0
M_4	5.0	4.5	5.0
M_5	4.0	4.0	1.0

* By an attendance irregularity is meant an absence from work or a deviation from the rules governing attendance.

** Includes 34 weeks' overtime.

year. Operator M_2 came the closest to duplicating the record of the relay assembly operators. The absences of M_3 increased during the two years of the test. Operator M_4 showed little change during the entire period of the study, and Operator M_5 improved materially only during the second year. These wide individual variations were quite different from the results in the Relay Assembly Test Room, where the attendance records showed a tendency toward marked improvement for all the operators. It could be argued, of course, that this difference in attendance was due to a difference in physical health, but in light of the physical examinations to which all the operators had to submit there was no evidence for any such conclusion. It seemed much more probable that the difference was due to a difference in attitude toward attendance. Among the mica operators there was no pressure for attendance except that which came from the individual's own personal situation.

(2) The mica operators did not join in common social activities

outside of working hours. They had no "parties" similar to the gatherings of the relay assembly girls.

(3) Their conversations during the day dealt mainly with personal topics from each individual's own particular social sphere.

(4) There was no evidence of willingness to help one another. Each girl's output seemed to be an individual problem, and while occasionally one operator did criticize another, this was never interpreted as bringing pressure to bear on that operator. This lack of pressure was in marked contrast to the effect that Operator 2 in the Relay Assembly Test Room had whenever she chided one of the other operators for low output.

(5) The weekly average hourly output gave no suggestion that the operators were pacing each other at work.

In short, no matter where the investigators looked, whether at the output changes, the attendance records, the recorded comments, or the interviews, the same essential difference was present. The Relay Assembly Test Room was a "group" story; the Mica Splitting Test Room was a story of "individuals." It was quite clear that the change in supervision was not solely responsible for the observed improvement in morale in the Relay Assembly Test Room, for with a similar change in the Mica Splitting Test Room the same effect had not occurred.

This result strongly suggested an essential difference between the two test rooms which might not have been given sufficient weight by the investigators when planning the experiment. Therefore, it might be well to ask: Had the conditions of work in the Mica Splitting Test Room been comparable to those in the Relay Assembly Test Room except with regard to one item, namely, that there had been no change in wage incentive? Of course, there were certain obvious differences in (1) the jobs, (2) the nature and length of the test periods, (3) the pay incentive systems, and (4) the personal situations of the operators.[1]

There was no evidence that the difference between the tasks of mica splitting and relay assembling could account for the difference in morale in the two groups. It is true, of course, that mica splitting was better paid than the job of assembling relays. It required more training. It involved fewer gross bodily movements and more manipulative discrimination. Although this in part might account for greater individual differences in the level of output among the mica operators and for the absence of pacing, it could not explain the fact that other mani-

[1] This difference will be discussed in the next chapter, in which an account of the personal situations of the different operators will be given.

festations of group solidarity had failed to appear among the mica operators.

A criticism frequently made of the Relay Assembly Test Room experiment was that the test periods had not been long enough. It was said that the Hawthorne investigators had not sufficiently taken into account the slow adaptation of the workers to the experimental changes, a factor which might have resulted in a cumulative effect on production.[1] In line with this suggestion, longer test periods were installed in the Mica Splitting Test Room, lasting in two cases 29 and 48 weeks. The interesting thing was that these longer test periods not only did not have the supposed advantage of measuring long-time effects due to slow adaptation to change by the workers,[2] but they did not function for the operators in the Mica Splitting Test Room in the same way as the shorter periods had for the operators in the Relay Assembly Test Room. It is, of course, difficult to say definitely what meaning these test periods had for the individuals in the different test groups. It seems probable, however, that in the Relay Assembly Test Room they served to separate the test room group from the regular department. They were one of the chief features which socially differentiated the test operators from their associates outside, and in so doing they functioned to create a solidarity among the members of the group. In the relay assembly group, during the first 18 months, twelve changes in conditions of work were made at frequent intervals, whereas in the Mica Splitting Test Room only two changes were made during an equal length of time. In addition, the test periods in the Relay Assembly Test Room introduced changes which made working conditions very different from those in the regular department. Quite the opposite was true in the Mica Splitting Test Room. Both in Period IV, when overtime was eliminated, and in Period V, when hours of work were shortened, the very same changes occurred in the regular mica split-

---

[1] Viteles, *Industrial Psychology*, p. 476: "The superior increase in production noted in Period 13 [Relay Assembly Test Room] may, for example, simply be due to the fact that observations in connection with this change were continued over a period of 31 weeks, a period almost three times as long as any other observed. Slow adaptation to changes may also account for the findings in Period 12. As a matter of fact, a study of the curves shows that the rise in productivity during this period was not as marked as in Period 13 and that, in a few cases, there is a tendency toward a drop in production at the end of the Period 12, a drop which, because of the slow adaptation to negative as well as positive changes in conditions of work, would naturally be expected only toward the end of this period of change."

[2] In theory, the notion was correct; in fact, lengthening the test periods also allowed new factors to creep in which counteracted the advantage it was hoped would be gained, as for example in Period IV.

ting department. These periods did not differentiate the girls outside the regular department from the girls inside. Here was one possible reason why the mica group in respect to morale [1] was different from the relay assembly group.

The difference between the pay incentive systems in the two rooms was recognized when the Mica Splitting Test Room was organized. In fact, the objective in planning this experiment had been to create a new test room situation wherein changes in working conditions similar to those imposed in the Relay Assembly Test Room could be introduced without changing the wage incentive method. The important consideration had been to reduce a department of workers to a group of five without effecting a change in the direction of an increased financial incentive, and therefore a department on individual piecework seemed to offer the best possibility. But the relation of type of payment system to the question of morale was overlooked. In the Relay Assembly Test Room the incentive was based on the output of five girls, whereas in the Mica Splitting Test Room the incentive was solely in terms of each individual's output. Under group piecework the operators in the Relay Assembly Test Room had a common interest around which they could organize. Under individual piecework each girl was self-sufficient; there was no need of working together.

SUMMARY AND CONCLUSIONS

What light did the data from the Second Relay Assembly Group and the Mica Splitting Test Room throw on the question of the effect of changing the wage incentive in the Relay Assembly Test Room? In view of all the evidence, the answer to this question was not simple. Although output had risen an average of 12 per cent in the Second Relay Assembly Group, it was quite apparent that factors other than the change in wage incentive contributed to that increase. The condition that all other things remain the same had failed of realization. There was some evidence to indicate that the operators in the Second Relay Assembly Group had seized upon this test as an opportunity to prove to everyone that they could do as well as the Relay Assembly Test Room operators. They were out to equal the latter's record. In view of this, even the most liberal estimate would put the increase in output due to the change in payment alone at somewhat less than 12 per cent.

Moreover, this substantial increase in output could be seen only by

[1] The word "morale" is used to refer to those characteristics, described on p. 154. by means of which the two test groups were differentiated.

comparing the average output of the group during the nine weeks of the test with the average output for five weeks three months before, a base period which had been chosen in order to make the two periods comparable with respect to hours of work. An increase was not evident in the weekly average hourly output for the nine weeks of the experiment. During these nine weeks no operator exhibited any tendency toward further increasing her output. On the contrary, output remained singularly steady, with the exception of that of Operator R_3, which showed a slight decline toward the end of the period. In other words, these data suggested that the effect of the wage incentive, for some inexplicable reason, had worked itself out rapidly. Once a point of equilibrium was reached, the opportunity for increased earnings ceased to function as an incentive.

The Mica Splitting Test Room, which was supposed to duplicate the Relay Assembly Test Room except for the change in wage incentive, also fell far short of the required experimental conditions. The differences which existed were due largely to the fact that the investigators did not realize their importance at the time. The experimental changes imposed in the Relay Assembly Test Room differed from those introduced in the Mica Splitting Test Room in character, duration, and frequency. Moreover, they functioned for the two groups in a different way. Those introduced in the relay assembly group were in the nature of special privileges in that they were not accorded anyone else, whereas those introduced in the Mica Splitting Test Room, except for the rest pauses, followed similar changes in the mica splitting department. The fact that the mica splitters were on individual piecework was another important factor. They did not have a vital interest in one another's output around which to organize as a social group. It seemed fair to assume, besides, that under straight piecework the operators would tend to work closer to their maximum capacity than they would under group piecework. In other words, the mica splitters probably did not have the same reserves of skill and energy to call upon at the beginning of the test as the relay assemblers had; consequently, the increase in output which occurred in the mica group was probably less than it would have been had the operators been on group piecework.

From the above considerations it is apparent that, apart from the wage factor, conditions in the Mica Splitting Test Room were not so conducive to an increase in output as they were in the Relay Assembly Test Room. Yet, in spite of this, output had risen an average of 15 per cent in 14 months. If this be allowed as the minimum due to changes in working conditions and supervision (all factors other than wage incentive), then this amount subtracted from the percentage increase in output in the Relay Assembly Test Room should leave the maximum amount to be attributed to the change in wage incentive. Inasmuch as output rose an average of roughly 30 per cent in the Relay Assembly Test Room, this leaves 15 per cent which might be attributed to the change in wage incentive. This deduction, however, depended on so many assumptions which might or might not hold true that it failed in any sense to be conclusive.

At least two conclusions seemed to be warranted from the test room experiments so far: (1) there was absolutely no evidence in favor of the hypothesis that the continuous increase in output in the Relay Assembly Test Room during the first two years could be attributed to the wage incentive factor alone; (2) the efficacy of a wage incentive was so dependent on its relation to other factors that it was impossible to consider it as a thing in itself having an independent effect on the individual. Only in connection with the interpersonal relations at work and the personal situations outside of work, to mention two important variables, could its effect on output be determined.

CHAPTER VII

THE TEST ROOM OPERATORS; THEIR INDIVIDUAL DIFFERENCES AND INTERPERSONAL RELATIONS

As THE Relay Assembly Test Room experiment continued, it became more evident that many significant variations either in the level of output or in the rate of improvement could not be related to physical working conditions alone. Some variations in output seemed to be closely associated with the workers' personal situations outside the shop; some expressed their interpersonal relations at work. It will be the purpose of this chapter to marshal all the evidence collected by the investigators relating to individual differences among the test room operators and their interpersonal relations inside and outside of the plant, in order to see what light this material will throw on their performance.

INDIVIDUAL DIFFERENCES AMONG THE RELAY ASSEMBLY TEST ROOM OPERATORS

It could be argued that the Relay Assembly Test Room operators were above the average operator both in native skill and intelligence, and that the increased output in the test room as compared with output in the regular department was a result of this superiority. Of course, no attempt had been made by the original investigators to select outstanding or exceptional workers for the experiment. It might be well, nevertheless, to examine this question of individual differences and see how one operator compared not only with her fellow workers in the test room but also with operators in the regular department.

Relative Ranking of Five Assemblers in Output

Table XVIII shows the relative ranking in output of each operator in each period. It is apparent that Operator 3 led in output for most of the first seven periods, while Operator 4 took second place in this same span of time. Operator 2A oscillated between third and fourth place, while Operator 5 ranked sometimes third and sometimes fifth. Operator 1A displayed the widest range of performance, going from first to fifth place during Periods I to III, climbing slowly back to third place in Period VI, but dropping back to fifth place again in Period VII. Taking Periods VIII to XIII, Operator 2 jumped immediately into

TABLE XVIII

RELATIVE RANK OF OPERATORS IN AVERAGE HOURLY OUTPUT FOR PERIODS I–XIII
RELAY ASSEMBLY TEST ROOM

Period Number	Op. 1A	Op. 2A	Op. 1	Op. 2	Op. 3	Op. 4	Op. 5
I	1	4			2	3	5
II	5	3			2	1	4
III	5	4			1	2	3
IV	4	3			1	2	5
V	4	3			1	2	5
VI	3	5			1	2	4
VII	5	4			1	2	3
I–VII	5	3			*1*	*2*	*4*
VIII			3	1	4	2	5
IX			2	1	4	3	5
X			2	1	4	3	5
XI			2	1	3	4	5
XII			2	1	4	3	5
XIII			3	1	4	2	5
VIII–XIII			2	*1*	4	3	5

the lead and maintained it throughout the experiment. Operator 1 took second place, Operator 3 fell back into fourth place, Operator 4 advanced (i.e., in relation to Operator 3) into third place, while Operator 5 was consistently last.

Relative Ranking of Five Assemblers in Dexterity and Intelligence

How does rank in output compare with individual differences in dexterity and intelligence? Figure 20 shows the relative ranking of the five test room assemblers in six different tests as compared with their relative ranking in output during Periods VIII to XIII. The six tests were as follows:

(1) A finger dexterity test referred to by the company as Pegboard I, which consists of picking up small pegs about .125 inch in diameter and 1 inch in length and placing one in each hole of a board containing two rows of 25 holes, each .133 inch in diameter. The subject is required to place the pegs one at a time in the holes during a specified period of time, first with the right and then with the left hand. The pegs are then removed and the subject is allowed to replace them, now using both hands. The score is the total sum of pegs the subject is capable of placing in three trials each with the right, left, and both hands respectively.

(2) A finger dexterity test developed by Johnson O'Connor at the General Electric Company and referred to by the company, for convenience, as

DEXTERITY TESTS

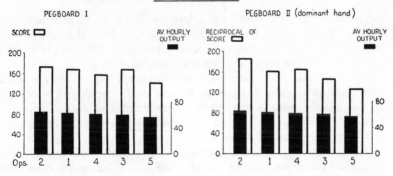

CANCELLATION TESTS

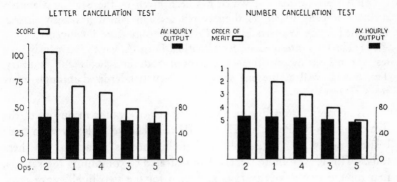

INTELLIGENCE TESTS

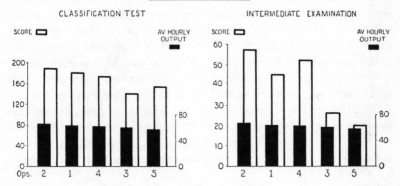

FIGURE 20

DIFFERENCES IN AVERAGE HOURLY OUTPUT COMPARED WITH DIFFERENCES IN
ABILITY AS MEASURED BY VARIOUS TESTS

RELAY ASSEMBLY TEST ROOM

Pegboard II. The test consists of a board with 100 holes, in which small pegs about .072 inch in diameter are to be inserted three at a time in holes .196 inch in diameter, arranged in square formation. The score is the time required to fill 100 holes using the dominant hand.[1]

(3) A standard letter cancellation test sometimes used to measure attention, visual perception, and perhaps to some degree rapidity of movement. In this test the score is determined by the number of cancellations of a particular given letter the subject is capable of performing in a given selection over a given period of time.

(4) A standard number cancellation test also used to measure attention and visual perception. In this test the score is expressed as the time taken to cancel certain specified numbers on a given page of numerals.

(5) A classification test which has been given by the Scoville Manufacturing Company to all its shop employees and which has been successfully used at the Western Electric Company to measure intelligence.

(6) The Otis Intermediate Examination, Form A, which is a widely used test for measuring intelligence employed both in schools and industry. This test, as well as the one above, has been standardized through many years of application.

It is apparent from Figure 20 that the relative ranks in output of the five operators for Periods VIII to XIII correlate very closely with their relative ranks in native skill and intelligence as measured by these tests.[2] This is even more clearly demonstrated by combining the ratings, first for the two dexterity tests and then for the two intelligence tests. In each case the ranking for the combined two tests correlates perfectly with the ranking in output, the order being Operators 2, 1, 4, 3, 5.

Since the Otis examination is more dependent upon the use of language symbols than the classification test, it is somewhat more influenced by language habits and reading ability. This is probably the reason why Operator 4, who had more education than any of the other operators, received second place in the Otis examination and third place in the classification test. Likewise, it probably accounts for the low rating in the Otis test of Operator 5, who had difficulty in reading English. All the girls had attended school in this country with the exception of Operator 5, who had received most of her education in Norway.

What these relative differences in scores mean can best be seen by referring to Figure 21, in which the test room operators are compared

[1] The score in Figure 20 is expressed as the reciprocal of the time taken multiplied by 1000.

[2] The results of the pegboard tests on the five operators were published in connection with another study. See Hayes, E. G., "Selecting Women for Shop Work," *The Personnel Journal*, Vol. XI, No. 2, 1932.

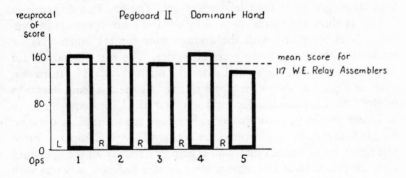

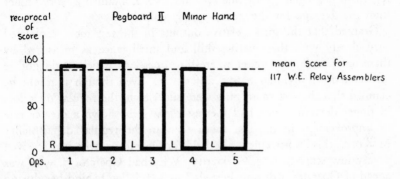

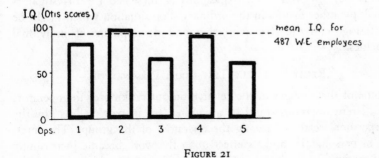

FIGURE 21

RELAY ASSEMBLY TEST ROOM OPERATORS COMPARED WITH OTHER OPERATORS IN THE PLANT IN RESPECT TO ABILITY AS MEASURED BY VARIOUS TESTS

with larger groups of their fellow workers. The first two diagrams in Figure 21 show the scores received by the test room operators in Peg-board II as compared with the average score for 117 other relay assemblers with two or more years of service. The first diagram is for the dominant hand; the second is for the minor hand. The third diagram in Figure 21 shows the scores received by the test room operators in the Otis Intermediate Examination, translated into equivalent intelligence quotients, as compared with the average intelligence quotient for 487 hourly rated employees at the Western Electric Company. From this figure it can be seen that with regard to dexterity all the operators, with the exception of Operator 5, were average or better, whereas with regard to intelligence only one operator, No. 2, attained a score higher than the average for the group of 487 employees.

Granted that the girls' relative outputs in the test room correlated very closely with their native skill and intelligence as measured by these tests, there were other interesting questions which could not be answered by individual native differences. Even though it might be claimed that the test room girls were superior to the regular operators in finger dexterity, why had the test room girls shown a greater rate of improvement in the test room than in the regular department? Moreover, this improvement also held for Operator 5, who had received a very low score in finger dexterity. Why had Operator 3, who was ahead of Operator 4 during Periods I to VII, fallen behind her during Periods VIII to XIII? Such questions as these led the investigators to look for other factors in the ordinary shop situation which might be interfering with the free expression and development of individual capacities.

RELAY ASSEMBLY TEST ROOM PERSONALITIES

Some of the changes in the relative output ranking of the operators on different occasions could be accounted for in part, at least, by the interpersonal relations among the operators of the group. The interplay of personalities and its effect upon the work became increasingly more noticeable to the investigators. Although at this stage of the inquiry they had attempted no systematic study of the problem, a number of interesting examples had come to their attention. Moreover, after two years of close association with the girls at work, a fairly clear and distinct picture of their personalities had been obtained.

With the exception of Operator 5, all the operators were single and approximately of the same age, about 18 to 20 years old, when they entered the test room. Only two operators, Nos. 2 and 4, had more than a grade school education. Both these girls had two years of high school training. Operator 3 had no work experience prior to coming to the Western Electric Company. All the other girls had approximately 6 months' to 1½ years' work experience in other companies. On entering the test room, all the girls had worked at Hawthorne not less than 1 year and not more than 3½ years. In short, then, with the exception of Operator 5, who was 29 years old and whose marriage took place while she was working in the test room, in July, 1928, the girls constituted a fairly homogeneous group in terms of age, marital status, education, and work experience.[1]

Operator 2

The test room personalities of the five operators can be illustrated best in relation to Operator 2, who became the acknowledged leader of the group. She was characterized by her supervisors as being not only the quickest and the most intelligent, but also probably the most ambitious and the most responsible, of any member of the group. She held all records in speed tests and in hourly, daily, weekly, and period output, and she received the highest scores in the various dexterity and intelligence tests. Her personal characteristics were displayed in other ways as well. When production lagged, it was Operator 2 who grew impatient. She often chided another operator who had an abnormal number of defective relays to repair or took an excessive amount of personal time out. Curiously enough, however, in the first two years of the test she herself averaged 27 per cent more personal time than the average for the group. Of all the operators she talked the most. She was the leader in suggesting changes or criticizing test room or company policies. Sometimes her comments to her fellow workers were rather caustic. But in spite of her occasional critical outbursts, most of the girls in the test room respected her, and she in turn seemed anxious to have their friendship. Although Operator 2 had been regarded as a problem by her supervisors before she entered the test room, she was considered one of the most co-operative and responsible members of the group by her supervisors in the test room.

Operator 1

In relation to Operator 2, Operator 1 always played a subordinate role. However, this characteristic was evident in most of her test room relations, for she was generally submissive to the will of the group. By her supervisors she was described as a kindly girl, highly gregarious,

[1] See Table I. p. 23.

and dependent upon her associates for motivation. She engaged in conversation only when her neighbors took the initiative and then she tended to agree rather than to argue with them. These characteristics were displayed in her work curves. Looking at either the average hourly output by weeks (Figure 6) or half-hourly output during the day (Figure 12), a striking similarity to her neighbor, Operator 2, is noticeable. Even when she acted as a substitute for Operator 1A in Period VII, her weekly average hourly output was similar to that of her neighbor, Operator 2A. It is still more interesting that when she returned to the test room as a regular operator only a few weeks later, she immediately jumped her output by approximately 7 to 8 relays per hour, keeping in step with her new neighbor, Operator 2.

Operator 4

Unlike Operator 1, Operator 4 was independent in thought and action and never allowed other operators to impose upon her. During the first two years she averaged 39 per cent more personal time out than the group, in contrast to Operator 1, who averaged 53 per cent less than the group. Operator 4 was described by her associates as a good-natured, sturdy girl, well liked by all the other girls. Her remarks in the test room, although brief, were always apropos. As the test room experiment continued, Operator 4 became more and more friendly with Operator 2, and they frequently went on parties together outside the plant.

Operator 3

Operator 3 played the part of the test room "jester," continually making witty remarks for the benefit of the group. In fact, in the opinion of the observers she played the role so much that it ceased to be effective. Although she gave the appearance of being a frivolous, light-hearted young girl, it was the opinion of the investigators that under this gay front she was very sensitive and unhappy. More than any other operator, she was dominated by her moods, which seemed to be reflected in her output.

During the first seven periods of the test Operator 3 led the group in output. With the coming of Operators 1 and 2 in Period VIII, however, Operator 3 immediately dropped into fourth place, even falling below Operator 4, to whom she previously had been superior. There is some evidence that she felt this loss of leadership keenly and tried to disguise her disappointment by playing the role of a clown. It was only after the arrival of Operator 2, who deprived her of first place, that she became the butt of considerable joking and raillery, to which she herself played up.[1] Most of her disputes were with Operator 2. It was after Period VIII that her progress began to diminish, and from Periods VIII to XIII she showed the least improvement of any girl in the group.

Operator 5

In sharp contrast to Operator 3 was Operator 5, noted for her quiet deliberation, sturdy persistence, and a firm but nonaggressive pursuit of whatever she decided to accomplish. She seldom spoke unless spoken to. Although she had no particular liking for Operator 2, she showed this, in her characteristic fashion, only by ignoring what Operator 2 said and did. With the other operators she was friendly in a quiet sort of way, content to get along without friction, and enjoying but seldom joining in their chatter. She participated less than any other girl in the social activities of the test room, her most intimate friendship being with the layout operator.

Operators 1A and 2A

Operator 1A was considered quiet, shy, and very responsive to, if not perhaps too easily influenced by, the opinions of other people. Operator 2A was considered nervous and irritable. During the early stages of the test room, Operator 2A was probably the most dominating personality in the group. About six months after the beginning of the test Operator 2A's nervousness and ill temper, which up to that time had been fairly well controlled, became increasingly more noticeable. She began remarking to the other girls that she did not intend to "work her head off" for anyone and made several other comments that were hard to reconcile with her previously co-operative attitude. She, more than any other girl, abused the test room privileges, especially by talking excessively. During this disturbance her output, as well as that of Operator 1A, began to drop, while the outputs of Operators 3, 4, and 5 were increasing. The other girls, particularly Operators 3 and 4, began criticizing her for not doing her share. The test room was split into two camps, with Operators 1A and 2A on one side and the rest of the group on the other. Although the investigators and even the superintendent had several talks with Operator 2A, they were unable to learn the cause of the trouble. The situation became more and more acute, and finally at the end of Period VII the investigators decided that it would be best to take both girls out of the test room and put them back in the regular department.[2]

It was not until four months later, when the case of Operator 2A

[1] See p. 74.   [2] See pp. 53–55.

was being discussed by the investigators and her physical examination records were being checked, that it was discovered that this girl had developed an anaemic condition, indicated by a red blood count of 3,500,000. It was thought that this anaemic condition might easily have been responsible for her apparent change in mental attitude. Her case was reinvestigated, and a new physical examination on May 4, 1928, showed a red corpuscle count of 3,640,000 and hemoglobin of 72 per cent. The investigators had a talk with her and suggested that she take some treatment from the medical department, to which she readily agreed. An examination about two months later showed a blood count of 4,600,000 and hemoglobin of 83 per cent. She was feeling much better.

At this time the girl herself stated that in the fall of 1927 she had noticed a decided loss of vitality. She could not seem to get started on her work, and when she came home from work at night she had no ambition to do anything. When her output began to slump in Period VII, and when the other girls began to criticize her, she became irritated and made the remarks she did. She also said that she had heard comments from girls in the regular department to the effect that what the company really was after in the test room was maximum output, and that the test room was not being run, as the investigators said, to determine the best working conditions.

These new facts made it possible to reconstruct what had probably happened in the case of these two operators. Operator 2A's reduced vitality, due to her anaemic condition, accounted for her inability to keep up with her fellow workers. Their criticism of her performance goaded her into making the remarks that she did and into an attitude of insubordination. This insubordination was reinforced by the doubts which were raised in her mind by the comments of the girls outside the test room. These doubts were readily accepted, for they allowed her to justify the difficulties she was having. The loyalty of Operator 1A to her friend had probably led her to adopt a similar attitude. Moreover, six months after entering the test room Operator 1A had been married; it might be expected that after this event her work had no longer its previous significance, and, being easily influenced, she followed the lead of her friend.

Personal Situations of Relay Assembly Test Room Operators

It was obvious that the personal situations of these operators influenced their behavior in the shop. The docile submission of Operator 1, the restless impatience of Operator 2, the moodiness of Operator 3, the sturdy independence of Operator 4, and the aloofness of Operator 5 were rooted in their personal and social backgrounds, which may be described as follows.[1]

Operator 1

Operator 1 lived at home with her parents, her younger brother, and older sister in an eight-room house which the family owned. Her parents, who had both been born in Poland, had come separately to the United States. After their marriage they had lived in a small town in Illinois, where the three children had been born. In 1925, the father, who was a carpenter, had brought his family to Chicago. Since that time, the family had lived in a Polish community in Cicero. Operator 1's life centered around the home, where she had few responsibilities except to turn over her pay check. Her sister, who had studied commercial art, was her chief companion. She was proud of her brother, a senior at high school. Unlike the other girls, Operator 1 seldom talked about her family or of herself in relation to them. In numberless small ways, nevertheless, she gave the impression of wishing to place her Polish antecedents behind her and of wanting to adapt herself to the American pattern of behavior. She was painfully self-conscious about violating even the minor social conventions. She dressed probably a little better than the other operators. Motion pictures were her chief diversion, and if given the opportunity she talked about them incessantly.

Operator 2

Operator 2 lived with her father and three brothers in an Italian quarter of Chicago, where she had been born and had spent most of her life. Just before she entered the test room, her younger sister died, and within three months her mother also died. After her mother's death she kept house for her father and three brothers and part of the time supported them too. Her father, a laborer, earned only about $18 to $20 a week when he worked. Not only was she the breadwinner and housekeeper in her family but she was also the financial manager. She was devoted to her family and valiantly strove to keep the home as her mother had kept it. But this dutiful acceptance of her family responsibilities, imposed on her by her Italian tradition, also involved certain personal frustrations. In order to take care of the family she had to give up an Italian boy with whom she had been "keeping company" for many years and who had been accepted by her mother

[1] It must be remembered that these situations are being described as of June, 1929.

and friends as the man whom she would some day marry. Although she had wanted more education, she had had to leave school at 14 years of age to support her family. The idea of working in a factory had always been distasteful to her, but the difficulty of obtaining office work and the smaller remuneration which such a change would have entailed had forced her to stay in the factory. There is no question that these frustrations of her personal ambitions had helped to develop her restless nature.

Operator 3

The family picture given by Operator 3 was on the whole not cheerful. Her family consisted of her parents, born in Poland, and five other children who lived in a rather small bungalow in the southwest section of Chicago. The father, who had a minor clerical job, an older brother, and Operator 3 worked and turned over their wages to the mother, who handled the family's finances. The father seldom spoke to his wife or children. The mother dominated the family, demanding strict obedience from her children, so that Operator 3's freedom was considerably hampered. Until after the age of 21, she had been required to be at home at an early hour in the evening. She longed for pretty clothes, but her pay check had to be turned over to her family and her allowance was too small for such indulgences. The preoccupations of Operator 3 were largely concerned with boy friends, "dates," and a good time. Her demands of men were so romantic that she was easily disappointed, and the loss of a boy friend made her silent and moody for several days. These conflicts were expressed in hypochondriacal complaints, worry over her eyes and weight, and fear of nervous breakdown. For these ills she resorted to various palliatives, from pink pills to fortune telling.

Operator 4

Operator 4 lived at home with her parents, her aged grandmother, four brothers, and two sisters. Like Operator 2, she had been born and had lived all her life in the same community, in this case a Polish community in Cicero, and she readily accepted the Polish traditions of her family. For the past 25 years, her father had had a secure job in a railroad yard. The mother seemed to be the vigorous and energetic member of the household. In addition to bearing and rearing her family of nine children and caring for her mother, she managed the family's finances and on occasions, by odd work, substantially contributed to them. She had made it possible for all her children, with the exception of the two oldest sons, to have a high school education.

One son had even graduated from college. She and her husband owned their six-room bungalow home, with an attic finished as an additional bedroom and a kitchen in the basement. They had invested also in a two-flat brick building on a lot in the same neighborhood. The picture this family gave was one of hard and steady work, frugality, economical management, and good health.

Operator 5

Operator 5 had come to this country from Norway at the age of 25. Her father had been a sea captain until he was 40, when his wife had persuaded him to give up the sea and take over the management of his father's farm. Fishing and farming had formed a large part of the economic situation in which Operator 5 grew up. Before coming to America, she had held a job in Norway in a sardine cannery. When she had saved enough money, she had told her family she was going to America. She had come alone, lived for a short while in Detroit, and finally settled in Chicago. Three or four years later she met at a party the man who had been her childhood sweetheart in Norway. They renewed their friendship and shortly afterward were married (July, 1928). She spent her week ends with her husband, a steam shovel operator, and during the week lived in Chicago with a family for whom she did some housework in exchange for her living expenses. She was very happy with her husband. Both were getting ahead financially and she was secure, because whether she worked or not her husband's income was sufficient for the standard of living to which she was accustomed. She and her husband rented a bungalow, drove their own Ford car, and were thrifty and congenial. Her two chief preoccupations were going back to Norway with her husband to live and having a baby.

Summary

From examining the family backgrounds of these five girls it is possible to make a few generalizations. Both Operator 2 and Operator 4 were well-integrated members of a foreign community in which they had been born and brought up. In both their lives this close relationship to a foreign culture had been a stabilizing force which had more or less ordered their existence, although this ordering had involved, as a consequence, certain conflicts with the surrounding American culture, of which they were also a part. In the case of Operator 2, it had meant considerable renunciation of her personal hopes and ambitions. Operator 4 had had to give up her boy friend who was not Polish in order to satisfy her family. Yet in neither case was the conflict so great as to disrupt the personality.

Operator 5 was in every sense still a foreigner who had not been noticeably influenced by the new culture. For her, America was a place in which to earn money in order that she might some day go back to Norway.

In the case of Operator 3, the situation was still different. She was a member of a family which had lost touch with its ancestral ties before it had become well adjusted to or assimilated by the new country. The result was a disorganized family, neither sustained by the traditions and customs of the foreign society to which it had belonged or by the new society in which it lived.

The situation of Operator 1 was less clear. She was probably more Americanized than any of the other operators. Both she and her brother and sister were showing signs of breaking away from the foreign traditions of the family. Operator 1's eagerness to conform to social conventions and her unwillingness to talk about her family appeared to be symptomatic of this tendency. Her sensitivity to group opinion and her docile submission to it looked like a "rite of passage" to an upper social stratum.

In short, in the test room there were three types of social situation, which are common among wage earners in this country:

(1) There was the foreign-born person who retained the traditions and values of her native land and resisted assimilation in the new culture. (Operator 5)

(2) There was the American-born person, of foreign-born parentage, living in a foreign section of a large metropolitan area, whose sentiments and values were dictated largely by the customs and traditions of a foreign culture. By these values her life was guided, and only on occasions did they come into conflict with the opportunities for personal development which this country afforded. (Operators 2 and 4)

(3) There was the first-generation American, whose family was cut away from its former social moorings and set adrift in a rapidly changing society which was not sufficiently organized to take care of its assimilation. (Operator 3)

PERSONAL SITUATIONS OF MICA SPLITTING TEST ROOM OPERATORS

The Mica Splitting Test Room presented two interesting personal situations: one was the case of a woman whose attendance and output, prior to joining the test room, had been extremely erratic and whose improvement during the first year of the test was very noticeable; the other was the case of a young girl whose fluctuations in output correlated in a marked degree with changes in her home situation. As both these situations offer striking examples of a relation between social conditions of work, home conditions, and work efficiency, they will be reported in detail.

Operator M_1

Operator M_1, at the time she joined the test room, was a widow, 40 years old, with a 16-year-old son and a 14-year-old daughter. She had been born in Massachusetts and had come to Hawthorne in 1909, at the age of 20. After her marriage four years later, she had stopped work for six years. In 1919, however, her husband had become ill and two years later died. From that time she had worked steadily for the company except for one ten months' leave of absence in 1922. For many years she had been in almost constant financial difficulties. Her attendance had been very irregular, since she had been out ill frequently for one reason or another. Her extreme nervousness was evident to all who knew her, and it was the opinion of the doctors that her troubles were more mental than physical. Her supervisors considered her a "personnel problem."

The favorable reaction of this operator to the test room situation was quite noticeable. For the first year after joining the test group she showed the most persistent gains in output of any one of the operators. She gained in weight, her absences decreased to one-third their former number, and she began subscribing to two of the company's savings plans. This improvement, however, did not last. During the second year of the test, she fell back into her old ways and finally was pensioned by the company. In spite of this relapse, there was no question that she had benefited by her association with the members of the test room group.

Operator M_5

The case of Operator M_5 was no less interesting. For the first five months in the test room, she showed an irregular output and a failure to keep pace with her fellow workers. She also constantly complained of a headache. Shortly after this, her output commenced to rise and her complaints ceased. At about the twelfth month, September 7, 1929, her production reached the highest point and remained at this new high level for a period of about fourteen weeks, that is, until about December 14, 1929, when again it started to decline (see Figure 17).

These variations were particularly interesting in light of her background. At the time she entered the test room Operator M_5 lived with her parents, three brothers, and one sister. When she was two years old, her family had moved from Vienna to America. She had attended grade school and had gone to work at the age of fourteen. She had worked at many different jobs for three years, finally coming to Hawthorne in January, 1927. Her mother, a nervous, easily irritated, and penurious woman, whose chief desire was to lay aside every cent so that she could return to Europe, was constantly finding fault with her husband and children and on occasions did not speak to them for a week at a time. Sometimes, when the oldest daughter had been out and did not return home until 11 o'clock in the evening, she found that her mother had locked her out of the house. Naturally, Operator M_5 frequently talked about leaving home.

As she became well acquainted with the other operators in the test room, Operator M_5 began to talk to them about her home difficulties. Comments such as the following were typical:

My mother bawled me out for coming home early Monday. She said it was too bad that overtime was discontinued, as I would be more of a bother around the house.

My mother was sore this morning. She wanted to know how much money I was going to bring home today and why I didn't bring home as much as I used to. She knows I haven't been working overtime and I have been working hard lately. She said I had too much taken out of my pay. The more money she gets, the more she wants. My brother, my dad, and I give her our pay checks, but when I want a new dress or a new pair of stockings she won't give me the money. She says I don't need it. She's told me before that if I don't like it at home I can pack up my things and go. The next time she tells me that, I am going.

My mother is always hollering at me not to go out and that I ought to stay home nights. She knows where I go and I don't stay out late. She makes me sore.

On August 17, 1929, she finally decided to leave home and go to live with a girl friend, which she did for a period of four months. On December 28, 1929, because of her mother's illness, she was forced to return home and help take care of her mother.

It was interesting to note that this operator's production in the test room began to increase as soon as she was able to express more freely her preoccupations with regard to her home situation. Since she was the youngest girl in the group, she was mothered by the older women, who listened to her troubles and gave her advice. Her output reached the highest point when she decided to leave home, and it remained at this high level practically the entire time she was living in more congenial surroundings. With the return home, however, her output began to fall.

Although it had been the intention of the investigators to set up in the Mica Splitting Test Room an industrial situation comparable to that in the Relay Assembly Test Room, the differences between the two groups became more noticeable as time went on. Only very superficially could the two group situations be described as comparable. This was most apparent when comparing the personnel of the two test groups.

Operators M_1, M_2, and M_4, in the Mica Splitting Test Room, were about 40 years of age; Operator M_3 was 28, and Operator M_5 was 18 years old. The three older women were widows with children. Operators M_4 and M_5 were foreign-born; all of them were of German or Bohemian parentage. None of them had had more than a grade school education. Four were Protestants; one was a Catholic. Most of them had considerable service with the company, ranging from 10 to 18 years.[1]

Only two of the operators, M_2 and M_4, had any similarity of interests. Both were hard-working, thrifty, and well-balanced women. Each had one child living, around whom her life was centered, and each had been forced to earn her own living in order to rear her child. Operator M_4, whose husband had disappeared, remarried while she was in the Mica Splitting Test Room, in July, 1929. Operator M_1, who has already been described, was a middle-aged hypochondriacal woman, seemingly out of touch with the social reality about her. Operator M_3 was a socially ambitious and independent young girl, with standards of living considerably above those of all the other operators. She was not considered the "typical shop girl" by her associates and she, herself, did not view herself as such, frequently commenting that the reason she remained at mica splitting was the high earnings she received. Outside the plant, her life was quite different from that of the other girls. She lived in a modernly furnished one-room kitchenette apartment with another girl. Her friends were young men and women who, like herself, were ambitious to raise their social status.

The social status of Operator M_5, whose situation has already been described, was below that of any other member of the group. It was interesting to see how the other operators took an interest in this girl and tried to lift her up to their level. They were constantly talking

[1] See Table XIII, p. 137.

to her about her appearance and manners. They offered constructive suggestions about her clothes and even arranged her hair. All these criticisms Operator M5 received with meekness. She tried to follow their advice, and the result was that her appearance improved considerably while she was in the test room.

In short, in the mica group there was a wide divergence of interests and outlook. This situation was very different from that in the Relay Assembly Test Room, where the operators with the exception of Operator 5 constituted a fairly homogeneous group in terms of age, marital status, education, and work experience. Working with the personnel of the Mica Splitting Test Room, the investigators could hardly have chosen more difficult conditions under which to test their hypotheses. That any social solidarity did develop in this heterogeneous group was astonishing and showed what could be accomplished through segregating workers into small compact groups.

CHAPTER VIII

THE RELAY ASSEMBLY TEST ROOM SUPERVISION

THE general improvement in output of the Relay Assembly Test Room operators was thought by some of the investigators to be closely associated with gradual changes in the direction of improved social conditions of work. Frequently in human and social situations the introduction of a single change brings in its train a host of other unexpected changes. The Relay Assembly Test Room was no exception to this rule. In setting the conditions for the test, numerous changes were brought about which at first either were taken for granted or were passed by unnoticed. The most important of these inadvertently introduced changes was the new method of supervision.

It will be remembered from the excerpts previously quoted from the daily history record that in the beginning of the experiment there were occasional misunderstandings with regard to supervisory control. The foreman of the regular relay assembly department still performed many of his supervisory functions for this group. On occasions, as when he talked to the group about their low output or when he called four of the girls into his office to reprimand them for talking too much, his actions, while they reflected a normal and sincere desire to improve output, nevertheless tended to disturb what the investigators regarded as one of the most important factors in a "controlled" experiment, namely, attitudes on the part of the operators which would not be subjected to this kind of external interference. It will also be remembered that as the experiment became more important and a thing in itself, supervision was gradually taken over by the experimenters themselves. From this shift of control to the experimenters two important consequences followed: (1) the test room operators were taken out of their shop setting and, informally at least, given a completely new set of superiors, and (2) the function of control as exercised by their new superiors was of a completely different order. The result was a radical alteration of the social situation. Let us trace this development in more detail.

(1) Originally, only one man had been in charge of the experimental work in the test room. He has been referred to as the "test room observer." The use of this title may have conveyed an inaccurate picture

of the personnel situation in the test room, for the test room observer had other functions to perform in addition to observing. His duties were to keep things running smoothly, to keep records of all the data, and to act to a certain extent in a supervisory capacity for the operators. As these duties and functions increased, several assistants were added to the staff. On February 1, 1929, a Division of Industrial Research was formed to take over the test room studies that have been described thus far, as well as other inquiries which will be reported in Parts II and III. This Industrial Research Division was divided into four departments, each with separate functions. One of these four departments was in charge of the inquiries in the two test rooms (Relay Assembly and Mica Splitting). The test room observer was made the head of this department. Under him were two young men: one was stationed in the Relay Assembly Test Room, the other in the Mica Splitting Test Room. Their duties were similar to those of the original test room observer. Each of them, in turn, had clerical assistants.

It would be incorrect, then, to think of the Relay Assembly Test Room as a small room in which there were only five girls, the layout operator, and, occasionally, an inspector. By Period XIII there was the newly created department chief (the original test room observer), who spent a good share of his time in the room. Assisting him was the now official test room observer, who acted also in a minor supervisory capacity and who spent all his time in the room. And further below him was the junior clerk and office boy, a young Italian boy in his late teens. At a later date, a young woman also was added to the group. Her duties were mainly related to statistical studies, but she in fact also contributed her observations about what was going on. Besides these daily contacts, a number of other people visited the room. In the beginning, the then superintendent of the Inspection Branch, who was extremely interested in the experiment, was a frequent visitor. There was an intermittent stream of other visitors or consultants: industrialists, industrial relations experts, industrial psychologists, and university professors.

All these changes resulted in altering considerably the test room situation from an ordinary shop situation. With the creation of a department chief in charge of the test room studies,[1] the Relay Assembly Test Room, informally speaking, took on the status of a department. The test room operators had an entirely new supervisory personnel

---

[1] It will be remembered from Figure 1 that a department chief in an office organization was equivalent to a foreman in the shop.

partaking more of an office than of a shop character.[1] In addition, they became the focus of considerable attention from top management.

(2) Let us now turn to the question of control. How did the experimenters exercise their supervisory function? To the average supervisor, control meant upholding all the rules and practices intended to maintain efficiency in the department. For the experimenters, however, control meant a "controlled experiment," which necessitated having willing and co-operative subjects who would respond to the different experimentally imposed conditions, uninfluenced by so-called "psychological factors." At first, the investigators were thinking of "fatigue." The experiment had been planned primarily to study the effect of changes in the number and length of rest pauses and of changes in the length of the working day on the worker. In order that the experiment would not be spoiled by varying attitudes on the part of the operators toward the experimental changes introduced, it was thought necessary to make certain that to every change each girl gave wholehearted co-operation.

Toward this end, then, the experimenters directed their efforts with the result that almost all the practices common to the shop were altered. The operators were advised of and consulted about changes to be made, and several plans suggested by the experimenters were not introduced because they met with the disapproval of the operators. The operators were questioned sympathetically about their reactions to the different conditions of work. Many of these discussions, in the beginning of the test, took place in the office of the superintendent. The girls were allowed to talk while at work. The "bogey" was eliminated. Their physical health and well-being became matters of great concern, and their opinions, fears, qualms, and anxieties were eagerly sought. The observer fostered a kind of relation with the operators that a busy supervisor in a regular department would scarcely have time or opportunity to develop.

For a while the chief supervisory problem of the experimenters was excessive talking among the operators at work. Were they to adopt the customary tactics and order the girls to stop conversing, or were they to adopt the attitude of a disinterested spectator and merely record the results? At the time, neither was a solution. To allow excessive talking to continue would spoil what was thought to be a controlled experiment. To discontinue the privilege of talking would be inconsistent with the general policy of allowing the girls to work as they

[1] The importance of this will become clear after certain findings arising from other inquiries are reported in Parts II, III, and IV.

pleased. To moderate the talking by disciplining the girls might work against a co-operative attitude, which was also a prerequisite of a controlled experiment. This conflict led to periods of indecision, followed by short periods of crisis, finally resolved by action.

Crises occurred in both Periods VII and XII. Let us see how each was handled. In Period VII, Operators 1A and 2A, the two girls who had been most prone to talk too much, were transferred out of the test room and replaced by two other operators. They were told that they had been inattentive and had failed to co-operate. No serious attempt was made to understand the reasons for their attitude. In other words, here the experimenters took the easiest road. Instead of looking for the causes of the operators' insubordination, which might have produced some interesting findings, the problem was settled by transferring the girls out of the test room. This action was taken with the idea of maintaining a controlled experiment.

In Period XII, however, when the problem of talking again flared up, the investigators took the girls into their confidence. They were not reprimanded. They were carefully told why excessive talking would spoil the experiment and that if the practice continued the experiment might be brought to an end. At the same time, the operators were reassured about certain of their apprehensions, particularly their fear that, should their previous performance be maintained or improved in this period, rest pauses might never again be reinstated.[1] On this occasion, the test room supervisor took account of the actual human situation instead of acting in accordance with certain abstract conceptions of how individuals should behave or scientific investigations should be conducted. He addressed himself to the total situation, which included the girls' hopes and fears, with the result that a difficult personnel problem was solved. The excessive talking among the girls diminished, and the problem never appeared again.

It is apparent that the logic of a controlled experiment was responsible for many strange occurrences in the test room. It prompted the experimenters on one occasion to transfer two operators back to the department and substitute two other operators. It caused them to interview the girls in the superintendent's office and otherwise to extend to them privileges hitherto unheard of in the ordinary shop department. In the endeavor to keep the major variables in the situation constant and the girls' attitudes co-operative, the investigators inadvertently altered the total social situation of the group. Thus, as

---

[1] It will be remembered that in Period XII the girls had returned to a full 8¾-hour working day without rests or lunch.

a consequence of setting up an experiment to study the factors determining the efficiency of the worker, they abrogated most of the rules
intended to promote and maintain efficiency. The "rules of the game,"
as they ordinarily applied in the shop, were changed.

The above statement implies no question whatsoever with regard to
the sincerity of the experimenters. They were themselves human beings with feelings and sentiments. The observer in his daily association with the girls grew to be very much interested in them. Although
he wanted them to be good human laboratory subjects (i.e., co-operative), he never treated them as nonhuman laboratory specimens. On
many occasions, as in Period XI when he arranged to have the girls
paid their basic hourly rates in order that they would not suffer
financially from the experiment with the five-day week, he displayed
almost too great a sympathetic identification with the girls' feelings and
sentiments.

The difficulty, however, went much deeper than the personal feelings of the investigators. They were entertaining two incompatible
points of view. On the one hand, they were trying to maintain a controlled experiment in which they could test for the effects of single
variables while holding all other factors constant. On the other hand,
they were trying to create a human situation which remained un-
affected by their own activities. By Period XIII it had become evident
that in human situations not only was it practically impossible to keep
all other factors constant, but trying to do so in itself introduced the
biggest change of all; in other words, the investigators had not been
studying an ordinary shop situation but a socially contrived situation
of their own making. The experiment they had planned to conduct
was quite different from the experiment they had actually performed.
They had not studied the relation between output and fatigue, monotony, etc., so much as they had performed a most interesting psychological and sociological experiment. In the process of setting the
conditions for the test, they had altered completely the social situation
of the operators and their customary attitudes and interpersonal
relations.[1]

With this realization, the inquiry changed its character. No longer
were the investigators interested in testing for the effects of single
variables. In the place of a controlled experiment, they substituted
the notion of a social situation which needed to be described and
understood as a system of interdependent elements. This situation in-

---

[1] This point will be elaborated in more detail in Chap. XXV, after other inquiries
have been described, and when its significance will be more fully realized.

cluded not only the external events but the meanings which individuals assigned to them: their attitudes toward them and their preoccupations about them. Rather than trying to keep these "psychological factors" constant, the investigators had to regard them as important variables in the situation. As much attention had to be given to these psychological factors as to output in assessing the external changes which took place.

The chief result of the first two years of experimentation in the Relay Assembly Test Room, then, had been to demonstrate the importance of employee attitudes and preoccupations. All attempts to eliminate such considerations had been unsuccessful. The importance of employee attitudes had been apparent in the "apprehension of authority" which had been common to all the operators, although in different degrees, in the early stages of the test room and which could be "lit up" at the slightest provocation. It had been evident in the effects of the experimentally introduced changes in working conditions, which had proved to be carriers of social meaning rather than mere changes in physical circumstances. It had shown itself in the output variations of certain operators, which could be related to their personal preoccupations, and which continued as long as these preoccupations persisted.

Over and above this, the results from a research point of view were negative. From management's standpoint, however, these experiments had many practical consequences, and it might be well to mention them briefly before turning to the next phase of the research program. Management regarded these experiments primarily as attempts to build up a sound body of knowledge upon which to base executive policy and action. It was clearly seen that research in management problems had to be regarded from a long-time point of view. This does not mean, however, that management was not alert to the possibilities of immediate application. Throughout the entire course of these experiments the results were followed with keen interest and with an ever-ready desire to make use of any findings which seemed sufficiently tested.

Rest pauses were the most important of such findings. Although the experiments did not succeed in determining the exact effect of rest pauses on output and employee well-being, all the available evidence suggested that they were desirable. Management therefore decided to experiment with them in regular shop departments. They were first tried out in the department from which the test room operators were selected. The results were favorable; the operators liked them, and output rose slightly during the four-month observation period. In June, 1928, rest periods were introduced in another large assembly department. In this department, the earnings of a representative group increased after the rests were put in, indicating, at the least, that rests did not decrease output. In October, 1928, a group of typists in an office organization were given rest periods, and again an increase in output occurred. Following these experimental studies, rest periods were introduced in other shop departments where the nature of the work seemed to warrant them. By March, 1929, 2,224 shop operators had rest periods. When the company reached its peak of activity about a year later, some 5,000 people were enjoying them. Of this number approximately 60 per cent were women. For the most part, these rests consisted of 15 minutes at 9:30 in the morning and 10 minutes at 2:30 in the afternoon. During these periods the operators were allowed to walk around and talk to others. They were permitted to play cards or checkers and to eat if they were hungry. They could do anything they were normally allowed to do at lunch hour except leave the section of the building in which their work was located. This provision was necessary to prevent interference with other employees who were not on rest periods at the same time.

Although rest pauses were one of the most practical results of these experiments, unquestionably the most important result was management's improved understanding of many of its problems. Throughout the course of the experiments matters vitally important to management, such as hours of work, wage incentives, and methods of supervision, had been examined. The mere fact that carefully conducted experiments failed to provide conclusive findings on these subjects was in itself very illuminating. Hitherto management had tended to make many assumptions as to what would happen if a change were made in, for example, hours of work or a wage incentive. They now began to question these assumptions and saw that many of them were oversimplified. They began to see that such factors as hours of work and wage incentives were not things in themselves having an independent effect upon employee efficiency; rather, these factors were no more than parts of a total situation and their effects could not be predicted apart from that total situation.

What impressed management most, however, were the stores of latent energy and productive co-operation which clearly could be obtained from its working force under the right conditions. And among the factors making for these conditions the attitudes of the employees stood out as being of predominant importance. All attempts to relate the experimentally introduced changes to the operators' performance, apart from their effect upon the operators' attitudes, had been inconclusive. Management decided, therefore, that everything pointed to the need for more research on employee attitudes and the factors to which they could be related. In Part II the methods which the investigators used and developed to study this problem will be reported.

PART II

A PLAN FOR THE IMPROVEMENT OF
EMPLOYEE RELATIONS

CHAPTER IX

THE GROWTH AND DEVELOPMENT OF THE INTERVIEWING PROGRAM

Its Origin and Objectives

THE interviewing program marked a turning point in the Western Electric Company research and, for a time, overshadowed the other activities of the research group. The program started essentially as a plan for improving supervision. The need for this improvement had been shown by the test room studies, which had clearly indicated that there was a close relation between employee morale and supervision. But how was the improvement to be accomplished? If it involved a re-education of the supervisors themselves, by what methods and with what material were the supervisors to be trained?

Supervisory training was not new at the company. For a number of years a systematic training in company routines and policies had been given to supervisors. But, although it was useful as far as it went, this kind of training did not enable the supervisors adequately to understand and to handle the personal and social situations under their care. The company tried to meet the supervisors' needs by organizing a series of discussions and conferences on "morale," but the outcome, as will be shown later, was not entirely satisfactory.

To this problem the investigators addressed themselves. The outcome was the interviewing program. This new plan for the improvement of supervision crystallized gradually out of two lines of thought.

In the course of the test room experiment, the one outstanding factor which challenged interpretation was the general improvement in the output of the operators, which rose independently of the specific changes in conditions of work made during the study. To what could this general improvement be attributed? One interpretation came from observing the operators' altered total responses to their new working environment. The girls lost much of their shyness and fear, or what came to be called their "apprehension of authority." They talked more freely among themselves and about themselves to officers of the company and to the observers. They developed greater zest for work. New personal relations between members of the group arose which developed into strong bonds of friendship. They visited one another's homes and went to parties, dances, and the theatre together. While the girls were at work, it was not uncommon to find one girl increasing her output so that her friend, who might not be feeling well, could rest. All this was described at the time as a general improvement in the girls' attitudes toward one another, toward their work, toward supervision in general, and toward the company. Moreover, it seemed clear that this change in mental attitude or morale could be associated directly with the improvement in output.

The comments of the operators suggested an explanation for this improvement in morale. Quite frequently while discussing their experiences they compared the test room situation with their previous working conditions in the shop. They talked about certain tactics used by shop supervisors, the existence of which had not been suspected by management. Their improved morale, therefore, seemed to be closely associated with the different supervision in the test room.

At about this time the company was conducting a training course for supervisors by the conference method. Those who were in charge of the course felt that the supervisors did not give sufficient attention to the matter of morale and suggested that several meetings be given over to this topic. A course of five meetings was prepared for this purpose, but after only two of them had been held it became quite clear that there were no factual data on which to base such conferences. Much of the material consisted of the personal experiences and opinions of different executives. These opinions were often conflicting and did not provide adequate information about what constituted an effective working together of supervisor and employee. It was apparent that a discussion of morale must be based on something more definite and factual before any improvement through supervisory training courses could be realized.

These two lines of reflection, independently developed, led to the interviewing program: On the one hand, the test room experiment suggested a close relation between supervision and morale. It suggested that some of the supervisory methods being employed in the regular shop departments were unsatisfactory. On the other hand, the supervisory training group, in attempting to improve supervisor-employee relations, had found many conflicting opinions and but few facts on which to base their course. It was evident that facts were essential. The problem was how such facts could be discovered. At this point one of the test room investigators made a pertinent suggestion: Why not gather the essential facts by approaching the employees themselves and asking them to express frankly their likes and dislikes about their working environment?

Out of this suggestion grew the plan of interviewing a group of employees in order to learn more about their opinions with respect to their work, working conditions, and supervision. It was decided to try this experiment in the Inspection Branch (representing about 1,600 skilled and unskilled employees in both shop and office work), with the expectation that the comments from a group so large and so varied in type of work would offer a fair idea of what the workers at the company liked and disliked.

The interviews were to be used in two ways. First, they were to be passed on to those organizations in the company responsible for plant conditions. These organizations were to investigate the conditions complained about and take the necessary corrective actions. Secondly, the interviews were to be given to the supervisory training group for use in their conference discussions.

Formulation of Plans

Since this project was new and different from anything previously tried by the company, it was necessary to lay careful plans in order to avoid unfavorable consequences. The co-operation of supervisors had to be sought, a group of interviewers had to be selected, explicit instructions for the interviewers had to be prepared, and a consistent approach toward interviewing the employees had to be developed.

The first step was to obtain the co-operation of the supervisors in the Inspection Branch. This was accomplished by calling them into conference and by explaining to them the nature of the proposed procedure. Their criticisms were invited, and various points in the plans were discussed at this meeting. They were told how the idea of interviewing had been evolved and why it seemed necessary to take this next step. It was carefully explained that this experiment was not motivated by any desire on the part of the company to spy or "get something" on any particular supervisor. On the contrary, complete anonymity was guaranteed to all parties. From the interviews any names or statements which might identify an employee who made a criticism or a supervisor who was criticized would be deleted. Most of the supervisors were in favor of such an experiment; only a few were doubtful of its value.

The investigator in charge of the experiment then selected five persons (three men and two women) to do the interviewing. In selecting these interviewers, one qualification considered essential was a thorough knowledge of shop conditions. The interviewer must know the routines and practices of the shop in order that the person interviewed should feel that his statements were being understood. Women were selected to interview women, and men to interview men.

Each interviewer was given a list of instructions recommending the method he should follow in establishing contacts with the supervisors and foremen of the various organizations in which he was going to interview. The procedure was as follows:

1. Each interviewer was assigned a certain territory to cover. From the foreman of each department in his territory he was to obtain a list of the employees' names.

2. When the interviewer was ready to start interviewing in any department, it was recommended that he go first to the foreman in charge and make known his presence.

3. It was recommended that the interviewer select the man he wanted to interview because otherwise the supervisor might be tempted to give the interviewer all his "problem cases" first. However, the interviewer should co-operate with the supervisor in such a way as to cause the least interference with the operation of the department.

4. The interviewer was to ask the supervisor's advice about where the employee should be interviewed, whether he should take him away from the job for a while, or whether he should interview him on the job. (Subsequent experience showed that it was usually advisable to take an employee away from his work for the interview. At this later date it was recommended that the interviewer ask the department chief for a bench or desk where he could conduct the interviews without interruption.)

5. The interviewer was to make sure that the necessary arrangements were made for paying the employee his average earnings for the time consumed in the interview.

6. In his contacts with the supervisors in the department the interviewer was to be very careful not to betray the confidence of any man in that department and to refrain absolutely from discussing the content of the interviews with the supervisors.

7. Only a few employees from any one location were to be interviewed on the same day, so that the work of the department might go on normally and without undue confusion or curiosity.

Careful instructions with regard to the conduct of the interview and the approach to the employee were also given to the interviewers:

1. Whenever possible, the employee was to be formally introduced to the interviewer by the supervisor. Interviewers were not to interview employees whom they knew, since their acquaintance might influence the employees' comments.

2. When the interviewer and employee were seated and ready to proceed with the interview, the employee was to be told the interviewer's name again.

3. The interviewer was to explain to the employee the purpose of the interview: i.e., why any comments the employee cared to make, either favorable or unfavorable, about his supervisors, working conditions, and job were being solicited.

4. The employee was to be told how the interviews were to be used: i.e., that any complaints the employee had to make with regard to working conditions would be investigated together with those of other employees, and that, in so far as practicable, remedial action would be taken. The manner in which the material gathered from the interviews was to be used in supervisory training conferences was also to be explained.

5. The interviewer was to make clear to each employee that the interviews were to be kept strictly confidential: i.e., the employee could say anything to the interviewer, no matter how bad it was, without getting into trouble himself or getting his supervisors or his co-workers into trouble. The interviewer was to explain that no names or organization numbers would appear on any interview and that the people who read the interviews or heard them read would not be told who the employee was or where he worked. Anything the employee said which might identify him with his supervisor would be deleted from his interview.

6. The employee was to be told that the company was as much interested in the things which he liked as in those things with which he was dissatisfied and which he thought needed to be corrected.

7. The interviewer was to take almost verbatim notes as the employee talked. The interviewer was to explain to the employee that he was writing down what was said word for word in order that there would be no possible chance of misrepresenting or forgetting anything said. (At first it was thought that taking notes might make the employee reluctant to talk, but it was found that this was not true.)

8. The interviewer was to be sympathetic, a good listener, and let the interviewee know that he was really interested in his problems and complaints.

9. Strict care was to be taken not to express any agreement or disagreement with the complaints the employee made. The interviewer was to let the employee know that he was in no position to judge the correctness or incorrectness of what the employee was saying.

10. The interviewer was not to inform the employee of the nature of the complaints made by other employees.

11. The interviewer was not to give the employee advice as to what he should do. In rare cases he might advise the employee to see his supervisor, or tell him about the various benefit plans, the Hawthorne evening school, and similar things. However, the interviewer was not to hesitate to offer encouragement to any employee if he thought that would do him any good.

12. The interviewer was to write up the interview under six headings. The opinions of the employee were first to be divided into three categories: working conditions, supervision, and job. Under each of these headings two subclassifications, likes and dislikes, were to be added.

The Reaction of the Employees to the Interviewing Program

Interviewing in the Inspection Branch was begun in September, 1928, and completed in February, 1929. In the next chapter the ways in which the interviews were utilized by the company to improve working conditions and train supervisors will be described. For the present, attention will be confined to the unexpected response which the program received from both employees and supervisors. This influenced the course of the program more than any other single factor.

There was no question that many employees enjoyed the opportunity of expressing their thoughts and feelings. A typical reaction after an interview was, "Gee, it's good to get this off your chest!" As the following comments illustrate, there were many different expressions of this feeling:

It's pretty good of the company to have this interviewing. If things don't go all right, we have someone to tell them to.

I think interviewing is a good idea. It helps some people get a lot of things off their chests.

It is a good idea to interview the operators, as they may have something on their minds that they want to talk over with someone and this gives them a chance to do it.

I think this interviewing is a fine idea. We certainly can talk more freely to you girls [the women interviewers] than to anyone else, and I feel it is going to do a lot of good.

Gee, I think it's swell of the company to give everyone a chance to tell someone how they feel about this place.

Oh, I'm so glad I'm going to be interviewed! The other girls who have already been interviewed said, "Well, that's once you can tell everything and get a load off your chest and feel better after it."

I surely enjoy a good talk like this once in a while. A fellow has to get rid of the gas some way.

Many of the employees commented upon the recognition by management of the worker's point of view which this program implied. They felt that the program allowed the employees to participate jointly with the company in its endeavor to improve working conditions and supervision. The following comments illustrate this attitude:

I think the program is going to do a lot of good, as it will help the supervisors. It will show them what good supervision is.

The reason I told you all this is because I know the interviews are used at the supervisors' conferences, and I hope they hear all I have told you.

I never really thought this interviewing amounted to very much, but since you have explained it to me I see where I can tell you something that may help in the supervisors' conferences.

If interviewing the employees will help to improve conditions, I think it is a wonderful thing. There are a lot of supervisors that need training.

I have waited for this opportunity of being interviewed because I feel what I have to say will be of benefit to my fellow employees as well as to the Western Electric Company.

This interviewing is very interesting. It looks as though the company thinks the laboring class should have a right to say something around here.

When you first brought me out here, I thought, "Well, here's a guy with a lot more company stuff who is going to ask me a few more questions, but I surely won't answer any of them." But after you had explained your program to me, I began to see that the proposition was going to do us a lot of good. I think we are all going to benefit by this program that you people are putting on. That's why I have told you what I have about the conditions over here.

Of course, some of the employees obtained a kind of satisfaction by imagining what would happen to certain supervisors if the company acted upon their complaints:

Now maybe some of the people will take a hint and learn that they have not been doing the right thing, especially some of these underhanded bosses. I hope that they get their share of this.

Now I guess the company means to take notice of some of the unfairness and dirtiness that goes on.

I would never think of going up to the office with the things I have told you because I know I would be found out. In this way I know the company is going to find out how many people are dissatisfied and why. I have a hunch that this man I had so much to say about is getting cold feet already, because he just hates to see the operators who are not his friends get called up to be interviewed for fear that he will be talked about, and every time one of us does get called, he gives us a dirty look as if to scare us.

I have enjoyed this talk with you, but I don't expect to see much of a change until they take this gang boss out.

Equally interesting were the many comments from employees who felt that supervision had improved because of the program. Although the company had not acted, and had no intention of acting, upon the complaints about any one supervisor, a change in supervision might have resulted from the supervisor's realization that his methods were being made the subject of research and that his subordinates were being invited to express their opinions about him. Although some of these comments, a sample of which follows, were probably the result of such a change on the part of a supervisor, nevertheless it was also probable that in many cases the change occurred in the attitude of the operator rather than in that of his supervisor:

Conditions have changed down here within the last few months. Up to that time the boss's friends got all the good jobs. Now we are getting a good break.

Our section chief used to be very crabby and often would bawl the men out for nothing at all. In fact, he made up excuses to pick on us and bawl us out, but since the interviewing began he has been a regular prince and we can't figure out what has happened to him.

It seems to me that the supervisors, particularly the section chiefs, have an entirely different attitude since you fellows started coming around.

I notice the difference in the supervision since the interviewing started. Our group bosses used to sneak behind trucks and try to catch operators doing something they shouldn't be doing. Since the interviewing started they cut that out.

The bosses are beginning to treat us with a little more consideration. I notice that they don't swear so much lately.

Of course, all the opinions were not favorable. Some employees could not see the benefit of such a program and expressed themselves accordingly. They wondered whether real expressions of opinion would actually be given and, if they were, whether management would act on many of them. Some were suspicious as to how the interviews would be used. Typical comments illustrating such skepticism follow:

I wonder how long I will have to wait before they take any action on transferring me now that you have heard my story.

This interviewing program is a good thing if it is carried out right.

What is this all about anyway? Do you think it will do any good?

You say this is confidential? Well, the way I understand it they take some of these interviews and discuss them. I told a certain story about a boss. He may recognize it, and although he may not say so, he will hold it against me. The boss may think he recognizes an interview and hold it against his help, whether it has anything to do with him or not.

The interviewing program will be a good thing if those higher up pay any attention to it.

I wish you could send someone down to investigate the complaints I am making. I would feel a lot better if I knew the company was going to take some action on these complaints.

[While one employee was being interviewed in a small room, he started looking around at the ceiling and all the walls. The interviewer asked

him what the trouble was.] I am looking to see where you have the dicta-
phone hidden so that everybody can hear what I am telling you.

I heard that if anybody makes a lot of complaints, they will get laid off.

When you first started to interview, we thought the company wanted to
find out who was giving information to the Communist paper, but after
the program progressed we were convinced the company was really interested in finding out the actual conditions in the shop, both as to the working
class and supervision. I believe this is going to help everyone.

What good is the interviewing going to do? About two or three months
ago I complained about bum tools. It seems to me that this interviewing
does not amount to much, as there has not been anything done about the
tools as yet.

Many times improvements made by the company were undeservedly
attributed to the interviewing program, or the program was credited
with having made improvements that had not been made. A typical
example of the latter was that of a woman who complained at great
length and with considerable feeling about the poor food being served
in the company restaurant. When, a few days later, she chanced to
meet the interviewer, she commented with great enthusiasm upon the
improved food and thanked the interviewer for having communicated
her grievance to management and for having secured such prompt
action. Here no change had been made in the thing criticized; yet the
employee felt that a change had been made. The following are examples of actual improvements in working conditions for which the
program undeservedly received credit:

I notice that since this interviewing started the wages are better. I know
several people who work in the next department who had not had a raise
in salary for a long time.

Have I heard about you? I'll say I have! You sure are doing a lot for us
over here. Say, don't we get clean overalls every day? How would we get
them if it wasn't for you reporting what we said about them?

The reactions of the supervisors to the program were favorable.
Many of them wished to participate in the program and made requests
to contribute their bit to the fund of information which was being
collected. This movement resulted in interviewing the two lower ranks
of supervisors in the Inspection Branch: group chiefs and section chiefs.
Supervisors were asked their opinion of the plan and its results as they
saw them, and the consensus of opinion was that the plan had in no
way embarrassed them. They were sure that most employees and
supervisors were in favor of it, and they were practically unanimous in

thinking that the interviewing program not only should be continued but also should be extended to other organizations in the plant.

Material gathered from the interviews was discussed in supervisory conferences, and the following opinions from supervisors were indicative of the interest in the new form of supervisory training. While the favorable comments far outnumbered the unfavorable ones, several of the latter are included to show the point of view of those supervisors who were not completely convinced of the plan's merits:

I wish they had started this interviewing program when I was first made a group chief as I sure am getting a lot of good out of the conferences. There are so many points brought out about supervision that I never thought of.

I don't think I am getting very much out of the conferences so far. We had an interview last week that brought out a few arguments, but I have been waiting for some of the problems that I have had to deal with in my section. I have been fighting for one thing for a good many years and I know that the only reason that nothing has been done about it is because the foreman has not taken it high enough. I would like to have them discuss this problem in an interview so that I could find out what some of the other fellows would do in a case of this kind.

Gee, my supervisors sure are getting a kick out of these conferences. This morning one of the men came to me and asked if he could attend a second conference on the same subject because he enjoyed the first one so much that he felt sure he would get enough out of the second one to pay for his time.

I really believe you are helping some of these hard-boiled foremen and group chiefs. You know after they come back from a conference they start thinking it over and I believe it begins to soak in. They begin to realize what may happen in the future, for your work is just new as yet.

The training conferences are the bunk as far as I am concerned. They don't give us credit for knowing anything around here. Why, it might be all right for a new group chief, but I wouldn't say it was worth the time for our old group chiefs. Say, do you think the employees are telling you everything? Far from it! There are many things that are brought up to the foreman that we take care of and never say anything about, but no one ever gives us credit for it.

I like the supervisors' conferences very much. You see, I am beginning to find out lots of things I was doing before which I know now were wrong. I did not do those things because I meant to, but I guess I just never thought about them. Now that some of these things have been called to my attention in the supervisors' conferences, I am sure doing things different.

Did you go to the last conference we had? Say, they are getting to be good. You know, I am getting a lot of help from them. I am learning to see the operator's viewpoint of things, and I really believe I am learning to do my job much better by attending these conferences.

The conferences have not helped me one bit. The interviews that we discussed have nothing to do with my job. I would like to see what some of the fellows in my group think about me. I would recognize an interview from my group in a minute. They all think that I am a son-of-a-gun here, and the worst crab in the department is making the most money. I would like to know how some of the other group chiefs would handle the bunch of crabs that I have to deal with.

Many unsolicited comments from supervisors indicated that they thought the program was having a good effect on employee morale:

I think this interviewing program is doing a lot of good among the group chiefs, and the operators seem to be more content.

Well, when are you coming to interview in my department again? It really does me a great deal of good to see the satisfaction the men get from being interviewed.

I think this is a good idea of the company's to interview the operators and I am sure we will all benefit by it.

We have been giving you the operators to interview who we felt had a real grievance of some kind. I have noticed that they seemed to be more contented after they talked to you. Personally, I think the interviewing program is going to help us all.

Of course, even the supervisors were not free from suspicions about the use to be made of the interviews. A department chief, for example, asked an interviewer, "What do you think is the real reason for this interviewing program? Do you think they are trying to pick out the Bolsheviks?"

The actual proportion of favorable to unfavorable comments is not indicated by the above illustrations. In total number, the favorable responses far outweighed the unfavorable. In fact, the quick way in which the program took hold and the keen interest shown in it, both by the workers and the supervisors, were astonishing to management. So much enthusiasm had not been expected.

The Extension of the Program and the Formation of the Industrial Research Division in 1929

Following this experimental period in the Inspection Branch, the plan was carefully reviewed by management and its value assessed. This consideration led to a decision to extend the program in two steps, the first one to be taken in 1929 and to include only the Operating

Branch, and the second to be taken in 1930 and to extend to all the eight branches in the Hawthorne Works organization. On February 1, 1929, the Industrial Research Division was formed to take over this work in addition to continuing the test room studies described in the first part of this book.[1]

The extension of the program necessitated a larger number of interviewers to undertake the work. For the most part, these additional interviewers were taken from those organizations in which interviewing was in progress. They were either of supervisory status or were recognized as potential supervisors and were assigned temporarily to interviewing work for a period of about a year. It was thought that they could do adequate interviewing with a certain amount of preliminary training and that the interviewing experience in itself would be excellent training for them as supervisors. For the latter reason, it was decided to give as many shop supervisors as possible the opportunity of participating, and consequently interviewers were kept for a limited time and were then replaced by others. All the personnel in the interviewing department, however, was not of this temporary order. A permanent staff was gradually being built up to take care of the work as a research activity.

An enlargement of the supervisory training program also occurred during this period. The staff of conference leaders was increased from two to six. The new men came from other organizations where they had had supervisory experience, and they were temporarily assigned to the Industrial Research Division. This staff was also changed from time to time. Conference leaders were selected on the basis of their supervisory and company experience and their natural ability to get along with people. Preparatory to their work as conference leaders they spent a short period taking interviews and interpreting them. Their experience and knowledge were then enlarged by studying the

---

[1] The Industrial Research Division was divided into four departments, each with a separate function: (1) Interviewing, (2) Interview Analysis, (3) Supervisory Training, and (4) Test Room. The function of the first department was to interview employees and record their likes and dislikes relative to their working environment. The function of the second group was to analyze the favorable and unfavorable comments of the employees so that the company could make use of this information. The third department was to conduct supervisors' training conferences based upon interview material. The test room group was to continue its studies of employee relations and efficiency. The activities of the first three groups were referred to at the time as "A Plan for Improving Employee Relations on the Basis of Data Obtained from Employees." A paper with this title was presented by M. L. Putnam at the autumn conference of the Personnel Research Federation in New York, November 15, 1929, and was later published in the official journal of that organization, *The Personnel Journal*, in its issue of February, 1930.

company organization, the history and development of supervisory training, books and articles on the technique of conference work, and finally by a period of observing the more experienced conference leaders at work.

Changes in the Interviewing Method

No part of the plan was more interesting than the growth and development of the method of interviewing. At first, the interviewers patterned their procedure on the existing techniques of interviewing. They knew something about, and had had experience with, the conventional type of interviewing done by supervisors, by employment departments, and by personnel people. Nevertheless, each interviewer began to suggest certain modifications, and these were discussed and criticized daily among themselves. The suggestions presented at informal gatherings offered so many interesting possibilities that it was decided to organize the discussions by having weekly conferences of interviewers. At these meetings certain observations were made which led to important changes in the interviewing method.

Under the plan of interviewing in the Inspection Branch, it had been the practice of the interviewers to ask the employees about their likes and dislikes, first with regard to supervision and then with regard to working conditions and the job. In each area the interviewer had in mind certain questions to be used for the purpose of eliciting the material. Such questions, however, were never used with the definite purpose of making the interview a questionnaire procedure. For example, if it was difficult to get the employee to talk about his dislikes with regard to supervision, such questions as the following were frequently resorted to: How does your boss treat you? Does your boss ever bawl you out? Has he any favorites? Is your boss a slave driver? Do you consider your boss to be reasonable?

It was found that merely asking an employee to state his likes or dislikes with regard to his working conditions was frequently misunderstood; the employee might begin to talk about his job or something else. For this reason, the interviewer was instructed to ask specifically about the lighting system, heat, ventilation, drinking water, toilets, lockers, treatment which the employee might have received in the hospital, as well as about safety devices and accident hazards in his department. One question which was found very useful in evoking opinions about working conditions was: What do you think of the company as a place to work? Other questions used were: Have you ever worked in any other factory? How did the working conditions there compare with those in this plant? What do you think of the thrift plans, insurance plans, and education plans? Opinions with regard to the job were elicited by asking the worker if the job was fatiguing or dirty, if he thought he had been on the job too long, if there were prospects for advancement, if he was being paid in accordance with what he thought he was worth, and so on.

In short, it was quite clear that, although it had been the intention of the interviewers merely to invite the employee to express his opinions, nevertheless each interviewer was mentally equipped with a set of questions which he expected to have answered by everyone. He was not satisfied until he had in some way solicited some comment from each employee about his supervision, working conditions, and job. It also became clear that by this method the interviewer was recording those comments of the employee which he rather than the employee thought important. The interviewer led the conversation; the employee followed.

This realization was forced on the attention of the interviewers by a number of experiences. They found that an employee might start talking about the topic suggested, but in a short time he would be way off the subject. Feeling that this material was irrelevant, the interviewer would try to lead him back to some other point, but in a few moments the employee would be back where he was before. Regardless of what the interviewer said, the employee's thoughts tended to gravitate toward one idea. There was some one thing uppermost in his mind which completely overshadowed everything else, and it was about this that he wished to talk.

It may be interesting to describe the first occasion on which such an experience was related. At a meeting of the interviewing staff a member was berating himself for being a poor interviewer because he had been unable to keep a certain employee on the specified topics. The worker had tended to wander and to talk about his personal life, his experiences, and other "irrelevant" topics. At this meeting there were several other interviewers who immediately confessed to numerous similar experiences. They had had cases in which several subjects predominated in the mind of the employee, and any attempt to lead him away from them had been unsuccessful. In other instances the interviewers had found that a particularly reticent person became remarkably communicative if just the right topic could be touched upon in the conversation.

This conference marked a turning point in the interviewing method. It revealed certain obvious defects in the direct-question method. Such a method tended to put a person in a "yes" or "no" frame of mind. Instead of obtaining the employee's spontaneous and real convictions, it tended to arouse a reaction of antagonism or a stereotyped form of response. Frequently the questions themselves suggested the answers. And, moreover, the method elicited opinions upon topics which the interviewer thought to be important but which the employee might never have thought of before.

It was finally decided, about July, 1929, to adopt a new interviewing technique, which at that time was called the indirect approach. After the interviewer had explained the program, the employee was to be allowed to choose his own topic. As long as the employee talked spontaneously, the interviewer was to follow the employee's ideas, displaying a real interest in what the employee had to say, and taking sufficient notes to enable him to recall the employee's various statements. While the employee continued to talk, no attempt was to be made to change the subject. The interviewer was not to interrupt or try to change the topic to one he thought more important. He was to listen attentively to anything the worker had to say about any topic and take part in the conversation only in so far as it was necessary in order to keep the employee talking. If he did ask questions, they were to be phrased in a noncommittal manner and certainly not in the form, previously used, which suggested the answers.

This change in method had an important effect on the duration of each interview. In the first stages of the program the interview was approximately 30 minutes long, but with the change in method the average time for a single interview grew to approximately $1\frac{1}{2}$ hours.

In October, 1929, a change in the method of writing up interviews followed the change in technique. The original method of grouping employee comments as likes and dislikes under the headings of supervision, working conditions, and job was supplanted by a method of recording entire interviews as nearly verbatim as possible, showing the comments made both by the interviewer and by the employee. This change lengthened the reports from an average of approximately $2\frac{1}{2}$ pages to 10 single-spaced typewritten pages.

The Extension of the Interviewing Program during 1930

In 1930 the plan reached its greatest development. On January 1, 1930, the Industrial Research Division began to interview employees in all organizations at the Hawthorne Works and to offer conference training for all supervisors in these groups. This extension of the program was in accordance with the decision reached by the management in 1928 after the Inspection Branch experience. Since the experience in the Operating Branch during 1929 had confirmed the value of the program, this decision had not been altered. Table XIX shows the number of employees interviewed in 1928, 1929, and 1930.

By March, 1930, sufficient material had been gathered to start supervisory conferences in all branches of the Hawthorne Works. The supervisory training department was expanded, and the conferences based on interview material were extended to include a total of 2,487 supervisors.

TABLE XIX

NUMBER OF EMPLOYEES INTERVIEWED IN EACH BRANCH IN 1928, 1929, AND 1930

Branch	1928	1929	1930	Total
Public Relations	....	.....	8	8
Industrial Relations	....	.....	130	130
Accounting	....	.....	637	637
Production	....	.....	963	963
Operating	....	10,300	5,109	15,409
Inspection	1,600	....	514	2,114
Technical	....	.....	1,166	1,166
Specialty Products	....	.....	699	699
	1,600	10,300	9,226	21,126

Changes in the Program during 1931

The year 1931 brought about a very important change in the interviewing program. As a result of the general decline in business it had already become necessary to lay off a considerable number of employees throughout the plant. In view of this uncertainty it did not seem practical to plan to interview all employees as had been done in 1930. It was therefore decided to suspend the general interviewing program until the business outlook was more favorable. In the meantime it was decided to continue some interviewing work for experimental purposes with the thought in mind that should the interviewing program be reinstated at a later date the benefits of these experiments could then be incorporated in the program.[1]

[1] It may be said here that conditions suitable to the resumption of a plan for interviewing employees did not occur until 1936, when a new program was begun on an experimental basis. Although it utilized the interviewing method as developed during the program here under consideration, nevertheless it differed considerably in emphasis and purpose. In the concluding section of this book a brief statement of the concepts and methods utilized in this new plan will be given. This new plan will be called "personnel counseling" to differentiate it from the interviewing program of 1928–1930.

The experiments in interviewing which were made in 1931 consisted of assigning a selected group of interviewers to different departments for the purpose of making intensive studies of the individuals in each department. In particular the investigators wished to compare the results of repeated interviews in a small group with the results of single interviews in a larger group.

The direction taken by the experiments in interviewing is of interest for two reasons: In the first place it reflected certain doubts as to the adequacy of the interviewing program which was being conducted. The nature of these doubts will become clear from the interpreted findings from the interviewing program which are reported in the chapters which follow. In the second place these experiments were of interest because they led directly to a study of the social organization of employees. These studies will be reported in Part IV.

CHAPTER X

THE PRACTICAL OPERATION OF THE PLAN; THE TRAINING OF SUPERVISORS AND THE INVESTIGATION OF COMPLAINTS

SUPERVISORY TRAINING

DURING periods of rapid increase in personnel, when a large number of employees were promoted to supervisory positions, the need for a systematic training in company routines and policies had become evident. Largely to fulfill this need, there had been intermittent efforts in supervisory training at the Hawthorne Works for a number of years. Up to 1927 these efforts took the general form of classroom meetings in which certain informative material was presented and discussed. For the most part, this material was confined to specific job subjects such as the use of various order blanks, waste elimination, and budgetary control. The training was done by the respective personnel organizations of the different branches in order that it would be adapted to the particular needs of each organization.

Type of Personnel Training before Introduction of Interview Material

A new development in supervisory training began in 1927. During that year, at the close of a series of job problem conferences, some of the supervisors suggested that a similar series dealing with their personnel problems might be formulated. To meet this need, a series of conferences on seventeen subjects was prepared. These subjects are listed below:

1. The supervisor and his job.
2. Hiring — placing the right employee in the right job.
3. The new employee.
4. Sizing up and rating employees.
5. Production — efficiency of the individual.
6. Training and upgrading.
7. Wages and rate revision.
8. Transfer — terminations.
9. Turnover.
10. Giving orders to subordinates.
11. Leadership.
12. Co-operation.

13. Keeping up the morale.
14. Safety.
15. Health.
16. Thrift.
17. Outside activities.

The supervisory training leaders discussed these subjects with the staff group [1] in each branch. In turn, each division chief or general foreman acted as a conference leader for the supervisors under him in his own department. The following outline of the subject "outside activities" illustrates the manner in which the material was prepared, the kind of discussion held, and the type of conclusions reached.

OUTSIDE ACTIVITIES
PREPARATORY OUTLINE

Outline of discussion
1. What results may be expected from employee participation in outside activities?
2. What outside activities do you classify as desirable? What ones as undesirable?
3. How far should the supervisor go in encouraging or discouraging outside activities of employees?

Hypothetical arguments to be considered
1. It has been our policy to discourage outside activities of employees. Our experience indicates that a man cannot serve two masters and we have found that employees who have other interests do not get on well with us.
2. It is well for a man to take his work seriously and perform his tasks industriously and conscientiously. But, there is such a thing as getting into a rut. In the long run he will do his work more effectively if his mind changes to other subjects after the whistle blows. In our plant we encourage employees to participate in some outside activity while off the job.
3. It should be the aim of every supervisor to do his part in relieving the worker's mind of job anxiety so that he can go out at the end of the day's work without carrying with him a mind full of worries and bitterness. He has then done his part in keeping the job from spoiling his worker's recreation hours. It is very questionable as to how far a supervisor should go in inquiring into and attempting to regulate the details of a man's life outside the plant. When a worker's outside activities result in an inability to deliver a fair day's

[1] The branch staff at that time included the superintendent, the assistant superintendents, and the division chiefs, or general foremen, of each branch.

work, his supervisor has a right and a duty to take a hand. The boss has another responsibility; he must set a good example himself.

Summary of discussion:

Results of employee participation in outside activities

1. Benefits which may be derived by the employee:
   Pleasure and recreation
   Improved health
   Financial gain
   Education
   Valuable experience
2. Benefits to be obtained by the company:
   Increased morale and satisfaction
   Reduction of lost time from poor health
   Good will and loyalty from activities sponsored by the company
   Increased efficiency on the job
3. Undesirable results:
   Overparticipation may result in poor health
   Loss of interest in work
   Lost time and divided attention
   Financial loss to employee
   Increased accidents

Activities which may generally be considered desirable

   Educational
   Recreational (athletics, hobbies, pastimes)
   Civic or political
   Social (organization parties, individual social activities)
   Or any activity which promotes company's as well as employee's welfare

Activities generally considered undesirable

   Outside business
   Outside work for others (in most cases)
   Excess in any outside activities
   Or any activity which reduces job efficiency or employee's future growth or health

Supervisor's position in encouraging or discouraging outside activities

   In general it is agreed that the supervisor should encourage activities considered desirable and discourage activities considered undesirable.
   The supervisor should remember that there is a difference between his own personal interest in employee activities and the interest he expresses for the company.
   Almost all cases in which employees have outside interests and activities must be handled individually.

Running through this conference report there is an underlying demand for a set of rules in terms of which the supervisors could judge the employees' conduct. It is also clear, and this became more apparent as the conferences continued, that only the supervisors' point of view was being given consideration. As a result, the conferences were chiefly expressions of the supervisors' own sentiments, and of what they thought the employees' sentiments were or should be. While there may have been some merit in discussions of this kind, it soon became apparent to the conference leaders that the meetings would be much more fruitful if they knew what ideas and feelings the employees themselves had on these subjects.

A New Type of Personnel Training for Supervisors Based on Interview Material

When interviewing was started in the Inspection Branch in September, 1928, a new kind of personnel training for supervisors began. A series of conferences based on material obtained from the interviews was introduced, only the supervisors of the Inspection Branch participating. As the interviewing program extended to other branches, supervisors in these other branches were given this new kind of training. Finally, in February, 1929, when the Industrial Research Division was organized, all supervisory training based upon employee interviews was centralized in a single department and became one of the activities of the newly created division.[1]

At first, conference groups were made up of several levels of supervision. After two or three conferences based upon the interview material, however, it became apparent that junior supervisors were reluctant to express their real opinions in the presence of their superiors. Because of this, the conferences were rearranged so that only people of equal rank were brought together.

How the Interview Material Was Used in Personnel Training for Supervisors

(a) *Selected Employee Comments*

Selected employee comments were first used as a basis for conference discussion. The method followed was to select from one or several interviews provocative comments on topics of supervisory interest and read them at the conference. The following comment is typical:

I feel that my supervisors do not do all they can to adjust our wages

[1] See footnote, p. 200.

properly. In my section we have a particular job a man with eight years' experience is working on. He gets $5 a week more than I do. I know I can do his job as well as he can but he can't do mine. Of that I am satisfied. I also have had experience on practically all the other jobs. This other man was changed around when working on overtime and put on some of the new work, but he can't seem to get on to it. He is always asking questions. Inasmuch as I have been here 10 years, the only difference between the two of us is that the other man is married and I am not, although I do have my mother to support. The other man does not have any more education than I and he is not attending an evening school and never has, as far as I know, and I am attending. No one seems to be able to explain why this inconsistency exists. I have asked my supervisor and he tells me they will look into it or they will help to make it up next time, but I have been told that before.

After presenting a problem such as this, the leader would give each supervisor an opportunity to express his opinions. He would then outline the points at issue. For example, in the case cited, the following questions would be asked: Assuming that this situation existed in your group, how would you talk it over with a person who complained to you about it? Would you attempt to explain the inconsistency? What would you tell him? What factors might account for the difference in rates? If the rates are inconsistent, how should they be straightened out? What factors in addition to those listed by the employee (length of service, home responsibilities, experience, attendance at evening school) should be considered at the next rate revision period? Which three factors should bear the greatest weight in rate revision?

Some of the conclusions reached and opinions expressed in the conference on the above case are given below:

1. The second employee may be overrated, depending on his job, or the first employee may be underrated.

2. Such an inconsistency in pay may be due to a man's being penalized for poor attendance or poor work. It may also be the result of advancement along different routes.

3. It was pointed out that if the second employee was overrated, the supervisor might be reluctant to tell him so. A discussion followed of the advisability of coming out frankly and explaining the circumstances and then asking the first employee if it would make him feel any better if the second employee's rate was cut. However, it was decided that if the employee should answer "Yes" it might lead to some difficulty with the second employee.

4. The group was of the opinion that the bogey would help to equalize the rates in time, assuming that the employee's statement was an accurate

recital of the facts. The conclusion was reached that the supervisor in this case was negligent and he should act as follows:

    a. He should gather all the facts.
    b. Weigh each fact considered.
    c. Decide the fair thing to do.
    d. Explain it to the employee.

5. Under 4a, the section chief should carry on the discussion concerning rate of pay with the employee, as the group chief usually does not have much to do with rates.

6. Under 4b and 4c, the section chief should go to his superior for advice if he needs it.

7. The difficult job for a section chief comes under 4d. It is especially difficult if he is not sure his course is the right one. Regardless of the reason for not increasing an employee's pay or for an inconsistency in pay, the employee must be told and not left "up in the air."

8. Some cases were then discussed in which supervisors had told employees directly that they could see no reason for giving them increases in pay. The advantage of doing this, it was thought, lay in the fact that it gave the employee a chance to express his views before it was too late for the supervisor to change his opinion. Also, the employee could perhaps be more thoroughly convinced if told beforehand. It was suggested that the employee might be told that, although a raise could not be granted at present, it would be considered at the next revision period. The disadvantage in this method, it was pointed out, was that the employee might only be silenced and not "sold." This would be especially true if others in the group were given raises.

(b) *Complete Interviews*

When the interviews began to be recorded verbatim and when the content of the interviews, as the technique of interviewing improved, became more interesting and varied, it became evident that the complete interviews themselves provided an excellent basis for discussion among supervisors. As an experiment, several interviews were selected, carefully edited to insure the anonymity of both employees and supervisors, and then tried out in conferences. This material was received so favorably that conferences in which complete interviews were used were continued for some time.

The usual experience in using material of this sort was that one supervisor after another began to discuss some phase of the employees' thought, so that very little guidance by the conference leader was necessary. The employees' comments kept the supervisors well on the subject. At first their zest in examining this "human interest stuff" was not unlike that of a group of boys watching a League baseball team through the cracks of a high board fence. But as they became more accustomed to the material, they settled down to serious discussion. Usually these discussions took the form of trying to determine why the employees said what they did and what could be done about it by supervisors.

An employee interview used in training conferences, shortened considerably to make it more convenient for use, follows:

Interviewer: Perhaps you might like to give me an idea of what you think a good supervisor should be like.

Employee: I think first of all he should be able to handle his men right, and should know how to show them courtesy. He should never bark at a man or talk in such a way that a man doesn't feel like taking it. You know, some men, there's no getting away from it, are quick-tempered, and they must be approached in the right way and if they are they will do anything for a supervisor, but if someone barks at them — well, then it is time to look out.

You hear employees say that this place is a jail, but it isn't, it's the supervisors every time. . . . Another thing: Supposing a man gets hurt. Maybe he lifts up something and slightly bruises his hand or makes a scratch or something like that. Well, you have to tell your boss about it or go to the hospital. You tell the boss about it and he growls, "Why are you so clumsy?"

You understand, of course, that he fills out a big report for some small scratch. You know how easy it is for blood poison to set in, and all you have to do is to have them bandage it up or put some antiseptic on it or something. The supervisor, as perhaps you know, has to make out a report of time lost through accidents.

Here is something else: In regard to this Personnel Department, I don't know whether that department is a bluff or a disgrace to the company. A man goes for a transfer and the first day that he goes up there they tell him that they will line something up for him, and then the next day they will say, "No, we are sorry that we haven't got anything." I don't know whether they have a conversation with the bosses over the telephones or not; but if they do, I think that is all wrong.

If you follow the rules, why you get bawled out for it because the rules aren't right; and if you don't follow them, you get bawled out. So . . . it makes a fellow wonder just what he should do. Why not have one rule which everyone abides by?

(c) *Selected Topics*

The conferences using complete interviews began to have a note of confusion in them because of the wide variety of subjects commented on in each interview and the cursory manner in which each topic was handled. At the end of about ten meetings, the conference leaders came to the conclusion that, although such material was exceedingly valuable in allowing the supervisors to gain an insight into the individual differences between employees and a better appreciation of their attitudes, there was also need for more complete discussion and understanding of particular subjects. Instead of presenting a whole interview and discussing the variety of topics it contained, it was decided to prepare for each meeting material on a single subject such as "health," "benefit fund plan," "vacations," or "A.T. & T. stock plan." From a number of interviews different opinions relating to a particular subject were selected. Mimeographed sheets containing from ten to twelve different opinions on the subject to be discussed were prepared and passed out to conference members at the beginning of the meeting.

(d) Combined Employee and Supervisory Comments

In addition to the problem of selecting interesting, helpful, and varied material, the conference leaders had other difficulties to meet. As more employee comments on supervision were taken into the conferences, there was a tendency for some supervisors to put themselves on the defensive and take refuge in saying that the employee was a "sorehead," a "failure," or just "didn't know what he was talking about." This attitude, while not general, was unfavorable to effective discussion of supervisory problems. A second problem was a feeling among some of the supervisors that they were continually attending conferences but were never getting anything settled, and that the employee's side of controversial items was emphasized to the neglect of supervisory opinion. The second criticism was particularly interesting in the light of the earlier situation when the opposite had been true, that is, when only the supervisor's opinions had been considered and those of the employee neglected. In endeavoring to correct this latter situation, the conference leaders had swung too far in the opposite direction.

For these reasons, it was decided to make two changes in the conference material. The first change was to arrange the material in a series of related unit subjects, that is, a major problem was selected and subdivided into four or five related parts, each of which was to be the subject of one conference. The advantage of this approach, it was thought, would lie chiefly in linking the conferences together, thus making it possible to develop in the participants a feeling of interest and progress and to conclude each series with a degree of finality.

The second change was to accompany each group of employee comments about a particular subject with a related supervisory problem drawn from some supervisor's experience, in which the attitudes, opinions, and questions of the supervisor involved were incorporated. The supervisors felt that this gave them a better opportunity to submit their own problems for discussion and to match an employee's criticism with a statement of the problem from their own point of view.

An illustration of this kind of material follows. This particular material was presented in the third of a series of conferences on "Orders, Directions, Suggestions, and Teamwork." The subject for each of these meetings was chosen in accordance with a guiding policy, namely, that the selection of a subject should be governed by the relative importance of that subject to employees, as determined by the frequency with which it was mentioned in the interviews.

It is well to remember that these problem cases were first discussed by the superintendent and staff of each branch. This arrangement insured a correct interpretation of company policies in the discussion. It also gave the staff members an opportunity to share in supervisory training and helped in securing their active interest.

SUPERVISORS' CONFERENCES
FALL — 1930

Series No. I   Conference No. 3

Principles of Successful Supervision   *Teamwork*

[The following remarks were based upon conversations with two supervisors. The comments of each told approximately the same story, so they were written up as though one supervisor did all the talking. All names are fictitious.]

Since our new supervisor, Jones, has been in our department, things have sure changed! I guess the whole problem is that he doesn't know how to get teamwork from us or from our employees.

When our former supervisor, Smith, was with us, there was a wonderful spirit among all of us. Our work was always "up to snuff" and everything was done so well they promoted Smith to a better job. We sure hated to see him go.

Since Jones took his place, things have gone down fast. In the first place, he came in here from a different kind of work, and knows practically nothing about our work. We sure got "sat on" when we old-timers who had been on the job for some time tried to help Jones over the "rough spots" by pointing out to him those items in our work on which we had to keep an eye if things were to keep running smoothly. The same thing happened when we told him what policies we had been following in dealing with our people. He let us know mighty quick that no subordinate could tell him anything about his job, and that he felt himself perfectly able to run the job, and that our job was to take orders and say nothing.

If he sees someone laughing or talking during working hours or if he sees someone take a minute after the starting whistle to finish reading a newspaper article, he rushes over to the employee's supervisor and sarcastically asks, "What's the matter with that loafer over there? Don't you have any work for him, or are you afraid to tell him that we start to work here as soon as the whistle blows?"

Perhaps I shouldn't be too severe. When he wants to be, Jones really can be a fine fellow, and some of his ideas are great, but some of them are all wet and he won't discuss them with us or in any way take advantage of our experience. On top of that, he seems to take a delight in continually making us realize that he is the boss.

Since he came here the old spirit of our bunch is pretty much gone. We all seem to have developed the habit of doing exactly as we are told and no more. He never tells us what he is trying to do, and our real interest in the job is dead. If we try to make suggestions, he simply says, "I'm not interested; I'm doing things in a better way."

Sometimes I'm ashamed to pass his orders along to my employees. I suppose they think I have lost any knowledge I used to have about how the jobs ought to be done. All I can say is, "That's the way the boss says to do it, so that's the way we'll do it." I try not to say even that, but sometimes my own self-respect makes me "alibi."

I'd like to know what my real responsibility is in this affair. I know this condition is bad for the department. I've tried to tell Jones, and it doesn't work. I have my family to support and can't take too much into my own hands. The big boss surely thinks Jones is O.K. for the job or he wouldn't be there.

I'd like to see this discussed in the conferences. I know of some other supervisors who have about the same problem, and I think it could be discussed so that we could all profit by the experiences of the other fellows.

[The following comments from employees were also included in this conference material.]

When our boss wants a certain job done, he don't tell us how to get it out. He can't — he don't know himself. He just tells you to have it done by four or five o'clock and then walks away, and sometimes it is utterly impossible to do this. It don't pay to reason with him. When he comes back, he wants to know why you didn't get it ready. He has no reasoning.

I don't know just why I like my boss. I guess we get along well together because he has a way of asking me to do a job that makes me feel good. Sometimes I don't like the work he asks me to do, but I do it willingly because he asked me to do it in a nice way.

The main thing I have in mind is the fact that our supervisors think we should know more than we do. They expect too much from us. They say we should work on our own hook and then if we do that and make a mistake, they say that we should have asked them for advice. The trouble is, we don't get any credit for doing good work, but they sure let us know when our work is bad.

That's the way the boss gets back at you. He gives you a rotten job or gives you just enough of an idea to make you wonder what the work is all about. You have to take a great deal of time to figure out how to go about the job.

This just burns me up — it isn't so easy to avoid accidents when you're not familiar with a job. They can't explain all about the job to you in one lump. Then, when you have an accident they say, "What's the matter?" About the only way we can learn anything about the hazards is through experience.

On this job, our supervisors actually baby us too much. I get so disgusted with it, but I suppose they think they have to because of the importance of this work.

One thing I have noticed more than anything else around here is the lack of co-operation between the supervisors and the fellows. I feel that the supervisors should talk more to the employees and try to understand the human side of this work. Of course, I realize that their time is limited and they have to get the job out, but I think they should get in and mix a little more and they will be better able to handle all situations.

When our supervisor has any occasion to correct or reprimand any of us, he does so in a decent way. He seems to have confidence in his people. He tells us what he wants us to do, and then he lets us alone.

Our supervisor is very funny sometimes. We are afraid to ask him anything twice because he gets so mad. He doesn't treat the girls so bad but he is terribly fresh to the men and he calls them mean names. I would report him, wouldn't you? One of the men in our organization is supporting a widowed mother, and he never answers the boss back because everything depends on his job and he don't want to lose it. One time this man made a lot of work bad because he did not want to ask the boss the second time how to work on it and then the boss bawled him out.

Results of Supervisory Training

What were the results obtained from the conference program? Naturally, the question the conference leaders would have liked to be able to answer was, "Had supervision improved because of the conferences?" This question obviously could not be answered conclusively. The conference leaders thought there was some direct evidence which pointed to a steady and perceptible improvement in supervision. First, they pointed to comments from employees which seemed to suggest such an improvement. Secondly, they presented the testimony of supervisors. And thirdly, they argued from their own observations and experiences in the conference room. Let us examine these three bodies of evidence.

(1) Most of the employees' comments were of a specific nature and referred to specific changes which they thought the training program had brought about in certain supervisors. Such comments as the following were typical:

Speaking of these supervisory conferences, I think they do a lot of good all right. I know it's helping this group chief. It's not so long ago he attended a supervisors' conference and when he came back he stood and talked with the section chief about what he had learned up there. I was standing near them doing my work and I overheard him say: "Well, I have learned a lot at conference today. There's one thing they told us that I'll try not to forget and that is, 'You can ask a man to do something, but you can't make a man do it.' I'm going to see if I can't keep that in mind."

Well, one thing, those conferences are doing the supervisors some good all right.

I don't think much of these supervisory training conferences because when the group chiefs come back from those conferences they'll blah-blah about them for an hour or two.

Well, what I wanted to say was that I think your program is certainly doing a lot of good things around here in the last couple of years. The reason why I mentioned that is because when Mr. Z, our foreman now, came into the department he tried to show how tough he was. He was always trying to bulldoze everyone in the department. Any time an employee done anything wrong, he always wanted to have something to say. It seems as though no one ever could get along with him. At times it was impossible to go up and ask him something. If you did, he would say to you, "Is that all you got to do is to bring something up to me that don't mean anything?" He would then say that if you stayed on the job and done more work instead of trying to find something to talk about all the time, we would be better. It seemed as though everyone in the department at that time was scared of him. Any time any one seen him coming up the aisle, or probably somewhere else, they would always duck from him. But now he is one of the best foremen that you can find anywhere. That fellow sure has changed. The way it is now, it seems as though he is always willing to help everyone out. You can go up to him now and ask him a question, and he is always willing to answer you. I think you will interview other men that will almost tell you the same as I am saying.

I tell you, I think they treat the girls mighty fine around here, especially since those meetings. The group chief treats everybody right. He is willing to listen to reason and if there is anything he can do to help them, I know he'll do it.

Supervision is different now than it was last year. I can't say the same things about my boss now that I said then. He's improved a lot.[1]

(2) What did the supervisors think they were learning from the conferences? On the whole, their reactions to the program were favorable, and a countless number of general statements expressing their approval were made. Many supervisors felt that they were learning a great deal from the program. Some felt it was more beneficial for others than for themselves. The personal benefits derived from the conferences, as expressed by certain supervisors, may be enumerated as follows:

(a) They were able to see their own practices through the eyes of employees.

(b) From the discussion they learned that their individual problems were not unique in the plant and that many other supervisors had similar problems. From the opinions of other supervisors on problems similar to their own they were able to see how other people handled such difficulties.

(c) They had acquired greater self-confidence and freedom of expression by talking before a group of men. It was a new experience to speak their own minds freely and to participate openly in discussing problems of management.

(d) The conferences gave them additional opportunity to become acquainted with their fellow supervisors.

Of course, not all the comments were of this kind. Some supervisors disapproved of the conferences, saying that they were filled with too much "ballyhoo," that nothing was learned or that nothing was ever settled. These supervisors wanted to be told specifically what to do, whereas in the conferences, they claimed, everyone did a lot of talking and at the end everything was "up in the air."

(3) According to the conference leaders, the best and most impressive evidence of what was happening in the training program lay in the "tone" of the meetings. As the conferences progressed, they noticed a tendency for the supervisors to become less dogmatic about supervisory practices and to be less sure of many of the techniques they had previously applied without analysis or question. There was a growing spirit of open-mindedness among many supervisors who, in

---

[1] Comments of this sort were very frequent in 1930, after the program had been in operation for more than a year.

the early stages of the program, were inclined to believe that good supervisors were born and not trained, and that supervisors could learn nothing from their subordinates. This type of supervisor was becoming more willing to seek the advice of others and to take into account the feelings of his own subordinates. The conference leaders also noticed that the supervisors had a growing appreciation of the effect which their methods of supervision might have on the attitudes, morale, and working effectiveness of the employees.

THE ANALYSIS OF COMPLAINTS

If management was to be provided with information from the interviews on the basis of which it could improve working conditions, it was necessary to develop a rough but effective way of analyzing the interviews. At first, only the unfavorable comments of employees were selected, as it was thought that such expressions would give a good picture of the conditions which needed to be corrected. After making a preliminary survey of a sufficiently large and representative sample of Inspection Branch interviews, a list of 74 topics, ranging from washrooms, lighting, and ventilation to advancement, fatigue, and monotony, was prepared. It was thought that most of the complaints could be classified under these topics. With this list as a basis, the interviews were reviewed and analyzed according to the number of times each item on the list received unfavorable mention.

This form of analysis, however, presented several difficulties. When the Inspection Branch began to investigate these complaints, they soon found that a simple numerical tabulation was inadequate because it showed only the number of unfavorable comments without giving any clue as to just what the employees' criticisms had been. The limitations of working with this restricted information brought out the need for obtaining not only a list of complaints but also a more complete account of the employees' thoughts on any one topic. This meant that the favorable as well as the unfavorable reactions had to be selected and that a more complete description of them had to be given.

The increasingly large number of interviews, accumulating as a result of the extension of the interviewing program to the Operating Branch in 1929, made it necessary to create a separate analyzing department.[1] This group soon became aware of the shortcomings of the method which had been tried and set about to remedy them. The analyzing procedure was changed, therefore, so that those who were to

[1] See footnote, p. 200.

correct the conditions complained about could have the advantage of working with as complete information as the interviews afforded. In addition, the analyzing department established a routine which enabled it to deal with the stream of interviews steadily increasing in volume.

How the Interviews Were Analyzed

The first step in analyzing the interviews was to determine the subject headings under which the comments might be classified. The original list of 74 Inspection Branch topics was reduced to 34 by grouping some topics together. Then approximately 1,000 interviews taken from the Operating Branch were reviewed and analyzed in accordance with these topics. This was done to check the list and to gain some experience in this form of analysis. Instead of attempting to force the employees' comments into the prepared list of topics, care was taken to make the list correspond with the conditions about which the employees actually talked. That this list included most of the things about which the employees talked was shown by the fact that by the end of 1930, when the 10,300 interviews taken in 1929 had been analyzed, only 3 new topics had been added to the original list of 34. The 37 topics with their subheadings are shown in Table XX.

In analyzing an interview the analyzer first read it through carefully to obtain a general impression of the employee's attitude. He then went back and indicated by marginal notations the subject headings under which the comments fell. In doing this, the analyzer at first accepted what the employee said at its face value, but later on, when the interviews were written up verbatim, he deleted any comments which clearly were suggested by the interviewer. Any comments which were obviously incongruous in the light of their context were also eliminated. Statements which concerned two or more topics were classed under each topic to which they pertained. If the same opinion was expressed several times in the interview, only the most representative expression was used. On the other hand, if different ideas were expressed about the same topic, they were all used.

When the marginal notations had been made, each comment was typed on a 3″ by 5″ slip of paper. Four copies, each copy on different colored paper, were made. Two of these copies were retained in the analyzing department for reference and study purposes. The third set included only those comments pertaining to plant conditions. These were filed by subject matter and subdivided by building location, and when a sufficient number had accumulated they were forwarded to

TABLE XX

Topics Discussed in Employee Interviews

Absence

Advancement

Aisles

Bogey

Club activities *
  General
  Entertainment
  Club store
  Educational
  Sports

Dirt

Fatigue

Floor

Furniture and fixtures
  Time clocks
  Drinking water and
    fountains
  Chairs
  Trucks
  Pans
  Elevators
  Fans
  Benches
  Miscellaneous

Hospital

Hours
  Standard
  Night
  Overtime
  Rest periods

Interest

Interviewing program

Light

Lockers

Material
  Quality
  Quantity
  Finished product
  Miscellaneous

Monotony

Noise

Payment
  Wages
  Group piecework
  Straight piecework
  Rate revision
  Piecework rate
  Piecework in general
  Pay roll routine
  Miscellaneous

Placement
  Company placement
  Job placement
  Transfers
  Personnel organization

Restaurant

Safety and health

Sanitation
  Spitting
  General

Smoke and fumes

Social contacts

Steady work

Supervision

Temperature

Thrift
  Stock purchase plan
  Building and loan
  Life insurance
  Ready money plan
  General

Tools and machines
  Tools
  Machines

Transportation

Vacation

Ventilation

Washrooms

Welfare
  General
  Benefit plans
  Employment
  Service (continuous)
  Publications
  Pensions
  Loans to employees
  Christmas welfare
  Legal service

Working space

General
  Miscellaneous
  Education

* Hawthorne Club

the central organization charged with the responsibility of investigating plant conditions. The fourth set, which included all comments, was filed by subject matter and subdivided by departments, and then routed to specially created organizations in the different branches, whose duty it was to study them, conduct investigations, and recommend changes.

In all their work the analyzers treated comments on supervision quite separately from comments on other industrial topics for the reason that the subject had no place in the regular routine for the disposition of interview material. Comments on supervision were regarded as too confidential to be routed back to the branches from which the interviews were taken. The company had promised the employees that their confidence would not be disclosed in any way that might react to their detriment, and although comments apart from the complete interviews might seem safe enough, it was thought best to be doubly sure and not circulate them outside the research division.

The Dual Function of the Analyzing Department

It will be seen from the preceding description of the analyzing routine that this department performed two functions. One of these was an integral part of the interviewing plan and consisted of breaking down the interviews into their component topics, classifying the comments and seeing that they were routed to the proper organizations. The department served as a clearinghouse into which interviews were poured from all parts of the plant and from which there issued periodically a classified list of employees' opinions ready for study and investigation by certain people in each branch.

The other function of the department was to study the comments which were steadily accumulating in its own files. This part of the work lagged because so much attention and effort had to be directed toward the practical aspects of the program. Largely for this reason, studies based upon the interview material scarcely got beyond the simple classificatory stage. But the classification itself, as will be shown later, yielded first rough approximations of great interest. For convenience in presentation, these two functions of the analyzing department will be discussed separately. In the remainder of this chapter, only the uses which the various investigating organizations made of the material will be described. The next chapter will be devoted to studies made of the comments themselves.

The Investigation of Complaints

Investigation of Individual Complaints from the Inspection Branch

During 1929 the Inspection Branch investigated individual complaints from 321 of the 1,600 interviews taken in that branch. In these 321 interviews, taken in 11 departments in the Inspection Branch, the analyzers found 471 unfavorable comments. Approximately 366, or 78 per cent, of the complaints were regarded as worthy of investigation, while the remaining 22 per cent could not be investigated because they were too vague and ambiguous. On about 40 per cent of the 366 complaints investigated, action was advised, considered, or taken. Action already had been taken on 30 per cent of the complaints before they were investigated. Action was not taken on about 30 per cent of the complaints because, in the opinion of the investigators, the conditions complained about were not serious enough to warrant action.

This attempt to consider each complaint as an individual case was too laborious to be of practical value. It was of interest, however, from the point of view of the reliability of complaints. Of the original 471 complaints, 22 per cent were so indefinite that it was difficult to tell whether the worker was really complaining and, if there was some dissatisfaction, just what it was.[1] In an equal number of complaints, the investigators did not think that the conditions complained about were serious. In about half the cases, then, there were substantial grounds for complaint. In the other half of the cases, there were some grounds for complaint, presumably, but these grounds were either not clearly stated or, in the opinion of another person, they were not serious.

New Procedure for Routing and Investigating Complaints

After the experience in the Inspection Branch, the attempt to consider each complaint separately was abandoned, unless, of course, a complaint was sufficiently serious to warrant action at once. A new procedure was instituted whereby after a number of complaints had accumulated they were forwarded to different organizations whose duties were to study them, conduct investigations, and recommend changes. These organizations may be divided into three groups according to the types of complaints they dealt with. One group was

---

[1] The change to recording the interviews verbatim helped materially, for the analyzer was then able to interpret the complaint in terms of its context. In the abbreviated form of recording the interviews, the analyzer's chief difficulty, in many cases, was to find out what a statement meant.

primarily interested in the regulation and maintenance of physical plant conditions. Such things as the condition of floors, lights, benches, and ventilation fell naturally within its scope. The second group, the Safety and Health Division, assumed responsibility for the investigation of complaints relating to dirt, safety, health, sanitation, and similar matters. The third group of organizations, the chief function of which was to maintain and improve employee relations, included the restaurant, the Hawthorne Club, the Employees' Service Division, and the hospital.

(a) *Investigation of Physical Plant Conditions*

During 1929, some 40,000 comments, including 28,000 complaints and 12,000 approvals, divided by location and subdivided by subjects, were sent to the organization responsible for the regulation and maintenance of physical plant conditions. These comments pertained to such things as aisles, floors, furniture and fixtures, and lockers. The usual procedure was to wait until a sufficiently large number of complaints about some condition in a particular location had accumulated and then investigate it.

The more important of the investigations on which action was taken concerned heating, light, drafts from outside corridors and stair wells, and smoke and fumes. In some cases, of course, the conditions complained about were known to exist and did not come to light merely through interviewing employees. Nevertheless, the consensus of adverse opinions from operators on such conditions went a long way in bringing about improvements. The following illustrations give an idea of the type of improvements made in working conditions as a result of the interviews:

(1) In a certain group of buildings many of the employees complained about the fact that these buildings were uncomfortably cold. Upon investigation it was found that at the time the heating system had been changed from steam to hot water these buildings were utilized as storerooms and, as they did not require additional heat, the radiation surface had not been increased. Later, when this location was used by the Operating Department, the fact that the heating was not up to standard was overlooked until the employees' comments stimulated investigation and the condition was corrected.

(2) Employees on a soldering operation continually complained about smoke and fumes. Even though an efficient exhaust system was installed, complaints were still voiced. Finally from the interviews came the clue which cleared up the difficulty. The system which had

been installed exhausted the air at the ceiling with the result that the smoke and fumes were drawn up past the operators' faces. At comparatively little cost the flow of air was reversed, drawing the fumes downward, and thus eliminating the cause for complaint.

(3) For a number of years drafts near doors opening onto the corridors between buildings had been the cause of much dissatisfaction, but seemingly no easy remedy could be found. When cumulative evidence of the extent of this dissatisfaction was studied, effort was concentrated on the problem and a very simple remedy was found. A vacuum was created in the corridor by means of exhaust fans, thereby causing a slight outflow of warm air rather than an inflow of cold air when a door was opened.

(4) Very soon after the interviewing of employees commenced, so many complaints about lockers had accumulated that an inquiry was immediately started. Expressions of employee dissatisfaction were not so convincing when viewed singly, but when viewed collectively it was clear that correction needed to be made, and steps were taken toward improvement.

(b) *Investigations Concerning Safety and Health*

All comments on safety and health were turned over to the supervisors of the Safety and Health Division. They, in turn, organized a series of conferences at which the comments were studied and various problems were assigned for investigation. The results of these investigations were reported and discussed at subsequent meetings. Many times it was found that other organizations were working on the same conditions, that the responsibility for the complaints belonged to another organization, that the condition existed but was not serious enough to warrant the expense of remedying it at the present time, or that the condition had been remedied since the date of interviewing. However, in this way each complaint was brought to the notice of the proper organization and served as an added incentive for correction. Investigations in 72 departments were made by this organization.

An interesting example of a serious accident hazard which was brought to the attention of this group by employee comments concerned the wearing of hairnets required of a particular group of women operators. These women attended coil winding machines that traveled at approximately 6,500 revolutions per minute. As it was possible for an operator to lean over and get her head too close to the relay coil head and have her hair caught in the revolving motor shaft, the women were required to wear hairnets. Even though this precaution was taken, an accident did occur. Interviews with the women in this group showed very clearly the root of the trouble, as the following two comments illustrate:

I don't see any sense in wearing the hairnets because the girls put them on so just the back of the hair is in the net and the hair on the front of the head is all out anyway.

Those hairnets are pesky things anyway. We just have them on the head, half the time they are hanging on one ear. I sure don't see any sense in having them on if they don't want to be strict with the girls, and make them wear them the way they belong.

Here was definite evidence that the hairnets were not being used in the proper way, and that the supervisors did not seem to realize the seriousness of the situation. Because of a natural carelessness brought about by familiarity with the situation, the employees fretted at the measures taken to guard them against accidents. But, in addition, the interviews showed the underlying reason for the accident hazard, namely, that the women objected to wearing the hairnets in the way they should be worn, largely on the ground that they were detrimental to their appearance.

(c) Studies by Groups Interested in Improving their Relations with Employees

There were a number of service organizations which also utilized the employee comments. Some of these groups were the psychological investigation department, the restaurant, the hospital, the Hawthorne Club, and the Employment Division. The psychological investigation department used the material primarily in connection with their studies of vocational placement and employee development. In determining the attributes or qualities which were essential to employees for certain jobs, extensive use was made of the comments to get the employees' reactions to certain types of work. Employee comments on "restaurant," although not showing many conditions that were not suspected, did give a fairly clear picture of the extent to which some of these conditions were considered objectionable by the employees. The service which the hospital provided was improved through use of information that could be gained from the interviews.

UNEXPECTED RESULTS FROM THE INTERVIEWING PROGRAM

There were many unexpected by-products of the interviewing program, some of which have already been mentioned in passing. Many comments received both from employees and supervisors seemed to suggest that there were effects from the program in addition to those which came directly from the investigation of complaints and the training of supervisors. Some of these effects played an important role in the research development of interviewing. They can be enumerated as follows: (1) the indirect effect of the plan on supervisors; (2) the educational value of interviewing for the interviewer; (3) the personal value of the interview for the interviewee.

(1) The mere existence of the interviewing program created a change in supervision over and above that which came from the participation of supervisors in conferences. This change, commented on by many supervisors themselves, resulted from the supervisor's knowledge that his methods were being made the subject of research and that his subordinates were being invited to express their opinions about him. There was no doubt that this stimulated an independent effort to improve the quality of supervision. In certain instances, probably, feelings of uneasiness and insecurity were aroused. But, on the whole, there was little fear on the part of any supervisor that his individual technique would be criticized. Nevertheless, the mere fact that the supervisor knew that his product was to be inspected stimulated him to greater effort.

(2) Another unexpected result of the interviewing plan was the training and education which the interviewer obtained. Nowhere in the program was there a more vivid interest shown than among the interviewers themselves. Those who experienced the interviewing of employees caught glimpses of intimate human situations hitherto unsuspected. They began to sense the importance of taking into account the intimate thoughts and reflections of the workers, and they were eager to develop a technique which would help them obtain this kind of information. They felt that they had acquired a new and improved way of understanding and dealing with their fellow men.

(3) The most unexpected results, however, were the personal values which came to the employees from being interviewed, and which in turn reflected to the benefit of the company. These values were twofold. In the first place, the employees appreciated being recognized as individuals who had valuable comments to make. They enjoyed the opportunity of offering their opinions and also of participating jointly with the company in its endeavor to improve supervision and working conditions.

In the second place, from the interview itself the employee seemed to obtain a certain "lift." Over and over again employees commented on the beneficial effect of expressing freely their feelings and emotions.

Comments of this sort from thousands of employees could not be overlooked. Moreover, it was startling to find the number of employees who had nursed for many years grievances which they never had had the opportunity of expressing to any person of authority in the company. Many of their grievances were trivial in nature, but they were of real importance to the worker. It was frequently found that employees' opinions tended to become exaggerated and distorted, probably because of continued preoccupation with unpleasant experiences, and that these distortions became modified when freely expressed to a sympathetic and critical listener. The interviewers received the impression that many employees when given an opportunity to express their thoughts and feelings to a careful listener discharged in the process emotional and irrational elements from their minds, and it was thought that many adverse attitudes had been improved by these emotional "abreactions" which the interviews afforded.

Evaluation of the Interviewing Program

It will be clear from the foregoing discussion that the interviewing program could not be evaluated in any simple manner. The benefits derived from it were roughly of four kinds: (1) the correction of unfavorable conditions of work; (2) material for training supervisors and personnel people; (3) psychological benefits accruing to the person interviewed; and (4) material for research. Considered from any one of these four points of view to the exclusion of the others, the program could be found lacking. For example, from the point of view of correcting unfavorable conditions of work, it is probable that other less laborious methods could have been utilized to achieve the same results in less time. Also, although the use of interview material as a basis for supervisory training had been very effective compared with the conferences conducted before such material was available, similar material could have been collected without undertaking such an extensive program. It is doubtful, however, whether any other program could have been devised by the company at the time which would have made equally substantial contributions from all these points of view. It was this consideration, together with the "lift" that management people themselves obtained from the program, that made the program in the opinion of management worth the effort and expense put into it. This does not mean that a similar program would be recommended for other concerns or that it would have been considered satisfactory by the Western Electric Company five years later. In fact, the program actually adopted by the Western Electric Company in 1936 was substantially different. The point is that the interviewing program was the best the investigators could devise in the light of their knowledge at that time. It remained for subsequent research to show wherein the program was deficient and wherein it could be improved. One of the purposes of the remaining chapters of this book will be to show what these limitations were.

CHAPTER XI

THE URGENCY AND TONE OF INDUSTRIAL TOPICS

Limitations of the Interview Data

In discussing the routine for classifying and disposing of interview material it was pointed out that the analyzing department, although it served at first mainly as a clearinghouse for incoming interviews, had accumulated in its own files data to be used for study purposes. With this material the present chapter will be concerned. The arrangement of this material had been dictated primarily by the plan for investigating complaints outlined in Chapter X, and for this reason it is well to understand the nature and limitations of these data.

From 10,300 interviews taken in the Operating Branch during 1929, about 80,000 comments pertaining to 37 common industrial topics[1] had been extracted. These 80,000 statements had been classified by (1) industrial topics and departments, (2) favorable and unfavorable tone, (3) men and women. The problem was: How could these statements be used? Some of the limitations of these data were obvious:

(1) The statements were no longer in the interview context.
(2) Because of the policy of keeping the interviews confidential, all personal material had been deleted from the statements.
(3) There was no way of going from the statement to the person who had made the statement.
(4) Although it was possible to go from the statement to the interview, in most cases the latter gave hardly any more information. It was not until October, 1929, that the form in which the interview was recorded had been changed to make it as nearly verbatim as possible.
(5) The two things known of the worker apart from the statement made were (a) the worker was either a man or a woman, and (b) he or she worked in such and such a department and hence was probably doing such and such work.

Although these limitations of the data were apparent, nevertheless the investigators thought it would be possible to gain from the data an over-all picture of the kind of industrial topics about which the workers

[1] For a list of these topics, see Table XX, p. 221.

expressed grievances. The frequency with which employees discussed certain subjects and the tone in which they discussed them might offer clues to those aspects of their industrial life which they considered important and significant. In short, the following questions could be asked:

(1) What subjects did employees talk about in discussing their work situation?

(2) How were the total comments distributed among these subjects? Which topics were the most emphasized and which were the least emphasized?

(3) What was the distribution of favorable and unfavorable comments on these topics and what significance, if any, could be attached to it?

(4) How did men's and women's comments compare (a) as to relative emphasis of subject discussed, (b) as to distribution of favorable and unfavorable comments? [1]

Basic Data Table for 1929 Operating Branch Interviews

Table XXI contains all the essential data which will be used in this chapter, and it may be referred to as a guide in following through the studies to be reported. It will be noted that wherever subdivisions of a topic heading occur, the subheadings are isolated and the data are compiled for each of them. The subject heading *payment*, for example, includes the following subdivisions: *wages, group piecework, straight piecework, rate revision, piecework rates, piecework in general, pay roll routines,* and *miscellaneous.* While it is true that all of these topics pertain to the general subject of *payment,* yet each of them is distinctly different and connotes a different set of factors. Many such subheadings are of great importance, especially in comparing data, and will be treated as major headings in some of the studies that follow.

Urgency and Tone Defined

Table XXII shows the different classes into which the interview comments can be divided. For convenience, symbols indicating the different classes will be used in this chapter. For the purpose of comparing the frequency with which topics are discussed, the ratio $S_T/T_I \times 100$ will be used, i.e., the number of comments on any one subject per 100 interviews. In using this ratio, caution should be taken

---

[1] If in the course of this presentation it seems that too much emphasis is placed on such things as, for example, comparing comments of men and women, it should be said that such comparisons were made largely because the data were originally filed in this way and not because the investigators thought such comparisons to be of paramount importance.

TABLE XXI

Number of Comments on Each Subject in 10,300 Interviews Taken from 6,800 Men and 3,500 Women

operating branch. 1929

Subject	Total			Men			Women		
	Number of Comments	Favorable	Unfavorable	Number of Comments	Favorable	Unfavorable	Number of Comments	Favorable	Unfavorable
Absence	46	25	21	34	17	17	12	8	4
Advancement	1,423	607	816	1,240	508	732	183	99	84
Aisles	379	8	371	221	6	215	158	2	156
Bogey	2,093	711	1,382	567	154	413	1,526	557	969
Club activities *	3,333	2,954	379	1,513	1,274	239	1,820	1,680	140
General	309	285	24	185	170	15	124	115	9
Entertainment	1,430	1,313	117	498	441	57	932	872	60
Club store	616	555	61	249	226	23	367	329	38
Educational	505	400	105	297	210	87	208	190	18
Sports	473	401	72	284	227	57	189	174	15
Dirt	2,699	1,402	1,297	1,589	784	805	1,110	618	492
Fatigue	2,275	964	1,311	1,011	447	564	1,264	517	747
Floor	319	78	241	185	21	164	134	57	77
Furniture and fixtures *	1,246	211	1,035	891	145	746	355	66	289
Time clocks	502	2	500	369	1	368	133	1	132
Drinking water and fountains	275	161	114	216	128	88	59	33	26
Chairs	121	39	82	48	8	40	73	31	42
Trucks	102	3	99	102	3	99	0	0	0
Pans	79	1	78	60	1	59	19	0	19
Elevators	36	0	36	10	0	10	26	0	26
Fans	27	0	27	7	0	7	20	0	20
Benches	25	1	24	19	0	19	6	1	5
Miscellaneous	79	4	75	60	4	56	19	0	19

Hospital	2,195	1,714	481	962	705	257	1,233	1,009	224
Hours *	4,285	2,012	2,273	2,097	957	1,140	2,188	1,055	1,133
Standard	594	259	335	422	182	240	172	77	95
Night	1,257	497	760	706	287	419	551	210	341
Overtime	1,366	448	928	675	249	436	691	199	492
Rest periods	1,058	808	250	284	239	45	774	569	205
Interest	1,968	1,850	118	981	905	76	987	945	42
Interviewing program	440	346	94	249	193	56	191	153	38
Light	2,598	909	1,689	1,767	613	1,154	831	296	535
Lockers	3,846	306	3,540	2,709	242	2,467	1,137	64	1,073
Material *	1,283	42	1,241	728	23	705	555	19	536
Quality	699	19	680	305	6	299	394	13	381
Quantity	440	17	423	313	11	302	127	6	121
Finished product	68	2	66	56	2	54	12	0	12
Miscellaneous	76	4	72	54	4	50	22	0	22
Monotony	603	219	384	405	126	279	198	93	105
Noise	104	32	72	60	18	42	44	14	30
Payment *	11,803	4,987	6,816	7,892	2,972	4,920	3,911	2,015	1,896
Wages	4,499	3,215	1,284	2,843	1,882	961	1,656	1,333	323
Group piecework	1,309	275	1,034	834	109	725	475	166	309
Straight piecework	509	392	117	260	222	38	249	170	79
Rate revision	1,767	226	1,541	1,236	137	1,099	531	89	442
Piecework rate	1,713	203	1,510	1,304	148	1,156	409	55	354
Piecework in general	1,225	102	1,123	850	58	792	375	44	331
Pay roll routine	159	30	129	118	24	94	41	6	35
Miscellaneous	622	544	78	447	392	55	175	152	23

* The amounts shown for the main subjects are the totals of those shown for the subheadings.

TABLE XXI (continued)

Subject	Total			Men			Women		
	Number of Comments	Favorable	Unfavorable	Number of Comments	Favorable	Unfavorable	Number of Comments	Favorable	Unfavorable
Placement *	8,827	7,321	1,506	5,072	4,018	1,054	3,755	3,303	452
Company placement	821	821	0	489	489	0	332	332	0
Job placement	7,755	6,437	1,318	4,393	3,493	900	3,362	2,944	418
Transfers	164	35	129	132	24	108	32	11	21
Personnel organization	97	36	61	65	17	48	32	19	13
Restaurant	543	357	186	201	129	72	342	228	114
Safety and health	4,029	821	3,208	2,463	552	1,911	1,566	269	1,297
Sanitation *	1,105	145	960	605	120	485	500	25	475
Spitting	863	10	853	419	9	410	444	1	443
General	242	135	107	186	111	75	56	24	32
Smoke and fumes	1,118	54	1,064	733	30	703	385	24	361
Social contacts	905	628	277	384	268	116	521	360	161
Steady work	813	600	213	552	459	93	261	141	120
Supervision	4,605	1,868	2,737	2,922	1,116	1,806	1,683	752	931
Temperature	1,345	225	1,120	955	165	790	390	60	330
Thrift *	5,809	5,504	305	3,181	3,000	181	2,628	2,504	124
Stock purchase plan	4,076	3,823	253	2,367	2,220	147	1,709	1,603	106
Building and loan	385	373	12	227	218	9	158	155	3
Life insurance	70	64	6	58	53	5	12	11	1
Ready money plan	441	431	10	162	156	6	279	275	4
General	837	813	24	367	353	14	470	460	10

Tools and machines *	1,584	303	1,281	1,286	258	1,028	298	45	253
Tools	592	44	548	558	42	516	34	2	32
Machines	992	259	733	728	216	512	264	43	221
Transportation	606	265	341	255	105	150	351	160	191
Vacation	3,723	3,550	173	2,167	2,055	112	1,556	1,495	61
Ventilation	2,561	1,037	1,524	1,602	626	976	959	411	548
Washrooms	2,352	308	2,044	1,374	222	1,152	978	86	892
Welfare *	2,121	1,799	322	1,249	1,030	219	872	769	103
General	135	118	17	66	51	15	69	67	2
Benefit plans	1,383	1,302	81	847	790	57	536	512	24
Employment	262	142	120	123	44	79	139	98	41
Service (continuous)	135	54	81	83	35	48	52	19	33
Publications	43	37	6	22	17	5	21	20	1
Pensions	82	70	12	79	68	11	3	2	1
Loans to employees	26	22	4	17	14	3	9	8	1
Christmas welfare	46	45	1	5	4	1	41	41	0
Legal service	9	9	0	7	7	0	2	2	0
Working space	1,042	88	954	662	37	625	380	51	329
General *	345	229	116	253	169	84	92	60	32
Miscellaneous	244	149	95	171	103	68	73	46	27
Education	101	80	21	82	66	16	19	14	5
Total	86,371	44,479	41,892	51,017	24,469	26,548	35,354	20,010	15,344

* The amounts shown for the main subjects are the totals of those shown for the subheadings.

not to interpret it incorrectly. Had each employee spoken only once on each subject, this ratio would express the percentage of the employees who expressed themselves on any given subject. But, inasmuch as two or more distinct opinions or thoughts expressed by an employee about any one subject were all counted, this ratio only states that *not more*

TABLE XXII

FORMAL CLASSIFICATION OF EMPLOYEE COMMENTS WITH RESPECTIVE SYMBOLS
FOR EACH CLASS

T_I	= Total number of interviews (10,300)
T_{I_M}	= Total number of men's interviews (6,800)
T_{I_w}	= Total number of women's interviews (3,500)
S_T	= Total comments *on any one subject*
S_M	= Total men's comments *on any one subject*
S_w	= Total women's comments *on any one subject*
S_{M_f}	= Total men's favorable comments *on any one subject*
S_{M_u}	= Total men's unfavorable comments *on any one subject*
S_{w_f}	= Total women's favorable comments *on any one subject*
S_{w_u}	= Total women's unfavorable comments *on any one subject*
S_f	= Total favorable comments *on any one subject*
S_n	= Total unfavorable comments *on any one subject*

than and *perhaps less than* that percentage of the employees expressed themselves on a given subject.

In order to express the relative standing of different industrial topics according to this ratio, S_T/T_I x 100, the word "urgency" will be used. Nothing more will be meant by this word, however, than what is represented by the relative position of industrial topics when arranged in the order of magnitude of their ratios. A subject of greater or less urgency to employees, for example, will mean only a subject having a relatively higher or lower number of comments per 100 interviews.

For the purpose of denoting the distribution of favorable or unfavorable comments on any one subject the ratios S_f/S_T or S_u/S_T will be used. It is apparent that between these two ratios the following simple relation holds: $S_f/S_T + S_u/S_T = 1$. The ratio S_f/S_T will be called the favorable ratio, or index of satisfaction. The ratio S_u/S_T will be called the unfavorable ratio, or index of dissatisfaction. Whenever it becomes necessary to compare the distribution of favorable and unfavorable comments for any one subject among men or women, the following ratios will be used: S_{M_f}/S_M, S_{M_u}/S_M, or S_{w_f}/S_w, S_{w_u}/S_w. The word "tone" will be used to indicate the relative position of industrial topics according to these ratios. A subject having a "favorable tone" will mean that it has an index of satisfaction of about .66 or higher; an "unfavorable tone" will mean an index of satisfaction of about .33 or lower; a "neutral tone" will mean that the favorable and unfavorable comments on any one subject are fairly equally distributed.

These ratios involve certain assumptions about what constitutes a "comment" or an "interview." It is, of course, difficult to determine when any statement ceases to be one idea or thought and can be called another idea or thought. In the early stages, the people who analyzed the interviews for the investigation of complaints were not psychologists or logicians; their classifications were made for the practical industrial uses described in Chapter X. The differentiations they made were based on the material content of the complaint rather than on its psychological or logical form. If a worker complained that his earnings were too low, then mentioned that his "bogey" was too high, and went on to say that in endeavoring to maintain his efficiency he was injuring his health, this statement was listed under three topics: *payment, bogey*, and *safety and health*. In other words, this statement was treated as three comments on three different subjects. If, on the other hand, a worker said that his work was too hard three different times in one interview, this was listed only as one comment on one subject (*fatigue*). If he complained about the drinking fountains on the grounds that (1) they were dirty, and (2) the water was too warm, this statement was treated as two comments on the same subject (*drinking water and fountains*).

A pertinent query may be raised about using the interview as a base in the ratio "number of comments per 100 interviews." Is not the number of spoken words or written words a better base? An employee who talks only 15 minutes has less opportunity of mentioning as many topics as one who talks 2½ hours. Although this suggestion is worth considering, it involves certain difficulties. In the first place, no record was kept of the actual length of the spoken interview, and it would be doubtful to assume that the length of the written interview bore any close relation to the length of the spoken interview. In the second place, the length of the interview, as a significant variable, can be disregarded on the ground that in each interview the same opportunity had been granted each employee to express himself on any topic under similar conditions and under the guidance of an experienced interviewer.

Distribution of Topics According to Urgency and Tone — Men

Figure 22 shows the distribution in terms of urgency and tone of 80 subjects discussed by men. There are several interesting points about this distribution:

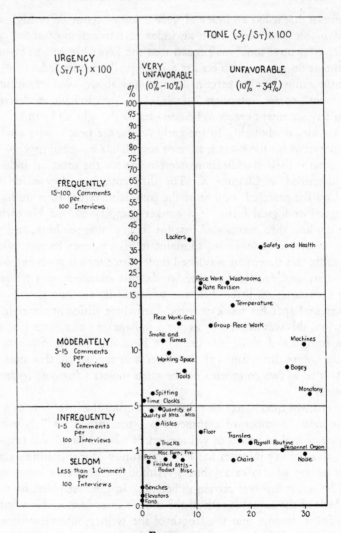

238

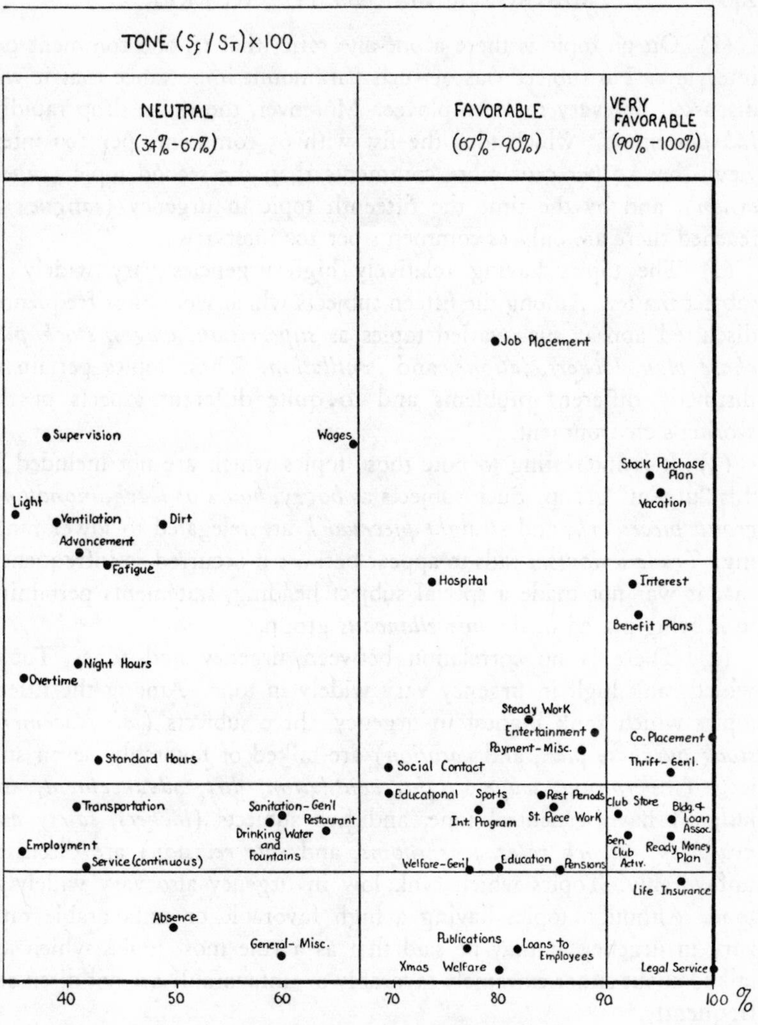

FIGURE 22 (continued)

DISTRIBUTION OF TOPICS ACCORDING TO URGENCY AND TONE FOR MEN,
BASED UPON 6,800 INTERVIEWS

OPERATING BRANCH, 1929

(1) On no topic is there a one-one ratio, that is, one comment per interview. No subject was of such paramount importance that it was discussed by every male employee. Moreover, the ratios drop rapidly. *Job placement*,[1] which tops the list with 65 comments per 100 interviews, has 50 per cent more comments than the second topic (*supervision*), and by the time the fifteenth topic in urgency (*fatigue*) is reached there are only 14 comments per 100 interviews.

(2) The topics having relatively high urgencies vary widely in subject matter. Among the fifteen subjects which were most frequently discussed appear such varied topics as *supervision, wages, stock purchase plan, lockers, fatigue*, and *ventilation*. These topics pertain to distinctly different problems and to quite different aspects of the worker's environment.

(3) It is interesting to note those topics which are not included in this "urgent" group. Such subjects as *bogey, hours of work, monotony, group piecework*, and *straight piecework* are relegated to lower ranking. *Trade unionism* fails to appear because it occurred so infrequently that it was not made a special subject heading, statements pertaining to it being placed in the *miscellaneous* group.

(4) There is no correlation between urgency and tone. Topics which rank high in urgency vary widely in tone. Among the fifteen topics which rank highest in urgency, three subjects (*job placement, stock purchase plan*, and *vacation*) are talked of favorably, seven subjects (*supervision, wages, light, ventilation, dirt, advancement*, and *fatigue*) have a neutral tone, and five subjects (*lockers, safety and health, piecework rates, washrooms*, and *rate revision*) are discussed unfavorably. Topics which rank low in urgency also vary widely in tone. Although topics having a high favorable or unfavorable ratio vary in urgency, it may be said that as a rule most topics which are talked about either extremely favorably or unfavorably are not discussed frequently.[2]

---

[1] No particular importance can be attached to the great frequency with which *job placement* was discussed, because some conversational remark about the job was a likely starting point for the interview. Moreover, many of these remarks also appeared under the categories of *monotony, fatigue*, and *interest*.

[2] The three exceptions to this statement (*lockers, stock purchase plan, vacation*) deserve special comment. The frequency with which these subjects were discussed by the workers arises primarily from the peculiar situation existing in the company with respect to these matters in 1929. In that year the company expanded its working force considerably. It was employing some 40,000 workers. As a consequence, there was a shortage of locker facilities, of which the company was quite aware and which it was trying to rectify as quickly as possible. Also in 1929 the market price of A. T. & T. stock was considerably higher than the price at which it was being sold to employees — a situation which pro-

(5) Although there is no correlation between urgency and tone, there is a relation between tone and the kind of subject mentioned. All subjects having an extremely unfavorable tone are chiefly concerned with plant conditions, whereas all subjects having an extremely favorable tone are, with one exception (*interest* [1]), concerned with employee relations activities such as *benefit plans, thrift,* and *club activities.*

(6) Among those topics having a neutral tone are found a number of controversial subjects such as *supervision, advancement, hours of work,* and *employment. Fatigue* also appears in this list and the debatable subjects of *dirt, light,* and *ventilation.* In short, this group includes most of those topics in terms of which human problems in industry are usually stated, both by employees and by management.

Distribution of Topics According to Urgency and Tone — Women

Did women differ significantly from men in respect to the urgency and tone of the topics they discussed? Figure 23 shows the same data for women that Figure 22 shows for men. It is apparent that in general all the remarks made about the distribution of topics for men apply equally well for women. No subject was of such paramount importance that it was discussed by every woman. The subjects talked about quite frequently by women are varied in type. There is no correlation between urgency and tone. However, there is a relation between tone and type of subject mentioned. Items connected with plant conditions tend to be unfavorable in tone; items connected with employee relations activities tend to be favorable. Topics with a neutral tone include more or less the same topics discussed in that manner by men.

There are, however, some interesting differences in the distribution of topics for men and for women; these differences are shown in Table XXIII. This table shows those subjects both more and less urgent for women than for men, those subjects on which women are more and less favorable than men, and those subjects on which women and men roughly agree in both urgency and tone. What arbitrarily has been taken to mean "more," "less," or "equal" is defined in the table.

---

voked a great deal of interest and comment. At about this time, perhaps a few years before 1929, the company had made several changes with regard to its vacation policy. The first change had been to lower the service requirements for a vacation with pay for shop employees and to lengthen the vacation period to two weeks for those employees with a specified amount of service. The second change had been to institute a common vacation period for all employees, a certain two-week period in the summer when the shop was shut down completely and all went on their vacations at the same time. These changes aroused considerable interest and favorable response from the employees.

[1] The one exception (*interest*) can be ignored on the ground that the negative side was probably expressed under two headings, *monotony* and *fatigue.*

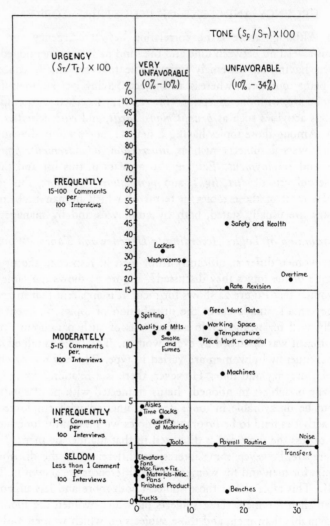

FIGURE 23

DISTRIBUTION OF TOPICS ACCORDING TO URGENCY AND TONE FOR WOMEN,
BASED UPON 3,500 INTERVIEWS

OPERATING BRANCH, 1929

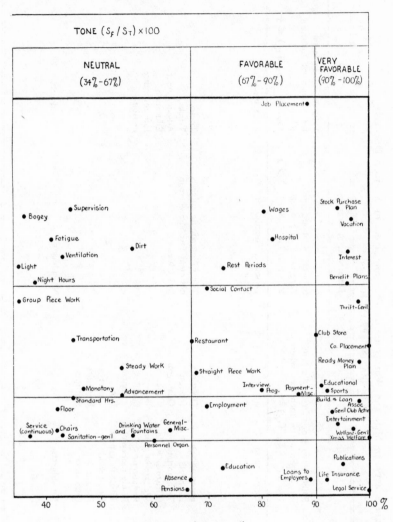

TONE $(S_f / S_T) \times 100$

NEUTRAL (34%-67%) FAVORABLE (67%-90%) VERY FAVORABLE (90%-100%)

Job Placement

Supervision
Bogey
Fatigue
Ventilation
Dirt
Light
Night Hours
Group Piece Work

Transportation

Steady Work

Monotony
Advancement
Standard Hrs.
Floor

Service (continuous)
Chairs
Sanitation-gen'l
Drinking Water and Fountains
General-Misc.
Personnel Organ.

Absence
Pensions

Wages
Hospital
Rest Periods
Social Contact

Restaurant

Straight Piece Work
Interview. Prog.
Payment-Misc.
Employment

Education
Loans to Employees

Stock Purchase Plan
Vacation

Interest
Benefit Plans
Thrift-Gen'l
Club Store
Co. Placement
Ready Money Plan
Educational
Sports
Build. & Loan Assoc.
Gen'l Club Activ.
Entertainment
Welfare-Gen'l
Xmas Welfare
Publications
Life Insurance
Legal Service

40   50   60   70   80   90   100 %

FIGURE 23 (continued)

DISTRIBUTION OF TOPICS ACCORDING TO URGENCY AND TONE FOR WOMEN,
BASED UPON 3,500 INTERVIEWS

OPERATING BRANCH, 1929

243

TABLE XXIII

Differences between Men and Women in Urgency and Tone of Subjects Discussed
Operating Branch, 1929

Differences in Tone	Differences in Urgency		
	Subjects twice or more as "urgent" for women as for men, i.e., where $(S_W/T_{I_W} \div S_M/T_{I_M}) \geq 2$	Subjects of about equal "urgency," i.e., where $2 > (S_W/T_{I_W} \div S_M/T_{I_M}) > \frac{1}{2}$	Subjects half or less as "urgent" for women as for men, i.e., where $(S_W/T_{I_W} \div S_M/T_{I_M}) \leq \frac{1}{2}$
Subjects on which women are more favorable than men $(S_{W_f}/S_W - S_{M_f}/S_M) \geq .33$	Employment	Personnel organization Floor	No subjects
Subjects on which women have about the same tone as men	Entertainment Hospital Transportation Christmas welfare Welfare in general Restaurant Ready money plan Thrift in general Rest periods Fatigue Club store Overtime Interest Quality of material Bogey Social contacts Fans Chairs Elevators Spitting	The 51 remaining subjects not mentioned elsewhere in this table	Tools Trucks Advancement Education Life insurance Pensions
Subjects on which women are less favorable than men $(S_{M_f}/S_M - S_{W_f}/S_W) \geq .33$	No subjects	No subjects	No subjects

244

From Table XXIII it can be seen that the outstanding difference between comments by men and by women is in the urgency rather than in the tone of the topics discussed. The tone of 77 of the 80 subjects is about the same for women as for men. On only three subjects (*employment*, *personnel*, and *floor*) are women appreciably more favorable than men. On no subjects are men appreciably more favorable than women.

From the standpoint of urgency, on the other hand, only 53 of the 80 topics are the same for women as for men. On 21 subjects women make twice as many comments as men, and on 6 of the topics men make twice as many comments as women. Women comment more than men about *thrift, welfare, overtime, rest periods, fatigue, bogey, social contacts, furniture and fixtures.* Men comment more than women about *tools, trucks, advancement, education, life insurance,* and *pensions.*

Some of these differences in urgency, of course, can be explained in terms of the extent to which men and women participated in the activities concerned. For example, the fact that men talked more about *trucks* and *tools* may be explained on the ground that the women did not operate trucks and had much less to do with tools than the men did. The remaining differences, however, seem to be fairly closely related to the differences between attitudes of men and of women toward the economic and social functions of work. *Life insurance, pensions,* and *employment* are closely associated with economic security, for which man, as head of the family, is traditionally responsible. Man's social status in the community is affected in no small part by the kind of work he does, and *advancement* and *education* are closely allied with this preoccupation. Woman, on the other hand, is not by tradition the breadwinner of the family, nor is her social status so dependent on her job. It would be natural, therefore, not to expect these considerations to dominate her preoccupations as much as they do those of men. An easy job, not too fatiguing, in pleasant surroundings, sufficiently well paid to support herself or to contribute something to the income of her parents or husband, and congenial hours which allow her to take part in the activities of the home seem, from Table XXIII, to be the woman's main interests.

Limitations of Interpretation

It is obvious that too many factors enter into the determination of the tone or urgency of an industrial topic to allow any simple conclusions to be drawn about conditions at Hawthorne or about their relative

MANAGEMENT AND THE WORKER

importance to employees. From the relative tone of these industrial
topics little can be concluded about the comparative state of different
working conditions at Hawthorne. The tone of an industrial topic is
affected by such factors as (1) the nature of the topic discussed,
(2) differences in working conditions in different departments at
Hawthorne, and (3) differences of sentiment among employees about
the subjects mentioned. Likewise, only in a limited sense can it be said
that the relative urgency of industrial topics reflects their relative importance for the workers. Urgency is affected by such factors as (1)
how widespread the conditions are, (2) the number of employees
coming in contact with the subject talked about, and (3) the degree to
which the topics lend themselves to the elaboration of social sentiments.

Determinants of Tone

The importance of these limitations in relation to any general conclusion that may be drawn from the tone of these data can best be
discussed with reference to Figure 24, in which the industrial topics
are divided into three groups for men and for women: (1) those with
an unfavorable tone, i.e., where $S_u/S_T = (100\%$ to $67\%)$; (2) those
with a neutral tone, i.e., where $S_u/S_T = (66\%$ to $34\%)$; and (3) those
with a favorable tone, i.e., where $S_u/S_T = (33\%$ to $0\%)$. Items within
each of these groups are then arranged in order of urgency. This
arrangement shows very clearly that three different kinds of topics
correspond to these three tone divisions. The unfavorable group includes topics more or less related to plant conditions; the neutral group
includes topics related to payment, supervision, hours of work, and
advancement; and the favorable group includes topics related to employee relations activities.

At first glance, these differences in tone may appear to suggest that
the company had "good" employee relations policies, "fair" policies
with regard to payment, advancement, and supervision, and "poor"
plant and technical conditions of work.[1] This conclusion, however,
fails to check with all the evidence. For example, plant conditions at
Hawthorne have always compared most favorably with those in other
industries. This judgment is based not merely on the opinion of the
officers of the company, who may be biased in its favor, but also on the
favorable showing of the·company in many contests, conducted by
such bodies as the National Safety Council and the Chicago Safety
Council, in which hundreds of plants competed.

---

[1] "Good" and "poor" are used here to mean above and below the customary standards of similar industrial plants in the neighboring community.

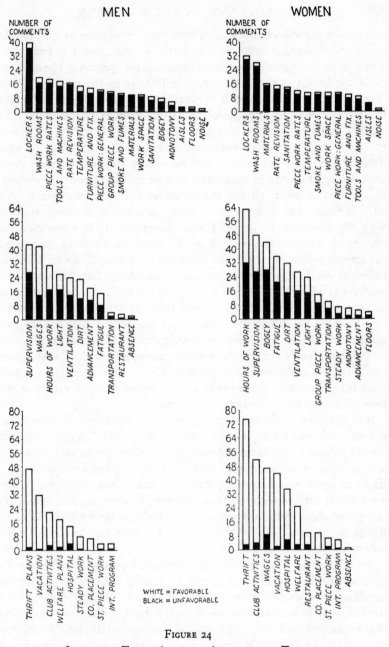

MEN

NUMBER OF COMMENTS

Lockers, Wash Rooms, Piece Work Rates, Tools and Machines, Rate Revision, Temperature, Furniture and Fix., Piece Work: General, Group Piece Work, Smoke and Fumes, Materials, Work Space, Sanitation, Bogey, Monotony, Aisles, Floors, Noise

Supervision, Wages, Hours of Work, Light, Ventilation, Dirt, Advancement, Fatigue, Transportation, Restaurant, Absence

Thrift Plans, Vacation, Club Activities, Welfare Plans, Hospital, Steady Work, Co. Placement, St. Piece Work, Int. Program

WOMEN

NUMBER OF COMMENTS

Lockers, Wash Rooms, Materials, Rate Revision, Sanitation, Piece Work Rates, Temperature, Smoke and Fumes, Work Space, Piece Work: General, Furniture and Fix., Tools and Machines, Aisles, Noise

Hours of Work, Supervision, Bogey, Fatigue, Dirt, Ventilation, Light, Group Piece Work, Transportation, Steady Work, Monotony, Advancement, Floors

Thrift, Club Activities, Wages, Vacation, Hospital, Welfare, Restaurant, Co. Placement, St. Piece Work, Int. Program, Absence

WHITE = FAVORABLE
BLACK = UNFAVORABLE

FIGURE 24

INDUSTRIAL TOPICS ARRANGED ACCORDING TO TONE,
BASED UPON 10,300 INTERVIEWS: 6,800 MEN, 3,500 WOMEN
OPERATING BRANCH, 1929

It can be argued, of course, that how plant conditions at Hawthorne compared objectively with the standards of other plants is irrelevant. The conclusion to be drawn should be that *in the opinion of the workers* plant conditions in the company were inferior to those under which they had worked elsewhere or to what they thought conditions "ought to be." But even this conclusion is not substantiated by evidence. In the first place, there were very few statements made by the employees in which they compared conditions at Hawthorne unfavorably with those of plants in which they had previously worked, whereas there were a large number of statements expressing the opposite sentiment. In the second place, all the comments on *company placement* (this term included any statement expressing satisfaction or dissatisfaction with the company in general) were favorable. It is a question, of course, of whether the worker in his intimate thinking associated the company in general with its employee relations policies or with the technical conditions of work which it afforded. That many of the workers at Hawthorne, when they spoke favorably of the company in general, were thinking of its employee relations policies seems probable. On the other hand, had there been a big discrepancy between the two areas, that is, had the company indulged in extravagant gestures in employee activities and yet allowed the employees to work in insanitary and inefficient conditions, it seems probable that this discrepancy would have been caught by the worker and expressed to some extent in the tone of comments on *company placement*.

It is clear, then, that the distribution of industrial topics by tone cannot be explained by saying that the company had "good," "fair," or "poor" policies in the three different areas. What can be said, however, is that subjects with a high index of dissatisfaction are topics more likely to be commented on unfavorably rather than otherwise. They are subjects such as *tools, machines, lockers, washrooms*, etc., which are not talked about unless there is some complaint to be made. Only when things fail to work smoothly or are out of order are they mentioned; otherwise, they are taken for granted. This is particularly true of most items relating to plant conditions; therefore, topics with a high index of dissatisfaction in this area do not necessarily indicate poor working conditions. To draw the conclusion that they do indicate poor working conditions is to assume that on all topics there is the same likelihood that employees will state their satisfactions as well as their dissatisfactions. This assumption is clearly false. In certain areas the employees tend to state only their dissatisfactions, whereas in other areas they express their likes as well as their dislikes. In short, there are two different kinds of topics: (1) topics which in general the worker takes for granted unless something goes wrong; (2) topics which he does not take for granted even if they are favorable.

This second class of topics covers two groups, shown in Figure 24: (1) a group of topics with a neutral tone, and (2) a group of topics with a very favorable tone. Examining the latter group first, it is apparent that this group includes most of the company's employee relations activities. But are these topics which the workers are likely to mention only if they regard them favorably? There is very little evidence to support this hypothesis. Had they disapproved of what might have appeared to them to be unwanted paternalism, it is likely that they would have said so. Of course, there is a question of whether the satisfactory reactions to these activities were spontaneous and real convictions or merely polite responses. Did the workers really think the company's employee relations activities were good, or were they merely registering attitudes of approval which they thought management wished to hear and which they thought it politic to manifest? That some of the employees were doing the latter is very probable, but that most of the employees should adopt the same attitude would be curious. As we shall see in a later chapter, the interviewers had developed a technique for detecting such ambivalences of attitude. They were on the alert for just such disclosures, and yet they were unanimously of the opinion that most of the employees were sincerely expressing their convictions. Moreover, it would be difficult to explain why the workers had decided to be politic in one area and not so in another. With regard to questions of *payment, advancement,* and *supervision,* they had not talked "with their tongues in their cheeks." The available evidence, in short, did not support the interpretation that the employees were shamming in this area.

Those topics with a more or less neutral tone form an interesting group. On these subjects the majority of employees did not agree in their opinions. Some of the reasons for this difference of opinion are evident. In the first place, this group of topics includes *supervision, wages,* and *advancement,* and in these matters there is a wider variation in interpretation and administration of company policy than in any other area of the worker's life. In no very definite sense can it be said that in regard to these matters the workers were enjoying the same conditions of work. Company policies with regard to *supervision, advancement,* etc., were being administered, in all probability, quite differently in different departments. In the second place, in these matters the personal hopes and fears of the employees enter in a greater variety of forms than elsewhere. The employees were not facing these aspects of their working life with similar sentiments. Roughly, it can be assumed that the workers were facing their technical conditions of work and their employee relations activities with similar sentiments and standards. But such an assumption with regard to conditions of *advancement* and *payment* is obviously too simple, for differences in personal and social situations enter too much into the determination of attitudes toward these subjects. In other words, the assumption that the employees were reacting to a similar universe with the same standards of expectation is more obviously fallacious in this area than in the others. For this reason, it seems probable that under ordinary conditions the tone of such industrial topics as *supervision, advancement,* and *hours of work* would tend to be neutral.

With these discriminations in mind, it may be well to look at exceptions. Five topics connected with plant conditions (*ventilation, dirt, light, monotony,* and *fatigue*) are not included in the group with a high unfavorable ratio. (Although *monotony* is unfavorable for men, it has a neutral tone for women.) At first glance, it might seem strange to find favorable comments on these subjects — for example, comments about the absence of dirt. But it is this peculiar fact which offers a clue to the function of such comments. *Dirt* is a word which can be used not only to indicate unsatisfactory conditions but also to express favorable as well as unfavorable sentiments. For instance, a person is likely to express satisfaction with a job because it is not dirty, but it is unlikely that anyone will express satisfaction with a door because the knob is not broken. The same use can also be made of the words *fatigue* and *monotony.* Similarly, the weather is a popular topic of conversation, partly because it can be used by people to communicate their moods and to convey sentiments in which others can participate.

Determinants of Urgency

To draw any conclusions from the relative urgencies of different subjects about their comparative importance to the worker may also lead to error. This is particularly true when comparing the urgency of a topic which tends to elicit expressions of dissatisfaction only with the urgency of a topic which tends to elicit both favorable and unfavorable comments. It would lead to such absurd conclusions as, for example, in the case of men, *lockers* are as important as *wages, washrooms* are as important as *advancement,* and *thrift* is more important than any other aspect of the worker's situation. It is evident that differences in urgency have significance only within each of the three groups in Figure 24.

Among those topics having a high unfavorable ratio, differences in urgency, it was thought, did reflect roughly how widespread were the conditions complained about. In the case of lockers, for example, the large number of comments reflected a shortage which had resulted from rapid expansion of personnel. A large number of complaints about *washrooms, dirt, light,* and *ventilation* also could be accounted for in part by this influx of new workers.

Among those topics having a high favorable ratio, on the other hand, differences in urgency seemed to correspond very closely to differences in the number of persons participating in these activities. The *stock purchase plan, vacations,* and *benefits,* for example, concerned a greater number of employees than *legal service, Christmas welfare,*[1] and *life insurance.*

In addition, many differences in urgency could be explained on the ground that some topics more than others afforded convenient symbols for expressing general and vague discontents arising from various stresses and strains that the worker himself might not be able to specify explicitly. Topics such as *supervision, hours of work, wages, safety and health,* and *stock purchase plan* all had emotional connotations around which solidarities and antagonisms could be expressed. *Wages* more than *absence, lockers* more than *aisles, washrooms* more than *floors,* lent themselves readily to the elaboration of social sentiments.

It is interesting to note that men and women differ markedly with respect to urgency in two of the three groups of subjects in Figure 24. In the first group, with the exception of *lockers, washrooms, tools and machines,* there is very little difference between men and women. In the second group, women have much more to say than men about *hours of work* and *fatigue.* In the third group, women are much more articulate than men in their praise of the company's employee relations activities. There is very little evidence to suppose that actual conditions of work for men differed from those for women as greatly as these differences in urgency might indicate. It is more plausible to suppose that differences in sentiment between men and women, because of differences in social situation, account largely for the differences in urgency of these topics.

---

[1] By *Christmas welfare* is meant the company's practice of distributing baskets of food, flowers, etc., to all employees who are sick at Christmas time. Ordinarily these gifts are distributed by the employee's foreman or department chief.

Conclusion

Although these studies did not go very far in the analysis of employee complaints, they did suggest a rather important consideration which was being brought more and more to the attention of the investigators. They suggested very strongly that employee comments had a dual character: they could be used just as readily to express sentiments as to communicate facts. The fact that all topics frequently mentioned had one thing in common, namely, that they were particularly adaptable to the expression and elaboration of social sentiments, seemed to suggest that these social sentiments, their nature and their interrelations with other factors, were of particular importance for the understanding of employee complaints and well-being. In Chapter XII the first step in the direction of clarifying this consideration will be taken.

PART III

A CONCEPTUAL SCHEME FOR THE UNDER-STANDING OF EMPLOYEE DISSATISFACTION

CHAPTER XII

THE ANALYSIS OF COMPLAINTS; FACT VS. SENTIMENT

The Reliability of Employee Comments

THUS far the practical operation of the interviewing program has been described: how the interviewing program provided concrete material about particular conditions in the company which could be investigated and sometimes corrected; how it supplied case material for the training of supervisors; and how it functioned, in a general way, for the employees, the supervisors, and the interviewers themselves. As has been shown, the successful practical operation of the plan depended, in part, on whether or not the complaints could be used by management at their face value as a basis for the improvement of working conditions, supervision, and employee relations policy. As the interviewing program continued, the utility of employee comments, in the direct fashion originally conceived, became more and more questionable. It was not that the employees were willfully telling falsehoods; the skilled interviewer was able to detect such responses fairly easily. But the use by management of the complaints made by employees depended on three conditions: (1) the extent to which the complaints were accurately stated; (2) the extent to which the complaints had an objective reference, and so could be verified independently of the individual who made the complaint; and therefore (3) the extent to which the conditions complained about could be stated in terms of standards which are generally accepted.

It was evident that for a number of complaints these conditions were only fulfilled in part. Practically all of them were stated in vague, indefinite terms such as hot, cold, heavy, damp, smoky, or dusty. There were practically no statements to the effect that "the temperature in the room at such and such a time was 67° F., and for me that is cold" or "on such and such an occasion I went into this washroom, and that washbowl had some dirt in it." These particulars were lacking in such general statements as "the room I work in is too hot" or "the washrooms are insanitary."

In short, the interview material did not supply comments which were reliable in the sense that they pictured accurately the conditions in the company. A group of men had to be used to investigate the conditions and to restate the problems which needed attention. For example, there were many complaints about the insanitary or dirty condition of the washrooms. An investigation in many instances revealed the following condition. The washrooms were cleaned and disinfected once each day. A matron was in constant attendance in the women's washrooms, and a monitor was assigned to the men's wash-rooms. Nevertheless, in spite of these precautions, the washrooms were occasionally left with paper strewn on the floor, etc. In the opinion of the investigators, the insanitary condition was largely due to the carelessness of some employees. The problem became one of education in hygiene. A general campaign against throwing papers, spitting on the floor, and similar practices was instituted. It was in this way that many of the complaints were reinterpreted and used to effect improvements.

Of course, it could be argued, and quite correctly, that scientifically exact statements about plant conditions from employees were not to be expected. But this was not the kind of reliability in question. Were the complaints reliable in the sense that there were objective conditions to which they referred? Was this reference sufficiently clearly indi-cated by the employees so that a competent engineer could determine the cause of the complaints without having recourse to the individuals who made them?

In regard to physical plant conditions, comments in this sense were fairly reliable. Even though a complaint was not explicitly formulated, there was something in fact to which it referred. The washroom was "dirty," not in the sense that it was never cleaned or attended to, but in the sense that it had been left dirty by another employee. A complaint about the temperature of a room or of drinking water could also be tested by some objective standard. The vague statements of the em-ployees could be reformulated in such terms as "when the temperature of the water in the drinking fountains is about 60° F., it is warm" (for a particular employee or group of employees). A complaint about overcrowded lockers could be investigated and expressed in terms of what happened to hats, overcoats, jackets, shoes, and lunches when two or three people had to share the same locker.

To repeat, in the case of complaints about plant conditions, there was the possibility of a restatement which would give a fairly accurate meaning to the complaint in terms of the object criticized. In addition, there was in most cases an implied agreement between the standards of the workers and those of the investigators, i.e., it was assumed that the workers and the investigators had in common approximately the same standards of bodily comfort, safety, and personal integrity. It is apparent that in many instances action was more dependent on this agreement than on any statement of fact. Although it might be interesting to know that some worker complained of the cold when the room was 72° F., something was done about the situation only if the investigators and other employees felt the same way about it. There were, on the whole, few statements made about plant conditions by employees which involved disagreement with the standards of the investigators. Of course, there were exceptions. In certain areas where social as well as physical standards were involved, there was some difference of opinion, as, for example, with regard to matters of health, sanitation, and dirt.

In criticisms of persons and of company policy, however, it was much more difficult to locate the reference and hence to administer the remedy. What appeared to be the same set of external conditions for a group of employees brought forth a host of differing opinions. An engineer could restate and clarify a vague complaint about plant conditions, but it was very difficult to say just what an employee who called his supervisor a "bully" meant, when the same supervisor was held in high esteem by other subordinates in his department and, moreover, when the employee upon being asked to amplify his complaint replied, "He doesn't say 'good morning' to the help."

Three Classes of Complaints

These considerations prompted the following question: Did the interviews elicit from the employees many statements having characteristics essentially different from the properties which are generally associated with common facts,[1] and, if so, how were these statements to be interpreted or understood? It is apparent that even from a practical point of view the answer to this question is rather important, for if some of the complaints made by employees have properties essentially different from those of facts, it is well to discriminate such complaints from those that can be regarded as statements of fact.

To answer this question, all the complaints taken from the 1929 interviews were examined. Analysis of the comments with this ques-

[1] By a "fact" will be meant a statement from experience involving sensory processes, and physical and logical operations, such that if the statement is challenged there exist certain generally accepted procedures by means of which the statement can be tested, verified, or corroborated. For those who wish a further discussion of this definition, see Henderson, L. J., "An Approximate Definition of Fact," *University of California Publications in Philosophy*, Vol. 14, 1932, p. 179. The extensive use which the authors have made of this paper will be apparent to anyone who has read it.

tion in mind showed that there are essentially three different classes of complaints. These classes can be differentiated from one another both on the basis of the kind of experiences which the statements involve and on the basis of the processes which enter into their verification.

Class A — Complaints involving terms which refer to objects that can be seen and touched, and for which there exist some operations which can be agreed upon as defining them.

Class B — Complaints involving terms which refer primarily to sensory experiences other than those of sight and touch, and for which there do not exist, at least in the case of one term, any operations which can be agreed upon as defining them.

Class C — Complaints involving terms which do not refer primarily to sensory experiences, and for which there exist no operations which can be agreed upon as defining them.[1]

Although the formal statement of these differences seems formidable, the distinction is in fact very simple. It involves the difference between such complaints as "the doorknob is broken," "this machine is out of order," "this tool is not sharp," and such statements as "earnings are not commensurate with length of service," "the supervisor is unfair," "the job is too hard," "rates are too low," and "ability is not rewarded." On

[1] Inasmuch as some readers may find it difficult to understand the purpose of the distinctions elaborated in this and the following chapter, the authors feel that some further explanation is perhaps desirable.

For some time the investigators were baffled by the problem of analyzing the interviews. What were these interviews telling them about the company, its supervisors, and employees? What uniformities were being revealed? They soon found that a mere statistical cataloguing of likes and dislikes was not the answer to their problem. They realized that they had been naive at first with regard to the phenomena of verbal behavior, and that the understanding of interview material, or verbal behavior, presents difficult problems which are frequently ignored. The search for uniformities among the statements made in an interview presupposes some simple conceptual framework in terms of which the interviewer can operate upon the statements made. Without such a framework, confusion is inevitable.

This chapter and the one that follows, therefore, will be concerned with the development of the conceptual framework necessary for the understanding of interview material. It happened that the first step in the development of this working hypothesis came to the investigators through the consideration of the reliability of employee complaints. (This development will be explained in this chapter.) The further elaboration came in connection with certain problems of interviewing method. (This development will be considered in the next chapter.)

Although this conceptual framework was developed in terms of employee interviews, it should be remembered that these distinctions express nothing peculiar to employee interviews alone. They are distinctions rooted in the properties of verbal behavior, and therefore distinctions fundamental to the thinking of an interviewer regardless of what person or groups of persons he is interviewing.

the basis of the kind of experiences which enter into the determination of these three classes of complaints, and consequently on the basis of means of verification, they differ as follows:

Class A complaints involve primarily sensory experiences and physical and logical operations. They are conclusions from experience about things which can be seen and touched, that is, they embody visual, tactual, and kinesthetic sensations. Physical operations, such as moving, turning, handling, lifting, assembling, as well as logical operations, such as counting, verifying, and establishing relations, enter into their determination. They involve terms which can be defined by a competent worker or engineer. Moreover, the definition implies physical procedures by means of which the statement can be tested. For example, such statements as "the tool is dull" or "the machine is out of order" involve standards that can be defined in terms of technological practice and that can be agreed upon by most people who are competent judges of such matters.

Class B complaints differ from those of Class A in that, although sensory experiences still play a large role, they are primarily experiences other than those of sight and touch. They involve such experiences as heat, cold, pain, nausea, thirst, and hunger, as well as sensations arising within the organism by movement or tension in its own tissues (feelings of fatigue). Moreover, such statements include terms for which no physical or logical operations exist which can be agreed upon as defining them. They are terms whose meanings are biologically or socially determined and hence vary with time, place, age, nationality, personality, social status, and temperament. Examples of such statements are: "the work is dirty," "the lockers are insanitary," "the job is dangerous," "the work is hard," and "the room is hot."

In Class C complaints sensory experience plays a small role. These comments involve the hopes and fears of the employees. Often they are reducible to verbal expressions of sentiment and reasonings in accord with sentiment. Frequently entering into their determination are such experiences as daydreaming, revery, fantasy, and preoccupation. They too contain terms whose meanings are socially determined and hence for which no physical or logical operations exist which can be agreed upon as defining them. Some examples of such complaints are: "rates are too low," "earnings are not commensurate with length of service," "ability doesn't count."

It is apparent that these three groups differ to a large extent on the question of verification. For Class A complaints there are certain procedures clearly defined, either explicitly or implicitly, by means of which the statement can be tested, verified, or corroborated. For the latter two groups no such clear procedures exist. In Class A, experiences of sight and touch can be brought in as witness; physical and logical operations can be used in verification. This possibility is not present in the case of Class B and Class C comments. If such statements are to be verified, the ambiguities of the terms require definition. But here is the difficulty: no definition can be agreed upon by all those concerned with their verification.

For example, let us take the employee who complains that piece rates are too low (Class C). A fair piece rate, of course, can be defined by fiat. Management assumes that a fair rate is one that is set in a systematic manner on the basis of motion and time studies and/or in accordance with rates paid by other concerns in the same territory for comparable work. But is this the definition of management or the definition of the employees? According to the employee, piece rates may be too low when the earnings therefrom are insufficient for his needs, or are not in accordance with his hopes and expectations. Depending on which definition is used, the complaint may or may not be justified. But agreement cannot be reached by logical definition. The test is very simple. Go to the employee who says his wages are too low and appeal to the fact that his rates have been set in accord with the most expert knowledge at the company's command. At the end of the discussion the employee is likely to reaffirm his statement, "the rates are too low." Where is there a court of appeal? For him the rates are too low. To him management's definition is arbitrary and management's reasoning appears equivocal.

The Properties of Class B Comments

But surely, it will be said, the statement "the room is too hot" (Class B) can be verified. People do agree on judgments of this kind, and it is quibbling to say that there is no definition which can be agreed upon as defining the word "hot." It may be, our dissenter continues, that a room at 68° F. is called comfortable by an Englishman, cold by an American, hot by a man who is doing muscular work, cold by a man who is sitting at a desk, cold by a hypothyroid person and hot by a hyperthyroid person, but such individual differences are not important. It still remains that for most people not doing heavy manual labor a room at 50° F. is cold and a room at 90° F. is hot.

The statement "the room is hot" still remains unverifiable. What is found from experience, however, is that a high correlation exists in many instances between the statement "the room is hot" and a set of physical conditions (temperature, humidity, and ventilation). This does not follow from definition but from the nature of the human organism as known by experience.

Let us take, as an example, three individuals who make the statement "the room is hot." In the case of *A*, the room is 68° F.; in the case of *B*, it is 72° F.; and in the case of *C*, it is 90° F. Let us further assume that the time of year is winter and that all three individuals are not doing heavy muscular work. It is probable that the third complaint would be considered justified, the second doubtful, and the first not justified. Note that determining the justifiability of the complaint does not change the experience of any one of the three individuals. The room still remains hot for *A* even though the temperature is 68° F.

But our dissenter objects. In spite of the fact that such statements are unverifiable, nevertheless they can be used by management in improving plant conditions. Should a large number of people in a room in which the temperature is 90° F. complain about the heat, the company has a basis for action. Here would be a situation in which an investigator of complaints about plant conditions could take action. But note that in such an instance action would follow not by verifying that the room is hot but by verifying the fact that when the room is 90° F. a large number of persons complain about the heat, a fact which fits in with everyday experience. In the case of a large number of similar complaints about plant conditions, a high correlation was found between the complaints and a certain set of physical circumstances. Moreover, it was assumed that by altering such physical conditions a large percentage of the complaints would be eliminated, and experience showed this assumption to be correct. However, it should be observed that action followed from treating "the room is hot" as a symptom in a way very similar to that in which a doctor handles a complaint about an ache or pain, except that the doctor refers the symptom to the organism whereas the company referred it to the physical environment. In the case of worker *A*, however, who complained of the heat when the room was 68° F. (and let us remember that the kind of action described above left his situation unaltered), it might be well to refer this complaint to his physical condition.

So far, then, it is clear that although Class B comments are not facts in the strict sense of the term, nevertheless this did not prevent their use by management within certain limits for the sufficient reason that, although they have certain properties already mentioned which differentiate them from Class A comments, they also have an added characteristic. Sometimes they can be referred to the relation between an organism and its physical environment, about which there is some knowledge (common and scientific·facts), and in terms of such knowledge action can be taken.

The Properties of Class C Comments

Although among Class B statements a fairly reliable correlation can frequently be obtained between a given set of complaints and a given set of physical circumstances, this does not happen so often among Class C statements.

Let us take the example of worker *A* complaining about the fact that worker *B*, doing a similar job, is earning more money than he is. He says, "I have as much or more service than *B*, my efficiency is as high or higher, my potentialities are as great or greater, my attendance record is as good or better, my home responsibilities are as much or more." In short, every factor entering into the determination of wages is to *A*'s advantage. *A* concludes by saying, "This is unfair." Here we have a case in which most people would agree that *A* has a justifiable complaint. That two people doing the same work, all other things being equal, should earn the same amount would be agreed upon by management and the worker. But note that in order to obtain agreement, an *atypical* case has to be presented. Actually, there were no complaints which fulfilled the condition "all other things being equal," and there were very few which even approximated it. The situation was more frequently something like this:

Worker *A* doing (what he thinks is) a similar job to that of worker *B* might complain in the following different ways because (he thinks) *B* is earning more money than he is:

Relation of A to B	A complains by saying [1]
A has less service than *B*.	Earnings are not commensurate with job.
A has more service than *B*.	Service is not being rewarded.
A is a man; *B* is a woman.	Woman's place is in the home.
A is a woman; *B* is a man.	Women are being discriminated against.

[1] There is no implication from these examples that the particular condition mentioned brought forth in every case the corresponding complaint. Human situations are never quite so simple as that. All we wish to show is that factors like those illustrated influenced the reactions of the workers.

Relation of A to B	A complains by saying
A is single; B is married.	Married employees are given preference over single employees.
A is married; B is single.	Home responsibilities should be taken into account by the company.
A has less education than B.	The company attaches too much importance to education.
A has more education than B.	Brains don't count.
A is, or thinks he may be, less efficient than B.	Piece rates are too low.
A is, or thinks he is, more efficient than B.	Ability is not rewarded.

It is obvious that most of these reactions are more than simple descriptions of experience involving receptor processes and physical and logical operations. None of these conclusions follows logically from the given premises, even assuming the situation was as worker A thought. No inference can be drawn from these examples, however, about the illogicality or irrationality of employees in particular. Similar illustrations can be found in all walks of life. Even the scientist outside his laboratory is not immune from this kind of thinking.

The important thing is that these conclusions involve a logic of sentiments. They are expressions of sentiment and reasonings in accord with sentiment, which are very common phenomena in all social life. They are neither facts nor errors. They are nonfacts, involving the sentiments of individuals, and as such verification in the strict sense cannot be applied to them.

It was difficult to see just how such expressions, taken at their face value, could be used to correct conditions in the company. Differences in jobs, abilities, length of service, age, marital status, and so on, would always exist. There would always be a group of employees (generally newcomers and single) who would be opposed to having such factors as service and marital status enter into the determination of earnings. There would also be another group of employees (generally people who had long service and were married) whose sentiments would be the opposite. But that employees were not expressing facts was nothing to be deplored. This made their statements no less important or useful. Difficulty only arose if fact were not discriminated from sentiment, and the latter were taken as the former.

A good example of this confusion of fact and sentiment is found in the logical debates that take place about straight, or individual, piece-work and group piecework. The problem is a question of equity. Which one of these systems of payment is more equitable to the worker? To the advocates of group piecework,[1] this system is more equitable than straight piecework because any one individual will suffer less from any discrepancies in rates between jobs within a depart-ment — a situation which may exist no matter how scientifically the rates are set. In a straight piecework department, some workers feel themselves to be unfairly discriminated against if they are assigned to a job which carries with it a "low rate," that is, a job on which they cannot earn so much as on some other job in the same department. As a consequence, in a straight piecework department complaints of partiality against the supervisor are prevalent. To eradicate these com-plaints, group piecework is proposed on the ground that each member of the group participates in the total group earnings, so that if a dis-crepancy in piece rates between jobs exists, no one individual is affected more than any other.

In the process of correcting these complaints by instituting group piecework, however, another deeply rooted sentiment is violated. The earnings of an individual do not correspond exactly to his efficiency or to the amount of work he does. By the very nature of group piecework the earnings of any one individual are bound to be affected to some degree by the day rate of each individual in the group and by the amount which each individual contributes to the output of the group. An influx of newcomers or of old-timers, or any change in the efficiency of any one individual, or lack of co-operation between individuals, affects the "percentage."[2]

But whether or not a change of personnel in a group piecework de-partment or the daily variations in efficiency of any one worker per-ceptibly affect the earnings of any one individual is irrelevant to the present consideration. The important phenomena are that some workers express such sentiments about group piecework and that some workers feel as they do about it. In short, the battle between advo-cates of straight piecework, on the one hand, and of group piece-work, on the other, is largely a battle of sentiments. And to treat complaints about the two systems as statements of fact is to cloud the real issue.

[1] In this discussion we are talking only of the group piecework system that was in operation at the company (see pp. 13–14). We are not referring to all group piecework systems.

[2] See p. 14 for a definition of this term.

It should be clear that Class C complaints have peculiar properties which differentiate them from the other classes of comments in that:

(1) They are complaints in which fact and sentiment are inextricably mixed so that verification in most cases is impossible. Any attempt at verification involves an arbitrary definition which frequently cannot be agreed upon, so that it ends in a meaningless process (a verbal argument). The worker's complaint still remains a complaint even though it may be unjustified from a certain definition. To apply arbitrary criteria is to miss the nature of the complaint.
(2) They are complaints which refer to the significant personal and social life of the worker, and apart from such a context they are meaningless. They cannot be assessed apart from the situation of the individual who makes them.[1]

It should also be clear that Class B comments have these properties to a lesser degree than Class C, and Class A less than Class B. In most cases Class A complaints are capable of being verified and hence are either facts or errors. Yet even in such statements there is always the possibility of a subjective reference. The complaint "the tool is dull" may be the complaint of a poor worker, as evidenced by the common saying, "a poor worker blames his tools."

Manifest vs. Latent Content of Complaints

This study of employee comments pointed to the need for reassessing the objectives of the interviewing program. The notion that from employee comments in themselves management could obtain an accurate and correct picture of industrial conditions had to be abandoned. It would be approximately true to say that from the interviews nothing had been learned about the physical plant conditions which was not already known by those in charge of such matters. However, it was also true that although the engineers were acquainted with plant conditions they were not acquainted with the reactions of the employees to them. What the interviewing program had provided was not an exact description of plant conditions but statements of how employees felt about such conditions. And this was, for the most part, the practical way in which the employee comments functioned. They offered additional evidence on which the engineer could act.

There was another body of comments which expressed the employ-

---

[1] It would be erroneous to conclude that because of these properties there may not exist in some Class C statements considerable agreement among the reactions of employees to a given set of conditions (a rate, policy, etc.). To the extent that they share the same sentiments, this uniformity will appear.

ees' feelings toward the policies of management, supervision, and certain social conditions of work, and these comments could not be used in so simple a way as those about plant conditions. Although they gave a picture of how the employees felt about such matters, they did not provide any immediate illumination as to why the employees felt as they did. Complaints such as these could not be handled in the simple and direct fashion considered possible in the early stages of the program, for they involved the sentiments of individuals and groups. There were no specialists in sentiments at the company to whom this material could be referred for interpretation and investigation. Of course, any skillful executive or administrator is constantly handling and manipulating such material, but his methods are largely intuitive and implicit. It was obvious that, strictly speaking, verification for this kind of material was not only impossible but irrelevant. Whether justified or not, hopes and fears, desires and sentiments, values and significances existed. To decide which were justified and which were not, to correct the former and to ignore the latter, was to lose sight of the real problem.

The difficulty lay in the reference of such complaints. To what did they refer? It was clear that frequently there was no simple and direct relation between the complaint and the object toward which the complaint was directed. This lack of relation had been noticed by the interviewers. Probably no group had become more aware of the dangers involved in a too simple acceptance of comments at their face value. Often they had good reason to believe that certain grievances, although directed toward some object or person, were not due to some deficiency in the object criticized but rather were expressions of concealed, perhaps unconscious, disturbances in the employee's situation. Such complaints had an inner as well as an outer reference, and the inner reference could be reached only by a further study of the person who made the complaint. To put it in other words, the latent content of a statement, that is, the attitude of the complainant, was, in many instances, just as important to understand as its manifest content. For example, although the manifest content of a complaint might shift and vary, sometimes being directed to this and sometimes to that object, the psychological form might remain the same. The same underlying complaining attitude might be present, even though the employee might on one occasion be complaining about smoke and fumes and on another occasion about his supervisor. Or, to cite a different example, two complaints which from the viewpoint of manifest content might appear to be the same, from the viewpoint of latent content might be quite different. Two workers might both find the same fault with the same supervisor. Yet, in one case the supervisor might be merely the object of a mild antagonism which is often present in any superior-subordinate relation and about which the worker is not greatly concerned, and in the other case the supervisor might have become an object of fear and hatred by means of which all the worker's personal failings and frustrations are expressed.

This need of differentiating the actual significance of the complaint from its manifest expression led to the first discrimination which the investigators used in studying and analyzing the interviews. This discrimination was sometimes referred to as (1) the *manifest* vs. the *latent* content of the complaint, and sometimes as (2) the *material content* vs. the *psychological form* of the complaint. A few simple illustrations will suffice to make this distinction clear.

Let us take, first, an instance which the reader may find it easy to duplicate in his own personal experience. *A* has an argument with his wife at the breakfast table, an argument, let us assume, in which *A* is worsted. Still rankling under his discomfiture, *A* comes to work in a surly mood. Some little thing goes wrong, something which under different circumstances *A* would "pass off" lightly. But this happening gives him an opportunity to "explode." Anyone or anything in the vicinity may bear the brunt of *A*'s irritation — the temperature or stuffiness of the room, the draft from the window, the condition in which his tools have been left, the trucker who fails to arrive with the necessary piece parts, the "silly grin" of the boss, the obsequious attitude of his subordinate. In this case it can be readily seen that the irritation displayed by *A* at work is closely related to the argument he had with his wife.

Suppose a worker, *B*, complains that the piece rates on his job are too low. In the interview it is also revealed that his wife is in the hospital and that he is worried about the doctor's bills he has incurred. In this case the latent content of the complaint consists of the fact that *B*'s present earnings, due to his wife's illness, are insufficient to meet his current financial obligations. This source of his dissatisfaction can be expressed in many different ways, one of which is to grumble about the piece rates.

The case of a worker, *C*, is slightly more complicated. In the interview *C* calls his supervisor a "bully." It is learned that *C* resents the fact that his supervisor passes him by in the morning without a nod of recognition. It is also apparent that this is only one of many ways in which *C* expresses the fact that he is sensitive about his place in the world. If he is told to do something, he interprets this as a "misuse of authority"; if he is left alone, he interprets this as a "slight" and a failure to recognize his true worth. In his preoccupations, which he begins to express freely in the interview, are to be found all sorts of fantasies about what he could have said or done or would have liked to have said or done to his boss. Under the skillful handling of the interviewer, C begins to relax and to discuss other topics not connected with the shop. He commences to talk about his family and early life. He talks a great deal about his overdominating father who brooked no insubordination on the part of his children. He relates incidents to show his father's inconsiderateness toward his mother and toward himself in particular. As the situation is gradually disclosed in the interview, a clearer picture of the real significance of C's dissatisfaction begins to emerge; it is rooted somewhere in his attitude toward authority as conditioned by the early parental situation. On anyone in a position of authority he tends to "project" the parental image.

Worker D, who complains bitterly about the temperature, ventilation, smoke, and fumes in his department, offers another example. Health is the dominating motif of the interview. This preoccupation is paramount, and a good deal of the interview is taken up with questions of diet, health, disease, and the deception of physical appearances (D is a robust, healthy-looking person). Gradually D tells about the case of his brother who had recently died from pneumonia. He compares himself to his brother: "Here I am a healthy, strapping fellow, just like my brother; yet tomorrow I too may be gone."

The first simple rule which the interviewers contributed to the analysis of complaints was this: *Consider the complaint not only in relation to its alleged object but also in relation to the personal situation of the complainant.* Only in this way is the richer significance of the complaint realized. The significance of B's grouch about piece rates is better grasped in relation to the increased financial obligation incurred by his wife's illness. C's attitude toward his boss is greatly illuminated by the experience he relates in connection with his father. D's complaint about smoke and fumes is more readily understood in relation to his fear of contracting pneumonia.

Of course, such an analysis did not settle the question of whether or not B's piece rates were "really" too low, whether or not C's boss was a bully, or what the "real" state of affairs with regard to smoke and fumes in D's department was. But the difficulties encountered in answering such questions, particularly the first two, have already been discussed. The investigators felt that more could be learned about the worker, his values and significances, by trying to find out more fully the emotional significance of the complaint for the complainant than by trying to judge the truth or falsity of the complaint, particularly in those cases where there was no sensory experience or common standard agreed upon by which to settle the matter. The important consideration was not whether his complaint was justified but why he felt the way he did.

This search for the latent content of the complaint afforded excellent training for the interviewers. Had this way of thinking not been developed early in the program, many interesting problems would have been overlooked, and an adequate conceptual scheme for the handling of personal dissatisfaction would not have been developed. What the interviewers found was that workers by themselves were not able to specify precisely the particular source of their dissatisfaction, but that if they were encouraged to talk freely, the effect was not merely emotional relief but also, in many instances, the revelation to the critical listener of the significance of the complaint. From a research point of view, this was the first finding of great importance which resulted from the interviewing program, and it had an important bearing on the future activities of the interviewing staff. It shifted the direction of the research from merely an exploration of industrial conditions to an exploration of human situations as well. *Certain complaints were no longer treated as facts in themselves but as symptoms or indicators of personal or social situations which needed to be explored.*

CHAPTER XIII

THE INTERVIEWING METHOD

STATEMENT OF THE PROBLEM

DURING the interviewing program the investigators had become more and more interested in interviewing as a method of industrial research. In the beginning, the interviewing method had been viewed as rather simple and incidental to the material which it was hoped such a technique could obtain. But as the inquiry progressed, it became apparent that to obtain the intimate thinking of the worker was no simple matter, but a tedious and arduous task requiring more special training than at first had been thought necessary. Only after some 20,000 employee interviews had been taken had a personnel capable of doing such a job been trained. The need for this training will be better appreciated when the viewpoint demanded of the interviewer, as well as the minute precautions he needs to take, are more fully described.

The investigators became more certain that the chief value of interviewing as a method of industrial research lay in the fact that such a method, when exercised with care and skill, could obtain with some accuracy the emotional significance to the worker of particular events and objects in his experience. For as the interviewers became more skilled, they were able to tap this source of material more and more often. If the interviewers, on the one hand, had become more sceptical of interviewing as a means of obtaining "objective information" or an accurate picture of "things as they are," they became, on the other hand, more enthusiastic about interviewing as a means of obtaining the implicit evaluations of his environment made by the person interviewed. Many of the interviewers came to regard these implicit meanings which the worker assigned to the reality about him as the only legitimate object of the interview, and as the only kind of material the interviewing method could accurately provide. Toward this end, then, the interviewers turned their attention, with the result that a method was developed which, although still called the "interviewing method," differed in many respects from interviewing as it was ordinarily conceived and used in industry.

As the interviewers became more aware of the kind of material they were trying to elicit from the worker, they found that for several reasons the questionnaire method, or direct type of interviewing, was unsatisfactory. There was the difficulty of framing a question without suggesting a significance to the individual which the object of the question might not have for him. The direct type of interviewing tended to elicit opinions on topics which the interviewer, rather than the employee, thought to be of importance. Also, the results obtained from such a method were frequently valueless because of the absence of a sufficient context for interpreting the response.

However, it was equally clear that the interviewer had to play some active role in the interview. Although the skilled interviewer allowed himself to be led by the topics which the employee chose to discuss, frequently he wished to have the employee express himself more fully on a particular topic or in certain areas where he felt there had been significant omissions. The skilled interviewer was not just listening without any ideas in mind. He was putting to himself certain questions; he had certain ideas and hypotheses; he attached more importance to certain matters than to others.

Here, then, was the difficulty which confronted those interviewers who were interested in developing their technique: On the one hand, an indirect type of interviewing was preferable if the spontaneous convictions of the worker were to be obtained, and these could only be obtained by not asking too many questions and by following rather than leading the interviewee. On the other hand, this method had its limitations, for if the interviewer asked too few questions, the interview tended to remain at the level of polite social conversation. Moreover, the interviewer often wished to break into critical zones. Naturally, such a problem taxed the ingenuity and intelligence of the interviewer. He had to guard against two errors: he had to guard against having fixed and preconceived ideas which would prevent him from catching anything new; on the other hand, he had to guard against allowing the interview to become incoherent because of no guiding hypothesis.

If the interviewers were to conduct interviews skillfully, it was necessary for them to have some simple conceptual scheme, that is, some framework in which their thought was set and by means of which they could operate on the material elicited in the interview. This conceptual scheme depended on some idea of what took place when two people were talking together, and the way in which an interview differed from an ordinary social conversation.

Rules of Orientation [1]

This conceptual scheme probably can be presented best by first listing and then discussing separately each of the rules which the interviewers found useful for the interpretation of what took place in an interview. These rules were as follows:

I. The interviewer should treat what is said in an interview as an item in a context.
    A. The interviewer should not pay exclusive attention to the manifest content of the intercourse.
    B. The interviewer should not treat everything that is said as either fact or error.
    C. The interviewer should not treat everything that is said as being at the same psychological level.
II. The interviewer should listen not only to what a person wants to say but also for what he does not want to say or cannot say without help.

---

[1] Since these rules imply a way of conceiving of human situations that is employed in certain fields of psychology and social anthropology, it may be well to state here that part of their conceptual equipment which the interviewers borrowed from these related fields of inquiry. From modern psychopathology the interviewers gained a good deal (Janet, P., *Les Névroses*, Flammarion, Paris, 1930; *Les Obsessions et la Psychasthénie*, 2 vols., Troisième Édition, Alcan, Paris, 1919. Freud, S., *Selected Papers on Hysteria and Other Psychoneuroses*, 3rd Edition, Nervous and Mental Disease Publishing Company, New York, 1920. Jung, C. G., *Two Essays on Analytical Psychology*, Dodd, Mead & Co., New York, 1928). Piaget, the child psychologist, with his excellent statement and discussion of the clinical method of interviewing as used with children, was extremely helpful (*The Child's Conception of the World*, Harcourt, Brace & Co., New York, 1929). The reader may also discern echoes from the French sociological school, who were eagerly read (Durkheim, *Elementary Forms of the Religious Life*, Allen & Unwin Ltd., London, 1926; *Le Suicide*, Alcan, Paris, 1930. Lévy-Bruhl, L., *Primitive Mentality*, Allen & Unwin Ltd., London, 1923). The functional school of anthropology did not go by unheard (Malinowski, B., "The Problem of Meaning in Primitive Languages," Supplement 1 in Ogden, C. K., and Richards, I. A., *The Meaning of Meaning*, Harcourt, Brace & Co., New York, 1927. Radcliffe-Brown, A. R., *The Andaman Islanders*, Cambridge University Press, Cambridge, England, 1933. Pitt-Rivers, G. H. L. F., *The Clash of Culture and the Contact of Races*, Routledge & Sons Ltd., London, 1927). To the first chapter in Bjerre's *The Psychology of Murder* (Longmans, Green & Co., London, 1927) they were also indebted for some illuminating remarks. Pareto's *The Mind and Society* (4 vols., Harcourt, Brace & Co., New York, 1935) contributed probably most to the systematic understanding of a social system. Three articles published by Lawrence J. Henderson helped considerably in the systematic statement of the method as described in this chapter ("An Approximate Definition of Fact," *Univ. of California Publications in Philosophy*, Vol. 14, 1932; "Science, Logic and Human Intercourse," *Harvard Business Review*, April, 1934; "Physician and Patient as a Social System," *New England Journal of Medicine*, Vol. 212, 1935). To Elton Mayo, in particular, the interviewers were most indebted (*The Human Problems of an Industrial Civilization*, Macmillan, New York, 1933).

III. The interviewer should treat the mental contexts described in the preceding rule as indices and seek through them the personal reference that is being revealed.

IV. The interviewer should keep the personal reference in its social context.

    A. The interviewer should remember that the interview is itself a social situation and that therefore the social relation existing between the interviewer and the interviewee is in part determining what is said.

    A_1. The interviewer should see to it that the speaker's sentiments do not act on his own.

Rule I *The interviewer should treat what is said in an interview as an item in a context.*

The relation between any item in an interview and "context" will become more clear as the following rules are discussed. It may be said here, however, that the interviewer is constantly seeking a context for every item in an interview. Although in this sense the context is that which the interviewer adds to the interview, this addition is not arbitrary. It is constantly being subjected to verification and modification as new items and interrelations appear. This first rule of interpretation has several important corollaries.

Rule IA *The interviewer should not pay exclusive attention to the manifest content of the intercourse.*

This rule warns the interviewer to guard himself against falling into a common attitude that he as a human being is likely to take in a social conversation. When two people are exchanging thoughts and sharing ideas, attention is likely to be directed exclusively to the manifest content of what is being said. In the heat of discussion, the emotional and personal significance to the participants of the topic being discussed, let us say, for example, the "cause of the depression," the "Supreme Court," the "equality of women," is missed. Frequently it is this ignored factor rather than any strictly logical consideration which accounts for the respective positions which the participants take on the question under discussion.

Here is an illustration. At an afternoon tea in New England, attended by members of both sexes, a woman made a remark to the effect that the English public school system tended to make men brutal. All in the group took sides, some agreeing and some disagreeing with the generalization. A heated and lengthy discussion followed in which the merits and demerits of the English public school system were thoroughly reviewed. In other words, the statement was taken at its face value and discussed at that level. No one, seemingly, paid attention to the fact that the woman who made the statement had married an Englishman who had received an English public school education and that she was in the process of obtaining a divorce from him. Had it occurred to the others, as it did to one person in the room, that the woman had expressed more clearly her sentiments toward her husband than she had expressed anything equally clear about the English public school system, and that the form in which she expressed her sentiments had reacted on the national and international sentiments of her audience, which they, in turn, had more clearly expressed than anything equally clear about the English public school system, such an idea would have been secretly entertained and not publicly expressed, for that is the nature of polite social intercourse.

But in an interview things are otherwise. Had this statement been made in an interview, the interviewer would not have been misled by the manifest content of the statement. He would have been on the alert for a personal reference, and, once he had learned about the woman's husband, he would have guided the conversation on this topic rather than on the English public school system. Furthermore, he would have been on his guard not to allow any sentiments which he as a social being might entertain toward the English to be acted upon by the form of the statement. This second point is of great importance and will be discussed more fully later.[1]

Rule IB   The interviewer should not treat everything that is said as either fact or error.

This is a favorite false dichotomy for the beginner in interviewing. He tends to be exclusively concerned with the truth or falsity of what is said in the interview. Everything for him is either fact or error. Now the majority of statements made in the interviewing program at the Western Electric Company were, strictly speaking, neither facts nor errors. They were more in the nature of nonfacts. To ask of such statements whether or not they are "true" involves a completely different kind of meaning than to ask the same question of a statement capable of verification.[2]

---

[1] See Rule IVA₁, pp. 285–286.

[2] According to some logicians, such a question is meaningless. See Bridgman, P. W., *The Logic of Modern Physics*, Macmillan, New York, 1928, pp. 28–30.

For example, take three very common statements made by employees during the interviewing program:

(1) My wages last month averaged only $35.00 per week. I used to make more.
(2) Working in this company is like being in a jail.
(3) This is the most wonderful company to work for.

If the interviewer doubts the truth of the first statement, he can easily verify it; not so with the second or third statement. Of course, the interviewer can ask, Do most employees agree with the second or third statement? He may find:

(1) The majority of workers agreeing with the second statement.
(2) The workers divided between the second and third statements.
(3) The majority of workers agreeing with the third statement.

Should the interviewer find that most of the workers agree with the third statement, can he conclude therefore that the third statement is "true" and the second is "false"? If he does, he is using "true" in a sense quite different from that in which he used it in verifying the first statement. If 99 people in a room agree that the temperature of the room is 72° F., with only one person claiming a temperature of 68° F., the question is not settled by a majority opinion.

For many readers this distinction will probably seem like splitting hairs, with perhaps some theoretical significance for the logical purist, but with no great practical value for the interviewer. But it is actually a distinction of the utmost significance for the interviewer engaged in the kind of interviewing here being described. Many of the common errors of interpretation arise from treating nonfacts as facts, or vice versa. As a result, what is being said is taken out of its mental context, an irrelevant context is substituted, and irrelevant questions are asked by the interviewer of the material elicited.

Of course, it is frequently very important for the interviewer to know what people agree and what people disagree with a nonfactual statement. But should the interviewer put such a question to himself, it is not with the purpose of establishing the truth or falsity of the statement made. He has a completely different purpose in mind, which will be discussed later.[1]

[1] See Rule IV, p. 283.

Rule IC   The interviewer should not treat everything that is said as being at the same psychological level.

This rule warns the beginner against another serious stumbling block. For no sooner does he stop asking of nonfactual statements whether or not they are true than he begins to ask, Is the speaker saying what he really thinks? Here again the interviewer is likely to over-simplify matters. There is always the tendency to take one of two extreme attitudes, either completely believing or completely disbelieving everything a person says. In the first case the interviewer takes everything that is said at its face value. In the other case he disbelieves everything he hears. Both attitudes arise from the fallacy of assuming that everything that is being said during the interview is at the same psychological level. This is very seldom the case. Sometimes the speaker is bored and is just making conversation. Sometimes he is poking fun at the interviewer. Sometimes he is nervous and appre-hensive and therefore he is guarded in the statements he makes. Some-times he is trying to make a favorable impression on the interviewer. At other times he is more earnest and is attending to and reflecting upon what is being said. Naturally, the meaning to be assigned to the speaker's remarks depends upon interpreting his responses in the light of the psychological context in which they occur.

The tendency completely to believe or disbelieve the speaker also arises in part from oversimplifying the relation between what the speaker says and what he thinks. It is commonly supposed, although there is very little evidence to warrant such a supposition, that there exists a simple and logical relation between what a person says and what he thinks. On this assumption, any deviation from a logically explicit statement is taken as implying a willful and conscious intent on the part of the speaker to distort and disguise what he really is thinking. Now there is the possibility that the speaker does not say what he thinks, not because he will not, but because he cannot express it. This is a very common situation and will be discussed more fully under the next rule.[1]

It has frequently been suggested that perhaps the workers in the Western Electric Company's interviewing program were "spoofing" the interviewers, that they were not telling the interviewers what they

---

[1] It will no doubt be apparent to the reader by now that all these rules are so inti-mately interrelated that it is difficult to discuss one without presupposing the others. For this reason, no importance is to be attached to the order in which the rules appear. In-asmuch as everything cannot be discussed at the same time, some order is necessary, and to the authors this order seemed the simplest and most convenient.

really thought and felt but what they thought management would like to hear. That this was the attitude of some of the employees some of the time goes without question, but that this was consistently the attitude of any one worker during an interview lasting from one to two hours is a proposition which can be maintained only by a person who has had no experience with interviewing.

It was the experience of the interviewers that the genuine hypocrite was rarely encountered. In order to realize how difficult it is for anyone consistently to play the role of hypocrite, it is only necessary to realize that if a person is to disguise completely his feelings and sentiments he must be aware of them explicitly and to an extent which few people can achieve.

Of course, it is possible for a person to say *x is white* when he really thinks *x is black*. But if the interviewer is looking for meaning not in the statement *x is white* as something which exists by itself, but rather in the situation of which the statement *x is white* is an expression, such discrepancies do not go by undetected.

Let us take, for example, a worker who comes into the interview apprehensive and nervous. He is afraid that if he says *x is black* he may lose his job. Hence he says *x is white*. But in an interview lasting an hour, assuming that this basic attitude remains unchanged, he will make a number of other statements all guided by the same considerations. For the interviewer on the alert for contexts, this context will be the most noticeable element in the interview.

Another common example is that of the worker who wishes to give a certain impression of himself to the interviewer. In the interview he therefore says and does those things which he believes will convey that impression. Here is another very common context, not very different from the first. The first worker gains a feeling of security by remaining passive and making only the proper and conventional remarks. The second worker gains his feeling of security by trying actively to "sell himself" to the interviewer.

But neither of these two workers can be called really a hypocrite. Although they may not be saying exactly what they think, the sentiments which guide them to do this become more obvious as the interview continues. As a matter of fact, in the interviewing program there were very few cases in which a worker said *x is white* when he thought *x is black* merely to "stuff" the interviewer as an intellectual pastime. If he did make such a statement, it was because he was apprehensive and endeavoring to make a good impression, or trying to show his equality with the interviewer. That this was a fact is not difficult to understand. For a worker to disguise his feelings and sentiments completely and consistently throughout an interview would have required an insight into himself and a capacity for the understanding of social intercourse that it would be difficult for anyone in his social position to have acquired. Moreover, had he acquired such insight and understanding, he would probably not have remained in that social position. The difficulty which confronted the interviewers was not that of hypocrisy on the part of the worker but the achieving of a relationship to the worker which would enable him to state things in the interview which he was unable to state to himself.

Rule II   The interviewer should listen not only to what a person wants to say but also for what he does not want to say or cannot say without help.

Although there are no precise rules for the interpretation of individual responses, there are three broad categories into which the verbal behavior of a person in an interview can be placed:

(1) What a person wants to say.
(2) What a person does not want to say.
(3) What a person cannot say without help.

During an interview the interviewer has many opportunities to note significant gaps and omissions in what a person is saying. The interviewer should note these omissions and ask himself whether these related topics have been omitted because (1) the speaker does not care to talk about them, or (2) he has never thought about them.

Things about which a person does not care to talk are often likely to be connected with unpleasant or painful experiences. There has already been occasion to mention examples of such omissions: the worker who did not want to say *x is black* because that assertion was associated in his mind with the possibility of losing his job, and hence with unpleasant feelings of insecurity; the woman who in a discussion about English public schools failed to mention her husband, with whom unpleasant memories were associated. Such omissions are likely to indicate areas of emotional significance, which, should the opportunity arise, should be explored. These explorations cannot be rushed. The interviewer has to wait for an appropriate time to break into such critical zones. Many times the procedure has to be indirect. Instead of trying to lead the interviewee directly into such critical areas, the interviewer tries to remove the "resistance," that is, the fears or doubts which he believes are preventing the interviewee from expressing himself freely. In the case of the previously mentioned worker who is afraid of losing his job, the interviewer does everything to assure the worker that what is said in the interview has no connection with the security of his position. In this way he hopes the interview will be directed into more fruitful channels.

However, most omissions that occur in an interview involve not only things about which the speaker does not wish to talk but also things which lie so implicitly in his thinking that they have not yet become conscious discriminations. A person may not want to talk about a particular topic and yet he may not be quite clear as to why he refrains. In the case of most omissions, therefore, the interviewer is on the alert for both contexts.

Take, for example, the case of an interviewee who changes the subject of conversation and begins to speculate (aloud, of course) on whether or not a psychologist can handle his personal affairs any better than most people, and whether or not a psychologist follows the advice he so freely gives to others. In such an instance the uncomplimentary things which the speaker thinks and feels about the interviewer, but which he does not choose to mention directly, are probably clear even to the speaker. But it is doubtful if the speaker could have stated explicitly the source of his antagonism toward the interviewer.

For the interviewer, therefore, it is important to note what the speaker regards in his own mind as obvious and of such universal application that it has never occurred to him to doubt or question it. By listening carefully to him as he discusses a variety of topics, the interviewer can frequently detect things which underlie what is said but are themselves not expressed. These implicit assumptions are of the greatest importance in assessing a person's ultimate values and significances, for, although they cannot be expressed explicitly by the person, nevertheless for that very reason they enter into the determination of his everyday judgments and thoughts.[1]

Rule III   The interviewer should treat the mental contexts described in the preceding rule as indices and seek through them the personal reference that is being revealed.

The previous rule makes a number of assumptions about the speaker and his mental processes. It assumes that he is not always at

---

[1] In this connection it is interesting to note that Rules IA, IB, and IC warn the interviewer against implicit assumptions frequently made by people in ordinary social intercourse.

attention or concentration, but that a good portion of his mental activity is spent in revery, daydreaming, wishful thinking, and preoccupation. It assumes that much of this "blind thinking" is concerned with the satisfaction of, rather than with the communication of, desires. It assumes that such thinking often remains inaccessible to the person so that it cannot be clearly expressed by him. It assumes that in what a person says there is a trace, but not an explicit statement, of this "blind thinking," and that for this reason it is not to be expected that between what a person says and what a person thinks there is a simple and direct relation.

Rule III follows from these assumptions. It warns the interviewer that the person whose situation he is assessing has a particular set of sentiments, desires, and interests which often are not clearly apprehended by him and which act in his thinking as a system of "absolute logics." Therefore, it is necessary to treat individual responses as symptoms, rather than as realities or facts, of the personal situation which gradually is disclosed as the interview progresses.

For example, let us take an evaluational judgment in the form *A dislikes B because B has the characteristic x*.[1] There are two attitudes which can be taken toward such a statement, one of which is more common than the other. The common attitude is to look at *B* and see if *B* has the characteristic *x*. The procedure adopted is generally one of "counting noses." How many people acquainted with *B* agree with *A* in his judgment of *B*? Implicit in this procedure is the notion of assessing the correctness or incorrectness of *A*'s judgment. If most of the people acquainted with *B* agree with *A* in his judgment of *B*, *A* is considered justified in having such an opinion. If the reverse is true, *A* is not considered justified and probably is dubbed "peculiar" or "abnormal." It will be noted that this procedure reveals directly only one thing about *A*, that is, the extent to which other people agree with him in his judgment of *B*.

The other, less common, attitude is to inquire what sentiments, desires, or interests of *A* are involved in *A*'s judgment of *B*. This attitude presupposes that any evaluational judgment is a composite of two elements: (1) the total effects from the object, and (2) the reaction of the person himself. Or, to put it in another way, satisfaction

---

[1] For those to whom this form of statement bears no resemblance to the worker as they know him in flesh and blood, let them picture a worker anxious and eager to tell the interviewer what a "helluva guy" his supervisor is and to make such statements as, "He's a bully; a slave driver; unfair; unjust; etc." The above statement is merely a formal way of expressing such remarks.

or dissatisfaction is treated as relative to the demands which the person is making of his environment, and the opportunities which the environment offers for their fulfillment. Many times these demands are not precise and definite. They are only vaguely apprehended by the speaker. For this reason, it is not to be expected that they will be explicitly expressed in the statements which he makes in an interview. Rather, they take the form of implicit assumptions. Therefore, the first question the interviewer asks is, What hopes and expectations on the part of the speaker does his evaluational judgment imply? The statement *A dislikes B because B has the characteristic x* is translated into the form:

(1) *A* has such and such expectations of *B*, or *A* has such and such sentiments toward *B*;

(2) *B* fails to come up to these expectations, or violates these sentiments of *A*;

(3) therefore, *A* dislikes *B*.

Such a translation is, of course, in many instances not easy to make. It demands a constant probing on the part of the interviewer for a detailed account by *A* of his many unpleasant experiences with *B* and other similar experiences.

Rule IV   The interviewer should keep the personal reference in its social context.

This rule warns the interviewer against considering the sentiments, desires, or interests of an individual as things in themselves. It cautions him to remember that he is looking at a person who has a past history and that here and now in the interview he is observing an end product of a particular historical route. That is to say, the interviewee has had particular experiences which, in turn, have aroused particular preoccupations. During the formative period of his childhood he has lived in a particular family which, in turn, has had particular social relations with the wider community. In terms of such factors the individual has been conditioned to a particular way of looking at and feeling about things.

But not only does the speaker have a social past; he is also enjoying a social present. Here and now he is having social relations with other people and groups of people. Moreover, these social relations are not of a chance character but for the most part are controlled by the codes, customs, and conventions of the community to which the individual belongs. If a person's feelings and sentiments are to be understood, they have to be related to his present social reality.

All the rules mentioned thus far can be briefly summarized in Figure 25, which roughly represents the configuration of interrelations which these rules warn the interviewer to keep in mind.

The verbal and overt acts (A and B) of the interviewee are to be kept in their contexts, the meanings of which are to be sought in terms

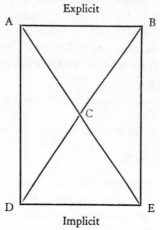

A = verbal behavior of person

B = overt behavior of person

C = sentiments, desires, interests, etc., of that person (personal reference)

D = the person's past history (social past) ⎫ social

E = the person's present interpersonal relations (social present) ⎭ reference

FIGURE 25

CONFIGURATIONS OF RELATIONSHIPS TO BE TAKEN INTO ACCOUNT BY INTERVIEWER

of the sentiments which such contexts express (personal reference, C). These sentiments, in turn, are to be seen in relation to their social reference: the speaker's past social conditioning (social past, D) and the present personal interrelations he has with the groups in which he is now living and working (social present, E).

Only by keeping together such a complex of interrelated factors can significant uniformities among the statements made by any one person, or among the statements made by different social groups, be obtained. For instance, the translation of statements in the form *A dislikes B because B has the characteristic x* into the form *A dislikes B because B violates such and such sentiments of A* frequently allows the interviewer to obtain uniformities which he otherwise would miss. Many times the interviewer finds, for example, that the sentiments A has toward B are the same as those A has toward any person having the same formal social relations that B has to A. For example, A has the same sentiments toward B, C, and D, his supervisors, as he has toward E, his father, that is, toward all people who in relation to him hold a position of superordination. Moreover, in interviewing groups of people, it sometimes can be seen that the sentiments A has toward B (a policy of the company, for example) are shared by all other people who are socially differentiated in the company structure in the same way that A is (in age grouping, service grouping, social and economic status, etc.).

It can now be seen in what sense it is important for an interviewer, particularly when interviewing groups of people, to be on the alert for those employees who agree and those employees who disagree with the evaluational judgment of any one employee about some particular aspect of his working environment. The purpose of such a procedure is not to verify the truth or falsity of the individual's judgment, but to see if any uniformities can be detected between the sentiments expressed by such a judgment and the social organization of the employees. To put it in terms of Figure 25, uniformities which exist between C and E or C and D might be only partially revealed by looking merely at the relation between A and E or A and D and would be entirely missed by examining A from the point of view of whether or not it is fact or error.

Rule IV A   The interviewer should remember that the interview is itself a social situation and that therefore the social relation existing between the interviewer and the interviewee is in part determining what is said.

This rule is implicitly recognized by most interviewers, and many of the practical rules of conducting the interview, which will be discussed later, follow from it. However, unless the beginner realizes explicitly certain consequences of this rule he is likely to fall into common misunderstandings of what frequently takes place in his relation to the person being interviewed.

In the first place, the speaker's attitude toward the interviewer is very likely to change in the course of the interview. To avoid errors of misinterpretation, the interviewer should be aware of this possible change in relation. Although changes of this sort are not so great in a single interview, they become increasingly more noticeable in a series of interviews with the same person.

In the beginning of the interview, the formal social setting is likely to dictate the relation between the two participants. In the Western Electric Company interviewing program, for example, the interviewers and the employees were members of the same company. In terms of that industrial organization, the interviewers, even though some of them were of nonsupervisory rank, were for many of the employees representatives of management. It might be expected that many employees in such a situation might have hesitated to express themselves freely and frankly to the interviewer. The astonishing thing, therefore, was to find how different from this expectation the actual results were. Many employees discussed with great frankness both personal and public matters concerning the policies of the company. Two conclusions seemed to be warranted from these results. One was that the frank relation of the employee to the interviewer reflected the basic confidence which the employee had in management. The second was that in the course of the interview the attitude toward the interviewer changed in such a way that things the employee might have hesitated to talk about in the beginning of the interview he later felt free to mention. There was considerable evidence that both factors operating together accounted for the general results. At present, however, only the second factor will be considered.[1]

As the interview progresses, an informal and sometimes quite unique social relation may develop between the interviewer and the person being interviewed. Although this social relation is more conspicuous in prolonged interviewing where a therapeutic element is involved than in the case of the single interview, it may take place in some degree even in the case of the latter, and it is important that the interviewer should be aware of this possibility. The interview is quite different from an ordinary social conversation or discussion. The interviewer is sympathetically listening to the person in a way that seldom occurs in an ordinary conversation. Nothing that the speaker says is too slight or too trivial for his attention. Moreover, the social personality of the interviewer, if he follows the rules prescribed, is quite different from that to which the interviewee is generally accustomed. The interviewer is not exercising authority in its many subtle forms. He is not ordering, advising, criticizing, interrupting, or in any fashion attempting to force his set of values and significances upon the interviewee. As a result, a relation develops which is quite different from

---

[1] Had it not been for the presence of the first factor, it is very unlikely that the interviewing program would have operated, from a practical standpoint, as successfully as it did.

any relation which the interviewee has ever experienced. The interviewee finds himself not only saying things which he never said to anyone else but in many instances saying things which he has not been able to express explicitly to himself.

Sometimes this relation becomes extremely trying to the interviewer, for the interviewer becomes an object ideally suitable to the speaker for the projection of his most deeply rooted hopes, fears, and expectations. What happens sometimes is that the interviewee begins to project on the interviewer that complex of sentiments related to authority to which he has been previously conditioned by his early training and experience. He constantly tries to force the interviewer into a position of authority, either by asking him his advice about this and that, or in a countless number of other ways. Unless the interviewer is dealing with a very neurotic person, these complications are not likely to arise in a single interview. If they do, such cases are better handled by specialists.

Between these two extremes, however — on the one hand, a formally prescribed social situation to which the interviewee is reacting and, on the other hand, a situation where quite a unique social relation is created — there are, of course, all possible combinations. For the interviewer, it is important to know more or less at which end of the scale the interview is being conducted. A great deal can be learned about the interviewee at either end of the scale, but only if the interviewer is somewhat aware of what his relation to the interviewee actually is. It is obvious that the interpretations he makes at one end of the scale are quite different from those he would make at the other.[1]

In the second place, it is well to remember that the relation between interviewer and interviewee is reciprocal. What the interviewer says and does affects the speaker, and what the speaker says and does affects the interviewer. This second relation is so frequently misunderstood that it deserves a special rule.

Rule IV A₁ The interviewer should see to it that the speaker's sentiments do not act on his own.

To the layman it may seem that the interviewer is advised to be a very superior person, devoid of all social sentiments. This is not so, for the interviewer is also a social being, with a social past and a social

---

[1] In this connection it may be well to mention the limitation of use of the interviewing method by supervisors because of their social relationship with the employee. This is necessarily an authoritative relationship, and such a relationship makes the employee reluctant to discuss his situation sufficiently frankly for a thorough appraisal of it to be

present. If he is to guard against mistakes, it is important that he does not pretend to be otherwise. The only way in which the interviewer can guard against having his own sentiments acted upon is not by denying their existence but by admitting and understanding them. Anyone who has had experience in interviewing realizes that often he learns more about himself than about the person being interviewed. Frequently he finds himself becoming irritated and annoyed at what a person is saying. It is not sufficient to brush these moods lightly aside; he must ask himself what sentiments of his own are involved. Otherwise, in a quite unexpected fashion, he may find himself doing and saying things which may evoke the very attitude on the part of the speaker that he is trying to avoid. The interview might then become a battle of opposing sentiments.

Rules for Conducting the Interview

The rules of orientation with which we have been concerned may be applied by the field worker in social anthropology as well as by the clinical psychologist or the social case worker. They can be used by the personnel manager of a large industrial corporation in his daily activities as well as in the more formal industrial relations interviewing. With regard to the rules for conducting the interview, however, this possibility of general application no longer holds, for they vary with the kind of personal and social situations being explored. It is evident that the interviewing of a child, a psychoneurotic, a native of a primitive community, or the normal adult of a civilized community involves different modifications in the way the interview takes place. For this reason, then, in discussing the rules of performance we shall limit ourselves to those rules which were found helpful in interviewing industrial workers.

There is always the danger for the beginner that he attach a significance to the rules of performance that they do not have. He tends to treat them as absolute prescriptions which should never be violated, and he tends to multiply them without end. This fetish about the rules of performance arises in part from a failure to understand the rules of orientation; ritualistic rules for conducting the interview are substituted for understanding. The rules of performance should play a secondary role to the rules of orientation. If the interviewer understands what he is doing and is in active touch with the actual situa-

---

made. All the experience at Hawthorne has pointed to the need of an impartial, non-authoritative agency whose function is that of interviewing employees, diagnosing their problems, and counseling with them.

tion, he has extreme latitude in what he can do. Whether or not the interviewee faces the light is not of first importance. What is important is that his rules of procedure should take into account the considerations discussed under Rule IVA. For if the interview is a social situation, involving a relation between two people in a particular social setting, the rules of performance must address themselves to that situation.

The interviewers formulated five rules for the conduct of interviews, to which they tried to adhere fairly closely. These were as follows:

1. The interviewer should listen to the speaker in a patient and friendly, but intelligently critical, manner.
2. The interviewer should not display any kind of authority.
3. The interviewer should not give advice or moral admonition.
4. The interviewer should not argue with the speaker.
5. The interviewer should talk or ask questions only under certain conditions.
   a. To help the person talk.
   b. To relieve any fears or anxieties on the part of the speaker which may be affecting his relation to the interviewer.
   c. To praise the interviewee for reporting his thoughts and feelings accurately.
   d. To veer the discussion to some topic which has been omitted or neglected.
   e. To discuss implicit assumptions, if this is advisable.

Rule 1 The interviewer should listen to the speaker in a patient and friendly, but intelligently critical, manner.

The attitude of the interviewer should be one of patiently listening to what the speaker has to say before making any comment himself. He should listen and not talk until the person has made a complete statement. Probably the quickest way to stop a person from sufficiently expressing himself is to interrupt. No matter how irrelevant the material may seem to be to the interviewer, he must remember that the person being interviewed probably cannot easily state what is really important to him. Of course, it follows that, besides actively listening and not interrupting, the interviewer should try to understand what is being said. Nothing irritates a person more than the feeling that he is misunderstood. Moreover, the interviewer should show his interest in what is being said. His attitude should be more than a pretense of being interested; he should be really interested.

Rule 2 The interviewer should not display any kind of authority.

The interviewer should do everything to help the worker to feel at ease. There are many different ways of accomplishing this end, but most of them are corollaries of the above rule. The worker is likely to be resentful of any display of authority, or of any indication of his social subordination. The interviewer, therefore, should guard himself against displaying authority in any of its forms. He should not give any orders to the interviewee, and, of course, he should never violate any confidence given to him. He should also avoid the more subtle forms of displaying authority, such as contradicting the worker, interrupting him, taking the role of the teacher, or treating his ideas lightly.

Of course, there is an element of subordination in the very process of interviewing, since the interviewee is in a position of subordination to the interviewer. The interviewer should not pretend that this element does not exist. The above rule does not deny the existence of the element of subordination, but it warns the interviewer not to misuse or make capital of the superordinate status that his position as interviewer gives him.

There are two forms of expressing authority which should be particularly avoided. They will be stated, therefore, as separate rules.

Rule 3 The interviewer should not give advice or moral admonition.

The interviewer must not suggest or imply judgments of value or of morals concerning the worker's overt or verbal behavior. If the worker says, "This is a hell of a company, and my supervisors are 'goddam' slave drivers," the attitude of the interviewer should not be, "Tut-tut, my good man, you are not displaying the proper spirit." Instead, he should prevail upon the worker to express himself more fully by asking such questions as, "Why do you feel this way?" or "Tell me more about this." In this manner the interviewer allows the person to express his opinions more frankly and in greater detail.

Rule 4 The interviewer should not argue with the speaker.

As a rule, it is wise never to argue with the speaker about his opinions, prejudices, or irrationalities. No attempt should be made at first to modify his opinions by suggestion or coercion. In fact, it is often a good plan to go in the opposite direction and to restate the speaker's position even more strongly than he has done himself. The effect of this procedure in many instances is to cause the interviewee to modify his own original statement.

The best way for the interviewer to avoid argument is for him to see that the speaker's sentiments do not react upon his own. The interviewer should not defend or justify himself. If the speaker criticizes him, he must be ready to ask, "Why do you think this?" For this reason more than any other, the interviewer should be aware of his own sentiments, for, otherwise, he is in a position of having them at times painfully violated.

Rule 5 The interviewer should talk or ask questions only under certain conditions.

a. To help the person talk. The main objective of the interview is to get the speaker to talk freely and frankly about himself and his environment, and there are a number of stock phrases that can be used for this purpose, such as, "Isn't that interesting?" "What do you mean?" "Why?" "Isn't that curious?" "For example?" and "Tell me more about it."

It has been said that the consistent use of three expressions, "Why?" "For example?" and "Define," can stop any conversation. Now, although this applies to the interview as well as to social intercourse, the interviewer sometimes can with discretion use two of these expressions, namely "Why?" and "For example?" In this way, generalizations can sometimes be brought to a more concrete level.

b. To relieve any fears or anxieties on the part of the speaker which may be affecting his relation to the interviewer. As we have said before, a person frequently enters the interview apprehensive that what he may say will be used against him. For this reason, in the Western Electric Company interviewing program the interviewers found it very helpful to start the interview by explaining carefully to the worker just what its purpose was, and that the statements made would in no way be identified with the person who made them. In most cases such reassurances at the beginning of the interview are sufficient. But frequently, in the case of rather suspicious persons, it is necessary to reassure them many times during the course of the interview.

c. To praise the interviewee for reporting his thoughts and feelings accurately. Although in general it is wise for the interviewer not to operate on the speaker's sentiments, there is one sentiment which he can use in order to facilitate the interviewing process, and that is to praise the speaker for trying to express freely and frankly what he regards as important.

d. To veer the discussion to some topic which has been omitted or neglected. Many times the interviewer would like to direct the discussion to a certain topic which has either been neglected or omitted by the speaker. In a fairly long interview opportunities sometimes arise which allow the interviewer to break into such critical zones. No specific rules can be stated. The more training an interviewer has, the more skill he develops in this direction.

e. To discuss implicit assumptions, if this is advisable. During an interview the interviewer frequently has occasion to note an assumption which underlies the conversation but which itself is not expressed. Sometimes it is helpful in stimulating further discussion to bring to the interviewee's attention such an assumption. In doing this, the interviewer has to exercise discretion. If calling forth such an assumption is likely to embarrass the speaker, it is, of course, better not to do it. But many times the person welcomes such a restatement of his thinking, and the interview starts out again with renewed vigor at a new level.

Summary

Perhaps a few words should be said about the abilities required of the interviewer. To some readers it may seem that the practice of the interviewing method requires unusual perspicacity, in fact, almost superhuman abilities. Although it is true that certain skills are demanded of the interviewer, it would be incorrect to suppose that these skills are acquired and developed differently from the way skills are developed by a competent worker in any scientific area. It is obvious, of course, that such a method cannot be applied by anyone, anywhere, and at any time. The interviewer needs to have a certain amount of intelligence, knowledge, training, and experience. But similar requirements apply to any person who wishes to become proficient in a particular technique or method.

The interviewer should be seriously and sincerely interested in human situations. At times he needs to exercise a certain amount of intelligence. But just as in a chemical laboratory there are some good technicians unable to state explicitly the grounds of their skill, so in the interviewing field there are some successful interviewers who would be unable to formulate a conceptual scheme. Equally important to the interviewer are training and experience. Several years of training at actual interviewing are almost essential before a person can become proficient. But, even though an interviewer may become very proficient in interviewing a certain class or group of people, the more experience he has with different kinds of personal and social contexts, the more proficient he becomes as an interviewer. Any successful executive, administrator, or politician implicitly makes use of many of the rules of orientation which we have more explicitly stated. Many of these rules are merely a more explicit statement of a point of view that persons who have to deal with people unconsciously take. It is not an opinion but an induction from experience that many people of moderate ability acquire considerable skill as interviewers.

In conclusion, it can be said that any conceptual scheme or method can best be judged in terms of its utility. Inasmuch as in the remainder of the studies to be reported the conceptual scheme outlined in this chapter will be applied, the reader will be in a position to judge from the results obtained whether or not the scheme is useful. At first the investigators were primarily interested in exploring the relation of complaints to the complainant's personal situation (see relation C–D in Figure 25). The results of these studies will be reported in Chapter XIV. Later the investigators explored the relation of complaints to the social organization of employees (see relation C–E in Figure 25). The results of these studies will be reported in Chapters XV and XVI.

CHAPTER XIV

COMPLAINTS AND PERSONAL EQUILIBRIUM

MORBID PREOCCUPATIONS AND PERSONAL SITUATION

THERE was one type of personal situation encountered in the interviewing program which particularly interested the investigators. This type of situation manifested itself in an exaggerated and morbid form of response, more particularly with regard to persons than with regard to things. For some employees a reprimand from a supervisor became the object of a great deal of morbid reflection. It would be only a matter of time before such an incident was elaborated in the employee's private thinking to such a degree that the supervisor took on all the aspects of a "fiend" whose sole purpose was to torment him. A supervisor of a rather strict demeanor became in the eyes of some timid employee an "ogre" constantly watching him, ready to pounce in case he made a mistake. Comments on supervision, more than those in any other area, could not be taken at their face value. It was not that these comments were completely fabricated; part of the story was probably correct. A supervisor may have been unduly severe; the employee may have been unjustly reprimanded. The interesting thing, however, was the way in which certain events grew to have such a distorted emotional significance for the employee that his capacity for effective discrimination was greatly reduced.

The following four interviews offer good examples of exaggerated and morbid thinking.[1] Although these interviews are not to be regarded as typical of those obtained from the majority of employees, they

[1] It is well to point out clearly that the "distortion" of which we are speaking is with respect to the role which the object of the complaint plays in the complainant's private and intimate thinking. For example, A calls B a "bully." "Is B really a bully?" is not the question of distortion that we are raising. The fact remains that for A, B is a bully. The questions are: (1) How does A come to regard B as a bully? (2) Does the kind of thinking by means of which A makes B a bully show tendencies such that other persons who stand in the same relation to A as B stands are also regarded as bullies? (3) By calling B a bully, does A distort to himself his own situation? (4) Does B become a "symbol" by means of which A is expressing unspecified fears, doubts, and anxieties? When we speak of "distortion," it is to these latter questions that we are addressing ourselves. In reading the interviews, therefore, the reader is urged to keep this latter viewpoint in mind; otherwise, irrelevant questions will keep intruding themselves. For example, the reader may conclude erroneously that because we have offered the following four interviews as examples of distorted and exaggerated thinking, we have justified at the same time the

set forth so well the nature of obsessive thinking that they make excellent material for purposes of illustration. The four employees in these interviews will be referred to as Mr. Brown, Mr. Green, Mr. White, and Mrs. Black.

The authors at first hesitated to introduce interviews such as these for two reasons: (1) these interviews are not typical of those obtained from the majority of employees; and (2) they may be read by the employees with whom they deal, whose feelings the authors did not wish to injure. Inasmuch as these interviews, however, are completely anonymous, neither the authors nor the company knowing the identity of the persons with whom they are concerned, and inasmuch as concrete illustrations were desirable, the authors finally decided to include them. All the interviews have been carefully reviewed to make sure that statements which might identify the employees to anyone other than themselves were deleted. In some cases the interviews have been considerably shortened. Parts of the interviews have been italicized for convenience in referring to them later. All names of persons or firms, except Western Electric Company, are fictitious.

An Interview with Mr. Brown

The interviewer was introduced to Mr. Brown at the latter's place of work by the group chief.

Interviewer: "How are you, Mr. Brown? Glad to meet you. Will you shut down your machine for a short while? I would like to have a little talk with you."

Employee: "All right."

Interviewer: "Suppose we go into the restaurant where we can be alone."

Employee: "That would be a better place to talk."

Interviewer: "Well, let's sit down. You make yourself comfortable and so will I. Then we can talk at ease. Have you heard about the plan the company is putting over in the various branches?"

Employee: "Yes, I have heard something about it, but nothing in detail."

Interviewer: "Have you talked to anyone who has been interviewed about the program?"

Employee: "No, I haven't."

Program explained.

---

behavior of certain supervisors. The behavior of the supervisor may have been "stupid," "justified," "brutal," "kind," "trivial," "unwarranted," etc. From the evidence presented, the reader is in as good a position as we are to make such judgments. Only let the reader be aware of the kind of judgment he is making. (See Chapter XII.)

Employee: "That's something new, isn't it?"

Interviewer: "Yes, it's new in this branch, but it has been in operation in other branches for more than a year."

Employee: "Well, I think it's a good idea, as we at least get a chance to express ourselves."

Interviewer: "Yes, you do. How long have you worked here, Mr. Brown?"

Employee: "Going on seven years. I started on St. Patrick's Day, 1917."

Interviewer: "Then you're not Irish, because if you were that's one day you wouldn't start to work on."

Employee: "No, I'm German."

Interviewer: "What is your rate of pay, Mr. Brown?"

Employee: "$1.03 an hour."

Interviewer: "I suppose you have been raised regularly?"

Employee: "I have done very well in that respect."

Interviewer: "Now, that's good. How is everything else in general?"

Employee: "Well, it seems to be all right now, as things are going along fairly well."

Interviewer: "Haven't they always been going on that way?"

Employee: "No, not exactly, as at times I was pretty much disgusted with everything and everybody."

Interviewer: "How's that?"

Employee: *"Between the hard luck at home and the unfair treatment around here, why I certainly would feel dumpy many a day."*

Interviewer: "Well, that's what I want to hear about. As I explained to you a little while ago, we want your criticisms and comments on everything in general, so what do you say?"

Employee: "I started here about six and a half years ago in another department doing general machine work. I took that job with the understanding that I would get in the tool and die game, as that is my line of work. In the summer of that year, during the vacation period, I was considered for a job of temporary supervisor; in fact, there were two other men besides myself in line for the job. I did not get it, as I was the youngest man in length of service amongst the three, but I felt rather good at even being considered, as I had only worked here a short time. A little later on I had an opportunity of going into the tool room, but I did not accept it, as I was given to understand that I had a chance of making good where I was.

"Things went along pretty good until the following year. Then the slack period came. Naturally, being one of the newest men hired, I was amongst those laid off first. I am not complaining about that, as I realize that they kept the men with longer service. I was off about three or four months when the Western sent for me again.

"I came back and was sent over to Department ——. That was around the time that the movietone job was beginning to get hot. A man that was on the job for the movietone parts that we made slipped up a couple of times and Mr. Jones asked me if I would handle it. I told him, 'Sure thing.' So I worked on those for a while until we got those things going pretty good. Then they put me on nights for a couple of months. As we were getting new machinery in, we had a better chance to set it up and get it in operation nights."

Interviewer: "I see."

Employee: "Things went along pretty well for a long time, although at times I was a little discouraged, as during the time I was laid off for three or four months there were quite a number of changes in supervisors; and when I came back to work in Department ——, I was very much surprised."

Interviewer: "How's that?"

Employee: "It seems that it was my destiny to be working for a man who had been my supervisor three times before on outside jobs. We had always got along together then, but there seemed to be a certain coolness developed between us — why, I don't know — but I did my work and said nothing. His attitude toward me did not get any better and many a time I had reasonable cause for complaint, but I kept still."

Interviewer: "Is that so?"

Employee: "Yes, he used some very abusive language at times. . . .

"Last year I was hit a terrible blow. My seventeen-year-old girl was taken away from me. She was sick not quite a week. She died of spinal meningitis."

Interviewer: "That's too bad."

Employee: "Yes, she was a dandy young lady. She would have graduated from high school this February.

"My daughter's death caused my wife to have a general nervous breakdown a week after my girl was buried. That meant I had to send her to the hospital right away. In the course of her treatment at the hospital, the doctors advised me that in addition to her nervous condition she was in a very delicate condition. I could hardly believe it, but later on I was convinced. Well, my wife was in the hospital for about nine weeks and then came home.

"About seven and a half months after that I was the father of twins, a girl and a boy, and the birth of twins, along with my wife's nervous condition, left her in a very bad shape. She came home from the hospital three weeks after the twins were born. She was unable to walk; in fact, she was almost an invalid. A week or two later, while my other girl who is fifteen years old went to the store and there was nobody else around, my wife made an attempt to walk, and in doing so she was so weak that she fell and knocked one kneecap out of place and injured herself internally. I had to send her back to the hospital. She was there from three to five weeks, I think, and now she is practically an invalid.

"I have been advised by the doctors that what she needs the most is rest and quiet, and I am saving every penny so that I may be able to send her to a sanitarium.

"Mr. Interviewer, aren't you getting tired of listening to me?"

Interviewer: "No, indeed I am not. Go right ahead. I am very much interested."

Employee: "*Well, all the time that I was having this trouble my supervisor, a man whom I worked with twelve years, treated me like a dog.*"

Interviewer: "In what way, Mr. Brown?"

Employee: "Why, I have been accused by him of not co-operating in any way, and one time he said to me, 'I'm going to see that you are transferred out of my group.' I asked him why. He said, 'You know too damn much and you are not helping me.' I told him I would do anything he asked. He said, 'You would like hell.' I said, 'Do you want me to get down on my knees and beg you?' He said, 'Never mind what I want you to do, you'll do it.' Well, Mr. Interviewer, I got pretty mad and I told him that he won, that I couldn't fight him; I had trouble enough at home. Therefore, I continued to take the abuse.

"Why, even when vacation time came around last year they were pretty busy on movietone parts and he asked me to postpone my vacation for three months. I told him that I didn't like to; that I wanted a little rest after all the trouble I had last year; but I told him if he couldn't get anybody else I'd stay on the job. He never said any more about it.

"Why, all the time my wife was in the hospital he kept continually asking me to work nights. I told him if it was at all possible I would appreciate it if he would let me have my evenings to myself, although I needed the money, because I had a wife in the hospital and a fifteen-year-old girl at home doing the work around the house, and I wanted to get home to help her. He always told me to stick on the job. Well, I had to do as I was told, that's all.

"I finally took the matter up with the general foreman, and after he listened to my story and later on talked to my group chief, why there seemed to be a change in him. I told my boss one time that some day a greater power would make him suffer the same way he made me suffer when my wife was nearly dead and my girl gone. He didn't say anything, as I think his conscience bothered him."

Interviewer: "Mr. Brown, it's almost noon now. Suppose I see you after lunch."

Employee: "All right."

Interviewer: "Say about 1:30?"

Employee: "All right — so long."

The following conversation took place after lunch.

Interviewer: "Here I am — back again."

Employee: "Yes, I see you're on the job all right."

Interviewer: "You bet."

Employee: "As I was saying before lunch, I thought my supervisor's conscience bothered him. I don't know what happened to him, as I have been treated wonderful by him since then. Sometimes I can hardly believe it's the same man. Maybe I'm not doing right by talking to you about him. I certainly would not care to work under those conditions again. I don't think I could, and I feel pretty sure that if the company knew such things were going on they would put a stop to it.

"I had to ask for a loan shortly after my wife was taken to the hospital for the first time, and I didn't have any trouble at all in getting it from the company, because when I told them my circumstances they did everything possible for me.

"I cannot in all my life remember what I did to my supervisor to make him act the way he did. There is only one instance that I can recall that we crossed each other, and that was when we both worked at the Simplex Company on the North Side. I am somewhat of a baseball bug and the day that the Cubs and Cincinnati opened the baseball season here, I wanted to see the game. Well, it so happened that I had a very unpleasant job in the machine that morning, and I don't know — I just got thinking about the game. I was born and raised in Cincinnati and every chance I get to see the team from my home town I take advantage of it, and when they were booked to open up here — why, you know, there's always a little extra thrill and so on at the opening game. I told Mr. Jones that I wanted to go and he didn't like it I know, but he said, 'Go ahead,' so I did.

"I came to work the next morning and the job that was in my machine had been taken out. Mr. Jones came over to me and said, 'You don't have to lay off when you don't like a job.' I told him I laid off to go to the ball game, not to get out of doing any job. Well, he is a very hard-hearted fellow and always has been. I kept still, and that is the first time we ever had any cross words, but that's over now, isn't it?"

Interviewer: "Yes, it is."

Employee: "You haven't had a chance to talk since I got going, have you?"

Interviewer: "I'm not supposed to talk."

Employee: "You've been a good listener. *I tell you it does a fellow good to get rid of that stuff.*"

An Interview with Mr. Green

Interviewer explained the program.

Employee: "Well, I have worked in five different departments, so I should know something about supervision. [Smiling.] Every time, I was transferred to a higher grade of work, but just before I came to this department I had trouble with the department chief and was transferred out of there for that reason."

Interviewer: "Is that so?"

Employee: "Yes, I sure had a lot of trouble in that department. The whole thing started when I got a rupture. I ruptured myself and they called it a company case and I went under an operation in the company hospital. After I got out of the hospital, I stayed home a few weeks and then the doctors told me to go back to work but not to lift over twenty-five pounds until they said it was all right for me to lift more weight. The boss gave me a job working on the bench assembling small parts for about three weeks. One day he came up to me and said: 'Starting tomorrow morning you are going back on the machine.' I told him that I was supposed to stay on light work, but he said that did not make any difference and that I had to do as he told me to.

"This job he wanted to put me on was a piecework job and to make any money you had to handle four pieces at one time. Each piece weighed twelve and a half pounds, so that was fifty pounds that I would have to lift. I told the boss that I was not going against the doctor's orders, but that if he wanted me to work that job I would take one piece at a time but would not work piecework. He did not like the idea of me taking that stand, but I was not going to take a chance of myself getting hurt, so I ran the machine but only handled one piece at a time.

"A few days after that, I had to go to the hospital for an examination. The doctor asked me what job I was on and I explained it to him and then he said: 'What the hell is the matter with your department chief? When we give you orders not to lift over twenty-five pounds we want them carried out, and whenever your boss asks you to lift over twenty-five pounds you tell him to go to hell.' Then the doctor sat down and gave me a note to bring back to my boss. I took the note back and gave it to him and went back to work on the machine. About fifteen minutes later the boss came over where I was working and bawled me out something awful.

"He said that I was nothing but a troublemaker for going over to the hospital and telling them what job he put me on. I told him that I was not a troublemaker but when the doctor asked me what job I was working on I thought I might as well tell him. A few weeks later, I went back to the hospital and the doctor said to me: 'Say, the last time you were down here you told me you were working on a heavy job. I sent a man up to your department to investigate and he came back and told me that you were doing nothing but light work.' I said: 'Probably they didn't show him the right job.' Again I explained my work to him and the doctor said that when they went up to check my job I was not around and the foreman must have showed them a different job and covered himself up. I offered to take the doctor back with me and show him the job, but he seemed satisfied that they put me on heavy work and that someone did not show them the right job. Along about this time was raise day and when the pay slips were handed out all the fellows received eight- and ten-cent raises and my rate was just the same. When I did not receive a raise, I went up to the department chief and asked him how it was that the other men all received good raises and I didn't get any. He said that as long as I was on light work and could only do certain jobs in the department that he did not think I was entitled to a raise, but as soon as I was released by the hospital and allowed to work on heavier work he said that he would give me the same raise that he gave the other men.

"When the hospital finally released me and told me that it was all right to lift seventy-five pounds, I went back and told my department chief that I had been released and was willing to work on any job. I said: 'Don't forget the promise you made to me when raise time was here. You said that as soon as I was released from the hospital you would give me the same rate you gave the other men.' He got very angry and said: 'Who the hell told you they would give you a raise?' I said: 'You told me.' He said: 'You're a goddam liar. I never promised you anything.' I said: 'All right, if you don't want to give me the raise I'm going up to see the assistant superintendent.' Then he said: 'Nothing doing. I won't let you go up there.' Well, then I said: 'If you don't give me permission, I'll go up there myself.'

"He would not let me go that day and I asked him the next day and he would not let me go, so the following day I went up to the assistant superintendent's office myself. I told him the whole story about the trip to the hospital, about being bawled out for telling the doctors just what job I was on and also the promise of a raise which I did not receive. He said to me: 'Well, you go back to your department and I will call for you to-morrow. In the meantime I will look into this.'

"The next day he called me up to his office and told me he was going to get me a transfer to another department and that he would also give me a fifteen-cent raise. That time my department chief bawled me out in front of all the men. I think he talked rough to me to get me to hit him, but I was too wise to do that. I knew that if I hit him I would be dismissed. He talked to me so rough that day that I was nervous all over. . . . After that I got some mysterious telephone calls. The first time I got one of these calls I answered the telephone and a man who would not tell me his name said that he wanted to see me at Halsted and Madison Streets. I asked him what he wanted and he said that he wanted to offer me a good job. I told him that I had a good job and that I did not feel like changing. He told me to go down there anyway and that we could talk it over. He wanted me to meet him at a certain time, but I told him that I would not go and hung up. Later on that evening, he called up again and I told him the same thing. The next night the phone rang again. It was the same man. I told him that I did not want to consider another job and that I did not want him to bother me by calling me up, so after that time I would not answer the phone. When the phone would ring my little girl would answer it and they would ask for her father. She would say that her father was not at home and then this fellow would say: 'Where the hell do you get that stuff? Tell your old man I want to talk to him.' They kept this up for five or six nights and finally I had the call checked and I found out it came from a pool room in the neighborhood of Halsted and Madison Streets. I know them fellows wanted to get me down there to kill me and I was so nervous that I did not sleep sound for six months. I was always afraid that they would throw a bomb at my house at night.

"At that time I worried so much that I could not eat and I was just about on the verge of having a nervous breakdown."

Interviewer: "Do you really think that they wanted to harm you?"

Employee: "Yes, I do. I think they wanted to get me down there so that they could kill me."

Interviewer: "Did you have any idea who it was?"

Employee: "No, I don't know who these men were that were calling up. Chances are they were gunmen. You know there are men in the city of Chicago that would kill a man for five dollars."

Interviewer: "How do you think they got your telephone number?"

Employee: "I don't know but I know that *my department chief knew where I lived* because I was off sick at Christmas time and he brought a basket to my house. I was never so scared in all my life because I was afraid he would not only harm me but harm my family. I was so scared that I got my gun out of the trunk and made sure that it was in good condition and I had it handy all the time. I would have killed the first one that would have started anything with me. One day these fellows called up and my daughter answered the phone. I told her that if it was that same bunch I wanted to talk to them. Sure enough, it was them calling up and my daughter called me to the phone. I told them that if they were looking for trouble that I was prepared for them. I told them that the sooner they got the thing over with the better. They hung up the telephone and they never called after that time. You know in this lodge that I belong to we have some very smart men. We have doctors and dentists and lawyers, and

I went up to see one of these lawyers and told him about this trouble. He listened to my story, and then he said: 'If you were sure you knew who was at the bottom of this and had any evidence, we could take this case to court. The way it stands now, you have no grounds to start court subpoenaing. My advice to you is to keep your mouth shut around the Western Electric Company or somebody is going to kill you. The chances are you have talked too much and you got someone in wrong and if you continue to talk they are going to get you, so from now on you keep your mouth shut around that place and don't say anything to anybody.' . . .

"If I had told the assistant superintendent everything I know, everyone in that department would have been fired."

An Interview with Mr. White

The interviewer was introduced to the employee by the department chief.

Interviewer: "How are you today, Mr. White?"

Employee: "Fine, thank you."

Interviewer: "Let's take a walk where we will be by ourselves and not disturbed."

Employee: "There's no damn use of you and I going anywhere because I refuse to talk. I talked out of turn once before and got myself in such a mess of trouble that I refuse to talk to you or anybody else."

Interviewer: "Do you understand what this program is about?"

Employee: "No, not all about it. But you can't get me to talk because I absolutely refuse to. Of course, if you want me to go somewhere with you I will, but it won't do you a damn bit of good."

Interviewer: "Why do you feel that way towards me? I have interviewed a great number of men in your division and I am certain that you haven't heard anything except maybe from the employees themselves."

Employee: "I've heard plenty. I don't know where it came from, but I am not saying anything anyway. Not until you prove to me that it is confidential."

Interviewer: "That's exactly what I would like to do if you allow me to have that opportunity. I think we should go somewhere by ourselves where I can have the opportunity of explaining this program to you, allowing you to see my side of the story; then if you do not choose to talk, that will be your privilege."

Employee: "Well, you know, when you have talked out of turn once and got yourself in bad, you are going to be darn careful how you talk thereafter, if you talk at all."

Interviewer: "I don't blame you a bit for feeling that way, but, **as I said** before, give me the privilege of telling you my story. Then probably we'll understand each other better."

Employee: "All right, I'll go with you wherever you say."

Interviewer: "All right. Would you care to smoke?"

Employee: "Sure."

Interviewer: "Get your hat and we'll take a walk over to the restaurant building."

Employee: "That's a good place to go."

On the way to the restaurant building:

Employee: "This sure is terrible weather. But I guess we can expect mostly any kind in March."

Interviewer: "Yes, I guess anything from a cloudburst to a snowstorm."

Employee: "They sure spend a lot of money on the grounds around the Western here, don't they?"

Interviewer: "The grounds are beautiful in summer."

Employee: "If we had half the money they spend on the gardens, we wouldn't have to work any more."

Interviewer: "No, I don't suppose we would. We would have to worry how we could spend it then." (Both laughed.)

Employee: "I wouldn't have a hell of a lot of trouble doing that."

Interviewer: "Well, here we are. We'll take an ash tray and sit over here by ourselves."

Employee: "All right, whatever you say."

Interviewer: "Have a smoke on me."

Employee: "All right. You go ahead and explain your program now. I'll listen. I promise to give you a chance to explain yourself."

Interviewer: "I'm certain that after I explain the program, you will see things in a different light."

The interviewer explained the program and its purpose.

Employee: "The only thing that gets my goat in this place is *this goddam personnel record*. That's the biggest injustice to the employees that the Western Electric ever had. I don't see how the company tolerates such an unfair method of keeping track of their employees. *It's just like a damn jail here.* If a fellow is sentenced to go to prison, say for fourteen years, his fingerprints are taken and a complete record too. After he has served his time, they tell him he is a free man, that he can now go and do as he pleases. He does go out into the world and get a job. He's probably.

getting along just fine when somebody knowing him reports to his boss that he is an ex-convict. Immediately he loses his job. That's the same damn thing they do here at the Western. No matter how many places you are transferred to, how many different supervisors you have, *you are marked*.

"Now, I know this to be an actual fact. Once I had a friend of mine that I was personally interested in. I went up to the department head to speak for this fellow. I told him his weaknesses, told him that he was an exceptionally good worker, and that I thought he could overcome these obstacles that stood in his way. The department head said: 'Oh, that's all right. You just go ahead and send him up here. We'll straighten him out on that.' This happened to be on a Wednesday. About two days after that, the personnel man came down with all of this fellow's record. Of course, we don't know what was said between the department head and the personnel man.

"This fellow happened to get wind of the personnel man coming down to see the department head, and he came to me and said: 'Red, I'll bet five bucks that I don't get that job.' I told him: 'Why, you're crazy, there's nothing in the world to stop you from getting that job.' He said: 'No, the hell there isn't! The personnel man was just down talking to the department head. I suppose if I ever had any black marks, this bird will bring it out.' Well, this fellow was to be transferred onto his new job Monday and already had been accepted by the department head. Saturday prior to the date of transfer, he was notified that there was no job open in that department. But the fact was that a new man from the outside had been hired and placed on that job.

"That's the same damn way that this personnel record follows and haunts a man all throughout his life. *I have been with this company twenty-four years and the company as a whole, I think, is the best place in the world to work. But the individuals who are supposed to carry out the policies of the company are a bunch of skunks.*

"This damn record just burns me up. I suppose you think I'm quite radical because I act and talk as I do. I am not telling you any hearsay. I've experienced this and have seen it with my own eyes. I am on the *S* list and have been on there for a damn long time. Just what it is, I don't know. I don't see how in hell the supervisors and the personnel division are permitted to refuse a man from seeing his personnel record.

"The department chief makes up a record about three times a month and sends it up to the personnel. You are never permitted to see this or know what it is all about."

Interviewer: "What makes you so sure that you cannot see this personnel record?"

Employee: "I am damn sure. I have asked to see it. They have flatly turned me down.

"Now this friend of mine that I told you about, that lost out on the transfer after the personnel man saw the new department head he was to work for, well, this friend of mine went to the personnel division and asked them just why it was that he didn't get this job, and that he would like to see his personnel record. They told him that he could not see it, that that was impossible. Now, why in hell should anything be put on that record that the employee cannot see? If it's on the square, why shouldn't the employee know it? Why should that be held over a man's head as a hammer for the rest of his life? That's just what it is. It's a hammer over your head.

"*I'll just give you my own case, for instance.* In 1925, when we had that slack period, I worked for Mr. Jones at that time. My department head told me that he was very sorry but he had no work for me, that I should go over to the employment department and see what they could do for me. At this time, I had about eighteen years' service with the company. I thought it was a mighty funny thing for him to say. Nevertheless, I had no choice, so I went over to the employment department. Mr. Johnson was in charge at that time and Mr. Smith was his assistant. I went to Mr. Johnson and told him that I had no work in my department and that I had come over to find out whether he had anything open. He asked me where I worked, who I worked for, how long I had been with the company. I told him I had been with the company about eighteen years. He wanted to know why I was to be laid off. I told him I didn't know. The only thing I knew was that I had a wrangle with my section head. I had some information that was·correct and my section head tried to tell me that I was wrong. I don't see any sense in a man admitting that he is wrong when he is absolutely sure that he is right. If I was wrong I would have been glad to admit it, but I was positive that I was right and consequently I held my own ground. Well, that's the only thing that I could figure he wanted to get rid of me for.

"Well, anyway, Mr. Johnson had Mr. Smith call up. He was in one of those booths and I assumed that he called up the division head. They had quite a lengthy conversation and when he came out he told me to go back to my department head and if he did not have a job for me, that I should come back tomorrow and he would find one. I went back there and they put me back to work under the same section chief that I had had an argument with. And, boy, did he give me a ride! I was on the verge of quitting when I came to the conclusion that they were purposely riding me to force me to quit. So I decided that, for that reason, I would show that I didn't have to quit and that I wouldn't.

"Well, they kept me in this department for about a year. They rode me something terrible. When they discovered that their method of riding me was not going to force me to quit, they transferred me. This sure pleased me when they told me that. Because I sure led a dog's life that year. No matter what I did, it was wrong. No matter how much I did, there was never enough. They can sure make it hot for you.

"I have been a supervisor myself. I always tried to give a fellow a break anyway. At least, be on the square; that's the least a man can do. We're not all built alike. I don't think we are here for likes and dislikes. If a man is producing by giving sufficient output, I think that's what the company is after.

"*The college men get a lot of preference around here.* I don't mean to say that they are never entitled to any opportunity; they should be. They spent a lot of time learning. I think a college education is a wonderful thing to have. But if our own condition forbade such education, through sickness or death of the father or something of that sort, I don't think that should have an important bearing on holding a man down. Of course, I'll admit that I'm not a college graduate, but I think with my experience that I am just as capable, if not more, of holding down a section as a lot of these college men. You take ten or fifteen years ago, college men were not known of in this company. Now I don't believe you could be hired unless you have at least two years of high school. What the hell is this all coming to? It will be so after a while that the poor man won't be able to get a job.

"Another unfairness that I want to call your attention to is that a college man will come in here, work for eight or nine months, and then become a section chief. In looking over his group of fellows, he forms an opinion immediately: 'Here's a fellow that has been a chaser for the past twenty years; well, he's no damn good.' *How can he form his opinion of a fellow if he has no idea of what his past performance has been?* That is one wrong that is done day in and day out here.

"Another thing that very often happens is this. At raise time the department head calls up three or four section chiefs and they in turn discuss the advisability of giving certain individuals an increase. My name, for instance, is brought up by my section chief, who wants to put me in for a raise, saying that I am a very good man, deserving of that increase. The next section chief says: 'Well, I don't think so much of that fellow. I've had an occasion to ask him for a certain job and he never gave me very good service.' The third man comes along and says: 'I think you are full of boloney. He is a man who is worthy of that increase.' The fourth man comes along and says: 'You're a damn liar. That fellow is no good. He has fallen down on two or three of my jobs so far.' Your judgment for the final vote is then left up to the department head. The two section chiefs, who are close friends of the department head, don't want to give me the increase; he is persuaded by this friendship, and the result is I am struck out for a raise. And this happens time and again."

Interviewer: "You feel that there is a little politics played, is that it?"

Employee: "*A little? Well, I think there is a great deal of it, if you are asking me. This friendship stuff, stepping out with the boss, goes a long way around here. A blind man could see that.*"

Interviewer: "You feel that stepping out with the boss gives a person a drag?"

Employee: "A drag? Say, he is sitting on top of the world. It doesn't make any difference whether he knows anything or not. He is put on a job and is sure to remain there as long as his friend remains a department head. Usually the man has ample time to get experience and with the department head coaching him along, he has probably developed himself well enough so that by the time his friend is transferred he is rather familiar with the job."

Interviewer: "You mentioned that you were a supervisor one time. What capacity were you in?"

Employee: "I was a section head in the X department at one time. I was later made a section head in charge of the Y department."

Interviewer: "Were you given any reason why you were taken off this supervising work?"

Employee: "No, they never told me a thing. They took me off and made me like it. That's what makes me mad. They do these damn things and they never give a fellow any explanation. *They put anything they feel like down on this personnel record*, and it goes upstairs and the employee never knows what is on that record. I don't see how they can do that. If they put anything on record, I don't see why the employee is not allowed to see it. I think if they would show these things to the employees, an employee would have an opportunity of correcting these wrongs if he only knew what they were. When raise time comes along, you don't get a raise and they never give you any reason why. They just tell you that you are doing a good job, to keep it up, that they are very sorry but they didn't have enough to go around. Of course, that's very possible, that everybody can't get a raise every time, but I think they should arrange it so that certain ones would get a raise one time and the others another time. They also tell you that you are not under limit of the job, but they don't give you any more money. I can't figure that thing out.

"If a fellow gets up around $50 a week, he is at a standstill. It's been two and a half years now since I have had an increase. I am working just as conscientiously as I ever did. I am always living in hope that the next time I'll get a raise. When a fellow is married and has a family, there are always certain places for your money every week."

Interviewer: "I assume from that that you are a married man."

Employee: "Yes, I have been married for fourteen years. *Another thing that I don't think is right here is that the company allows these married women to work after they become married*. A lot of these poor girls that really need a job walk in the streets without work. If a woman is working on account of sickness or the loss of her husband, or something like that,

I think it's O.K. for a woman to work. But in these cases where the husband and wife are both working and hoarding up the money, I think it's very unfair. A woman never gets any enjoyment out of life if she has to work all the time. What usually happens, either one of them may pass out, and the result is she may die and never has had an opportunity to enjoy all the money that she has been working for.

"Another thing, when a woman works it makes her rather independent. Did you ever notice all the married women around here? I don't truthfully believe that they produce as much as a single girl that really has to work. A girl that has to work is afraid of losing her job and is always turning out the highest efficiency. Things are considerably different now than they used to be. When I was married it was a disgrace for a man to marry a woman and allow her to work. My wife has never worked since we have been married. But nowadays it seems that it is agreed upon before they get married.

"Marriage isn't looked upon today the way it used to be. A couple get married nowadays and never have any children. What is going to become of this nation if they all do the same thing? There's people dying off all the time and they must be replaced. It's the same thing as a forest. If you keep cutting down the trees and do not transplant any, you will not have a forest. It's the same with the people. Of course, some women can't have them, but the majority of them won't have them because they'd have to give up their job if they did."

Interviewer: "In a great number of cases, the man doesn't make enough for the woman nowadays. In a number of cases, it is almost compulsory that the woman work."

Employee: "I think it is all right for a woman to work a year or two, until they get a start. Then quit and give a chance to some other single girl that has to work. I suppose if my wife would have worked for a few years after we were married, I'd be a lot better off than I am today. Of course, we manage to get along, but we have no luxuries. What pleasure is there in being married if you have to get up in the morning, eat breakfast, then eat your dinner out? In a great number of cases these couples of today eat their supper at the restaurant. The woman is too tired to come home and prepare a meal for a man."

An Interview with Mrs. Black

The supervisor asked the interviewer what girl she wanted to see. When told, he remarked, "Oh, say! You ought to get a good story out of her."

Interviewer: "Is that so?"

Supervisor: "Yes. I don't know what it is that is the matter with that girl, but she's what you call a chronic kicker. You ought to get a lot out of her. We regard her as a problem case."

Employee was introduced to interviewer. On the way to the conference room they talked about the weather.

Employee: "I don't know what's the matter with me, I've always got a cold. [Employee spoke in a very calm and uncomplaining manner throughout the interview, with only occasional exceptions.] You know, it seems like I didn't used to get colds that way, but the last couple of years I can't turn around without getting a cold. You know, I get just a little bit of a draft on me, and I've got a cold. It's almost gone now though.

"You know, when Mr. Jones, my group chief, called me, I was scared I was going to get laid off. I saw the chief stand down at the other end of the department talking with him just before you came in and I didn't see you, see? You were standing way ahead there, and I couldn't see you from where I was sitting, and I thought sure I was going to get laid off. I says to myself when he says, 'Come here,' I says, 'Well, here's where I get it,' and I really thought I was going to get laid off, but then when I saw you out there I knew different." (Laughed.)

Interviewer: "Oh, you knew who I was?"

Employee: "Yes, I've seen you around. Didn't you talk to Mary yesterday?"

Interviewer: "Yes, I did."

Employee: "Well, she's a friend of mine. I saw you with her. I knew you were the interviewer. *Say, you know, that Mr. Jones is not so good.* You know, he never goes around smiling. He gives you the awfullest looks. I don't think he's such a good boss. You know, Mr. Smith [former group chief] is so different. He comes around you all the time and says little jokes and makes you feel good, but Mr. Jones is kind of mean like. He's so mean-looking."

Interviewer: "You mean it's just his looks?"

Employee: "Well, he talks that way too. If it happens that just one coil is bad — by gosh, that happens once in a while — he comes over and wants to know why it happened. Gee, he just has to tell you all about it. Well, it's not like that in other groups. You know, like yesterday, after you got through talking to Mary, he came over to her and wanted to know what she was talking so long about, and she said it was on business. She wasn't going to tell him; it was none of his business. You know, with Mr. Smith when things would go wrong, you'd just feel like telling him, but not with Mr. Jones. You'd sooner suffer than tell him. You know, he just came off nights, and all the night girls say the same thing about him. They all feel the same; they haven't much use for him. It seems like he just likes to hurt people. He just wants you to know that he's the boss, I guess. . . .

"You know, this is the third time I've been interviewed. I was interviewed once about a year ago and then before that. I don't remember their names; they were awfully nice ladies. . . .

"Gee, it's a good thing I didn't get laid off. I don't know what I would have done if I had been laid off because, you know, it's only a year since I've been married. It will be a year next week, and my husband's been out of work most of the time. He got laid off just two weeks before the wedding and he couldn't find anything for a long time, and after a couple months he found something that lasted just a few weeks, and he's had a few short jobs like that just off and on. He's been working the last couple months. Then he got a job sawing in a box factory. They have a circular saw and it broke on him. It's not very big, you know, but when they break, they break hard, and the saw broke on him and cut his hand right here. [Employee pointed to thumb and forefinger.] He cut the vein in here in both these fingers. He had to go to the hospital for four or five days, and they put him on piecework. He can't earn much that way, because they don't have many orders. Maybe he'll go and work two hours and then come home, and maybe he won't work for two or three days. Then he'll go down and work four hours or something like that, and you know what that means. Why, I don't know what I would do if I was called to the office and laid off. I sure got trouble when I got married.

"I've always had a lot of trouble. You know, I've had to help my mother a lot because things aren't so good at home. I have a stepfather, and he's a mean man. Gosh, he's the meanest man I ever heard of. Gee, and my mother is the sweetest woman! She's got to take so much dirt from him; I feel so sorry for her. That's why I stayed home as long as I did. I wanted to help her."

Interviewer: "How do you mean stayed home?"

Employee: "Well, I mean before I was married, see? I would have left home long before if it hadn't been for her, but, you know, she is the kindest person. She would take a thing into her heart and cry over it before she would say anything. *I never could stand my stepfather.* I think that's the reason he was so mean to me, because I used to stick up for my mother, see? I used to argue for her and fight, and that would make him mad, of course. You know, the trouble with him, I think, was prohibition. You see, he's a drunkard. He always has to drink and then it makes him so mean, and if he hasn't anything, it makes him mean. It seems like he just can't be mean enough when he hasn't any, because he wasn't that way before prohibition. I can remember in the days of the saloons that he wasn't that way. We had a lot of trouble with him, because he used to get it from a friend of his who made it, and this fellow lived right next door, so it was kind of hard. Then when that fellow moved away, he'd get it somehow. He'd go out and buy it and sometimes he'd go to some friend of his that was making it. He'd get it some way. Gosh, he's mean to my little brothers and sisters too. You know, my mother's got a big family. There are seven children. When I was home there were eight, and I still try to help my mother. My own father died when I was about six and a half. My mother had three children then besides me. There were three little boys; one of them was three, and one was two, and one was only about six weeks old, just a little fellow, when my father died, and then it wasn't long after he died, a couple years, that my mother lost one. She lost the one that was two, and then five years ago the other one died, the older one."

Interviewer: "Oh, the one that was three when your father died?"

Employee: "Yes. He was so young. He was only seventeen and, gee, he was the nicest kid. He was the only one that my stepfather was scared of and, you know, he wasn't mean at all. He never argued. He just couldn't stand to argue. He was always singing and whistling, and the minute he would come into the room it just seemed like my stepfather would stop being mean. I don't think it was because he liked him; I figured it was because he was scared my brother might beat him up. You see, he was awfully well built for his age. He was tall. He was a lot bigger than my step-father, and I think the only reason that my stepfather stopped when he was around was that he was afraid he might get beaten up. Of course, there was never no thought in any of us to beat each other up. My stepdad has never beat my mother. If he had, I think we would have all beat him up so that he'd never have done it again, but he used to be mean in other ways, you know, saying things to her mean that would make her cry. Well, finally I decided I couldn't stand it any longer, so I told her that she had to tell him that he had to cut that out or I was going to leave home. Well, of course, she couldn't stand to have me leave home, so she went and told him, and after that he was always mean to me, because he was mad that my mother would listen to me and not to him. Gosh, it makes me feel so sorry for my mother when I think what she has to suffer. You see, she was real young when my father died. She was only twenty-three and she married my stepfather to have someone to take care of our family. She's real young now; she's only forty-one. Her baby is six years old now, and the oldest one will be seventeen in a couple of months, in December. My own brother is nineteen, but he's not working now; he can't find a job. He has been working, but he got laid off. He goes every day, but you know you can't find anything nowadays. The other one is still going to school, so he can't earn anything. Maybe he couldn't get work if he wasn't going to school, so he might as well get an education. . . .

"You know, I think the reason that I can't stand Mr. Jones is because every time I look at him he reminds me of my stepfather."

Characteristics of Obsessive Thinking

Let us look more carefully at what the investigators found of interest in these four interviews. In the case of Brown, for example, several things are noticeable. Brown's "unfair treatment by his super-visor" coincides with his "hard luck at home" and "feeling dumpy many a day." All the illustrations which Brown gives of unfair treatment ("being treated as a dog," as he calls it), such as the supervisor's request that he work overtime and postpone his vacation, are suggestions which at any other period in Brown's life might have been welcomed. The supervisor did not force the issue when he asked Brown to postpone his vacation. In fact, after seeing that Brown was unwilling, "he never said any more about it." It looks very much as if Brown were caught in a vicious circle in which his "hard luck at home" and "feeling dumpy" helped to increase his conviction of unfair treatment.

Whereas we obtain in terms of Brown's personal misfortune a partial illumination of why he felt that his supervisor was "treating him as a dog," the various interferences at play in the case of Green are not so clear; yet the distortion is even more apparent. Green paints an extremely unpleasant picture of his "boss" and, although there is a slight suggestion of malingering, the story is perfectly straightforward until he comes to the part where he suggests that his supervisor was "out to kill him." At this point one begins to suspect an unduly heavy preoccupation about the matter, particularly after he finishes his story, for Green is still alive and no attempts have been made on his life; he received only certain mysterious telephone calls. The interesting thing about this interview is the skillful way in which the interviewer allows Green to state his case and to expose the exaggerated role which the "boss" plays in his thinking. For Green his superior had become a "fiend," who in face of opposition would go to the length of physical extermination. Had the story been stopped short of the end, a completely different impression would have been gained. As the story is expanded, however, it looks as if Green's mental health has been somewhat shattered by the altercations he has had with his supervisor. It would be interesting to speculate on just what function this building up of the "gangster-killer" supervisor played in Green's psyche. On the assumption that Green had toyed with the idea of malingering — an idea, let us assume, that was not pleasing to Green's conscious moral code — it would be natural to expect that he would endow the supervisor with attributes which might occasion his unpleasant feeling.[1] The fear that the supervisor had detected any overt behavior or even

---

[1] This mechanism, called "projection," has been well studied by psychoanalysis. Its application is not confined to the pathological. Illustrations can be found in the thinking of the child, of the primitive, and of the normal civilized adult. An interesting discussion of this mechanism can be found in Piaget, J., *The Child's Conception of the World*, Harcourt, Brace and Co., New York, 1929, p. 34 et seq.

any wishful thinking in the direction of malingering was to Green an unpleasant feeling. By emphasizing the bad character of the supervisor this fear could be justified, accounted for, and ultimately put out of consciousness.

White attributes all his troubles to one thing, namely, the personnel records kept by the company. It is clear that by this means he justifies to himself his own demotion from supervisor to operator. White's interview is interesting for a number of different reasons: (1) The way the interview starts is significant: "There's no damn use of you and I going anywhere because I refuse to talk." Curiously enough, this did not stop the interviewer from obtaining an interview of more than average length. For, once White started talking, the interviewer had no difficulty in keeping him talking. (2) It is interesting to note that White first undertakes to illustrate his grievance with the case of a friend. Not until some time later does he say, "I'll just give you my own case, for instance." It was the experience of the interviewers that the more subjective a person's judgments were, the more objective he tried to make them appear to be. (3) It is difficult to understand the complete mystery which White makes of his demotion and of just what it was on his personnel card that had prevented his advancement in the company. That a person with White's capacity to overthink his situation should fail to have any theories on this matter is curious. It suggests very strongly that this was a matter about which White did not wish to talk. The interviewers had learned the importance of listening not only to what a person wished to say but also for what he did not wish to say. (4) One of the most interesting rationalizations comes in the middle of the interview, when one is beginning to wonder why White ever worked so long in a company of which he was so critical: "I've been with the company twenty-four years and the company as a whole, I think, is the best place in the world to work. But the individuals who are supposed to carry out the policies of the company are a bunch of skunks." This distinction between the company and its visible representatives was one made frequently by the workers at Hawthorne and one about which more will be said later, in Chapter XVI. (5) It is obvious that White is very alert to "unfairness." Once he finishes talking about the unfairness of keeping personnel records, he points out a number of other unjust practices: (a) College men get too much preference. (b) College men, when they become supervisors, do not judge their subordinates on the basis of past experience. (This argument is particularly interesting in the light of White's former contention that too much emphasis was placed by the company in their personnel records on past experience.) (c) The fore-man is influenced by those subordinates with whom he has personal friendships. (d) Married women should not be allowed to work.

Mrs. Black was characterized by her superiors as a "chronic kicker." Her interview not only offers an excellent illustration of distorted think-ing but also shows how the interviewee herself gradually comes to see the irrational source of her dislike of her supervisor. She begins by describing the "meanness" of her group chief. The second stage of the interview is concerned with her family and in particular with her "mean" stepfather. It is not until the end of the interview that she comments on the resemblance between her stepfather and her supervisor.

It was evident that all these interviews had at least one characteristic in common: a tendency on the part of the complainant to project all his troubles on one object and in such terms to overthink his situation. This morbid overelaboration of an oversimplification in fact was con-sidered by the investigators to be one of the chief characteristics of what they called "obsessive response." Such situations as these gen-erally revealed an habitual chain of preoccupation which persisted long after the provoking occasion had passed. Brown, Green, and White were still preoccupied with events that had happened some time in the past. In the case of White, this brooding about the past was par-ticularly obvious. Mrs. Black's preoccupations about her stepfather still persisted in her married adult situation, after her childhood and adolescent surroundings had ceased to exist in fact. Her response to her supervisor could be understood only in relation to her personal history and private thinking. Such persons as these had lost in part their capacity for adequate discrimination. The meanings they as-signed to the reality about them were "colored" too much by their personal experiences. It was evident that the complaints of this type of person could not be taken seriously as criticisms of company policies or conditions. Moreover, in many such situations the responses were determined in part by factors outside the immediate control of management.

The Psychopathological Interpretation and its Limitations

For a long time during the period when the employees were being interviewed, the main interest of the interviewers was in the preoccupa-tions of the worker and the relation of these preoccupations to the worker's personal background and history. For this approach there was a school of thought to which they could turn, and consequently the concepts and methods of psychopathology were studied. Psychopathology has demonstrated that there is an important relation between the total orientation of the individual to the reality about him and his earlier childhood experiences. Distortions of attitude, of which the psychoneurotic offers a good example, are the product of long trains of dispersed rather than concentrated thinking. The history of an adult psychoneurotic generally reveals an habitual chain of preoccupations conditioned by the early family situation. These preoccupations persist into adulthood, long after the childhood surroundings cease to exist in fact, and as a consequence the psychoneurotic's responses to the adult situations with which he is faced are not likely to be entirely adequate. From the interviews there was evidence that the responses which some workers made to their associates and superiors in the factory were determined in part by factors relating to their personal histories. However, although there was a great deal to be gained from the psychopathological approach, it had several limitations.

Interest in the personal situation drew attention away from the immediate work situation. It put the "cause" for the employee's dissatisfaction in the "individual" and in factors beyond the control of management. Moreover, it seemed contrary to common sense to assume that for the majority of workers their likes and dislikes were unrelated to their immediate work situation and merely rooted in factors in their personal histories. Few of them were candidates for a mental hospital. The obsessive thinking which characterized their reactions to their environment, although somewhat similar to that found in the psychoneurotic, was occasioned by a different total situation. Their responses to slight alterations in their immediate environment were quite different from those of a psychoneurotic. In the case of a psychoneurotic, little benefit is obtained solely by a change in the conditions of living and working. His cure requires a thorough overhauling of his preoccupations; otherwise, by his faulty thinking he tends to break down any new situation in which he is placed. In the case of most "obsessive" workers at Hawthorne, this was not true. Frequently, such a worker responded at once to any slight betterment in his social conditions of work. This experience, which the interviewers met again and again, suggested a restatement of the problem.

A study of those normal human situations in industry which carry with them an obsessive consequence in the thinking of the worker was indicated. In such cases as these the relation of working conditions to different kinds of personal situations is important. To study the employee's reactions only in terms of his early childhood experiences, the preoccupations that have persisted, and the way in which such habitual preoccupations tend to fix a stereotyped response to superiors and associates, although important, provides only a partial account of the situation. It assumes the overwhelming importance of one set of relations which the individual has with the socio-reality to the neglect of all other social structures in which he participates. In the case of the psychoneurotic, with his relatively stereotyped attitudes and fixed responses, this assumption can be made without leading to any great error. The psychoneurotic's relation to the socio-reality can be viewed as an extension of the familial configuration. But in the case of the normal individual, whose responses are more plastic and who is capable of "learning," of correcting his attitudes, and of "adjusting" himself to the society in which he lives, this assumption is far too simple.

In Chapter XVI the kinds of social relations which workers had in the plant, and which went into the determination of their complaints, attitudes, and work behavior, will be considered. For the present, however, attention will be confined to the relations existing between work effectiveness and personal situations in which there was a tendency to morbid reflection. Two questions can be raised: (1) How do such preoccupations affect the worker's output? (2) In what way do conditions of work tend to exaggerate or diminish the worker's morbid preoccupations?

PREOCCUPATION AND OUTPUT

In the Relay Assembly and Mica Splitting Test Rooms, many variations in output could be related to the personal preoccupations of the workers, and these variations continued as long as the preoccupations persisted. Whenever any pessimistic preoccupation emerged for any reason whatsoever, there was an observable adverse effect on output. Although several cases were cited in Chapter VII, it is only necessary for the present purpose to recall Operator M_5, whose output record can be roughly divided into four phases corresponding very closely with preoccupations about her personal affairs. This correspondence is tabulated in Table XXIV; Figure 26 gives the weekly variations of output for Operator M_5.

This operator's case was not the only illustration of a relation between personal preoccupation and output. In another segregated group, the Bank Wiring Observation Room, in which it was possible to compare output records with personal situations, a similar relation was found in the case of a wireman, W_7, who was also engaged in a semi-

TABLE XXIV

PERSONAL PREOCCUPATION AND VARIATIONS IN OUTPUT, OPERATOR M₅

Length of Phase (see Figure 26)	Personal Preoccupations and Events	Variations in Output
Phase 1 (from October 22, 1928, to point A)	Operator M₅ nurses a great resentment against strong parental control and her inability to live as other girls do, the general effect of which takes the form of complaining frequently about a headache.	Operator M₅'s output is characterized by pronounced irregularity and a failure to keep pace with her fellow workers.
Phase 2 (from A to B)	She begins to express more freely her preoccupations about her home to the older women in the group, who listen to her troubles and give her motherly advice.	Her output commences to rise and is less irregular.
Phase 3 (from B to C)	She finally comes to the decision to live away from home and takes an apartment with a girl friend.	Her output steadies significantly and remains at a high level.
Phase 4 (from C to end)	Because of her mother's illness, she is forced to return home and help take care of her mother.	Her output starts to decline and develops its former irregularity.

316

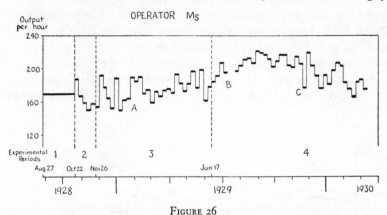

FIGURE 26

VARIATIONS IN AVERAGE HOURLY OUTPUT PER WEEK, OPERATOR M₅

MICA SPLITTING TEST ROOM

repetitive task. The work curve for W₇ (Figure 27) can be divided into five phases:

Phase 1 (from B to C), when his output shows a steady decline.
Phase 2 (from C to February 6), when his output shows an abrupt rise which is sustained for three weeks.
Phase 3 (from February 6 to D), when his output starts to go down again.
Phase 4 (from D to E), when the highest rate for the entire period is achieved.
Phase 5 (from E to end), when his output rate takes a precipitous drop.

In an interview with W₇ on December 7 (see B in Figure 27), which was shortly after his rate began to decrease, he made quite a point of the fact that he was turning out more work than W₉, but was getting less money. He was also disgruntled because he had not been regraded, which he thought he deserved. Although W₇ had been interviewed before, this was the first time that he expressed this complaint. Yet the discrepancy between the earnings and output of W₉ was not a new discovery to W₇. In fact, it was fairly common knowledge among all the associates of W₉. Why, then, did W₇ become so disgruntled at this time?

In the first interview with W₇, which took place in early November (see A), W₇ said that he was going with a girl who was living alone in the city and earning her own living. He was thinking of marriage, but he said that he needed to earn more money before he could get married. At the time, this situation did not worry him greatly because both he and his girl were working and they saw each other frequently. When the interviewer saw W_7 the second time (see B), this situation had changed. His girl had been placed on shorter hours, and she was faced with the possibility of unemployment. This meant a great deal to W_7. If his girl were to be laid off, he would be faced with an alternative of letting her go back to North Dakota and live with her parents,

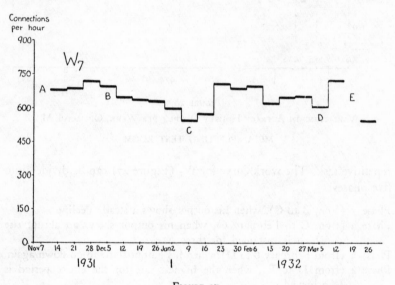

FIGURE 27

VARIATIONS IN AVERAGE HOURLY OUTPUT PER WEEK, OPERATOR W_7

BANK WIRING OBSERVATION ROOM

thus risking the possibility of never seeing her again, or of marrying her. Since he was in love with her, the latter choice seemed to be the more desirable solution. His output curve started downward at about the time he was first confronted with this situation. His earnings had now taken on a new significance. It was no longer simply a question of whether he could support himself, but a question of whether he could through his earnings preserve a relationship which meant a great deal to him. This growing preoccupation probably accounts for the fact that at this particular time he became disgruntled with his own earnings, especially as compared with W_9's earnings. The downward trend in W_7's output continued all during the period of indecision. Finally, on January 7 (see C), after sitting around most of the day and being unable to work, he announced his intention of getting married.

He did so two days later. During the next week his output curve started upward, and in the second week thereafter it reached its highest point up to that time. The conflict had been resolved.

During Phase 3, when his output again became irregular and low, W_7 was interviewed once more (see D). In this interview he related certain difficulties of an intimate nature which he was experiencing with his wife. Two or three times since their marriage she had threatened to leave him. He revealed these troubles to the interviewer on Tuesday, March 8. Because of their urgency, the interviewer made certain recommendations, a practice which in other cases he scrupulously avoided. By the end of that week W_7's output rate reached its highest point during the study (see E).

The low output of W_7 in his last week in the observation room can be associated with the fact that W_7 was notified that he was to go back to the regular department and that he would work only alternate weeks.

It was through such cases as those of M_5 and W_7 that the interviewers began to understand better the relation between personal preoccupation and output. There were only a few instances in which a relation could be objectively demonstrated, but it is obvious that only in the test rooms had there been prearranged routines which made it possible to relate personal factors to output. In the interviewing program, the daily or weekly variations in output of the employees interviewed had not been recorded. It is clear, however, that had there not existed in the test rooms an arrangement for the observation of factors other than those in the immediate work situation, many of the changes in output, such as those that occurred in the cases of M_5 and W_7, might have been attributed to "learning," "fatigue," or "monotony." Therefore, it seemed plausible to assume that wherever obsessive preoccupations were divulged in the interviews, a set of factors similar to those revealed in the test rooms was operating: (1) some circumstances interfering with the worker's total orientation, and (2) a reduced capacity to attend to work.

The investigators marked off a set of symptoms as diagnostic of some interference in the worker's total equilibrium: (a) obsessive verbal response, (b) a reduced capacity for attending to work, and (c) marked or pessimistic preoccupations. But, although in the cases just cited the interferences arose from conditions outside of the work situation, there was no reason to believe that all interferences affecting the worker's equilibrium are confined to this source. There was also evidence that interferences arising from immediate working conditions, in connection with certain types of personal situation, can exaggerate or diminish the above-mentioned symptoms (a), (b), and (c). Let us therefore examine four factors in the immediate work situation which may assist or prevent the emergence of morbid preoccupations: (1) fatigue or organic unbalance, (2) repetitive work, (3) supervision, and (4) interhuman relations at work.

Contributing Interferences within Work Situation

Fatigue or Organic Unbalance

Psychiatrists have commented on the intimate relation that seems to exist between fatigue and a tendency to morbid reflection. Janet has remarked on the fact that anyone suffering from fatigue displays symptoms of psychasthenia such as "motor agitations, tics, irritability, and obsessive revery." [1] Several industrial investigators have observed that a worker who is constantly employed upon a job of an extremely repetitive type shows neurotic symptoms after the advent of fatigue. Or, to state the observations more broadly: Whenever there exists an organic incapacity for adequate response to established conditions of work, whether it is due to the deficiency of the individual or to abnormal conditions of work, a situation is created which, if it does not lead completely to the organic breakdown of the individual, will manifest itself in its first stages, at least, in hysterical and abnormal reveries.

A good example of this is the case of Operator 2A in the Relay Assembly Test Room. In the early stages of the experiment she began to show signs of restlessness and ill temper, which took the form of excessive talking and open criticism of the experiment and the company. Her attitude baffled the investigators. They made several attempts in talking with her to find out the source of the trouble, but she remained unresponsive and negativistic. It was not until later that an organic unbalance (low red blood cell count and low hemoglobin percentage) suggested itself as a possible clue to her changed mental attitude. She was given medical treatment and her health rapidly improved. Upon her recovery, she was again interviewed. Her former attitude had disappeared. She talked freely to her former supervisor and openly disavowed her former criticisms of the company and the experiment and gave a plausible explanation of what had happened.[2]

Of course, the case of Operator 2A is only one of many types of organic unbalance which may be included under the term "fatigue."

---

[1] Janet, P., *Les Névroses*, Flammarion, Paris, 1930, p. 358.
[2] For a complete account of this case, see Chapter VII, pp. 169–170.

But at this stage of the inquiry, from their observations in the Relay Assembly and Mica Splitting Test Rooms, the investigators came to the following conclusion: Inasmuch as fatigue in its popular sense is not essentially the same ill in all instances, it is best to restrict the word "fatigue" to one type of organic unbalance. In this type there are present not only the previously mentioned symptoms, (a) obsessive verbal response, (b) a reduced capacity for attending to work, and (c) marked or pessimistic preoccupations, but also certain changes in the blood stream, that is, an increase in lactic acid, a diminution of alkali reserve, and "oxygen debt." [1] For all other cases of "unbalance" it is best to state the nature of the interference (internal or external conditions) and the nature of the disequilibrium (organic, mental, or both).

It was apparent that in failing to make this discrimination industry had confused its problem in two ways. By lumping together in one class under "fatigue" all cases which had symptoms (a), (b), and (c), it treated them all as susceptible to the same kind of remedy. Furthermore, because of the confusion it failed to see that the preponderance of interferences which occur in modern industry are not of an organic nature. By dropping the popular notion of fatigue, it becomes clear that: (1) There are very few instances of organic fatigue in the strict sense among workers engaged in repetitive tasks, for such cases tend to be eliminated. Workers suffering from disability of this kind either stop work or are transferred to other jobs where it is possible for them to maintain a steady state.[2] (2) There are only sporadic instances of organic unbalance induced by some interference in the nature of unusual external physical conditions such as high temperatures and other climatic conditions. These instances occur mostly in certain industries and localities, for example, in steel mills or at Boulder Dam.[3]

Repetitive Work

In the interviews employees frequently stated grievances about which they had brooded for many years. Not only was it astonishing to find how far back in the past the worker could go in stating his dissatisfac-

---

[1] This kind of fatigue, generally referred to as "physiological or muscular fatigue," is a well-recognized variety and has been studied by many physiologists. See Hill, A. V., *Living Machinery*, Harcourt, Brace and Co., 1927; Bock, A. V., C. Van Caulaert, D. B. Dill, A. Fölling and L. M. Hurxthal, "Studies in Muscular Activity. III. Dynamical Changes Occurring in Man at Work," *Journal of Physiology*, Vol. 66, 1928, p. 136.

[2] For a further discussion of this point, see Mayo, Elton, *The Human Problems of an Industrial Civilization*, Macmillan, New York, 1933, pp. 1–27.

[3] For studies on such kinds of "organic unbalance," see Talbott, J. H., and Jost

tions, but also it was astonishing to find that he could speak about them with all the feeling and emotion of things that had just recently occurred. Through such experiences as these the interviewers began to understand the relation of repetitive work to personal preoccupation.

The important role repetitive work plays in creating an ideal setting for the development of discontent has been frequently overlooked. Work in modern industrial organizations consists not so much of hard manual labor as of repetitive jobs which require a minimum of skilled attention and allow a great deal of time for preoccupation. It is apparent that for many workers engaged in repetitive or semirepetitive tasks the point of proficiency is soon reached, that is, the amount of attention the job can carry for the worker is less than the amount of attention the operator is capable of giving. In such a situation, where it is no longer possible for the worker either to elaborate or change his job, he can either switch his attention to other things in the immediate surroundings or indulge in revery. In the absence of any real social situation in which to participate, his reveries frequently take the form of brooding futilely about his personal problems.

Of course, it was not the investigators' intention to imply that repetitive work in itself was the cause of abnormal reveries. They merely saw that under certain conditions of work any pre-existing tendency toward anxiety, apprehension, pessimism, or suspicion could be exaggerated. Repetitive work in itself could not bring this about. It did, however, give the worker long periods for revery thinking. The form which his reveries took depended not only on the individual's personal situation but also on the nature of the human surroundings in which he worked.

Supervision

The extent to which indifferent methods of supervision could provoke irrational responses was well illustrated in the cases of Brown and Green. Had the supervisor been more sympathetic with Brown's home situation and made allowances for his "feeling dumpy," Brown's reaction might have been quite different. Brown might have become a more responsive and responsible worker. Likewise, in the case of Green the supervisor might have handled the situation with better results if he had tried to understand it. Had either supervisor listened sympa-

Michelsen, "Heat Cramps. A Clinical and Chemical Study," *Journal of Clinical Investigation*, Vol. 12, 1933, p. 533; Dill, D. B., B. F. Jones, H. T. Edwards and S. A. Oberg, "Salt Economy in Extreme Dry Heat," *Journal of Biological Chemistry*, Vol. 100, 1933, p. 755.

thetically and attentively to his subordinate, he might have found out what the trouble was. Instead, the supervisors delivered futile ultimatums, which had little result other than to make any kind of effective working together impossible. Both the test rooms and the interviewing program showed the importance to morale of good first-line supervision. The situation has been well described by Elton Mayo:

The fact that one man has been set in control of others has usually been taken to imply that he is expected to give orders and to have them obeyed. So supervision has frequently come to mean "ordering people about." There is only one objection to this, and the objection is not in any sense political, it is simply that the method is exceedingly stupid. If there is difficulty or delay in obedience, or eccentricity, or "slackness," the supervisor is expected to yell and bawl and swear or, what is even worse, to indulge in lengthy admonition. So he "talks" and does not "listen"; and he never learns what is really wrong. The workers are often terrified, they harbour a grievance and at last, if they express it, they tend to overstate or to distort. At once the overstatement is seized for attack, and the possibility of understanding is lost.

Perhaps in this, I am myself indulging in overstatement. But at least I can claim that where the good supervisor listens and becomes acquainted with personal eccentricities of attitude — and the causes of such eccentricity — the usual supervisor does not; he prefers to talk and to give futile orders.[1]

The recognition of the need to understand personal situations was for a long time the central idea of supervisory training at Hawthorne. The purpose of this training was to convey to supervisors the technique that the interviewers had developed and had found to be so effective: that is, to listen rather than to talk, and to exclude from their personal contacts with employees any moral admonition, advice, or emotion. It was believed that by using this technique supervisors would be able to become better acquainted with the employees they supervised and to handle more intelligently those complex human situations the general results of which were unsatisfactory to the worker.

Interhuman Relations at Work

Another set of social relations, those which the employee had with his fellow workers, also had something to do with the development of morbid preoccupations. It was found that employees who were in a work situation which prevented or diminished their opportunity for

[1] Mayo, Elton, "Changing Methods in Industry," *The Personnel Journal*, Vol. VIII, 1930, p. 331.

social participation were inclined to indulge in pessimistic reflection. Even for persons otherwise capable and socially well adjusted, such a situation had a debilitating effect. Moreover, it was apparent that persons in human surroundings at work which suited and sustained them were able to carry a burden of domestic difficulties without becoming depressed.

A good illustration is the case of Operator M1 in the Mica Splitting Test Room. She was a woman 40 years old who had been a serious problem to her supervisors for many years because of attendance irregularities and frequent "nervous breakdowns." [1] After joining the test room she showed over a period of a year the greatest improvement of any one of the operators. This improvement was apparent not only in her output but also in a decrease in her absences to one-third of their former frequency. Her change of attitude seemed to be closely associated with the more intimate human associations which the test room afforded. Moreover, it was particularly striking in view of the fact that this was a case bordering very closely on a "neurosis," where any slight alteration in environment could not be expected to bring about any permanent improvement.

Probably even more striking is the case of Operator 2 in the Relay Assembly Test Room. She had also been considered a "problem case" by her supervisors before her entrance into the test room. [2] Her family situation showed that she was carrying a burden of domestic problems which could easily account for her frequent displays of temper and irritability. She was practically the sole support of her family. Her mother was dead and she had to take care of her three younger brothers. These responsibilities did not leave her much opportunity to develop her own interests. Nevertheless, after joining the test room Operator 2 showed unusual capacities for leadership, loyalty, and friendship. During the whole five years of the experiment, there was no girl in the test room more popular than she, both among her fellow workers and her supervisors. When she found an appropriate niche in the social structure, so that she could intimately identify herself and her work with a social function, she became an enthusiastic and co-operative worker.

The case of Operator M5 in the Mica Splitting Test Room also offers confirmation of the importance to morale of appropriate human surroundings. Operator M5's improvement started when she first began to express her preoccupations to her fellow workers and before any real change in her living arrangements had occurred. Opportunity for

[1] For a more complete account of this case, see Chapter VII, p. 175.
[2] For a more complete picture of this girl's personal situation, see Chapter VII, p. 167.

human comradeship and social conversation played an important part in helping her to meet her personal difficulties. It gave her a sense of social support without which she could not have decided to take the step that she did take.

Summary and Conclusions

A certain class of statements in which there was a tendency toward exaggeration and distortion, and in which these responses seemed to be directed more toward persons than toward things, suggested to the interviewers the problem of the relation between complaints and personal equilibrium. Interviews have been presented in this chapter to illustrate the relation between the tendency toward obsessive response and factors in the worker's personal background. Personal situations in which there was a serious disorientation of general attitude were frequently accompanied by a reduced capacity for work and an increase in morbid reflection. It also became evident that, in addition to difficulties in personal situations, there were certain factors in the immediate work situation which could relieve or exaggerate a tendency toward distortion. In the case of Operator 2A, an example was given of how an organic unbalance could find expression in criticism of company policy. It was apparent that repetitive work offered an ideal setting for brooding and overthinking one's situation, although repetitive work did not in itself bring about abnormal preoccupations. Social surroundings played an important role in this respect. Indifferent methods of supervision and an impoverished socio-reality at work left the employee without social support. In such a situation it was easy for him to interpret anything or everything as a threat to his security.

In order to fit their findings into a coherent whole, the investigators had to evolve a new way of thinking about the worker and those things about which he complained. Their conclusions emerged in terms of a conceptual scheme for the interpretation of employee complaints, which can be stated as follows:[1]

(1) the source of most employee complaints cannot be confined to some one single cause, and the dissatisfaction of the worker, in most cases, is the general effect of a complex situation;

(2) the analysis of complex situations requires an understanding of the nature of the equilibrium or disequilibrium and the nature of the interferences;

[1] These conclusions have been reported in an earlier statement of the Western Electric researches by Elton Mayo, in *The Human Problems of an Industrial Civilization*, Chapter V, pp. 99–121.

(3) the interferences which occur in industry can come from changes in the physical environment, from changes in the social environment at work, or from changes outside the immediate working environment, and the "unbalances" which issue from such interferences may be organic (changes in the blood stream), or mental (obsessive preoccupations which make it difficult to attend to work), or both;

(4) therefore, to cloak industrial problems under such general categories as "fatigue," "monotony," and "supervision" is sometimes to fail to discriminate among the different kinds of interferences involved, as well as among the different kinds of disequilibrium;

(5) and if the different interferences and different types of disequilibrium are not the same ill in every instance, they are not susceptible to the same kind of remedy.

For purposes of convenience, this way of interpreting complaints has been roughly depicted in Figure 28, which shows the major areas from which interference may arise in industrial situations and the kinds of responses which can be expected if unbalance results. It is apparent that this way of thinking substitutes for a simple cause and effect analysis of human situations the notion of an interrelation of factors in mutual dependence: that is, an equilibrium such that any major change in one of the factors (interference or constraint) brings about changes in the other factors, resulting in a temporary state of disequilibrium until either the former equilibrium is restored or a new equilibrium is established. The interconnections between the boxes in the diagram express the futility of trying to determine what is cause and what is effect. For example, in the case of Operator M_5, which of the following factors is cause and which is effect:

(a) situation at home,
(b) the nature of her social relations with fellow workers and supervisor,
(c) preoccupations of futility,
(d) frequent complaints about headaches,
(e) irregular and low output?

More particularly, with regard to the different types of interference and different kinds of equilibrium to be found among the workers at Hawthorne, the investigators concluded:

(1) the interferences which occur among the workers at Hawthorne and which diminish their capacity to attend to work are not chiefly confined to the physical conditions of work; and for the average worker engaged in repetitive or semirepetitive tasks, that type of organic unbalance characterized by changes in the blood stream such as an increase in lactic acid, a diminution of alkali reserve,

and "oxygen debt," and generally called physiological or muscular fatigue, is not of frequent occurrence (see relations *G, C, D, A,* and *B* in Figure 28);

(2) although in the case of some employees the constraint or interference can be traced to factors in their personal history, that type of mental unbalance which has been studied by psychopathologists and ordi-

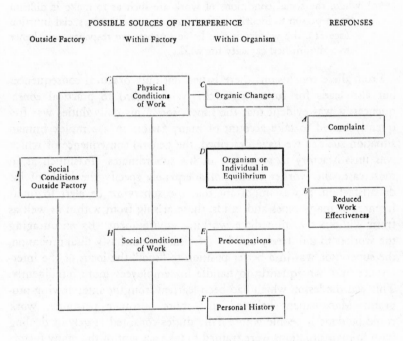

POSSIBLE SOURCES OF INTERFERENCE   RESPONSES

Outside Factory   Within Factory   Within Organism

FIGURE 28

SCHEME FOR INTERPRETING COMPLAINTS AND REDUCED WORK EFFECTIVENESS

narily referred to as "psychoneurosis" does not occur with sufficient frequency to constitute a major problem at Hawthorne (see relations *F, E, D, A,* and *B* in Figure 28);

(3) a very common form of induced unbalance in the worker which diminishes his capacity to work effectively can best be understood in terms in which (a) capacity to work, or to fix and sustain attention, is to be regarded as a product of the personal equilibrium of the worker with the socio-reality about him (see relations *I, H, E,* and *D* in Figure 28); and (b) any circumstance adversely affecting this personal equilibrium is likely to reveal itself in a reduced

capacity for active work, in obsessive reveries, and in irrational responses (see relations E, D, A, and B in Figure 28):

(4) workers whose personal unbalance is due to factors in their personal history (F) or social situation (I) are less capable of standing any pressure at work (overtime, repetitive work, indifferent methods of supervision, etc. (see G and H)) than those workers who have more satisfactory personal or social situations;

(5) where the social conditions of work are such as to make it difficult for a person to identify himself or his task with any social function (see H), the worker is also liable to obsessive responses and hence to a diminished capacity for work.

From these conclusions there issued not only practical consequences but also leads for future research. With regard to practical consequences, it was evident that the supervisor in his daily duties was frequently forced to take account of many factors in a complex human situation such as we have described, the general consequence of which was unsatisfactory to some one of his subordinates. Inasmuch as in most cases the worker could not adequately specify the locus of his dissatisfaction, it was important that the supervisor be alert to interferences of many types and kinds, those arising from within as well as from without the immediate working environment. By encouraging the worker to talk freely and by refraining from hasty disapprobation, the supervisor was in a better position to "spot" the locus of the interference and consequently to handle his employees more intelligently. This was the lesson which had been learned from the interviewing program. Management believed that more adequate personnel work could be done if people whose daily duties consisted largely of dealing with human situations were trained to take account of the many factors which went into the determination of employee dissatisfaction and particularly to understand those complaints which were more symptoms of the complainant's situation than accurate statements of the particular interference or disability. The supervisory training program was therefore directed toward this end.

With regard to plans for future research, it was evident that as yet too little was known about those interferences which arose within the area of human interrelations at work. All the evidence pointed strongly toward the importance of appropriate social surroundings to the morale of the worker. Therefore, the investigators believed that the next phase of the research program should be directed toward a study of those everyday relations which the workers had with one another and with their supervisors.

CHAPTER XV

ATTITUDES WITHIN THE SUPERVISORY ORGANIZATION

IN FEBRUARY, 1931, the superintendent of the Operating Branch sent a questionnaire, from which their names were to be omitted, to all the supervisors in his branch asking them, along with other questions about the interviewing program, "Do you think supervisors should be interviewed on the same basis as employees?" This question was included in the questionnaire because of the numerous requests received from supervisors in the company training program that they be interviewed on the same basis as employees. About three-fourths of the supervisors replied to the question in the affirmative. Because of this favorable response, and because it was felt that such a program would provide a valuable picture of supervisory problems and attitudes, management decided to extend the interviewing program to the supervisors of the Operating Branch, commencing May 15, 1931.

Although in general this interviewing was done on the same basis as that for employees, there were some differences. First, in order to make sure that there would be no possibility of misusing the information obtained, it was decided to have the interviewing done by two men outside of the Western Electric Company organization.[1] Moreover, in fairness to those supervisors who discussed a great variety of problems involving both personal and company matters, it was decided to have the original data kept by the Industrial Research Department of the Harvard Business School, of which the two interviewers were members. From this body of data, the interviewers were asked only to prepare reports showing the major kinds of satisfaction and dissatisfaction and to indicate, in their opinion, what the sources of dissatisfaction might be, without in any way revealing the identity of the individual supervisors.

Secondly, there was a slight difference in the method of arranging for interviews with supervisors. All the supervisors in the Operating Branch were notified by letter from their superintendent of the decision to extend the interviewing program to them. In each letter a card requesting an appointment for an interview was enclosed, which each supervisor who wished to participate in the study could use. In response

[1] O. S. Lovekin and F. J. Roethlisberger, of the Graduate School of Business Administration, Harvard University.

to this letter there were approximately five hundred requests for an interview. Each interviewer was assigned a room in a location removed from the general offices, and appointments were made in advance to avoid waiting time. Two interviews were scheduled in the morning and two in the afternoon. At the specified time the supervisor came to the office of the interviewer, who introduced himself and explained the program to the supervisor.

Thirdly, the interviewing situation which confronted the supervisors was somewhat different from that which had originally confronted the employees. All the supervisors had heard of "interviewing" for a year or more. Their employees had been interviewed, and the topic had been discussed many times in supervisors' conferences. Although they never had been formally interviewed themselves, they were acquainted with the essential features of the procedure.

Fourthly, the chief way in which the interviewing of supervisors differed from the regular interviewing program was in its objective. The interviewing program had been primarily a plan for the improvement of plant conditions and employee relations; the interviewing of supervisors was more in the nature of a research program to find out if by means of an improved technique of interviewing the interviewers could determine more precisely the meanings, and those factors entering into their determination, which the supervisors assigned to their working environment. In the plan for interviewing of supervisors, therefore, no provision was made for investigating the complaints.

This chapter will deal only with the attitudes of the supervisors toward various aspects of their working environment as these attitudes were expressed in the interviews.[1] It will be essentially descriptive. In the next chapter an interpretation of these attitudes, which will attempt to show their meaning and function, will be given.

The distribution of the supervisors interviewed was as follows:

Assistant Superintendents	6
General Foremen	5
Foremen	47
Assistant Foremen	49
Section Chiefs	166
Group Chiefs	219

Because relatively few supervisors in the upper ranks of the organization were interviewed, practically no use was made of interviews ob-

---

[1] "Attitude" is being used here in a very general sense to include the beliefs about and the feelings of expectancy toward, certain objects, events, and practices.

tained from those above the foreman level, except to observe that the attitudes expressed at these higher levels were not inconsistent with the general picture. The conceptions which the lower ranking supervisors had of these higher executive positions will be considered.

The beliefs and attitudes of supervisors as expressed in the interviews will be described under five headings:[1]

(1) Attitudes toward visible authority.
(2) Attitudes toward invisible authority — the policies and practices of the company.
(3) The supervisor's conception of his job; attitudes toward subordinates.
(4) Attitudes toward personal advancement and progress in the company.
(5) Attitudes toward the interview.

Attitudes toward Visible Authority

Supervisory attitudes toward authority can be discussed more concretely by considering what attitudes were expressed by supervisors from each rank in the supervisory organization toward each position superordinate to them. Inasmuch as the discussion of every one of these relations would involve considerable repetition (since the interviewers were not able to discern significant differences, for example, between the attitude of group chiefs toward foremen and the attitude of section chiefs toward foremen), these relations will be discussed under four headings, where significant differences could be noted:

(a) The attitude of group chiefs toward section chiefs.
(b) The attitude of group chiefs and section chiefs toward assistant foremen and foremen.
(c) The attitude of assistant foremen toward foremen.
(d) Varying attitudes toward higher levels of supervision.

[1] Before reading the following description, the reader should be warned against drawing any hasty conclusions about the supervisory force at the Western Electric Company until he has read Chapter XVI, in which the attitudes described will be interpreted. The authors realize that among the possible readers of this book there may be some industrialists who are unfamiliar with the data and methods of social science and also some social scientists who are unfamiliar with industrial situations. There is always the danger that interview material, when summarized, may convey a false total impression of the human situation to those readers unacquainted with the handling and interpreting of such material or unacquainted with the contemporary industrial scene. Such readers may tend to take the statements made in the interview at their face value and to make value judgments in light of their own personal experiences. As a result, a completely erroneous picture of the company and its supervisory and working force may be obtained.

In this and the following chapter, it will be well for the reader to keep in mind that (1) the purpose of interviewing supervisors was not to make a personnel inventory but to try to understand better the meaning of their complaints, (2) the interviewers did not see these men actually at their work and therefore were not in a position to make any

The Attitude of Group Chiefs toward Section Chiefs

Personal criticisms made by group chiefs of their superiors were usually directed toward foremen or assistant foremen. A group chief never talked of the section chief as his "boss." The foreman, or the "Old Man" as he was frequently called, for most of them was the "boss." Any accusation made about a section chief by a group chief usually had a reference to the foreman, such as "he [the section chief] could do anything he wanted to because he was in strong with the boss [the foreman]."

Often it was difficult to understand the group chief-section chief relation apart from the other interrelations in the department. Not infrequently it was found that the personal relations existing between group chiefs and section chiefs in the same department reflected the relation between the foreman and his assistant. In certain departments where the foreman and the assistant foreman did not work in harmony with each other, the junior supervisors in the department were split into two camps; one faction sided with the assistant foreman, and the other sided with the foreman. In such a situation there was a tendency for the group chiefs to ally themselves with the assistant foreman and for the section chiefs to ally themselves with the foreman, as shown in Figure 29A. In departments where there were very strong bonds of solidarity between the foreman and assistant foreman, there was a tendency for the junior supervisors to be allied in opposition to both the foreman and the assistant foreman, as shown in Figure 29B.

The Attitude of Group Chiefs and Section Chiefs toward Assistant Foremen and Foremen

The foreman of the department and his immediate assistant were usually regarded as the "bosses." Whenever a first-line supervisor criticized methods of supervision, and this was not often, his remarks were generally directed toward men in these positions. Criticisms of a boss could be put into three categories:

(1) There was the boss who was accused of being a "slave driver" or "bully." This accusation was generally applied to a supervisor who "bawled out" his subordinates without a hearing and, in many cases, before other

---

valid judgment about their abilities, (3) the very nature of the research as conducted tended to bring to light chiefly the complaints of supervisors and to leave unmentioned those attributes of supervisors which in the opinion of management made the supervisory staff at Hawthorne outstanding in character and ability.

employees, — a man who was arbitrary in his instructions and promiscuous in his reprimands.

(2) There was the boss accused of being ignorant, unprogressive, or un-co-operative. This accusation was generally made of an "old-timer" who was set in his ways and refused to change, — a supervisor whose attitude was, "What was good enough 20 years ago is good enough now."

(3) There was the boss accused of being a "watchdog," unfair, and secretive. This accusation was generally applied to a supervisor who played politics, who had favorites among his workmen, who was likely to distrust his subordinates, and who was always on the lookout for infractions of the

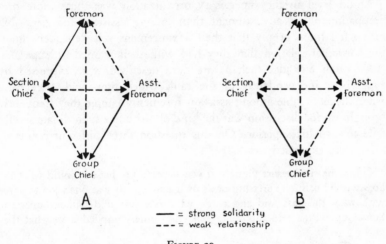

FIGURE 29

TWO COMMON CONFIGURATIONS OF SUPERVISORY RELATIONSHIPS

rules, — a man who was meticulous in his demands and who did not pass on to his subordinates information sent to the department by his superiors or by other organizations.

Two rather common statements made about foremen were: "There was one man who had it in for me" and "He was like a father to me." Although comments such as these were made by supervisors in all ranks, the greatest number were made by assistant foremen and section chiefs. A rather typical expression was: "I am going along all right now, but there was one guy who had it in for me once. Now that I have gotten away from him, things are O.K." Not infrequently this sort of comment continued: "It is a funny thing, you know; you might say he was the fellow who got me started in the first place." Statements of affection and of particular loyalty to one foreman, either now or at some previous time, were also fairly common.

For the section chief, the step to assistant foreman was considered much more difficult than his promotion from group chief to section chief. As one section chief expressed it: "The thing that bothers me is how one makes the step from section chief to assistant foreman. A section chief is similar to being a noncommissioned officer in the army. An assistant foreman is like a commissioned officer. And you know how hard it is to go from one step to the other in the army."

The Attitude of Assistant Foremen toward Foremen

At no level in the supervisory organization was there more preoccupation about advancement than among assistant foremen. No group felt more keenly that their advancement was dependent upon the particular relation that they had with their immediate superiors.

Although attitudes such as are here described were expressed by supervisors independently of the rank which they held, they were especially noticeable among assistant foremen. A topic they frequently brought up for discussion was the kind of attitude a subordinate should take toward his superior. On this question three different points of view were expressed:

(1) Some supervisors thought it was necessary to have in mind what the boss wished before expressing one's own opinion. It was one's job to agree with what the boss said and to do what one was told without question. Some supervisors said this quite explicitly; others implied it in what they said.

(2) There were some supervisors to whom being a "yes-man" was objectionable; nevertheless this, they claimed, was the attitude the boss demanded of them and it therefore led to the best results. These supervisors might disagree with the judgments and instructions of their superiors, but they thought it unwise openly to express disagreement. Although they might question the orders that the boss gave, nevertheless they did what the boss said. Their attitude was, "If things go wrong, it's the boss's funeral and not mine."

(3) Some supervisors strenuously objected to "yessing" their superiors. These supervisors expressed themselves somewhat as follows: "Those birds [the yes-men] get along all right around here, but I'll be damned if I kowtow to my boss. I tell him what I think whether or not he likes it or wants it. I suppose that makes me unpopular, but at least I am not a hypocrite."

There were two rather interesting assumptions in these attitudes. In the first place, all the supervisors who brought up this problem spoke as if the need to agree with the boss and to do without question what they were told was an attitude forced upon them by their superiors. If they hoped to get along in the company, this was what was expected of them. In the second place, no supervisor explicitly stated that the "yes" attitude was the one he demanded of his subordinates, although in some cases this was implied indirectly in what he said.

Varying Attitudes toward Higher Levels of Supervision

The terms "big boss" or "big shot" were generally applied by a supervisor to a person at least four or five ranks higher than he. For a group chief the "big boss" might be anyone from a general foreman up. In most cases he was a man with whom the supervisor had little personal contact. He knew he existed and had an office somewhere in the plant from which rather important orders or instructions were issued. Few personal criticisms were expressed about the "big bosses." The attitude of a first-line supervisor toward such men was generally one of curiosity as to how they had achieved their success. Some of the younger supervisors expressed grave doubts as to the alleged merits by means of which certain "big shots" had risen to their positions. There was a tendency on the part of junior supervisors to fabricate myths, little substantiated in fact, about some of the higher executives. These myths related the spectacular methods used or the "accidental strokes of good fortune" which had entered into the rise to prominence of some person. Many of the old-timers spoke with pride of some men who were now "big shots" but who in the old days had been their immediate supervisors or perhaps had worked alongside them at the bench.

For the assistant foremen and foremen, the superintendent of the branch was the important figure. Just as authority in the department was localized in the office of the foreman and his immediate assistant, so authority in the branch was localized in the superintendent and his assistants. Whenever the men mentioned the branch conferences, at which the superintendent spoke, it was always with approval. They evidently valued the chance of seeing the whole branch organization together and of hearing their superintendent.

Many supervisors when severely criticizing a particular superior would frequently end their statements by saying, "This is no reflection on the company. The company is O.K." Or, "The policies of the company are fine, but some of the supervisors who are responsible for carrying them out are poor representatives of the company." Many group chiefs who spoke bitterly of the foremen commented favorably about the "big bosses," who, they said, acted "like gentlemen." In some instances, but very rarely, the "big shots" were spoken of unfavorably in contrast to more immediate bosses.

ATTITUDES TOWARD INVISIBLE AUTHORITY — THE POLICIES AND PRACTICES OF THE COMPANY

Criticisms directed against the policies and practices of the company involved chiefly the topics of shorter hours, payment, layoffs, advancement, and demotion. It should be remembered that during the period in which the supervisors were being interviewed the employees were being subjected to stresses and strains of an unusual order. For the first time the depression was beginning to be felt, and there was considerable activity on the part of the company in the direction of retrenchment and curtailment of operations in line with the rapidly falling volume of business.

It might be thought that during such a critical period it would be difficult to obtain a representative picture of the supervisor's attitudes. On the other hand, it could be argued that those sentiments which tend to lie dormant and hence might be overlooked in a period of normalcy become more clear and distinct in a period of crisis. Those who have studied the social life of primitive communities have said that the tribal structure and organization are more clearly revealed during moments of great social activity, on the occasion of some important ceremonial or ritual, than during more quiescent periods. Be that as it may, the evidence from the interviewing of supervisors seemed to indicate that during this period of upheaval the basic sentiments of the supervisors, instead of being distorted, were being more vividly expressed.

The policies [1] and practices of the company about which the supervisors spoke will be considered under six headings:

    (a) The system of promotion and demotion.
    (b) The system of retrenchment.
    (c) The system of remuneration.
    (d) The system of supervision.
    (e) The system of industrial relations activities.
    (f) Plant conditions.

[1] It should be remembered that many of the matters to be discussed under these headings may or may not, strictly speaking, be company policy. In this section we shall be discussing the "rules of the game" as the supervisors conceived them to be and which, in some way not clearly specified, they felt were sanctioned by the company. As we have mentioned before, however, it was not uncommon for a supervisor to absolve the company from blame and to accuse a particular representative of the company of not living up to the "letter of the law."

The System of Promotion and Demotion

Discussions of the company's system of promotion usually dealt with the varying degrees in which different factors should be considered important in determining advancement. The factors mentioned most frequently were (1) personality, (2) education, (3) length of service, (4) ability, (5) personal friendship, (6) loyalty.

(1) According to some supervisors, "personality" or "personal salesmanship" was necessary in order to get anywhere in the company. To succeed, one had to "sell himself" to his subordinates, to his superiors, and to management. Some supervisors told of the various methods they used to accomplish this end. In general, these methods consisted in trying to draw attention to themselves by identifying themselves in a conspicuous way with whatever they thought management or their superior was emphasizing at the moment, whether this was a matter of putting over a thrift or safety campaign, signing up for a course in psychology at the Hawthorne Club, or being a "leader among men." Another group of men repudiated this personal salesmanship as being hypocritical. According to them, too high a value was placed on personality in determining advancement, to the detriment of other qualities which were more important, such as loyalty and "doing a good job."

(2) Lack of education was often cited as a reason for not having progressed. Some of the lower ranking supervisors spoke of their limitation in this respect quite bitterly, feeling that the company, or certain of its representatives, was placing too much emphasis on education and college training. On the other hand, others who had little formal education felt that they had been able to advance without it, getting what education they needed as they went along. If they mentioned the topic, they were likely to remark that complaints about lack of education are merely alibis and that in the long run men always find their own level. Younger men with more schooling than their seniors were likely to deplore the ignorance among many men in the higher ranks of supervision.

(3) Discussions about too much or too little emphasis on education were generally coupled with statements about too little or too much emphasis on length of service. Instances in which it looked as if a supervisor had been advanced largely because of his education were cited as violations of the principle of seniority.

(4) Ability was sometimes opposed to length of service in discussions of progress in the company. Particularly among the junior

supervisors there was a feeling that ability was not being sufficiently rewarded and that too much emphasis was being placed on length of service. This question of ability was practically never brought up by anyone other than a young man who had a relatively short service record.

(5) Some supervisors who were dissatisfied with the progress they had made in the company said that personal friendships with superiors counted too much. In their opinion the importance attached to personal friendships worked against ability, education, experience, or knowledge. A very popular form of expressing this sentiment was, "It is not what you know but whom you know around here that counts."

(6) Many supervisors who were dissatisfied with their progress in the company thought that loyalty to the company was not sufficiently recognized. They expressed themselves in the following way: They would argue that they had done everything that had been expected of them; they had always obeyed all the rules, and in every way they had attempted to do everything that had been asked of them; they had always been faithful to company policy and had tried to conduct themselves accordingly; yet, in this or that department, they could point to men who were selfish, dishonest, egotistical, unfair, etc., who had been advanced over their heads. They were perplexed by the injustice of things. Those who had qualities and attributes of which the company ought to disapprove were being rewarded, and they, on the other hand, who had done everything according to company policy, had been left at a standstill.

A variation of this attitude was expressed this way: Some supervisor had finally come to the conclusion that justice did not prevail in the company. He claimed that should he use rather questionable tactics, he too could progress, but of course his conscience would not allow him to do such things. The gist of his remarks was to the effect that he would rather be honest and remain a group chief than be dishonest and become a foreman.

The interesting thing about these two attitudes was the unexpressed assumption that a supervisor should be rewarded merely because of his implicit obedience to the written rules of the company. The supervisor in question assumed that he was doing everything that the company wanted merely by not doing anything that the company explicitly prohibited.

In general, whereas most supervisors when discussing advancement would try to talk of it in terms of company policy and not as a personal matter, the topic of demotion, on the other hand, was usually discussed in a personal way and was brought up only by men who had actually been demoted. During the period when the supervisors were being interviewed, some section chiefs had been demoted to group chiefs and some group chiefs had been demoted to benchwork.[1] Dissatisfaction among the demoted section chiefs was never so great as it was among the demoted group chiefs. Many group chiefs, however, accepted their demotion with a certain amount of resignation. They were glad to have their jobs. Those who were dissatisfied never expressed their dissatisfaction against the company but always against a particular superior who, they claimed, had demoted them when they thought there were others in the department who should have been demoted first.

The System of Retrenchment

During the period when the supervisors were being interviewed, all questions relating to the way in which the company was meeting the depression loomed very large as topics of discussion. Two topics were particularly stressed: (1) shorter hours and (2) layoffs. The lower their rank, the more frequently did supervisors mention these topics.

(1) Before listing the kinds of criticisms made, it might be well to review the situation with regard to hours of work in the early summer of 1931, when most of these complaints were voiced. At that time, most of the workers in the Operating Branch were still on a 5-day, 40-hour week. All group chiefs and section chiefs working in shop departments were also on a 5-day, 40-hour week. Some section chiefs in the Operating Branch, because of the nature of their work, were on a 4½-day week. Everyone from assistant foremen up in the Operating Branch was on a 5½-day, 48-hour week, that is, full time.[2]

There was very little criticism of the principle of shorter hours as such. All criticisms were directed against what they felt was the unfair way in which the cut was being applied, that is, the unfair discriminations that were being made between ranks, or between departments, or between branches. Some section chiefs in the Operating Branch who were on a 4½-day week were disturbed because section chiefs in other branches took only a half-day cut, while they had to take a full-

---

[1] It should be remembered that these demotions did not arise as disciplinary measures "for cause." They were the result of the severe decline in business activity, which necessitated a shrinkage in the supervisory organization.

[2] As the depression continued, this disparity of working time between workers on the bench and the supervisory force became much less.

day cut. Group chiefs and section chiefs in shop departments could not understand why they were asked to take a 16 per cent cut in hours when they, of all supervisors, could least afford it. They wished to know, "Where the hell does this company get this two-class system anyway?" Group chiefs argued against the "two-class system" on the ground that they were put on the same level as the operators. Some felt that their social prestige had been injured. Friends and neighbors to whom they had proudly boasted of being supervisors at the Western Electric Company would no longer believe them and taunted them by saying, "Oh, I thought you were a supervisor, but I see your hours were cut like the operators'."

No supervisor complained about shortening hours of work as a means of curtailing expenses. There was no question that many group chiefs and section chiefs were being financially affected by the cut. Many men whose incomes had been reduced had not been able to effect a corresponding reduction in their own "fixed charges." Homes had been bought on which first and sometimes second mortgages still had to be paid. Taxes, street assessments, and other levies for improvements had to be met. As a result, many supervisors' savings were being depleted in an attempt to keep up their standard of living. Many of them had dependent parents or married sons and daughters toward whose support they had to contribute. There was considerable worry about what might happen if their earning capacity did not soon improve. Nevertheless, most of them accepted this load with a certain amount of resignation. Only in a very few cases were any accusations made against the capitalistic economy or against a political government which allowed such a condition to arise. In no case was the company held responsible for the situation. The chief complaint against shorter hours was that the cut applied unfairly in one case as compared with another, and that they as supervisors of a particular department, branch, or rank were being discriminated against.

(2) Although in the summer of 1931 no supervisors were being laid off, most of them having had at least six years' service, the topic of layoffs was frequently discussed with regard to the laying off of employees. Most of the supervisors agreed that as long as ample consideration was being given to length of service, layoffs were being made on a fair basis. However, there were a few exceptions.

Among some of the senior executives, who were more directly concerned with laying off employees, there was considerable discussion with regard to the difficulty of selection, particularly at this stage, when all the "lemons" had long since been let go and only good men remained.

Many of these supervisors praised the company's policy of holding long-service employees but bewailed the loss of many bright young people who would be difficult to replace.

Some group chiefs and section chiefs who did not have much service with the company felt that old-timers among the employees were being unduly favored. Among the long-service supervisors, however, there was only one situation in which the importance of length of service was ever questioned, and that was with regard to married women. Many supervisors felt very strongly that married women should be discharged before single girls in spite of the fact that the former might have longer service records. "Married women ought not to be working in times like these," was a frequent comment. For most supervisors there seemed to be no doubt that every single girl needed her job more than any married woman. If pressed into a discussion, a man usually would admit that each case had to be decided on its own merits, and that some single girls were only working for "pin money," whereas some married women needed every cent they could get. But the general idea seemed to be that if a single girl lost her job she would be thrown "onto the street," and that if a married woman worked she was maintaining too high a standard of living. Many did not like to see their fellow supervisors whose wives were working enjoy a higher standard of living than they were capable of maintaining. In several instances supervisors who strongly advocated giving priority or preference to single women had a daughter working in the company.

The System of Remuneration

Shorter hours of work because of the depression had resulted in lower and fluctuating earnings for many supervisors both on and off group piecework. A considerable portion of the discussion about wages, therefore, was related to the reduction in earnings resulting from the introduction of shorter working hours. In general, unfavorable comments about the reduction of earnings were more numerous in the lower ranks, and the lower ranks were more preoccupied with the general topic of remuneration.

Most of the supervisors who commented about having had their earnings reduced spoke of the matter in a personal way. They usually told the interviewer how they were managing to make "both ends meet" now that they had less income than that to which they had been accustomed. Some were having difficulties; others were not. But no matter in which way they spoke of their personal financial situation, supervisors seemed to agree that the wage level of the company was high and compared favorably with that of other companies in the vicinity. Of course, there were a few supervisors who thought that certain rates on certain jobs in certain departments were too low, but such criticisms were by far in the minority. Most criticisms about the payment policy of the company were of the following kinds:

(1) Among some group chiefs and section chiefs in group piecework departments there seemed to be a feeling that although wages had not been actually cut, the same result had been achieved by keeping only the long service, high-rated men, and thus reducing the "group percentage." [1] When this feeling found specific voice, it was in a comment such as, "Even if we got raises, they wouldn't mean anything. It's taking money out of one pocket and putting it in the other."

(2) Some group chiefs and section chiefs in straight piecework departments who earned less than many of the operators in their departments commented upon this as unfair and unjust. They were being asked to take a position of greater responsibility and yet they were not being paid as much as the operators they were supervising.[2]

(3) Some assistant foremen of group piecework departments who were earning less money than some of the group chiefs or section chiefs in the same department expressed the same grievance as in (2) above.

(4) Among those group chiefs and section chiefs in a few group piecework departments where a change in the design of the product or method of manufacture had been introduced and new piece rates had been established which resulted in a lowering of the "group percentage," there were feelings of injury and resentment.

(5) Some group chiefs and section chiefs of group piecework departments who participated in the piecework earnings commented quite frequently about fluctuating earnings. As one section chief expressed it: "I never know how much I'm going to take home at the end of the week. If anyone asks me how much I'm making, I have to say, 'Oh, between $30 and $40.' I never really know. I think it would be much better if supervisors were on a straight salary. Then they would always know at least how much they made." [3]

It is interesting to note that the majority of these complaints were from first-level and second-level supervisors. In all the complaints there was a faint trace of resentment against being treated like the

---

[1] The first two lines of supervision — group chiefs and section chiefs — in some group piecework departments shared in the "percentage" (see p. 14). Their earnings therefore fluctuated with the output of the operators. However, an allowance had been made in the piece rates for supervision so that in no sense were these supervisors "carried" by the workers.

[2] In straight piecework departments, the supervisors were paid on a daywork rate, which meant that their earnings did not fluctuate with the output of the operators.

[3] Because of these and similar expressions, the company decided later to remove all

operators. This attitude was expressed by a section chief as follows: "They say around here that the group chiefs and section chiefs are the backbone of the supervisory organization. But how can management expect that they will be treated with respect by the operators? Whatever authority they gain by their title they lose when they are treated in the same manner as the operators."

The System of Supervision

In contrast to the number of unfavorable comments about particular supervisors were the relatively few unfavorable comments about supervision in general. Supervisors of all ranks agreed that supervision had improved greatly since earlier days when they had first started work. The consensus of opinion seemed to be that a new type of leadership had arrived. Supervisors of today, they claimed, were as different from those of former years as "day is from night." They were no longer so "hard-boiled" as they had been in the old days. As one poetical supervisor described the difference, "Them are the days of yore, we ain't got them days no more." However, there were a few who were not so favorable in their attitude toward the change that had taken place. A few foremen, in particular, thought that supervision had "gone soft." They liked to talk of the old days when you did not have "to handle people with kid gloves."

The longer-service men viewed one change in the methods of supervision with disfavor: "There's too much paper work and red tape nowadays" was a frequent remark made all through the line, from group chief to foreman. Some of the foremen were particularly preoccupied with the mass of reports and records which they had to keep and memoranda which they had to write. They could not see how such things could be of any use; they wanted to see and touch the machines and talk directly to the men.

The System of Industrial Relations Activities

(1) Interviewing employees

About 85 per cent of the supervisors who commented on this topic talked favorably about interviewing employees. Frequently they mentioned the fact that it was "good for a man to have a way of getting things off his chest." Occasionally such a favorable comment would be qualified by a statement, "But you know a lot of that stuff that they

---

group chiefs and section chiefs from piecework groups and pay them on a straight day-work basis.

got in the interviews must have come from the chronic kickers. Some of these guys will kick no matter what you do for them. I don't see that what they say means very much."

Unfavorable comments were of various types, such as: (a) interviewing undermined the supervisors' authority (expressed largely by long-service supervisors); (b) interviewing was bad for morale because it made people think about how many complaints they had (expressed largely by higher-ranking supervisors); (c) nothing had been done by the company about the things of which the employees had complained anyhow (expressed solely by group chiefs and section chiefs); (d) interviewing was a waste of money, a horrible example of useless overhead, and "the whole idea was just a lot of boloney."

(2) Supervisors' conferences

About 75 per cent of the supervisors who commented about the supervisors' conferences based on the interviewing program spoke favorably of them. A number felt that they had profited from the discussions. Others commented on the fact that the conferences had allowed them to become acquainted with supervisors from other departments.

Criticisms directed against supervisors' conferences were: (a) they were not definite enough, that is, they did not tell the supervisors just what they should do, and no conclusions were ever reached; (b) the conference leaders did not know enough, that is, they were not sufficiently well acquainted with shop practices to instruct the supervisors (expressed mostly by group chiefs and section chiefs); (c) they had no effect on anyone anyhow, that is, "these guys talk one way in conferences and act just the opposite on the floor" (expressed by some foremen).

(3) Thrift and benefit plans

On the whole, the supervisors were highly in favor of the policies of the company with regard to the various thrift and benefit plans. Most supervisors could not speak highly enough of them. No supervisor objected to what might have been regarded as a paternalistic attitude on the part of the company. Unfavorable comments mostly centered around the decline in the market price of the A. T. & T. stock purchased under a pay roll deduction plan.[1]

---

[1] An employee was eligible to subscribe to American Telephone and Telegraph Company stock if he had worked for the company six months. The subscription price was considerably below the market price of the stock. An employee who wished to purchase stock could choose between two methods of subscribing for it. Under one plan he could subscribe for one share for each $400 or fraction of it in his annual rate of pay,

Because of the usual discussions in textbooks on corporation finance of the benefits of employee stock ownership, the interviewers were watching to see whether the supervisors expressed any unusual amount of concern about the profits of the company. They were impressed by the fact that opinions on the subject never came out voluntarily, although they may perhaps have been inferred. When a supervisor was questioned specifically on this point, he always affirmed that because he was a stockholder he took a greater interest in seeing that work was done efficiently and therefore with profit to the company, but the interviewers felt that this was merely said because it was the obvious thing to say in reply to the question. Favorable comments were almost entirely to the effect that the stock purchase plan helped men save by taking money out of their pay before they got a chance to spend it, that A. T. & T. was safe in contrast to other investments, and that the difference between the subscription price and the market price was "easy money."

(4) Pensions

This topic was brought up mostly by older men. Unfavorable comments were not directed at the principle of pensions but were criticisms of the amount to be paid at the time of retirement.[1] Foremen on the whole were satisfied with the pension provisions; long-service men in the lower ranks were more likely to be dissatisfied. They felt that old-timers who had served just as long and faithfully as others whose ability had taken them farther were to be retired on relatively penurious amounts. They felt that a pension should be a reward for faithfulness in years of service rather than for ability and that payments should be more nearly equal for all.

---

and make weekly payments at the rate of $1.00 a share, or $4.00 per month. Under the other plan he could subscribe to one share for each $300 or fraction of it in his annual rate of pay, and make weekly payments at the rate of $.75, or $3.00 per month. Under both plans, therefore, the subscription price was spread over several years. The only difference between these two plans was that under the first an employee with a given salary could purchase fewer shares than under the second plan, but he could acquire the shares sooner under the first plan. For the convenience of those participating in the stock purchase plan a pay roll deduction system was established whereby, with the employee's authorization, his weekly payments on the stock to which he had subscribed were deducted from his weekly pay. Any employee could cancel his subscription at any time and receive what he had paid in, plus interest. This plan was discontinued during the depression.

[1] Under the company pension plan, which is noncontributory, the annual pension is computed on the basis of one per cent of the employee's average annual pay during the ten years preceding retirement (or, at the discretion of the Benefit Fund Committee, of the average annual pay during the ten consecutive years of service during which the retired employee was paid the highest rate of wages) multiplied by the number of years of credited service.

(5) *Personnel activities*

Favorable and unfavorable comments on this topic were approximately equal in number. However, the number of favorable comments was greater in the higher ranks; unfavorable comments came largely from the lower ranks. The latter were mostly charges that the personnel department was "in cahoots" with the foremen, and that it always sided with them and against the men. This condition existed, it was sometimes said, because of the fact that personnel department workers did not regard their jobs as permanent. Since they never knew when they might be shifted back under some foreman, they endeavored to keep in the good graces of all of them. Some men complained about the fact that because there was a personnel department in each branch, and each personnel department was concerned only with its own people, it was almost impossible to get a transfer from one branch to another.

Plant Conditions

Probably one of the most striking differences between employee interviews and supervisory interviews was that employees were far more concerned with plant conditions than were supervisors. Supervisors above the rank of assistant foreman hardly mentioned this topic at all, except to talk about general policies of safety and health for employees at the bench. Among group chiefs and section chiefs there were some complaints in this area, although not nearly so many as there were among the workers. Inasmuch as employees and these first two levels of supervision shared the same general physical environment, this difference is interesting. The comments were as follows:

(1) Some first-line supervisors complained because they were not furnished a towel a week by the company. Junior supervisors in office departments received such service. "It wasn't fair" was a typical reaction.

(2) Some first-line supervisors complained because they had to share their lockers with fellow supervisors. Such complaints were generally followed with the remark, "In the office the supervisor has an individual locker."

(3) Some complained about the difficulty they had in getting operators to use safety devices. Many of them shared the operators' feelings about such "gadgets." They were just a source of nuisance and irritation to the worker.

(4) Some felt that too much emphasis was put by the foreman on "housecleaning." Many of them thought that it was just done to make a good impression on the "big shots" when they "paraded" through the shop.

(5) Some of them complained that the washrooms and drinking fountains were insanitary.

The Supervisor's Conception of His Job; Attitudes toward Subordinates

In this section we shall consider the different conceptions supervisors had of their duties. How and to what extent did they differentiate their functions, and what relative degrees of importance did they attach to them? Did they talk as if their duties were connected primarily with maintaining low costs? Were they primarily concerned with maintaining authority and discipline? Were they concerned with the efficiency of the employees at the bench, or were they more concerned with keeping their subordinates happy and contented? Just as in the first two sections of this chapter we investigated some of the subordinate-superior types of attitude, so in this section we shall look at some of the superior-subordinate types of attitude.[1]

In the course of the interview it was frequently possible, without disrupting the continuity of the discussion, to ask the supervisor what he considered his chief job to be. To this question the lower-ranking supervisors gave innumerable answers. But from the higher-ranking supervisors this question invariably brought forth one type of response. Their chief problem, they said, was connected with matters of personnel administration, of handling subordinates, of handling people.

The Attitude of Group Chiefs and Section Chiefs

In the opinion of most group chiefs and section chiefs, their main job was to keep certain records, to see that the workers were supplied with materials, to attend to the machines when they were out of order, and to know more than the operators about the job being performed. These men displayed little interest in costs of production. For most of them budgets were requirements of management. Of course, there were a few who had an interest in, if not an accurate knowledge of, the costs of production in their department, and some of them even complained that they never saw the budgets and that they never knew how their department stood. But such statements were not common among supervisors of these ranks. Most of them felt that their chief job was to help the workers in their group to earn as much money as possible by keeping them supplied with piece parts and seeing that their machines were in good working condition. In other words, their chief function was to facilitate the task of technical production. By so doing they achieved their own economic purposes as well as those of their

---

[1] It should be remembered that this dichotomy is being made only for convenience in presentation. In fact, these attitudes are inextricably intertwined.

subordinates. Otherwise, their function seemed to be a protective one, that is, to resist any changes in technical production which might affect themselves or the operators.

This protective attitude was brought out in connection with the "group percentage."[1] It might be thought that inasmuch as group chiefs and section chiefs in many departments shared in this "percentage" they would have been extremely concerned with the efficiency of the employees. But this did not seem to follow. Although they were concerned with the "group percentage," it was never from the viewpoint of the efficiency of particular operators. No criticisms were ever made of particular operators who by limiting output decreased the "percentage." Criticisms were always directed toward outside interferences, such as cost reduction studies,[2] an influx of new, inexperienced operators, or an influx of old-timers with high hourly rates, which might serve to lower their "percentage."

For some group chiefs and section chiefs there was a problem of whether one should be a company man or an employees' man; that is, whether one should look at things from the viewpoint of the company or from the viewpoint of the employees. But the supervisors who mentioned this were far in the minority. Whatever conflict of loyalties their jobs entailed was for most of them far below the level of verbal discrimination.

In discussing the problem of handling people, most supervisors advocated a humane policy. The consensus of opinion was that the day of the "bully" and the "slave-driver" had gone, and the day of the "gentleman" and "leader" had arrived. It was rather difficult, however, for most of the supervisors to articulate this new conception of leadership. For some of them, it meant "to get around and say a cheery word"; for others it meant "to treat the employees as you would wish to be treated"; and for still others it meant "to treat them as human beings," "to treat them all alike," "to show no favoritism," "to give them a square deal," "to allow them to talk to you," "to interview them occasionally," "to listen to their grievances," "to give them service," "to give them a fair hearing," "to allow them to express their own ideas," "to sell yourself to them," "to encourage them," and "to keep them satisfied."

There were, however, a few minor variations from this general thesis. According to some supervisors, there were always a few persons whom

[1] See p. 14.
[2] Changes in the design of the product or the method of manufacture which might result in a change in the piece rates.

you could not "handle with kid gloves." If you did, they would "walk over you." To such persons you had to talk "straight from the shoulder," occasionally "bawling them out" and swearing at them. These exceptions were brought up generally in connection with the old-timer and the chronic kicker. Each of these had to be handled in quite a different fashion from the ordinary operator. In most cases, it was better to handle the old-timer by leaving him alone. To the chronic kicker, however, you had to "lay down the law," or occasionally you had to "bawl him out."

The problem of handling men in comparison with women was also discussed. Although there was a difference of opinion with regard to which sex was easier to supervise, most of the supervisors agreed that women had to be handled quite differently from men. What was generally meant by this statement was that you could not talk to women in the same fashion as you could talk to men. You had to approach a woman and give her orders more indirectly. Moreover, you had to be more careful about the language in which you couched your instructions.

In all discussions of the treatment of subordinates, first-line and second-line supervisors were interested not so much in raising questions as in disposing of them. They had very little curiosity as to why people felt or acted in certain ways and what the significance of their feelings or behavior might be. One supervisor expressed this attitude very well when he said: "They told me at some conference that one of the workers hated his foreman because his father used to kick him about when he was a child, or some such idea. Well, even if it is true, what of it? I've got to do something with such birds."

That these supervisors were expressing fundamental sentiments and not discussing principles of supervision at a logical level was attested to by a number of incidents. One of the most amusing occurred in connection with the naivety of one of the interviewers himself. In the beginning, failing to realize the nature of the phenomenon he was observing, he asked several supervisors whether there was not an inconsistency between treating all employees alike and treating men differently from women. Or on other occasions he asked, "How do you treat human beings?" or, "How would you like to be treated?" or, "What constitutes a square deal?" These questions had such a devastating effect in reducing the interviewee to stony silence that they were quickly discontinued.[1]

---

[1] It is important to remember that these observations have nothing to say one way or the other about whether a person was or was not a good supervisor. There is no evidence to suggest any correlation between capacity to handle people effectively and capacity to articulate the means by which it is done.

The Attitude of Assistant Foremen

The assistant foremen as a group were far more concerned with their relations to their immediate superiors than they were concerned with their relations to their subordinates. For many of them the important problem was "how to handle your superiors" or "how to do what the boss wanted." Some of them spoke about the difficulty of obtaining co-operation from their subordinates and from supervisors of other departments or of other organizations. Specifically with regard to handling subordinates, however, they expressed the same sentiments as did the first-line and second-line supervisors, with one interesting exception. Whereas no group chief or section chief talked about the problem of restriction of output among employees, this problem was mentioned by several assistant foremen, who told of the methods they used to overcome it.

The Attitude of Foremen and Higher Supervisors

In general, it can be said that whereas supervisors below the rank of foreman talked more about their relations to their superiors and less about their relations to their subordinates, supervisors of the rank of foreman and above talked more about their relations to their subordinates and hardly at all about their relations to their superiors. The further removed a supervisor was from the worker, the more interest he seemed to show in matters of personnel administration. However, a supervisor of the rank of foreman or above expressed few distinctions of attitude toward the different levels of rank below him; he tended to group all below him as subordinates and discuss them together. Unlike the group chief who differentiated chronic kickers from loyal employees, women from men, and old-timers from newcomers, a foreman never differentiated the way one handled a section chief from the way one handled a group chief, or the way one handled a group chief from the way one handled an operator at the bench.

The higher-ranking supervisors frequently mentioned the importance of good first-line supervisors, men who not only had practical knowledge of the job but who were also capable of handling the personnel problems that came up in their groups. Some foremen spoke about the problem of restriction of output. Others felt that they were so overburdened with paper work that they were unable to give as much time as they wished to personnel matters.

The Attitude of Supervisors in General

In one respect, all supervisors expressed the same sentiments. With very few exceptions, they all seemed to agree in denouncing the old-time, hard-boiled, slave-driving methods of handling subordinates. Although the capacity to articulate this point of view improved with rank, from the point of view of the sentiments expressed group chiefs could not be differentiated from assistant superintendents. The gist of all their remarks was that subordinates could not be forced into co-operation. Strategy (for some), psychology (for others), and understanding (for a few) had to be substituted for force in human relations. Satisfied and contented employees were a necessary prerequisite for effective collaboration.

The fact that the higher supervisors, in discussing their methods of handling subordinates, did not distinguish between the different ranks below them was interesting. There was very little reason to believe, for example, that the foreman treated the assistant foreman exactly as he treated the first-line supervisors, or that he treated the latter, in turn, as he treated the workers. Yet, if the statements of the higher supervisors were taken at face value, this was the situation.

This absence of expressed differentiation was particularly interesting in view of the fact that it was considered improper for a supervisor to jump a rank in the organization in the course of his work, that is, "to go over somebody's head." It was understood that a group chief should discuss his problems with his section chief before taking them to the assistant foreman. Likewise, the foreman should issue instructions to the workers only through his staff of subordinates. In practice, of course, these codes were frequently disregarded. Although "going over the head" of either a superior or subordinate was a technical violation, it was more common for a supervisor "to go around" his immediate subordinate by dealing directly with a man two or more ranks below him than it was for a supervisor "to go over the head" of his immediate superior by dealing directly with a man two or more ranks higher. Many group chiefs and section chiefs complained that they had no real authority, "because the foreman goes around us directly to the men with every little thing."

Of course, having social contacts with subordinates two or more ranks below did not necessarily mean that the supervisor in question was "going around" his subordinate. Such contacts were inevitable in a situation where supervisors of different ranks had face-to-face relations, and it can be seen that such a situation was bound to lead to differences in personal relations among men of different ranks. A supervisor might express attitudes toward a subordinate two ranks below him that were quite different from those which he could express toward his immediate assistant. Toward the former he need never be in a position of giving direct orders, as was necessary in the case of his immediate assistant. For this reason it was not uncommon to find attitudes of the "kindly benefactor" or of friendly banter on the part of a foreman toward the workers or his junior supervisors which he did not show toward his own immediate assistant.

The problem of how much a supervisor should mix socially outside the plant with his subordinates was sometimes brought up for discussion. Some supervisors argued against the practice on the grounds that it was likely to be misunderstood and to provoke criticisms of partiality and favoritism from other subordinates. Foremen on the whole were more likely to argue in this fashion than section chiefs or group chiefs, some of whom felt that association outside the plant helped rather than hindered co-operation in the work situation. It was the impression of the interviewers that it was not uncommon to find group chiefs, section chiefs, and operators associating outside of working hours.

ATTITUDES TOWARD PERSONAL ADVANCEMENT AND PROGRESS IN THE COMPANY

In the interviews the supervisors made many statements in which they expressed their personal feelings about their own positions and progress in the company. Let us look at some of the more common attitudes.

(A) Some supervisors had no desire to improve their positions in the company, but only a wish to maintain the positions that they had achieved. Such supervisors, however, unlike the ones to be described later, had no fear of being demoted. There were several variants of this general type of supervisory situation.

(1) There was the supervisor who expressed complete satisfaction with the progress he had made in the company. The attitude of this satisfied supervisor can best be described by the remarks which one group chief made. He said: "During my 15 years of service, I have been able to buy 48 shares of stock, pay off my home, and raise and educate my children. My position is steady. Each year I get two weeks' vacation, and when I get sick or have an accident the company takes care of me and pays my expenses. Why should I kick?" The guarantee of a socially secure position, in which nothing happened to jeopardize the occupational status which he had achieved, was the chief demand which this supervisor made. As long as

that demand was fulfilled, he was satisfied. Anything which tended to alter his status was viewed with apprehension. This attitude was found in all ranks of supervisors but was particularly conspicuous among foreign-born supervisors of the lower ranks who had long service.

(2) There was the supervisor who claimed that he was not satisfied with his progress, adding, "But then, of course, nobody is." Such a man was reluctant to admit being satisfied, inasmuch as such an admission might imply stagnation and a total loss of ambition. Actually, this supervisor's attitude toward his position in the company did not differ very much from the one above. Steady work and a guaranteed income were his chief demands. There was little demand for new experiences or responsibility. This attitude was also expressed by supervisors from all ranks.

(3) There was the supervisor who seemed to show no concern about his position or progress in the company. Some of these unconcerned supervisors held only minor positions in the company and to all appearances might easily have gone higher. Yet they seemed perfectly satisfied with the positions they had. All of them had active interests (social, economic, or political) outside of the plant. Their wish for recognition and new experiences was fulfilled outside. The interview was largely taken up with lengthy accounts of their extra-work activities. These men were found in all ranks of the supervisory organization.

(4) There was the supervisor who in his youth had served an apprenticeship and learned a definite trade. Most of these supervisors were satisfied with their rank. Such men seemed to have a feeling of security that did not depend on their relation to the company alone. Their feeling had a maturity that seemed to be lacking in some other supervisors who had no particular trade, had never worked anywhere but at the Western Electric Company, and had lived all their lives in the Chicago area. As one supervisor expressed it: "The trouble with a lot of these young fellows nowadays is that all they are after is the money. They don't care what kind of job they have. It is the money they want. When I was a boy, it was quite a thing to learn a trade. You had to be in good character, and your family had to be known. It wasn't the money so much; it was the trade."

(5) There was the supervisor who had been many years in the same department and who felt that he was getting "into a rut." This man was quite satisfied with his present rank and did not want to go any higher. What he wanted was new experiences, and he would have welcomed a transfer to another department at the same level. This attitude was expressed by some foremen.

(6) There was the supervisor who was dissatisfied with his position, not so much because of a wish for public recognition which his present rank failed to satisfy but more because he felt he was not obtaining the friendly and intimate appreciation from his associates that he wished to have. His good qualities, his honesty, trustworthiness, and loyalty, were not being recognized.

(B) Some supervisors were ambitious to rise higher in the ranks of the company. However, all these men were not dissatisfied with the positions they held at the time.

(1) There was the supervisor who was satisfied with his present rank because he felt that his advancement was guaranteed. According to the "grapevine," he was "on the make." His present job was just a "grooming" for one that was higher. He was willing to bide his time; ultimately his advancement was assured. Of course, there were not many supervisors with this attitude.

(2) There was the supervisor whose hopes had been raised by having been sent to a particular department or assigned new duties for purposes of training, and who then failed either to get promoted at all or to be promoted as rapidly as he had expected to be. The attitude of this supervisor was likely to be something like this: "I used to be all steamed up over my work. They told me I was an outstanding man, put me through a training course, and then promoted me to this job I am on now. But it doesn't seem to have gotten me anywhere. Whenever I try to get a move, they say they need me here. I don't believe it pays to be too good on your job. You will get frozen to it for life."

(3) There was the earnest and conscientious supervisor who was taking every advantage of improving himself by going to night school. Many younger supervisors were taking courses in engineering, business, English, psychology, economics, or electricity. These men were satisfied with their present rank only in so far as it was not being viewed as a ceiling. Some of them were a bit disgruntled because it took so long to progress in the company. However, they still had expectations that their day would come sooner or later. They were ambitious men, eager to learn, and were taking every advantage to prepare themselves for a better position. This attitude was conspicuous among some of the younger men in all ranks of the organization.

(4) There was the supervisor who was trying to cultivate personality or personal salesmanship. In general, he belonged to the "it's not what you know but whom you know . . ." school of thought. For many such supervisors personality was a sort of magical substance which adhered to certain individuals and which accounted for their success. Personality was to a supervisor what "it" was to a movie actress, an indefinable and elusive quality which some people possessed. Toward this elusive something-or-other two attitudes were displayed: for some of them personality was something you were born with; for others it was something you could develop. Of those who held the first view and who felt that personality had not been included in their native endowment, some were resigned, while others became bitter. Those who held the second view were trying to develop personality.

(C) Some supervisors expressed dissatisfaction with their present rank as if they were extremely desirous of promotion. Actually such supervisors as these were more preoccupied with the possibility of being demoted and losing the status they had achieved than they were concerned with advancement. Their yearnings for advancement were largely in the nature of rationalizations and disguised their real situation. This attitude was expressed in a number of different ways.

(1) There was the supervisor who said he was satisfied with his position when what he meant was that he was resigned. Men of this type had come to the conclusion that their progress was definitely limited. Many of them felt that there were men in the company better qualified for advancement than they were, men with more education than they had had the opportunity of receiving, and hence in a better position for promotion. Many of these men were anxious to give their sons and daughters the education of which they had been deprived. This attitude was common among group chiefs and section chiefs who had remained in the same position for many years.

(2) There was the supervisor who felt that he had done everything that had been expected of him. He had obeyed all the rules and done everything that had been asked of him, and yet other men had been put over his head. This supervisor sometimes expressed the idea that he easily could have risen higher in the ranks had he been willing to play the game differently, but such a procedure would have gone against his own personal code of ethics.

(3) There was the supervisor who accounted for his failure to be further advanced on the ground that he had been a victim of prejudice on the part of some one supervisor in the company. Had it not been for this particular man, he would be further ahead by this time, but this man had held him down. This attitude was expressed by supervisors from all ranks.

(4) There was the supervisor who had been offered promotion to a higher rank on a job that would have involved moving from Hawthorne to another plant of the Western Electric Company at Kearny, New Jersey, and who had refused to go for personal or social reasons. Some of these supervisors were afraid that this refusal would be held against them and that their possibility of advancement was slim.

(D) There was the supervisor who had no desire to maintain his position. A man of this type frequently expressed the wish to be back at the bench where he could earn more money. This wish was expressed by only a few group chiefs and section chiefs.

To summarize, it is apparent, from examining these different attitudes, that a supervisor's satisfaction or dissatisfaction with his position did not depend upon his rank alone. There was no evidence that dissatisfaction increased the lower the rank held in the supervisory organization. Nor did satisfaction increase the higher the position. It is true that at the foreman level there were a number of satisfied and contented individuals. But then there were more dissatisfied assistant foremen in proportion to the total number interviewed than there were dissatisfied group chiefs or section chiefs.

It is also evident that a supervisor's satisfaction or dissatisfaction with his position in the company was not unrelated to factors outside the immediate working environment — to the kind of relation he had with the wider society, to the demands he was making of his work and the opportunities which were afforded for their fulfillment. Recognition through advancement was only one, and frequently not the chief, demand that he was making.

Attitudes toward the Interview

In conclusion, it might be well to comment on the attitudes of supervisors toward the interview itself. Some supervisors welcomed the interview as a chance "to blow off accumulated steam," others were neutral or came out of a sense of duty only, and still others were definitely antagonistic. Of this latter group some remained antagonistic throughout the interview, while others became more co-operative as the interview progressed. In making these judgments the interviewers were not entirely dependent on the verbal behavior of the supervisor; overt behavior helped materially in forming an opinion of a man's attitude. For example, when a supervisor arrived ten minutes late, refused to smoke a proffered cigarette only to pull out a package of the same brand a few minutes later, it seemed safe to conclude that the supervisor was not very glad to be there and would leave as soon as his idea of politeness allowed him to, even though he was effusive in his praise of interviewing in general. On the other hand, it might be concluded that a man who arrived early and stayed for a long time welcomed the opportunity of being interviewed.

There were only a few, about 5 or 10 per cent, who seemed to be worried and were glad for a chance to unburden themselves in the interview. In this group there were a number of assistant foremen, some group chiefs and section chiefs, but no representatives from the higher ranks.

There was a larger group who seemed to welcome wholeheartedly the chance to be interviewed, although this does not imply that the men had any particular grievances or preoccupations. This group did not always include men who talked freely and easily. Many rather inarticulate persons seemed genuinely glad to be interviewed.

A comment not infrequently heard went something like this: "I don't see why they wanted to interview supervisors. I think the plan is a good one for the workers because they have no one to go to with their complaints, but a supervisor has always got his foreman to go to if he has a kick." The general opinion seemed to be that the worker could not get the satisfaction from his group chief or section chief that the latter could get from his foreman, and that the worker could not go to the personnel department without antagonizing the supervisor. This comment was made by supervisors from all ranks, with a slightly higher incidence among the higher ranks.

Probably the greatest number of supervisors were neutral, expressing no strong attitude one way or another toward the interview. If asked for an opinion, they would almost always express approval of interviewing in general. This attitude was displayed by supervisors from all ranks.

There were some supervisors who said or implied that they would not have come had the program not been a company policy. They would deny that they were antagonistic or suspicious, but they could not see the point of being interviewed when they felt they had nothing to say.

And lastly, there were a few supervisors who stated or plainly inferred that they were suspicious of the motives behind the interviewing plan, that they thought the whole idea was a "lot of bunk." When the interviewer admitted ignorance of their particular job in the shop, they could see no point in talking to him and decided that he was an incompetent theorist who lacked "practical experience." Some of these antagonistic people changed their attitude in the course of the interview. Evidently some had expected it to be a sort of examination, concluding with a lecture from the interviewer on "how to be a supervisor." Some of them expressed disappointment because they had not been given any advice. They intimated that the interviewer was a funny kind of "professor"; professors were supposed to give lectures and they had come ready to take notes.

CHAPTER XVI

COMPLAINTS AND SOCIAL EQUILIBRIUM

In this chapter some of the favorable and unfavorable attitudes of supervisors, as these attitudes have been described in the previous chapter, will be interpreted. By interpretation is meant the discovery not of the origin of these attitudes but of their meaning.[1] Their meaning, or function, can be discovered by understanding, first, the sentiments which these attitudes express and, secondly, the social interaction to which the sentiments can be related.

In Chapter XIV it was concluded that a common form of induced unbalance in the worker could be regarded as a disturbance in his personal equilibrium with the socio-reality about him. The importance to the individual employee's morale of the interpersonal relations which he enjoyed at work was recognized, but these relations were considered only when they were weak or were not operating effectively. At the time, the investigators were primarily interested in the individual complainant and the particularities of his personal situation. Their attention was fixed upon his deviation from the norm rather than upon the norm itself. As a result, they failed to see some of the more general uniformities which existed among employee complaints, and they missed the intricate web of social relations which determined the employee's situation in the plant.

As the research continued, it seemed to the investigators that individual disturbances of personal equilibrium could not be understood apart from the more general social setting at work in which the employee participated, for many complaints were expressing the interpersonal relations inherent in the social organization of workers, supervisors, and higher executives within the company. From interviewing supervisors there was a great deal of evidence to support this hypothesis. Stated briefly, the hypothesis is as follows:

(1) that the attitudes of employees are regulated and controlled by a certain system of sentiments;

(2) that this system of sentiments expresses the social organization of the employees, supervisors, and higher executives within the company;

[1] For the approach taken in this chapter, the authors are particularly indebted to Radcliffe-Brown, A. R., *The Andaman Islanders*, Cambridge University Press, Cambridge, England, 1933.

(3) that every feature and event in the working environment becomes an object of this system of sentiments; and

(4) that, therefore, in order to understand an employee's satisfactions or dissatisfactions with certain features or events in his working environment, it is necessary to understand these features or events in relation to their interactions with and effects upon

    (a) his position in the social organization of the company,

    (b) the social organization to which he has grown accustomed, i.e., the system of sentiments by means of which his position is defined, differentiated, and ordered from other positions, and

    (c) the demands which he is making of his work, as determined by his temperament and past social conditioning, or by the kind of relation he has to the wider community.

Social Distinctions Expressed in Interviews

The supervisors expressed or implied a number of distinctions in terms of which they evaluated their problems. In discussions of problems connected with advancement, payment, layoff, shorter hours, how to handle people, pensions, vacations, etc., these distinctions occurred over and over again and were expressed in innumerable ways. There were distinctions with regard to differences of rank in the supervisory organization, distinctions between office and shop, distinctions with regard to length of service, and distinctions between men and women. It will be the purpose of this section to examine these distinctions with a view to a better understanding of their function.

Distinctions between Different Ranks in the Supervisory Organization

Let us start first by examining the attitudes expressed by supervisors toward different ranks in the supervisory organization. In practically every interview distinctions such as those depicted in Figure 30 were expressed. Using the concept of "social distance,"[1] some of these distinctions can be expressed as follows:

(1) Social distances between any two consecutive levels in the supervisory organization are not equal. For example, between section chief and

---

[1] "The concept of 'distance' as applied to human, as distinguished from spacial relations, has come into use among sociologists, in an attempt to reduce to something like measurable terms the grades and degrees of understanding and intimacy which characterize personal and social relations generally." — From "The Concept of Social Distance," by Robert E. Park, in *Journal of Applied Sociology*, Vol. VIII, 1924, p. 339.

If, as we shall assume, grades of understanding and intimacy between persons or groups, or between a person and a group, are dependent upon the degree to which they assistant foreman there is greater social distance than between group chief and section chief, or between assistant foreman and foreman.[1]

(2) In terms of social distance, there is a more marked cleavage between foreman and general foreman than between any other two consecutive steps in the supervisory organization.[2]

(3) Authority tends to be localized in three ranks of the organization: in the office of foreman, of superintendent, and of works manager. All other supervisors tend to be regarded as adjuncts of these offices.

(4) For the lower members of the supervisory organization there is a marked distinction in sentiment between visible and invisible authority, personal and impersonal authority: (a) there are those visible representatives of management with whom the supervisor has actual daily contact; (b) there are those representatives of management who the supervisor knows exist and whom on special occasions he may even see, but with whom he has no actual daily contact; (c) there is the company and its policies.

Distinctions between Office and Shop

Besides sentiments relating to different ranks of the supervisory organization, there were sentiments attaching to the Operating Branch

share the same sentiments and interests, "social distance" measures differences in sentiment or interest which separate individuals or groups from one another or an individual from a group.

[1] In order to avoid misunderstanding, this statement probably needs to be amplified. It does not mean that there was more conflict and antagonism between a section chief and an assistant foreman than there was between a group chief and a section chief or between an assistant foreman and a foreman. In fact, in some instances the personal relation between a foreman and an assistant foreman was quite bitter, while the assistant foreman was quite cordial and friendly toward one of his section chiefs. What is meant is that, in spite of these personal relations between individuals, there are, nevertheless, social distinctions maintained between ranks, such that a group chief acts toward his workers in the presence of his section chief quite differently from the way he would behave were his assistant foreman or foreman (the "bosses") present. It means, likewise, that a foreman does not treat his assistant in quite the same way as he treats his first-line supervisor. In spite of his personal feelings, there are things that he can say to his assistant that he cannot say to his group chiefs or section chiefs.

[2] This statement means that with the passage from the rank of foreman to that of general foreman a supervisor has passed, in the eyes of the worker, from visible to invisible authority. He ceases to have daily contacts with the worker at the bench. For the first time he has weekly, if not daily, work associations with the assistant superintendents and superintendent of the branch. His functions become more administrative and less immediately concerned with the task of technical production in one department. As a result, the general foreman takes on an occupational personality quite different from that of the foreman. He has definitely passed into a new set of duties, responsibilities, and associations which differentiate him clearly from all ranks below and identify him more intimately with those ranks above. From the point of view of the bottom, he is a "big shot"; from the point of view of the top, he is in the upper levels of management and a member of the branch staff.

as opposed to other branches in the company, or attaching to one department in the Operating Branch as opposed to other departments in the same branch. These sentiments differentiated office workers from shop workers and were most clearly expressed in connection with the company's policies of retrenchment: layoff and shorter hours. The distinctions between workers in office and shop departments can be expressed as follows:

(1) A person's status in the company is not determined entirely by his rank in the supervisory organization; it also depends upon the kind of work he is doing. Certain jobs carry with them more social prestige than others. On the whole, a worker in an office department has a higher social status in the company than a worker in a shop department.

(2) This distinction carries through the first few ranks of the organization, so that the ranks of group chief and section chief in a shop department carry with them little more prestige than the rank of an individual worker in an office department. A section chief in an office department has a higher social status than a section chief in a shop department, etc.

Distinctions of Seniority and Sex

Distinctions between newcomers and old-timers and between men and women were expressed.[1] These distinctions were made by people enjoying the same formal status in the supervisory organization. They can be stated as follows:

(1) All other things being equal, two group chiefs in the same shop department are not regarded as of equal status unless they have the same length of service and are of the same sex.

(2) On the whole, occupations performed by men are of a higher social status than occupations performed by women.

(3) All other things being equal, employees with long service have a higher status than employees of the same sex with short service.

A SYSTEM OF SENTIMENTS REFLECTING THE SOCIAL ORGANIZATION OF THE COMPANY

What do these distinctions mean? What are they expressing? In the first place, they constitute a framework in which the supervisor's thought is set. They are not distinctions of fact but distinctions of

---

[1] Among the supervisors interviewed there were only about half a dozen women. Because of this small number, their statements have not been reported. However, their interviews have been carefully examined to see that their statements are consistent with the interpretation being given.

sentiment, and they do not coincide with the technical discriminations of the organization. From a technical standpoint, that is, from the standpoint of manufacturing telephones efficiently, these distinctions are not implied. The supervisory organization as a method of control

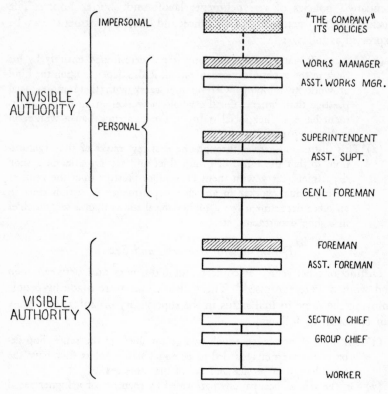

Legend: ▭ RANKS IN WHICH AUTHORITY TENDS TO BE LOCALIZED

FIGURE 30

THE INFORMAL SUPERVISORY ORGANIZATION

OPERATING BRANCH

involves no such discriminations about social distance between ranks as are shown in Figure 30. There is, from a strictly technical standpoint, no difference in importance between the work done by men and the work done by women, or between the work done by clerks and the work done at the bench.

In the second place, therefore, these are distinctions implied in the social organization; they do not arise solely from the technical or economic organization of the company. They arise because the company is not merely an organization for the manufacture of telephones in the most efficient manner; it is also a human organization in which the needs, hopes, and desires of human beings are trying to find expression. These distinctions form a system of sentiments which expresses the values and significances residing in the social organization of the company. This system of sentiments refers to the different ways in which persons and groups of persons are differentiated from one another, as well as the manner in which they are ordered and integrated. The status of each individual in the company is determined in terms of this system. Status depends not only on rank but also on such things as sex, length of service, and on whether or not the individual is in an office or a shop organization.

In the third place, however, a good portion of a person's working environment does reflect these distinctions: Office workers are differentiated from shop workers in terms of method of payment, conditions of work, and hours of work. Supervisors are differentiated from workers in terms of method of payment, privileges, and duties. Supervisors of one rank are differentiated from supervisors of another rank in terms of the degree in which they participate in the function of management. Old-timers are differentiated from newcomers in terms of hourly rates and possibilities for promotion or layoff.

In the fourth place, by means of this system of sentiments not only are certain persons and groups of persons in the structure differentiated from one another but they are also integrated. The lowest worker and the highest executive can share the same feelings about length of service. A supervisor and a worker in a shop department can share the same sentiments with regard to office workers. Old-timers and newcomers can have a common bond in being either shop workers or office workers together. The lower status generally assigned to women can be improved upon by working in the office rather than in the shop.

And, lastly, these distinctions are not of equal importance to all ranks of supervision. Although they are expressed or implied by all supervisors, they do not apply to each supervisor in the same way. Their significance for any individual supervisor depends upon his position as defined by his particular rank, length of service, sex, and on whether he works in one branch or another. The social distance between a section chief and an assistant foreman is expressed by a section chief in one way and by an assistant foreman in another. The social distance between men and women has a different significance for men from that which it has for women. Length of service is more important to the lower ranks than it is to the higher ranks of supervision. The office and shop distinction is not important to the general foreman.[1] The social distance between a group chief and his operators has a more important significance to the group chief than it has to the general foreman.

An Interpretation of Some Supervisory Problems

Let us now see if, in terms of this system of sentiments, the supervisors' grievances, problems, and difficulties can be better understood.

(1) *What does a supervisor mean when he calls a policy of the company unfair?* In all the criticisms of company policy one common theme ran throughout, namely, the question of fairness. About shorter hours, for example, it was said that so-and-so of such-and-such a department, branch, or rank did not get so great a cut as somebody else of a different department, branch, or rank. With regard to method of payment, criticisms were expressed in the form that a supervisor of a certain department did not get paid so much as an operator in that department. In some instances the aggrieved persons were not seriously affected; nevertheless, so long as they thought that someone else in the company was benefiting more than they, they were sure to express this grievance. It was this attitude which attracted the interviewers' attention.

At first it might seem as if all these complaints were demands for equality and protests against the company's showing any kind of discrimination among its employees. But this hypothesis does not quite explain all the evidence. What did the group chief mean by saying, when complaining about a cut in his hours of work when those of his assistant foreman were not cut, "Where the hell does the company get this two-class system anyway? It puts me on the same level as the help." Why didn't the assistant foreman whose hours of work were not cut so much as those of his subordinates comment on this favorably instead of complaining about the fact that he earned on occasions less money than some of them? Do not these statements and omissions express a disguised demand for privilege, a demand to be differentiated from those below but not from those above?

---

[1] But it is well to remember that it is that very distinction which in the eyes of subordinate supervisors gives the office of general foreman its "mana" and prestige. Although still a member of the Operating Branch, the general foreman definitely is "off the floor."

When a supervisor says that a policy of the company is just or unjust, fair or unfair, what he means is that the policy is either acceptable or offensive to his sentiments, as his sentiments stand either in relation to the actually existing social equilibrium [1] to which he has become accustomed or in relation to an ideal equilibrium which he desires. A person who by his rank and service has achieved a certain social status regards anything, whether real or imaginary, tending to alter this status as unfair or unjust. The assistant foreman whose earnings are less than those of some of his subordinates sees in this situation an undermining of his prestige. The group chief whose hours of work are cut "like the help" interprets this move as a lowering of his social status.

Any move on the part of the company, such as cutting of hours of work, tends to disrupt the existing social equilibrium. Immediately, this disruption is manifested in expressions of sentiments of resistance to the real or imagined alterations in the social equilibrium. If the company cuts hours of work of supervisors below the rank of assistant foreman, the group chiefs and section chiefs, who in their sentiments have been identifying themselves with management, see the alteration in the form of having their social status reduced to the rank of "help." As a consequence, they voice sentiments which for them have the effect of tending to restore the equilibrium to what they wish it to be.

(2) *What does a supervisor mean when he calls his superior a slave-driver or a bully?* The supervisory organization can be considered from two standpoints: from the point of view of the company, it is a mechanism for technical control and discipline; from the point of view of any one supervisor, it is also a mechanism by means of which he can rise and gain social prestige and dominance. According to the company point of view any supervisor has two functions to fulfill: (a) he has to control the task of technical production, and (b) he has to maintain authority and discipline. For the individual supervisor this situation has certain psychological consequences. The supervisor can easily fall into one of the four fixed attitudes which are depicted in Figure 31.

Attitude A: He can emphasize the social distance between himself and his subordinates, as well as that between himself and his superiors. In popular parlance, this is the attitude of the

[1] We are intentionally referring to the social organization as a social equilibrium in order to emphasize what we conceive the chief character of a social organization to be: an interaction of sentiments and interests in a relation of mutual dependence, resulting in a state of equilibrium such that if that state is altered, forces tending to re-establish it come into play.

supervisor who "crawls on his belly" before the boss and handles his subordinates with an iron fist.

Attitude B: He can emphasize the social distance between himself and his subordinates and minimize the distance between himself and his superiors. This attitude is frequently described by the worker as that of the supervisor who, although he goes out to play golf with the boss, insists on having his subordinates show him the "proper" deference.

Attitude C: He can minimize the social distance between himself and his subordinates and emphasize the distance between himself and his superiors. This attitude is depicted by the supervisor who treats his boss with deference while putting himself on an equal plane with his subordinates (for example, by allowing them to call him by his first name).

Attitude D: He can minimize the social distance between himself and his subordinates, as well as that between himself and his superiors. This attitude is depicted by the supervisor who refuses to recognize any social distinctions.

Although supervisors representing all four of these attitudes could be found in the organization, there was no evidence to suggest that supervisors in any one of these four groups were more frequently selected for promotion than those in any other group. However, there were certain uniformities. In the first place, it can be said in general that any supervisor who tries, or is thought to be trying, to maintain authority and discipline by emphasizing either through speech or by action the social distance between himself and his subordinates is disliked by his subordinates. This generalization may or may not define the actual situation between a supervisor and his subordinate. It may be that the superior who is being called a bully is in fact adopting methods tending to emphasize social distance. On the other hand, it may be that the subordinate, because of feelings of insecurity or inferiority, tends to misinterpret and distort the significance of certain actions of his superior.

(3) *What does the insistence of all supervisors on leadership versus driving mean?* Attitudes A and B (Figure 31) were being repudiated under the new concept of leadership. The slogans under which the new method of supervision was being organized, and which differentiated the existing methods of supervision from those of the hard-boiled supervisor of two decades before — "to give the workers service," "to treat them as human beings," "to show no discrimination" — were all expressing the same sentiment: the superior is not to maintain authority

and discipline by emphasizing the social distance between himself and his subordinates. It is apparent that this sentiment tends to reduce social distance between the supervisory group and the nonsupervisory group, and between a supervisor of any particular rank and his immediate subordinates. In this way it functions as a corrective of the misuse of authority which is likely to manifest itself in any hierarchical system. It tends to reduce social distance down the line which has been created up the line by an elaborate scale of privileges and distinctions.

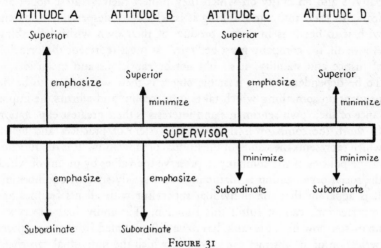

FIGURE 31

FOUR COMMON SUPERVISORY ATTITUDES

OPERATING BRANCH

Only in this way can the slogans expressing the new method of supervision be interpreted. To take them as beliefs in accordance with which supervisors logically and consistently behaved would be to miss their function. Although there was considerable evidence that a subordinate likes to be treated as an equal by his superior, there was no evidence that a subordinate likes to be treated by his superior as equal to those ranks subordinate to him — in fact, all the evidence was to as an equal by his foreman, but he resents having the foreman treat the contrary. An assistant foreman, for example, likes to be treated the section chiefs, group chiefs, or employees as equal to him.

(4) *Why is a supervisor's attitude toward the company different from his attitude toward its visible representatives?* Why is the supervisor insistent on differentiating the company from his superiors? What does this differentiation mean? From the interviews it was apparent

that the supervisor wanted his superior to treat him as an equal and not as a subordinate, or, to use the family analogy, to treat him as an adult and not as a child. Toward the company, however, there were no accusations of paternalism. The employee was only too willing to project on the company his wish for a just parent.

For most of the supervisors the company represents more than the "big bosses," New York, the stockholders, or board of directors. It is more than an economic unit with merely economic functions. The company is also an entity on which they project their greatest hopes and fears. In their intimate thinking it is what they desperately hope and wish it to be; it is in part a product of their own wishful thinking. Above all, the company must be "fair." It must represent the principle of justice and stability; it should not be capricious and inconsiderate. To be dependent on an unstable object is their worst fear; to be dependent on something which takes into account and affirms the importance of their own sentiments and interests is their greatest expectation. In short, the company is that abstract system of practices and beliefs which represents the values of the human organization. It is the function of the policies of the company to preserve the values by means of which the social organization is maintained in a steady state of equilibrium.[1] It is apparent that the individual supervisor with all his frailties and imperfections cannot fulfill this function. The individual supervisor, no matter how high his rank, has to be differentiated from the supposed perfection of an abstract collectivity to which the individual can cheerfully and willingly submit.

(5) *Why is the foreman the butt of the first-line supervisors' criticisms about supervision?* As a visible representative of authority, the foreman is deprived of that prestige which comes from distance. Yet, more than any other supervisor, he is responsible for maintaining discipline in his department and for upholding the rules of the technical organization by means of which efficiency is maintained. More than any other of his subordinate supervisors, he has to think in terms of cost, efficiency, and output. In spite of his best intentions, he is always in a position of violating the feelings of personal integrity of his subordinates. He is, in short, an ideal scapegoat for the expression of any disturbances in the social equilibrium.

Moreover, the foreman's position can also be complicated by psy-

---

[1] It might be worth while in this connection for the reader to refer back to Chapter I, footnote, pp. 7–9, and examine the ten points of the company's employee relations policies — interestingly enough, referred to by the employees as the "Ten Commandments" — in order to see how closely these policies express the values of the human organization and the symbols by means of which these values are organized.

chological factors. Any immaturity of attitude on the part of a particular subordinate can be easily expressed toward the foreman, for, as the head of the department, the foreman is somewhat in the position of father with regard to his junior supervisors. Any complexes toward authority arising from the early familial conditioning of the individual are therefore likely to find expression with reference to the "Old Man."

(6) *Why are the preoccupations of the group chiefs and section chiefs so similar to those of the worker?* In their preoccupations about their superiors and about the company and its policies, group chiefs and section chiefs could be little differentiated from the nonsupervisory group. Essentially they talked the same language. This similarity is not so startling if it is remembered that in terms of the social organization group chiefs and section chiefs were very little differentiated from the worker. In many respects important to their status they were treated more as workers than as representatives of management. In most group piecework departments they participated in the earnings of the group. They shared more or less the same material environment; they had only a few privileges and distinctions, such as toilet and locker facilities, which differentiated them from the operators. Many of their duties with reference to the work at the bench, such as providing the operators with piece parts and sometimes trucking, placed them in a subordinate role to the worker. In many instances they were supervising men who had at least as much service as they had. They were treated as essentially shop people by supervisors from office organizations with whom they came in contact.

(7) *Why are assistant foremen more preoccupied with their personal relations to their immediate superiors than are supervisors of any other rank?* Assistant foremen were more preoccupied with advancement than were supervisors of any other rank. Moreover, it was the impression of the interviewers that in this rank there was a somewhat higher incidence of worry and neurotic troubles and a greater proportion of men who were glad to unburden themselves in the interview. Are not these manifestations of irrational preoccupations partly explicable in terms of the peculiar position in which the assistant foreman is placed with respect to his lines of authority and his personal relations in the department? The foreman is the recognized head of the department. He is spoken of as the "Old Man" by the section chief and group chief, whose relation toward each other may be compared to that of brothers in a family. The assistant foreman, however, is neither quite the head nor quite the junior subordinate. Because of the social distance between the section chief and assistant foreman, analogous to

the distinction between noncommissioned and commissioned officers in a military hierarchy, the assistant foremanship is regarded as the first step in real executive rank. Men who have taken this step have left the ranks of the subordinates and yet are still on trial by their superiors, who may not quite accept them.

Besides these difficulties residing in the social setup, there are opportunities for psychological complications. Carrying out the family analogy a little further, it is apparent that the close relationship between foreman and assistant foreman may be of the father-favorite son type, with the natural internal conflict that such a relationship implies. The assistant foreman may feel affection and loyalty toward his foreman and still want to get him out of the way in order to have a chance to step into his shoes.

(8) *Why are some supervisors more disturbed than are others of the same rank about questions of unfairness in matters of company policy?* In the last three questions which we have discussed, some of the supervisors' problems have been considered in terms of the social implications inherent in the ranks which they occupy in the supervisory organization. But it is impossible to state the satisfactions or dissatisfactions of a particular supervisor merely in terms of the social factors involved in his rank. The personal attitude of the individual toward his position is also an important factor.

For example, it was evident from the interviews that all the supervisors who held the same rank did not express themselves in the same way with regard to the policies of the company. There were a number of group chiefs and section chiefs whose hours of work had been cut who did not comment on the unfairness of the way in which the cut had been applied. There were some group chiefs who did not complain because supervisors in office departments were provided with towels by the company and they were not. Now, of course, it may be that these men felt the same way as their fellow supervisors and had merely failed to express themselves on these matters. On the other hand, the very fact that, given the opportunity to express themselves freely, they had failed to mention these matters suggests the possibility that they did not have the same significance for them as for others.

The attitude of an individual toward his job in the company plays an important part in determining his attitude toward such questions. To a group chief who is only trying to conserve the position he has achieved and has no desire for further advancement, changes introduced by the company mean something quite different from what they mean to a group chief who sees himself some day as a foreman or higher. For the former, all changes which in any way seem to be altering his status adversely are viewed with feelings of apprehension and insecurity. He is envisaging an ideal social equilibrium in which there will be no alteration in those factors which differentiate supervisors from nonsupervisors. For the latter, however, similar changes do not have the same significance, or do not arouse the same preoccupations. Distinctions which separate him from those above are not a source of irritation. In fact, they are a necessary prerequisite for his desire for recognition and rise to social dominance. He is envisaging an ideal social equilibrium in which there is always room at the top.

It is apparent, therefore, that dissatisfaction arises not only from changes in the actual existing social equilibrium to which an individual has become accustomed, but also from alterations occurring, or thought to be occurring, in an ideal social equilibrium which he is contemplating and desiring. The ideal equilibrium which an individual is envisaging depends on the fundamental demands he is making of his work. For a supervisor of any rank whose demand for recognition is still unsatisfied, the ideal equilibrium is envisaged as one which gives full scope for the expression of this demand. The policies of the company are judged good or bad in terms of this configuration. For a supervisor of any rank whose chief demand is only to retain and hold the position he has achieved, the ideal social equilibrium is envisaged as one in which at least those factors differentiating him from those less privileged are strictly maintained. He judges the policies of the company in terms of this configuration.

In these terms the preoccupations of many supervisors about personality, education, loyalty, and length of service can be understood. The supervisor expresses in such preoccupations those values of the social organization on which his own personal integrity and position depend. For the middle-aged group chief with grammar school education, long service, and a number of dependents, any actions on the part of the company which seem to him to depreciate those values by means of which the security of his position is assured violate his feelings of personal integrity. Naturally, he talks about the importance of service, experience, and loyalty. For the young group chief with high school education and short service, who is unmarried and ambitious, the ideal type of social organization is one in which advancement is dependent on factors other than time, age, and experience. He stresses the importance of education and personality. These are the vehicles of rapid vertical social mobility. Any action on the part of the company which tends to depreciate those values by means of which rapid advancement can be assured are viewed by him with disillusionment and frustration.

(9) *On what factors does satisfaction or dissatisfaction with progress in the company depend?* If the analysis has been correct so far, it is evident that all the factors determining satisfaction or dissatisfaction at work do not arise within the walls of the factory. The attitude which the supervisor brings with him to work and the basic demands which he is making of his job are extra-occupational factors making for satisfaction or dissatisfaction. These demands are a product of his social relations outside of the plant and of his previous life history. From single interviews with supervisors it was possible to obtain only a faint notion of the relation between these demands and the supervisors' social life outside of the plant.

One generalization, however, can be made. The more impoverished the social reality for the supervisor is, the greater are his feelings of insecurity and the greater are his demands for recognition and security. For some supervisors the company is father, mother, society, and state all rolled up into one, and strivings for success are a compensation for lack of normal and adequate personal interrelations. Such supervisors as these are attempting to substitute the company for the wider social reality. They are less likely to stand pressure of any kind and are more likely to make excessive and distorted demands. Any act on the part of the company is apt to be misconstrued and to arouse sentiments of resistance to the alteration. On the other hand, the more lines of loyalty extending outside of the plant the supervisor has, the less urgent are his feelings of insecurity and the less excessive are the demands he projects on the company. Men with trades, foreign-born supervisors living in foreign settlements, and supervisors with active political or social affiliations seem, on the whole, more contented.

It was also evident that there is a close relation of mutual dependence between social status in the community and occupational status in the company. With some exceptions, status in the community corresponds very closely to status in the company. In the beginning of employment, social status more or less determines occupational status within the plant; but as changes in occupational status occur, they are likely to be accompanied by social changes outside. These adaptations do not take place entirely without friction, and some of the problems discussed by supervisors were connected with such adjustments. In these terms, the importance of continuous employment can be understood. In a community where occupation plays such an important role in ordering the relation of an individual to the community, to lose one's job is to be dislocated in the community.

CONCLUSION

With the study concluded in this chapter, the phase of the investigation which began with the interviewing program in 1928 was culminated. The investigators felt that they had finally developed an adequate conceptual scheme for understanding factors determining satisfaction or dissatisfaction at work. In order to make clear what this conceptual scheme was, it may be helpful to go back and review the steps leading up to its formulation.

In the early stages of the interviewing program, statements reflecting employee satisfaction and dissatisfaction were referred to the employees' physical environment. It was thought that by examining those objects, plans, or policies about which employees expressed themselves, either favorably or unfavorably, management could arrive at some basis for making improvements. Actual investigation showed, however, that relatively few employee comments could be used in this straightforward manner. People working in similar surroundings did not react in the same way to those surroundings. Some expressed satisfaction, some dissatisfaction with similar plant conditions, wages, and working conditions. In addition to this sort of disagreement, the problem of using the interview material was made still more difficult by the baffling and complex nature of the comments themselves. The great majority of the comments received, far from being simple, clear statements of fact, were couched in vague terms. These terms, while excellent for conveying feelings and emotions, were by their very nature indefinite.

The more the investigators worked with this interview material, the clearer it became that they were dealing with essentially two kinds of statements: factual and nonfactual. It also became clear that nonfactual statements, or expressions of sentiment, had to be handled quite differently from factual statements. Before nonfactual statements could be used they had to be interpreted, that is, they had to be related to some context other than the explicitly stated one. The first context suggested to the interviewers was the personal situation of the employee. This discrimination led the investigators to concentrate upon the exploration of the personal situations of the people interviewed as a source of complaints. For a time, this point of view determined the activities of the members of the research organization. They became extremely interested in employee satisfaction and dissatisfaction as related to the previous social conditioning of the individual. The limitation of this approach, the investigators found, was that it led them farther and farther away from the immediate industrial situation and to an overemphasis of irrational responses.

The particular contribution of the study of supervisory attitudes, just reported, to the formulation of an adequate conceptual scheme for understanding the factors determining satisfaction at work was that it revealed another context to which complaints could be related. If the former context could best be described as psychological, this new context could best be described as social. It became clear that many employee comments which had formerly been interpreted in terms of the interviewee's personal situation could be better understood if they were interpreted in the light of the employee's existing social relations within the plant: the social organization of the group with which he worked and his position in that group. The advantage of this concept, the investigators felt, was that it enabled them to return from the study of personal situations to the study of factory situations. It was not that they had been unmindful of the importance of a study of concrete situations within the plant. The significant thing for them was that they could now return to the study of shop situations with an entirely different and more fruitful point of view. This point of view, furthermore, was consistent with the concepts which had been developed in the interviewing program and, it may be added, will be substantiated in the study to be presented in Part IV.

As a way of summarizing the conceptual scheme for understanding employee satisfaction or dissatisfaction which was evolved in the studies reported thus far, Figure 32 has been prepared. This figure attempts to show in terms of their relations to one another those factors which have to be taken into account when considering employee content or discontent. According to this interpretation, it is not possible to treat, as in the more abstract social sciences, material goods, physical events, wages, and hours of work as things in themselves, subject to their own laws. Instead, they must be interpreted as carriers of social value. For the employee in industry, the whole working environment must be looked upon as being permeated with social significance. Apart from the social values inherent in his environment the meaning to the employee of certain objects or events cannot be understood. To understand the meaning of any employee's complaints or grievances, it is necessary to take account of his position or status in the company. This position is determined by the social organization of the company: that system of practices and beliefs by means of which the human values of the organization are expressed, and the symbols around which they are organized — efficiency, service, etc. In these terms it is then possible to understand the effect upon the individual of — or the meanings assigned by the individual to — the events, objects, and features of his environment, such as hours of work, wages, etc. Only then is it possible to see what effect changes in working environment have upon

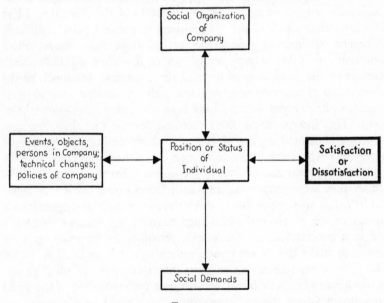

FIGURE 32

SCHEME FOR INTERPRETING COMPLAINTS INVOLVING SOCIAL INTERRELATIONSHIPS OF EMPLOYEES

the social organization to which the employee has become accustomed, or upon that ideal type of social equilibrium which he desires. In terms of his relative position in the social organization it can be seen what values such changes overemphasize or underemphasize.

But the relation of the individual employee to the company is not a closed system. All the values of the individual cannot be accounted for by the social organization of the company. The meaning a person assigns to his position depends on whether or not that position is allowing him to fulfill the social demands he is making of his work. The ultimate significance of his work is not defined so much by his relation to the company as by his relation to the wider social reality. Only in terms of this latter relation can the different attitudes of satisfaction or dissatisfaction of individuals who are presumably enjoying the same working environment and occupational status be understood.

Although this interpretation has been given solely in terms of interviews taken from supervisors, it seemed clear to the investigators that it applied equally well to the comments of workers. For example, the meaning of many employee complaints about plant conditions could be understood only when they were interpreted in the light of the employee's position in the social organization of the company. More than any other aspect of the work situation, physical plant conditions differentiated supervisory and office groups from shop groups. Plant conditions, in other words, served partly to define an individual's position in the social organization of the company. Inasmuch as the lower status of the shop employee was indicated by the kind of plant conditions he enjoyed, he may have been somewhat more conscious of them. This interpretation would account for the fact that shop employees commented a great deal about plant conditions whereas the supervisors who were interviewed mentioned them relatively little.

However, it was also evident to the investigators that, with the techniques they were employing and with interviewing as it was being conducted, it was impossible to catch the more subtle and spontaneous aspects of the employees' social organization. By interviewing once and in a general fashion over a wide territory, the interviewers were unable to make the detailed studies they would have liked to make. There was every indication that more intensive studies of small groups would have to be made before an adequate understanding of the social situation in which the employees functioned could be obtained. Accordingly, plans were laid for achieving this objective, and with this departure the research program entered upon its final phase, which will be reported in Part IV.

PART IV

SOCIAL ORGANIZATION OF EMPLOYEES

CHAPTER XVII

METHOD AND PROCEDURE IN STUDYING A
SHOP DEPARTMENT

Early Studies of Shop Departments

THE final phase of the research program consisted of a detailed study of a shop situation from a sociological point of view. This study will be reported in its entirety, first, because it illustrates an application of the conceptual scheme developed in the previously reported researches and, secondly, because it gives a picture of a spontaneous, informal social organization functioning within the formal framework of the company's structure.

By a series of studies which were conducted by members of the interviewing staff early in 1931, the investigators' attention had been called to the fact that social groups in shop departments were capable of exercising very strong control over the work behavior of their individual members. At that time, partly because the onset of the depression made the interviewing program somewhat unfeasible and partly because it was felt that a change of procedure would be beneficial from a research point of view, management approved the assignment of specialized interviewers to small groups for the purpose of interviewing each person in the group as often as seemed necessary. Prior to this time the investigators had been interviewing people not more than once a year, and the people interviewed by any one investigator were frequently scattered over a wide territory. By assigning interviewers to more concentrated activity, it was felt that the interviewing method as a therapeutic measure could be better adapted to the needs of each individual case. It was also felt that the investigators could obtain a better picture of the human problems in any one department and thereby enhance the possibilities of practical application of findings.

It was while the investigators were working in this way that their attention was first called to problems of employee interrelations and group organization. Their reports showed very clearly that they were encountering several related phenomena, the importance of which had escaped them before this time. Chief among these was restriction of output. Although restriction in some form is not an uncommon occurrence and most industrialists recognize its existence in varying degrees, the investigators had hitherto been unaware of its implications for management practice and employee satisfaction. Some of the evidence obtained suggested that the wage incentive systems under which some of the groups worked had been rendered ineffectual by group pressure for controlled output. Informal practices by means of which certain operators were placed under pressure and kept in line were brought to light. There was evidence of informal leadership on the part of certain persons who took upon themselves the responsibility of seeing that the members of a group clung together and protected themselves from representatives of other groups within the company who could interfere with their affairs.

In order to make clear the manner in which the above phenomena were manifested, it may be well to quote at length from the reports of three interviewers. One interviewer who was assigned to a group in a large department reported:

They [the employees] firmly believe that they will not be satisfactorily remunerated for any additional work they produce over the bogey, or that if they do receive more money it could only be for a brief period, at the end of which the job would be rerated. Because of the belief that rates may ultimately be lowered if output is too great, there seems to be a tacit agreement among the members of this group to limit their production to the bogey requirements on each operation. Seldom do they exceed the bogey by a large margin. Most of the work is turned out in the morning in order that they can "take it easy" during the latter part of the afternoon. When questioned as to whether or not their earnings would be greater if they turned out more work, they claimed that the difference, if any, would be negligible because the percentages made by the other groups tend to pull theirs downward. To this general scheme all their attitudes and behavior are related.

The leader in this group is one of the two group chiefs, undoubtedly a very significant factor in giving the group a strong feeling of security. This supervisor, *A*, was at one time on the bench in the same group which he now supervises, but he refused to allow the change to alter his relations with the men. From observing the group one can hardly draw a line between supervisor and employees. It is obvious that he is very popular with them; no one has any adverse criticism to make of him. He is very close to the men, keeping them well informed at all times as to the group standing in the department, i.e., relative percentages, rates, output, etc. When asked why they consider him a good supervisor, his men replied with such statements as: "He knows his stuff," "He's fair and impartial," "He'll go to hell for you and make sure you get plenty of work." In short, all their statements implied a firm conviction that this group chief would protect their interests. By way of contrast, while *A* was on sick leave, another supervisor, *B*, took over the group. Toward *B* the employees expressed strong antagonism. *B* is an older man, further removed from the interests and sentiments of his subordinates. He is not quite trusted by the men and commands very little respect. As one employee sized him up, "When he bawls you out, he is more nervous than you are." This group is only vaguely conscious of the other supervisors in the department; in fact, a confusion of the supervisory ranks is quite evident. For example, *C*, a section chief, has held the same position for a number of years; but the men cannot figure out what position he holds in the department, who reports to him, or what his duties are.

An attitude common to this group, but existing in varying degrees of intensity, may be characterized as a lack of ambition and initiative and a complacent desire to let well enough alone. Most indifferent is their attitude toward advancement, referring, of course, to promotion or higher-grade work. Whereas it is usual in any group to find several employees striving to improve their position, here only one or two seem to be interested. The others merely say, "All we are here for is the old pay check." Sometimes they speak of the department as the "Old People's Home" because, quoting one man: "The fellows get in here and don't seem to want to get away. Take a fellow like me. I have been on this job ten years. If I was transferred out, I would have to start all over again and I would have a pretty tough time."

In their group life they are congenial and happy-go-lucky. This is obvious not only during rest periods but also while they work. Side play is frequent, and good-natured bantering constantly flashes back and forth. During rest periods everyone either plays cards or stands by as an interested spectator, and in these games rivalry is always keen but congenial. Several of the newer men express the consensus of opinion by describing their associates as "a swell bunch of guys."

Another investigator, interviewing a different group, described the response of the group to one worker who defied their pattern. The workers of this group are identified by the letters, *A*, *B*, *C*, *D*, etc.

A says *B* gets mad because he [*A*] does too much work: "*B* sometimes tries to do as much as I do, and whenever he can't make it he gets mad and swears about it. Then he will go over to some of the others and say that I am trying to kill the bogey." The girl assemblers in the group tell *A* that he should not stand for the treatment he gets from the group chief. They tell him he does the most work and gets the least recognition.

A mistrusts *D* because *D* represented himself as a sort of a supervisor to *A* and took the easy jobs when *A* first came to work here. He is not friendly with *E* because *E* does favors for everyone but him. His friends are an old man, *G*, and the girls. When *B* was called to the office because his production was too low, *A* told him it was his own fault. *B* then said, "What! Do you expect us to come down here and slave?"

B is 36 years of age, a rather stocky, well-built, athletic type. Although he supports his father and mother, their dependence apparently serves to accentuate his own manhood. He says that the supervisors are all satisfactory. He knows them well because he has worked here so long. He takes a senior position in the group and gets along well with everyone but *A*. His attitude toward *A* is indicated by the incessant "kidding" to which he subjects him. He attributes to himself all the best characteristics of virile manhood and attributes to *A* feminine characteristics. He says that *A* is an hermaphrodite. He demonstrated in the first interview how *A* swings his hips and carries himself like a woman. *B* thinks that *A* works hard because he is "dumb," and that nobody likes *A* because he does so much. He explains that *A* sits all by himself (in reality he sits next to *B*) and nobody will talk to him, so all he can do is work from the first whistle to the last. *B* was once offered a position as supervisor which he refused.

In commenting about these interpersonal relations within the group, the investigator said:

There seems to be little doubt in the group and in the department that *A* is the best worker in the group. It is equally evident that he is not the pace setter. On the other hand, by producing more than the other operators he lays himself open to direct criticism. For instance, *B* at times tries to equal *A*'s record. He finds himself unable to do this in spite of having been with the company longer than *A*. The question arises: What does he do when he finds he cannot compete with *A*? He does a number of things. He "kids" *A* about wearing red neckties, thereby implying that he is not a man. He elaborates this thesis in any number of ways. He tells him he ought to get married. He asks him if he will come and live with him and be his wife. He "kids" him about the girls. His apparent contempt for *A* is transmitted to other members of the group. Because *A* disregards the group standard of output, they in turn begin to hold *A* in contempt. They lose sight of the fact that *A* is really a good workman and capable of doing as much labor and more than any of the rest of them. The latent feud between *A* and *B* in time becomes a pattern for the way the whole group thinks of *A*. They begin to call him "Mary Lou," a name which originated with *B*.

The supervisor then complicates this situation by using *A* to find out whether or not the other operators are doing as much work as they can. In one instance, *D* was working on a job and could not make a reasonable percentage. The supervisor put *A* on the job to see if he could do better. *A* made the bogey. This intensified the antagonism between *A* and the rest of the group and made an overt enemy of *D*. For example, when *D* got tickets through a friend for a prize fight, he distributed them to everyone except *A*. The supervisor realizes that *A*'s superior performance causes trouble in his group. He gives *A* additional jobs to do, in the belief that they will reduce his efficiency and thus tend to appease the group. The outcome, however, is that *A* is further stimulated to show up the group.

In reality, then, the attempt of the supervisor to cope with the problem merely serves to give *A* an opportunity to express further his superiority. We are witnessing a vicious circle in which *A* works hard because the group derides and attempts to frustrate him; but the harder he works the more intense becomes the antagonism.

A third interviewer reported his findings with regard to another group as follows:

They [the employees] went on at great length explaining that adjustments were almost impossible in many cases because of variations in the quality and quantity of piece parts available, until I wondered how they were able to accomplish anything. I also noticed a general dissatisfaction or unrest. In some, this was expressed by demands for advancement or transfers; in others, by a complaint about their lot in being kept on the job.

These serious continuous defects, about which they talked a great deal, were not reflected by variations in their output curves. In other words, it looked as if they were limiting their output to a figure just below the bogey, and evidently this ouput could be accomplished even though machines were running poorly.

I then noticed that two of the workers in particular held rather privileged positions in the group and were looked up to by the rest of the members. On these two the group seemed to place considerable responsibility. Of *A* they said: "He can handle the engineers, inspectors, and the supervisors. They have to come to him if they want to know anything." In speaking of *B* they expressed admiration for his work habits and capacities. The common remarks about him were: "He taught me my job," "When he adjusts a machine, he never raises his eyes until it works," "So-and-so talked too much a while ago, and *B* shut him up." Quite frequently *B* shows them an easy way to make an adjustment that is difficult because of a variation in the piece parts. All expressed appreciation of his willingness to help them.

A, in his interviews, told of fights with supervisors and arguments with engineers and inspectors which usually resulted in their making the changes he recommended. In referring to one case he said, "I made several machines work after an expert from the East said an adjustment was impossible." *B* told of helping other adjusters. He said that he threatened to punch one operator in the nose because he had let the supervisor know that he had finished early.

From observations and from conversations with the supervisors I observed that the group chief consults with either *A* or *B* when a change is contemplated. The group chief defends the group in general whenever the foreman expresses dissatisfaction with their work, and he never bawls them out. On one occasion the foreman asked him why he didn't bawl them out when the quality chart showed an increase in defects. The group chief answered that he passed the quality record around the group so that they all could see it: "They know when they are slipping without my telling them." The bulk of the group chief's time is occupied in obtaining an even flow of work so that all are kept busy. The section chief and the assistant foreman have adopted a "hands off" policy. They say that the group has a "union" and that it could turn out much more than it does, but they don't know what to do about it, so they leave the men alone.

This, in general, is the picture which this investigator obtained from his interviews with and observations of the employees of this group. The investigator concluded:

The supervisory control which is set up by management to regulate and govern the workers exercises little authority except to see that they are supplied with work. It is apparent that the group is protected from without by A. He absorbs the brunt of the arguments which might upset the group's morale. The behavior of the group itself is regulated by B. He teaches them their work and sees to it that their behavior does not jeopardize the group security. For instance, he sees that they look busy even though they are through work, that they do not tell others that their work is easy or that they are getting through work early. Several of the workers told the interviewer to look out for B. "He's hard-boiled," they said. It is apparent that he protects the group from internal indiscretions. We can summarize the situation as a group protected from without by one (A) capable of obtaining security for the workers and protected from within by one (B) capable of administering punishment for any violation of the group standards.

The Need for a More Systematic Inquiry

The foregoing illustrations of social organization among employees were derived almost entirely from interviews with the men in the different groups. The investigators had little opportunity to observe the groups at work, they knew little about their output except what could be learned from departmental records, which were kept for practical rather than research purposes, and they knew almost nothing about the overt behavior of the employees toward one another and their supervisors.

The statement that little was known about the overt behavior of the people studied implies a distinction which should be made more clear. By overt behavior is meant the manner in which the employees acted toward one another. In the interview situation the investigators obtained only statements of how the employees said they acted. The interviewers had no means of relating these statements to what actually transpired. This distinction between actions and words, or between overt and verbal behavior, is emphasized here because it led to an innovation in method which distinguished the study to be reported from all the others dealt with so far, namely, supplementing the interviewing method with direct observation.

The Bank Wiring Observation Room study, then, was planned with two purposes in mind: to develop the new method and to obtain more exact information about social groups within the company. It was conducted with a group of fourteen male operators who were working, as they were accustomed to work, under standard shop conditions. The study lasted from November, 1931, to May, 1932, when it had to be terminated because of lack of work. The investigators spent the period of six and one-half months in observing the situation before them. No intentional changes were made in the situation once the group was so placed that observation was possible.

Difficulties in Studying Shop Departments

One need not have an intimate acquaintance with shop departments to anticipate many of the problems which arise in studying them. There is, for example, the question of size. Many departments in the plant contained one hundred or more employees exclusive of supervisors. To study such a large group carefully would not only require a large staff of investigators and entail a great deal of expense, but it would also require an unusual amount of tolerance on the part of the supervisors and employees.

Closely connected with the question of size is that of complexity. Technical, administrative, supervisory, and personal problems are all mixed up into one interacting whole. It is practically impossible to study all of these factors in detail; some selection is essential. The selection made, of course, must be determined by the questions one has in mind. In this study, for example, the investigators were interested in the technical aspects of the work to a certain extent, but they were not interested in engineering problems as such. It was enough for them to know that the workers used certain materials and were supposed to carry through certain specified operations. Whether or not the workers' routines and the layout of the job were organized in the best possible way was a question with which they were not concerned. They were, however, very much interested in administrative and supervisory practices because these deal with the organization and motivation of the personnel.

A third problem is that of change. Most departments are exceedingly dynamic. The personnel is frequently increased or decreased, technical changes are made, and people are often shifted from one job to another. The keeping of records becomes very difficult in such a situation, especially if they are to be kept individually and with precision.

Quite apart from problems like these is one related to the sociological nature of working groups. This problem is too frequently ignored or considered unimportant by investigators in industry. A protective or defensive attitude surrounds many shop departments. It may be brought into play whenever the employees feel that their security is being threatened. Any person unknown to them who expresses more than a casual interest in their work or affairs is likely to be regarded with suspicion unless he takes pains to make clear to them just what he is doing and why. Even then, they may not believe him and may alter their work habits and behavior in defense. This attitude has a parallel in the suspicion of the stranger manifested by many closely knit groups in modern and primitive societies. It was especially important to overcome such resistance as this in the present study because the success of the study depended on establishing a situation in which the employees would feel free to work and behave as they were accustomed to, even though the investigators were looking on. To illustrate the manifestation of such a protective attitude, the following case may be cited:

One day an interviewer entered a department unobserved. There was a buzz of conversation and the men seemed to be working at great speed. Suddenly there was a sharp hissing sound. The conversation died away, and there was a noticeable slowing up in the work pace. The interviewer later discovered from an acquaintance in the department that he had been mistaken for a rate setter. One of the workmen, who acted as a lookout, had stepped on a valve releasing compressed air, a prearranged signal for slowing down.

The problem of allaying the attitude of distrust had been handled exceedingly well in the interviewing program, and by continual demonstration of the company's good faith the same end had been achieved in the Relay Assembly Test Room. It was felt, however, that the problem would be much more difficult in studying a whole or a vertical section of a department because the entire departmental structure, including the supervisory organization, would be brought into focus. To the apprehensions of the employees would be added those of the supervisors, from the foreman on down. One false step might ruin the relation between the investigators and the department. Accordingly, this aspect of shop situations had to be kept constantly in mind throughout the study.

Closely related to the above problem is that of what constitutes a change in a situation. It is one thing to overcome defensive attitudes; it is quite another thing to do so without introducing a fundamental change in the situation. This difficulty arises from the fact that the importance of a change in a worker's situation, however insignificant it may appear to an outsider, can only be judged in terms of the meaning attached to it by the employee. Changes unwittingly made in a situation while experimenting with rest pauses or hours of work, for example, might have more effect on efficiency than the experimental change itself; yet the investigators might attribute the entire result to the experimental change. The success of this study really depended upon being able to study a situation without at the same time introducing major changes in it. Those things which the investigators were careful not to alter will be discussed later. The foregoing discussion is intended to emphasize certain difficulties in studying shop departments which otherwise might be overlooked or considered negligible. The importance attached to them by the investigators was such that every step they took was in some degree guided by consideration of them.

The Method of Study

In view of the size and complexity of the average shop department, the investigators decided that it would be better to concentrate on one small group engaged in one type of work rather than to spread their efforts over a number of groups with dissimilar jobs. Inasmuch as departmental rules, policies, and practices applied to every worker, it was believed that they could be assessed in relation to one group as well as another. The same was true of the departmental supervisory organization. Accordingly, the investigators decided to study a vertical section of a department. It was assumed that one vertical section was essentially the same as another and that any vertical section, considered separately, would reveal the same type of factors as would be revealed by a study of the whole department.

Secondly, it was decided to place the group to be studied in a separate room. This was done reluctantly, because it meant a change in the workers' environment. The alternative of allowing the workers to remain where they were was unfeasible. In the first place, it would have been extremely difficult for an observer to keep adequate records of behavior without making a nuisance of himself. The ordinary shop was not so arranged that an outsider could mingle readily with the workers or sit at a desk near them. In the second place, it was felt that the group studied might feel uneasy in the presence of acquaintances not included in the study. They might feel obliged to do or refrain from doing certain things in order to keep in good standing with the remainder of the group. Such problems would not arise if the group to be studied were segregated.

Thirdly, in order to assess the effect of placing the group in a separate room, base period studies were to be made before either the workers or their immediate supervisors knew anything about the study.

Fourthly, nothing was to be said or done in selecting the group to be studied, in explaining the study to them, or in removing them from the department which might alter their status in any way.

Fifthly, no records were to be taken which might tend to make the workers apprehensive or too consciously aware that they were being studied. For example, they were unaccustomed to having their output recorded at short consecutive time intervals. It was decided at the outset, therefore, not to take such readings. To do so might arouse many apprehensions which would be difficult to allay. Similarly, records of such things as diet and hours of sleep were not to be taken because of the antagonism which such personal inquiry might arouse.

The investigating work itself was functionally divided between an observer and an interviewer. This was done in the belief that the types of material to be obtained by the two people were quite different and, furthermore, that both types of material could not be obtained equally well by one person.

The observer was stationed with the group in the role of a disinterested spectator. His function was to keep necessary records of performance as well as records of events and conversations which he considered significant. The role of a disinterested spectator was a difficult one to maintain. In order to obtain the confidence of the group, the observer had to establish friendly relations with everyone in it. This inevitably meant that he became a part of the situation he was studying. To keep his own feelings and prejudices from coloring the material recorded and to keep his own personality from affecting the situation under observation required a high degree of personal insight and objectivity.

It was decided beforehand that the observer should adhere to certain general rules: (1) He should not give orders or answer any questions which necessitated the assumption of authority. (2) He should not enter voluntarily into any argument. If forced to do so, he should be as noncommittal as possible. (3) He should not force himself into a conversation or appear to be either anxious to overhear what was going on or overinterested in the group's behavior. (4) He should never violate confidences or give any information to supervisors, whatever their rank. (5) He should not by his manner of speech or behavior set himself off from the group. It was recognized, of course, that rules like these could only help the observer to define his role; what measure of success he was to achieve depended upon his own ability and personality.

Apart from the observer's relations with the group, there was the question of what constituted a significant event. The observer had to make some selection of material to record, but what should he select? Of course, common sense determined part of the selection; for example, a heated argument between two operators or a clash between an operator and a supervisor would be noted by anyone. But the question goes much deeper. The point is that observation, if it is to be at all scientific, must be guided by a working hypothesis which enables the observer to make active discriminations in the complex interplay of factors before him. Without such guidance he is likely to miss much of significance and become lost in a welter of irrelevancies. It may be well, therefore, to state what the investigators agreed upon as being important for the observer to look for and record.[1]

First of all, the observer had to have clearly in mind what the situation was demanding of the supervisors and employees. In other words, he had to know the formal and technical organization of the department. The formal and technical organization provided an object of reference to which observations of performance and behavior could be related. Every item which indicated a similarity or difference be-

---

[1] The investigators were fortunate in having the counsel of William Lloyd Warner, at that time Assistant Professor of Social Anthropology at Harvard University and now Associate Professor of Anthropology and Sociology at the University of Chicago, who had become interested in the research program about the middle of 1930. The general methodological concepts employed throughout this study were chiefly derived from Mr. Warner; however, he should not in any sense be held responsible for their detailed application to this industrial situation. Mr. Warner frequently discussed the investigators' problems with them and called their attention to the similarity between the problems confronting them and those confronting the anthropological field worker. He also directed their attention to the works of such people as Durkheim, Malinowski, Radcliffe-Brown, and Georg Simmel, from which a wealth of background material was obtained. With the exception of the work of Georg Simmel (Spykman, N. J., *The Social Theory of Georg Simmel*, The University of Chicago Press, Chicago, 1925), reference has already been made to publications of these authors in Chapter XIII, footnote, p. 272.

tween the actual situation and the way it was supposed to be was to be recorded.

Secondly, he was to look for evidences of any informal organization which the employees in their face-to-face relations consciously or unconsciously formed. To this end he was to watch for (a) recurrent verbal utterances or overt acts which were indicative of the relations between two or more people; (b) manifestations of the kind and extent of a person's participation in the immediate group situation; (c) evidences of the existence of a group solidarity (the importance of crises in bringing out the group organization was stressed); (d) if there was such a group solidarity, to what occupational groups it extended and how it was expressed.

Thirdly, should the observer detect evidences of an informal organization, he should attempt to understand the functions it fulfilled for the employees and how it was related to the formal company organization. It was assumed here that every group organization fulfills functions both for the people participating in it and for the larger structure of which the group is a part. Sometimes these functions are explicitly stated, but more frequently they are not. For the most part, they can be assessed only after a careful, objective study of the group and its relation to other organizations.

It may be well to add a few words regarding the attitude required of a person doing the kind of observational work being discussed. He must above all else refrain from evaluational judgments. His function is to observe and to describe. Whether or not the conduct of those he is observing is right or wrong is entirely irrelevant to his function. The reason for this is that, as soon as one becomes involved in questions of right or wrong, attention is diverted from the only significant areas, personal and social, in which an explanation of a given action can be found. The observer's attitude toward the situation he is studying should be exactly the same as that of the interviewer toward the interviewee or of the doctor toward his patient. Instead of asking, "Is this man's conduct such that it should be stopped?" he should be asking such questions as, "Why does he act this way? What do his actions indicate his position in the group to be? How do his actions affect the interpersonal relations of others in the group?" Such questions provide fruitful leads for further research; they lead the investigator directly to a consideration of the personal and social contexts to which the actions are related, whereas evaluational judgments merely lead to a statement of the observer's own sentiments and to the formulation of irrelevant questions.

The interviewer, as contrasted with the observer, was to remain an outsider to the group as much as possible. Although he was to be in daily touch with the observer, he was not to enter the observation room unless it was necessary. It was felt that if the interviewer was an outsider the workers would feel more like telling him about themselves, their work, and occurrences in the observation room. In other words, the mere fact of talking to an outsider gave point to their relating certain events and experiences in the immediate work situation which they might otherwise pass over as being common knowledge. The interviews were to be held by appointment and conducted in privacy.

The function of the interviewer, as contrasted with that of the observer, who was to describe the actual verbal and overt behavior of the operators, was to gain some insight into their attitudes, thoughts, and feelings. He was to look for the values and significances for them of their situation. In addition, the interviewer was to learn what he could about each person's personal history, family situation, and social life outside the plant. The technique of interviewing to be employed was essentially the same as that previously described.[1]

The method of study developed can be summarized by visualizing a simple diagram consisting of three concentric circles: the innermost of which represents the department; the second, the company as a whole; and the outermost, the total community. The workers to be studied participated in all three areas. Their active participation in the department and, to a certain extent, in the larger company structure was subject to direct observation. Their participation in the wider community and their subjective attitudes, beliefs, and feelings toward their immediate surroundings in the plant could not, however, be observed. Such material had to be elicited from the individual and the best available technique was the personal interview. The functions of the observer and interviewer, therefore, were complementary. Their attention was fixed upon the same group, and one simply attempted to get information which the other, because of his relation with the group, either could not get as well or could not get at all.

Selecting the Department to be Studied

Having decided upon the method of study and the necessity for segregating the group for purposes of observation, the next step was to determine which department to study. This was really decided by the kind of job the department performed. It was essential that the

[1] See Chapter XIII.

job chosen should fulfill the following requirements: (1) that the operators be engaged in the same task, (2) that the output for each operator be capable of being exactly determined, (3) that a comparatively short time, preferably not more than one minute, be required for the completion of one unit, (4) that the operator's work pace be determined by his own effort and not controlled by a machine or conveyor, (5) that there be assurance of reasonable continuance of employment of those selected, (6) that the group could be removed from the department without inconvenience, (7) that the removal to a separate room would not require the installation of bulky or costly equipment, and (8) that the operators be experienced at their work. It also seemed desirable to study a group of male operators.

An extensive survey of the most likely departments showed that these requirements were difficult to fulfill. It was especially difficult to find a group which was reasonably sure to remain intact. Orders were being curtailed, and the company was finding it necessary to reduce its force. The department finally chosen was engaged in the assembly of switches for step-by-step central office equipment. One operation performed in the department, that of connector and selector bank wiring, was particularly suitable, and from men employed at this task the group to be studied was finally selected.

The task of selector and connector bank wiring was divided among three groups of workmen: wiremen, soldermen, and inspectors. Each of these groups performed a specific task and collaborated with the other two in the completion of each unit of equipment. The work rate of a workman in any one of these groups was necessarily related to the rates of two other workmen. The output of an inspector, for example, was limited to the number of wired and soldered terminals completed. So, also, the solderman's output was limited to that of the wiremen with whom he worked. The wiremen, as a rule, did set the pace for the other two groups, but it was quite possible for the latter to limit output by refusing to work as fast as the wiremen.

Tools, Equipment, and Piece Parts

The photograph in Figure 33 shows the kind of tools, equipment, and piece parts used by a wireman. The metal workbenches were three feet high and twenty inches wide. Upon them heavy cast-iron fixture supports were fastened. Two such supports were required for each fixture. The fixture consisted of a wooden board about one inch thick, eight inches wide, and six feet long. This fixture was placed upon the supports and extended lengthwise on the workbench. The supports

Figure 33

Photograph of a Section of the Bank Wiring Department, Showing Banks at Different Stages of Completion

were constructed so that the fixture was tilted toward the wireman at an angle. Projecting upward from the wooden base of the fixture was a row of eleven pairs of iron pins which were high enough to hold three 200-point banks. The banks were slipped down over the pins, which held them conveniently before the wireman at a height of four feet.

The banks were about one and one-half inches high and four inches long and were convex in shape. Projecting fanwise from the faces of them were the terminals or "points" which were to be connected by the wireman. From the workman's point of view there were two kinds of banks, depending on whether they had 100 or 200 terminals. The dimensions of the two types were the same, the difference being in the spacing of the terminals. On a 200-point bank there were ten rows of twenty terminals, whereas on a 100-point bank there were five rows. The distribution of the terminals on the two types of banks differed in that the terminals were staggered more and were spread farther apart on the 100-point banks. Wiremen preferred to work on 100-point banks because of the larger space around each terminal. Soldermen preferred the 200-point banks because the terminals were all on the same level and could be soldered by sliding the soldering iron along the row. The terminals on a 100-point bank were spaced so far apart that they had to be soldered separately.

The finished product was called an equipment. An equipment could be either ten or eleven banks long and two or three banks high. A two-bank equipment could have either two rows of 200-point banks or one row of 200-point banks and one row of 100-point banks. The latter type was more common. A three-bank equipment always had three rows of 200-point banks. Where 100-point banks were used, they always constituted the second and top row.

A wireman alternated between two equipments, the second being placed either adjacently to the first on the same bench or on the bench immediately in front. After the first level on one equipment had been wired, he shifted to the first level on the second equipment.

A tool was sometimes used for spreading the levels on 200-point banks. A small pair of pliers was used occasionally to straighten bent terminals. A large spool holding a pair of colored wires, which were twisted together, was attached to a horizontal bar under the bench in such a way that it unwound when pulled by the wireman. The wire had been previously run through a machine which stripped off portions of insulation at regular intervals. A small claw-like tool was used to comb the attached wires out straight so that they would lie flat. Fiber insulators were inserted between the levels of each bank.

The Wiring Process

A fixture was taken from a near-by storage rack and placed in position on the support. Banks, wire, and fiber insulators were next obtained. Then a cable with a wired terminal strip was obtained and placed in position on one end of the wooden fixture immediately behind the row of upright pins. Ten or eleven 200-point banks, as the equipment required, were then slipped down over the upright pins and the wiring task proper was begun.

First, certain colored wires in the cable with the wired terminal strip were attached to the bottom level of terminals of the end bank immediately in front of the cable. These were fastened in accordance with a color code. Then, starting at one end of the equipment and using the pair of wires on the spool under the workbench, the wireman attached them to the first two terminals in the lower level of an end bank. He then attached the wire in sequence to the corresponding terminals of the other nine or ten banks. This was accomplished by looping the bare wire, where the insulation had been removed, over the terminals and pulling it tight. When the last bank had been connected, the operator broke the wire and, going back to the first bank, secured it to the second pair of terminals in the bottom level and proceeded as before. This was repeated ten times, which completed the wiring of the first level. The wireman then moved to his other work station and wired the first level of that equipment in the same manner. While he was working on the second equipment, the solderman and inspector performed their respective functions on the completed level of the first equipment. Before wiring the second level, fiber insulators were placed over the first level. When the ten levels of the 200-point banks had been completed, a second row of banks was placed on top and the operation was continued.

Two kinds of errors had to be guarded against by the wiremen: reverses and wire breaks. A reverse occurred when a wire was attached to other than the specified terminal. Reverses might occur either in attaching the cable to the end bank or in connecting the terminals in sequence. The wireman was solely responsible for reverses and partly responsible for broken wire. Wire breaks which occurred where the wire was looped around a terminal might be caused either by the wireman or by the machine which stripped off the insulation. The gauge on the stripping machine might be set so small that a portion of the wire was taken off with the insulation or, as was usually the case, the gauge might be set correctly but the diameter of the wire might vary slightly. In either case, the wire would break easily when twisted. Wire breaks within the insulated portion usually resulted from defects in the wire itself.

The Soldering Process

Each solderman soldered the work of three wiremen. The soldermen were equipped with an electrically heated soldering iron and solder in the form of a wire, the center of which consisted of resin. The solder was melted by pressing it against the tip of the iron, from which it flowed onto the terminals. The soldering irons were equipped with detachable copper tips which had to be filed several times a day. Each solderman filed his own tips.

The Inspection Process

Each completed level of an equipment was thoroughly inspected. The inspector was equipped with a test set with which he detected any serious defect in the equipment. The test set was attached to an equipment, and when a contact was made with a terminal it made a buzzing sound. If the set failed to buzz when a terminal was touched, it meant that the circuit was not completed. The cause might be a cable reverse, a wiring reverse, a broken wire, or a short circuit caused by solder spanning the gap between two terminals. It was up to the inspector to determine which one by visual inspection. Having tested for these four defects, he then examined the equipment visually for other defects.

The inspector filled out a quality form for each equipment inspected. An identification number stamped on the equipment was entered on the form. Each defect and the terminal upon which it occurred were entered on this record. The two inspectors in the observation room divided the work of the nine wiremen equally between them.

Obtaining the Co-operation of the Department Officials

Following the selection of the job, the next step was to obtain the co-operation of the supervisors concerned. First, a detailed statement of the proposed study was presented to the general foreman within whose jurisdiction the department came. He was asked to voice his approval or disapproval of having the study conducted in one of his departments and he was also encouraged to offer any suggestions or criticisms he might have. The general foreman was very much interested in the project and at a conference with the research group offered several valuable suggestions. He then took the initiative in laying the plan before the foreman concerned. The research group suggested that he offer it to the foreman as a tentative plan and ask the foreman not to discuss it with his subordinates until something more definite was decided upon. It was felt that if the first-line supervisors and the group selected knew that they were to be studied it might cause a great deal of unnecessary speculation and uneasiness. Furthermore, the research group wished to make a preliminary investigation in the department before anything about the study was made known.

During the whole of the planning period, the foreman was consulted and his permission was obtained on every move. He gave his wholehearted co-operation, as did every other supervisor once the study had been explained to him. It should be pointed out here that none of the supervisors was ever formally included in the group to be studied. However, the supervisors' frequent contacts with the group and their immediate presence in the department made it necessary to include them to a certain extent in the material recorded by the observer.

Base Period Studies

The research group was now in a position to go ahead with its plans. Because they felt that if the operators knew they were to be studied they might alter their customary work habits and behavior, they decided to make certain preliminary investigations before the study proper began. The investigators also wished to find out to what extent segregation in a separate room might alter the behavior and performance of the operators. To this end, three different types of material were collected. First, departmental records of production and earnings of the group over a period of eighteen weeks prior to the beginning of the study were obtained. Secondly, interviews were taken with thirty-two men in the regular bank wiring department to obtain their attitudes toward their jobs, supervisors, and departmental working conditions. Thirdly, for ten days prior to the time the men were informed of the study an investigator was stationed in the department to observe their behavior and work habits. The foreman provided him with a desk near his own from which the observer could obtain a general impression of their work behavior.

The Size of the Group Selected

The number of wiremen in the group selected had to be some multiple of three because each solderman was assigned the work of three wiremen. The investigators believed that one observer could carefully observe six wiremen best, but the work of a group of six was more than one inspector could manage. It was decided, therefore, to select nine wiremen and to include three soldermen and two inspectors. Six of the wiremen worked on "connector" equipments and the other three worked on "selector" equipments. These two types of equipment differed in that a connector equipment was eleven banks long and a selector equipment ten, and in that a connector fixture was less heavy than a selector fixture. The technique of wiring was the same in each case, so that for the purposes of computing output records the types did not need to be differentiated.

Informing the Group of their Selection for the Study

The men selected were first informed of the study by the foreman. He told them that he had promised to co-operate with the research department in making the study and solicited the co-operation of the men in carrying out his pledge. He also stressed the point that they would still be members of his department and responsible to their regular supervisors. Then the foreman took them to the observation room, where they were met by one of the research directors and the person who was to be the observer.

The research director explained the purpose of the study in detail. He told the men briefly about the work of the research department and how it had become necessary to study an ordinary department more closely. They had been selected, he said, because the type of work they were doing was particularly suited to measurement and because the department supervisors had promised their co-operation. The men were told that the research department would not interfere in any way with their usual routines. Two points were stressed: first, that no one in the research group would have any jurisdiction over them and, secondly, that whatever they did or said in the presence of the investigators would in no way be used to their detriment. They were introduced to the observer and were told that he would be in the room most of the time to record output and to make any other observations he considered important. The operators were asked to express their opinions and ask any questions which might occur to them.

Obtaining the Co-operation of the Employees

When the study was first planned, the investigators believed that it would be exceedingly difficult to obtain the co-operation of the employees without special inducements of some kind. The people who had planned the Relay Assembly Test Room had sensed this problem and had dealt with it in the following manner: First, the members of the group were given the considerate attention of supervisors of high rank, a recognition rarely accorded employees of nonsupervisory status. They were also visited by outsiders of high executive and academic rank. Secondly, they were made a separate group for the purposes of payment and were thus assured a wage more nearly proportional to their output than their previous wage had been. Thirdly, their customary supervision was gradually replaced by that of the man in charge of the study. Under his leadership they were excused from certain annoying rules, such as being required to pick up piece parts when they dropped on the floor. Finally, the experimental changes themselves (rest pauses, lunches, and shorter hours) were in the nature of special privileges inasmuch as they were not at that time accorded other employees in the plant.

However, the problem of obtaining co-operation in the Bank Wiring Observation Room was not so difficult as it first seemed. Comparison of the objectives of the two studies brought out the fact that there was a fundamental difference between the types of co-operation required in the two cases. In the bank wiring group all that was required was a willingness on the part of the employees to carry on in their usual way and to express themselves freely in the presence of the interviewer and the observer. The investigators did not expect them to work harder or do anything to which they were unaccustomed. They were interested in performance only in so far as it could tell them something about the departmental situation. If, upon entering the observation room, the group's output had suddenly increased, the investigators would have felt that they had failed in their objective of keeping the situation unchanged. In the relay assembly group, on the other hand, it had been desired that the group would respond as they felt to changes introduced, and certain special inducements had been given to insure a natural, wholehearted response.

Acting upon this distinction, the investigators decided that the bank wiring group would be accorded no special favors. The employees would continue to report to their regular supervisors, they would still be paid out of the departmental earnings, and they would be subject to the same rules and regulations as before. In order to control the factor of attention from outsiders or people of high rank, it was decided that such people should not be allowed to enter the room during working hours unless it was necessary.

The problem of obtaining the co-operation of the employees, therefore, became purely one of establishing the right kind of relation between the investigators and the group. In this the observer had much the most difficult task. During the first few days the men were in the observation room, they behaved quite differently from the way they had behaved in the department. There was much less talking and they worked steadily until quitting time. The observer was apparently regarded with distrust. The men did not talk to him except to voice complaints. They all complained about the lighting and the ventilation. The observer listened to their complaints and occasionally asked them for suggestions, but each time he made it clear that he could do nothing to rectify the conditions complained about. They were told to take all such matters up with the group chief. The group chief also besieged the observer with questions. The observer talked things over with him but refrained from recommending action, and the group chief was thus gradually made to see that he was free to make decisions without consulting the observer.

Of particular interest were the conversational habits of the men during the first week. From a distance one could not see whether they were talking or not. They neither looked up from their work nor slowed down in their work paces. Only a barely audible murmur indicated that they were conversing. If the observer got up and walked about, the murmur stopped. The observer felt that their attitude toward him was similar to their attitude toward the foreman. Whenever the foreman entered the room, the men became absolutely quiet and cast furtive glances at him as he moved about. Whenever he talked to a worker, those near made an effort to overhear what he said. This attitude was not so evident in the department, where the foreman seemingly could move about as he pleased without arousing unusual curiosity. The observer noticed that whenever he himself left the room the volume of conversation increased and that as soon as he came back the men all became quiet just as they did when the foreman came in.

Toward the middle of the week the tension lessened. The men began to talk more loudly and occasionally someone would laugh. Any unusually loud noise, however, whether it was a laugh, a whistle, or the dropping of a spool of wire or solder, seemed to cause embarrassment to the person responsible and several of the others would glance over their shoulders toward the observer. With each unusual occurrence they apparently expected something to happen. By Friday the group had become less timorous. Someone might start a popular song, a few would join in, and they would sing it over and over.

At the close of the second week the observer reported that the wiremen near his desk no longer appeared to be constrained by his presence. Occasionally one of them would attempt to assist him in taking the output count by telling him what level he was wiring. At times one of them would sit in his chair when he was not using it. By the end of the third week the observer was on fairly good terms with everyone in the group and he was being included in conversations which would be considerably altered at the approach of a supervisor. This was taken as a sure sign that he had gained their confidence.

The interviewer also played an important part in dispelling the fears and uncertainties aroused by placing the group under observation. In the first round of interviews with the men he discovered that almost every one of them had misinterpreted the purpose of the study and that they were in a state of considerable anxiety. This misunderstanding was not easily detected; it came out first in an interview with W_1 after the interviewer had talked to him about the study at some length. The interview began with W_1's complaining about poor illumination:

Int: "Well, how are things going?"

W_1: "I would rather work where I was before. There is something about this place; I don't know what it is. I don't like it as well as the other room."

Int: "What seems to be the trouble?"

W_1: "It's the lights. Over there where I am working there is a lot of shadow and I can't do my work as well. It isn't so bad over by the window, but even there it's not so good as it was in the other room. I have been sort of expecting to get a headache from that eyestrain, but I haven't yet. I sort of feel like I might get one today."

Int: "I should think dim lights might be harder on the solderman than on you."

W_1: "Well, he is kicking plenty. A lot of them down there are kicking about it. . . . It slows me down too. That is another thing. I work just as hard as I ever did before, and I have to work longer. Out in the other room I used to get through about twenty minutes to four.[1] You know, I had a few minutes to sit down and take it easy. In here I have to work right up to four o'clock and I have to keep my fingers going to get through in time. I used to turn out around 6,200 a day. Now it keeps me jumping to get out 5,600."

Int: "Is that so? I didn't think poor lights would make that much difference."

W_1: "Well, it's just the way you feel about it, you know. The other fellows are slowing up too. They all have to work longer. That goes for W_6 too, the Speed King. He says that he has to work harder and longer to turn out his 6,600."

---

[1] When this study began the operators were working forty hours per week. Their working day was 7:30 A.M. to 12:00 M. and 12:45 P.M. to 4:15 P.M.

Thus far the employee had given no hint of the fact that he had misunderstood the purpose of the study. Lights were poor, and because they were poor he couldn't get as much work done. Later on, the interviewer explained the purpose of the study to him simply and in detail. At the conclusion of the explanation W_1 made the following revealing remarks:

W_1: "Gee, I think I see what you are driving at now. You know I had the idea that what you people were trying to do was to see if you could get us to do just as much work in six hours as we are doing now."

Int: "For less money too, probably."

W_1: "Yes, for less money. I am not the only one either. About everybody down there who has talked about it has the same idea. Some of them have a vague idea of what it's all about but I don't think very many of them understand it at all. . . . I'll bet if you could explain it to them like that they would say so too."

These remarks strongly suggested that the men were only pretending to work harder and longer in the observation room, and that they justified this pretense on the ground that the lighting was poor. Although the lighting may have been inferior in that it cast shadows, the investigators felt that this was a minor instead of a major difficulty. This belief was substantiated by the fact that after the confidence of the group had been obtained complaints about illumination disappeared.

The Method of Designating the Operators and their Bench Positions

Numbers were assigned to the operators for convenience in recording observations and to preserve the employees' anonymity. Throughout this study the following abbreviations will be used:

W	stands for		Wireman
S	"	"	Solderman
I	"	"	Inspector
GC	"	"	Group Chief
SC	"	"	Section Chief
AF	"	"	Assistant Foreman
F	"	"	Foreman
Int.	"	"	Interviewer
Obs.	"	"	Observer

Different wiremen, soldermen, and inspectors were designated by subscript numbers. Thus the nine wiremen were designated by the letter "W" with the numbers 1 to 9 as subscripts. The soldermen were designated by the letter "S" with the numbers 1, 2, 3 as subscripts.

Numbers were also assigned to the bench positions normally occupied by each worker. This was done for the sake of accuracy in recording output and for convenience in indicating changes in work positions. The workmen instead of always working in the bench positions to which they were assigned sometimes traded jobs or helped a neighbor at his position. Each work station or bench position was given the same number as that of the worker who originally occupied it. Thus W_1 worked in position W_1, S_1 in position S_1, and so on. If W_1 traded jobs with S_1, this would be indicated by the observer as follows: "W_1, in position S_1, said or did so-and-so." Or take the following entry: "W_5, in position S_3, traded jobs with W_8." This means that wireman W_5 had been soldering in position S_3 (i.e., soldering for W_7, W_8, and W_9) and while in that position had exchanged places with W_8. The solderman who normally occupied position S_3 was wiring in position W_5.

From time to time in the material to be presented, it will be con-

TABLE XXV

Work Units
BANK WIRING OBSERVATION ROOM

Soldering Units	Inspection Units
Soldering Unit A	Inspection Unit A
W_1	W_1
W_2	W_2
W_3	W_3
S_1	W_4
	W_5 *
Soldering Unit B	S_1
W_4	S_2 *
W_5	I_1
W_6	
S_2	Inspection Unit B
	W_5 *
Soldering Unit C	W_6
W_7	W_7
W_8	W_8
W_9	W_9
S_4 †	S_2 *
	S_4 †
	I_3 ‡

* One-half of the work done in positions W_5 and S_2 was inspected by I_1, the other half by I_2, and later by I_3.

† S_4 replaced S_3 early in the study. See p. 405.

‡ I_3 replaced I_2 early in the study. See p. 405.

venient to refer to the different work units in the observation room. There were two kinds of work units, the soldering unit, consisting of three wiremen and a solderman, and the inspection unit, consisting of half the wiremen, their respective soldermen, and one inspector. These different units, and the men who comprised them, are shown in Table XXV.

The Observation Room

Figure 34 is a diagram of the observation room showing the wiremen's bench positions. This room was approximately 40 feet long and 20 feet wide and was located about 200 feet from the regular department, this being the nearest available space. In order to avoid the

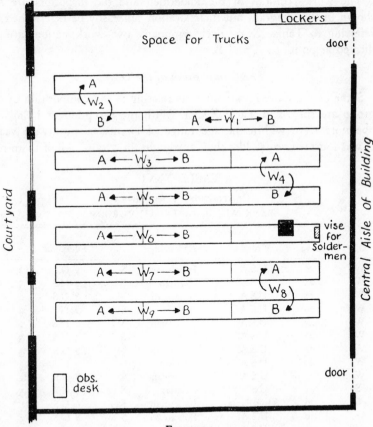

FIGURE 34

DIAGRAM OF OBSERVATION ROOM SHOWING WIREMEN'S POSITIONS (A & B)

necessity of installing costly ventilating equipment, the walls were not extended to the ceiling but were left with about four feet of space at the top. The room was equipped with standard workbenches taken from the regular department. Ample space was left at the front of the room for trucks of material to come in and out. At the rear of the room, space was left for the observer's desk. Inasmuch as a position in front of a group, especially if the occupant sits while the group stands, may imply superordination of some sort, care was taken to have the observer's desk in the rear. When he was seated, he faced toward a side wall and could not look directly at the group without turning to one side. It was believed that this arrangement would mitigate any feeling the operators might have of being watched.

The work positions of the soldermen and the inspectors are not shown in this diagram but their location can easily be determined by referring to Table XXV. Each wireman's two work stations are indicated as positions A and B.

The Composition of the Group

Some of the more important facts relating to the composition of the group are shown in Table XXVI. With the exception of I_3, all the operators were within the age range of twenty to twenty-six years. I_3 was fourteen years older than anyone in the group. All of them had

TABLE XXVI

COMPOSITION OF THE GROUP

BANK WIRING OBSERVATION ROOM

Operator	Age	Birthplace	Nationality	Marital Status	Education	Service Yrs.	Mos.
W_1	22	U.S.A.	Polish	S	7 G.S.	3	2
W_2	25	U.S.A.	German	S	2 H.S.	5	5
W_3	26	U.S.A.	American	M	8 G.S.	2	5
W_4	20	U.S.A.	Irish	S	2 H.S.	3	7
W_5	24	U.S.A.	Bohemian	M	4 H.S.	2	8
W_6	21	U.S.A.	Polish	S	2 H.S.	3	1
W_7	22	U.S.A.	Bohemian	M	8 G.S.	3	2
W_8	22	U.S.A.	German	S	4 H.S.	3	8
W_9	21	U.S.A.	American	S	8 G.S.	2	10
S_1	21	U.S.A.	German	S	8 G.S.	5	4
S_2	26	Yugoslavia	Bohemian	S	6 G.S.	9	8
S_4	20	U.S.A.	Bohemian	S	8 G.S.	3	0
I_1	23	U.S.A.	American	S	4 H.S.	3	0
I_3	40	Turkey	Armenian	M	3 Col.	7	0

two or more years' service with the company, the average being four years. S_2 had been with the company longest, with ten years to his credit; I_3 was next with seven years. Half of them had an eighth grade education or less. Of the other half, three had completed two years of high school, three had graduated, and one had the equivalent of about three years of college education. Six nationalities were represented: Bohemian, Polish, German, Irish, Armenian, and American. With the exception of S_2 and I_3 they were all born in this country. Of those who were born in the United States, all but three were of foreign-born parents. Four were married and all but one of the others had someone in their families dependent, wholly or in part, upon them. As a group they had more economic responsibilities than most young men of their age and marital status.

Changes in Personnel during Period of Observation

The group of fourteen men originally selected for the study did not remain intact very long. In less than three weeks one of the soldermen, S_3, was operated upon for a ruptured appendix; pneumonia developed, and he was not yet able to return to work when the study was concluded. S_3 was replaced by a person who will be referred to as S_4. Two weeks after this happened, the Inspection Branch removed one of the inspectors, I_2, and substituted another person, I_3. There were no other changes in personnel until a few weeks before the study ended. Then GC_1, who had a short service record, was demoted because of the general decline in business activity and another group chief in the department, GC_2, took over the group. About the same time, the department was consolidated with another department and the foreman was transferred to still another department. The new foreman took no direct part in the study, so there will be no further reference to him. Inasmuch as S_3 and I_2 were in the observation room such a short time, they too, for the most part, will be omitted from further consideration.

Records Obtained by the Investigators

The following records were obtained by the investigators:

1. *Quantity of output.* Output readings were taken by the observer at noon and at night after the men had quit work. These were taken with precision and were based upon an actual count. They were kept for each wireman and were entered on a form which showed the exact number of terminals wired by each man in each of his two work positions. They

showed the level upon which the wireman started and stopped, the type of banks used, and the number of banks in the equipment.

In addition to these independent readings, the investigators obtained the outputs reported by the wiremen to the group chief at the end of each day. These were kept for comparison with the observer's count. The investigators also obtained from the group chief a record of the amount of lost time claimed by each wireman and the reasons they gave for lost time.

2. *Quality of output.* Each day the observer obtained the inspectors' quality ratings of each wireman's work. These inspection records showed the equipment, the level, and the terminal upon which the defect specified occurred. They were copied onto a form which recorded the above information and, in addition, showed who wired the equipment, who soldered it, and who inspected it.

3. *Record of observations.* The observer kept a daily record of significant happenings in the observation room, of conversations of the employees, and of his own impressions. This record, completed, consisted of some three hundred single-spaced typewritten pages and ranged in content from occurrences in the observation room itself to fragmentary information concerning family life and past experiences of the operators.

4. *Record of interviews.* With the exception of the inspectors, each man was interviewed before the study began, and all the men were interviewed two or more times during the study itself. The interviews lasted from one to two hours. They were dictated in as nearly verbatim form as possible, giving both the interviewer's and the employee's conversation. The interviewer's own impressions were recorded separately. Typewritten, single-spaced, this material occupied well over three hundred pages.

5. *Physical examination records.* Each person was given a thorough physical examination at the company hospital. These records will not be presented in this report. All the men were found to be in good health and no disabilities were found which might interfere with their work.

6. *Mental and dexterity tests.* Toward the close of the study each man was given the following tests: Pegboard I, Pegboard II, a battery of soldering tests, and an Otis Intermediate or Higher Examination, depending upon educational attainments. The tests were administered by a psychologist well trained in the field.

Plan of Presentation

With the removal of the group to the observation room, the period of planning and preparation was over and the study proper began. The investigators felt that they had succeeded fairly well in laying the groundwork for the study. There were two major differences between the group's situation in the observation room and what it had been in the department. These, which were unavoidable, consisted of their segregation in a separate room and their knowledge that they were being studied. The investigators had to await developments in the observation room before the influence of either factor could be assessed. This will be done in the concluding chapter of this study. It is enough to point out here that neither factor appreciably altered the findings of the study. The output of the group remained practically unchanged, and their attitudes toward their work and supervision remained basically the same during the time they were in the observation room.

There was, however, one important difference which, while it in no way altered the value or significance of the data obtained, nevertheless should be mentioned at this time. In the following chapters the behavior of this group while they were in the observation room will be described and analyzed in detail. The description of some of these occurrences may convey a false impression of the regular departmental situation to the reader. There is no doubt that the members of this group were boisterous and that they said and did many things in the observation room which they never would have said or done in the regular department. The fact that they were in a small room by themselves gave them considerable freedom to do as they pleased and, being fairly young and energetic, they frequently took advantage of the situation. The members of the group did not regard either their group chief or section chief as possessing much authority and, inasmuch as their foreman and assistant foreman could spend very little time in the observation room, this in effect removed them from disciplinary authority during the greater part of the day. The important point to be made here, from a research point of view, is that the group's behavior was of the same general pattern in the observation room as in the department though less subdued than in the department. In other words, the changes which occurred in their behavior were changes in degree rather than in kind. The same basic attitudes were finding expression in their behavior in both situations, but the expression of these attitudes was more free and even somewhat exaggerated while they were in the observation room.

The data to be presented here have been divided into four parts, corresponding to the next four chapters, each of which seems to possess sufficient unity to warrant separate treatment. In the next chapter (XVIII) the various records relating to output are presented and analyzed. The following three chapters (XIX, XX, and XXI), which are based chiefly upon the observer's records, consider the operators in their daily relations with their supervisors and with one another. These four chapters complete the description of the human situation in the Bank Wiring Observation Room. In two subsequent chapters (XXII and XXIII) the investigators' interpretations and conclusions will be given.

CHAPTER XVIII

THE OUTPUT SITUATION IN THE BANK WIRING OBSERVATION ROOM

THE WAGE INCENTIVE SYSTEM

BEFORE describing the output situation in the Bank Wiring Observation Room, it is necessary to describe in some detail the wage incentive system under which this group worked.[1] The men were working under a system of group piecework according to which the entire department was considered a unit for purposes of payment. For each unit of equipment the department assembled and shipped out it was paid a fixed sum. The amount thus earned each week constituted the fund out of which all wages were paid. The greater the number of units completed each week by a given number of employees, the larger would be the sum to be distributed among them.

The allocation of the weekly departmental earnings to the individual employees in the department was based upon their hourly rates. The hourly rates differed for individuals, depending largely upon differences in efficiency, and were guaranteed by the firm in case piece-rate earnings were insufficient to cover them. An employee's hourly rate multiplied by the number of hours he worked per week was called the daywork value of the work he accomplished. By adding together the daywork value of the work done by all the employees in the department, and subtracting the total thus obtained from the total earnings of the department, the excess of piece-rate earnings over the total daywork value was determined. This surplus divided by the total daywork value was called the "percentage." Each individual's weekly daywork earnings were then increased by this percentage and the resulting figure constituted his actual weekly wage.

Inasmuch as the employees were paid weekly and it took some time to compute the amount due each workman, the foreman estimated the number of units his department would complete in a given week one or two days before the end of the week. The pay roll organization computed earnings on the basis of these estimates. At the end of each

---

[1] The purpose of this description is solely to provide the reader with information on the basis of which he can understand the material to be presented in this study. Certain technical details of the payment system in operation have been omitted as being extraneous to this purpose.

four-week period the amount of work actually accomplished was compared with these estimates and the difference, if any, was paid to the employees along with their usual checks. The amount thus paid every four weeks was called a "monthly balance."

Under this system of payment, differences in the earnings of different operators, hours of work remaining the same, depended entirely upon differences in individual hourly rates. A uniform increase in the hourly rates of all the employees in the department, output remaining the same, would have resulted in no change in individual earnings. It would simply have lowered the "percentage" or the excess of piece-rate over daywork earnings. However, an increase in the hourly rates of a few people, output remaining the same, would have lowered the earnings of those whose rates were not changed. The only way the group as a whole could increase its earnings was by increasing total output. Partly because of this, a "bogey" was established for each job. The bogey was simply an output standard in terms of which an individual's efficiency could be measured. It was something "to shoot at" and was intended to serve in much the same way as a record does for an athlete. The closer to it the employees came, the higher their earnings would be. It will be readily seen that a raising or lowering of the bogey would in no way affect earnings except in so far as it might influence output. Raising a bogey had none of the effects of reducing a piece rate or hourly rate. This point is emphasized here because it is well to keep it in mind throughout this study.

It is apparent that under this system the earnings of any one individual were affected by the output of every other person in the group. If a person did an unusually large amount of work one week and the other operators did not increase their output proportionately, his earnings would be but slightly higher than if he had not increased his output at all. The results of his increased efforts would be spread among all the workers in the department. Conversely, if a person were unusually low in output for a time, the output of the other operators would serve to sustain his earnings at about their ordinary level.

In order to bring about a rough correspondence between output and earnings, then, adjustments in hourly rates of the operators were based largely upon individual outputs. Records were kept of each person's production for guidance in adjusting rates. These records were based upon the person's weekly average hourly output. In computing them, the individual's total weekly output was divided by standard working hours, from which time lost on account of stoppages beyond the operator's control or time spent on unfamiliar work was deducted. If such time were not deducted, the efficiency ratings of those people who for some reason were delayed would suffer in comparison with those of people who had lost little time. The time thus deducted was called a "daywork allowance" by the people in the department and was used solely for computing efficiency records.

Inasmuch as these daywork allowances will be discussed a good deal in this study, it may be well to describe them further at this time and to differentiate them from "daywork credits," with which they may be confused. The difference between a daywork allowance, as the term is used in this study, and a daywork credit is simply that the former pertains solely to the computation of efficiency records and has nothing to do with payment, whereas the latter pertains primarily to payment. This distinction can best be made clear by an illustration. Suppose one of the wiremen in the observation room spent six hours wiring, one hour soldering, and one hour cleaning solder off the workbenches. Let us assume further that the wiring and soldering jobs were on a piecework basis but that miscellaneous work like cleaning solder off the benches was on a daywork basis and was not included in the piece rate on the soldering job. Now in this case the wireman, in reporting his ouput for the day, would report the number of terminals he had wired, the time spent in wiring them (six hours), and then he would enter a daywork allowance claim for the two hours he had spent soldering and cleaning solder off the benches. The group chief in computing this wireman's efficiency for the day would base his computation solely on the time spent at wiring. In other words, he would divide the wireman's output by six hours instead of eight so as not to lower unduly his efficiency rating on the wiring job.

Now let us look at this same case from the standpoint of payment. Inasmuch as both the wiring job and the soldering job were on a piecework basis, the wireman, or more accurately the payment group to which the wireman belonged, would receive piecework earnings for the seven hours spent on these two jobs. In other words, no adjustment would need to be made for the hour spent at soldering. An adjustment would have to be made, however, for the hour spent at cleaning the benches. For this hour spent on daywork the wireman would be credited with his hourly rate. He would, in other words, receive a daywork credit of one hour for purposes of payment and a daywork allowance of two hours for purposes of computing his efficiency. For the most part, these daywork credits were pooled with the piecework earnings of the payment group and were distributed on a prorata basis.

It is apparent that this system, in order to function satisfactorily, required a high degree of collaboration between employee and employee and between employees and management. It demanded that each employee look constantly toward increasing or at least maintaining total output and that every other employee do the same. It demanded that each employee think not alone of his own personal interests but also of those of his fellow workmen. Thus if a person, once having achieved a high hourly rate, deliberately slowed up, he could, for a short time at least, receive in payment more than he contributed to the earnings of the group. The chief thing which would prevent him from doing this was his regard for the well-being of his co-workers and for their attitude toward him. Indeed, it could be easily understood, in fact it was expected, that the employees would group together informally to bring pressure to bear upon the slower workers.

The group chief and the section chief were also assigned an hourly rate, and they shared in the departmental earnings on the same basis as the operators. The assistant foreman and the foreman were paid on a salary basis. An allowance was made for supervision in the piece rate so that the employees in no sense "carried" the supervisors.

This, in brief, was the wage incentive plan under which the group worked. Every aspect of it was based upon some logical reason and could be defended on the grounds, first, that it should promote efficiency and, secondly, that it provided an equitable means of apportioning earnings among the employees. Both of these claims were true, however, only if the plan worked as it was supposed to and the employees acted in fact as they were presumed to act in theory. In what follows, we shall inquire to what extent these assumptions held true.

BELIEFS OF EMPLOYEES REGARDING PAYMENT SYSTEM

The Concept of a Day's Work

In interviews with the operators in the department before the study began, the investigators encountered certain beliefs which the employees seemed to hold in common. Chief among these was the concept of a day's work. This idea kept cropping up in interview after interview. Of the thirty-two men interviewed in the department before the study began, a group which included the nine wiremen later selected for the study, twenty-two discussed rates of output. Of these twenty-two, twenty said that the wiring of two equipments constituted a day's work. The other two men said they were supposed to try to make the bogey, which they correctly stated as 914 connections per hour. The following comments, quoted from interviews with members of the group under observation, are typical:

W_1: "6,600 is the bogey. You see, that's two sets. There are 3,300 connections on a set. Now on selector wiring the bogey is only 6,000, because there are only 3,000 connections on a set. In order to turn out 6,600 there, you have to wire three levels on a third set."

Int: "6,600 is your bogey then?"

W_1: "Yes, it's 6,600. You see they told us if we got out two sets a day it would be all right. That's a pretty good day's work too."

. . . . . .

W_2: "You know, some of those fellows stall around for three months before they turn out 6,000. There's no reason for that at all. I could turn out 6,000 in three weeks. I think the rest of them could if they wanted to. . . . I'm making around 7,000 every day. . . . I don't mind that [their fooling around] as long as it doesn't interfere with the work. I never fool around until I have my bogey out. That is the first thing. When I get my bogey out, then I don't mind loafing around a bit."

. . . . . .

W_3: "I turn out 6,600 regularly. That's about what is expected of us. Of course you could make out less and get by, but it's safer to turn out about 6,600."

Int: "And is 6,600 your bogey?"

W_3: "No, our bogey is higher than that. It is 914 an hour."

. . . . . .

W_4: "I think connector wiring is the better job. The boards aren't as heavy [as on selectors] and you have an extra bank. You see, the rate on connectors is around 6,600 and on selectors it's only 6,000."

. . . . . .

W_5: "I turn out 100 per cent efficiency right along. That means I turn out 6,600 a day."[1]

Int: "Is the bogey 6,600 a day?"

W_5: "No, that's not the bogey. The bogey is 7,200, I think."

. . . . . .

W_6: "Well, the bogey is pretty high. I turn out 6,600 a day right along and that is pretty good, I think, for the average."

Int: "Is that the bogey?"

---

[1] In order to have an efficiency of 100 per cent, a wireman would have to wire 7,312 terminals a day.

W₆: "I think it is."

Int: "Then you are making 100 per cent efficiency?"

W₆: "Well, I don't know about that. I don't think I am turning out 100
per cent. You see the bogey was 914 an hour for an 8¾-hour day,
so I suppose it will be about 6,600 for an 8-hour day."

. . . . . .

W₇: "6,000 a day is the rate. I guess there's another rate that's higher than
that, but the bosses tell us that 6,000 is a day's work."

. . . . . .

W₈: "I make between 5,500 and 6,000. On selectors they don't have to
turn out as many. I think they are supposed to turn out 6,000 a
day. We have an extra bank on each set so that if we wire two
sets a day we would be making 6,600 a day."

Int: "Is that the bogey?"

W₈: "Yes, I think it is."

From comments such as these it was apparent that the operators
were accustomed to thinking of two equipments a day as a day's work.
This was verified by the observer, who found that the operators frequently stopped wiring when they had finished their quotas even though
it was not official stopping time. This concept of a day's work was of
interest for two reasons. In the first place, it did not refer to the bogey
or to any other standard of performance officially imposed. As compared with the day's work of which they spoke, which amounted to
6,000 or 6,600 connections depending upon the type of equipment, the
bogey was considerably higher. If asked what the bogey was, some of
the men could give the correct answer. Many of them, however, spoke
of the day's work as being the bogey. Others said that they were
supposed to turn out about two sets but they thought the bogey was
higher. Still others spoke of the day's work as being the rate on the
job, and the rate was held to be synonymous with bogey. Technically,
the word "rate" had three quite different meanings depending on
whether it referred to piece rates, hourly rates, or rates of working;
yet frequently the employees made no distinction. Whatever else this
confusion of terminology meant, one conclusion was certain. The
bogey was not functioning as a competitive standard for this group.

In the second place, the idea of a day's work was of interest because
it was contrary to one of the basic notions of the incentive plan. Theoretically, the incentive plan was intended to obviate the problems
attendant upon the determination of a day's work. The chief draw-

back to paying stipulated monthly, daily, or hourly wages is that there is no accurate way of determining how much work should be done for the wages received. Some criterion there must be, but if its determination were left up to the workers it is possible that they might fix upon a low standard. On the other hand, standards arbitrarily imposed by the employer might possibly be too high and entail detrimental physiological results. Where the amount of work to be done in a given time for a given wage is determined by custom, such problems may be present but they do not come to the fore. In modern industry, however, jobs are subdivided and changed so frequently that whatever influence custom might bring to bear is lost. There is no customary standard to which to appeal. One of the chief arguments to be advanced in favor of incentive plans is that under an incentive system a day's work will be determined at that point where fatigue or "pain costs" balance the worker's subjective estimate of the added monetary return. The amount of work done by different individuals should, theoretically, vary as individual capacities vary, and for any one individual variations from day to day might be expected. Under such a system, the concept of a day's work, of a specified number of units to be completed each day by every worker, has, strictly speaking, no place. In the Bank Wiring Observation Room, then, there was evidence that the wage incentive plan was not functioning entirely as it was intended to function.

The question of how two equipments came to be fixed upon as a day's work is an interesting one, but it cannot be definitely answered. Among the possible explanations, four may be mentioned. First, it might be argued that the hourly rates of the people who wired 6,000 or 6,600 terminals a day were at the maximum of the labor grade established for this kind of work. If this were so, the supervisors could not offer the men, except in unusual cases, increases in hourly rates for further increases in output, and therefore the men would tend to fix their output at that level. This explanation failed to be in any sense conclusive, however, simply because the majority of the people in the observation room had not reached the maximum of the labor grade.

Secondly, it might be argued that 6,000 or 6,600 terminals per day, or two equipments, represented the balance point between fatigue or "pain costs" of work, on the one hand, and the satisfactions to be derived from the monetary returns for that amount of work, on the other. There were, however, no evidences of fatigue among the operators in the observation room. Furthermore, some of the operators wished to turn out more work, but they were reluctant to do so in the face of the attitudes prevailing in the group. Their concept of a day's work, in other words, did not represent a personally calculated equilibrium between work and monetary return.

A third explanation is that the supervisors might have mentioned some figure as a desirable day's work when attempting to stimulate some of the slower men. They might have said, for example, "Your output is too low, you should be turning out 6,000 connections a day." The figure thus mentioned might then have become, in the operators' thinking, the standard of acceptable performance. This explanation, however, fails to explain why the supervisors should have chosen this figure instead of some other or why the operators agreed among themselves that it was wrong to exceed it. In practice the supervisors did tell some of the slower men that they should have been turning out two equipments a day, but they also told some of the other wiremen that they should have been doing more. In view of the fact that different figures were given different operators, it is difficult to understand how this explanation could account for their concept of a day's work.

Finally, it might be claimed that the wiring of two equipments was a "natural" day's work in that a wireman could complete two but not three equipments. Rather than start on a third unit he might, for the sake of tidiness and good workmanship, prefer to complete only two and start out on a new one the first thing in the morning. Although some of the operators claimed that they did get a certain satisfaction out of finishing an equipment and seeing the resulting colorful pattern of interlaced wires before them (one of them likened it to the pleasure a woman must derive from knitting), the fact is that they stopped work during the wiring of an equipment more frequently than at the end.

None of these four explanations, then, is satisfactory. There is no way of telling whether one is more plausible than the others. For this reason, the question will be dropped from further consideration. It may be well to point out, however, that one could not hold to any one of the above explanations without admitting, implicitly, that the wage incentive was not functioning as it was supposed to. For, if it were functioning as it was supposed to, the conditions assumed in these arguments would not exist.

The Day's Work as a Group Standard

As the study progressed, it became more and more apparent that the operators' conception of a day's work had a much wider significance than has thus far been implied. The interviewer, while inquiring further into this belief, found that it was related to other beliefs which the operators held quite generally. These other beliefs, which incidentally are quite common and more or less familiar to everyone, usually took the following form: "If we exceed our day's work by any appreciable amount, something will happen. The 'rate' might be cut, the 'rate' might be raised, the 'bogey' might be raised, someone might be laid off, or the supervisor might 'bawl out' the slower men." Any or all of these consequences might follow. It is difficult to produce evidence in which such apprehensions were articulated as clearly as here represented. This statement represents the summation of a variety of employees' remarks in which these fears were more or less implied. The following quotations are given to show the type of evidence upon which the above observation is based:

W_2: (After claiming that he turned out more work than anyone else in the group) "They [his co-workers] don't like to have me turn in so much, but I turn it in anyway."

(In another interview) "Right now I'm turning out over 7,000 a day, around 7,040. The rest of the fellows kick because I do that. They want me to come down. They want me to come down to around 6,600, but I don't see why I should. If I did, the supervisors would come in and ask me what causes me to drop like that. I've been turning out about that much for the last six months now and I see no reason why I should turn out less. There's no reason why I should turn out more either."

. . . . . .

W_3: "No one can turn out the bogey consistently. Well, occasionally some of them do. Now since the layoff started there's been a few fellows down there who have been turning out around 7,300 a day. They've been working like hell. I think it is foolishness to do it because I don't think it will do them any good, and it is likely to do the rest of us a lot of harm."

Int: "Just how do you figure that?"

W_3: "Well, you see if they start turning out around 7,300 a day over a period of weeks and if three of them do it, then they can lay one of the men off, because three men working at that speed can do as much as four men working at the present rate."

Int: "And you think that is likely to happen?"

W_3: "Yes, I think it would. At present we are only scheduled for 40 sets ahead. In normal times we were scheduled for over 100. If they find that fewer men can do the work, they're going to lay off more of us. When things pick up they will expect us to do as much as we are now. That means they will raise the bogey on us. You see how it works?"

   •   •   •   •   •

Int: "You say there is no incentive to turn out more work. If all of you did more work, wouldn't you make more money?"

W_4: "No, we wouldn't. They told us that down there one time. You know, the supervisors came around and told us that very thing, that if we would turn out more work we would make more money, but we can't see it that way. Probably what would happen is that our bogey would be raised, and then we would just be turning out more work for the same money.[1] I can't see that."

   •   •   •   •   •

W_5: "There's another thing; you know the fellows give the fast workers the raspberry all the time. Work hard, try to do your best, and they don't appreciate it at all. They don't seem to figure that they are gaining any by it. It's not only the wiremen, the solder-men don't like it either. . . . The fellows who loaf along are liked better than anybody else. Some of them take pride in turning out as little work as they can and making the boss think they're turning out a whole lot. They think it's smart. I think a lot of them have the idea that if you work fast the rate will be cut. That would mean that they would have to work faster for the same money. I've never seen our rate cut yet, so I don't know whether it would happen or not. I have heard it has happened in some cases though."

   •   •   •   •   •

W_6: (Talking about a relative of his who worked in the plant) "She gets in here early and goes ahead and makes up a lot of parts so that when the rest of the girls start in she's already got a whole lot stacked up. In that way she turns out a great deal of work. She's money greedy. That's what's the matter with her and they shouldn't allow that. All she does is spoil the rate for the rest of the girls."

Int: "How does she do that?"

W_6: "By turning out so much. When they see her making so much money, they cut the rate."

   •   •   •   •   •

W_7: "There's one little guy down there that turns out over 7,000 a day. I think there's a couple of them. And we have to put up with it."

   •   •   •   •   •

---

[1] It should be remembered that raising the bogey could not have this effect unless it resulted in lower output. See p. 410.

W_8: "Some people down there have had lots more experience than others and they can't possibly turn out the rate. I know a fellow who came in there just a few months ago and he is up above average already. It won't be long before he will be turning out 7,000 or 8,000 of them."

Int: "Do you think he will?"

W_8: "Well, I think so. Some of them do it. Of course, the slower men don't like that so well."

Int: (After a discussion of a large vs. a small gang for purposes of payment) "Your earnings would probably increase as much under your present system of payment, provided everyone increased his output proportionately."

W_8: "That would mean that somebody would be out of a job. We've only got so much work to do, you know. Now just suppose a person was doing 6,000 connections a day, say on selectors, that's two whole sets. Now suppose that instead of just loafing around when he gets through he did two more rows on another set. Well, then, when he comes to work the next morning he would have two rows to start with. Then suppose he did another whole set and two additional rows. On the third day, let's see, where would he be? On the third day he would start on the equipment that was already wired up six levels. Before long he would have an extra set done. Then where would you be? Somebody could be laid off."

Int: "Are you conscious of that when you are working? Are you consciously thinking that if you turn out over a certain amount somebody will be laid off?"

W_8: "That only stands to reason, doesn't it?"

Int: "That if you increase your output they're going to lay somebody off?"

W_8: "Yeah. Now just suppose the fellows in that room could increase their output to 7,000. I think some of them can. That would mean less work for others."

Int: "On the same basis, why do you work at all? If you turn out only 3,000 a day, you're just doing work that someone else might do."

W_8: "Yeah, but I think it should be spread around more."

Statements like these indicated that many apprehensions and fears were centered around the concept of a day's work. They suggested that the day's work might be something more than an output standard, that it might be a norm of conduct. The data obtained by the observer provided additional evidence in support of this interpretation. He found that men who persisted in exceeding the group standard of a day's work were looked upon with disfavor. This was manifested in subtle forms of sarcasm and ridicule which can best be illustrated by quoting from the observer's record:

W_6 and W_4 were kidding each other about working hard. W_6 was working very fast. W_4 was working faster than usual.

W_4: (To W_6) "Go on, you slave, work. You're enough connections ahead now to take care of Friday."

Obs: (To W_4) "Is W_6 going too fast to suit you?"

W_4: "He's nothing but a slave. A couple more rows and he'll have 8,000."

W_6: "No, I won't. I haven't got today's work out yet."

W_4: "You should have quit when you finished that set."

W_6: "I'm good for another 6,000 connections. If they'd pay me for it, I'd turn 'em out."

. . . . . .

GC_2 was taking the output count.

W_4: (To W_6) "How many are you going to turn in?"

W_6: "I've got to turn in 6,800."

W_4: "What's the matter — are you crazy? You work all week and turn in 6,600 for a full day, and now today you're away an hour and a quarter and you turn in more than you do the other days."

W_6: "I don't care. I'm going to finish these sets tomorrow."

W_4: "You're screwy."

W_6: "All right, I'll turn in 6,400."

W_4: "That's too much."

W_6: "That don't make any difference. I've got to do something with them."

W_4: "Well, give them to me."

W_6 did not answer.

. . . . . .

W_2: (To S_1) "Come on, get this set."

S_1: "All right." (To Obs.) "I want to introduce you to Lightning [W_2] and Cyclone [W_3]. When these two get going it's just like a whirlwind up here. Give W_2 a big chew of snuff and he just burns the solder right off the terminals."

. . . . . .

S_1: (To Obs.) "What's a guy going to do if these fellows won't quit work?"

Obs: "That's it, what?"

S_1: "Keep right on working."

Obs: "There you are. Now you've got it."

S_1: "W_2 has got 8,000 and he don't know enough to quit. Well, if he wires 8,000, I must solder 8,000. That's it, isn't it?"

Obs: "Sure."

W_6 and W_2 were the first in output and it was toward them that most of the group pressure was directed. W_6 was designated by such names as "Shrimp," "Runt," and "Slave." Sometimes he was called "Speed King," a concession to his wiring ability. W_2 was called "Phar Lap," the name of a race horse. W_1 was nicknamed "4:15 Special," meaning that he worked until quitting time. W_5 was also called "Slave" occasionally.

One of the most interesting devices by which the group attempted to control the behavior of individual members was a practice which they called "binging." This practice was noticed early in the study. The observer described it as follows:

W_7, W_8, W_9, and S_4 were engaging in a game which they called "binging." One of them walked up to another man and hit him as hard as he could on the upper arm. The one hit made no protest, and it seems that it was his privilege to "bing" the one who hit him. He was free to retaliate with one blow. One of the objects of the game is to see who can hit the hardest. But it is also used as a penalty. If one of them says something that another dislikes, the latter may walk up and say, "I'm going to bing you for that." The one who is getting binged may complain that he has been hurt and say, "That one was too hard. I'm going to get you for that one."

In the following incident binging was being used as a simple penalty:

W_9 suddenly binged W_7.

Obs: (To W_9) "Why did you do that?"

W_9: "He swore. We got an agreement so that the one who swears gets binged. W_8 was in it for five minutes, but he got binged a couple of times and then quit."

Obs: "Why don't you want W_7 to swear?"

W_9: "It's just a bad habit. There's no sense to it, and it doesn't sound good. I've been getting the habit lately and sometimes I swear when I don't want to. I never used to swear until I got next to W_8, there, and now I find myself doing it all the time."

Another time binging was advocated as a means of expressing a mutual antagonism and settling a dispute:

W_7 had his window open. W_6 walked over and opened his window wide. W_9 went over and closed W_6's window. W_6 ran over and grabbed the chain. He insisted that the window stay open. W_9 insisted that it was too drafty.

W_6: "You run your own window, I'll take care of this one."

W_9: "It's too drafty. You leave that window closed or I'll bing you."

W_6: "Go ahead, start."

W_9 glanced up to see if he could take the chain off the top of the window. W_6 held the chain tight so that W_9 couldn't loosen it. They had quite an argument.

W_6: (To W_8) "How about it? Is it too drafty over there?"

W_8: "No, it's all right."

W_6: "There you are. Now leave the window alone."

S_4: (To W_8) "What's the idea of lying?"

W_8: "I'm not."

S_4: "You're lying if you say you don't feel the draft."

W_8 did not answer.

W_7: (Tired of the argument) "Why don't you bing each other and then shut up?"

In addition to its use as a penalty and as a means of settling disputes, binging was used to regulate the output of some of the faster workers. This was one of its most significant applications and is well illustrated in the following entry:

W_8: (To W_6) "Why don't you quit work? Let's see, this is your thirty-fifth row today. What are you going to do with them all?"

W_6: "What do you care? It's to your advantage if I work, isn't it?"

W_8: "Yeah, but the way you're working you'll get stuck with them."

W_6: "Don't worry about that. I'll take care of it. You're getting paid by the sets I turn out. That's all you should worry about."

W_8: "If you don't quit work I'll bing you." W_8 struck W_6 and finally chased him around the room.

Obs: (A few minutes later) "What's the matter, W_6, won't he let you
work?"

W_6: "No. I'm all through though. I've got enough done." He then went
over and helped another wireman.

From observations such as these and from interviews the investigators
concluded that they had come upon a set of basic attitudes. Beliefs
regarding a day's work and the dangers involved in exceeding it were
not confined to a few persons but were held quite generally, both by
the men in the observation room and in the regular department. It
was apparent that there existed a group norm in terms of which the
behavior of different individuals was in some sense being regulated.

The Demand for "Straight-Line" Output Curves

Another idea frequently expressed, directly or indirectly, by the employees in their interviews was that their weekly average hourly output
should show little change from week to week. This did not mean that
all of them should try to achieve identical average hourly outputs each
week. It did mean that each of them should try to be fairly consistent
week after week irrespective of differences in the absolute levels of
their outputs. Their reasons for this were similar to those they advanced
for not exceeding their day's work. They felt that if their output
showed much change either from day to day or from week to week
"something might happen." An unusually high output might thence-
forward become the standard their supervisors would expect them to
maintain. The men felt it would be a way of confessing that they were
capable of doing better. On the other hand, they felt that a low output
would afford their supervisors a chance to "bawl them out." If output
were kept fairly constant, they thought, neither possibility could
happen.

If the wiremen acted as one might infer from their statements, it was
to be expected that their weekly average hourly outputs would, when
plotted, approximate a horizontal line. To verify this point the departmental performance records were examined. These are shown in
Figure 35. The time period over which these records extend includes
the observation period proper as well as the base period of eighteen
weeks just prior to the time the study began. These curves will be
referred to again in connection with other questions; for the time being,
they will be examined only in relation to the question of "straight-line"
output curves. In passing, certain omissions in the curves should be
explained.

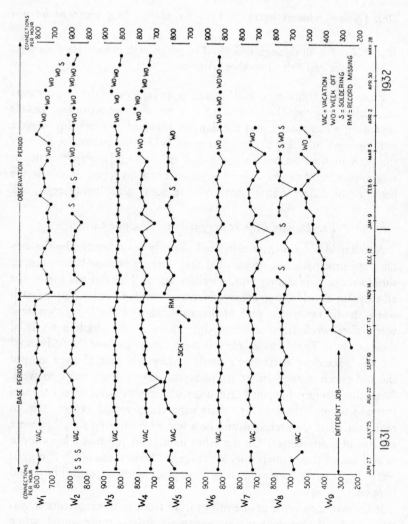

FIGURE 35

REPORTED AVERAGE HOURLY OUTPUT PER WEEK FOR BASE PERIOD AND
OBSERVATION PERIOD

BANK WIRING OBSERVATION ROOM

It will be noted, first, that W_9 was employed at bank wiring during only six of the eighteen weeks of the base period. W_9 was looked upon as a problem case by the supervisors. According to them, he had been tried out on every job in the department and had had previous experience at wiring. Therefore, the fact that he was on a different job during the first twelve weeks of the base period does not mean that he was a beginner at wiring. It does mean, however, that he was out of practice. Secondly, following the week ending January 9, 1932, all employees in the Operating Branch had to take some time off. This was necessitated by the company's policy of spreading available employment over a larger number of employees than could be employed on a forty-hour work week. From that time until this group was finally laid off, the amount of work to be done steadily declined. On January 11, the work week was shortened from five eight-hour days to four. Following the week ending February 27, it was decided that each employee should take off one week in four. On March 28, working time was cut to every other week. This arrangement continued for only four weeks. It then became necessary to reduce working time to seven days in every four weeks. Two weeks were taken off, three days were worked the third week, and four days the fourth week. The broken lines, marked WO (week off), indicate these gaps in employment. Thirdly, W_5, W_7, W_8, and W_9 were not in the observation room so long as the others. The department chief could not allow the entire group to be away at one time, and these four men worked while the others were away. Inasmuch as they did not do enough work to keep one inspector busy, it was necessary to move them back to the department. The investigators kept in touch with them during this time, but output records were not taken.

Confining attention to the shape of these curves, i.e., to the extent to which they change direction from week to week, it is apparent that although, strictly speaking, they are not horizontal lines, nevertheless they approximate horizontal lines and are certainly devoid of individuality. No upward or downward trend is apparent except in the case of W_9. In the curves for W_2, W_3, and W_6 there is remarkably little fluctuation. These three curves, in fact, can be called "straight-line" output curves. Furthermore, it is apparent that the fluctuations which occur are ordinarily either gross changes or very minor ones. In this respect, as well as in their lack of trend, these curves contrast sharply with those of the Relay Assembly Test Room group, which show marked week-to-week variations as well as pronounced individual characteristics. On the basis of these observations it was concluded that the operators' output curves were in fact expressing the ideas and beliefs they held with respect to output.

DEVICES FOR ACHIEVING UNIFORMITY IN PERFORMANCE RECORDS

In their attempts to maintain uniformity in their output curves, the operators resorted, in varying degrees, to two practices. The first consisted of reporting sometimes more and sometimes less than they actually accomplished. The second, and more important, device was that of manipulating the amount of net working time (a figure used by the department in computing output rates) by claiming daywork allowances. These mechanisms for keeping average hourly output rates fairly constant can best be understood by remembering that average hourly output equals total output divided by hours of work. A given hourly output rate could be maintained by manipulating the dividend, i.e., reporting more or less output than the actual amount, or by manipulating the divisor, i.e., claiming more or less daywork allowance. These two devices will be examined in some detail.

Actual Output vs. Reported Output

In their interviews some of the employees remarked that they sometimes "saved up connections" on days when their output was high and reported them on days when their output was low. They said that having some work saved up made them feel better. The group chief was supposed to take individual output counts at the end of each day. In practice, however, instead of actually counting the number of terminals each person wired, which would have been a laborious task and an almost impossible one considering his many duties, he had the operators themselves report their outputs to him. He knew that they did not always report exactly what they produced and he took this as a matter of course. "They like to have a few saved up in case things don't go so good," he said. The observer kept track both of the outputs reported by the men and of their actual outputs. The latter he obtained by an actual count, taken at noon and at night.[1]

The observer's record showed that no wireman reported exactly what he actually produced each week. Sometimes the two figures did agree but more frequently they did not. Moreover, the fact that a balance

---

[1] It should be pointed out here that the group was not paid on the basis of reported output. Payment was based on an accurate count of the completed equipments actually delivered by the department. Inaccuracies in the amount of output reported by individual operators affected only the efficiency records, upon which changes in hourly rates of individuals at regular rate review periods were based.

was achieved at the end of the week did not mean that the wireman concerned had reported exactly what he produced each day within the week. More often it meant that there were daily differences which canceled out at the end of the week. During the first part of the study the weekly differences tended to be smaller than during the last part. This was probably because the operators were at first uncertain of the use which the investigators might make of these figures. As time went on and the men began to have more confidence in the investigators, there was less tendency to cover up the actual situation. The weekly balances of some of the men were almost always negative. Thus, during those weeks in which their actual and reported outputs did not balance, W_2, W_7, and W_9 almost always reported more work than they accomplished. Their deficits were, therefore, cumulative throughout the study. W_3 and W_6, on the contrary, tended to report less than they produced. The others fell in between these two extremes, reporting sometimes more and sometimes less than they produced each week.

Table XXVII shows the average hourly difference between each wireman's actual and reported outputs. In computing these figures the

TABLE XXVII

AVERAGE HOURLY DIFFERENCES BETWEEN ACTUAL AND REPORTED OUTPUTS
BANK WIRING OBSERVATION ROOM

Wireman	Actual Output Higher than Reported Output (no. of connections)	Actual Output Lower than Reported Output (no. of connections)
W_6	1.7	..
W_3	1.4	..
W_5	..	1.2
W_2	..	2.6
W_4	..	3.1
W_8	..	4.2
W_1	..	4.9
W_9	..	18.7
W_7	..	22.3

difference between each wireman's total actual and reported outputs over the entire study period was determined and then divided by the total number of hours each person was wiring during that period. These figures show that W_3 and W_6 actually turned out more work than they reported. All the others reported more work than they accomplished. The average deficits were not large except in the cases of W_7 and W_9, the two slowest wiremen.

The question of whether the wiremen were aware of the fact that they were producing more or less than they reported may be raised. Perhaps most of these surpluses and deficits could have resulted from inaccuracies in their daily estimates of output or from losing track of where they stood over the week end. Although mistakes such as these might have occurred, especially toward the end of the study when the men were away from their work for one or two weeks at a time, the investigators found little evidence in favor of this interpretation. One of the most interesting things about the group was that each man seemed to know just where he stood at any time. The men could tell not only how much they had accomplished at a given time, but also, and with a startling degree of accuracy, how much their neighbors had accomplished. Some of them could even calculate the other way and tell the time of day by the number of connections they had wired. At the close of an interview with W_8 the interviewer asked him if he knew what time it was when he came up. He replied, "Just a minute and I'll figure it out. Let's see, how many levels have I wired this morning?" After a moment's thought he said he came up at 8:45, which was not more than two minutes off.

As far as the observer knew, the men kept no written records; yet they frequently carried rather difficult figures over from day to day. Thus, during one week W_2 had surpluses on Tuesday, Wednesday, and Thursday of 440, 432, and 1,128 respectively, making a total of 2,000. On Friday he reported exactly 2,000 connections more than he had wired, thus achieving an even balance for the week. Again, on the first three working days of the week ending March 5, W_6 had surpluses of 286, 1,386, and 352 respectively. On the fourth day, Friday, he reported 1,804 connections more than he had wired, thus leaving a surplus of 220, which was a comparatively easy figure to carry over to the next week. These observations are significant in that they show how enormously preoccupied these men were with the quantity of output.

Daywork Allowance Claims

The department permitted employees to claim daywork for unusual stoppages which were beyond their control. It did not, however, define what an unusual stoppage was or attempt to state which stoppages were and which were not beyond the employees' control. Such a definition would have been very difficult to make because practically all delays were in some sense subject to employee control. Moreover, if the wage incentive plan functioned as it was supposed to, there was no need for such a definition. It was assumed that the employees would resent any stoppage which interfered with their work and, as long as the opportunity of doing piecework was present, that they would never either deliberately bring about a situation in which they could get only daywork or claim more daywork than they were entitled to. Yet that is exactly what happened. Some of them claimed more daywork allowances than they were entitled to or contrived to bring about occurrences which would justify their claims. The interesting thing about these claims is that they meant nothing to the operators in terms of payment. The operators were here addressing themselves not to financial gain but to the security they felt came from uniform output curves. They saw, of course, that the more daywork they were allowed, the less output they would have to produce in order to maintain a given output rate.

As a rough measure of the amounts of daywork claimed by different wiremen, the average time per hour claimed by each man was computed. These figures are shown in Table XXVIII. They were computed by summing up the total daywork time claimed by each person

TABLE XXVIII

AVERAGE HOURLY DAYWORK ALLOWANCE TIME CLAIMED BY EACH WIREMAN
DURING THE STUDY
BANK WIRING OBSERVATION ROOM

Wireman	Average Time Claimed per Hour (mins. secs.)	
W_3		18
W_5		30
W_4		36
W_6		42
W_2	1	00
W_1	1	06
W_8	2	06
W_9	3	42
W_7	3	48

during the study and dividing by the number of hours each worked. Here again there were marked differences. W_7, W_8, and W_9, the three slowest wiremen in the group, together claimed over twice as much lost time as the other six wiremen combined. W_3, one of the fastest wiremen, claimed least, averaging only 18 seconds per hour.

Each time a wireman claimed daywork, he was supposed to give the group chief the reason for the delay as well as the amount of time lost.

The reasons offered by each wireman were interesting because they showed which factors in the total work situation were regarded as offering sufficient justification for a daywork allowance claim and they also showed where most of the blame was placed. The reasons and the frequency with which they were given by each wireman are shown in Table XXIX.[1]

TABLE XXIX

REASONS FOR DAYWORK ALLOWANCES AND FREQUENCY WITH WHICH THEY WERE GIVEN

BANK WIRING OBSERVATION ROOM

Reasons for Daywork Allowances	Frequency with Which Reasons Were Given									
	W_1	W_2	W_3	W_4	W_5	W_6	W_7	W_8	W_9	Total
Shortage of cables ..	3	2	..	1	1	1	6	2	6	22
Shortage of banks ..	4	3	2	4	3	3	6	3	4	32
Defective wire	1	1	1	1	..	..	8	4	1	17
Defective solder	1	..	..	..	..	..	..	..	2	3
Cable reverses	4	..	..	..	1	..	1	..	3	9
Waiting for trucker .	..	..	..	1	..	..	..	1	..	2
Waiting for solderman	..	..	..	..	2	1	10	2	5	20
Waiting for inspector	..	..	..	..	1	6	17	8	22	54
Making repairs	..	..	..	..	..	..	1	..	31	32
Soldering	2	..	..	.	1	..	1	..	1	5
Power off	..	..	..	..	..	..	1	1	1	3
No reason given	5	3	1	3	.	1	4	3	5	25
Total claims	20	9	4	10	9	12	55	24	81	224

Table XXIX shows that eleven different reasons were given for daywork allowances. They may be divided into four classes: shortage of parts, defective materials, slowness of co-workers, and miscellaneous.

[1] In reporting their claims some of the wiremen frequently gave two or more reasons, but the time claimed was always given in a lump sum. It was impossible, therefore, to determine the amount of time claimed for each reason. In comparing the total number of reasons offered by different wiremen, it must be remembered that W_6, W_7, W_8, and W_9 were not in the observation room so long as the other wiremen. The totals for these men, therefore, are relatively lower than they would have been if comparable periods of time had been taken. This error, however, does not affect the conclusions that will be drawn from the table, inasmuch as comparisons will be made only between the three fastest wiremen, W_2, W_3, and W_6, and the three slowest wiremen, W_7, W_8, and W_9. It is apparent that the frequency with which claims were made by the members of the latter group far outweighs the frequency of those made by anyone else, in spite of the fact that a shorter time period was involved.

The first class includes shortages of cables and banks. Together, these two reasons were given 54 times. Everyone in the group except W_3 gave both reasons at least once and there was doubtless some basis in fact for them. It should be noted, however, that W_7 and W_9 gave these reasons more frequently than anyone else. Twenty-two of the 54 claims originated with these two people, a number in excess of the combined claims of W_2, W_3, W_4, W_5, and W_6.

The second class includes defective wire, defective solder, and cable reverses. Cables reverses were included in this class because cables were among the piece parts used by a wireman, and if they contained reverses they were defective. Reverses were detected by the inspector's test set and there could be no question of their existence. In this respect they differed from defective wire or defective solder, which were matters of personal judgment; wire judged defective by one wireman might be acceptable to another. Because of the fact that cable reverses were detected by the inspector's test set, there was no opportunity for the wireman to exaggerate their incidence. They will, therefore, be omitted from future discussion. The other two reasons, defective wire and defective solder, were offered 20 times. W_7, W_8, and W_9 together entered them 15 times, whereas W_2 and W_3 together entered them only twice.

The third class includes waiting for the trucker, the solderman, and the inspector. This group differs from the others in that it includes reasons which placed the blame for delays upon people instead of upon things. All three of the occupational groups with which the wiremen were supposed to collaborate were held responsible for delays. A total of 76 different claims were made for these three reasons. This number was in excess of the total for any other class. The trucker was held responsible twice, the solderman 20 times, and the inspector 54 times. The inspector was cited about two and one-half times as frequently as the trucker and solderman combined. Of the 76 claims in this group, 65 were entered by the three slowest wiremen, W_7, W_8, and W_9.

The fact that certain wiremen entered more claims in the third class than others meant that certain soldermen and inspectors were being charged with more delays than others. S_1, who soldered for W_1, W_2, and W_3, was not once held responsible. S_2, who soldered for W_4, W_5, and W_6, was cited 3 times. W_7, W_8, and W_9 blamed the solderman 17 times. I_1, who inspected the work of W_1, W_2, W_3, and W_4, and one-half that of W_5, was never held responsible for a delay. All 54 claims on account of inspection were entered against one inspector, I_3, who inspected the work of W_6, W_7, W_8, W_9, and the other half of W_5's work. Thirty-nine of these claims were made by W_7 and W_9.

The miscellaneous class includes making repairs, soldering, and power off. Of these reasons, only two necessitate comment. Making repairs was a duty officially assigned to W_9, and it consisted of repairing cable reverses. "Soldering" meant that a wireman replaced a solderman while the latter was called away from his work temporarily. The reasons in this class were similar to those in the first class in that they had more foundation in fact than those in the second and third classes. But, as with the first class, it was known that the number of claims made for reasons in the fourth class was inaccurate. W_9 sometimes claimed daywork for repairing when he made no repairs. Wiremen sometimes did, but more frequently did not, take soldering time while substituting for a solderman. This was particularly true if the solderman was away without leave.

To summarize, the wiremen offered eleven different reasons for daywork allowances, which could be divided into four classes. The first and fourth classes contained fairly sound reasons. They could have been verified by the group chief, had he had time, and they were the kind of delays over which the wiremen had no control. The second and third classes contained reasons which involved the wiremen's personal judgment and which were more or less subject to their control. Delays of the third class, particularly, could be made larger or smaller depending upon the extent to which the different occupational groups voluntarily attempted to collaborate. The wiremen could, if they wished, so arrange their work that no solderman or inspector could keep up with them. For example, if all five wiremen agreed among themselves to finish a level simultaneously, they could easily "get time" on the inspector. They could do the same with a solderman. Of the 199 claims for which reasons were given, 105 were of the kind which involved the wiremen's personal judgment.

ACTUAL VS. REPORTED OUTPUT RATES

From the foregoing evidence it is apparent that the departmental efficiency records, while perhaps sufficiently accurate for practical purposes, could not be taken as sufficiently reliable for purposes of research. They were based upon the output reported by the wiremen and were computed by dividing these reported output figures by gross working time, from which all lost time claimed by the wiremen was deducted. Inasmuch as both the reported output and the lost time records were somewhat distorted, the efficiency figures derived from them were also distorted. The problem was how to construct a more accurate measure of actual work rates. The investigators' output figures were accurate, so there was no question about them. They also had an accurate record of the operators' daywork allowance claims and of nonproductive time.[1] The difficulty was that of determining how much lost time should be deducted, that is, of determining the extent to which the operators were actually delayed as contrasted with the amount of time they claimed they were delayed. Clearly, nonproductive time should be deducted, but how should daywork allowance claims be treated?

Some wiremen claimed a great deal of daywork; others claimed very little. A workman might enter on some days claims which he would ignore on other days. Furthermore, there was considerable evidence that some of the men tried to bring about delays so that they could claim daywork. In view of these facts, it was clearly inadvisable to recognize all daywork claims and deduct them from standard hours if an accurate output rate was to be obtained. It was also unfair to ignore all daywork claims because there were occasions when real stoppages occurred. Either alternative would lead to some distortion of the facts; yet any compromise would be purely arbitrary and might not approximate the facts any more closely. The course chosen, in computing the actual work rates shown in Figure 36, was that of disregarding all daywork claims. Technically, each worker should have been affected to about the same degree by stoppages beyond his control. To rule out all daywork allowances, therefore, would not greatly alter the relative standings of the different operators. It would, however, increase the discrepancy between the resulting figures and those compiled by the department. This must be kept in mind while examining the two sets of figures. The extent to which the investigators' figures were too low was difficult to ascertain. It was their belief that the error involved was sufficiently small to be negligible, this in view of the facts cited relative to work behavior in the Bank Wiring Observation Room and the further observation that no stoppage need have affected a workman's daily output to any great extent.

The weekly average hourly outputs obtained by the investigators, then, were based on actual weekly output and gross working time less nonproductive time. Any half days worked during the week were omitted from these calculations. This was done because there were

[1] Nonproductive time consisted of absences from work which were officially authorized, such as time required for interviews and hospital appointments. Accurate records were kept of nonproductive time and for it the operator was paid his average hourly earnings.

wide discrepancies between morning and afternoon output rates. Hereafter the figures obtained by the investigators will be referred to as the "actual" output rates as contrasted with the departmental figures, which will be called the "reported" output rates.

Figure 36 shows both the actual and the reported output rates for each operator during the observation period. Actual rates are indicated by the starred lines, reported rates by the solid lines. The solid horizontal lines are drawn to indicate the output rate the operators would have had to maintain in order to produce what they conceived to be a day's work. These lines should be disregarded for the time being as their significance will be brought out later. Examination of the curves shows: (1) The two curves do not coincide for any operator. (2) They more nearly coincide among the faster wiremen, W_2, W_3, W_4, W_5, and W_6, than among the slower wiremen. The greatest discrepancy between the curves is in those of the two slowest wiremen, W_7 and W_9. (3) The curves representing actual output rates are more irregular than those representing reported rates. (4) In some weeks actual rates exceed reported rates, but on the whole the latter tend to be higher, particularly among the slower wiremen.

Table XXX has been compiled to show the relative ranking of the wiremen in actual and reported average hourly output rates and to show how these rates differed for each person. The average hourly outputs shown are the means of the weekly average hourly outputs,

TABLE XXX

COMPARISON OF ACTUAL AND REPORTED AVERAGE HOURLY OUTPUTS *
BANK WIRING OBSERVATION ROOM

Wireman	Reported A.H.O.	Actual A.H.O.	Difference	Rank Based on Reported A.H.O.	Rank Based on Actual A.H.O.
W_1	740	724	−16	7	6
W_2	877	860	−17	1	1
W_3	821	823	+2	3	2
W_4	769	757	−12	5	5
W_5	812	804	−8	4	4
W_6	824	822	−2 †	2	3
W_7	711	651	−60	8	8
W_8	741	710	−31	6	7
W_9	468	416	−52	9	9

* Based upon the means of the actual and reported weekly average hourly outputs during the observation period.

† Both W_3 and W_6 reported less output than they produced, but W_6 claimed sufficient daywork to lower his actual output *rate* below his reported output *rate*.

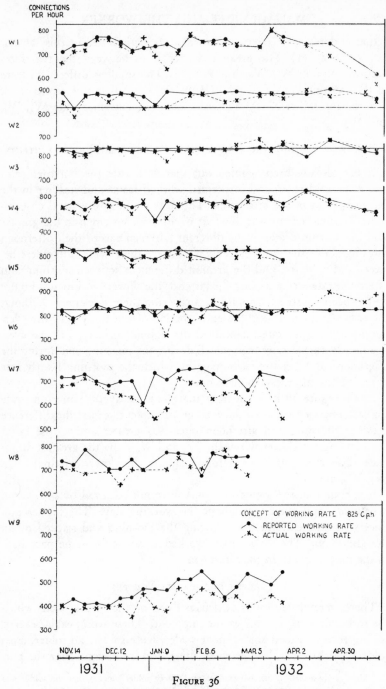

CONNECTIONS
PER HOUR

W 1
W 2
W 3
W 4
W 5
W 6
W 7
W 8
W 9

CONCEPT OF WORKING RATE   825 C.p.h.
REPORTED WORKING RATE
ACTUAL WORKING RATE

NOV.14   DEC.12   JAN.9   FEB.6   MAR.5   APR.2   APR.30

1931   1932

FIGURE 36

ACTUAL VS. REPORTED AVERAGE HOURLY OUTPUT PER WEEK

BANK WIRING OBSERVATION ROOM

435

actual and reported, over the entire study period. From this table it can be seen: (1) The greatest discrepancies between the two rates occurred among W_7, W_9, and W_8. (2) The smallest differences were in the rates of W_6, W_3, and W_5; in fact, the differences are so small as to be insignificant. (3) Between these two extremes were W_4, W_1, and W_2.

Comparison of Morning and Afternoon Average Hourly Outputs

It has already been pointed out that as a rule the wiremen, and hence the soldermen and inspectors, worked faster and steadier in the morning than in the afternoon. This was made as a general observation. To what extent was this true of different wiremen in the group? Did the morning rates of the different wiremen exceed their afternoon rates by about the same percentage or were there wide differences between individuals? Did the greatest differences between morning and afternoon rates occur among the faster or the slower workmen? Figure 37 has been constructed to aid in answering these questions. It shows for each wireman during the entire period of the study: (1) the average hourly output rate maintained throughout the day; (2) the average hourly output rates maintained during the morning and during the afternoon; and (3) the percentage by which the morning hourly rate exceeded the afternoon hourly rate.

From Figure 37 it is apparent that: (1) the average morning rate for each operator exceeded the average afternoon rate; (2) the difference between morning and afternoon rates was greater among the faster than among the slower wiremen. W_2 and W_6 show the greatest difference. The least difference is found among the slower wiremen, W_1, W_7, W_8, and W_9.

It is clear that the greatest outputs were not achieved by steady and consistent application throughout the working day. The higher producers worked extremely fast during the morning and slacked off in the afternoon. The slower men worked at about the same pace both in the morning and in the afternoon.

Analysis of Quality Records

There were eleven kinds of defects listed on the quality form which the inspector filled out for each equipment. These were: cable reverse, wiring reverse, excess solder, poor solder, loose solder, no solder, cross solder, splash solder, broken wire, dress, and insulation.[1] For the pur-

[1] Most of these defects are self-explanatory. "Poor solder" meant that the solder was poorly placed on the terminal; "loose solder," that the wire was not soldered securely;

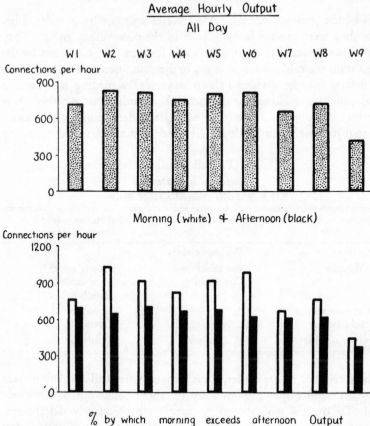

Average Hourly Output
All Day

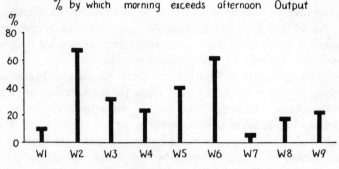

FIGURE 37

COMPARISON OF MORNING WITH AFTERNOON AVERAGE HOURLY OUTPUT

BANK WIRING OBSERVATION ROOM

poses of the present analysis, cable reverses will not be considered because they were not made by anyone in the observation group. They were made by another group, the cable formers, but could not be detected until the cables were attached to the equipments. The remaining ten defects may be divided in two ways: (1) according to who was responsible for making them, and (2) according to whether their detection was objectively determined or depended upon the inspector's personal judgment. In Table XXXI the defects are classified according

TABLE XXXI

CLASSIFICATION OF DEFECTS
BANK WIRING OBSERVATION ROOM

Responsibility for Defects	Defects Determined Objectively	Defects Determined by Personal Judgment
Wireman	Wiring reverses	. . . .
Solderman	No solder	Excess solder
	Cross solder	Poor solder
		Splash solder
Wireman and/or		Loose solder
Solderman	. . . .	Dress
Indeterminable	Broken wire	Insulation

to these criteria. Loose solder, dress, broken wire, and insulation were of such a nature that responsibility for them could not be definitely fixed. Of the six which remain, three were objectively determined. Wiring reverses and cross solders were detected by the inspector's test set. No solders were not so detected, but, inasmuch as two or more people can agree when there is no solder on a terminal, a judgment of no solder is independent of personal opinion.

Individual quality ratings for the three objectively determined defects are shown in Table XXXII. Those for the wiremen are based on wiring reverses, whereas those for the soldermen are based on no solders and cross solders. In computing the wiremen's scores, the total number of wiring reverses made by each person was divided by the total number of terminals wired by him during the study. A similar procedure was followed in computing the soldermen's scores, the output count in this case, however, being the combined outputs of the

---

"no solder," that the solderman had overlooked a terminal; "cross solder," that the solder joined two terminals, thus causing a short circuit; "dress," that the wires were not neatly arranged; and "insulation," that the insulation on the wire was either pulled back or pushed up too far on the terminal.

wiremen in each soldering unit. Days on which a solderman was absent or on which he wired during part of the day were omitted from the calculation of his quality rating. Because the resulting quotients were fractional, they are expressed here in terms of 100,000 connections.

The main conclusion to be drawn from this table is that the three wiremen who stood out above all the others in their output rates (W_2,

TABLE XXXII

Quality Ratings of Wiremen and Soldermen Based upon Objectively Determined Defects

BANK WIRING OBSERVATION ROOM

Operator Number	Defects per 100,000 Connections	Rank in Quality	Rank in Actual Average Hourly Output
W_1	14.0	8	6
W_2	4.6	2	1
W_3	5.4	3	2
W_4	6.4	5	5
W_5	9.8	7	4
W_6	3.0	1	3
W_7	9.3	6	8
W_8	6.0	4	7
W_9	41.2	9	9
S_1	11.0	1	1
S_2	13.6	2	2
S_4	56.3	3	3

W_3, and W_6) also rated highest in quality. The same is true of the soldermen. However, it does not follow that the slower men rated lowest in quality. W_9 did, but W_7, who ranked eighth in output, held sixth place in quality. W_8 ranked seventh in output and fourth in quality. Before leaving this topic, one interesting characteristic of wiring reverses should be pointed out. Wiring reverses represent gross errors. They are not the kind of error that would be made if the operator watched what he was doing. In fact, it is difficult to understand how they could be made without pronounced inattention. If this be true, it follows that W_9, W_1, W_5, and W_7 found greater difficulty than the others did in fixing their attention on their work.

Defects which were determined by the inspector's personal judgment were not included in making up these quality ratings because it was found that different inspectors did not always agree upon either the existence of a particular error or classification of it. One inspector might disregard what another would mark up as a defect. Again, one inspector might tend to list the majority of judgment defects as poor solders, whereas another might class them as excess solders. Such differences as these made it impossible to include judgment defects in an accurate quality rating. However, this group of defects could be used in other ways. It was reasoned that inasmuch as the inspector's judgment entered into their determination, they might reflect differences in the relations between him and the individuals whose work he inspected. For example, if he were strongly antagonistic toward a certain wireman or solderman, he might find more defects in the work of that person than in the work of a person toward whom he was favorably inclined. Again, if one inspector tended to write up an unusually large number of defects on all the work he inspected, it might mean that he felt insecure and consequently wished to list everything which might possibly be construed as a defect by the check inspector.

To test these ideas the investigators worked out the quality scores shown in Table XXXIII. These scores are based upon those defects

TABLE XXXIII

QUALITY SCORES OF SOLDERMEN BASED ON DEFECTS DETERMINED BY
PERSONAL JUDGMENT *

BANK WIRING OBSERVATION ROOM

Solderman-Inspector Combinations	W_1	W_2	W_3	W_4	W_5	W_6	W_7	W_8	W_9	Mean
S_1-I_1	414	440	245	...	...	...	...	...	...	366
S_2-I_1	...	...	...	471	444	...	...	...	...	458
S_2-I_2	...	...	...	...	363	297	...	...	...	330
S_2-I_3	...	...	...	...	474	537	...	...	...	506
S_3-I_3	...	...	...	...	...	...	327	282	325	311
S_4-I_2†	...	...	...	...	...	...	372	430	344	382
S_4-I_3	...	...	...	...	...	...	606	664	514	595

* Scores are expressed as the number of defects per 100,000 connections.
† Based on one week's output only.

determined by personal judgment for which the solderman alone was responsible. They were computed as follows: First, only those days on which a given inspector-solderman-wireman combination occurred were selected. Theoretically, it made no difference whether the wireman in each combination was always the same person, because he was not supposed to have any responsibility for this kind of defect. However, in the absence of any definite proof of the correctness of this reasoning, the investigators decided to include the wireman as a necessary part of each combination. Secondly, the total number of such defects occurring on these days was determined and then divided by the total output. The results, as in the previous table, are expressed in terms of 100,000 terminals. The scores for S_3 and S_4 are, of course, based on fewer days than those for S_1 and S_2. S_3 was in the observation room only 15 days in all.

In Table XXXIII the solderman-inspector combinations are listed at the left of the chart and the different wiremen are indicated at the top. This table reads as follows: When S_1 was soldering for W_1, the inspector, I_1, detected 414 defects per 100,000 terminals. Similarly, when S_1 was soldering for W_3, I_1 detected only 245 defects per 100,000 terminals. Passing on to the column for W_5, three figures will be found, 444, 363, and 474. This means that while S_2 was soldering for W_5 three different inspectors rated his work. I_1 found 444 defects per 100,000 connections, I_2 found 363, and I_3 found 474.

The first question to be asked in reference to this table may be stated as follows: If the solderman was solely responsible for these defects, then one would expect his ratings to be about the same irrespective of who did the wiring. But if it is found that his ratings do vary with different wiremen, either of two conclusions may follow. Either the personal relations between the different wiremen and the solderman were affecting the solderman's work, or the personal relations between the wiremen and the inspector were influencing the inspector's judgment of the solderman's work. In either case it may be concluded that the personal attributes of the wiremen were affecting the solderman-inspector relation. With this point in mind, it is apparent that: (1) I_1 detected fewer defects in S_1's work when S_1 was soldering for W_3 than when he was soldering for W_1 or W_2, and he found more defects in S_1's work when S_1 was soldering for W_2 than when he was soldering for W_1. (2) I_3 found considerably fewer defects in S_4's work when S_4 was soldering for W_9 than when he was soldering for W_7 or W_8. This evidence strongly suggests that the various interpersonal relations in this group did affect either the quality of the solderman's work or the inspector's judgment of the solderman's work.

The second question to be asked in reference to this table pertains to the differences between different inspectors' ratings of the work of the same solderman, the wiremen remaining the same. S_2's work for W_5 was rated by all three inspectors, I_1, I_2, and I_3. His work for W_6 was rated by two of them, I_2 and I_3. S_4's work for W_7, W_8, and W_9 was inspected by both I_2 and I_3. If it is assumed that there were no pronounced changes in the soldermen's abilities during the observation period, then differences in their ratings by different inspectors reflect differences in the inspectors' judgments. It is apparent that there were pronounced differences in the judgments of the different inspectors. In the work done by S_2 for W_5, I_2 found 363 defects per 100,000 connections, I_1 found 444, and I_3 found 474, over a hundred more than I_2. On W_6's work S_2 was charged with almost twice as many defects by I_3 as by I_2. I_3 charged S_4 with many more defects than I_2 did, regardless of whether S_4 was wiring for W_7, W_8, or W_9. Unfortunately, I_2's ratings of S_4 are based on only one week's work and do not, therefore, afford a very reliable comparison; yet the difference between his ratings and I_3's is so large that it might be taken as significant.

To summarize, by dividing the different defects detected by the inspectors into two groups, one of which contained only objectively determined defects and the other subjectively determined defects, two different sorts of measures were found. The first reflected the relative differences in the quality of the operators' work. The second reflected the interpersonal relations in the group under observation. This was particularly clear cut in the case of I_3. I_3, as will be shown later,[1] aroused the antagonism of the group whose work he inspected, and they expressed their antagonism by charging him with exorbitant amounts of daywork. This analysis shows that he reciprocated by charging them with large numbers of defects. He was able to do this because so many of the defects depended upon his personal judgment. This does not mean that he did it consciously; it means that a person is likely to be more critical of the work done by an opponent than of that done by a friend.

INDIVIDUAL DIFFERENCES IN OUTPUT

It has been shown that the operators in the Bank Wiring Observation Room agreed not only on what constituted a day's work but also on what might happen to them if they exceeded that standard. It would seem logical, therefore, that each and every one of the wiremen would turn out approximately two equipments a day, their standard of a day's work. According to their way of thinking, this would give them the maximum amount of earnings consistent with security. The curious fact, however, is that they did not do this. There were marked differences in the output levels of different wiremen. How were these differences to be accounted for? To what did they relate? The most plausible explanation was that they might reflect differences in ability as measured by tests of dexterity, aptitude, and intelligence. Conse-

[1] See pp. 486–492.

quently, each person in the group was given two tests: a combined soldering and dexterity test, and the Otis Intermediate or Higher Examination, depending upon educational attainments.

In the combined soldering and dexterity test the subject was required to solder as many terminals in a bank as possible in a fixed time. The efficiency rating of each person was computed by subtracting the total number of errors from the number of contact points completed and dividing by the latter. Errors consisted of touching contact points with iron without solder, with solder without iron, or touching the board. The resulting efficiency score was then combined with the individual's quality score, as measured in errors detected, and with his scores in two pegboard tests.[1] Each of these four measures was weighted before they were combined. The resulting weighted composite scores are shown in the bottom diagram of Figure 38. Ability as measured by these scores showed no relation to actual performance. Three of the slower wiremen, W_8, W_1, and W_9, scored higher than W_2, W_3, and W_6, the three fastest men.[2]

Each operator's Otis Examination score, translated into terms of an I.Q., is also shown in Figure 38. The average Binet mental age of 487 hourly rated employees in the company was 14 years, 11 months, equivalent to an I.Q. of 92. In terms of this mean, four of the nine wiremen in the group were average or above. It should be pointed out that the very low score for W_2 should not be considered reliable. W_2 was a very difficult person to deal with, and it is more than likely that he did not co-operate in the test. This assumption is substantiated by the fact that he graduated from high school, an almost impossible feat for a person with such a low I.Q. Comparison of the relative ranking of the wiremen in intelligence and in average hourly output showed no relation between the two. W_9, the lowest man in output, ranked first in intelligence. W_4, whose I.Q. was about equal to that of W_9, ranked fifth in output. With the exception of W_3, the faster wiremen scored rather poorly on the test.

From the foregoing analysis it can be concluded that there was no direct relation between performance in the Bank Wiring Observation Room and capacity to perform as measured by dexterity or intelligence tests. The lowest producer, W_9, ranked first in intelligence and third in the weighted soldering scores. The man who scored highest on the

[1] For a description of these pegboard tests, see pp. 162–164.

[2] It may seem strange to the reader that the wiremen should be given a soldering test. Actually, this was not merely a trade test; it was used by the company as a test for many different jobs requiring steadiness and dexterity. Two of the soldermen came out poorly in the test; S_1 had a combined score of 79 and S_2 of 91.

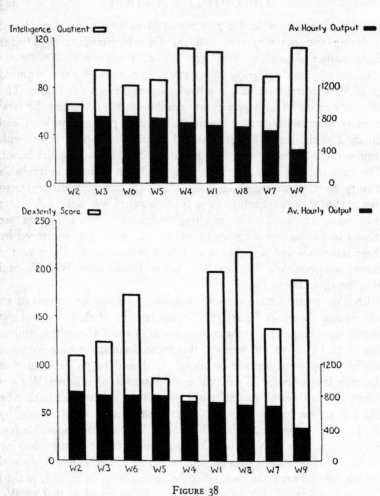

FIGURE 38

DIFFERENCES IN AVERAGE HOURLY OUTPUT COMPARED WITH DIFFERENCES IN
INTELLIGENCE AND DEXTERITY

BANK WIRING OBSERVATION ROOM

soldering test ranked seventh in intelligence and seventh in output. W_4 ranked last in the soldering test and shared first place with W_9 in intelligence; yet he ranked fifth in output. W_3 ranked relatively low on the soldering test and quite high in intelligence, whereas W_6 ranked fairly high on the former and low in the latter; yet their output rates were equal. This, then, was a situation in which native ability as measured by these tests was not finding expression in work. It contrasted sharply with the situation in the Relay Assembly Test Room, where there was a direct relation between tests of ability and output.

Summary

Because the foregoing analyses were given in such detail that the main points were sometimes obscured, it may be helpful to bring them together in summary form. No attempt will be made to interpret these findings at this time.

(1) Each individual in the group was restricting his output.

(2) Restriction of output manifested itself in two ways: (a) the group had a standard of a day's work which was considerably lower than the "bogey" and which fixed an upper limit to each person's output. This standard was not imposed upon them, but apparently had been formulated by the workmen themselves. Furthermore, it was in direct opposition to the ideas underlying their system of financial incentive, which countenanced no upper limit to performance other than physical capacity. (b) In each individual case it manifested itself in an output rate which remained fairly constant from week to week. The departmental output curves were devoid of individuality and approximated a horizontal line in shape.

(3) The departmental output records were distorted. This was found by comparing the observer's count with the figures compiled by the department during the study period.

(4) The inaccuracies in the departmental records were traceable to two factors. These were (a) differences between actual output and reported output, and (b) differences between standard working time and reported working time. The first factor was assessed by comparing the observer's output count with that reported to the group chief by the wiremen. It was found that no wireman reported exactly what he produced each day; some days he reported more and some less. The second factor was studied by recording and analyzing claims for daywork allowances. It was apparent that most of the wiremen frequently claimed to have been prevented from working by stoppages beyond their control when in reality there was little justification for their claims because (i) the stoppage was shorter than claimed, or (ii) the stoppage was brought about by the operators themselves, or (iii) there was in fact no delay, or (iv) there was a real stoppage but it could have been compensated for by working a little harder or decreasing spare time.

(5) Analysis of quality records showed that they reflected not only the quality of the work done by the wiremen and soldermen but also the personal relations between them and the inspector. This was found by separating objectively determined defects from those which were determined by the inspector's personal judgment. Analysis of the former showed that the faster operators rated highest in quality. Analysis of the latter showed that an inspector's rating of a solderman varied with different wiremen even though the solderman was solely responsible for the defects. It also showed that different inspectors differed widely in their gradings of a specific solderman's work.

(6) Differences in weekly average hourly output rates for different wiremen did not reflect differences in capacity to perform. This conclusion was based on the following observations: (a) Most of the wiremen stated definitely that they could easily turn out more work than they did. (b) The observer said that all the men stopped work before quitting time. Frequently, a wireman finished his work quite early and stalled until quitting time. In general the men who ranked highest in output were the first to be finished. This point was verified by a comparison of individual morning and afternoon output rates, which showed the greatest differences in the cases of the faster wiremen. (c) Tests of dexterity and intelligence showed no relation between capacity to perform and actual performance.

In addition to these findings, a number of interesting questions were raised which could not be answered by analyses of performance records alone. These may be listed here for future reference:

(1) Why did every person in the group feel that it was necessary to maintain a fairly uniform rate of output? The reasons given by the wiremen were indicated early in this chapter, but these attitudes and beliefs themselves needed explanation. None of the men had ever experienced any of the things they claimed they were guarding against; yet they acted as though they had.

(2) Why, if they all agreed on what constituted a day's work, did they not try to turn out that amount? If security were the key to their actions, why didn't they continue to do exactly the same amount of work each day? This would have obliterated all individual differences and their supervisors could have made no unfavorable comparisons. Yet W_2 persisted in exceeding the standard figure and W_1, W_7, W_8, and W_9 were quite content to fall far short of it. W_3, W_4, W_5, and W_6, however, managed to approximate the standard fairly closely. If differences in capacity did not account for these differences in performance, what did?

(3) Why did W_2, who stood at the top in performance, report more work than he produced, and why did W_3 and W_6, who ranked next lower than W_2, report less work than they produced?

This list could be extended, but these are sufficient to indicate some of the more interesting questions that might be asked. An attempt to answer these questions will be made in the following chapters. It will require first, however, a thorough understanding of the interpersonal relations existing between supervisors and employees and among the employees themselves. Therefore, the next three chapters will be concerned with describing these relations.

CHAPTER XIX

THE SUPERVISORY SITUATION IN THE BANK WIRING
OBSERVATION ROOM

THE chief function of the supervisory organization of the bank wiring department was to maintain order and control. To maintain adequate control two things were essential: (1) orders had to be transmitted from top to bottom essentially as they were originally given; and (2) information about what transpired at each level, particularly at the work level, had to be transmitted upward without distortion. Only with the help of accurate information could the foreman act intelligently. The success of the first function was fairly well assured because orders had the weight of authority behind them, and whether or not they were carried out could ordinarily be observed to some extent. Whether the second function worked equally well was a matter of doubt; there was nothing to force information upward. In this chapter, the manner in which these two functions were performed by the supervisory organization in the Bank Wiring Observation Room will be examined.

Before taking up this problem, however, the limitations of the data obtained should be mentioned. In the first place, the data did not cover the entire scope of any one supervisor's daily activities. Both GC_1 and GC_2, the man who replaced GC_1 during the last two weeks of the study, spent only about half their time in the observation room. The remainder of their time was taken up in supervising the work of people who were located in the department. The section chief to whom the group chiefs reported spent, on the average, only about an hour a day in the observation room, and the assistant foreman and the foreman had so much of their time occupied elsewhere that they could visit the observation room only once or twice a day.

In the second place, the supervisors were functioning in a somewhat unusual situation when they were in the observation room. The group chiefs were accustomed to working in the regular department, where the higher-ranking supervisors were located, and this made their jobs easier from the standpoint of maintaining order and discipline. The higher-ranking supervisors, on the other hand, were accustomed to more casual relations with the operators than were possible in the observation room. Their trips to the observation room were in the nature of visits; everyone was clearly aware of their presence, and consequently the relations between supervisors and operators were more formal. Furthermore, when the foreman and the assistant foreman did enter the room they were ordinarily there in the role of disciplinarians rather than in their major role of shop executives. In other words, the investigators obtained a rather one-sided view of their functions.

Because of these limitations the material obtained by the investigators could not be used for appraising the supervisors as such. In fact, any conclusion as to the abilities of any of the supervisors mentioned would be not only misleading but extraneous to the purposes of the study. The objective of this study was not to evaluate or rate the different supervisors. The investigators were interested solely in the kinds of problems the supervisors were confronted with, the nature of the relations between the supervisors and the operators, and the significance of these findings for the problem of human control in industry. They were regarding the supervisory organization as a configuration of social relations and they were seeking, by observing the behavior of the different people in that configuration, to discover problems which seemed to inhere in such relations. They were, in short, looking for the limitations not of individual supervisors but of the social structure in which the supervisors functioned.

The Group Chief's Situation

Under this heading only GC_1, the man who supervised the observation group during the greater part of the study, will be considered, leaving GC_2 to be considered later. The situation in which the group chief found himself can best be described by taking up some of the problems with which he was confronted in his daily work of supervising the men. Chief among these was the problem of daywork allowance claims. The operators frequently entered excessive daywork claims in order to maintain steady output rates. The group chief was aware of the fact that many of their claims were excessive, but he found it very difficult to reduce them. For example, the workers might claim that they were delayed because of defective materials. As soon as the group chief had proved to his satisfaction that the materials were of standard quality, he might find that they were no longer blaming defective materials but had shifted the cause of their complaints to the slowness of the solderman or the inspector. If he questioned the solderman, the latter could maintain either that he was not too slow or that the wiremen had so arranged their work that no one could keep up with them. The wiremen, on the other hand, could claim that the solderman was just defending himself and that they were in the right. The group chief had so many other duties that he did not have time to determine whether the claims were justified or not. To do so, he would have had to stand over the workers with a stop watch all day. But he could not refuse daywork claims without inciting an argument and appearing arbitrary to his men. He knew that some claims were justified and that to suppress all of them would be unjust. On the other hand, if he attempted to honor some and refuse others, he would be open to charges of partiality. The difficulty here, as with many of the other problems he encountered, was that there were no objective criteria in terms of which the validity of the men's statements could be tested.

The tendency of the employees to insist upon being credited with daywork placed the group chief in an awkward position. He saw that as a representative of management he should do everything possible to keep daywork claims at a minimum. As the immediate supervisor of the wiremen, however, he was under pressure from below to report the claims as they were given to him. Because of this pressure, he usually acknowledged the employees' claims for daywork. What this meant, in effect, was that the group chief shouldered the responsibility for excessive daywork claims himself in order to keep on congenial terms with his men. Having done so, he was practically forced to find some way of defending himself and this he was able to do in two ways. First, the departmental efficiency records did not reflect the real state of affairs. What the foreman saw when he looked at the efficiency charts was an average hourly output rate and not the actual output and hours of work upon which the efficiency records were based. Secondly, if anyone did investigate the daywork claims being made, the group chief could place the blame wherever he wished. Although the employees had to give the group chief reasons for the claims they made, and he entered these reasons in a record book which he kept for that purpose, no one except himself and the investigators ever referred to the book. He regarded it as his private property. If, therefore, anyone should ever ask him why his men were claiming daywork, he could attribute the reason to defective materials or to some other factor for which he was not responsible. He could not, of course, say that the solderman was too slow, because he was responsible for seeing that such a situation did not occur. He might, however, place the blame on the inspector because the inspector was a representative of an outside organization and reported to a different set of supervisors.

The group chief encountered the same sort of difficulty in dealing with the problem of job trading. The employees were supposed to work only at the jobs assigned to them. They were not supposed to trade off unless it was absolutely necessary. Almost the only reason the department officials recognized as a legitimate excuse for a wireman's trading with a solderman was sore fingers. But when were a wireman's fingers sore? The group chief had no way of telling and, since he was responsible for the safety and health of the operators, about the only thing he could do was to allow them a change of jobs. Here, of course, the group chief was well protected. If the foreman asked him why certain people had traded jobs he could reply that the wireman had sore fingers. This reason was acceptable to the foreman and, even if he wished to, he had no way of proving it false.

In addition to the problems of daywork allowance claims and job trading, the group chief encountered difficulties in enforcing some of the housekeeping rules, in making the men work after they had completed their "day's work," and in trying to get them to use materials which they claimed were defective or inferior in quality.

In the face of such problems as these the group chief could either let the employees do as they wished and say nothing about it, or he could report their conduct to the foreman and attempt to force them to do his bidding, or he could steer a middle course. In practice he did choose a middle course. He tried his best to make the men obey his orders, sometimes successfully, but he never on any occasion "told the Old Man on them." Then, again, not all of his orders were disputed. Those which obviously originated higher up were carried out without question. If the men were told to report to the hospital or to the foreman, they obeyed immediately and without protest. Only in his attempts to enforce certain rules and practices did he meet with resistance. The investigators felt that he countenanced disobedience to some rules largely because he himself thought them unimportant; yet his position demanded that he give lip service to them. His chief interest was in seeing that the men turned out an acceptable day's work, and this they unquestionably did. If they liked to talk and "cut up" a bit while doing it, he did not strenuously object.

By acting in accordance with the sentiments of the group, the group chief won the friendship of the men. They genuinely liked him. This was testified to by them in their interviews and was shown in countless little occurrences in their day-to-day contacts with him. The most illuminating expression of their feeling toward him came when he notified them that he was to be demoted and would no longer be their boss.[1] One man said he was going to quit. Another said they were losing the best boss they had ever had. Others expressed themselves in similar fashion.

The group chief's attitude toward the foreman was practically indistinguishable from that of the operators. Like them, he was afraid he would be caught, or, more precisely, that they would be caught and. he would be held responsible. With the assistant foreman he was much less distant than with the foreman. He sometimes criticized the foreman in the assistant foreman's presence, and occasionally joked with the latter about certain minor things, such as housekeeping rules, upon which he felt the foreman laid undue emphasis.

GC$_1$ seemed to get along fairly well with the section chief and did not appear to be at all apprehensive of him. Certain things the section chief did irritated him a good deal. Chief among these was what the group chief interpreted as "passing the buck." If the foreman wanted something done, he usually told the section chief to do it. The section chief, in turn, would pass the foreman's orders on to the group chief and leave to him the task of seeing that they were carried out. This was frequently very difficult for the group chief to do, especially if the order related to the enforcement of housekeeping rules or to other disciplinary measures which the operators resented.

Group Chief 2

Although GC$_2$ supervised the men in the Bank Wiring Observation Room for only a short time, his methods of dealing with people differed so markedly from those of GC$_1$ that they afforded an interesting contrast. GC$_1$ typified the tolerant, sympathetic supervisor. GC$_2$, on the other hand, tended to be more abrupt in handling his subordinates. Although he was not unsympathetic, he placed much more emphasis on discipline and obedience than did GC$_1$. His chief interest, as he himself said many times, was the perfectly legitimate one of seeing that the "percentage" stayed up. GC$_1$, of course, was quite as much interested in a high percentage as anyone else, inasmuch as the size of his pay check also in part depended on it. The important difference between these two men in this matter, their subordinates felt, was that GC$_2$'s interest in the percentage was purely personal while GC$_1$ was interested in the percentage as much for their sake as for his own.

[1] This demotion, it will be remembered, was due to the general decline in business activity. Fewer supervisors were needed. GC$_1$, along with many others, was demoted because his service with the company was comparatively short.

In matters of discipline the same sort of difference was apparent. GC_2, much more than GC_1, tended to think of himself as a member of management. Consequently he laid a great deal of stress upon efficiency and rules of conduct. In doing so he unconsciously tended to subordinate the operators, sometimes in ways which they resented, and to increase the social distance between himself and them. As a result several of the operators felt that GC_2 was not "one of them," in other words, that he did not share their interests and sentiments.

Although the operators were much more circumspect in what they did and said in GC_2's presence, it did not follow that they obeyed him more readily than they had obeyed GC_1. They did not admit authority merely because he exercised it. To them it seemed that GC_2 was laying claim to more authority than his actual position entitled him to; they felt that what he was upholding to them was not so much the company as himself.

To the investigators, the supervisory methods employed by GC_2 were of interest because they were, in effect, a test of those employed by GC_1. If GC_1 was too lenient, as some readers might suppose, then GC_2's methods should have afforded proof of such an hypothesis. The results, however, tended to show that GC_2's methods were less effective than those used by GC_1. Unfortunately GC_2 was not in charge of the group long enough to warrant taking output as a criterion of his success and, moreover, so many factors affect output that in any case it would be a measure of doubtful validity. What the investigators did observe was that the operators tended to conceal from GC_2 what they frankly expressed to GC_1. GC_1 was well acquainted with the actual work situation at all times. He knew what the sentiments of the group were and, therefore, was in a better position to elicit their co-operation than was GC_2.

The Section Chief

The section chief spent much less time in the observation room than the group chief. His participation differed from the group chief's in that it had to do more with "official business" than with the routine functioning of the job. He helped the foreman and the assistant foreman prepare the lists of people to be laid off and he had some voice in determining who should or should not go. He did some of the work on the pay roll records and was well informed about changes in output schedules. He was "in the know" more than the group chief. Each week he distributed the pay checks to the operators and the group chiefs reporting to him. It was the section chief who announced the various courses being offered by the evening school and urged the men to attend. He also solicited attendance at the "safety meetings," which were held after hours from time to time. When the assistant foreman or the foreman came in to talk to the men, if they were accompanied by anyone it was the section chief and not the group chief. He, in short, partook in the functions of management much more than the group chief.

The attitude of the operators toward the section chief was very similar to their attitude toward GC_1. They did not obey an order any more readily simply because it was given by the section chief. Neither did they refrain from arguing with him in case they disagreed. There was, however, some evidence which indicated that they regarded him as possessing more authority than the group chief. For example, when W_6 thought his pay was figured incorrectly, he asked the group chief to get the section chief to refigure it. When S_1 wanted his stock subscription canceled, he saw, not the group chief, but the section chief.

Although the section chief was always busy, his duties were difficult to define. He performed a variety of jobs, none of which appeared to have the functional significance of, for example, wiring the banks. Unlike the group chief, the section chief was removed from the work line; yet he was not sufficiently advanced in supervisory rank to be a bona fide member of the managerial group. This may account for the fact that he felt his position insecure. As the effects of the depression became more noticeable in the department, he became increasingly worried over "where it would all end."

The Assistant Foreman

The assistant foreman was regarded by the group as possessing much more authority than the first-line or second-line supervisors. When he gave an order or advised them, they listened to what he had to say with respect and never ventured to argue with him. They might protest as soon as he left the room but never in his presence. His chief concern with the group was in seeing that they maintained satisfactory output standards and that they conformed to rules and regulations. He entered the observation room less frequently than any other supervisor, and his comings and goings were always matters of interest to the group. When he came in, they "expected" something in the form either of criticism or of news which would affect them vitally, perhaps notification of a change in working hours, of transfers, of layoffs, or other official business. The assistant foreman's relations with the group were pleasant, and the employees, as well as the first-line and second-line supervisors, felt that they could get certain things done better by going to him rather than to the foreman.

Some of the things the assistant foreman said indicated that there was a certain amount of friction in his relations with the foreman. If he had his way, he sometimes said, he would see to it that each workman's base rate was altered periodically so that he would be paid no more than he contributed to the group earnings. He thought it was unjust for the better workmen to be penalized on account of the slower ones. Moreover, he did not think the regular departmental records were much good for rating men, and so he kept one of his own which was more detailed and helpful. More than anyone else in the department, the assistant foreman was concerned with matters of cost and efficiency.

The Foreman

The foreman seemed to be a kindly, well-meaning person with a good deal of tolerance toward youth. He was very proud of his "boys," as he called them, and thought they were distinctly better than the average workman in the plant. Both he and the assistant foreman felt that if a man consistently wired more than 6,600 connections a day, "he would wear his fingers out." He placed a good deal of emphasis on education and believed that no man should stay in his department more than five years. The men should have worked themselves to the top of the labor grade by that time, he thought, and then should be transferred to higher-rated work. "I don't want any old men getting their beards tangled up in the wire, not in my department," was the way he expressed it. He felt that inasmuch as most of the employees in his department were young, they should be allowed considerable latitude in matters of discipline. He said that although they "cut up" a good deal and were sometimes boisterous, he didn't mind. They did a good day's work and that was what counted. The employees, in their interviews, talked very little about the foreman, but when they did it was always favorably. He was more or less taken for granted.

In view of their favorable attitude toward him and the foreman's privately expressed attitude of tolerance and sympathy toward them, it was interesting to note that in their daily relations with one another these attitudes rarely found expression. Because of the foreman's position of prestige and authority, he felt compelled to maintain an outer mask or social personality which effectively concealed his real attitudes and sentiments toward his subordinates. Whenever he entered the observation room, the behavior of the group underwent a sudden change. Talking and singing stopped immediately, and the operators scuttled back to their positions or, if too far away to return, they pretended to be where they were for some purpose. When he moved about or talked to someone, the men cast furtive glances at him and attempted to overhear what he was saying.

The foreman came into the room about once each day, if for no other reason than to look around. Frequently he just came in and watched the men for a while and after exchanging a few words with the observer went out again. When he did have some other purpose in mind, it almost invariably had to do with the enforcement of rules of work, safety, or conduct. If he saw the men helping one another, he told them that they were supposed to wire on their own equipments. If they had traded jobs, he might ask the group chief why. If they were talking or making too much noise, he put a stop to that because, technically, they were not supposed to engage in purely social conversation while working. If the men were sitting down or were not working during hours, they might "get in bad." Unless they had some good excuse, they at least had to pretend to be working. If the solderman was not wearing his goggles, the foreman would tell him to put them on and remind him of the dangers in not wearing them. If the room was untidy or if he thought there was too much solder or wasted wire on the floor, he would order that it be cleaned up and give a lecture on waste. Inasmuch as some of the many rules were almost constantly being violated by the group, the men had to "watch their step" when the foreman made his appearance.

Summary

Examination of the attitudes and behavior of the employees toward the different supervisors did not reveal a simple, sharp dichotomy between supervisor and employee. Most of the employees looked upon the group chief very much as one of themselves. They did not regard him as possessing much authority and they thought nothing of disobeying him. Although they recognized the section chief as possessing more authority, they did not always obey him either and they frequently argued with him. But toward the assistant foreman their attitude was quite different. They never disobeyed him or argued about his orders. Their behavior when he was in the room was much more restrained than when only the section chief was present. Toward the foreman they were still more apprehensive. They not only obeyed him with alacrity but also when he was present refrained from doing anything that was not strictly according to rules. The difference between their attitude toward the group chief and toward the foreman was well illustrated by the fact that a mild caution from the foreman was regarded as a "bawling out," but the group chief would have had to lecture them very severely before they would have felt that they were being "bawled out."

Just as the degree of apprehensiveness exhibited by the operators increased with the rank held by the supervisors, so the degree of strictness shown by the latter varied also. The group chief was most tolerant, the foreman least. Implicit in the foreman's attitude and in his every judgment was the "logic" of management, the pattern in accordance with which the department was technically organized. He was constantly insisting that the "rules of the game" as conceived by management be carried out. To the group chief many of these rules were just as annoying as they were to the operators, and he did not try to conceal that fact from them. The employees had their own rules and their own "logic" which, more frequently than not, were opposed to those which were imposed upon them.

It has been pointed out that the chief function of the supervisory organization was to maintain order and control, and, furthermore, that to maintain control it had to perform two functions: first, orders had to be transmitted downward essentially as they were given, and, secondly, accurate information about what happened on the working line had to be transmitted upward. Examination of the facts showed that both of these functions fell short of their technical fulfillment. Orders, in the narrow sense, were carried out. But if orders include the way in which a person is supposed to execute them and the way he is supposed to conduct himself, the actuality fell far short of the ideal. Those rules and regulations which related specifically to conduct were, on the whole, disregarded by the employees.

But it was in its performance of the second function that the supervisory organization was found most deficient. The root of the difficulty here was that the employees did not act as it might be assumed they would. Had they acted in accordance with the logic of their wage incentive plan, the difficulties encountered by the group chief would not have existed. There would have been no job trading, helping one another, exorbitant daywork claims, or stalling. The method of control which had been set up by the company was based upon the assumption that, given certain inducements or incentives, employees would act in certain ways. That they might act differently was a possibility with which neither the incentive plan nor the supervisory organization was prepared to cope.

The employees were making certain demands of the group chief which he could neither recognize nor repudiate without either betraying the trust placed in him by the company or arousing the hostility of the workers. If their demands could have been tested or verified objectively, the situation might have been different. As it happened, however, none of them could be verified. It was simply a matter of one man's word against another's. Largely because he did want the good will of his men, the group chief acquiesced to their demands. He, in effect, became one of the group he was supervising. Having taken that position, he then had to conceal from the foreman everything which was contrary to the logic of management he, as well as the foreman, was supposed to represent. This he did in the various ways described. The foreman had little opportunity to find out what the situation was for himself. When he entered the room, the behavior of the men underwent a sudden change; they acted as they were supposed to while he was present. The group chief and section chief sided with the men and did not dare to give the foreman an objective account of the facts. It is even doubtful if they could have done so; their own hopes and fears were too much involved. The outcome was that the departmental performance records became distorted and the foreman remained ignorant of much that was going on. There was something in the relation between subordinate and superior which inhibited the free upward passage of facts necessary for intelligent control.

CHAPTER XX

INTEREMPLOYEE RELATIONS IN THE BANK WIRING OBSERVATION ROOM

THE study of the output situation and of the supervisory situation in the Bank Wiring Observation Room raised many questions in the minds of the investigators which could not be answered apart from a more thorough analysis of the interpersonal relations existing among the operators themselves. It will be the purpose of this and the next chapter, therefore, to make such an analysis. In this chapter, only the descriptive material pertaining to the relations which existed among the fourteen operators will be presented. The purpose of this chapter, in other words, is to present the data upon which the investigators based their analysis. Then in the next chapter, the method used in analyzing this material and the conclusions reached will be presented.

Before discussing the relations which existed among the operators, a task which can best be accomplished by considering each person separately and describing his social participation in the observation room, in fairness to the operators and supervisors concerned a word of caution should be inserted here lest the reader draw erroneous inferences from the material which follows. In the description of the relations among these operators only those data will be presented which show what their relations were and how they were expressed. The reader might conclude from the material that either the supervision or the management or both were at fault in permitting many of the occurrences which will be related. It is just such a conclusion against which the authors wish to warn the reader. The incidents herein described were scattered over a period of some six months. For purposes of presentation, however, the time lapse between many of the events has been omitted; consequently, the net effect may be to give the reader an exaggerated impression of the amount of talking and horseplay that occurred. Secondly, it is well to keep in mind the fact that these operators and their supervisors were, throughout the study, doing a good day's work and that many of the events to be cited, although they clearly reflected relations between people, were of very short duration. This point can be readily appreciated by imagining having one's own behavior throughout every day carefully observed and described over a six-month period. It is likely that few people would care to have a summary of such a record submitted to a superior. The person thus described might agree that the record reflected his relations with other people, but he no doubt would also feel that a summation of isolated occurrences presented him in a false light, that the events described were incidental, and that in spite of the record he was doing a good day's work anyway. It is well to remember, therefore, that the material presented here pertains to and is meant to pertain to only one aspect of the total work situation, that it covers a long period of time, and that any conclusions based upon it relative to management or supervision are likely to be erroneous.

Wireman 1

W_1's chief social contacts in the Bank Wiring Observation Room were with the other three people in his soldering unit, W_2, W_3, and S_1. He entered into social relations with I_1, W_6, and W_4 also, but to a lesser extent. With the remaining seven individuals he maintained little more than a speaking acquaintance. His best friend was W_3, with whom he conversed a great deal. They frequently associated outside of working hours, going to dances and card games. Late in the afternoon they usually sorted insulators together.

W_1's relation with W_2 was difficult to describe. When the group was first moved to the observation room, there was a dispute between these two over who should occupy a certain bench position. The matter was taken up with the foreman, and in spite of W_1's protests he made him change with W_2. This incident made W_1 quite antagonistic toward W_2, but his antagonism seemed to wear off in time. He felt that W_2 was superior to himself as a wireman and gave him credit for that.

With S_1 he was friendly. He traded jobs with him and frequently soldered for him while he was absent without leave. He did not claim daywork for time thus spent. Between W_1 and S_1 a great deal of "kidding" went on, most of which was instigated by S_1. In some of their verbal interplay, W_1's nationality figured prominently. The nature of these arguments, which afforded a good deal of amusement to the nonparticipants, can best be illustrated by quoting from the observer's record:

S_1 and W_1 have been kidding each other this afternoon. S_1's family is going to move. He told W_1 that they're moving to a neighborhood where no Polacks are allowed.

W_1: "I suppose they won't allow *any* white people there."

. . . . . .

I_1: "Two of the boys in the other room made a trip to the Gulf last week."

Obs: "They must have covered some ground."

W_3: "I guess they did. They claim they made over three thousand miles."

W_2: (To S_1) "What do you say we take the Studebaker and make that trip next week?"

S_1: "I'm afraid the Studebaker wouldn't go that far. How about taking your Chrysler? The only trouble is we can't take W_1 along with us. They don't allow Polacks down below the Mason-Dixon line."

W_1: "No, they just allow niggers down there."

. . . . . .

At 1:30 the Inspection section chief and the Operating section chief came in and told the group that they had to take some intelligence tests.

W_1: "Can I take my chew along? I can't take a test without a chew."

S_1: (To SC) "You can't take W_1 over there. They ain't got no tests for Polacks."

W_6: "What do they want to test us guys for? We can't use any brains on this job."

S_1 and W_1 became really angry with each other only once, when they got into an argument about religion, but even that soon blew over. Quoting again:

The group in the front of the room were having a heated argument about the Knights of Columbus and several other Catholic organizations. The trucker, S_1, and W_1 started the argument. W_1 was upholding the Catholic organizations and S_1 was ridiculing them. The trucker was doing all he could to get somebody angry. W_1 lost his temper early in the argument. When it became apparent that he was getting angry, the trucker danced around the front of the room and shouted: "W_1's cork's out. Now we've got him, fellows. He's burned up."

W_3: "What do you say we call a truce?"

They made fun of W_1 until he felt better. Then the argument started again. All this time W_4 and I_3 had their heads together and were discussing the Masonic order and the Knights of Columbus.

I_3: "A Catholic can never be a Mason because a Mason has to keep secrets, and the Catholics have to confess everything to the priest."

The argument between W_1 and S_1 hadn't been going long this time before S_1 got angry. The trucker enjoyed this. When it was over, S_1 was still angry. W_1 sent the trucker to him with a message. The trucker went over and looked at S_1's face and said: "Nope. I won't tell him. If you want him to hear that crack, you tell him yourself."

W_3: (To Obs.) "Religion is a bad thing to argue about."

Obs: "They seem to be having a lot of fun, though."

W_3: "Yes, that's what makes the wheels go round. Arguments are all right if they don't get too serious."

W_1 lagged coins and matched nickels with S_1, W_2, W_3, W_4, and I_1. This group also bought candy together, which they divided among themselves. When W_1 helped another wireman, it was always W_3, with the exception of one occasion when he did help W_9. Sometimes he acted as a conciliator. When W_2 and S_1 quarreled one day, it was W_1 who stopped them. On another occasion, when S_1 was swearing at I_3, W_1 tried to get him to go back to work. In both these instances, of course, he was trying to protect S_1 from "getting in bad" with the supervisors. Each time if the foreman had witnessed S_1's behavior, he might have subjected him to heavy penalties or at least to a "bawling out."

Compared to the men near him, W_1 was a slow wireman. Frequently he worked right up until 4:15, which was quitting time. This earned him the nickname of "4:15 Special," which was used derisively. He was the only person in the group who attended any of the meetings of the Safety Council, attendance at which was solicited by the supervisors. W_1 felt that the "group in back," W_7, W_8, and W_9, appropriated the best wire, and so he and W_2 sometimes sent S_1 out into the department to get wire for them.

Wireman 2

W_2 was not a talkative person. He rarely participated in the arguments going on about him. The other operators, on the whole, tended to leave him alone. He could not be said to be friendly with anyone in the group. He was most nearly so with S_1 and W_3. With I_1, W_1, and W_4 he talked occasionally in a casual way, but with the rest of the operators he had little to do. He was particularly contemptuous of the "group in back," W_7, W_8, and W_9. When he was soldering in S_4's place one week, for example, he claimed that he could solder for a dozen men like W_9.

It was W_2's custom to work steadily and at top speed until he got his work finished; then he was content to loaf. While working he brooked no interference. If the solderman or the inspector was not right there to solder or inspect his levels as they were completed, he would tell him to do so in no uncertain terms. The speed and concentration with which he worked earned him such nicknames as "Cyclone" and "Phar Lap," the latter the name of a race horse.

His habit of demanding service irritated both S_1 and I_1 occasionally. One day when S_1 made him wait several times, W_2 became very angry and retaliated by trying to make S_1 work right up until quitting time. This made S_1 angry and they began to quarrel. Suddenly, W_2 stamped over to one corner of the room and challenged S_1 to fight it out then and there. The group chief was not in the room at the time. Only the timely intervention of W_1 prevented a fight. W_2 and S_1 did not speak to each other for a week afterward. On another occasion I_1 accused him of working too fast and tried to get him to slow down. W_2 answered everything I_1 said in southern dialect. He jeered at him with the words "yo' all" so much that I_1, who was a southerner, became angry and refused to talk to him.

Although he was not very sociable, W_2 did take part in games of chance such as lagging coins and matching nickels. His participation was limited to games in which S_1, I_1, W_1, W_3, and occasionally W_4, took part. Once in a while he told outlandish stories which he tried to make the others believe. He spent a lot of time one day trying to convince them that he had seen a blind basketball team play. On one occasion when the group chief was out of the room his conduct was not at all in accordance with his usual demeanor. W_6 was strutting around the room with his chest stuck way out, claiming he was "Pop-Eye the Sailor." W_2 joined W_6 in imitating the character. After a while W_2 tired of this and rolled up his trousers so that they looked like plus fours. He then cavorted around claiming he was Bobby Jones. On the whole, however, W_2 was apt to be serious.

W_2 traded jobs with S_1 quite frequently and sometimes voluntarily soldered a row to help him. On one occasion he helped W_3; W_3 had helped him once previously. On the whole, however, he helped no one. When he was "on the outs" with S_1, he traded jobs with S_4 instead of with S_1. One day W_2 traded jobs with S_4, and immediately afterward S_1 traded with S_4. The investigators thought this incident was a significant reflection of the differences in status among the operators. Their interpretation of it was that by trading with S_4, who was looked upon as a poorer solderman than S_1, W_2 was in effect saying: "No matter what you think of yourself or what the others think of you, S_1, I don't think you are any better than S_4 and to prove it I, a superior wireman, am going to trade jobs with him." S_1 by trading off with

S_4 said in reply: "You think you are hurting my feelings by trading with an inferior solderman and making me solder for him. But I'll fool you. I won't serve him as a solderman. I'll trade jobs with him and make him serve me."

Wireman 3

W_3 was on good terms with every person in the group. He never once aroused antagonism or did anything intended to irritate another person. His closest friends were W_1, S_1, and W_4, all three of whom he invited to his wedding. But he was also friendly with the others. He was always willing to take part in the games and sports of the group and to contribute his share to their various pools on horse racing, baseball, and the like. All the men in the observation room had a standing invitation to play poker at his home. Those who attended these parties were S_1, W_1, W_4, W_6, W_8, and W_9. W_6, W_8, and W_9 did not attend so frequently as the other three. While at work he had little to do with W_7, W_8, and W_9, yet his relations with them were pleasant enough.

W_3's performance was consistently good. He worked at a rapid, even pace day in and day out, slowing down only when he had finished his quota. His work was done so well that S_1, who soldered his work, and I_1, who inspected it, claimed he was the best wireman they had ever worked with. He never once traded jobs with anyone; he was a wireman. A good indication of the way the other wiremen regarded him was the extent to which they helped him. Although he did not need it, he was helped more than any other operator in the group, W_1, W_2, W_4, W_5, and W_6 joining with him at one time or another. They liked to work with him. Once when W_3 was away for an interview, W_1, W_4, and W_6 collaborated in wiring ten levels on his equipments, which they let him report as his own. No other wireman was ever helped in this way. W_3 did not need the count, he was paid his average hourly earnings while being interviewed, but they worked for him anyway. W_3 did not always reciprocate by helping other people. In another person such behavior might have been regarded as selfish, but with W_3 the men did not mind.

W_3 was an indefatigable talker. Whether working or not, he kept up a continual stream of chatter which he directed chiefly toward W_1, S_1, and I_1. He seldom lost an argument whether it was about baseball, horse racing, movie stars' salaries, the interest rate on postal savings, or the cost of shipping a dozen eggs a hundred miles by express. His superiority was demonstrated not only by the fact that he usually won out in arguments but also by the way in which he advised and cautioned the men. Thus when S_1 said he was thinking of getting a transfer to a subsidiary of the Western Electric Company, W_3 told him that he should consider his chances of getting back on his present job in case he didn't get along well on his new job. He told W_5 which horses to bet on in the races. When W_6 and some of the others got too boisterous, it was W_3 who warned them to "pipe down." If he thought an argument was going too far, as in the argument about religion between W_1 and S_1, he tried to put a stop to it.

The following incident serves well to show W_3's position in the group. The men were complaining about poor wire, but the group chief told them they had to use it up. Contrary to his orders, W_1 and W_8 went out to the department and got some wire for themselves. They were rather proud of themselves and thought they had "got away with something." W_3 then went out to the department and in a short time came back accompanied by the trucker, who had a whole truck-load of wire.

Wireman 4

W_4 felt that the people at his end of the room were superior to those in back. He told the interviewer there were two groups in the observation room. There was the superior group, with which he identified himself, consisting of W_1, W_2, W_3, S_1, and I_1. The inferior group, he said, consisted of W_7, W_8, W_9, and S_4. He also thought that W_6 should be included in that group. He said that W_5 did not fit in either of them very well.

W_4: "We have sort of got together. We're a group all by ourselves. It seems like we are apart from the department now. We're really two groups down here, the group in front and the group in back."

Int: "What do you think brought that about?"

W_4: "Well, the fellows up in front talk about one thing all the time and the group at the other end of the room talk about different things. It seems like most of us up in front talk about the same thing together."

Int: "What do you talk about? I would be interested in knowing."

W_4: "Well, we talk about different things, but they are of some importance. There's a whole lot of arguing. Gee, how we argue! Everybody gets in on it too."

Int: "What does the other group talk about?"

W_4: "I don't know just what they do talk about — I don't talk to them very much. They mostly horse around so. You see, there is W_7, W_8, and W_9. They are the slowest wiremen in there. Not only in there but in the whole department. The rest of us up in front turn out all the way from 6,000 to 7,000, and those fellows never get up to 6,000."

Int: "Would you say, then, that all the faster wiremen are in your group?"

W_4: "Oh no. There's W_6, he's with the other bunch. He's a good wireman too. Then there's W_5. He keeps to himself pretty much, though. About all he does is turn out the work."

W_4 was particularly antagonistic toward W_5. Speaking to the interviewer, W_4 said:

"There's only one guy I don't like. That's W_5. It wouldn't make any difference to me if he was dead or alive. Nobody likes him. It's funny too. It's all on account of the way he acts. The reason I don't like him is that one time I didn't have any banks, so he said, 'Come over and help me out a little bit, will you?' I went over and wired about 4,000 connections for him that day and didn't turn them in. Then another time I helped him out about eight levels. I always thought he would help me out when I needed it, you know. But he never did. I never asked him to. I thought if he was any sort of a fellow at all he would do it without being asked. But no sir! If he was waiting, he never helped me out. I'll never have anything to do with him again. W_2 and W_3 are not like that. They help me out right along and I help them out. That way you get along better. If something happens that you can't go ahead on your own equipment, why you can go over and help them. W_5 seems to be all for himself and he doesn't care about anyone else."

W_4 was friendly with W_3, S_1, W_1, and W_2 in the order mentioned. In his interviews he expressed admiration for W_3's work. He thought S_1 was the best solderman in the room and he liked the way he carried gossip from one wireman to another and kept the arguments going: "He sort of goes along when there's an argument on and carries it from one person to another. I think that's what a solderman should do." Evidence of the antagonism between W_4 and W_5 came to the observer's attention when they quarreled over the windows and on one occasion when W_5 changed the sequence of a row of cables lying on a truck so that a particularly difficult equipment would have to be wired by W_4 instead of himself. The group chief arranged the cables in the order he wanted the equipments wired and the first wireman through was supposed to begin anew on the equipment indicated by the order of the cables. When the group chief noticed that the order of the cables had been changed, W_4 told him that W_5 had done it. This was considered "squealing" and was something W_4 would not have done to any of the other operators.

W_4 did not trade jobs with anyone, but he helped W_1, W_3, W_6, and the trucker on occasions. He was the only wireman in the group who ever helped the trucker. He participated in the games and betting that went on among the wiremen in front, but to a lesser extent than the others. Unlike W_1, W_2, and W_3, who did not enter into the controversies about the windows, W_4 frequently argued about them. His arguments were chiefly with W_5 and W_6, and particularly with the latter. No matter how cold it might be, W_6 would not allow W_4 to close his window. One time he offered to loan W_4 his sweater and vest rather than let him close the window. There was only one exception to this. One day both W_5 and W_6 had their windows open. W_4 complained of being cold and closed both of them. W_5 reopened his and told W_4 to leave it alone. W_6 was about to open his also, but as soon as W_5 started to argue with W_4 he changed his mind and left it closed. The antagonism between W_6 and W_5 was stronger than that between W_6 and W_4. W_4 sometimes vied with W_6 in output, but W_6 was much too fast for him. W_4 referred to him as a "slave" and several times told him to slow down because he shouldn't turn out so much. When W_4 argued about the windows with the other wiremen, W_3 "kidded" him about it as if to say, "If you're one of us you shouldn't do that. It isn't done by our group." W_4 was the only participant in these controversies who was "kidded" by the wiremen in the front of the room.

Wireman 5

When W_5 was wiring he gave the appearance of being relaxed; there was nothing tense about either his facial expression or his movements. The ease with which he wired gave a false impression of slowness. He was in fact a very efficient wireman and was just as fast as many who seemed to expend a great deal more energy. He worked smoothly and with precision, seizing his wires and slipping them over the terminals without hesitation. As he moved steadily along, he shifted his weight alternately from one foot to another with a rather slow rhythmic motion of the body. Frequently, after he had finished his day's work he idly fastened wires here and there on his equipment, scattering the connections in such a way that no one level was completed and so that neither the solderman nor the inspector could work on the equipment. The next morning all he had to do was to connect up the unfastened wires and in a very short time he would have several levels completed. This trick of fastening wires here and there was practiced by some of the other wiremen also, and it required considerably more skill than fastening them in sequence because there was a greater chance of error. W_5 was easily irritated by anything that broke his "swing" once he got started and he was quick to complain if banks were not handy or if the wire was not just right.

W_5 was without doubt the most disliked wireman in the group, probably because he was critical of anyone who didn't work as hard as he did and, still more, because he did certain things which the group felt were wrong. Several times he took it upon himself to bawl out W_9 because he wasn't doing enough work. He thought S_1 did too much "horsing around" and should work harder. He referred to W_7 as a "fairy," and frequently he petulantly commanded W_6 to shut up. To show his contempt for W_7, W_8, and W_9 he one day did the soldering for all three positions in addition to trying to do as much wiring as W_8 ordinarily did. W_8 was absent and S_4 changed jobs with W_5 that day. The group did not object to these activities of his so much as to his willingness to "squeal" if he saw fit. Thus, one day he purposely made a number of derogatory remarks about I_3 so that I_3's supervisor, who was in the room, could hear him. W_6 joined with him in "razzing" I_3, but he was not aware that I_3's supervisor was in the room. When W_6 saw the supervisor he stopped short, and after the latter left he tried to make up to I_3 by helping him. The following incidents illustrate W_5's relations with the various people in the group:

W_5 was wiring for W_8. W_8 was soldering for S_4, and S_4 was wiring for W_5.

W_5: (To S_4) "I'm coming back up there tomorrow. I can't do anything up here. Monkey around all day."

A little later the group chief came in.

W_5: "I want to go back in my old position."

GC: "What for?"

W_5: "Aw, too much monkeying around. First W_8 went over to the hospital. He got lost then and I had to solder. Then he went over to the Service Division and got lost again. Then he goes out to see you and he don't come back."

W_9: "Shut up, you. You talk too much. You don't know when to keep your mouth shut."

W_5: "Never you mind about that."

GC: "How about it, W_8?"

W_8: "I didn't waste any time I didn't have to."

. . . . . .

W_5 and W_6 were talking about the card game they have every noon.

W_6: "Well, there's one thing certain. You can't play cards with me any more — you're scummy."

W_5: "I don't want to play cards with you. I wouldn't if you wanted me to."

W_6: "You think you're a card shark, but you don't know anything about cards."

W_5: "I can beat you any time."

W_6: "You can't win anything unless you have me as partner, and I won't play any more."

. . . . . .

W_6: (To GC) "Say, how long will it be before W_5 gets his transfer?"

GC: "I don't know."

W_6: "It sure will be a relief to have him out of here."

. . . . . .

W_5: (Walking back to W_7's position) "Say, what's the idea, coming down and taking my wire?"

W_7: "What do you care? How do you know it was me?"

W_5: "I know it was you. You're the only one scummy enough to take a fellow's wire."

W_7: (Angrily) "All right, it was me. What are you going to do about it?"

W_5 did nothing.

. . . . . .

W_5 was soldering in position S_4. W_7, W_8, and W_9 were all wiring 100-point banks and were trying to get waiting time on W_5. W_5 had a hard time keeping up with them. They razzed him for being slow and he resented it. It ended up in an argument between W_5 and W_7. W_5 told W_7 he was scummy. W_7 told him to shut his mouth or he would punch his nose, and he meant it. That ended the argument.

. . . . . .

S_1: (To interviewer) "I won't work for some of those guys. Take W_5, I can't stand that fellow. All he does is crab and crab. If you're not right there to solder his level as soon as he's finished it, he'll go up and tell the boss about it. I haven't any use for a guy like that. Lots of times the solderman simply can't be right on the job when he is needed because he is somewhere else. A guy who goes and crabs to the boss at a time like that I don't like."

$\cdot \quad \cdot \quad \cdot \quad \cdot \quad \cdot$

W_4: (To interviewer) "S_2 ordinarily gets his work done in time. He's very good that way. Nothing will interfere with him as long as he's got work to do. He doesn't like to keep people waiting, but once in a while W_5 is too much for him. I've seen him deliberately go ahead and do everybody else's soldering and leave W_5 until the last just to make him wait."

In addition to W_4's testimony about S_2's attitude toward W_5, there was the fact that W_5 traded jobs not with S_2, his solderman, but with S_4. S_2 traded with W_6, and both S_1 and S_4 traded more frequently with men in their own units than outside of them. This, then, might be taken as a reflection of the relation between W_5 and S_2.

The only people with whom W_5's relation approached friendship were W_1 and W_3, both of whom got along with him fairly well. W_5 helped W_3 wire a few times, but he himself was not once helped by anyone. W_5 did not enter very much into arguments. He took some part in the gambling games of the group, but usually bet by himself on the horse races.

The observer noticed that W_5 rarely smiled. He seemed unhappy and very discontented with his job. He was constantly asking his supervisors for a transfer, and once when he thought he was going to get one he was more cheerful than he ever was before or afterward.

Wireman 6

W_6 was so short in height that only with some difficulty could he wire the upper levels of his equipments. Equipments which were three banks high were especially difficult for him. This led the foreman to suggest that the group chief hang him up by the heels to stretch him out a little. It was also in part responsible for various nicknames, such as "Shorty," "The Shrimp," and "The Runt," by which he was called from time to time. In spite of his size, however, W_6 was an extraordinarily fast wireman. Working "like a human dynamo" earned him the comparatively respectful title of "Speed King." He was always in action, whether working or not. He simply couldn't stay still; he had to be doing something. When he had finished his work, which he usually accomplished fairly early, he either helped other people or stirred up trouble. Like W_5, but to an even greater extent, he complicated his job by fastening wires here and there on his equipments after his day's work was finished.

W_6 entered into direct social relations with everyone in the group. He talked to everyone. While no one of the men really disliked him, neither could it be said that anyone was particularly friendly with him. He did and said many things which in themselves would indicate strong antagonisms toward the people concerned, but he usually tempered the effect by overtures in the other direction. Thus he "rode" W_9 even more than did W_5, but unlike W_5 he sometimes helped W_9 wire and engaged in friendly conversation with him.

More than any other person in the group, W_6 liked to draw attention to himself. This he did in various ways. His imitation of "Pop-Eye the Sailor" was one example. At other times he told long yarns in which he pictured himself as a hero or as possessing extraordinary virility. He shared honors with W_8 in the art of "cracking wise" and telling off-color stories. When his jokes fell flat, he said he got them from the trucker. W_6's behavior is illustrated in the following excerpts from the observer's record:

W_6 was waiting for banks. He entertained the group by telling of his experiences, in which he always takes the part of a hero. He told them of a fight in which he knocked out several fellows. A while later he told them about the time he was manager of a big company. He pictured himself as a hard-boiled executive. He gets a lot of fun out of telling these stories. W_3 and W_1 asked him what he had for lunch that made him feel this way. They said he must have taken some kind of dope. S_1 decided that it must be "Roo Hee," an Indian tonic.

. . . . . .

The group were talking a lot about war this morning. They were laughing and talking of going to Shanghai. The section chief came in with the pay checks and joined in the conversation.

SC: "Maybe if a lot of you guys would get pulled over to that mix-up there'd be work for everybody."

W_6: "If I went over there, they wouldn't need any of the rest of you guys. You fellows never saw me in action. If I'd get over there, those Japs would go right and left. I'd make mincemeat out of them."

W_6 manifested a strong desire for leadership, which took the form of trying to tell the others what to do or of arguing with the group chief or section chief. He often argued another person's cause for him. Thus one of the men might present certain objections or complaints to a supervisor. The supervisor would reply and the issue would be almost settled when W_6 would "butt in," bring it out in the open again, and try to convince the supervisor that the objections or complaints were justified. Some of the various ways in which W_6's desire for leadership manifested itself are illustrated below:

W_5 and W_8 were waiting for banks. When two pans of them came in, W_6 ran to the rear of the room to get his. W_9 jumped over and took the remaining ones and put them on his bench. W_9 did not need them for another half-hour. W_5 grumbled because W_9 took them and then went over and started helping W_3. W_6 then went back to W_9's bench, took the banks and gave them to W_5. W_5 accepted them without a word and started working in his own position.

. . . . . .

W_6: (To substitute wireman) "No wonder you're getting laid off the way you work."

W_8: "There's no use working today. That won't do me any good. I used to be able to wire right up with the best of them. One day I had two equipments finished by noon."

W_6: "You never did that. There ain't nobody around here can do that."

W_8: "I suppose you think you're the fastest man around here."

W_6: "No. W_2 can't do it, I can't do it, and there ain't nobody in the other room can do it."

. . . . . .

W_6 made some remark while he was looking for his spectacles.

S_1: "What do you know about it, you little runt?"

W_6: "Shut up. When I say something, you just button up. Don't say a word back to me." (To group) "He's talking back to me when I'm blind; I haven't even got my glasses."

. . . . . .

The section chief came in with the pay checks. After distributing them he spoke to W_9.

SC: "Do you know that you are farther in the hole than anybody in the department?"

W_9: "I suppose I am."

SC: "How many are you turning out?"

W_9: "Oh, I don't know. Some days I get 4,000."

SC: "You ought to be getting that every day. All of you guys ought to be turning out more than what you're doing. There are some guys in the other room that are turning out just about as much as you fellows are and they haven't been here as long."

W_6: "Yes, but don't forget that they are getting their $\$.43$ an hour."

W_7: "Maybe if we'd get more we could turn out more work."

SC: "I know there's some of those guys out there, but there's not many of them."

W_6: "I could use a little more money right now, but I suppose when I get it I'll have to fight for it."

W_7: (To W_6) "You don't know what it is to need money. You're only a kid."

W_8: "You can live on those Polish sausage, that kind they sell by the yard."

W_6: "Yes, but I don't eat that stuff." (To SC) "I had to fight for every penny I ever got out of this place. Now if I want any more I suppose I'll have to fight for it."

The section chief left the room without answering.

$\cdot$ $\quad$ $\cdot$ $\quad$ $\cdot$ $\quad$ $\cdot$ $\quad$ $\cdot$ $\quad$ $\cdot$

W_9 and W_7 went out for a drink of water.

W_6: "I don't think that guy W_9 will ever learn to wire."

W_8: "He hasn't been here hardly long enough to be good yet."

W_6: "Yuh, but he doesn't want to wire. I'll bet if they put him in my charge he'd learn to wire in a hurry."

W_8: "Who are you, the boss?"

W_6: "I don't mean that. I mean if they gave me all the privileges, that is, put him under my control, he'd learn to wire. I'd get over him with a big club and every time he'd stop wiring, I'd sock him."

S_4: "That would be no good. You would be a driver."

$\cdot$ $\quad$ $\cdot$ $\quad$ $\cdot$ $\quad$ $\cdot$ $\quad$ $\cdot$ $\quad$ $\cdot$

GC_2, who has charge of the machine which strips the insulation off the wire, was called in by GC_1 to look at the wire which the wiremen claimed was no good. He picked up a roll, looked at it, and then brought it over to the observer's desk.

GC_2: "Now what's the matter with this wire? Not a thing wrong with it. These guys are just like kids. Shove all their bum wire out there for the other fellows to use." (To group) "Listen, you guys, after this when wire comes out here you use it up."

W_6: "Yuh, you send out all the bad wire and then you tell us we got to use it up. How can we make our bogey with that kind of wire?"

GC_2: "You're not getting any worse wire than anybody else. Wire can't be perfect, I know that, but if you guys'd use it up you wouldn't have so much."

W_6: "Why don't you let those guys in the other room use some of it?

Your guys out there pick out all the good spools and then you send us the rest."

GC_2: "No, they don't. They use the wire just as it comes and when they get a spool with a few bad places in it they use it up."

W_6: "What do you know about wire? You oughtta get in here and wire for a while. If any of you bosses would wire for a day you wouldn't be out here trying to tell us to use wire that's no good. You'd know what we're up against."

GC_2: "Say, I was wiring when you guys were in short pants."

W_6: "I suppose you're gonna tell me you wired when they used to skin the wires with flats."

GC_2: "No, I didn't wire then."

W_6: "Well, if you know so much about wire, come here and tell me if this is any good."

GC_2: "No, that isn't so good, but you don't get a spool like that very often. When you get a spool like that, let me know."

W_6: "When you want to know something about wire, come out and ask me. I've used up more bum wire than any guy in this place."

Although W_6 showed a strong desire for leadership, the group did not accord him the position of leader. The men constantly tried to belittle him by calling him all sorts of nicknames and by making fun of him and of his nationality. The incident, quoted above, in which W_7 and W_8 made fun of him while he was arguing with the section chief over his rate of pay offers a good example of how they tried to keep him in his place.

At the beginning of the study W_6 frequently traded jobs with S_3, but as soon as S_4 replaced S_3 he no longer soldered in position S_3. Toward the end of the observation period he traded with S_2 a few times. This was significant for two reasons: it reflected the relation between W_6 and S_4, which was one of mild antagonism, and it reflected the change which had taken place in S_2's relation with the group. S_2 was beginning to take part in the social activities of the group. The people W_6 helped most frequently were the members of the group in the rear of the room, W_7, W_8, and W_9. He also helped W_3 occasionally. W_6 needed help as little as anyone in the group, yet he was helped by W_4, W_8, and S_2 on occasions.

Although W_6 tended to associate with those in the rear of the room more than with those in front, he was not fully accepted in either group. This was manifested in many subtle ways. For example, on one occasion W_7, W_8, and W_9 ordered some candy from the Hawthorne Club store and asked W_6 to contribute to the purchase price, but when the candy came they would not give him his share. Again, when W_6 tried to "bawl out" W_9 for not working fast enough, W_7 and W_8 sided with W_9 against W_6. The group in the front of the room, W_1, W_2, W_3, and S_1, also showed some resistance toward W_6, as in such incidents as the following:

The group chief was sitting at the observer's desk. Suddenly W_6 came running in and sat down beside him. S_1 was chasing him. The group in the front of the room accused W_6 of taking S_1's orange. W_6 tried to convince them that someone else took the orange and put it in his locker, but he didn't have much success.

W_8: "That's right. Go and sit on GC's lap, that's the kind of a guy you are."

W_6: "I tell you I didn't put the orange in there."

S_1: "You did it all right."

Wireman 7

If W_6 was too short to wire the upper levels of his equipments easily, W_7 was too tall to wire the lower ones comfortably. He had to stand in a tiresome stooping position with his head bent down.[1] W_7 was a slow worker and his nickname of "Jumbo" was suitable. He was easily distracted from his work and, unlike W_2, W_3, W_5, and W_6, even welcomed some interruption which would allow him to "take it easy" for a while. The observer recorded that W_7 was very clever at getting out of a chair and into a working position unobtrusively when someone entered the room suddenly. He had an enormous appetite and frequently ate a sandwich during the morning. At noon he sometimes ate a large lunch at a near-by restaurant in addition to the one he brought from home.

W_7 was friendly with W_8, W_9, and S_1, particularly with the latter two. With S_1 he went to dances and drinking parties and participated in other forms of amusement. At noon they ate lunch together. He frequently went out to get a drink of water with W_9 or S_1, and he took more time out in this way than any person except W_9. In the following incident S_1 expressed his solidarity with W_7 by ridiculing S_4, with whom W_7 had been arguing:

---

[1] The foreman noticed that there were difficulties due to differences in height and thought that the workbenches should be adjustable.

W_7: (To S_4) "Learn how to solder. If you can't solder, throw the iron away."

S_4: "Learn how to shut up."

The Group: (To W_7) "That's telling you."

W_7: "I guess so."

S_4: "I'm not afraid of any army shirt." (W_7 was wearing an army shirt.)

W_8: (To W_7) "I guess he knows you."

    S_1 came over to file his iron.

S_1: "What do you think of a guy like S_4 that wears his Sunday suit to work?"

S_4: "This ain't my Sunday suit."

W_8: "Maybe he's going to sing."

S_4: "Maybe I'm going to the opera."

W_7's friendliness with W_9 was expressed in several ways besides going out for drinks of water together. Thus when the group chief told W_9 to "snap out of it" and get busy on a certain set of difficult banks, W_7 and W_8 told W_9 not to take them, that he should insist that the group chief give them to W_2, who was just finishing a set. W_7 also allowed W_9 to close his window after he had refused that privilege to others.

    W_7 was trying to keep the window open. The others objected.

W_9: (To I_2) "Close that window, will you? I'm about froze."

    I_2 was leaning against the radiator near the window but he would not close it. W_9 did it himself.

W_7: (To W_9) "Do you know me?"

W_9: "No, I don't know you."

W_7: "Then it's all right to close the window."

W_8: "Yes, it's all right to close them and then leave them closed. After this if any of you boys want to open the windows, you come to me. I'll tell you whether to open them or not."

I_2's refusal to obey W_9 reflects the superordinate position of the inspectors. W_7's question, "Do you know me?" and W_9's reply in the negative were of interest because through the use of this verbal device W_7 retained his jurisdiction over the window. If W_9 had said he did know him, W_7's response would have been the same. It was simply a way of granting permission. There was some evidence which indicated that W_7 felt superior to W_9. When the group chief ordered each man to clean the solder off his bench W_7 protested, saying that it would be a good job for W_9.

Ordinarily W_7 did not argue with W_8 over the windows, but on one day when W_7 was in an ill temper because of an itch from which he was suffering, he very stubbornly refused to let W_8 close his window. When the group chief closed it part way, W_7 told him also to leave it alone. Later he apologized to W_8 for his behavior. He frequently "kidded" W_8 about his appearance, particularly about his curly hair, telling him that he would not dare to let him meet his wife.

W_7 did not get along well with W_5 or W_6. With W_1, W_2, W_3, and W_4 he had little contact. He thought that W_6 turned out too much work and he also disliked him because he was Polish. His attitude toward Poles is clearly shown in the following excerpt from one of his interviews:

"I think most of them would turn out more work if they were on straight piecework. . . . Of course, some of them Poles don't mind. They keep right on chewing their tobacco and spitting all over the floor and trailing their wire through it. I think it sort of numbs their minds so they can work without thinking of anything else."

Wireman 8

W_8 preferred soldering to wiring and spent a good deal of time at it. He always soldered in position S_3. More than any other person in the group, he complained about not feeling well or not feeling like working. The cause of his feeling poorly he usually attributed to drinking too much the previous night or to staying up too late. He frequently told the group about his escapades with women and the difficulties he got into with them. He also liked to impress them with his boxing ability and compared himself to Jack Dempsey.

He was friendly with W_7 and W_9 and got along well with S_4. Although he mingled with the other people in the room, his relations with them were distant. The one exception was W_6, with whom he scuffled and argued a good deal. He took delight in scuffing W_6's shoes after he had had them shined and in tussling with him over whether the windows should be kept open or not. Their relation was not unfriendly, however, as is shown by the fact that they sometimes helped each other wire and entertained each other with stories. W_8 also helped W_7 and W_9, and was helped by S_4.

Wireman 9

W$_9$ was more easily distracted from his work than anyone else. The slightest disturbance was sufficient to cause him to stop work and look around. He worked very slowly and, although he stopped frequently, he persevered throughout the day fairly well. His lack of interest in his work was shown not only by the ease with which he was distracted from it but also by the frequency with which he went out to get a drink of water. He always asked someone to go with him, usually W$_7$, W$_8$, or S$_1$. Frequently he complained of being tired and of his lack of interest in the work. The former complaint was probably closely allied to the latter, because his physical examinations showed that he was in good health, he looked healthy and strong, and he always had enough energy to participate in strenuous sports after working hours.

W$_9$ was considered intelligent and well-read by his associates. He frequently used "big" words which impressed some of them favorably.

W$_7$, W$_8$, W$_9$, and S$_4$ took time out to admire a girl who was sitting across the aisle and could be seen through the open door.

W$_9$: "Well, boys, I'll tell you. That girl has got what I call voluptuous hips."

W$_8$: "What did you call them?"

W$_9$: "Voluptuous. I don't suppose you know what that means."

W$_8$ tried to pronounce the word but failed.

W$_8$: (To Obs.) "Say, did you hear what he called that girl's hips?"

Obs: "No."

W$_8$: "Hey, W$_9$, come here. Stop laughing and pronounce that word again."

W$_9$ was doubled up with laughter.

. . . . . .

W$_9$: "Oh say, W$_7$, I got a new word when I was reading last night."

W$_7$: "What was it?"

W$_9$: "Diagnostician."

W$_7$: "Oh boy, is that a word! What does it mean anyway?"

W$_9$: "It's one who diagnoses something."

W$_7$: "Tell it to W$_8$ before you forget it."

W$_9$: "Don't worry. I won't forget it."

W_7: "I've got to start reading some of those books and see if I can't get a few words."

Because of his poor job performance W_9 was frequently "razzed" by other people in the group. The people who took occasion to tell him how poor he was were W_2, W_6, W_5, W_8, S_1, S_4, and I_1. W_1, W_3, and W_4, although they may have privately held a poor opinion of him, did not tell him so. W_9 took criticism good-naturedly; he admitted that he was slow and warned the others not to expect anything better of him. He said he could do better if he wanted to, but he didn't care to. There the matter ended. He never changed jobs with anyone and the only person he tried to help was S_4. W_1, W_6, and W_8 helped him on occasions. He joined in the purchase of candy with W_7, W_8, and S_4 and talked with them a great deal. Although the members of the group looked down upon him as a wireman, no one except W_5 really disliked him. His personality served to offset, in part at least, any odium attaching to him as a workman.

The following quotations from the observer's record illustrate the way in which some of W_9's associates tried to bring pressure to bear upon him, their feelings toward him, and his attitude toward them and his work:

W_9 has just returned from the assistant foreman's office.

W_7: "Well, did you get bawled out?"

W_9: "No. He just showed me how much money I was losing [for the group] and then he told me to come back and earn some."

A little later, W_5 came to the back of the room for some banks.

W_5: (To W_9) "How many are you turning out now?"

W_9: "Oh, about 3,000 or 4,000."

W_5: "Then you are losing [us] $.09 an hour."

W_6: "How do you figure that?"

W_5: "Well, his rate is $.37."

W_7: "It is, like hell; it's $.39."

W_5: "Well, then he's losing $.11 an hour."

W_8: "Watch him tear, now that he got bawled out."

W_9: "Don't worry. I won't do any more."

W_6: "He's got the same rate as I got. I'd just like to see what would happen to you if they should ever make this a group by ourselves. I'll bet you would work. Just like I said the other day, we'd make you work."

W_9: "I don't know whether you would or not."

W_6: "Well, you wouldn't be turning out any 3,000."

W_9: "Well, I suppose I would get beat up a couple of times and then I'd quit."

W_6: "You would either work or quit, one or the other."

. . . . . .

GC: "What are you sitting there for, W_9? Why don't you get to work?"

W_9: "How can I? I'm waiting for the inspector."

GC: "You sit around too much anyway. You could be putting your cable wires on."

W_9: "Yes, suppose there is a cable reverse?"

W_8: "You can take a chance. There won't be."

GC: "You're too doggone lazy for any use."

W_9: "I'm not lazy — I'm tired."

GC: "You make me tired just looking at you."

W_6: "Why don't you fire him?"

W_9: "He isn't the foreman."

GC: "It's a good thing for you I'm not. I'd like to be the foreman for one day. If I was, you wouldn't be around here any more."

W_9: "That would be all right with me. It wouldn't make me mad. I hate to work anyway."

W_6: "Why don't you transfer him to that —— job?"

GC: "They wouldn't have him down there."

W_9: "Yes, and I wouldn't go either. It'd cost me $14 a month for carfare."

W_8: "Why don't you move in from ——? Maybe that's what's the matter with you, living out there in the sticks."

GC: "If you could have any job you liked, what kind would you take?"

W_9: "I don't know, but it wouldn't be a wiring job."

GC: "What kind of a job would you want?"

W_9: "I'd like a job reading. Some job where I could sit and read all day."

Solderman 1

S_1 was well liked by everyone in the group except W_5 and possibly W_2. He was particularly friendly with W_7 and almost as friendly with W_3. With W_1 he had a relation characterized by "kidding," sarcasm, and funmaking. S_1 did more clowning than anyone in the group and was a source of constant amusement to his associates.

The observer had been in the room only a few minutes this morning when W_7 stopped to wait for the inspector. He looked toward the observer, caught his eye, and then locked his fingers. This gesture was to signify that he had been married.

Obs: "Congratulations."

W_7: "Yes, I guess I need some. We went out to —— and got buckled. It's nice out in that town. It wouldn't be bad living there."

Obs: "How did the wedding go?"

W_7: "Fine. No trouble. Six of us went up to the justice of the peace and he buckled us. That fellow was pretty good. He picked us out of the crowd. You see, we had another fellow and a girl go up and give him the license, but he picked us out as the ones that were supposed to get married. I guess we had a goofy look on our faces."

Obs: (To S_1) "Did you go with him?"

S_1: "No, I wouldn't help him do anything like that."

W_7: "Well, it's done now. There you are. I'm buckled, that's all there is to it. Well, I got out of it pretty cheap, anyway. It only cost me sixteen dollars. Eight dollars for the ring, two dollars for the license, five dollars for the bird that married us, and then one dollar that I spent."

S_1: "With all this stuff going on, I've got to get a better job. Here W_7 gets married and I've got to buy him a present. Then there's I_3 over there. He's going to have a baby — I should do something for him."

The group thought this was a great joke.

. . . . . .

S_1 talked to a visitor until the quitting whistle blew. He had forgotten to file his irons and began doing so just as the others were about to leave. They kidded him about working late.

S_1: "Well, boys, in a few years I'll be writing magazine articles, 'from solderman to president.' If you want to get ahead in this company, just work hard. You guys who watch the clock never will amount to anything." (Here S_1 was taking off a certain supervisor who sometimes gave them advice like this.)

When working time was shortened and it became more and more apparent that some, if not all, of the men would have to be laid off, it was S_1 who through his jokes and antics kept the group in good spirits. He made light of the situation in numerous ways. Early in the year he bought a calf which he said he was going to fatten on his uncle's farm so that he would have a good supply of meat the next winter. This calf figured prominently in the group's conversations and speculations. Soon thereafter some of the others began raising rabbits and chickens and they talked endlessly about ways of saving money. S_1 was largely responsible for the good-hearted attitude with which the group received the news of their layoff. He seemed to set the tone of their reactions. They thought of their layoff as something for which no one in particular was responsible and felt that there was no use in moaning about it.

The only person S_1 helped was W_7. He himself was assisted occasionally by W_1 and W_2. He traded jobs with W_1 and W_2 and on one occasion, mentioned previously, with S_4 while the latter was wiring for W_2.

Although S_1 got along well enough with S_2 and S_4, some of the things he said and did indicated that he felt he was superior to them. Thus he referred to S_2 as his helper when speaking to GC_2. Several times he told S_4 that he was not soldering properly and offered to give him lessons. These offers were rejected in no uncertain terms. One evening S_1 attempted to force S_4 to file his irons for him. S_4 refused. The next morning S_1 traded jobs with W_2 so that he would not have to file the irons. W_2, in turn, traded with S_4. In this roundabout way, S_4 finally had to file S_1's irons.

Solderman 2

S_2 rarely spoke, partly because of a speech difficulty, and did not enter at all into the games and other activities of the group. He traded jobs only toward the end of the study and then always with W_6. He also helped W_6 wire a few times, but he himself was helped by no one. Even though he did not take part directly, he seemed to enjoy the arguments and horseplay of the others. According to W_4, the men did not talk to him because he didn't seem to understand and they were not sure how he would react if he did understand. Toward the end of the study, according to W_4, he seemed to be less backward, and the men occasionally "kidded" him about women. This he took good-naturedly. He also began to express an interest in horse racing and would sometimes ask, "What horse, what horse?" in order to learn which horse the group was betting on that day. It was at about this same time that the job trading between him and W_6 began to take place. S_2 was a good solderman and rarely kept anyone waiting. When he did, he was usually told to "snap out of it."

Solderman 4

Just as S_1 conversed and "carried on" mostly with the wiremen whose work he soldered, so S_4's social activities were largely confined to his own soldering unit, W_7, W_8, and W_9. Although not so fast as S_1 or S_2, he was fast enough to keep up with his group provided they did not deliberately arrange their work in such a way that he could not keep up. This they frequently did in order to get an excuse for claiming daywork.

S_1 looked down on S_4, and S_4 tended to concede that he did occupy a lower occupational status. This was apparent when he took over the job of getting lunches for the group after S_1 had done it for a week. He kept the job until he was transferred back to the department, when it reverted to S_1. His inferior status was also indicated by the fact that he would almost always agree to trade jobs with anyone. During the study he traded jobs with W_2, W_5, W_7, and W_8. Sometimes, however, he complained that he did not like to trade jobs so frequently, and on one occasion he flatly refused to trade with W_8, saying that he was a solderman and not a wireman. Indeed, much of S_4's behavior indicated that he did not like the position in which his job placed him. He resented anything which seemed derogatory either to himself or to his work. When W_6 once made a slurring remark about the neighborhood in which S_4 lived, he resented it and criticized W_6's neighborhood, saying that it had a bad smell. When W_7 criticized his soldering, he became angry.

Unlike the other soldermen, who were quite content to allow the wiremen to set their work pace, S_4 sometimes tried to set the pace for the wiremen. This he did by starting to solder a level before it was finished — "pushing the wiremen" this practice was called. The wiremen did not like to be pushed, but they had no compunctions about pushing the solderman. In fact, pushing the solderman was to them a kind of game. The idea was not to get more work done but to annoy the solderman.

When S_4 traded jobs with W_2, the observer noticed that he felt ill at ease while working in the front of the room. He talked very little and did not act like himself. S_4 said that he felt isolated working in position W_2, that it was like being in a cell with nothing but four walls around him. It was true that this particular workbench was the most isolated one in the room and S_4's reaction to it constituted an interesting commentary upon W_2's preference for being by himself. S_4's feeling of isolation, however, was probably also due to the fact that he was not a member of the group in the front of the room.

Inspector 1

I_1 talked freely with the men in his inspection unit and argued a great deal with W_3 and S_1. In some of his arguments with W_3 a certain desire for dominance was noticeable. Sometimes he flatly contradicted everything W_3 said, but even their more serious arguments did not disrupt their friendship. I_1 frequently joined in lagging coins or matching nickels. He also placed bets on the "Test Room Horse" along with the operators. In many ways he appeared to be one of the group; yet certain things he said and did indicated that he regarded himself as being apart from them. His behavior toward the foreman, for example, differed from that of the operators in that he did not have their attitude of submissiveness toward him. One day the foreman came in to see W_5, apparently on business; the observer thought it might be about a stock cancellation. While he was in the room, the operators worked at top speed, hardly daring to look up. I_1, in the midst of this great activity, went over and talked to the observer. He said he thought that the foreman was really in the room to get a tip from W_5 on the horse race. When the foreman stayed on and on and I_1 noticed that the work was piling up too fast, he turned to the observer and said in a voice loud enough to be heard by the foreman: "I wish the Old Man would get out of here. These guys will never quit work if he hangs around. Look at 'em go." The observer did not know whether or not the foreman heard the remark, but the foreman did leave the room immediately. The operators, of course, would not have dared to stand around talking to the observer at such a time, much less make the remark that I_1 did.

On another occasion the section chief and the group chief were in the room soliciting attendance at a safety meeting. None of the men would sign up to go. The only names on the list were those of the assistant foreman, the section chief, and the group chief. When S_1 asked why the foreman's name wasn't on the list, the section chief said he didn't know. He said the foreman told him that he tried to get into the last meeting but couldn't because the seats were all filled. The section chief couldn't understand this because he was there and saw that half of the seats were empty. No one said anything for a while and then I_1 remarked: "He wouldn't go to those meetings. He was out playing poker." The point here is that I_1 spoke what was on everyone's mind. The others might have wished to make some such remark but they refrained from doing so.

Another incident which might be interpreted as a reflection of I_1's status was that when he became quite sure that he would be laid off in the near future he quit immediately; this in spite of the fact that he needed his earnings quite as much as any of the others. The operators hung on as long as possible.

One of the games which I_1 originated was of interest because it tended to improve the quality of the operators' work and was thus strictly in accordance with the aims of management. It incidentally tended to make his own work easier. The game took place between I_1 and W_1, W_2, W_3, and W_4. I_1 would offer to take bets that a certain one of these wiremen would make fewer reverses during the day than any of the others. After the bets were placed, the race was on. During the day I_1 kept them informed of one another's standing.

I_1's relation with I_3 was not very friendly. One day the group chief ordered W_6 and W_7 to wire two equipments which were three banks high and of a type which was not familiar to anyone in the room:

W_6 objected to wiring the equipment because he was so short. W_7 objected to wiring the one assigned to him on the ground that he didn't know how to do it. The group chief apparently did not know how to wire them either. He gave W_7 a rather hazy explanation of how to do it.

W_7: "Well, who's going to inspect these? I_3 don't know anything about them."

I_3: "I won't inspect those things. I don't know anything about them."

GC: "I'll go out and see your boss and find out what he wants to do."

The group chief left the room. The group kidded I_3. They asked him what he was going to do with "triples." The group chief came back.

GC: "We're gonna have to move you fellows down on the other end. I_1 is going to inspect them. W_6, you can change places with W_3. W_7, you bring your board down to position W_5."

The Group: (To I_1) "Boy, are you chiseled! You are gonna have to do the triples."

I_1: "How is that?"

GC: "I'm going to move these equipments down to these positions."

I_1: "Like hell! I'll not do 'em."

I_3 came back. He had been out talking to the inspection group chief. He came into the room with a smile on his face.

W_8: "What are you laughing at?"

I_3: "Triples are going to be moved."

W_8: (To I_1) "See, I_3 is laughing at you."

I_1: "He isn't laughing at me. I'm not gonna do 'em." (To GC) "He can just as well inspect those. We haven't any test set, so all he can do is give them a visual inspection. He can pass up reverses as well as I can." (I_1 did not want to get a poor quality rating.)

GC: "Well, go straighten it out with your boss."

I₁ left the room. In a few minutes he came back.

I_1: "I_3 is going to inspect them. He only has to give them a visual inspection."

GC: "All right. I'll leave them where they are."

I₃ protested but he had to inspect them.

This incident shows not only that I₁ thought I₃ should be given the "bum" jobs but also that he had better standing with the inspection group chief than I₃ had. It is also of interest because it shows the relation between the Operating Branch and the Inspection Branch. The group chief had no authority where I₁ or I₃ were involved; he had to take matters up with their supervisors and do what the latter recommended. That the operators were subordinate to the inspectors was indicated by the fact that instead of changing the inspectors around, which would have been simple, the group chief ordered the wiremen to change places, which meant that they had to go to a great deal of trouble moving their boards, piece parts, and other equipment.

I₁'s relation with I₃ and also with the operators is further illustrated by the fact that when he learned that I₃ had "squealed" on the observation group he immediately told the men. This information had been kept from them by the group chief and other Operating Branch supervisors. I₁ also informed the operators of other things which directly or indirectly affected their welfare, and he frequently repaired defects without charging the operators with them. The attitude of the operators toward I₁, in turn, is shown by the fact that on one occasion when he was away for about twenty minutes, no one, not even W₅ or W₂, protested.

Inspector 3

Although I₃ had been engaged in inspection work for over seven years, he was a newcomer to the department. Because he was unfamiliar with the test set used on the wiring job, he was given some experience in the regular department before he was moved to the observation room. During the first few days in the observation room, however, he experienced many difficulties with his test set and consequently held up the operators a good deal. His slowness in "catching on" irritated the operators, and soon their attitude toward him became definitely antagonistic. This antagonism, however, was only partly attributable to I_3's slowness, because it persisted and grew more intense as time passed and I_3 became more proficient. The men, instead of standing by and allowing him to work as best he could, contrived to arrange their work in such a way that he could not possibly keep up. Under the guise of helping him, they fixed his test set so that it would not work and in other ways impeded him. I_1's attitude was much the same as that of the operators; he tried to help out on one or two occasions but on the whole was content to let I_3 work out his own salvation. As time went on, the group became more and more solidly opposed to I_3 until finally a crisis was reached and he was transferred from the department. The way in which friction grew, and was ultimately resolved, is best illustrated by quoting excerpts from the observer's record throughout this period.

On the second day I_3 was in the observation room, the observer reported:

I_3 was trying to operate his test set. I_1 explained it to him and so did his group chief, but he didn't seem to understand. W_6 was trying to help him hook up the set, but he didn't know much about it either. They called I_1, who showed them how it should be connected. When I_3 went to another equipment, he again failed to connect the test set properly. W_6 went over to help him, but they finally had to call I_1 again. On the next three or four sets W_6 was able to hook it up. I_3 still did not understand how to do it.

About a week later, the group began to make fun of I_3 and tried to confuse him in the manner illustrated below:

I_3 ran into two more reverses which he could not locate. He was now so far behind that four wiremen were sitting along the radiator watching him. He was standing by one of W_7's units waiting for I_1 to come and find the trouble.

W_5: "Come on down here and work my unit while you're waiting."

W_8: "No, come on over and work mine."

I_3 unhooked the set and started back toward W_8's unit. W_6 and W_5 both called to him to work on theirs. He turned around and went over to W_5's unit.

W_7: "Hey, inspector, you can't walk off on me like that. That's no way to treat me."

I_3 continued down to W_5's unit. The group all thought this was an immense joke. I_3 was so befuddled that he didn't know what he was doing. I_1 came back to see what the trouble was with W_7's unit. I_3 then started to unhook his set from W_5's unit, even though it was only half inspected, in order to watch I_1. W_5 urged him to finish, but the others all called for him to come to their units. He finally finished W_5's unit.

W_7: "That's the kind of a guy you are. Walk out on a fellow after you start his unit." The group laughed.

W_6: (To GC) "Well, I got four hours waiting time now."

W_5: "Well, I did twenty-five rows and I waited twenty-five times."

GC: (To Obs.) "I can't do anything about this inspector. I talked to his group chief and told him he'd have to get somebody else out here, and then I talked to the section chief. I suppose I better go and see the assistant foreman."

Obs: "The boys had him all mixed up for a while there."

GC: "Yes, if they'd kept quiet and left him alone, he'd got along better."

With time, I_3's work improved so that without too much difficulty he could keep the men working. Their attitude toward him, however, remained much the same. From "kidding" and making fun of I_3 the group went on to interfering with his work.

I_3 kept W_8 waiting a few times this morning. W_8 said he was going to have some fun. He walked over to the unit I_3 was inspecting and while he was not looking pulled the plugs out far enough so that the set would not work. It took I_3 several minutes to find out why his set did not work. Shortly thereafter W_8 pulled the jig in such a way as to cause a short circuit. A little later I_3 went over to inspect W_7's equipments. W_8 was standing near W_7. This time the set failed to buzz because of a cross solder, one of the defects the inspector was looking for. I_3, however, thought W_8 had again done something to his set. He became so confused that he didn't know where to look for the trouble. W_8 then really tried to help him, but I_3, thinking he was causing the trouble, tried to make him go away.

· · · · · ·

Instead of completing the soldering of a unit, S_4 had only partially completed it and then had started soldering on another equipment.

I_3: (To S_4) "Go over and solder those two sets. You are going to make me behind."

S_4: "What are you trying to do, tell me what to do?"

S_4 was sitting down and did not move. The inspector went over to the group chief and asked him to make S_4 solder the sets.

GC: "What's the matter, S_4? Have you got sets to solder?"

S_4: "Yes, there's two of them."

GC: "Well, get over there and solder them."

S_4: "Well, you tell that inspector to mind his own business and not to be putting his nose in mine. He can't tell me what to do."

. . . . . .

Later the same day, S_4 soldered three-fourths of W_7's equipment and then went over to work on W_9's. I_3 thought he had finished and started to inspect it. Just as he started S_4 said:

S_4: "Get off that set. Wait till I get through with it."

I_3: "You are supposed to be through with it."

S_4: "Well, I'm not."

S_4 came back and finished soldering the set. When he left, I_3 picked up a soldering iron to repair some defects.

S_4: "Leave that soldering iron alone. All you gotta do is pull up the connection. I'll fix it."

I_3: "If you were any kind of a solderman I would do that, but I can't trust you."

S_4: "Leave that soldering iron alone from now on or I'll hit you right between the eyes."

I_3: "Go ahead, punch."

W_7: "Poor I_3. He's getting it today."

It was obvious that the antagonism between I_3 and the operators would soon come to a head. The crisis came one day when I_3, unable to tolerate the situation any longer, went to the Inspection Branch Personnel Division and laid the whole matter before them. The Personnel Division got in touch with the foreman and asked him if I_3's charges were true. The observer first learned about what had happened from the foreman:

F: "Say, did that inspector say anything to you about the fellows picking on him in there?"

Obs: "No."

F: "Well, he went up to the Personnel with a long story. He said that they were calling him names and pushing him around when he tried to work. He said that the fellows were done at 2 o'clock in

there, and that they told the group chief to go to hell and a lot of
stuff like that. They got me first thing this morning and I went
in there and found W_7 and S_4 sitting down, waiting for that guy,
and then we took his test box out and we found that the thing
had been grounded with solder and screws. Some one of those
fellows must have been monkeying around with it. I think it was
W_8. I've had trouble with him that way before, but I think that guy
lied about this other stuff. I checked up on the efficiency in there
and they're turning out about as much work as they did out here,
and I know that when a fellow is turning out between 6,000 and
7,000 connections he hasn't got much time to fool around. Those
boys in there are a little noisy, but I don't expect a man to stand
there and work all day without saying anything. Take W_6, it
comes natural for him to be noisy. I used to come over to him
once in a while when he was out here and say, 'For heaven's sake,
don't talk so loud.' He'd tell me he couldn't help it. He talks
that way every place. I know, I watched him play pool across the
street and I could hear him as soon as I came in the room. I don't
mind that, but I would like to find out who put solder in that
test set."

When news that I_3 had "squealed" reached the operators through
I_1, they were furious. They cursed him roundly and threatened to
"punch him in the nose." The group chief too was much incensed over
the charge that his men had told him "to go to hell"; he maintained
that they never had or that if they had he had never heard them. When
the foreman came into the observation room to check up on I_3's story,
the section chief was present. He sided with the operators in opposition
to the inspector:

F: "Show me this inspector who's causing so much trouble here."

SC: "It's the short guy with the potbelly. He's not any good on this job.
He's too slow for these young fellows. The whole trouble started
because he makes them wait when they want to work, and then
they get on him and get him so flustered that he don't know what
he's doing. He's all right as long as everything goes well, but if
he gets a case of trouble he is helpless. These lads are really good
eggs. They turn us out a good day's work, and they don't have
much trouble."

Apparently the foreman was convinced that the fault lay largely
with I_3, for shortly thereafter I_3 was taken out of the observation room.
Some time later, after the study was over, the interviewer saw I_3 out in
the department:

Int: "Well, I_3, I didn't know you were around here any more."

I_3: "I was loaned out to another organization for a while."

Int: "So they have taken to bartering around here, have they?"

I_3: "That's what it comes to. Trading me around like a slave. I wish I could have stayed on that other job. It was a good job." (Referring to the one he had before coming to the department.)

W_7: (Interrupting with a grin) "But this is a hell of a job, eh, I_3?"

Int: "Are you going to be around here for a while?"

I_3: "I guess I am. I don't know for sure, but they told me I was going to stay here for a while."

W_7: (After looking at one of his equipments) "Hey, I_3."

I_3: "Go ahead, that's O.K."

W_7: "O.K., is it? Well, come here and look at this. A cross solder as big as your fist, and you say you're an inspector."

I_3 grinned sheepishly and picked up a soldering iron. Soon cries of "Hey, I_3" could be heard in various parts of the room. A number of wiremen were calling for him at the same time. He was still having the same troubles he had had in the observation room.

I_3 did not participate in any of the group's extra-work activities. He did not enter into their gambling games, their purchases of candy, or any of the other things which I_1 entered into. He told the observer that he felt he was an outsider. One time when he stayed after hours to see if he could get his test set connected properly, he talked with the observer until nearly five o'clock. In his conversation he placed the responsibility for his failure on the job, first, on the difference between his nationality and the operators', and, secondly, on the inspection department for not training him properly. He then said that he could not get along with the boys because they were just irresponsible kids. He felt that he could work better with mature people.

Although I_3 did not enter into the group's social activities, he did occasionally take part in their arguments. In his conversation he tended to adopt the role of one possessing superior knowledge. Indeed, his general demeanor was a bit pompous. The following is a good example of the way he participated:

I_3 was by himself in a corner of the room. He had been walking back and forth thinking about something. Suddenly, he stuck out his chest and strutted over to W_9's position.

I_3: "W_9, I'm going to give you a test. You claim you've got an extensive vocabulary. I'm going to find out just how good you are."

W₉: "I think my vocabulary is more extensive than the average."

I₃ wrote down a list of words.

W₉: "What kind of a test is this?"

I₃: "Oh, it's something like the Alpha Test. It's a test for your intelligence."

W₉: "I thought you said vocabulary."

I₃: "That's what I mean, vocabulary. Now, here it is. You write down opposite these words the word that I'm thinking of. It is a word that pertains to these words."

W₉: "That's no test. How do I know what word you're thinking of?"

I₃: "If you know the word, you can write it."

W₉: "That's no test. There are a lot of words that pertain to 'trees.' How do I know what you're thinking of?"

I₃: "All right, then, you get zero. You don't know."

W₉: "Well, what word are you thinking of?"

I₃: "Arboreal."

CHAPTER XXI

THE INTERNAL ORGANIZATION OF THE GROUP IN THE BANK WIRING OBSERVATION ROOM

METHOD OF ASSESSING INTERPERSONAL RELATIONS

In CHAPTER XVII the method and procedure of obtaining the data of this study were described at some length, but methods of analyzing the data were not discussed. The problem of analysis proved to be the more difficult of the two. The questions the investigators were asking of their data, more particularly of the observation material, can be stated as follows: Do we have here just so many "individuals," or are they related to one another in such a way that they form a group or configuration? If they do form a configuration, how are they differentiated from or integrated with other groups? In short, do we have here evidences of social organization? Clearly, the method of analyzing the data had to be designed to bring out whatever evidences of social organization there might be. The procedure adopted may be summarized briefly.

First, each person entering into the study, whether operator, inspector, or supervisor, was considered separately. The observation material and interview material were examined carefully and every entry in which a particular person was mentioned or referred to was lifted out and listed under his name. Through this method of classification, the degree and kind of social participation of each individual in the Bank Wiring Observation Room became apparent.

Secondly, the material thus listed for each person was examined for evidence of the extent of his participation. Two questions were asked: (1) To whom do this person's relations extend? Does he associate with everyone in the group, or are his social activities restricted to a few? (2) Does he enter a great deal or relatively little into social relations with the people with whom he associates? In other words, if S_1 converses and associates with the men in his soldering unit to the exclusion of everyone else, does he do so frequently or infrequently?

Thirdly, an attempt was made to determine the kind of participation manifested by each person. Such questions as the following were considered: Does he assume a superordinate or subordinate role? Does he strive for leadership? If so, is he permitted to do so, or are his attempts in that direction opposed by others? Are most of his social contacts related to his job, or are they in the nature of arguments, conversations, or games which have no immediate relation to his work?

Fourthly, each occurrence in which a person entered into association with another person was examined to see whether the relation thus manifested expressed an antagonism, a friendship, or was merely neutral. Each incident, of course, had to be related to its social context before its significance could be determined. Take, for example, the following entry: "S_4 spent most of his spare time today drawing pictures. He drew an elaborate picture of a ship which he called 'Old Ironsides'." A conclusion which might be drawn from this statement as it stands is that S_4 apparently preferred to spend his time in drawing pictures rather than in mingling with the other operators. This, then, might be construed to reflect a negative relation between S_4 and the group, that is, that he preferred his own company to theirs. But when considered in connection with other factors in the situation, this interpretation is seen to be the opposite of that finally assigned to it by the investigators. S_4 at the time was a newcomer, having just replaced S_3. He was not well acquainted with anyone in the group. Furthermore, after he had been in the room a week and had become better acquainted, he no longer spent his spare time drawing pictures. The investigators concluded, therefore, that drawing pictures was a means by which S_4 attracted attention to himself, excited comment, and thus tended to integrate himself with the group. It was a way of approach rather than of avoidance.

In the two preceding chapters the results obtained from analyzing the material according to this procedure have been given. The participation of each individual in the social activities of the group has been described. After having analyzed the data in this manner, however, the question arises: Are there any similarities in the participation of certain individuals? For example, does W_1 almost always associate with W_2 and W_3 to the exclusion of W_7, W_8, and W_9, and, likewise, do W_2 and W_3 both associate with W_1 to the exclusion of W_7, W_8, and W_9? Do the members of one occupational group look up to or down upon the members of another? Do the employees arrange themselves in any social order with regard to games, job trading, controversies over windows, and other matters? In this chapter these and similar questions will be considered.

Relations between Nonsupervisory Occupational Groups

The first question the investigators asked was this: There are four occupational groups in the department: wiremen, soldermen, inspectors, and trucker. From a purely technical standpoint the members of these groups are all "operators," [1] that is, they are of nonsupervisory rank. Are they differentiated only from the standpoint of the jobs they perform, or have these technical divisions of labor become the basis of a social stratification? Do workmen in one group look upon themselves as superior or inferior to workmen in another group and, if so, how is this social distinction manifested? In order to answer this question, similarities in the behavior of different people in each occupational group, which could be said to be independent of the personalities involved, were noted. Wiremen as a group were considered in relation to soldermen as a group, and so on.

Connector Wiremen in Relation to Selector Wiremen

The wiremen in the department worked upon two types of equipment, one type called "connectors," the other "selectors." The technique of wiring was exactly the same for both types. The only differences, apart from the names, were (1) that a connector equipment might be and usually was eleven banks long, whereas a selector equipment was never more than ten, and (2) that a connector fixture weighed only about half as much as a selector fixture. In the observation room W_7, W_8, and W_9 ordinarily worked on selectors, and the other operators worked on connectors.

Some of the wiremen interviewed in the regular department expressed a preference for connector wiring. The reasons given usually related to the lightness of the fixture. In reality, however, the weight of the fixture was inconsequential. The fixtures were easily lifted, and only two of them had to be carried during an average day. The effort required was scarcely great enough to be felt by healthy young men who frequently engaged in strenuous sports after work. This explanation, therefore, could hardly be taken as the reason for their preference. Further study revealed the real significance of the preference for connector wiring. In the department the connector wiremen were all placed together toward the front of the room, the direction the men faced while working, and the selector wiremen were located back of them. They were, therefore, spatially arranged in such a way as to suggest

---

[1] This word was commonly used at Hawthorne to designate employees of nonsupervisory status. See pp. 11–12.

that the connector wiremen, since they were in front, were somewhat superior to those to whom their backs were turned. From talking to the supervisors and some of the wiremen the investigators learned that the newer members of the wiring group and some of the slower ones were located "in back." As these men "in back" acquired proficiency and new men were added, they were moved forward. Inasmuch as increases in efficiency were usually rewarded by increases in hourly rates, this meant that the people who were moving forward spatially were also moving upward socially. An individual's location roughly reflected his relative standing in efficiency, earnings, and the esteem of his supervisors. The connector wiremen represented the elite. Indeed, some of the wiremen looked upon "going on connectors" as a promotion even if their hourly rates were not changed. Conversely, some of the connector wiremen felt injured if they were "put back on selectors" and regarded such a change as a demotion even though their hourly rates were not changed. Here, then, a minor technical distinction had become so elaborated that it provided a basis upon which the wiremen were in some measure socially differentiated.

Wiremen in Relation to Soldermen

The position of wireman was regarded in the department as somewhat superior to that of solderman. Beginners were usually started as soldermen, and from soldering they passed on to wiring. The change in job was usually accompanied by an increase in hourly rate. This, together with the fact that the wireman's job required more specialized abilities than that of the solderman, gave the wiremen a slightly higher status in the department, which was expressed in numerous ways, some of which will be described below.

One of the most frequent ways in which the wiremen demonstrated their superior standing was in job trading. Theoretically, there was supposed to be no job trading. Wiremen were supposed to wire and soldermen were supposed to solder. The purpose of this rule was, of course, to promote efficiency through specialization. In spite of the rule, however, the men did trade jobs. The important point here is that in practically every case the request for trading originated with a wireman and the soldermen almost always traded without protest. Sometimes the wiremen presented their requests to trade to the group chief but more frequently they did not. Though occasionally the soldermen protested over trading, they usually gave in. In other words, the wiremen ordered and the soldermen obeyed.

In the task of getting lunches for the group the difference of status

between wiremen and soldermen was apparent. It was common practice in the department for one of the men to go out to one of the near-by
lunch counters and get lunches for those in the department who wanted
them. This practice prevented congestion at the lunch counters, and
it saved the people in the department a great deal of trouble. The
person who got the lunches was called the "lunch boy," even though he
was a grown man and was not assigned the duties of an office boy.
When the men were moved to the observation room, they continued
with this practice until the regular "lunch boy" was transferred. The
group chief, after announcing the transfer, asked if anyone in the group
wanted to take over the job. After some discussion S_1 said that he
would. On the first day the group chief went with S_1 to assist him. On
the second day, however, the group chief refused to go, saying that
there was no use in wasting two men's time. As long as the group chief
lent his prestige to the task the group said nothing, but as soon as the
solderman had to go alone they started "kidding" him. S_1 kept on
getting the lunches for about a week, and then S_4 started getting them
as a regular part of his job. Toward the end of the study, when S_4
was moved out to the department, the job reverted to S_1. He kept the
job until the group chief himself took it over. The group chief, however, was careful to explain to the observer that he was not actually
getting the lunches but merely taking the orders and giving them to
a man in the department. He apparently felt that the job was a bit
below his dignity. In the observer's record there was no instance of a
wireman's getting the lunches. One day W_1 went around and took the
orders for lunches and collected the money, but when he had done so
he turned the orders over to S_1. As soon as W_1 started taking the
orders, I_1 shouted, "Look who's getting the lunches today," which may
be taken as an indication that it was an unusual thing for a wireman
to do. W_1 continued taking the orders for some time, but S_1 always
bought the food and brought it back to the room.

The following illustration also serves to show that the wiremen felt
themselves a little superior:

The section chief came in and found S_1 soldering without goggles. He
told S_1 to stop until he put them on. S_1 had mislaid them and spent about
five minutes looking for them. He grumbled about having to wear goggles
as he looked for them.

S_1: "I don't know where the hell those glasses are. I suppose one of you
guys hid them. There ain't no sense to wearing them anyway.
I soldered for four years before they ever thought of glasses. Now
you've gotta keep them on. There ain't no solder gonna splash in

a fellow's eye. That's just the damn fool notion somebody's got. I've gotta go around here all day in a fog just because some damn fool wants us to wear goggles."

SC: "Never mind why you've got to wear them, just get them and put them on."

W₂: "I worked on a job for three years where I had to wear goggles and it didn't kill me."

S₁: "Yes, and I suppose you wore them all the time."

W₂: "Well maybe I didn't, but it didn't hurt me to wear them when I had to. There's one thing you have to remember, S₁. Do you hear? Don't do as I do — do as I say. Get that?"

S₁: "Why don't you guys wear glasses when you fix repairs?"

W₃: "We don't have to put them on for that little bit of soldering, but you're a solderman. You've got to wear them."

S₁: "Aw, you guys are all a bunch of damn fools."

Wiremen and Soldermen in Relation to the Trucker

The trucker's job was to keep the group supplied with piece parts and to remove completed equipments from the room. Before loading the completed units on his truck, which was pushed by hand, he stamped each one with an identification number, the purpose of which was to enable the Inspection Branch to trace the work back to the inspector who had passed upon it.

During the first few weeks nothing happened to indicate the relation the trucker had with the group. However, when the men felt more at ease in the presence of the observer, certain events began to occur which seemed to reflect the trucker-operator relation. For example, the group started referring to the trucker as a gigolo and as "Goofy." They annoyed him in numerous small ways: by spitting on the place where the identification number was supposed to be stamped, by jogging his arm just as he was about to affix the stamp, by holding the truck when he tried to push it out of the room, or by tickling him in the ribs while he was lifting an equipment onto the truck. That these incidents reflected a relation between occupational groups and not special personal relations is attested to by the fact that most of the wiremen and soldermen behaved in the same way toward the trucker, and by the fact that they displayed the same attitude toward a second trucker who replaced the first one about the middle of the study. Their general attitude was independent of the personalities involved.

Wiremen and Soldermen in Relation to the Inspectors

The inspectors belonged to an outside organization, the Inspection Branch. They reported to a different set of supervisors, were paid on an hourly basis, and on the whole had more education than the men whose work they inspected. Their function as inspectors gave them a superordinate position to the operators. This was manifested in many ways. For example, when the wiremen and soldermen came to be interviewed they invariably appeared in their shirt sleeves, or, if it were chilly, in sweaters. The inspectors, however, always came dressed in coats and vests. The significance of this cannot be understood without knowing something about the subtle distinctions in dress in the Operating Branch. The foreman and his assistant usually wore ordinary business suits with coats and vests, the vest being optional. The section chiefs and group chiefs usually wore vests but not coats. Their shirts were usually white, and they wore neckties. Operators as a rule wore neither coats nor vests. They might wear white shirts and a necktie, but ordinarily left their shirts open at the throat, or if they wore a tie, the knot was not pulled up tightly around the neck and the collar button was usually left unfastened. This was the general pattern. There were many exceptions and deviations from it, but the fact remains that dress did have some social significance. Thus, the fact that the inspectors wore coats and vests when they came to be interviewed might be taken as a reflection of their social status in the company.

The inspectors were considered outsiders, and this was indicated in many ways other than by the fact that they did not report to the Operating Branch supervisors. That they did not trade jobs or go for lunches was evidence of this relation between the operators and the inspectors, but perhaps the best demonstration of it was in the matter of control over the windows. The wiremen who were situated on the side of the room facing the court took a proprietary interest in the windows opposite their workbenches. If W_6, for example, wanted the window open, he opened it even though other people protested. The people who were farthest removed from the windows protested a great deal, because the draft was thrown on their side of the room. Endless controversy resulted. The point to be brought out here is that an inspector entered into one of these controversies only on one occasion, and it was this one occasion which demonstrated clearly the relation between operators and inspectors. The inspector involved was a man who was substituting for I_3. He complained that the room was cold. Someone had turned the heat off and one of the windows was open.

Since his complaint went unheeded, he walked over to close the window. As he was about to release the chain which held it open, W_9 ordered him to leave it open and seized the chain. The inspector then tried to turn on the heat, but W_9 scuffled with him and finally took the handle off the valve. During all this the other men lent W_9 their verbal support. Finally, after the operators had convinced the inspector that he had no jurisdiction over the window and he had given up, one of the soldermen walked over and closed the window. The inspector thanked him, and the controversy ended. Wiremen and soldermen might fix the windows if they pleased, but the inspectors could not do so without getting into trouble. The other inspectors probably sensed the situation and never attempted to overstep.

Social Stratification in the Observation Group

The foregoing analysis of the relations among the occupational groups in the observation room shows that social significance did attach to the occupations the several groups performed. An ordering process had taken place in the organization of the human element in the department, and social significance had become attached to the various tasks. From an informal standpoint, then, the observation group was differentiated into five gradations, ranging from highest to lowest in the following order: inspectors, connector wiremen, selector wiremen, soldermen, and trucker.

THE INFORMAL ORGANIZATION OF THE OBSERVATION GROUP

The first question the investigators asked of their data was answered in the affirmative: the workmen were socially differentiated along occupational lines. But did this mean that only the people within each occupational group tended to associate together? Did the workmen tend to form occupational cliques, or were they organized on some other basis? If occupation was not the basis of their integration, just how were they organized? The answer to this question, it was thought, could be obtained by observing how the members of the group were differentiated in terms of such informal social activities as games, controversies over the windows, job trading, and helping one another.

Games

From the beginning of the study the observer noted and recorded a variety of activities which may be subsumed under this heading. For the most part, these were games of chance which included the following: matching coins, lagging coins, shooting craps, card games, bets on combinations of digits in the serial numbers on their weekly pay checks, pools on horse racing, baseball, and quality records, chipping in to purchase candy, and "binging." The men usually engaged in these games during brief respites from work or during lulls in activity resulting from interruptions in the flow of work. The games were extremely varied and were seemingly elaborated spontaneously with reference to anything into which the element of chance entered. Financial gain was not the main inducement, for most of the wagers were small, ranging from one to ten cents. However, those who participated in the betting on the horse races usually did so seriously. They dubbed their favorite the "Test Room Horse" and bet on him fairly consistently.

Figure 39 shows the people who joined in these games and the people with whom each person participated. The symbols indicating the

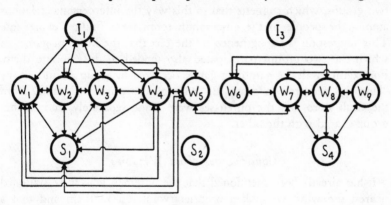

FIGURE 39
PARTICIPATION IN GAMES

BANK WIRING OBSERVATION ROOM

different operators are enclosed in small circles. The operators are arranged roughly by soldering units, which are indicated by the spacing of the wiremen. Thus, W_1, W_2, W_3, and S_1 constitute soldering unit A; W_4, W_5, W_6, and S_2 constitute soldering unit B; and W_7, W_8, W_9, and S_4 constitute soldering unit C. The inspectors are placed above the groups for which they inspected. The arrows connecting the different circles indicate that the people thus connected participated in one or more games either as pairs or as members of a larger group.

The significant point brought out in Figure 39 is that participation in games was confined to two groups and, furthermore, that each group participated to the exclusion of the other. One group, which for convenience will be referred to as group A, comprised W_1, W_2, W_3, W_4, W_5, S_1, and I_1. These people were in adjacent work positions and were all located toward the front of the room. The other group, referred to as group B, was composed of W_6, W_7, W_8, W_9, and S_4. These people were also in adjacent work positions and were located toward the rear of the room. Two people, S_2 and I_3, never took part in these activities. Although the frequency with which each person participated in games is not shown in this diagram, it should be stated that W_5 participated in only one game with the people in group A, whereas all the others in group A took part in a variety of games. It should also be noted that W_5 on one occasion took part with W_7. He was the only person in group A who participated with a member of group B.

Participation in games, then, was not at random. It was confined to two groups, which suggests that in this way the interpersonal relations among the people in the observation room were finding expression. This suggestion is strengthened by the fact that the kinds of games in which the two groups participated also tended to differentiate them. For example, all the gambling games occurred in group A, and all the "binging" occurred in group B. Both groups purchased candy from the Club store, but the purchases were made separately, and neither group shared with the other.

Controversies about Windows

It has already been mentioned that the wiremen who were stationed nearest the windows took a proprietary interest in them and that a great deal of controversy resulted over whether the windows should be open or closed. That this activity also expressed the interpersonal relations in the group is apparent from the following excerpt from the observer's record:

W_6 had his window open and W_5 closed it.

W_6: "You leave that window open. I want some fresh air in here."

W_5: "It's too cold. I want it closed."

W_6: "You take care of your own window. This one is mine and if I open it, it's going to stay open."

They opened and closed the window several times and had a heated argument over it. W_6 told W_5 that if he closed it again he would punch him in the nose.

S_1: (From the side lines) "That's right, W_6, stick up for your rights. If he closes it again, hang one on him. We've got to have a good fight in here before long."

W_5 left the window alone. This disappointed S_1, so he implied that W_5 was yellow.

S_1: "I'll tell you what you had better do if he closes that window again, W_6, sue him. He won't fight, so the only way you can do anything with him is to sue him."

The group had a lot of fun over this. W_5 and W_6 did not speak to each other during the rest of the morning.

This quarrel between W_5 and W_6 not only expressed their mutual antagonism but also gave S_1 an opportunity to express his antagonism toward W_5.

Figure 40 shows the men who joined in these controversies and those with whom they participated. This diagram is to be interpreted in the

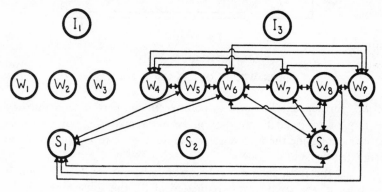

FIGURE 40

PARTICIPATION IN CONTROVERSIES ABOUT WINDOWS

BANK WIRING OBSERVATION ROOM

same way as that for games. A person was judged to be involved in these disputes even though he participated only verbally. The chief point brought out in this diagram is that most of the controversies over windows centered in group B (W_6, W_7, W_8, W_9, and S_4). The quarrels among the members of this group and between this group and other people in the observation room accounted for 90 per cent of the controversies. Their quarrels with people outside of their group were with S_1, W_4, and W_5. There was very little controversy over the windows among the members of group A, and what little there was occurred between W_4 and W_5 and between S_1 and W_5.

Job Trading

Job trading has already been mentioned in connection with the relation between wiremen and soldermen. Accurate records of this activity were kept throughout the study and are summarized graphically in Figure 41.[1] The inspectors are omitted from this diagram because they

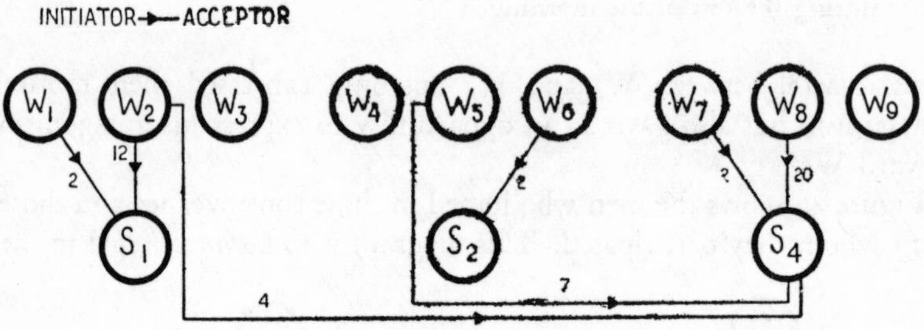

INITIATOR➤—ACCEPTOR

FIGURE 41

PARTICIPATION IN JOB TRADING

BANK WIRING OBSERVATION ROOM

did not participate. The arrows point from the person who initiated the request to trade to the person who accepted the request. The numbers alongside the arrows show the number of times the people so designated traded.

Perhaps the most interesting point brought out in this diagram is that most of the trading was requested of S_4, the solderman for the three selector wiremen. Thirty-three of the forty-nine times job trading occurred were with S_4. Furthermore, it will be noted that, whereas connector wiremen from soldering units A and B traded with S_4, none of the selector wiremen (W_7, W_8, and W_9) ever traded outside of their own soldering unit. In other words, the connector wiremen apparently felt free to change jobs either with their own soldermen or with the solderman for the selector wiremen, but the latter did not feel free to trade outside of their own unit.

[1] For the sake of simplicity, trading between wiremen and S_3, who was in the observation room only a short time, and trading between wiremen while one of them was soldering have been omitted from this figure. These omissions do not alter in any way the conclusions to be drawn from this figure.

Helping One Another

While there was no written rule to this effect, helping one another, like job trading, was in practice forbidden.[1] In spite of this rule, however, it was done a good deal when technically there was no justification for it. The wiremen said that it made them feel good to be helped. Their attitude is best expressed in the following excerpt from an interview with W₄. W₄ had just said that he liked working in the observation room because he felt more free to move around than in the regular department.

Int: "You do move around quite a bit, do you? Then you don't always work on your own equipment?"

W₄: "Oh no, not always, but most of the time. That is, once in a while if a fellow gets behind someone will go over and help him out."

Int: "Do they do that for anyone who is behind?"

W₄: "No. You know, it's a funny thing about that gang. It seems like if a fellow is loafing and gets behind, nobody will help him out, but if he is making an honest effort he will be helped. I've seen that happen time and again. Somebody who has been working along hard all day and has had a lot of tough luck will be helped out."

Int: "Do you find that certain people help certain other people all the time, or do they change around quite a bit?"

W₄: "Well, some people are friendlier than others, you know, and where that's the case you will find them helping each other out. Once in a while a fellow will get behind who ordinarily is a good worker. That sometimes happens to anyone. I know one fellow down there who did that and two other fellows went over and started helping him out. That was around a quarter to four. They had their job done and thought they would give him a hand. He didn't say anything, he let them go ahead and help him out, but you know he never helps anyone else out. Since then he has never given a hand to anybody. Do you think they would help him out again? No sir! They're off of him. They don't like a guy that does that. I think it's a good idea to help a fellow out once in a while. I know I appreciate it. It makes all the difference in the

---

[1] The operators were permitted to help one another only when for observable technical reasons, such as a shortage of parts, they were prevented from working on their own equipments. The reason for this rule was that a wireman should be able to work faster when unmolested by another wireman's presence. In practice there were very few occasions when helping one another was technically justified and for this reason the greater part of this activity was against the rules. This point will be discussed later in Chapter XXIII, pp. 547–548.

world. It's a funny thing, I'll be working along and be behind, and I'll feel all fagged out. Then somebody comes over and starts in wiring on my equipment with me, and you know I perk up to beat the band. I don't know; it just seems to put new life in you, no matter if he only helps you for a couple of levels. I can pick up and work like the deuce then, up till quitting time."

Int: "I wonder why."

W_4: "I don't know why it is. You have a feeling when you're behind that you've got so much work behind it's going to be impossible to get it done, anyway. Then when somebody helps you out it gives you a fresh start, sort of."

Records were kept of this activity and are summarized graphically in Figure 42. The inspectors are again omitted because they did not

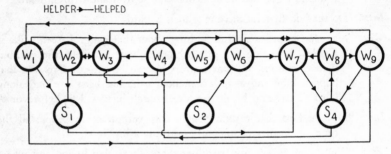

FIGURE 42

PARTICIPATION IN HELPING

BANK WIRING OBSERVATION ROOM

participate. The arrows in the diagram point from helper to the person helped. The chief points brought out are, first, that everyone participated in helping and, secondly, that it was not confined within work groups. In these two respects this activity differed from the others thus far described. It seemed to integrate the whole group rather than parts of it.

The frequency with which different people helped one another is not shown in Figure 42 because only two people stood out from the group in this respect. They were W_3 and W_6. W_3 was helped more than anyone else in the observation room, even though he did not need it. W_1, W_2, W_4, W_5, and W_6 helped him at one time or another. They liked to work with him. W_6, on the other hand, gave more help than anyone else in the room. His help was always accepted but it was rarely reciprocated. Two people, W_5 and S_2, gave help a few times, but on no occasion did they receive help.

Friendships and Antagonisms

The friendships and antagonisms which existed in this group were described at length in the last chapter. To summarize these interper-

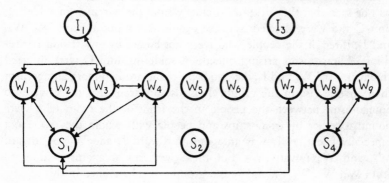

FIGURE 43

FRIENDSHIPS

BANK WIRING OBSERVATION ROOM

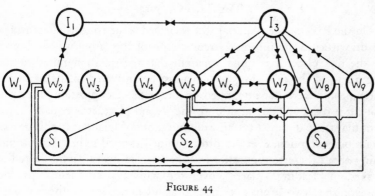

FIGURE 44

ANTAGONISMS

BANK WIRING OBSERVATION ROOM

sonal relations, Figures 43 and 44 have been prepared. Figure 43 shows friendships; Figure 44 shows antagonisms. The three soldering units are arranged as in the previous diagrams.

Looking first at Figure 43, representing friendships, it will be seen that they tend to cluster in two groups. One group includes five people who were in the front of the room, W_1, W_3, W_4, S_1, and I_1. The other group comprises the members of soldering unit C, the four people in the rear of the room. Outside of these two groups the only strong friendship was that between S_1 and W_7. Five people, W_2, W_5, W_6, S_2, and I_3, were not bound by any strong friendships.

Looking next at the diagram representing antagonisms, Figure 44, it will be seen that they originated chiefly from the wiremen in soldering unit C and were directed by these people as a group toward W_2, W_5, and I_3, three of the people who were not bound by any strong friendships. Antagonisms arising outside of soldering unit C were directed chiefly toward W_5 and I_3, the two people who aroused more antagonism than anyone else in the group. It is also apparent that there were no antagonisms between the people in the front of the room who were bound together by friendships and people with whom they were not especially friendly. I_1 was antagonistic toward I_3 and W_2, S_1 toward W_5, and W_4 toward W_5, but there were no antagonisms directed from W_1, W_3, W_4, S_1, and I_1 as a group toward anyone. In this respect the wiremen in soldering unit C were unique: they possessed an internal solidarity, a certain cohesion among themselves, and strong external antagonism or opposition to certain persons outside of their group.

THE TWO CLIQUES

On the basis of the material just reviewed some conclusion can now be drawn as to the informal organization of this group of workmen. In the first place, it is quite apparent that the question raised at the beginning of the preceding section must be answered in the negative: these people were not integrated on the basis of occupation; they did not form occupational cliques. In the second place, it is equally apparent that there did exist certain configurations of relations in this group. With one exception, every record examined seemed to be telling something about these configurations. Whether the investigators looked at games, job trading, quarrels over the windows, or friendships and antagonisms, two groups seemed to stand out. One of these groups was located toward the front of the room, the other toward the back. "The group in front" and "the group in back" were common terms of designation among the workmen themselves. The first of these groups will be referred to as clique A, the second, the group toward the rear of the room, as clique B.

What was the membership of these two cliques? This question can be answered only approximately. Clique A included W_1, W_3, W_4, S_1, and I_1, and clique B included W_7, W_8, W_9, and S_4. W_5, S_2, and I_3

were outside either clique. With W_2 and W_6, however, the situation was not so clear. W_2 participated in the games of clique A, but beyond this the similarity of his behavior to theirs ceased. He entered very little into their conversations and tended to isolate himself from them. Much of his behavior suggested that he did not feel his position in the group to be secure. He was the only wireman in soldering unit A who traded jobs with S_4, the solderman in clique B, and he traded jobs with his own solderman more than anyone else did. In so far as the social function of job trading was to differentiate wiremen from soldermen, this could be interpreted as meaning that W_2 felt rather keenly the necessity of constantly emphasizing his position by subordinating the soldermen. Taking all the evidence into consideration, then, it may be concluded that W_2 was not a bona fide member of clique A. W_6 tended to participate in clique B. He was continually "horsing around" with the selector wiremen and had relatively little to do with

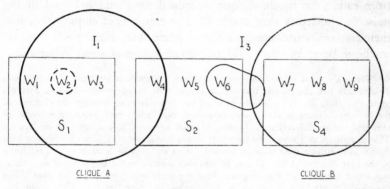

CLIQUE A   CLIQUE B

FIGURE 45

THE INTERNAL ORGANIZATION OF THE GROUP

BANK WIRING OBSERVATION ROOM

the members of clique A. That he was not entirely accepted in clique B was shown in many ways, chief of which was the way in which clique B co-operated in resisting his attempts to dominate anyone in their group. Yet he participated in clique B much more than W_2 did in clique A. It may be concluded that although W_6 tended to participate in clique B, he was still in many ways an outsider.

As a means of summarizing the results of this inquiry, Figure 45 has been prepared to represent diagrammatically the internal organization of the observation group. The soldering units into which the members of the group were divided are shown by the three rectangles.

The two large circles demarcate the two cliques, A and B. There were three individuals, I_3, W_5, and S_2, who were clearly outside either clique.[1] The line around W_6 has been made to intersect that of clique B to indicate his partial participation in it. The instability of W_2's position is indicated by the broken circle around his number.

That the members of clique A regarded themselves as superior to clique B was indicated in many ways. Clique A did or refrained from doing certain things which were done by clique B. They did not trade jobs nearly so much, and on the whole they did not enter into the controversies about the windows. Clique A engaged in games of chance, whereas clique B engaged more often in "binging." Both groups purchased candy from the Club store, but purchases were made separately and neither clique shared with the other. Clique A bought chocolate candy in small quantities, whereas clique B bought a less expensive kind in such large quantities that W_9 one time became ill from eating too much. Clique A argued more and indulged in less noise and horseplay than clique B. The members of clique A felt that their conversations were on a higher plane than those which went on in clique B; as W_4 said, "We talk about things of some importance."

[1] Perhaps a word of caution is necessary here. When it is said that this group was divided into two cliques and that certain people were outside either clique, it does not mean that there was no solidarity between the two cliques or between the cliques and the outsiders. There is always the danger, in examining small groups intensively, of overemphasizing differentiating factors. Internal solidarity thus appears to be lacking. That this group, as a whole, did have very strong sentiments in common has already been shown in discussing their attitudes toward output and will be brought out more clearly in the next chapters. It should also be said that position in the group is not so static as one might assume from this diagram. Had the study continued longer, membership in the cliques might have shifted. Also, if the group had been larger, or if the group had been allowed to remain in the regular department, it is quite probable that the people who appear to be outsiders here would have formed cliques with others who had similar sentiments.

CHAPTER XXII

SOCIAL CONTROL OF WORK BEHAVIOR

THE PURPOSE of this and the next chapter will be to consider the many unanswered questions raised in the preceding chapters, questions which could not be discussed adequately until all the data had been presented. It is necessary for clarity to keep separate two points of view. Any group can be regarded: (1) as a collectivity in and by itself, with certain internal functions; and (2) as a unit in a wider organization, with certain external functions. In other words, a group can be considered either from the point of view of its "internal function" or from the point of view of its "external function." These distinctions are useful in that they allow one to confine attention to one body of data at a time and to proceed in an orderly fashion.

In this chapter, the observation group will be considered from the point of view of its internal function. It has been shown that the fourteen men were organized into two cliques. Two questions can now be asked: (1) What factors determined clique membership? (2) What was the function of this clique structure for its members?

In the following chapter the group will be considered from the point of view of its external function. The questions are: (1) What external factors gave rise to the situation described in the observation room? (2) How did this type of informal organization function in relation to the total company organization?

The Group's Internal Organization and Spatial Relations

In examining the way the fourteen men in the observation room were grouped together, the first suggestion that comes to mind is that perhaps their formation into cliques simply resulted from spatial relations. It will be well, therefore, to consider this as a possible explanation at the outset. The spatial relations of the men were roughly as indicated in Figure 45. An accurate picture of the spacing of the work positions assigned to the wiremen may be obtained by turning back to Figure 34. Three explanations might be offered from this point of view: (1) The soldering unit was the social unit. (2) The inspection unit was the social unit. (3) Mere spatial proximity was the deciding factor. Each of these will be considered in turn.

The operators were divided into soldering units, each of which consisted of three wiremen and one solderman. There were three such units in the observation room. They are shown in Figure 45 by the three rectangles. Several factors make plausible the explanation that the soldering unit was the social unit. One is the fact that some of the operators spoke of the soldering unit as being the "natural" unit. The very nature of their work might tend to draw the people in each unit together, for it was necessary that the three wiremen arrange their work so as not to delay the solderman, and vice versa. Furthermore, the solderman was constantly circulating among the people within his unit and could carry conversation from one to another. It is apparent that from a technical standpoint the soldering unit should have been the social unit, and theoretically there was every reason to believe that it might be.

Looking now at Figure 45, it will be seen that the men did in fact tend to organize in this way. Clique A centered around soldering unit A, and clique B consisted of soldering unit C. But soldering unit B did not form a separate clique. This unit disrupted: W_4 was assimilated into clique A and W_6 tended to gravitate toward clique B, leaving W_5 and S_2 outside either clique. In order to hold, therefore, this interpretation must provide a plausible explanation for the disruption of soldering unit B.

Such an explanation might be based on the sociology of numerical relations. The argument might run as follows: Each unit consisted of four members, but in unit B the solderman, S_2, was so handicapped by his speech difficulty that his effectiveness as a social being was virtually zero. In other words, it might be argued that unit B, from a sociological standpoint, consisted of three members instead of four. Now it is claimed by some sociologists that triadic relations are exceptionally unstable.[1] The tendency is for a pair to separate out in opposition to the third member. This, then, might be one explanation for the instability of soldering unit B. It does not, however, account for the fact that instead of forming a pair, W_4 gravitated toward clique A and W_6 gravitated toward clique B. It is not, therefore, an entirely satisfactory explanation.

Let us next consider the plausibility of the second hypothesis, that the inspection unit was the social unit. The two inspectors in the room divided the inspection work equally between them. I_1 inspected the work of W_1, W_2, W_3, W_4, S_1, and half of that of W_5 and S_2. I_3 inspected the other half of the work of W_5 and S_2 and all that of W_6,

[1] Spykman, N. J., op. cit., pp. 133–135.

W_7, W_8, W_9, and S_4. The two people not completely within an inspection unit were W_5 and S_2, whose work was divided between the two inspectors. According to this theory, soldering unit B disrupted because part of it was in one inspection unit and part of it in the other. W_4 was assimilated in clique A because he was in I_1's inspection unit and W_6 gravitated toward clique B because he was in I_3's inspection unit. W_5 and S_2 were excluded from both cliques because the division of their work between I_1 and I_3 placed them half in and half out of each inspection unit. This explanation, however, fails to account for the exclusion of W_2 from clique A and of I_3 from clique B. Beyond these two exceptions it does provide a fairly good explanation.

The third suggestion to be considered is that membership in either clique depended upon whether or not the operators happened to be working in adjacent positions. The members of each clique were in fact spatially contiguous. This, for example, would account for W_6's tendency to participate in clique B instead of in clique A. It would also explain why W_4 was included in clique A. It does not, however, provide a satisfactory explanation for the exclusion of W_2, W_5, or I_3. Neither does it explain why the dividing line between the two cliques occurred where it did.

All the above explanations — there may be others — are based upon spatial relations. The difficulty with them is that they do not take into account the nature of the individual's participation. For example, it may be true that triadic relations are very unstable, but that does not explain why a certain two of the three people concerned form a pair in opposition to the third. In dealing with small groups such particularities are very important and cannot be ignored. Furthermore, and of chief importance, the concept of spatial relations fails to get at the underlying uniformities in the behavior of the members of the group.

Although not a satisfactory explanation of clique membership, the spatial situation was a significant factor in connection with the relation between the two cliques. Clique A was in the front of the room and clique B was in the back of the room. Thus the spacing of the cliques suggested the superior-subordinate relation which in fact existed between the two cliques.

The Relation between Position in the Group and Occupation

One of the significant points brought out in the preceding chapter was the fact that the members of the observation group were socially stratified on the basis of occupation. Their ranking, from top to bottom, was: inspector, connector wireman, selector wireman, solderman, and trucker. The second point brought out in that chapter was that instead of forming occupational cliques, as one would have expected, their association was as represented in Figure 45. The cliques actually formed tended to cut across occupational lines. In Chapter XXI these two observations were merely stated as findings, and no attempt was made to show the relation of the one to the other. Let us therefore begin this analysis by attempting to see how occupational stratification was related to clique membership.

Examining the internal organization of the group from this point of view, it will be seen that there was some correspondence between occupation and position in the group. This undoubtedly accounted for the position held by the trucker. He was relegated to the most subordinate position in the room, not because of any personal characteristic but simply because he was a trucker. This, incidentally, suggests the strength of the sentiments attaching to jobs. This same factor accounted, in part at least, for membership in cliques A and B. There were no selector wiremen in clique A. The three selector wiremen who were in the room were shunted off by themselves. An internal solidarity developed among them and they formed the nucleus of clique B. It seemed probable, therefore, that occupation was one of the factors entering into the determination of position in the group.

At this point an objection might be raised. If occupational status precluded the possibility of a selector wireman's becoming a member of clique A, how does it happen that S_1, whose occupational status was even lower than that of a selector wireman, became a member of that clique? The answer lies in the fact that the soldermen were subordinated to the wiremen in a way quite different from that in which the selector wiremen were subordinated to the connector wiremen. The soldermen served the wiremen, but there was no such relation between the two classes of wiremen. The position of connector wireman was in no sense jeopardized by the inclusion of S_1 in clique A. He was included not as an equal but as a subordinate whose position was well defined and accepted. He not only traded jobs with connector wiremen when asked, but he also got their lunches and tried to get good wire for them when requested to do so. In other words, S_1's behavior was in accord with the sentiments of the connector wiremen with respect to the occupational position he held, and he was therefore acceptable to them. Selector wiremen could not be included in clique A without destroying the social value of the connector wiring job, that is, placing it on a par with selector wiring. It might be added that although the inclusion of S_1 in clique A did not affect the prestige of connector wiring, it did have an effect upon S_1's standing as a solderman. It very definitely elevated him above the other two soldermen in the room and gave him an informal status approximately equal to that of the selector wiremen. This was indicated in two different ways. In the first place, he demonstrated his superiority to S_4 by passing the job of getting lunches for the group on to him, by asking him to file his irons, and by telling him that he was an inferior solderman. In the second place, his equality with the selector wiremen was suggested by the fact that he was very friendly with W_7 and spent a good deal of his spare time mingling with clique B. It may be concluded from this that the social standing of the soldermen was determined in large part by the status of the wiremen whom they served.

Was there any relation between the informal position of the inspectors in the group and their occupation? At first glance it would seem not. I_1 became a member of clique A and the other inspector, I_3, was eventually ousted from the department. Yet this apparent contradiction is explainable in terms of the attitudes of the operators toward the job of inspection. Among themselves the operators desired occupational differentiation, but their attitude toward the inspectors was quite different. They acted as though they wanted to reduce the social distance between themselves and the inspectors. This attitude was probably attributable to the fact that the inspectors were outsiders and were superordinate to them.

The relation between inspector and operator was fundamentally one of antagonism or opposition. The inspector could, if he chose, exercise considerable power over the operators. By marking up a large number of defects he could ruin a solderman's quality rating, and by being too meticulous in his inspecting he could become a source of irritation to wiremen and soldermen alike. The operators, of course, were well aware of the fact that an unfriendly inspector could make things difficult for them. What they wanted was a man who would work along with them and keep their interests as well as his own in mind.

The positions assigned to I_1 and I_3 in the group can only be explained by examining their overt behavior in relation to the sentiments of the operators. Entries in the observer's record indicate that nearly everything I_1 did served to lessen the social distance between himself and the operators. He, in effect, relinquished the status which his job conferred upon him and became one of the group. He conducted himself as one of them, entering into their games, arguments, and informal activities. His behavior, in other words, was in accord with the sentiments of the operators. This was brought out clearly by the fact that he sometimes called their attention to defects without charging them against them. This was something no inspector was supposed to do. By resorting to this practice at the risk of penalty, I_1 showed the operators that he shared their sentiments. Many of his other activities, such as siding with them against his colleague, I_3, and keeping them informed about what was going on outside the department, also served to integrate him with the group. The strength of the position he achieved is indicated by the fact that he could absent himself from the room without fear of being charged with daywork.

On the other hand, I_3's behavior served to increase rather than decrease the natural antagonism of the operators. In his conduct he constantly emphasized the fact that he was an inspector. He tended to remain aloof from the group. When he did participate in its activities, he usually did so in the role of one possessing superior knowledge. The facts that he was older than the others, that he was better educated than they, and that he was of a different nationality were no doubt contributory factors. If he had tried to identify himself with the group, he would probably have found it more difficult than I_1 did. But his personal characteristics were not an insurmountable obstacle; they assumed significance largely through the fact that he was an inspector. Had he been a wireman, it is quite certain that he would have been treated differently. It follows from this that the position of the inspectors was determined by the relation of their behavior to the sentiments the group held with respect to the inspection job. I_1's behavior was in accord with those sentiments and he was regarded favorably; I_3's behavior was not in accord with those sentiments and he was ousted by means of the social process previously described.

It may be concluded that occupational status was one of the important factors entering into the determination of the individual's position in the group. The trucker did not belong to either clique. The selector wiremen belonged to clique B but not to clique A. It is doubtful if a selector wireman could have become a bona fide member of clique A because these cliques apparently functioned, in part, to emphasize the difference between connector and selector wiremen. That occupation was only one factor is shown by the fact that all the connector wiremen were not included in clique A. Some other factor must have accounted for the exclusion of the outsiders. Let us, therefore, turn to output and investigate its bearing upon position in the group.

The Relation between Position in the Group and Output

At the end of Chapter XVIII, certain puzzling questions were raised concerning the output of this group. These questions were of the following order: Why did W_3 and W_6 report less output than they produced, and why did they claim less daywork than they were entitled to? Why did W_2, who ranked higher in output than W_3 or W_6, report more output than he produced, and why did he claim more daywork than he was entitled to? Finally, what accounted for the relative ranking of these operators in average hourly output? If these differences in rank were not related to differences in capacity to perform, as measured by tests of intelligence and dexterity, what were they related to? More particularly, why did W_7, W_8, and W_9, who ranked relatively high in the aptitude tests, continue to produce at a low level even though they were thereby lowering their own earnings and those of their associates?

In answering these questions, considerable reference will be made to differences in the performance of the various wiremen. Figure 46 has been constructed to facilitate comparisons and also to show the relation between performance and position in the group. The internal organization of the group is shown at the top of the diagram. At the bottom of the diagram, directly under each wireman's number, is shown the relative size of (1) his average hourly output, (2) the difference between his reported and actual outputs, and (3) the amount of daywork allowance claimed. The geometric figures are drawn in proportion to the size of each person's rating. The broken circles under W_3 and W_6 indicate that their actual output exceeded their reported output.

In considering the output of the members of the group it is necessary, first of all, to recall their general attitude toward output. It has been shown that the official "bogey" meant nothing to the operators. In its stead they had an informal standard of a day's work which functioned for the group as a norm of conduct, as a social code. They felt that it was wrong to exceed this standard.

W_3 and W_6 in refraining from reporting all the work they produced were expressing their adherence to this code. Both of these men were good workers and both of them liked to work. Occasionally they produced too much, but instead of reporting all their output, which would have affected their standing in the group, they refrained from doing so. The fact that they claimed less daywork than they could have is explainable in the same terms. If they had claimed the daywork they were entitled to, they would have raised their reported average hourly output too high. Their adherence to the group standard also accounts for their remarkably constant output rate. As can be seen in Figure

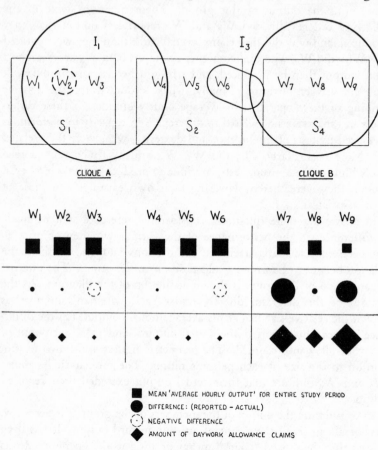

FIGURE 46

THE INTERNAL ORGANIZATION OF THE GROUP AND OUTPUT

BANK WIRING OBSERVATION ROOM

36, both of these men kept their reported output rate almost exactly on the line representing the day's work.

But here an apparent contradiction arises. Why, it might be asked, if these two men were so <u>mindful of the</u> group's sentiments regarding output, did they not occupy the same position in the group? W_3 was a member of clique A and was the best-liked person in the group, whereas W_6 was excluded from clique A and tended to associate with clique B. Unlike W_3, W_6 was subjected to sarcasm and ridicule and given such nicknames as "Runt" and "Shrimp." This was in spite of the fact that he conformed to the output standards of the group and helped more people than anyone else in the group. What, then, accounts for this apparent contradiction? The answer is that output, like occupational status, was not the only determinant of position in the group. One of the things which made W_6 objectionable to clique A was his irrepressible tendency to "horse around." Moreover, he had no compunctions about telling another person what he thought of him. Of still more importance, however, was his striving for leadership of the group. This was an honor no one was willing to confer upon him; yet he persisted in attempting to achieve it. The result was that he became a constant source of irritation. W_6, in other words, conformed to the group's sentiments attaching to output but violated those attaching to personal conduct. This was reflected in the position assigned him in the group, which was by no means an unfavorable one. He got along with everyone fairly well. It is quite likely that his adherence to the group's rules of output served to sustain him in the eyes of his associates. The sentiments he violated were much weaker than those attaching to output.

Let us next examine the relation between W_2's position in the group and his output. W_2, as interviews with him indicated, was not the type of person to conform to another's wishes. He was hard, enigmatic, self-reliant, and entered very little into relations with other people. In the observation room he tended to isolate himself, and his attitude toward his associates was one of mild contempt. This found expression in his output. By keeping his output high, he was expressing his disregard for the sentiments of the group. He knew he was doing something the others disliked and commented on it in his interviews. "They don't like me to turn out so much," he said, "but I turn it out anyway." He seemed to get a certain satisfaction from doing so. W_2's high output, then, which was consistently above the group's standard, was a means by which he expressed his antagonism toward his associates. They reciprocated by excluding him from clique A. Social isolation was the only measure at their command for bringing pressure to bear upon a member of the wiring group. But, unfortunately for them, it did not work as they wished it to in the case of W_2.

The above explanation accounts not only for W_2's high output but also for the fact that, unlike W_3 or W_6, he reported more output than he produced and claimed a good deal of daywork. The net effect of this was to boost his reported output even higher than it should have been, thus doing even more violence to the group's standard.

Let us next examine the wiremen in clique B to see if their output was related to the position they held in the group's informal organization. Clique B was looked down upon by clique A. The actual average hourly output rates of the members, as shown in Figure 46, were lower than the output rate of any other operator. W_7 and W_9 ranked unusually low. For this group, therefore, there was a direct correspondence between rate of output and informal standing in the group.

The same general relation held for other aspects of their performance. They tended to report more unearned output than the other wiremen. W_7 claimed more unearned output than anyone else, with W_9 a close second; W_8 ranked third. W_8's relatively good rating in this respect must be interpreted in the light of the fact that he spent a great deal of time soldering. It was less necessary for him to pad his figures in order to make a good showing because he could always use soldering as an excuse. W_7, W_8, and W_9 also claimed a great deal more daywork than any of the other wiremen. W_8 claimed an average of over 2 minutes lost time per hour. W_7 and W_9 each claimed an average of more than $3\frac{1}{2}$ minutes per hour. The most claimed by any other wireman was about 1 minute per hour. But these three not only claimed more lost time, the character of their claims differed also. Table XXIX shows that of the 160 claims entered by these three men, 64 were charged against their solderman and inspector. The members of clique A never once blamed a solderman or inspector for delaying them.

It may be concluded that the various performance records for the members of clique B were reflecting their position in the group. There was a clear-cut relation between their social standing and their output. But, it may be asked, did their low output determine their position in the group, or did their position in the group determine their output? The answer is that the relation worked both ways; position in the group influenced output, and output influenced position in the group. In other words, these two factors were in a relation of mutual dependence. Let us attempt to show more clearly just how this was so.

The selector wiremen, being differentiated from the connector wiremen, banded together and achieved a certain amount of solidarity among themselves. This internal solidarity resulted in increased opposition to those people who were not members of their group. Some such process usually occurs when a group becomes unified. The very process of unification entails a drawing away from those who are not members of the group. The entity retains or increases its unity by opposing other entities. In the case of the selector wiremen, opposition was expressed toward those occupational groups who stood in a relation of superordination to them; to those groups, in other words, in comparison with whom they were subordinated. These were the inspection group, represented in their case by I_3, and the connector wiremen. Their inspector, I_3, experienced the most forceful and the most personal expression of their opposition, and he eventually had to be removed from the room. The medium through which they expressed opposition to the inspector was daywork allowance claims, but with respect to the connector wiremen there was no such medium at their disposal. However, they could express their opposition to connector wiremen indirectly through output, and that is what they did. By keeping their output low, they not only lowered the earnings of the connector wiremen but at the same time they themselves managed to draw a wage quite out of proportion to their own contributions. They were, to use one of their own expressions, "chiseling" the other wiremen. This was, of course, resented particularly by W_2, W_5, and W_6. The bona fide members of clique A may have been equally annoyed, but they said nothing about it. W_2, W_5, and W_6, however, time and again tried to get clique B to raise their output. For the most part, their tactics were indirect. Frequently they traded jobs with S_4 and while in that position heckled the wiremen. They bragged that they could solder for a dozen men like W_9. Sometimes they finished their soldering very quickly and then made elaborate gestures of enforced idleness. At other times they subjected the members of clique B to direct personal criticism. The interesting thing about these tactics was that they served to subordinate clique B still further and as a result to strengthen their internal solidarity still more. So, instead of increasing their output, the members of clique B kept it low, thus "getting back" at those who were displaying their superiority.

The Relation of Employee to Supervision as a Determinant of Position in the Group

So far, all the operators except W_5 have been considered. He was the most disliked person in the group. Was this because he violated the output standard of the group? The answer is no. His output only rarely exceeded the standard of a day's work, and on the whole he conformed to this norm just as well as W_3 or W_6. Furthermore, he conformed to the group's practice of reporting more or less daywork and more or less output than he should have. In this area his conduct, from the standpoint of the group, was satisfactory. But in his relations with the foreman his conduct was anything but satisfactory. The operators, on the whole, were decidedly apprehensive of the higher supervisors in the department, partly because of the authority vested in them, and partly because much of their own conduct was contrary to the rules of management. It was an interesting fact that nearly all the activities by means of which the operators related themselves to one another, all their social activities in other words, were "wrong." They were contrary to the rules of management. Therefore, it was important that these activities be concealed from the foreman. To act as informer was an unpardonable breach of conduct. Yet this is what W_5 did, and his action explains the group's opposition to him. By "squealing" he violated a very strong sentiment intimately connected with the relation of subordinate to superior. Here, then, is still another factor which entered into the determination of the individual's position in the group's internal organization.

Determinants of Clique Membership

From the foregoing analysis it is apparent that this group of operators held certain definite ideas as to the way in which an individual should conduct himself. These sentiments, which were connected chiefly with occupation, output, and supervision, may be summarized as follows:

(1) You should not turn out too much work. If you do, you are a "rate-buster."

(2) You should not turn out too little work. If you do, you are a "chiseler."

(3) You should not tell a supervisor anything that will react to the detriment of an associate. If you do, you are a "squealer."

(4) You should not attempt to maintain social distance or act officious. If you are an inspector, for example, you should not act like one.

It may be concluded that the individual's position in the group was in large part determined by the extent to which his behavior was in accord with these sentiments. The members of clique A, the people who held the most favored position in the group, conformed to the group's rules of behavior in all respects. Members of clique B conformed to rules (1), (3), and (4). Indeed, they attached more importance to these rules than anyone else. This is easily understood because the higher the output of their associates, the more unfavorable their own output appeared. "Squealing" was more objectionable to them than to the others because more of their actions were wrong from the standpoint of management. Finally, they resented any show of superiority more than the others did because they were in the most subordinate position.

The Function of the Group's Internal Organization

The social organization of the bank wiremen performed a twofold function: (1) to protect the group from internal indiscretions, and (2) to protect it from outside interference. The same mechanism sometimes served to fulfill both functions.

The mechanisms by which internal control was exercised were varied. Perhaps the most important were sarcasm, "binging," and ridicule. Through such devices pressure was brought to bear upon those individuals who deviated too much from the group's norm of acceptable conduct. From this point of view, it will be seen that the great variety of activities ordinarily labeled "restriction of output" represent attempts at social control and discipline and as such are important integrating processes. In addition to overt methods, clique membership itself may be looked upon as an instrument of control. Those persons whose behavior was most reprehensible to clique A were excluded from it. They were, in a sense, socially ostracized. This is one of the universal social processes by means of which a group chastises and brings pressure to bear upon those who transgress its codes.

The operators attempted to protect themselves from outside interference by bringing into line those outsiders, supervisors and inspectors, who stood in a position of being able to interfere in their affairs. The chief mechanism by which they attempted to control these people was that of daywork allowance claims. The manner in which this weapon was brought into play against I_3 shows how formidable it could be. The operators did not use this weapon against I_1 or the group chief because they did not have to; both of these people submitted to group control. I_3, however, refused to be assimilated, and they helped to bring about his removal by charging him with excessive amounts of daywork. This was the most effective device at their command. Interestingly enough, it was a device provided them by their wage incentive plan. The mechanism by which they sought to protect themselves from management was the maintenance of uniform output records, which could be accomplished by reporting more or less output than they produced and by claiming daywork.

It can be seen, therefore, that nearly all the activities of this group may be looked upon as methods of controlling the behavior of its

members. The men had elaborated, spontaneously and quite unconsciously, an intricate social organization around their collective beliefs
and sentiments. The question as to what gave rise to those sentiments
and beliefs, whether they arose from actual or potential threats to their
security, as the operators claimed, is an important one and will be dealt
with at length in the following chapter.

CHAPTER XXIII

FORMAL VS. INFORMAL ORGANIZATION

So FAR it has been shown that the members of the Bank Wiring Observation Room group possessed an intricate social organization in terms of which much of their conduct was determined. Restriction of output was the chief outer manifestation of this complex of interhuman relations. Let us now turn from the particularities of the bank wiring situation to a consideration of the relation of the group as an entity to the wider company organization of which it was a part.

The problem to be considered in this chapter can best be defined in terms of the external function of the bank wiremen's organization. It has been shown that the internal function of this organization was to control and regulate the behavior of its members. Externally, however, it functioned as a protective mechanism. It served to protect the group from outside interference by manifesting a strong resistance to change, or threat of change, in conditions of work and personal relations. This resistance to change not only was reflected in all the wiremen's tactics to keep output constant but also was implied in all the reasons they gave in justification of their actions. Had it been explicitly stated, their behavior could be said to have been guided by the following rule: "Let us behave in such a way as to give management the least opportunity of interfering with us." There is no doubt that the most pronounced over-all characteristic of the interhuman activities described was their peculiarly protective or resistive quality. The problem, therefore, becomes that of discovering those external factors which gave rise to this resistance.

When stated in these terms, a number of answers to this problem are immediately suggested. Perhaps the wiremen were apprehensive of the investigators. Did not the study situation itself encourage the type of behavior observed? Or were not the operators simply attempting to stave off the effects of the depression, which were becoming noticeable within the factory at that time? Or, finally, were they not, in restricting their output, simply attempting to protect their economic interests? Inasmuch as any of these possibilities might have accounted for the situation, they must be considered at the outset.

The Effects of Placing the Group Under Observation

Did the situation in the observation room result from segregating the operators from the main department so that they were no longer under the direct surveillance of the foreman and the assistant foreman? This possibility was anticipated by the investigators when they planned the study, and it was this consideration which led them to make the base period studies referred to in the first part of this study. It was reasoned that if there were an appreciable change in the behavior of the operators it could be determined by comparing: (1) their output in the observation room with their output in the department; (2) their attitudes toward their work situation while in the observation room with their attitudes while in the department; (3) their overt behavior in the observation room with their overt behavior in the department. In addition to these comparisons which the base period studies made possible, the investigators felt that they should also consider their own relations with the operators as possible contributory factors. It may be well to repeat that the base period studies were made before the operators or their immediate supervisors knew that this study was to be made. They therefore provide a sound basis for comparison.

Weekly Average Hourly Output in the Observation Room Compared with That in the Department

The question here is whether or not average hourly output changed when the group was placed under observation. If it did change appreciably, either upward or downward, the investigators fell short of their objective. The reported average hourly output figures, both for the observation period and the eighteen weeks immediately preceding it, have been shown in Figure 35. Inasmuch as it has been shown that the output figures during the observation period were distorted, a question might arise as to whether or not they are sufficiently reliable to be compared with the base period figures. The only answer is that in all probability the base period figures were also distorted. In other words, the amount of distortion, whether due to excessive daywork allowance claims or to falsified reported outputs, may be regarded as a constant in both sets of figures and, for comparative purposes, may therefore be disregarded. Whether the amount of distortion was the same in the two periods is a question which cannot be answered, but it is more reasonable to assume that the same errors had occurred in the departmental records before the study began than to assume that they had not. The following analysis is based upon that assumption.

Table XXXIV shows the reported weekly average output of each wireman during the observation period and during the base period, and the amount it increased or decreased in the observation period as compared with the base period. It will be seen from this table that there were significant increases in the mean rates of W_4 and W_9 and pronounced decreases in the rates of W_7 and W_1 during the observation period. The mean rates of the other wiremen remained about the

TABLE XXXIV

RELATIVE RANK AND MEAN WEEKLY AVERAGE HOURLY OUTPUT DURING THE BASE PERIOD COMPARED WITH THE OBSERVATION PERIOD

BANK WIRING OBSERVATION-ROOM

| | Average Hourly Output | | | Rank | |
Wireman	Base Period	Observation Period	Increase or Decrease during Obs. Period	Base Period	Observation Period
W_1	791	740	−51	5	7
W_2	883	877	−6	1	1
W_3	828	821	−7	2	3
W_4	749	769	+20	6	5
W_5	800	812	+12	4	4
W_6	824	824	0	3	2
W_7	736	711	−25	7	8
W_8	732	741	+9	8	6
W_9	332	468	+136	9	9

same; whatever differences there were might have occurred even if the group had not been segregated. But how about the more significant changes in the outputs of W_1, W_4, W_7, and W_9? Could these be attributed to their being placed in the observation room? Referring back to Figure 35, it will be seen that the curve for W_4 shows a slight upward trend during the base period, and that this trend continues throughout the major part of the observation period. In other words, the increase in his output rate was already foreshadowed in his base period performance. It is reasonable to conclude, therefore, that being placed under observation did not account for the increase in the output rate of W_4. The same argument holds for W_9. His output rate was rising rapidly during the base period. That most of the increase which took place in his output rate during the observation period represented not an increase in rate of working but an increase in distortion does not affect this conclusion, for the departmental figures for his base period performance might have contained the same proportion of distortion. The curve for W_7 remained fairly steady up until the observation study began and then gradually declined, reaching its lowest point during the week ending January 2, 1932. In the absence of other data one might conclude that W_7's being placed under observation surely accounted for this change. Other available data, however, suggest that the decline which set in at that time was intimately related to his personal situation. This case has been reported in detail[1] and need not be repeated.

With W_1 the situation is different. It is definitely known that his dissatisfaction increased immediately upon entering the observation room. He attributed his dissatisfaction to poor illumination but, as previously shown,[2] that could not be considered the real reason. Perhaps his quarrel with W_2 over who should occupy the preferred bench position had something to do with it. Whatever the reason, it is quite likely that had he remained in the regular department he would not have become so dissatisfied. In the case of this one operator, therefore, it may be concluded that events associated with his removal to the observation room did have an adverse effect upon his attitude, and indirectly upon his output rate. The output rates of the other eight wiremen were not greatly affected.

Attitudes of the Men while in the Observation Room Compared with their Attitudes while in the Department

Were the attitudes of the operators toward their work, supervision, working conditions, and fellow workmen altered greatly by placing them under observation? In general, no. Their attitudes, as revealed in interviews taken before and after the study began, remained substantially the same. Some of the men claimed that the observation room was exactly the same as the department. Others said that the illumination was inferior, but that they felt freer to do as they pleased. Some of them said that the room was small and made them feel shut in, but these same people, after they had been placed back in the department, asked to be taken back to the observation room, saying that they liked it much better. The most pronounced change resulting from their being segregated seemed to lie in their relation to the workmen in the regular department. They felt further removed from them and that they were a group by themselves. This growing internal solidarity and increasing opposition to the outside department were manifested in many ways. For example, they felt that the men out in the main room used up all the good wire and sent them the "bum"

[1] See pp. 315, 317–319.
[2] See pp. 400–401.

wire, that they took all the *Microphones* (a weekly house organ), and in other ways discriminated against them. Much similar evidence has been quoted in the preceding chapters.

Overt Behavior in the Observation Room Compared with Overt Behavior in the Department

Did the overt behavior of the operators change much in the observation room compared with their behavior in the department? The observer, who had been in the department for ten days prior to the time the men were informed of the study, reported that in the department, even though the men were located directly across the aisle from the supervisors' desks, they seemed to feel remarkably free. They talked a good deal, and singing and horseplay were not at all uncommon. During the morning hours the men as a rule were very business-like and worked rapidly. In the late afternoon they began to work more slowly and to talk more. Job trading was quite common, and frequently the men helped one another. About fifteen minutes before quitting time most of the men were to be found sorting insulators into boxes in preparation for the next day's work. While doing this, they sat at their benches and were frequently arranged in pairs or small groups. The observer's impression was that most of the men regarded the last half-hour of the day somewhat as a social period. They did not stop work, but they conversed more. There were usually some people, however, who remained at their work stations and worked rapidly until stopping time. The behavior of the men in the observation room did not differ from this very much. It is true that the men in the observation room were more boisterous and talkative than those in the regular department, but the difference in behavior was more one of degree than of kind.

The Relations of the Interviewer and Observer to the Group

Inasmuch as the interviewer and the observer were a part of the situation they were studying, their relations with the operators and supervisors must also be considered. Of the two, the observer was much more closely associated with the operators and therefore was more likely to influence their behavior.

It has already been pointed out that the observer was apparently regarded with distrust at first but that in time he became friendly with all the operators. That they had not the slightest fear of him is attested to by the kind of material he was able to obtain. Many of the incidents he observed would not have taken place had he been regarded with suspicion or distrust. Some of the material in his record reflected the attitude of the men toward him. For example, one day the foreman stopped him and said: "You're getting to be a regular father to these fellows. I heard a couple of them arguing the other day with some of the boys out in the other room. They were telling the boys out there that they were wrong about something. They said: 'We asked — [Obs.] and he told us.'" The observer was quite sure that he had never been asked the question about which the argument had taken place. But whether he had or not makes little difference. The important point is that the operators respected the observer and liked him. Frequently after he had been absent from the room for a few hours his appearance was greeted with such remarks as: "Where have you been?"; "We thought you were lost"; "Been out having a smoke, have you?" If something had happened while he was away, they might greet him with, "You sure missed it. While you were out . . .", and then they would go on to tell him what had happened.

How did the operators regard the interviewer: as someone who had authority over them, as an equal, or just as someone to talk to? This is a difficult question to answer. The interviewer entered the observation room only two or three times, since, in accordance with the plan of study worked out, the interviewer was not to enter the observation room during working hours except when absolutely necessary. He was rarely mentioned by the men in their conversations in the observation room. However, what evidence there was indicated that they regarded him as a person who had some "say" in things. Thus, at the end of the study W_5 appealed to him to see what he could do to prevent his layoff. Again, W_8 asked him if he were the person I_3 "squealed" to and implied that he thought the interviewer was a "big shot." No employee acted in the interview, however, as though he were trying to create a favorable impression upon the interviewer.

In general, the men seemed to like to be interviewed. They did not "kid" a person who was leaving for an interview or returning from one. In fact, they vied with one another to see who could be interviewed longest and spoke of W_9 as holding the interviewing record. This, of course, played in well with the interviewer's aims, because he wanted them to be willing to meet him and to talk. It also indicated, and this was the important thing, that they were not apprehensive of the interviewer. They felt free to talk about many things in the interview which they would not have discussed with their supervisors or co-workers.

It can be concluded that the investigators surely were not observing a situation of their own making. Their relations with the group were very satisfactory. There was no evidence after the first few weeks that the operators were afraid of them or distrusted them. This is not to say they had no influence on the situation. They probably did have, but it is very unlikely that the investigators were merely observing a situation of their own creation.

The Effects of the Depression

Did not the situation in the Bank Wiring Observation Room reflect the response of the operators to the business depression? Was this not merely their way of warding off unemployment? In part, yes. There could be no doubt that the depression and fear of layoff occupied an increasingly important place in their thoughts, particularly after the beginning of 1932. In their interviews and in their daily conversations with one another and the observer they speculated endlessly upon when the depression would end, whether they would be laid off, and what would happen to them if they were. All but one of them were in very poor financial condition and if they were unemployed could not escape public support for long.

Although this was true, the investigators believed that fear of unemployment was only one among many factors determining the situation. It is doubtful if their formation into cliques and their attitudes toward their supervision had any relation to it. As for restriction of output, it may have been related to the effects of the depression but even that is doubtful. The output figures available, which stretched back before the depression, did not reflect any major interference. Furthermore, it is fairly generally conceded that restriction in one form or another occurs in good as well as bad times. It may grow more or less pronounced, but the basic pattern remains. The interviewers had detected suggestions of this pattern even in 1929, the year in which the company reached its peak of activity. It is fair to conclude, therefore, that this was not a "depression story," and that any conclusions derived from an analysis of such a situation might have relevance to periods of prosperity as well as to periods of depression.

Restriction of Output and Economic Interest

Perhaps the most common way of interpreting situations like this is to argue that the employee, in acting as he does, is simply protecting his economic interests. It is argued that if he does not restrict his output at some level his piece rate will be cut, the less capable workers will be reprimanded or discharged, or some of his co-workers will be laid off. These reasons are the same as those the worker himself gives for his behavior and are taken as explanatory and self-evident. It is assumed that the worker, from a logical appraisal of his work situation or from his own past experiences, formulates a plan of action which in the long run will be to his own best interests and then acts in accordance with that plan. This theory is based upon two primary assumptions: first, that the worker is primarily motivated by economic interest; and, second, that work behavior is logical and rational. In what follows, these assumptions will be examined in the light of the facts of this study.

Let us begin by examining the reasons the employees gave for their own behavior. These reasons, which have been quoted in Chapter XVIII, may be summarized in the belief the men held that if output went too high something might happen — the "bogey" might be raised, the "rate" might be raised, the "rate" might be lowered, someone might be laid off, hours might be reduced, or the supervisors might reprimand the slower workers. Now one of the interesting things about these reasons is the confusion they manifest. In talking about "rates," for example, many of the employees were not clear as to whether they were talking about piece rates, hourly rates, or rates of working. The consequences of changing a rate would vary depending upon which rate was changed; yet the operators did not discriminate. Again, raising the bogey would have none of the consequences they feared. If it induced them to increase their output, the effect would be to increase their earnings; otherwise, there would be no effect whatsoever. The result would be the opposite of cutting a piece rate; yet some of the operators felt that the result would be the same. It is clear, therefore, that their actions were not based upon a logical appraisal of their work situation.

Another important observation which supports the above conclusion is that not one of the bank wiremen had ever experienced any of the things they claimed they were guarding against. Their bogey had not been raised, their piece rates had not been lowered, nor had their hourly rates; yet they acted and talked as though they had. Their behavior, in other words, was not based upon their own concrete experience with the company. In this connection it might be pointed out that from a logical standpoint the operators should have wanted hourly rates to be flexible. They should have wanted them raised or lowered depending upon changes in the levels of an individual's efficiency, for only in that way could earnings be made to correspond with output.

Yet all of them, the highest and lowest alike, were opposed to a lowering of hourly rates.

Another illustration of the nonlogical character of their behavior is found in an incident which occurred before the study began. Hours of work had been shortened from 48 to 44 per week. The supervisors told the men that if they turned out the same amount of work in the shorter time their earnings would remain the same. After a great deal of persuasion, the men agreed to try, and they were very much surprised to find that their earnings did stay the same. Not one of the men who commented upon this in an interview could see how it could be, in spite of the fact that their supervisors had tried to explain it to them.

At this point an objection might be raised. Granted that the employees did not clearly understand their payment system, were they not, nevertheless, acting in accordance with their economic interests? Even though none of them had experienced a reduction of piece rates, was it not a possibility? And were they not at least guarding against that possibility by controlling their output?

In considering this objection, let us assume for the time being that many of their fears were justified. Let us suppose that the piece rate was endangered if their output exceeded their concept of a day's work. Then what would follow from this if we assume that they were motivated primarily by economic interest? It would seem that each and every worker would push his output up to 6,600 connections per day and then hold it at that point. If all of them maintained that level of output consistently, they would be securing the maximum of earnings possible without endangering the piece rate. The facts are, however, that there were wide differences in the outputs of different individuals and that some of the operators were far short of 6,600 connections per day. If earnings had been their chief concern, differences in output levels should not have existed unless the operators were working at top capacity, and that was far from being the case. Furthermore, in these terms it would be impossible to account for the amount of daywork claimed. Had they been chiefly concerned with earnings, they would have seen to it that there was very little daywork. It follows that this group of operators could not be said to be acting in accordance with their economic interests even if we assume that the reasons they gave for their actions were supportable by experimental evidence, which, of course, was not the case.

Two other fallacies in the economic interpretation of restriction of output may be mentioned. One of them is the implied assumption that a fixed, unchanging piece rate is desirable on economic grounds It is argued that a firm should maintain piece rates once they have been established, that this is the only way defensive reactions on the part of employees can be prevented. The general validity of this statement is scarcely open to question. Rapid change in piece rates is likely to undermine the workers' confidence in management and may in itself defeat the purpose of the most carefully constructed incentive plan. The justification of the fixed piece rate, however, is not so much economic as social. From a strictly economic viewpoint, it is to the advantage of the workers to have piece rates change with changes in the cost of living. The firm that takes pride in piece rates of long standing in the belief that it is thereby protecting the economic interests of the workers may be misplacing its emphasis. What it is really doing may lie more in the social than in the economic area.

The other fallacy lies in the assumption that the worker can effectively control the actions of management by acting in certain ways. Changes in piece rates, hours of work, number of people employed, and so on, frequently lie completely outside the control of the worker and even of management. Furthermore, changes in piece rates at the Western Electric Company, for example, are not based upon the earnings of the worker. The company's policy is that piece rates will not be changed unless there is a change in manufacturing process. Changes in process are made by engineers whose duty it is to reduce unit cost wherever the saving will be sufficient to justify the change. In certain instances such changes may be made irrespective of direct labor cost per unit. Again, where labor is a substantial element, increased output tends to lower unit cost and thus tends to obviate the need for a change in process. Restriction works precisely opposite. Restriction tends to increase unit costs and, instead of warding off a change in the piece rate as the worker believes, may actually induce one.

From this analysis it may be concluded that the ideology expressed by the employees was not based upon a logical appraisal of their situation and that they were not acting strictly in accordance with their economic interests. Rather, the situation was as represented in Figure 47, in which A stands for the sentiments of the group, B for their behavior in restricting output, and C for the reasons they gave for acting as they did. The economic interest argument which we have been considering assumes a causal relation between C and B. It assumes that B follows from C. Actually, we see that for these operators B was an expression of A, the group's sentiments. Their behavior was a way of affirming those sentiments which lay at the root of their group organization. C, far from being the "cause" of their actions, was merely the way in which they rationalized their behavior. They attempted to give logical reasons for their conduct and to make it appear as though the latter was directed toward some outside inter-

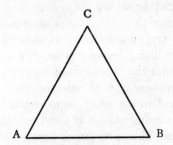

A = sentiments of the group

B = behavior in restricting output

C = reasons given for their behavior

FIGURE 47

MUTUALLY INTERDEPENDENT RELATIONS BETWEEN BEHAVIOR,
SENTIMENT, AND BELIEF

ference, whereas in fact B was primarily directed toward and expressed A.

OTHER MISINTERPRETATIONS OF RESTRICTION OF OUTPUT

In addition to the three major arguments so far considered, there are a host of other ways of interpreting restriction of output, most of which are based upon an inadequate understanding of human behavior.

One common way of misinterpreting such a situation is to blame the worker on the ground that he is deliberately and willfully opposing management. It is said that for malicious reasons he refuses to co-operate, that he is ungrateful or just plain lazy. This interpretation, however, is not supported by the facts of the situation under discussion. First, there was nothing in the behavior of this group that even faintly resembled conscious, planned opposition to management. The activities of the men in this group were directed inward toward maintaining their own social organization. They were not primarily directed out-ward toward management, as a casual observer might suppose. Of course, their endeavor to preserve their internal organization did result in a certain amount of opposition to management. This opposition came about indirectly and quite inevitably; there was no conscious intent. Secondly, with the exception of W_9, these men could hardly be called lazy. As we have shown, the men stopped work earlier than they were supposed to because they felt impelled to and not just to waste time. They were yielding to a pressure far stronger than financial incentive. Instead of saying they were lazy, it would be more accurate to characterize their behavior as abstention from work. This constrained idleness was unsatisfactory to some of the workmen who were aware of a discrepancy between what they should do as members of the group and what they could do if they felt free to work.

Another very common way of misconceiving this situation, one which is closely allied to the above, is to conclude that the behavior of the employees is a manifestation of overt hostility between management and employees. This error arises because of a failure to relate the behavior of the employees to their social situation. Instead, their behavior is judged in terms of what it should be according to the formal organization. It is contrasted with an ideal and, of course, is found wanting. Here it is relevant to point out that the company had a long record of fair dealing with its employees; and its attitude, as reflected in its socially directed employee relations policies, was distinctly sympathetic. Moreover, verbally in the interviewing program and overtly in their continued connection with the company, as shown by an exceptionally low labor turnover, the employees gave ample evidence of their appreciation of, and friendliness toward, the company. In the interviews of 1929, where over 40,000 complaints were voiced, there was not one single unfavorable comment expressed about the company in general.

A third common error is to assume that the immediate supervisor was responsible for the situation. For instance, it might be argued that in the Bank Wiring Observation Room the group chief was to blame because he sided with the workers rather than with management. Supervisory training is inevitably suggested as a remedy. The error here is the assumption that the supervisor, by sheer force of personality, can make his actual situation correspond to what it is theoretically held to be. The logic of industrial organization conceives of the supervisor as management's representative, and hence as having the necessary power to see that the policies of the company are carried out. It is only too clear that the supervisor could be pictured more accurately as victim than as contriver of the situation in the observation room. In the instances studied, the group chief had two alternatives. Either he had to side with his subordinates or he had to try to represent management. Both courses, however, had unpleasant consequences to him.

If he tried to represent management, he would lose sympathetic control of his men, and his duties as supervisor would become more difficult. If he chose to side with his subordinates, the job of handling them would become easier, but his relations with his supervisors would become more insecure. The difficulties he encountered resided in the nature of the situation itself, in the interrelations of human beings with different duties, obligations, and interests. Furthermore, these difficulties could not be easily solved by supervisory training. This is illustrated by the fact that GC_1 in the observation room was well trained and had real ability in handling men; yet he was forced into the position above described.

Still another error lies in assuming that situations in which restriction of output occurs are examples of inefficiency and poor management. In describing human situations of this sort there is always the danger of making them seem worse than they really are; that is, there is a tendency to judge them in terms of a logic of efficiency which is considered an ideal to be sought. Judged by customary standards, the output of the workers was acceptable and satisfactory. In the bank wiring department, output per worker was considered high. According to the foreman, it had risen over a period of years from an average of some 4,000 connections a day to 6,000. The bank wiring department also ranked high when its output was compared with the output of men in other concerns doing the same kind of work. The average output per man in outside concerns was about 4,000 connections per day as compared with 6,000 for this group. The department officials were proud of these accomplishments, and some of them commented that if the men consistently turned out more than 6,000 connections a day they would "wear their fingers out." Any outsider watching the men work, especially during the morning hours, would have concurred in this statement. The speeds attained by some of the men were in fact astonishing.

It is well to remember, therefore, that only with reference to an abstract logic of efficiency could the phenomenon described be called "restriction"; that is to say, the workers were not producing so much as they might have had physiological fatigue been the only factor limiting output. Instead of describing such behavior as "restriction," it could be described equally well as behavior which was not strictly in accordance with the logic of efficiency. Inasmuch as fewer moral implications attach to the statement that the workers' behavior did not conform to some abstract logic, the latter description is perhaps preferable.

The Social Organization of the Company

Since the preceding considerations do not provide a satisfactory explanation of the situation in the Bank Wiring Observation Room, let us now turn to an examination of the relation between the social organization of the wiring group and the company structure, of which the wiring group was a small part. This relation can best be shown by first describing the social structure of the company and then showing the position of the bank wiremen in that structure.

Before beginning this analysis a word of caution is necessary. The investigators never undertook a systematic study of the social organization of the company, and it is therefore impossible to characterize it in detail or entirely accurately. Because of this, what is said here is necessarily oversimplified and might need to be modified in the light of a more careful study. The general outlines are, however, fairly clear, and while they may not represent the total organization accurately they are sufficient to show the worker's position in that organization.

Differentiating Factors

The first thing to note about the total personnel of the company is that it was differentiated in many ways. One of the most important distinctions was the division of the personnel into office workers and shop workers. The social status of the individual varied considerably depending upon the group in which his job placed him. There were a variety of differentiating factors, other than the type of work itself, which may be looked upon as subheadings under the office and shop distinction. These fell into three groups: working conditions, method of payment, and privileges.

The working conditions of the shop worker differed in many ways from those of the office worker.[1] His hours of work were different. He started to work at 7:30, took 45 minutes off for lunch, and quit at 5:00, whereas the office worker started at 8:30, took an hour off for lunch, and quit at 5:15. Thus hours of work tended to set one group off from the other. This distinction between office and shop, generally speaking, extended to many other aspects of the material environment: to building location, locker facilities, toilet facilities, and so on.

Method of payment was another way in which office and shop groups were differentiated. Shop workers were, on the whole, paid time or

---

[1] The conditions herein described are as of the time of these studies. Since then many changes have been made, most of which tend to reduce the social difference between office and shop.

piece rates, whereas the office workers were, again generally speaking, paid a weekly salary. Practically all the company's devices for promoting efficiency — time study, motion study, and incentive plans — applied only to the shop force.

The privileges of the office worker also differentiated him from the shop employee. This distinction applied not only to such things as penalties for being late or absent, payment for holidays and vacations, but also to such things as freedom to move about and converse at work. It also appeared in the unwritten code which induced most shop workers to eat their lunches on the ground floor of the company restaurant instead of on the top floor, where the office forces gathered.

From the foregoing evidence, it may be concluded that within the company itself there were at least two major social groups. The point should be emphasized, however, that in some respects there was no sharp cleavage between these two groups. It should also be clearly understood that these differences were not imposed for the purpose of differentiating classes of employees. They existed for other reasons and could be explained or justified on the basis of economy and usefulness. In other words, their social function differed from their logical, explicit function. It may be concluded that the individual's position in the organization of the company was in the first instance determined by the kind of job to which he was assigned.

Another main differentiating factor which tended to cut across office and shop groups was the division of the employees into supervisors and nonsupervisors. Every person, irrespective of his vocation, was in either one or the other of these groups. The nonsupervisor in the office and the nonsupervisor in the shop were alike in that they were at the bottom level of a hierarchy. These bottom levels also differed in social status.

There were many other differentiating factors. There was, for example, differentiation based on sex. In addition, there were many informal distinctions based upon such things as nationality, age, education, and service.

The significance of these differentiating factors lies in the fact that the more bases there are for differentiation within a collectivity, the less likelihood there is for any one group to separate out. Thus nonsupervisory office employees have something in common with nonsupervisory shop employees, but their interests and sentiments are by no means identical. Similarly, the shop employee and the shop supervisor have a common ground in relation to the office employee and the office supervisor, and the supervisory group as a whole has something in common in relation to the whole nonsupervisory group. This criss-cross of relations creates communities of interest which only partially coincide. Individuals are thus integrated with and differentiated from one another. The result is not a dichotomous classification into office and shop workers, or into supervisors and nonsupervisors. It is instead a complex configuration of relations in which different groups are separated out and yet tied together.

Integrating Factors

Let us turn now to another set of factors which, unlike those just mentioned, extended to all groups irrespective of rank or job. These may be called "integrating factors," to distinguish them from those factors which applied to some groups but not to others. Perhaps the secret of this company's history of favorable labor relations lies in the fact that it possesses a remarkable number of social processes by means of which the individual is integrated or identified with the collective whole. In the absence of such rituals, one group is likely to separate out in opposition to another group from which it is too widely differentiated.

A large number of these integrating factors were to be found in the activities sponsored by the Hawthorne Club. This club, whose membership comprised every employee and which was run by the employees themselves, engaged in a wide variety of activities. It sponsored eight different clubs, with regularly elected officers, and twelve kinds of athletics, in addition to informal parties, dances, and entertainment programs. These activities interested a large number of employees of all ranks and served to create personal relations of great variety and endurance outside of the immediate work situation. The integrative character of these activities can best be shown by considering two sports, interbranch baseball and bowling. In interbranch baseball, competition was always keen. Teams were recruited within each branch, and just as the college team in some sense represents the school, so the team represented the branch. One effect of these games was to stir up the sentiments of the people within the branch, to arouse their loyalty, and to increase their solidarity. The other effect was to give a socially controlled expression to the antagonisms between branches. In games between the inspectors and the operators, or between the operators and the office workers, an opportunity was afforded for the expression of any feelings they may have had. The result was satisfactory from all standpoints, especially from the standpoint of control. The wise administrator recognizes that antagonisms inevitably result from human organization. His problem is to handle them in such a way that they neither endanger the organization nor result in repressed grievances. He must find ways of allowing them to be expressed in a socially integrative manner, and games are one of the means by which this may in part be achieved.

Just as interbranch games served to drain off antagonisms between branches, so the game of bowling served to lessen the constraints inherent in the supervisory organization. For the most part, bowling games were organized among workers within the branches. There was considerable social pressure brought to bear upon a person to join in these games. This pressure came not from the supervisors but from fellow workers. One of the interesting things about bowling was that employees and supervisors participated on a common footing. Here the shop worker might be found competing with his foreman on a common ground. The supervisory organization, on these occasions, was in effect collapsed and all, irrespective of rank or title, participated alike. Thus it can be seen that all these games and social activities were, from a sociological standpoint, important integrating processes. They served to cut across the differentiating factors previously mentioned and to identify the employee with a larger group, the company.

Another important integrating factor was service or seniority. The peculiarity of seniority is that it is acquired not by ability, education, personality, rank, or nationality, but through time. It is simply age with the company. It is the one basis upon which men are differentiated by an impartial process, a process free from human contrivance or feelings of prejudice. In this one respect, if in no other, every employee shares something in common with his superiors. That seniority was recognized as an important factor in the social organization of the company is seen by the importance attached to it by the employees and by the number of social rituals and privileges organized around it. Important service anniversaries were celebrated by dinners and parties given by friends, by "write-ups" and pictures in the *Microphone*, by public congratulations from someone in high authority, and by the conferring of certificates or buttons symbolic of the "age" attained.

Another group of important integrating factors included the thrift program, sickness, accident, and death benefit funds, pension funds, hospital care, financial and legal service, and so on. These activities were begun by the company through necessity and may be looked upon as the taking over by the company of social functions not adequately performed by society. They reflect, in some measure, the breakdown of the social milieu in a concentrated industrial population. The effect upon the industrial establishment is to make it an important source of stability. It becomes a highly complex and comprehensive social institution. The employees find within the company itself not only a source of income but also, and to a marked extent, a source of advice, friendship, and aid as well as a source of amusement and recreation.

SOCIAL GROUPS IN THE COMPANY ORGANIZATION AND THEIR INTERRELATIONS

It is clear that no simple dichotomous classification of the company's personnel could be made. The personnel could not be divided into an employer and an employee class because there was no employer class. Every person in the company from top to bottom was an employee. This point is emphasized here because many of the problems which have been encountered in these studies are commonly attributed to a conflict between employer and employee. To find them in a company that has no employer other than a scattered group of stockholders, many of whom are themselves employees of the company, suggests that these problems may be related to some other factor or factors. Also, although one could with some justification divide the personnel into supervisors and nonsupervisors, even this would misrepresent the actual situation. The study of the supervisors in the Operating Branch showed that the supervisory group was far from homogeneous.[1] The lower grades of supervision had more in common with the nonsupervisory group than with the higher grades of supervision. Furthermore, the nonsupervisory group itself was exceedingly heterogeneous.

Although the total personnel could not be divided into two classes, this does not mean that certain groups did not have more in common than other groups. In general, five main groups could be distinguished: management, supervisors, technologists, office workers, and shop workers. These may be spoken of as groups with some accuracy, provided it be remembered that the dividing lines were indistinct and that all these groups had many things in common. For the time being, attention will be confined to four of these groups, omitting the office workers. The latter group will be brought in only in so far as it is relevant to a point under discussion.

The general relations between these four groups are represented in Figure 48. Management, by which is meant the group in whom responsibility for the concern as a whole is vested, exercises control through two main subgroups, supervisors and technologists. The supervisory

[1] See Chapter XV.

category includes those lower-ranking supervisors whose chief concern is with getting a job done and carrying out the purposes of the managerial group. The technologist group includes all people with specialized training, such as the trained engineer, the efficiency expert, the cost accountant, and the rate setter. With these rough definitions in

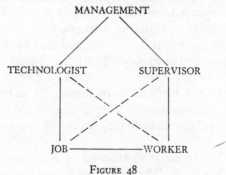

FIGURE 48

INTERRELATIONS AMONG FOUR GROUPS IN INDUSTRY

mind, let us now proceed to a more careful examination of the functions and interrelations of these different groups.

The Relation between the Worker and His Job

Inasmuch as much of what is to be said depends upon a clear understanding of the relation between the worker and his job, this will be considered first. This relation is ordinarily discussed in such terms as fatigue, monotony, learning, education, aptitudes, and so on. These are, of course, highly relevant problems, but they will not be discussed here. Rather, attention will be confined to some neglected aspects of the relation between the worker and his job.

As has been shown, the worker's social status in the company depends in large part upon his job. Also, a given job carries with it many related factors which have social significance. Wages, for example, vary with occupations, and these wage differentials frequently serve to reinforce occupational stratification. The results of the interviewing program showed very clearly that the worker was quite as much concerned with these differentials, that is, the relation of his wages to the wages of other workmen, as with the absolute amount of his wages. In short, the job and all the factors connected with it, such as the pay, the method of payment, working conditions, and privileges, together serve to define the social position of the worker. As one goes up in the occupational hierarchy, there is a change in these related factors which roughly corresponds to the change in status of the job.

That jobs are socially ordered is a fact of the greatest importance. For it will be seen that, in so far as this holds true, any change in the job may very likely alter the existing routine relations between the person whose job it is and other people within the factory. This process is thrown into high relief when a person is promoted to supervisory rank. Such a change modifies his relations with other people within the plant whether he wants it to or not and may even carry over into his social life outside the factory. The latter process is best observed in communities largely made up of employees of a given concern. Frequently when the husband is promoted, for example, the wife's associations in the community change. She is given access to new groups and, if socially mobile, may break off previously established relations.

But changes in the social significance of work are not confined to changes in the job alone. The physical task may remain the same, but its social significance may be altered by changes in working conditions. For instance, if the only visible difference between two levels of super- vision is the size or arrangement of the desk, the color of the carpet, or the kind of calendar pad each supervisor has, that difference, as anyone who has lived in such situations knows, assumes considerable signifi- cance, not only to the supervisors but to the people reporting to them. The following incident illustrates how important such small things become in situations permeated with social significance.

The personnel of one of the departments interviewed was moved from one building to another. In the new location, because of lack of space, it was found necessary to seat four people across the aisle from the remainder of the group. It happened that there were three women in the department who were to be transferred to other work. These women were given desks across the aisle so that their going would not necessitate a rearrangement of desks. The fourth person, a man, was given a desk there simply because there was no other place for him to sit. In choosing the fourth person, the supervisor was undoubtedly influenced by the fact that he was older than the rest of the group and was well acquainted with the three women. But, beyond that, nothing was implied by the fact that he was chosen. Now see how this employee interpreted the change in his seating position. He felt that his super- visor evaluated him in the same way in which he evaluated the women. The women were being transferred to other types of work; conse- quently, he felt that he too would be transferred before long. Two of the women were being returned to jobs in the shop. He felt that he himself might be transferred to the shop; and there was nothing he dreaded more. Having dwelt on speculations like these for a while, the employee recalled with alarm that his name had been omitted from the current issue of the house telephone directory. This omission had been accidental. The house telephone directory, however, constituted a sort of social register. Names of shop people below the rank of assistant foreman were not printed unless they were employed in some special capacity requiring contacts with other organizations. With the exception of typists and certain clerical groups, the names of all office people were listed. The fact that his name had been omitted from the directory now took on new significance for the employee. It tended to reinforce his growing conviction that he was about to be transferred to a shop position. He became so preoccupied over what might happen to him that for a time he could scarcely work.

The Relation between the Technologist and the Worker

Having indicated the social significance of the job to the worker, let us now examine the relation between the technologist and the worker. Modern industry has found it necessary to employ a large number of specialists. The primary function of these specialists is to make improvements in machines, technical processes, methods, and products. The indirect result of this activity is a high incidence of change in jobs and related conditions of work.

Perhaps the chief characteristic of the specialist group is that they are experimentally minded. They think in terms of their specialized logics and they scrutinize everything that comes within their scope from the point of view of their specialty. Frequently their attention is directed to the worker himself. For example, when it is found that the employee does not have the best possible work patterns and routines from a logical point of view, a highly logical plan may be introduced in terms of which he is supposed to govern his actions. Technologists frequently devise ingenious procedures to bring the worker's actions into line with a logic of efficiency. If the assumptions upon which such plans are based be granted, the plans themselves are sound. Certainly the technologist has no intention of foisting an arbitrary set of rules upon the worker. In fact, many of his plans are designed to help the worker. Carefully thought-out wage plans are intended to reimburse the worker with a wage proportional to his efforts. The simplification of his job, whether through a change in process, division of labor, or elimination of random movements, is supposed to make his work easier and less fatiguing. If fatigue is eliminated, the worker, theoretically, can produce more and can thereby earn more money. Indeed, some proponents of "rationalization" in industry see in it the solution of all labor troubles.

Why is it, then, that sometimes these logical plans, as in the case of the Bank Wiring Observation Room, do not work out as intended? The answer would seem to lie in the fact that frequently plans which are intended to promote efficiency have consequences other than their logical ones, and these unforeseen consequences tend to defeat the logical purposes of the plan as conceived. Let us consider some of these possible nonlogical consequences.

First, technical innovations make for changes in the worker's job and through the job may have profound consequences to the employee. For in so far as his job is changed, his position in the social organization, his interpersonal relations, his traditions of craftsmanship, and his social codes which regulate his relations to other people may also be affected.

Secondly, the worker must frequently accommodate himself to changes which he does not initiate. Many of the systems introduced to improve his efficiency and to control his behavior do not take into account his sentiments. Because of his position in the company structure, at the bottom level of a well-stratified organization, he cannot hold to the same degree the sentiments of those who are instituting the changes.

Thirdly, many of these same systems tend to subordinate the worker still further in the company's social structure. For instance, some of the incentive schemes and the procedures connected with them — job analysis, time and motion studies — apply for the most part only to the shop worker.

In summary, it may be said that the technologist is related to the worker in two ways. First, and more important, he is related to the worker indirectly through the job the worker performs. The indirect effects of technical innovation must be assessed not only in terms of fatigue and monotony but also in terms of their social consequences for the worker as a member of a social organization. Secondly, the technologist is related to the worker directly through those activities, such as time and motion studies, which are intended to supply him with standardized skills. The consequences of these activities must be assessed not only in terms of their logical objective, but also in terms of their effects upon the worker's sentiments of personal integrity. Thus it is seen that the technologist may be unwittingly a source of interference and constraint. Resistance to such interference was the chief external function of the bank wiremen's informal organization.

The Relation of the Supervisor to the Worker

To attribute the formation of the bank wiremen's informal organization solely to the indirect, social consequences of the activity of technical specialists would clearly be an oversimplification. The relation between the supervisory group and the worker must also be considered.

Unlike the technologist, the supervisor is related to the worker in a direct, personal, face-to-face way. He has disciplinary authority over the worker. To say that one person has disciplinary authority over another is a shorthand way of saying that one person is under the obligation of seeing that another person's conduct is in accord with certain generally accepted norms. The father-son relationship resembles the supervisor-employee relationship in that it contains an element of disciplinary authority. But the norms of conduct with reference to which discipline is exercised are of an entirely different nature in these two cases. In the case of the father-son relationship these norms are set by society at large. The father disciplines his son into socially controlled and socially approved modes of behavior, and he is aided in that process by numerous social institutions, such as the church and the school. But in the case of the supervisor-employee relationship no similar social codes exist. The criterion in terms of which the supervisor must exercise discipline is not the convention of ordinary social living but a logic of efficiency. His duty is to see that the worker's behavior corresponds to rules of efficient conduct. It is this insistence upon a logic of efficiency, this continual attempt to force the human organization into logical molds, that creates constraint.

This point was illustrated time and again in the Bank Wiring Observation Room. There it was seen that most of the problems encountered by the supervisors were problems of inducing the workmen to conform to the rules of the technical organization. The worker's conduct was considered right or wrong in so far as it corresponded to these rules. The supervisor's success was evaluated by his superiors in terms of how well he succeeded in achieving this objective. Theoretically, these rules were supposed to promote efficiency, and adherence to them was supposed to redound to the worker's advantage. From the point of view of the worker's sentiments, however, many of them were annoying and seemingly functioned only as subordinating or differentiating mechanisms.

Consider, for example, the unwritten rule that wiremen should not help one another wire. This rule received its sanction from the belief that employees could turn out more work by working only on the equipments to which they were assigned. There would be less opportunity for talking, less likelihood of their getting in one another's way, and less likelihood of their delaying the solderman and the inspector. There was, in other words, no logical reason why workmen should want to help one another in this fashion. To the wiremen, however, this was just another arbitrary rule. Many of them preferred to work together occasionally. It was one of the ways in which they expressed their solidarity; it was one of the integrative mechanisms in their internal organization. Furthermore, they knew that working together did not necessitate slowing down. In fact, the evidence showed that sometimes when they were refused the privilege of helping one another, they became less efficient.

It can be seen that one of the chief sources of constraint in a working group can be a logic which does not take into account the worker's sentiments. Any activity not strictly in accordance with such a logic (and sometimes this means most forms of social activity) may be judged "wrong." As a result, such activity can only be indulged in openly within the protection of an informal group, which, in turn, may become organized in opposition to the effective purpose of the total organization.

SUMMARY

In the studies reported it has been shown that in certain departments at the Hawthorne plant there existed informal employee organizations resulting in problems such as have been described. An attempt has been made to point out that to state such problems in terms of "restriction," "faulty supervision," or "mismanagement" is to mistake symptoms for causes and to neglect the social factors involved.

The significant problem for investigation appeared to be that of specifying the factors which give rise to such informal organizations. In attempting to answer this question, the external function of one group, the bank wiremen, was examined. This function could be characterized as that of resisting change. Following this lead, the position of the Bank Wiring Observation Room group in relation to the total company structure was then examined. This analysis led to the general conclusion that the informal organization of the bank wiring group resulted primarily from the position of that group in the total company structure and its consequent relations with other groups within the company.

PART V

APPLICATIONS TO PRACTICE OF
RESEARCH RESULTS

CHAPTER XXIV

AN INDUSTRIAL ORGANIZATION AS A SOCIAL SYSTEM

WE SHALL now attempt to state more systematically than was possible in a chronological account the results of the research and some of their implications for practice. Each stage of the research contributed to the development of a point of view in terms of which the data could be more usefully assessed. In presenting the studies, this aspect of the research program was given primary emphasis and an effort was made to show how each successive step in the research resulted in the discovery of new facts which in turn brought forth new questions and new hypotheses and assisted in the development of more adequate methods and a more adequate conceptual scheme. The point of view which gradually emerged from these studies is one from which an industrial organization is regarded as a social system. In this chapter a statement of this point of view will be made. In the next chapter various management problems which have been discussed in connection with the various research studies will be restated in terms of this new point of view. In the concluding chapter the application of the concept of an industrial concern as a social system to problems of personnel practice will be considered.

The study of the bank wiremen showed that their behavior at work could not be understood without considering the informal organization of the group and the relation of this informal organization to the total social organization of the company. The work activities of this group, together with their satisfactions and dissatisfactions, had to be viewed as manifestations of a complex pattern of interrelations. In short, the work situation of the bank wiring group had to be treated as a social system; moreover, the industrial organization of which this group was a part also had to be treated as a social system.

By "system" is meant something which must be considered as a whole because each part bears a relation of interdependence to every other part.[1] It will be the purpose of this chapter to state this conception of a social system, to specify more clearly the parts of the social system of

---

[1] "The interdependence of the variables in a system is one of the widest inductions from experience that we possess; or we may alternatively regard it as the definition of a system." Henderson, L. J., *Pareto's General Sociology*, Harvard University Press, 1935, p. 86.

which account has to be taken in an industrial organization, and to consider the state of equilibrium which obtains among the parts.

The Two Major Functions of an Industrial Organization

An industrial organization may be regarded as performing two major functions, that of producing a product and that of creating and distributing satisfactions among the individual members of the organization. The first function is ordinarily called economic. From this point of view the functioning of the concern is assessed in such terms as cost, profit, and technical efficiency. The second function, while it is readily understood, is not ordinarily designated by any generally accepted word. It is variously described as maintaining employee relations, employee good will, co-operation, etc. From this standpoint the functioning of the concern is frequently assessed in such terms as labor turnover, tenure of employment, sickness and accident rate, wages, employee attitudes, etc. The industrial concern is continually confronted, therefore, with two sets of major problems: (1) problems of external balance, and (2) problems of internal equilibrium. The problems of external balance are generally assumed to be economic; that is, problems of competition, adjusting the organization to meet changing price levels, etc. The problems of internal equilibrium are chiefly concerned with the maintenance of a kind of social organization in which individuals and groups through working together can satisfy their own desires.

Ordinarily an industrial concern is thought of primarily in terms of its success in meeting problems of external balance, or if the problems of internal equilibrium are explicitly recognized they are frequently assumed to be separate from and unrelated to the economic purpose of the enterprise. Producing an article at a profit and maintaining good employee relations are frequently regarded as antithetical propositions. The results of the studies which have been reported indicated, however, that these two sets of problems are interrelated and interdependent. The kind of social organization which obtains within a concern is intimately related to the effectiveness of the total organization. Likewise, the success with which the concern maintains external balance is directly related to its internal organization.

A great deal of attention has been given to the economic function of industrial organization. Scientific controls have been introduced to further the economic purposes of the concern and of the individuals within it. Much of this advance has gone on in the name of efficiency or rationalization. Nothing comparable to this advance has gone on in the development of skills and techniques for securing co-operation, that is, for getting individuals and groups of individuals working together effectively and with satisfaction to themselves. The slight advances which have been made in this area have been overshadowed by the new and powerful technological developments of modern industry.

THE TECHNICAL ORGANIZATION OF THE PLANT

In looking at an industrial organization as a social system it will first be necessary to examine the physical environment, for this is an inseparable part of any organization. The physical environment includes not only climate and weather, but also that part of the environment which is owned and used by the organization itself, namely, the physical plant, tools, machines, raw products, and so on. This latter part of the factory's physical environment is ordered and organized in a certain specified way to accomplish the task of technical production. For our purposes, therefore, it will be convenient to distinguish from the human organization this aspect of the physical environment of an industrial plant and to label it the "technical organization of the plant." This term will refer only to the logical and technical organization of material, tools, machines, and finished product, including all those physical items related to the task of technical production.

The two aspects into which an industrial plant can be roughly divided — the technical organization and the human organization — are interrelated and interdependent. The human organization is constantly molding and re-creating the technical organization either to achieve more effectively the common economic purpose or to secure more satisfaction for its members. Likewise, changes in the technical organization require an adaptation on the part of the human organization.

THE HUMAN ORGANIZATION OF THE PLANT

In the human organization we find a number of individuals working together toward a common end: the collective purpose of the total organization. Each of these individuals, however, is bringing to the work situation a different background of personal and social experiences. No two individuals are making exactly the same demands of their job. The demands a particular employee makes depend not only upon his physical needs but upon his social needs as well. These social needs and the sentiments associated with them vary with his early personal history and social conditioning as well as with the needs and sentiments of people closely associated with him both inside and outside of work.

THE INDIVIDUAL

It may be well to look more closely at the sentiments the individual is bringing to his work situation. Starting with a certain native organic endowment the child is precipitated into group life by the act of birth. The group into which the child is born is not the group in general. The child is born into a specific family. Moreover, this specific family is not a family in isolation. It is related in certain ways to other families in the community. It has a certain cultural background — a way of life, codes and routines of behavior, associated with certain beliefs and expectations. In the beginning the child brings only his organic needs to this social milieu into which he is born. Very rapidly he begins to accumulate experience. This process of accumulating experience is the process of assigning meanings to the socio-reality about him; it is the process of becoming socialized. Much of the early learning period is devoted to preparing the child to become capable of social life in its particular group. In preparing the child for social participation the immediate family group plays an important role. By the particular type of family into which the child is born he is "conditioned" to certain routines of behavior and ways of living. The early meanings he assigns to his experience are largely in terms of these codes of behavior and associated beliefs. As the child grows up and participates in groups other than the immediate family his meanings lose, although never quite entirely, their specific family form. This process of social inter-action and social conditioning is never-ending and continues from birth to death. The adult's evaluation of his surroundings is determined in a good part by the system of human interrelations in which he has participated.

THE SOCIAL ORGANIZATION OF THE PLANT

However, the human organization of an industrial plant is more than a plurality of individuals, each motivated by sentiments arising from his own personal and private history and background. It is also a social organization, for the members of an industrial plant — executives, technical specialists, supervisors, factory workers, and office workers — are interacting daily with one another and from their associations certain patterns of relations are formed among them. These patterns of relations, together with the objects which symbolize them, constitute the social organization of the industrial enterprise. Most of the individuals who live among these patterns come to accept them as obvious and necessary truths and to react as they dictate. Both the kind of behavior that is expected of a person and the kind of behavior he can expect from others are prescribed by these patterns.

If one looks at a factory situation, for example, one finds individuals and groups of individuals who are associated at work acting in certain accepted and prescribed ways toward one another. There is not complete homogeneity of behavior between individuals or between one group of individuals and another, but rather there are differences of behavior expressing differences in social relationship. Some relationships fall into routine patterns, such as the relationship between superior and subordinate or between office worker and shop worker. Individuals conscious of their membership in certain groups are reacting in certain accepted ways to other individuals representing other groups. Behavior varies according to the stereotyped conceptions of relationship. The worker, for example, behaves toward his foreman in one way, toward his first-line supervisor in another way, and toward his fellow worker in still another. People holding the rank of inspector expect a certain kind of behavior from the operators — the operators from the inspectors. Now these relationships, as is well known from everyday experiences, are finely shaded and sometimes become complicated. When a person is in the presence of his supervisor alone he usually acts differently from the way he acts when his supervisor's supervisor is also present. Likewise, his supervisor acts toward him alone quite differently from the way he behaves when his own supervisor is also there. These subtle nuances of relationship are so much a part of everyday life that they are commonplace. They are taken for granted. The vast amount of social conditioning that has taken place by means of which a person maneuvers himself gracefully through the intricacies of these finely shaded social distinctions is seldom explicitly realized. Attention is paid only when a new social situation arises where the past social training of the person prevents him from making the necessary delicate interpretations of a given social signal and hence brings forth the "socially wrong" response.

In the factory, as in any social milieu, a process of social evaluation is constantly at work. From this process distinctions of "good" and "bad," "inferior" and "superior," arise. This process of evaluation is carried on with simple and ready generalizations by means of which values become attached to individuals and to groups performing certain tasks and operations. It assigns to a group of individuals performing such and such a task a particular rank in the established prestige scale.

Each work group becomes a carrier of social values. In industry with its extreme diversity of occupations there are a number of such groupings. Any noticeable similarity or difference, not only in occupation but also in age, sex, and nationality, can serve as a basis of social classification, as, for example, "married women," the "old-timer," the "white-collared" or clerical worker, the "foreign element." Each of these groups, too, has its own value system.

All the patterns of interaction that arise between individuals or between different groups can be graded according to the degree of intimacy involved in the relationship. Grades of intimacy or understanding can be arranged on a scale and expressed in terms of "social distance." Social distance measures differences of sentiment and interest which separate individuals or groups from one another. Between the president of a company and the elevator operator there is considerable social distance, more for example than between the foreman and the benchworker. Social distance is to social organization what physical distance is to physical space. However, physical and social distance do not necessarily coincide. Two people may be physically near but socially distant.

Just as each employee has a particular physical location, so he has a particular social place in the total social organization. But this place is not so rigidly fixed as in a caste system. In any factory there is considerable mobility or movement. Movement can occur in two ways: the individual may pass from one occupation to another occupation higher up in the prestige scale; or the prestige scale itself may change.

It is obvious that these scales of value are never completely accepted by all the groups in the social environment. The shop worker does not quite see why the office worker, for example, should have shorter hours of work than he has. Or the newcomer, whose efficiency on a particular job is about the same, but whose hourly rate is less than that of some old-timer, wonders why service should count so much. The management group, in turn, from the security of its social elevation, does not often understand what "all the fuss is about."

As was indicated by many of the studies,[1] any person who has achieved a certain rank in the prestige scale regards anything real or imaginary which tends to alter his status adversely as something unfair or unjust. It is apparent that any move on the part of the management may alter the existing social equilibrium to which the employee has grown accustomed and by means of which his status is defined. Im-

[1] See Chapter XVI.

mediately this disruption will be expressed in sentiments of resistance to the real or imagined alterations in the social equilibrium.

From this point of view it can be seen how every item and event in the industrial environment becomes an object of a system of sentiments. According to this way of looking at things, material goods, physical events, wages, hours of work, etc., cannot be treated as things in themselves. Instead they have to be interpreted as carriers of social value. The meanings which any person in an industrial organization assigns to the events and objects in his environment are often determined by the social situation in which the events and objects occur. The significance to an employee of a double-pedestal desk, of a particular kind of pencil, or of a handset telephone is determined by the social setting in which these objects appear. If people with double-pedestal desks supervise people with single-pedestal desks, then double-pedestal desks become symbols of status or prestige in the organization. As patterns of behavior become crystallized, every object in the environment tends to take on a particular social significance. It becomes easy to tell a person's social place in the organization by the objects which he wears and carries and which surround him. In these terms it can be seen how the introduction of a technical change may also involve for an individual or a group of individuals the loss of certain prestige symbols and, as a result, have a demoralizing effect.

From this point of view the behavior of no one person in an industrial organization, from the very top to the very bottom, can be regarded as motivated by strictly economic or logical considerations. Routine patterns of interaction involve strong sentiments. Each group in the organization manifests its own powerful sentiments. It is likely that sometimes the behavior of many staff specialists which goes under the name of "efficiency" is as much a manifestation of a very strong sentiment — the sentiment or desire to originate new combinations — as it is of anything strictly logical.

This point of view is far from the one which is frequently expressed, namely, that man is essentially an economic being carrying around with him a few noneconomic appendages. Rather, the point of view which has been expressed here is that noneconomic motives, interests, and processes, as well as economic, are fundamental in behavior in business, from the board of directors to the very last man in the organization. Man is not merely — in fact is very seldom — motivated by factors pertaining strictly to facts or logic. Sentiments are not merely things which man carries around with him as appendages. He cannot cast them off like a suit of clothes. He carries them with him wherever he goes. In business or elsewhere, he can hardly behave without expressing them. Moreover, sentiments do not exist in a social vacuum. They are the product of social behavior, of social interaction, of the fact that man lives his life as a member of different groups. Not only does man bring sentiments to the business situation because of his past experiences and conditioning outside of business, but also as a member of a specific local business organization with a particular social place in it he has certain sentiments expressing his particular relations to it.

According to this point of view, every social act in adulthood is an integrated response to both inner and outer stimuli. To each new concrete situation the adult brings his past "social conditioning." To the extent that this past social conditioning has prepared him to assimilate the new experience in the culturally accepted manner, he is said to be "adjusted." To the extent that his private or personal view of the situation is at variance with the cultural situation, the person is called "maladjusted."

THE FORMAL ORGANIZATION OF THE PLANT

The social organization of the industrial plant is in part formally organized. It is composed of a number of strata or levels which differentiate the benchworker from the skilled mechanic, the group chief from the department chief, and so on. These levels are well defined and all the formal orders, instructions, and compensations are addressed to them. All such factors taken together make up the formal organization of the plant. It includes the systems, policies, rules, and regulations of the plant which express what the relations of one person to another are supposed to be in order to achieve effectively the task of technical production. It prescribes the relations that are supposed to obtain within the human organization and between the human organization and the technical organization. In short, the patterns of human interrelations, as defined by the systems, rules, policies, and regulations of the company, constitute the formal organization.

The formal organization of an industrial plant has two purposes: it addresses itself to the economic purposes of the total enterprise; it concerns itself also with the securing of co-operative effort. The formal organization includes all the explicitly stated systems of control introduced by the company in order to achieve the economic purposes of the total enterprise and the effective contribution of the members of the organization to those economic ends.

The Informal Organization of the Plant

All the experimental studies pointed to the fact that there is some-thing more to the social organization than what has been formally recognized. Many of the actually existing patterns of human inter-action have no representation in the formal organization at all, and others are inadequately represented by the formal organization. This fact is frequently forgotten when talking or thinking about industrial situations in general. Too often it is assumed that the organization of a company corresponds to a blueprint plan or organization chart. Actually, it never does. In the formal organization of most companies little explicit recognition is given to many social distinctions residing in the social organization. The blueprint plans of a company show the functional relations between working units, but they do not express the distinctions of social distance, movement, or equilibrium previously described. The hierarchy of prestige values which tends to make the work of men more important than the work of women, the work of clerks more important than the work at the bench, has little represen-tation in the formal organization; nor does a blueprint plan ordinarily show the primary groups, that is, those groups enjoying daily face-to-face relations. Logical lines of horizontal and vertical co-ordination of functions replace the actually existing patterns of interaction between people in different social places. The formal organization cannot take account of the sentiments and values residing in the social organization by means of which individuals or groups of individuals are informally differentiated, ordered, and integrated. Individuals in their associations with one another in a factory build up personal relationships. They form into informal groups, in terms of which each person achieves a certain position or status. The nature of these informal groups is very important, as has been shown in the Relay Assembly Test Room and in the Bank Wiring Observation Room.

It is well to recognize that informal organizations are not "bad," as they are sometimes assumed to be. Informal social organization exists in every plant, and can be said to be a necessary prerequisite for effec-tive collaboration. Much collaboration exists at an informal level, and it sometimes facilitates the functioning of the formal organization. On the other hand, sometimes the informal organization develops in oppo-sition to the formal organization. The important consideration is, therefore, the relation that exists between formal and informal organizations.

To illustrate, let us consider the Relay Assembly Test Room and the

Bank Wiring Observation Room. These two studies offered an interesting contrast between two informal working groups; one situation could be characterized in almost completely opposite terms from the other. In the Relay Assembly Test Room, on the one hand, the five operators changed continuously in their rate of output up and down over the duration of the test, and yet in a curious fashion their variations in output were insensitive to many significant changes introduced during the experiment. On the other hand, in the Bank Wiring Observation Room output was being held relatively constant and there existed a hypersensitivity to change on the part of the worker — in fact, what could almost be described as an organized opposition to it.

It is interesting to note that management could draw from these studies two opposite conclusions. From the Relay Assembly Test Room experiment they could argue that the company can do almost anything it wants in the nature of technical changes without any perceptible effect on the output of the workers. From the Bank Wiring Observation Room they could argue equally convincingly that the company can introduce hardly any changes without meeting a pronounced opposition to them from the workers. To make this dilemma even more striking, it is only necessary to recall that the sensitivity to change in the one case occurred in the room where no experimental changes had been introduced whereas the insensitivity to change in the other case occurred in the room where the operators had been submitted to considerable experimentation. To settle this question by saying that in one case the situation was typical and in the other case atypical of ordinary shop conditions would be to beg the question, for the essential difference between the two situations would again be missed. It would ignore the social setting in which the changes occurred and the meaning which the workers themselves assigned to the changes.

Although in both cases there were certain informal arrangements not identical with the formal setup, the informal organization in one room was quite different from that in the other room, especially in its relation to the formal organization. In the case of the Relay Assembly Test Room there was a group, or informal organization, which could be characterized as a network of personal relations which had been developed in and through a particular way of working together; it was an organization which not only satisfied the wishes of its members but also worked in harmony with the aims of management. In the case of the Bank Wiring Observation Room there was an informal organization which could be characterized better as a set of practices and beliefs which its members had in common — practices and beliefs which at many points worked against the economic purposes of the company. In one case the relation between the formal and informal organization was one of compatibility; in the other case it was one of opposition. Or to put it in another way, collaboration in the Relay Assembly Test Room was at a much higher level than in the Bank Wiring Observation Room.

The difference between these two groups can be understood only by comparing the functions which their informal organizations performed for their members. The chief function of the informal group in the Bank Wiring Observation Room was to resist changes in their established routines of work or personal interrelations. This resistance to change, however, was not the chief function of the informal group in the Relay Assembly Test Room. It is true that at first the introduction of the planned changes in the test room, whether or not these changes were logically in the direction of improvement, was met with apprehension and feelings of uneasiness on the part of the operators. The girls in the beginning were never quite sure that they might not be victims of the changes.

In setting up the Relay Assembly Test Room with the object of studying the factors determining the efficiency of the worker, many of the methods and rules by means of which management tends to promote and maintain efficiency — the "bogey," not talking too much at work, etc. — were, in effect, abrogated. With the removal of this source of constraint and in a setting of heightened social significance (because many of the changes had differentiated the test room girls from the regular department and as a result had elevated the social status within the plant of each of the five girls) a new type of spontaneous social organization developed. Social conditions had been established which allowed the operators to develop their own values and objectives. The experimental conditions allowed the operators to develop openly social codes at work and these codes, unhampered by interference, gave a sustained meaning to their work. It was as if the experimenters had acted as a buffer for the operators and held their work situation steady while they developed a new type of social organization. With this change in the type of social organization there also developed a new attitude toward changes in their working environment. Toward many changes which constitute an unspecified threat in the regular work situation the operators became immune. What the Relay Assembly Test Room experiment showed was that when innovations are introduced carefully and with regard to the actual sentiments of the workers, the workers are likely to develop a spontaneous type of informal organization which will not only express more adequately their own values and significances but also is more likely to be in harmony with the aims of management.

Although all the studies of informal organization at the Hawthorne Plant were made at the employee level, it would be incorrect to assume that this phenomenon occurs only at that level. Informal organization appears at all levels, from the very bottom to the very top of the organization.[1] Informal organization at the executive level, just as at the work level, may either facilitate or impede purposive co-operation and communication. In either case, at all levels of the organization informal organizations exist as a necessary condition for collaboration. Without them formal organization could not survive for long. Formal and informal organizations are interdependent aspects of social interaction.

THE IDEOLOGICAL ORGANIZATION OF THE PLANT

There is one aspect of social organization in an industrial plant which cuts across both the formal and informal organizations: the systems of ideas and beliefs by means of which the values residing in the total organization are expressed and the symbols around which these values are organized. Both the formal and informal organizations of a plant have systems of ideas and beliefs. Some are more capable of logical and systematic expression than others. Those of the formal organization in general are more logically explicit and articulate than those of the informal organization, but they are not for that reason more powerful in their effects than those of the informal organization. The sentiments underlying the beliefs and ideas of informal organizations are often very powerful determinants of overt behavior.

Some of these systems of ideas and beliefs represent what the organization should be; that is, what the relations of people to one another should be or how people should behave. Some express the values of one part of the total organization, for each specialist tends to see the total organization from the point of view of the logic of his own specialty. Still others express the values residing in the interhuman relations of the different social groups involved.

Some of these ideas and beliefs represent more closely the actual situation than others. In all cases, however, they are abstractions from the concrete situation. In this respect they are to the concrete situation as maps are to the territories they represent.[2] And like maps these

---

[1] Barnard, C. I., *The Functions of the Executive*, Harvard University Press, 1938, pp. 223–4.

[2] This distinction has been borrowed from Korzybski, A., *Science and Sanity*, The Science Press Printing Co., New York, 1933.

abstractions may be either misleading or useful. They may be misleading because sometimes the person using them fails to realize they are representing only one part of the total organization. Sometimes in the minds of certain individuals these abstractions tend to become divorced from the social reality and, in effect, lead an independent existence.

In their studies the investigators frequently ran into these different systems of ideas and beliefs. Although they were never made the object of systematic study, three general systems which seemed to cling together could be discerned.

The Logic of Cost

In the industrial plant there is a certain set of ideas and beliefs by means of which the common economic purposes of the total organization are evaluated. This we shall call the "logic of cost." Although the logic of cost is applied mostly to the technical organization, it is also sometimes applied to the human organization. When applied to the human organization it is frequently done under the label of "efficiency."

The word "efficiency" is used in at least five different ways, two of which are rather vague and not clearly differentiated: (a) sometimes when talking about a machine it is used in a technical sense, as the relation between output and input; (b) sometimes when talking about a manufacturing process or operation it is used to refer to relative unit cost; (c) sometimes when referring to a worker it is used to indicate a worker's production or output in relation to a certain standard of performance; (d) sometimes its reference becomes more vague and it is used as practically synonymous with "logical co-ordination of function"; (e) sometimes it is used in the sense of "morale" or "social integration."

We shall use the term "logic of cost" to refer only to the system of ideas and beliefs which are explicitly organized around the symbol of "cost" and are applied to the human organization from this point of view.[1] This logic represents one of the values of the formal organization: the system of ideas and beliefs which relates the human organization to the task of technical production.

The Logic of Efficiency

Closely associated with the logic of cost is another system of ideas and beliefs by means of which the collaborative efforts of the members

[1] According to this definition, "logic of cost" does not conform to any single one of the above uses of the word "efficiency" but conforms most closely to a combination of (b) and (c).

of an organization are evaluated. This we shall call the "logic of efficiency." [1] This system of ideas and beliefs, which is organized around the symbol of "co-operation," represents another value of the formal organization. It is addressed primarily to the problem of how co-operation between individuals and groups of individuals can be effectively secured and is manifested in plans, such as wage payment plans, designed to promote collaboration among individuals.

A system of beliefs and ideas such as this is usually based upon certain assumptions about employee behavior. In the case of the wage payment plan in the Bank Wiring Observation Room, for example, it was assumed that the employee was a logical being and therefore could see the system, as its creators saw it, as a logical, coherent scheme which he could use to his economic advantage. It was assumed that, given the opportunity, the employee would act in such a way as to obtain the maximum of earnings consistent with his physical capacity. Carrying this basic assumption still further, it followed that the slower workers, who would interfere with the logical functioning of that system, would be disciplined by the faster workers and that daywork claims would be kept at a minimum. It was assumed that the division of labor would permit the employees to increase production through specialization. The possibility that division of labor might result in social stratification, which in turn might generate nonlogical forces that would interfere with the logical functioning of that system, was unforeseen. Practically every aspect of the wage plan followed from the basic assumption that nothing would interfere with the economic motives. It is such assumptions as these that go to make up the "logic of efficiency."

The Logic of Sentiments

There is another system of ideas and beliefs which we shall give the label "the logic of sentiments." It represents the values residing in the interhuman relations of the different groups within the organization. Examples of what is meant here are the arguments employees give which center around the "right to work," "seniority," "fairness," "the living wage." This logic, as its name implies, is deeply rooted in sentiment and feeling.

Management and Employee Logics

At first glance it might seem that the logics of cost and efficiency are the logics of management groups, whereas the logic of sentiments is the

[1] The "logic of efficiency" conforms most closely to a combination of uses (c), (d), and (e) of the word "efficiency" as given in the previous section.

logic of employee groups. Although in one sense this may be accurate. in another sense it is an oversimplification. All groups within the industry participate in these different logics, although some participate to a greater or less extent than others. One has only to interview a supervisor or executive to see that he has a logic of sentiments which is expressing the values residing in his personal interrelations with other supervisors or executives. Employee groups, moreover, are not unknown to apply the logic of cost.

However, it is incorrect to assume that these different logics have the same significance to different groups in an industrial plant. The logics of cost and efficiency express the values of the formal organization; the logic of sentiments expresses the values of the informal organization. To management groups and technical specialists the logics of cost and efficiency are likely to be more important than they are to employee groups. In form the logic of sentiments expressed by an executive is indistinguishable from that expressed by a worker, but in content it is quite different. As anyone knows who has had industrial experience, much time is spent in industry in debating the relative weights attaching to the logics of cost, efficiency, and sentiments when they are applied to a particular concrete situation.

DEFINITION OF TERMS

For convenience, it may be well to summarize the different parts into which the industrial plant as a social system can be divided and the way in which the labels attaching to them will be used in the two final chapters. The following outline will help the reader to see the levels of abstraction of the different parts of the system:

1 Technical Organization
2 Human Organization
  2.1 Individual
  2.2 Social Organization
    2.21 Formal Organization
      2.211 Patterns of Interaction
      2.212 Systems of Ideas and Beliefs (Ideological Organization)
        2.2121 Logic of Cost
        2.2122 Logic of Efficiency
    2.22 Informal Organization
      2.221 Patterns of Interaction
      2.222 Systems of Ideas and Beliefs (Ideological Organization)
        2.2221 Logic of Sentiments

1 The term "technical organization" will refer to the logical and technical organization of materials, tools, machines, and finished products, including all those physical items related to the task of technical production.

2 The term "human organization" will refer, on the one hand, to the concrete individual with his rich personal and social background and, on the other hand, to the intricate pattern of social relations existing among the various individuals and groups within the plant.

2.1 The term "individual" will refer to the sentiments and values which the person is bringing to the work situation because of his past social conditioning and present social situation outside of the plant; i.e., the past and present patterns of interaction in which he has participated or is participating outside of work.

2.2 The term "social organization" will refer to the actual patterns of interaction existing within and between employee groups, supervisory groups, and management groups in a plant here and now. It will include those relations that remain at a common human level (friendships, antagonisms, etc.), those that have been built up into larger social configurations (social codes, customs, traditions, routines, and associated ideas and beliefs), as well as those patterns of relations formally prescribed by the rules, regulations, practices, and policies of the company.

2.21 The term "formal organization" will refer to those patterns of interaction prescribed by the rules and regulations of the company as well as to the policies which prescribe the relations that obtain, or are supposed to obtain, within the human organization and between the human organization and the technical organization.

2.22 The term "informal organization" will refer to the actual personal interrelations existing among the members of the organization which are not represented by, or are inadequately represented by, the formal organization.

2.212 and 2.222 The term "ideological organization" will refer to the systems of ideas and beliefs by means of which the values of both the formal and informal aspects of the social organization are expressed and the symbols around which these values are organized.

2.2121 The term "logic of cost" will refer to that system of ideas and beliefs by means of which the common economic purposes of the total organization are evaluated.

2.2122 The term "logic of efficiency" will refer to that system of ideas and beliefs by means of which the collaborative efforts of the members of the organization are evaluated.

2.2221 The term "logic of sentiments" will refer to that system of ideas and beliefs which expresses the values residing in the interhuman relations of the different groups within the plant.

A Condition of Equilibrium

The parts of the industrial plant as a social system are interrelated and interdependent. Any changes in one part of the social system are accompanied by changes in other parts of the system. The parts of the system can be conceived of as being in a state of equilibrium, such that "if a small (not too great) modification different from that which will otherwise occur is impressed on the system, a reaction will at once appear tending toward the conditions that would have existed if the modification had not been impressed." [1]

Some parts of the system can change more rapidly than others. The technical organization can change more rapidly than the social organization; the formal organization can change more rapidly than the informal; the systems of beliefs and ideas can change more rapidly than the patterns of interaction and associated sentiments, of which these beliefs and ideas are an expression. In the disparity in the rates of change possible there exists a precondition for unbalance which may manifest itself in many forms.

In their studies the investigators identified two such possibilities of unbalance. One was the disparity in the rates of change possible in the technical organization, on the one hand, and the social organization, on the other. This condition was manifested in the workers' behavior by distrust and resistance to change. This resistance was expressed whenever changes were introduced too rapidly or without sufficient consideration of their social implications; in other words, whenever the workers were being asked to adjust themselves to new methods or systems which seemed to them to deprive their work of its customary social significance. In such situations it was evident that the social codes, customs, and routines of the worker could not be accommodated to the technical innovations introduced as quickly as the innovations themselves, in the form of new machines and processes, could be made. The codes, customs, and traditions of the worker are not the product of logic but are based on deeply rooted sentiments. Not only is any alteration of the existing social organization to which the worker has grown accustomed likely to produce sentiments of resistance to the

[1] For a discussion of equilibrium, see Pareto, V., *The Mind and Society*, Harcourt, Brace & Co., New York, 1935, pp. 1435–1442. The quotation used above is Dr. L. J. Henderson's adaptation of Pareto's definition of equilibrium.

change, but too rapid interference is likely to lead to feelings of frustration and an irrational exasperation with technical change in any form.

Another possibility of unbalance lies in the relation of the ideological organization to the actual work situation. The logics of the ideological organization express only some of the values of the social organization. They frequently fail to take into account not only the feelings and sentiments of people within the plant but also the spontaneous informal social groups which form at all levels of the organization. Thus they tend to become divorced from the concrete situation and to lead an independent existence. As a result of failing to distinguish the human situation as it is from the way it is formally and logically represented to be, many human problems are stated either in terms of the perversities of human nature or in terms of logical defects in the formal organization. The facts of social organization are ignored, and consequently the result in terms of diagnosis or remedy is bound to be inadequate.

It became clear to the investigators that the limits of human collaboration are determined far more by the informal than by the formal organization of the plant. Collaboration is not wholly a matter of logical organization. It presupposes social codes, conventions, traditions, and routine or customary ways of responding to situations. Without such basic codes or conventions, effective work relations are not possible. In the chapters that follow, the implications of this point of view for management and personnel practice will be considered.

CHAPTER XXV

A RESTATEMENT OF THE HUMAN PROBLEMS
OF MANAGEMENT

In the preceding chapter an industrial organization as a social system was outlined. In this chapter the application of this point of view to the human problems of management will be considered. The function of management, stated in its most general terms, can be described as that of maintaining the social system of the industrial plant in a state of equilibrium such that the purposes of the enterprise are realized. To achieve this objective, management has two major functions: (1) the function of securing the common economic purpose of the total enterprise; and (2) the function of maintaining the equilibrium of the social organization so that individuals through contributing their services to this common purpose obtain personal satisfactions that make them willing to co-operate.[1] These functions are interrelated and interdependent. Failure to achieve the first objective will in time make co-operation of any kind unnecessary. Failure to obtain satisfaction from co-operation will prevent in time the effective achievement of the common economic purpose of the organization. If the enterprise is to survive, the effective performance of these two functions is necessary. This is the major problem of management.

A Need for Reformulating Human Problems

In terms of the concept of an industrial organization as a social system many of the human problems of management can be reformulated. A traditional statement of these problems frequently distorts the actual human situation in the industrial plant. The workers, supervisors, or executives are often considered apart from their social setting and personal history and are treated as essentially "economic men." Simple cause and effect analysis of their behavior is substituted for the richer situational context in which their lives are lived and in which the relation of mutual interdependence obtains. As a result, abstractions are treated as facts and an atmosphere of "misplaced concreteness" [2] results. This point can be illustrated by the early research studies.

[1] This distinction is similar to Barnard's distinction between the effective and efficient purposes of a co-operative system, op. cit., pp. 55–61.

[2] See Whitehead, A. N., *Science and the Modern World*, Macmillan, New York, 1925, p. 82.

Fatigue

The results of the early experiments in the Relay Assembly Test Room showed clearly that fatigue, in the sense of an organic unbalance, was not a major problem among the workers at Hawthorne engaged in semirepetitive tasks such as those observed in the test and observation rooms. It became clear that the term "fatigue," in its popular sense, did not mean the same thing in each instance. Because there is a word, there is not necessarily one thing to which it refers. Instead of one fatigue, there are "fatigues." Some are "organic"; some are not. Moreover, "feelings of fatigue" can be associated with different kinds of unbalances arising from different kinds of interferences. From these observations the investigators concluded that in each case it is necessary to describe the particular human situation, and the interaction of those factors (organic, personal, or social) making for or against balance. By lumping together in one class under "fatigue" all cases of unbalance which had similar symptoms, the investigators had not only failed in the early experimental work to discriminate among the different kinds of interferences but they had failed to see that the preponderance of interferences which occur in modern industry are not solely physiological.

The investigators made many studies of the relation between output rate and fatigue. Output curves arranged in different ways were carefully examined. Some of these output curves behaved as "fatigue curves"; others did not. To be more exact, some of these curves varied in the manner it is commonly understood that such curves should vary when work is having a direct physiological effect on the behavior of the worker; the majority did not. The interesting thing, however, was that many of both types of curves, when examined more minutely, tended to reflect factors not ordinarily associated with fatigue. In some instances (as in the cases of M_5 and W_7) they reflected the personal situation of the operator; in some instances (as in the Bank Wiring Observation Room) they reflected the social control of work behavior; in some instances (as in the case of Operator 3 in the Relay Assembly Test Room) they tended to form a work pattern unique for a particular individual — a pattern which continued irrespective of the different work conditions imposed. These results indicated quite clearly the danger of using only output data as a test for fatigue. Although such a use may be fruitful in the case of heavy muscular work where organic unbalance is induced, it has little relevance for those cases of work where it is organically possible to maintain a steady state.

The investigators concluded that an inadequate conception of the many factors affecting work rate leads to an overemphasis on fatigue and associated organic and physical factors. As a result, the worker is regarded as essentially a physiological machine hindered and limited by his organic make-up and his physical surroundings. Although, to be sure, there are cases of organic unbalance in industry, these cases do not constitute a major problem for industrial organizations where heavy muscular work is not involved in most of the occupations.

Rest Pauses

If fatigue is not a primary factor limiting output in most repetitive or semirepetitive tasks, how can the beneficial effects of rest pauses found by many investigators and substantiated by the results of the Relay Assembly Test Room be explained? As long as the investigators conceived of rest pauses as having only physical effects, it was, of course, difficult to explain their beneficial results other than in terms of a reduction of fatigue. But once the social meaning to the worker of his environment was appreciated, it became clear that the beneficial effects of rest pauses could be explained equally well in terms of their social function. From this point of view, it could be seen that the introduction of rest pauses reflected an interest on the part of management in the health and well-being of its workers. Moreover, rest pauses allowed the workers to get together and to converse. They offered relaxation and relief from tension. For the time being, at least, the "logic of efficiency" was in abeyance and the workers were permitted normal social interaction. Unlike many of the changes which are introduced to improve efficiency, rest pauses, if properly assigned and administered, appeal to the employees' sentiments of individual integrity. It is to this total situation that the workers react favorably.

According to this interpretation, the meaning of rest pauses rather than the rest pauses in themselves is of chief importance. Their meaning is largely determined by the social setting in which they occur. If the employee thinks that rest pauses have been introduced as a disguised form of "speeding up" work, he will meet the innovation with apprehension and resistance. If, on the other hand, he feels that they express a real and sincere interest on the part of management in his well-being and health, and the total social situation reinforces this belief, he is likely to respond to them positively and with a heightened interest in his task.

This is the most tenable explanation of the results of the experiments in the Relay Assembly Test Room. At first the girls were apprehensive of the different changes introduced. Their uncertainties were expressed in different ways: Could they make up for the time lost? If they did earn more money, would they receive it? Were the changes being made in order to increase output? As soon as their apprehensions were allayed, however, a more loyal and co-operative group of employees could not be found.

Physical Conditions of Work

Although all the studies showed very clearly that conditions of work cannot be treated as things in themselves, none of them demonstrated this more conclusively than the Relay Assembly Test Room. In this study it will be remembered that the success of the experiment depended upon "keeping co-operative" (i.e., constant) the attitudes of the operators toward the experimental changes introduced. In spite of all attempts to control or to keep these psychological factors constant, however, they persistently crept in to modify the results. Instead of being a "constant" the attitudes of the operators were the major variables in the situation. In comparison to them, the physiological effects of the changes in working conditions were minor. After two years of experimentation, the investigators concluded that for their purposes it was not useful to conceive of work behavior as essentially a response to physical conditions. Changes of physical circumstance were not significantly responsible in themselves for variability of work behavior as judged by output rate. Variations in work behavior could be related far more closely to variations in personal attitude toward the changes introduced. The notion that a simple change in working conditions would be followed by a simple response in output, apart from the attitude of the workers toward the change, was consequently abandoned. In this statement there is, of course, no implication that alterations in environment produce no alterations in response. It means that in the situations studied at Hawthorne the attitude of the workers was such an important variable that those changes in working conditions which were introduced did not produce by themselves any predictable effect capable of measurement in terms of output.

A similar conclusion with regard to the verbal behavior of employees was reached in the interviewing program. In the beginning the investigators hoped to get "facts" by means of which they could improve working conditions. Instead, a large part of the interview material was composed of an inextricable mixture of fact and sentiment. This kind of material could not be used in the simple manner originally conceived. Further study showed that the likes and dislikes of employees often have to be treated as symptoms or indicators of a personal or social situation which must be studied further to be understood. They found that expressions of sentiment have properties different from those of facts. Strictly speaking, they are neither true nor false. They refer to the significant personal and social situation of the individual, and apart from such a context they are meaningless.

Repetitive Work and Monotony

There is a popular conception that the worker through minute division of labor and specialization has become increasingly an automaton. It is claimed that the repetitive and semirepetitive tasks which result from the mechanization of work offer little opportunity for the expression of his skills, initiative, and "instincts" of workmanship. He loses his interest in work, and as a result boredom and monotony ensue. The research offered no evidence in favor of this conception. Most of the tests were conducted with workers engaged in semiautomatic tasks in which boredom, according to some, is most likely to appear. Yet there was little evidence, from a study of either their work behavior or verbal behavior, that monotony in any simple sense could characterize their responses to the work.

Early in the interviewing phase of the inquiry the investigators came to the conclusion that monotony, like fatigue, is a term which can be applied to many different kinds of personal situations and that the attitude of workers toward repetitive work cannot be covered by any one term such as monotony. Monotony, or boredom, is only one of many responses to work. Moreover, like many other expressions of dissatisfaction with work, it is a response to a total situation which includes not only the job but also the worker, with his own peculiar hopes and expectations, in relation to the collective life of the factory and the wider community. Repetitive work is only a part of this total situation and not the total situation itself.

It became evident to the investigators that a study of total personal situations in relation to repetitive work was the more important problem. For many workers engaged in repetitive or semirepetitive tasks the point of proficiency is soon reached, at which time the amount of attention the job demands of the employee falls short of the amount which the operator is capable of giving. When it is no longer possible for the worker to elaborate or change his job, he can either switch his attention to other things in his immediate environment or indulge in daydreaming or revery. In the latter case the social situation at work is likely to determine the character of the revery. Where the work situation is such that it does not allow the worker's preoccupations or attention to be socially expressed or directed by conversation or by other activities, an ideal setting is created for the development of morbid preoccupations. He is likely to spend his time brooding about his personal problems or his relations with his co-workers and supervisors. Where the social situation is such that it does allow for the social expression of preoccupation, much brooding about factors incidental to the worker's personal history can be alleviated.

Later studies of the social organization of work suggested a consequence from the mechanization of labor which is seldom mentioned by those who contrast the modern mechanized worker with the vanished craftsman. The differences between the modern worker and the old-time shoemaker or carpenter, for example, are generally discussed in terms of differences in the amount of skill, intelligence, ingenuity, or interest entailed. None of these generalizations, however, has received much support from the Hawthorne studies. In modern industry there are jobs which call for as much skill and intelligence as those of previous days. Moreover, it is generally agreed that repetitive work was not unknown before the industrial revolution. There is, however, one difference which should be mentioned. It is very doubtful if anyone outside of the Western Electric Company knows what Relay E901 represents, what a bank wiring equipment looks like, or just what in skill and training the performance of these jobs entails. Modern industry has created literally thousands of such new occupations, for which there exist no occupational names that have any social significance outside of the particular industry, factory, or even department, in many cases. As a consequence, the wages attaching to these jobs become the most important outer symbol of their social value in the community. This in part may account for the worker's preoccupations over wages and wage differentials, and also may account for complaints of monotony in work.

Complaints and Grievances

The interviewing studies revealed very clearly that the locus of many employee complaints cannot be confined to a single cause, and that whenever things are unsatisfactory to the worker his dissatisfaction is in most cases the general effect of a complex situation. In place of a simple cause and effect analysis of human situations, this way of looking at things substituted the notion of a number of factors in a relation of mutual dependence. Overt or verbal behavior at work was no longer regarded as an effect of some simple cause (fatigue, monotony, or supervision) but as the resultant of the interaction of a number of variables making for or against equilibrium. The problem of the investigators now became one of studying the different kinds of unbalance which occur in the worker, and which are expressed as complaints and grievances, as well as the different kinds of interferences which may induce the unbalance.

It was found that a very common form of unbalance in the employee manifests itself in obsessive thinking and a diminished capacity for work. The interferences inducing this unbalance arise from the social conditions of work. Where social conditions of work are such as to make it difficult for the employee to identify his task with a socially meaningful function, he is liable to obsessive response and diminished capacity for work. This discovery had a marked effect on the direction of the inquiry. No longer were the experimenters solely interested in factors of personal history as inducing personal unbalance; their attention was redirected to the immediate work situation. This time, however, they were not so much concerned with items in the material environment as with the social environment of work.

From examining the social environment within the factory, it became evident that the worker is far from being an isolated individual at work. He is in constant association with other workers and his superiors; he is a member of a particular social group. These social groups are related to one another in various ways. The individuals in the various groups and the various groups themselves are bound together by certain codes of behavior. These codes and customs define the attitudes of the workers to one another, to their supervisors, and to the company as a whole. The investigators were discovering the phenomenon of "social organization." They concluded that both the behavior and beliefs of the members of an industrial plant were at any given time in a relation of mutual dependence to a system of sentiments expressing their social organization. Many of their complaints had to be understood in terms of disturbances of this social equilibrium. It became clear that what the experimenters had been observing in the different test rooms and in the interviewing program was essentially neither logical nor irrational behavior. It was essentially social behavior.

Wage Incentives and Wage Incentive Systems

The results from the different inquiries provided considerable material for the study of financial incentive. None of the results, however, gave the slightest substantiation to the theory that the worker is primarily motivated by economic interest. The evidence indicated that the efficacy of a wage incentive is so dependent on its relation to other factors that it is impossible to separate it out as a thing in itself having an independent effect. The studies provided examples of a number of situations in which the wage incentive had either lost its power to motivate or functioned differently than is frequently assumed.

(1) In the interviews, for example, most of the dissatisfaction with wages implied that the employee is just as much concerned with wage differentials, that is, the relation of his wages to the wages of other workmen, as with the absolute amount of his wages. Complaints arise when wage differentials do not express appropriately the differences in social significance which the different jobs have to the employees themselves. Many workers who expressed a grievance about wages went on to say that the reason for their complaint was not that they were dissatisfied with their own wages but that "it isn't fair."

(2) In the Bank Wiring Observation Room a wage plan particularly designed to appeal to the employees' monetary interests failed to work as it should because it was not in line with the dominant social values of the situation.

(3) In the Mica Splitting Test Room output dropped in the last year of the experiment when the operators first began to fear that the business depression would lead to a reduction of available work. Logically it might have been expected that in this situation the monetary incentive would have been at the peak of its efficacy. The operators should have wanted to earn as much money as they could before they were laid off. However, output dropped. The wage incentive in the face of these doubts and fears had lost its power to motivate.

In this connection there was no more interesting experiment than the Second Relay Assembly Group. This experiment, it will be remembered, was designed to test the effect of a wage incentive. In the Second Relay Assembly Group, unlike the Relay Assembly Test Room, the only change made was in the direction of an increased financial incentive. This was done in the same way that it had been accomplished in the Relay Assembly Test Room, not by changing the wage incentive system in itself, the system still remaining group piecework, but by reducing the size of the group. The operators were not segregated in a separate room but remained in the regular department. They were supposed to be a "group" in name only. A closer scrutiny, however, revealed a new element, which had not been considered important at the time. Actually the operators had not been left in their respective positions at different benches; they had been moved to one common bench in the regular department in order to facilitate the keeping of records.

When the change was made, the investigators were not alert to its social consequences. It seemed of minor importance inasmuch as supervision had not been altered by the move, but the investigators failed to take into account the competitive attitude which existed in the regular department toward the Relay Assembly Test Room operators. When the girls were moved together to form the Second Relay Assembly Group this rivalry was brought to a focus. Their output rose rapidly. This in turn jeopardized the security of their fellow workers in the regular department, and processes were set in motion which ultimately led to the discontinuance of the study. This experiment, designed to test the effect of a single variable, succeeded only in exposing a most complex social situation. Conclusions about the efficacy of a wage incentive drawn from it, unrelated to the basic social situation, would have been entirely misleading.

Efficient Work Patterns

Many investigators hold it as self-evident that much ineffectiveness at the work level results from a poor logical and technical organization of work and that, left to his own resources, the worker does not build up the best work patterns and routines (i.e., from a logical viewpoint). According to this point of view there is much random movement and wasted effort which needs to be better directed. The concept of "fatigue" helps to give a "scientific" justification to this belief. If the work can be made easier, it will be less fatiguing. The concept of the "economic man" also helps to give it sanction. If the worker can be made more efficient, he can earn more money.

There is no question that much of value to both the work and the worker has come from the movement to secure better work patterns and routines. However, as the Hawthorne studies progressed, the investigators grew more convinced that the problem was not quite so simple as this logic represented it to be. Many of their observations indicated that this conception of work behavior failed to consider adequately the informal organization and the logic of sentiments. Sometimes attempts to make the employees more efficient unwittingly deprive them of those very things which give meaning and significance to their work. Their established routines of work, their cultural traditions of craftsmanship, their personal interrelations — all these are at the mercy of "logical" innovations. As a result, they are able neither to retain their former traditions and codes nor to evolve new ones of any duration.

THREE MAJOR HUMAN PROBLEMS OF MANAGEMENT

Although more "problems," as traditionally stated, could be considered in terms of the findings of the research, the conclusions reached would not be very different. The results all pointed to the need for a reformulation of such problems in terms of the concrete human situations in the plant. Too often the human problems of an industrial organization are discussed in terms which ignore the social realities of the situation. It was the opinion of the investigators that the research work reported in this book revealed three general human problems of major significance to management, in terms of which many of the subjects discussed and implied in the early part of this chapter could better be stated. These are:

(1) Problems of change in the social structure.[1]
(2) Problems of control and communication.
(3) Problems in the adjustment of the individual to the structure.

These three problems are interrelated and may be regarded as subheadings under the general problem of maintaining equilibrium in the internal organization of the plant. The manner in which they relate to this more general problem will be clarified in what follows.

PROBLEMS OF CHANGE IN THE SOCIAL STRUCTURE

We may think of an industrial organization as a social structure through which individuals are moving in time and place. The social structure itself is relatively stable and is not greatly altered by the movement of individuals through it. Certain parts of the structure, of course, change more rapidly than others, but if these changes are not too rapid, the equilibrium remains fairly stable.

In industry there are likely to be changes in parts of the structure which have consequences for the general problem of internal balance. That there is such a relationship will readily be seen when it is understood that the social structure includes all the intergroup relations within the company. In these relations there are processes which make for differentiation as well as for integration and solidarity, and the character of these relations has a direct bearing upon the manner in

---

[1] The term "social structure" will be used in place of "social organization" when we wish to emphasize particularly the stable character of the state of equilibrium which obtains among the interdependent parts of the social system.

which these various groups function together or collaborate. Any change in the structure, therefore, is likely to have consequences in terms of the existing equilibrium among these various groups as well as within each group. Two kinds of change in particular may be specified. These are: (1) technical change, and (2) change in formal organization.

Technical Change

Perhaps one of the most important ways in which the internal equilibrium of a company may be disturbed is through the introduction of technical change. In every organization there are groups of technologists and specialists whose attention is focused on the general problem of securing the effectiveness of tools and machines for the purpose of manufacturing a better product at the same or lower cost. These specialists are constantly seeking new methods and new combinations for improving the effectiveness of the technical organization. As a result, this aspect of the total organization is subject to frequent and rapid change.

These changes in technical organization, of course, have consequences in terms of the social structure of a concern. They frequently result in the social dislocation of individuals and groups and disrupt the interpersonal relations which tend to give these individuals and groups their feelings of security and integrity.

A general management problem, therefore, is that of determining the rates at which change may be introduced without disrupting the equilibrium of the social organization. Theoretically, at least, there may be a "best" rate of change for each organization; that is to say, a rate of change which will not result in serious unbalance in the structure. In practice, however, there is a continuous problem of ascertaining empirically, and keeping in touch with, the nature of the social equilibrium, on the one hand, and the rates at which change may be introduced without upsetting this equilibrium, on the other.

In addition to the general problem already indicated, there is the important problem of determining when the change should be introduced. The timing of a change may be very significant depending upon a number of considerations, such as whether business is expanding or contracting, the general state of morale within the plant at a given time, and the precise manner in which the change will affect specific individuals and groups.

The problem of how change should be introduced is equally important. In considering this problem the sentiments of the people affected are of primary importance. If the change is introduced abruptly and without sufficient consideration of these sentiments, there may be a reaction of resistance to the change, which in turn may have serious consequences not only for the management-employee relationship but also for the task of technical production. In introducing technical change, therefore, it is important: first, that the sentiments of the people directly affected be determined; secondly, that the sentiments of other people related to them be determined; thirdly, that problems arising from the new pattern of interpersonal relations be anticipated and understood; and finally, that an understandable and acceptable explanation of the change be made before it is introduced.

Change in the Formal Organization

The problems of making changes in formal organizations are similar to those involved in making technical changes and the same considerations apply to them. One of the major considerations in making changes in the formal organization is that of ascertaining the extent to which the formal organization is an accurate representation of the actual situation. If the informal organization of the concern is quite different from the way it is represented to be in the formal organization, then of course changes in the latter will have unpredictable consequences unless the informal organization be accurately determined beforehand.

A change in formal organization may, of course, have serious consequences for the entire social structure within the company. Typical of such changes are: (1) changes in the supervisory structure, such as increase or decrease in the number of levels of supervision; (2) changes in the functional interrelations among various groups, such as a change from a functional organization to a straight-line organization; (3) changes in the relations between major groups, such as office and shop; (4) changes in the wage structure; and (5) changes in policies and practices.

In summary, it may be said that changes in the technical and in the formal organization of the company are intimately related to the general problem of maintaining internal balance. These changes cannot be regarded as occurring in isolation from the total situation. They are intimately related to the social organization of the company and have profound consequences not only in terms of the effectiveness with which the organization as a whole functions but also in terms of employee relations.

Problems of Control and Communication

The formal structure of the industrial plant specifies the manner in which control shall be exercised. In general, this function of control is performed by the supervisory structure and by staff organizations such as accounting, cost control, personnel, and other specialist groups. The basic problem in all of these control agencies may be designated as that of communication. The problems of communication vary depending upon which group is being considered. A detailed description of the problems peculiar to each of these agencies is beyond the scope of the present discussion. For our purposes we shall treat problems of communication within the supervisory structure as one general subject and then will comment upon some of the problems of communication which seem to be characteristic of the other agencies of control.

Transmission of Accurate Information through the Supervisory Structure

In order to exercise intelligent control, the management of a concern must be continually provided with accurate information as to the manner in which the total organization is functioning. This is one of the major functions of the supervisory hierarchy and depends for its successful functioning upon the accurate transmission of information down through the structure, on the one hand, and of information pertaining to the work level and successive levels of supervision up through the structure, on the other. The problems involved in transmitting information from the top to the bottom are fairly well recognized, but some of the problems arising in communication from the bottom to the top have not been so clearly indicated; consequently, we shall be chiefly concerned with the discussion of these latter problems.

That important problems may arise in the process of communication up through the supervisory structure was clearly shown in some of the studies which have been reported, particularly the Bank Wiring Observation Room. There it was seen that the picture of the work situation obtained by the investigators as a result of their detailed observations was in many respects quite different from what management assumed it to be. It was seen that many controls, particularly the wage payment structure, failed to function in accordance with the logic upon which such controls were based. Yet this disparity between the actual situation and the way it was theoretically supposed to be was not clearly understood by management. In this study it was also seen that the employees had many sentiments and feelings which, to a considerable extent, controlled their work behavior. These sentiments pertained to such things as seniority, nationality, social responsibility, occupation, and position in the group, and extended to many factors in the immediate physical and social environment which were symbolic of the social status the individual had attained. It was also seen that management frequently had to act in ignorance of these sentiments. The supervisory structure did not function to communicate facts of this kind upward, and as a result there was always the danger that management practices and procedures might collide with the sentiments of the employees and result in many unforeseen consequences.

The information which flows through the supervisory structure should theoretically be an accurate representation of the situation. At successive steps in the supervisory structure a selection process takes place. Some of the information is pertinent only to the first level and not to higher levels; consequently, such information stops at the first level. The remaining information is transmitted to the next higher level, where another selection process takes place, and so on up to the highest level. In order to function effectively there must be a sorting-out process; otherwise, the top levels of supervision would be swamped with details and would be forced to make decisions which could be better made by supervisors lower in the organization.

In carrying out its function of communication it is important that the proper selection of information be made at each level in the supervisory structure; otherwise, erroneous impressions of the actual situation will be conveyed. If the first appraisal of a situation is inaccurate, then a distorted picture of the situation is transmitted all through the structure. It is important, therefore, that an accurate representation of the situation be made in the initial stages of communication, and that at successive stages useful simplification of the information be made for transmission to higher levels. It is impossible for a top executive to know all the facts or to comprehend fully all the details of every situation. He has to depend on a useful and accurate simplification of the situation which will enable him to grasp the major variables without becoming lost in detail.

Inadequate Orientation of Supervisors

There are various ways in which the channels of communication can become blocked. Two possible difficulties in the supervisory organization may be mentioned:

One of the common sources of faulty communication results from an inadequate orientation of the supervisor to his situation. Inasmuch as the supervisor's primary responsibility is to see that his organization fulfills its technical purpose satisfactorily, he is likely sometimes to appraise his situation in rather narrow terms. He may be able to communicate with his superiors in terms of the usual criteria of efficiency but he may not be able to comprehend or communicate explicitly the informal social processes within his group. In appraising his situation he may focus his attention upon only a few of the variables in the situation and ignore the others. Or again, he may make an adequate statement of the various factors operating in his situation but may not see their interrelations, with the result that what he considers as being of primary importance is actually of secondary importance. It can be readily seen that any failure on the part of the supervisor to make adequate discriminations in fact or adequate interpretations of the facts selected will automatically lead to a faulty communication of the actual situation.

Discrepancy between Formal and Informal Organization

A second important problem in communication relates to the nature of the informal organization of the work group and the extent to which the informal organization is at variance with the formal organization. Any marked discrepancy between the actual situation and the formal organization may place the supervisor in an awkward position. This problem was clearly seen in the Bank Wiring Observation Room. In order to maintain his own position the supervisor in such situations may tend to convey an inaccurate picture of the actual situation to his superiors. This possibility, of course, is not confined to the first level of supervision. This problem, as well as that relating to the orientation of the supervisor, may occur at any level in the supervisory structure.

Even though no marked disparity exists between the formal and the informal organizations, similar problems in communication may appear. A defective relation between a first-line supervisor and his employees may prevent the supervisor from obtaining an intimate understanding of many problems in the actual work situation. Similar difficulties arise when the relations between any two levels of supervision are unsatisfactory. In addition, any feeling of insecurity on the part of a supervisor may induce him to edit everything that he passes up the line.

From the foregoing discussion it will be seen that many problems of communication arise from the relations which exist between supervisors and employees and between the various levels of the supervisory structure. The problems arising in this system of relations are sometimes difficult to detect and to diagnose. Furthermore, they are exceedingly difficult to correct in any simple, direct manner. These are essentially problems in human interrelations.

Limitations of Specialist Logics

As has been pointed out, the administrator in exercising control relies not only on the supervisory organization but also upon the services of specialized control agencies. The general problem in considering the effectiveness with which these control agencies perform their functions of communication would seem to be that of how accurately the specialized logics of these agencies represent the total human organization. Each of these specialists is assigned a specific function and occupies a certain position in the total company structure. In performing his function the specialist tends to select from the total work situation only those aspects for which he is functionally responsible. The engineer is likely to be oriented to engineering problems and not to the total organization as such. The cost accountant is oriented primarily to those aspects of the total situation which can be included under the symbols of cost. The same is true with all other specialist groups. Each expert tends to appraise the work situation in terms of his specialty, which means that some part of the total situation is left out. As a consequence, the total group situation is never accurately represented as a functioning whole and the specific relations which obtain between the various specialist functions and the total organization are frequently ignored or inaccurately stated. Some of these specialist agencies fail to take systematic account of the social organization, particularly that part of the social organization which is informal. This means that the control which is exercised by management tends to be based upon an incomplete analysis of the entire situation, and unless that part which is ignored is intuitively understood and taken into account by management the control exercised is likely to be inadequate.

Another aspect of this problem can best be described as the "emotional identification" which is likely to occur between the specialist and his "logics." Theoretically, the logics in terms of which these specialists perform their functions are merely abstractions from the concrete situation. If they are so regarded by the specialist and their useful limitations of application clearly understood, no difficulties arise. Instead, however, these logics sometimes tend to become dominant in the thinking of the person who uses them, and he comes to regard them as being "right" for all occasions. As a result of this emotional identification with certain abstractions an experimental attitude is not achieved. Any evidence not in keeping with these systems of logic comes to be regarded as "wrong" and the possibility of understanding is thereby diminished. This emotional attachment of the person to his logic comes about in part because of the fact that by exercising his logic the specialist maintains his position in the social organization; consequently, any threat to it is interpreted as a threat to his integrity and security. The logic thereby becomes not merely a tool for investigation but also a weapon of defense.

In summary, it is apparent that the successful functioning of the agencies for control established in the management structure depends upon two factors: (1) the extent to which the evaluational systems being applied correspond to the actual situation, and (2) the extent to which these evaluational schemes are explicitly stated and freed from an emotional significance to the person who uses them. These are essentially human problems and are closely bound up with problems of social organization.

Problems of the Individual's Adjustment to the Structure

Within the structure of an organization there is a continual movement of people. This movement takes place in point of time and social space. A man is hired, he remains a member of the organization for a time varying in length from a few hours to a lifetime, and then moves out of the structure to another organization or to retirement. There is thus a continual income and outgo of people, or, as we shall say, movement in point of time.

During the time the person remains in the company he undergoes movement in terms of social space. As is sometimes the case, he may move over a period of time from the very bottom to the top of the structure. Again, he may move up a certain distance and stop, or he may ascend and then descend in the social scale. Movement which alters the person's position in relation to other individuals within the concern will be referred to as "movement in terms of social space." Of course, the individual need not actually move from one job to another in order to move in social space. The structure or social organization in terms of which his position is defined may itself change, thus altering the person's position in the structure.

Orientation

Movements within the structure of industry are significant from many points of view, but they are especially important for the personnel administrator, for each time movement takes place the individual must orient himself to a new or changed situation. This process can best be understood by imagining a stranger in a city. The situation is baffling to him and for a time he hardly knows what to do. Gradually, however, he gets his bearings and after a time he becomes acquainted with the new situation. When he has accomplished this, he can move about in the city with little conscious thought and direction. The newcomer to an industrial plant is in a similar situation except that it is more complex. The process through which he must go involves an orientation to the job and its technical requirements, to the norms of conduct required of him by the formal organization, to the immediate group with whom he works, and to the broader company structure, its policies and opportunities.

This process of orientation is clearly seen in relation to the newcomer, but similar processes take place with any movement in time or social space. As the employee grows older he moves from one age or service group to another and must reorient himself to the change in his relations with older and younger groups. As the employee moves from one job to another or from one social group to another he again must reorient himself. It will be seen, therefore, that there is a continual process of orientation within the industrial structure.

The problems which arise in connection with this process are apparent. The newcomer may make a faulty orientation to the job, the group, or the broader company structure. In the first instance he may lose his job, in the second he may become a problem case, and in the third he may develop preoccupations over his progress because he fails to understand the social ladder provided for his advancement. Faulty orientation on the part of a supervisor who has moved up a step may result in problems not only to himself but all up and down the line. Both from the standpoint of efficiency in production and employee satisfaction, therefore, this process of orientation is extremely important and may be marked out as one of the chief human processes within the industrial organization.

Evaluation

Closely related to the process of orientation is another process which will be called evaluation. Every individual in an organization evaluates or appraises himself in relation to his situation and is, in turn, evaluated by others. The individual worker evaluates his situation in terms of the extent to which it does or will satisfy his desires and ambitions. In this process he includes not only his immediate job and the satisfaction of economic and social desires which it provides but also his personal relations with his co-workers, supervisors, and management. Conversely, each individual employee is evaluated by his co-workers in terms of their codes and sentiments and by his supervisors in terms of their criteria of effectiveness.

This same process occurs with every individual in the structure from the bottom to the top except that the criteria of evaluation shift and vary with individuals, occupations, and ranks. Thus the supervisor evaluates the organization under him in terms of the logics of management and he evaluates himself in relation to such an appraisal. On the other hand, the supervisor is himself evaluated in terms of certain criteria: those of his subordinates, his co-workers, and his superiors. The process of evaluation extends to all levels of supervision and may therefore be characterized as a general social process. More often than not, the process of evaluation, except in the case of the logics of cost and efficiency, is not very explicit, in the sense that the person who is making the evaluation is often unconscious of the criteria in terms of which his evaluation judgments are made.

The problems arising in connection with the process of evaluation are extremely varied. Typical of one kind of problem is the individual who because of his personal history tends to demand more of his situation than it can possibly provide. In this case the individual has a mistaken evaluation of his situation because of a personal maladjustment. Another kind of distorted evaluation is seen where the individual in appraising his situation fails to understand or take into account certain aspects of the total situation. For example, an individual may become dissatisfied with his work situation because he sees no opportunity for advancement; yet the opportunity may be there and he has failed to see it. In this case he has misinterpreted his situation because he has omitted or failed to comprehend significant factors in the work situation.

Still other problems of evaluation occur at supervisory levels. The supervisor in evaluating his organization may overlook significant variables in it, or, what is perhaps more frequent, he may misinterpret much of what he sees and hears. In either case his evaluation of his organization is faulty and may lead to inappropriate decisions and actions. Sometimes the supervisor's evaluation of his people and of his organization is governed in large part by what he considers his superiors' evaluation of himself to be. If he feels that his superiors evaluate him adversely, this may determine his appraisal of the organization reporting to him. In such a case the supervisor may fall back on the formal organization for protection and insist that his organization function strictly in accordance with it. He hopes to avoid personal criticism from above by adhering strictly to the logic of management. By so doing he may disrupt the informal organization of his group and incur serious losses in efficiency.

It may be said, therefore, that every person in the industrial structure evaluates himself and is, in turn, evaluated by others. The criteria of evaluation in each instance determine the selection of factors entering into these appraisals. These criteria vary with the position of the individual in the structure, with his personal history, and with the stresses which he is experiencing at the moment. The adequacy of these evaluations is of utmost importance in the successful functioning of the concern, since they relate to the work satisfactions of the individual, the selection of people for promotion, and, in part, to all the major decisions made by employee, supervisor, and management.

Orientation and Evaluation in Relation to Personnel Practices and Maintaining Equilibrium

The problem of maintaining equilibrium within a concern depends in large part upon these processes of orientation and evaluation. These processes, in turn, are closely related to all the important aspects of personnel administration. The problem of maintaining equilibrium is closely related, for example, to the problem of hiring new people, for it will be seen that the kind of people employed has a direct relation to the composition of the various social groups, and indirectly may affect the normal channels of upgrading and promotion. An illustration may make this clear.

As a hypothetical case, let us imagine a concern in which the people who set piece rates are recruited from shop organizations. In such a situation movement from the shop group to the piece-rate group would undoubtedly have considerable significance to the people in each group. Assume, now, that the concern decides that only college-trained people are qualified to perform the task of setting piece rates satisfactorily. The introduction of college-trained people into such a situation would have consequences to both the piece-rate group and the shop group. Not only would it be likely to upset to some extent the equilibrium within the piece-rate group but also it would serve to block up the channel from the shop group to the piece-rate group. In connection with the problem of hiring, therefore, the personnel administrator has to be aware of the social consequences resulting from the selection of new employees. The above case has been cited to illustrate the relation between the ordinary functions of the personnel administrator and the broader problem under consideration.

Some such relation also obtains between most of the other processes of personnel administration and the function of maintaining equilibrium. The movement of people, both within an organization and between organizations, has a direct bearing upon this function. Within every concern there is a hierarchy of jobs. This hierarchy may be formally recognized or it may be entirely informal. In either case the job hierarchy determines the social ladder within the concern. The selection process which determines who shall move upward or downward on this social ladder is of the utmost importance not only to the person so selected but also to the group from which the selection is made. If the people selected for upgrading or promotion are those whom the other employees feel merit such recognition, the results are likely to have a positive influence upon the attitudes and work behavior of everyone concerned. The selection of people who stand in an unfavorable position in their respective work groups, however, is likely to have just the opposite effect. Also, if there is an accustomed channel of progression from job to job, deviation from this accepted procedure tends to weaken the social ladder and if carried to an extreme may destroy its significance to employees entirely. Thus it will be seen that the processes of placement, transfers, upgrading, and downgrading are intimately related to the general problem of maintaining balance in the social organization of the concern.

In this chapter an attempt has been made to restate the major human problems with which management is concerned and to show the relation of these problems to the general functions of personnel administration, such as employment, placement, transfers, upgrading, downgrading. The problem still remains of relating these problems to the more specific function of personnel practice. How are these problems to be handled in concrete situations? The purpose of the next chapter will be to discuss this question.

CHAPTER XXVI

IMPLICATIONS FOR PERSONNEL PRACTICE

IN THE preceding chapter the function of management has been described as that of maintaining the social system of the industrial plant in a state of equilibrium such that both the external and internal purposes of the enterprise are realized. In order to carry out this responsibility management makes use of various specialists — the engineer, the accountant, the chemist, etc. — each of whom has a formally defined place in the total system and contributes what he can within the limits of his specialty. The administrator synthesizes the reports of these different staff specialists, and this synthesis together with the "understanding" the administrator has of the situation continually determines his decisions.

One of the specialists frequently included in the technical staff is the personnel man. His advice is sought and given consideration in making the final decisions. As yet, the personnel man does not have the scientific knowledge or tools which would place his specialty on the same footing as that of the engineer or physical scientist. Consequently, his function tends to vary from one concern to another and his contribution to the management function likewise varies. A question may therefore be asked as to whether the research studies reported here throw any new light on the function of personnel work and the effective organization of that function. In this chapter we shall be concerned with this problem.

THE SPECIFIC FUNCTION OF PERSONNEL WORK

In discussing the human problems of management it was suggested that the customary statement of these problems in terms of fatigue, monotony, working conditions, and so on, is inaccurate and misleading in so far as the context in which the problem occurs is ignored. As a result, generalizations are made about these broad topics and it is assumed that they are applicable to any situation. In terms of the research studies it was shown that any human problem, in order to be understood, must be referred to its context and that the basic consideration, both for personnel research and personnel practice, is that of understanding the various work situations in which these problems occur and of specifying the factors making for or against equilibrium in the total situation. Thus attention is directed toward the analysis and understanding of specific work situations as a functioning whole, and whatever corrective action may be taken will be determined by this analysis.

From this point of view it follows that there is a function to be performed in an industrial organization which has not as yet been clearly recognized. There is the need for the explicit recognition and systematic application of a specialty which is addressing itself to the adequate diagnosis and understanding of the actual human situations —both individual and group—within the factory. The exercise of this specialty will be referred to as "the specific function of personnel work in industry" to differentiate it from the general functions of personnel administration, such as the administration of employment and placement routines.

An illustration may help to make the nature of this specialty clear. When a personnel specialist is addressing himself to the "average" or "typical" employee or "what is on the worker's mind in general," he is not exercising "the specific function" as defined here. However, when he is thinking of what is on some particular employee's mind in terms of a worker who has had a particular personal history, who was brought up in a particular family that had certain specific relations to the community, and who because of this particular "social conditioning" is bringing to his job certain specific hopes and fears; when he is thinking in terms of an employee whose job is in some particular place in the factory which brings him into association with particular persons and groups of people, i.e., a particular social setting which is making certain specific demands of the employee; and when he is thinking in terms of how these particular demands which the job is making of the person and the particular demands which the person is making of the job are producing either equilibrium or unbalance—when he is thinking in this way and oriented in this manner toward the employee, he is exercising "the specific function of personnel work."

The orientation of this specialty, unlike that of the statistician, is away from abstractions and toward concrete human situations. It is an orientation the purpose of which is to find what is present in some particular place and at some particular time. It also can be seen that this specialty can be and often is exercised, perhaps intuitively, by any executive or administrator or practitioner of human relations whenever he is called upon to handle a complex situation. The question, however, can be raised: Should not this specialty be applied systematically and explicitly by the personnel man to the human situation in industry?

Skills Required for Fulfilling the Specific Function

The exercising of any specialty presupposes certain skills. In diagnosing any human situation there are two prerequisites: a conceptual scheme and a method. By a conceptual scheme is meant a framework in which one's thought is set and by means of which one can operate usefully upon the data. In this sense a conceptual scheme is neither "true" nor "false." It is only a useful and convenient way to think about the data. A useful conceptual scheme for the human diagnostician is one which enables him to obtain relevant data, to see uniformities in his data, and to formulate fruitful hypotheses that will allow him to take more intelligent action because he can make predictions as to what will occur if certain kinds of action are taken. Unlike a set of preconceived ideas, a conceptual scheme does not prevent him from seeing something "new" when it arises. It was the opinion of those involved in the research that the conception of the industrial plant as a social system is a useful scheme for the personnel specialist when fulfilling his specific function with regard to particular individuals or groups in the organization.

In addition to having an adequate conceptual scheme, the personnel investigator must have techniques for eliciting the kind of data his conceptual scheme indicates to be relevant. His techniques must enable him to understand and describe the social situation at work as well as the personal situations of the individuals in it. The two techniques which enable him to accomplish this purpose are the technique of interviewing and the technique of observation. As both of these techniques have been previously described, they need not be discussed here again in detail. It will suffice to say that the technique of observation is common to all the empirical sciences; the technique of interviewing is a particular tool of the social sciences where diagnosis is involved. For this reason it is especially useful to the personnel specialist when he is exercising his specific function, for the interview is a diagnostic and therapeutic tool which assists him in specifying and handling adequately particular human situations. It is a tool which is similar to that employed by the medical practitioner when he has to go from the symptoms to the realities behind them. It is a skill which assists him to analyze a complex human phenomenon into the elements that have produced it. The skill addresses itself directly to something in the concrete and not to "something or anything but nothing in particular."

A Plan for Fulfilling the Specific Function of Personnel Work

So far we have stated and defined the specific function to which personnel people can address themselves, the need of a conceptual scheme and of techniques by means of which that function can be fulfilled. It is now relevant to ask how people possessing these skills can apply them in a work situation. It was to this problem that the research investigators at the Western Electric Company addressed themselves in 1936 when business conditions, in the opinion of management, warranted the resumption of interviewing work similar to that which had been conducted in 1928 to 1931. The work begun at that time is continuing and, although it is still undergoing development, it may be briefly described as one way of organizing to carry out the specific personnel function.

This work will be called "personnel counseling" to differentiate it from the interviewing program described earlier in the book. Under this program people trained in the concepts and methods described above are assigned on a continuous, full-time basis to territories in the shop. The size of these territories varies but on an average each counselor covers about 300 people. These counselors report to an organization in the Industrial Relations Branch and have their desks located in the office, but the larger part of their day is spent in the shops to which they are assigned. As in the interviewing program, men interview men and women interview women.

Mechanics of the Program

The mechanics of the program are simple. Before introducing the counselor in an organization, the consent of the supervisors is first obtained. If, as is often the case, the supervisor in charge, after the objectives of the program have been explained to him, feels that he would like to have the program in his organization, he then takes the initiative of explaining it to his subordinate supervisors. Ordinarily he does this by calling a conference of all his supervisors to which the people who are to do the counseling work are invited. At this meeting the senior supervisor explains the program and tells his junior supervisors why he wishes to have it tried in his organization. The counselor is then introduced to all of the supervisors and they may ask any questions they wish. These questions are answered by the senior supervisor or by the representatives of the personnel counseling activity who are present in the group. As a result of these discussions, the supervisors go away with a fairly good idea of how the program will be conducted and what its objectives are.

Following this kind of introduction, the counselor then gets acquainted with each of the supervisors in the organization in order to learn what he can about his problems. The time spent in these preliminary contacts varies depending upon the number of supervisors in the organization and the kinds of problems each of them is experiencing. During this period the counselor also becomes acquainted with the work being done, the mechanical processes involved, the kinds of work problems which the supervisors face, the flow of work through the organization, and other similar details. A fairly good understanding of the technical organization is considered essential to an adequate understanding of what the supervisors and employees talk about. Also, the counselor is interested in the manner in which the various departments perform their manufacturing functions, for he recognizes that the success with which these functions are performed has a direct bearing upon the various human problems he is likely to encounter in each organization. Of course, a good deal of this technical information is obtained from the interviews he has later on with the employees, but it is considered important that he have a general idea of how the department functions, or is supposed to function, before he interviews.

In addition to obtaining an understanding of the technical organization of each of the departments in his territory, the counselor also obtains considerable information about the formal organization. He must have a clear understanding of the supervisory structure and of the formal lines of authority. He also tries to pick up a general understanding of the various kinds of formal reports prepared and the flow of paper work through the organization to outside organizations.

When the counselor has a general idea of the technical organization of work and the formal organization of the various departments, he is then ready to start interviewing the nonsupervisory employees. Before this is done, however, he obtains as much personnel data as he can regarding the people in each organization. He obtains lists of employees in each supervisory unit and tabulates such data as their age, service with the company, service in the department, previous work history, the occupations to which they are assigned, the labor grades in which their work falls, their hourly rates, their average earnings, changes which have occurred in hourly rates, and the kind of payment plans under which they are working.

When the counselor feels that he has sufficient information about each department he then begins interviewing. The people selected for interviewing may be determined in a variety of ways. Frequently, in his talks with the supervisors they indicate certain employees whom they regard as problem cases. Sometimes the supervisors wish the counselor to interview the more perplexing of these cases. This he may agree to do. However, if he feels that employees may get a wrong impression of the program if he interviews problem cases first, he may ask to interview someone else. The employee selected is chosen with the consent of the supervisor and the employee. An employee is not interviewed if he objects. Such cases, however, are rare.

Having through agreement with the supervisor selected an employee to be interviewed, the counselor is then introduced to the employee by the supervisor. In this introduction the supervisor explains the purpose of the interview. The employee then goes with the counselor to an interviewing room located near by. When they reach the interviewing room the counselor gives a more thorough explanation of the program and the interview commences. When the interview is over the employee returns to his work. He is paid his average earnings during the time spent in the interview. There is no time limit to these interviews but they last an average of about eighty minutes.

Following the interview, the counselor writes it up in as nearly verbatim fashion as possible. This record is his personal property and is in no way considered an official company record. The counselor has a code system which enables him to identify the interview with the employee but the counselor alone holds the key to this code.

In addition to conducting formal interviews with employees, such as have been described, the counselor also spends considerable time in the department. Time spent in this manner is taken up in discussions with supervisors and informal contacts with employees. Also, during these intervals spent with the various work groups, he is alert to detect and describe the various patterns of interaction among employees and supervisors. These observations assist him in understanding the informal organization of the various groups.

Relationship between Counselor and Line Organization

One of the major considerations determining the mechanics of the program concerns the relationship between the counselor and the line organization he serves. The research studies tended to show that most shop departments are, in a sense, closed organizations; that is to say, they may resist outsiders who stand in a position to interfere with their internal affairs. One of the major problems in introducing the counseling program, therefore, was that of developing a relationship with the employees and supervisors in the line organization such that the interviewer would have free access to each group continuously over a long period of time. Also, it was essential that everyone in the situation should feel free to discuss problems with him. It was therefore decided that the relationship of the counselor with the line organization should be a nonauthoritative one.

It was felt that if the counselor possessed any formal authority a number of unsatisfactory consequences might follow. In the first place, the employees and supervisors might not feel free to discuss their problems with him. They would tend to communicate to him only those aspects of their situation which would place them in a favorable light. It can be seen that this in itself would defeat the major purpose of the program.

In the second place, it was felt that vesting authority in the counselor would tend to weaken the supervisor-employee relationship because it would inevitably take from the supervisor some of his responsibilities in dealing with his people. One of the major objectives of the counseling program was to strengthen rather than weaken this relationship. This consideration was based upon the observation that in the last analysis the supervisor is and must be responsible for the handling of his employees. The problems of employee relations are intimately associated with all phases of management practice. The supervisors stand in the position of translating these practices and policies into action at the work level. As a result, practically everything that is done by the supervisor in the shop has consequences in terms of personnel. The technical requirements of the job, the flow of work, the condition of tools and equipment, the movement of people from one job to another, the manner in which orders are given, and how comments and suggestions from employees are received — all these matters have direct or indirect consequences for employees and go to make up the major employee relations problem. It can readily be seen, therefore, that the function of the counselor could not be performed if he were given formal authority.

A third consideration affecting the decision to give the interviewer no formal authority follows as a corollary from those already discussed. The counselor, like any other technical specialist, is primarily oriented to only certain aspects of an organization. He is primarily oriented to the human problems of the organization. The supervisor, on the other hand, must regard this as only one aspect of his total function, the other function being the task of technical production. Consequently, the supervisor is in a better position to make decisions than the specialist. What might appear to be correct action from the point of view of the counselor might not appear to be the best action from the point of view of the total organization. Decisions made by the counselor, therefore, might eventually lead to resistances both from supervisors and employees. Should this continue for any length of time, defensive processes might be built up by means of which the counselor would become excluded from the organization. Thus the purpose of the program would be defeated.

Maintaining an Interview Relationship

In setting up this program it was seen that not only must the counselor abstain from taking any authoritative action but also he must provide positive guarantees to employees and supervisors before they would feel free to talk to him without reservation. It was therefore regarded as essential that each employee and supervisor be guaranteed that everything he said would be regarded by the interviewer as confidential and that nothing the interviewer would do would react to his detriment. This guarantee had been given in the interviewing program previously conducted and was one of the chief reasons for its success. Consequently, this was adopted as the second guiding principle in determining the counselor's relationship to employees and supervisors.

Here questions may arise in the minds of some readers: What assurance does the interviewer have that this guarantee will be accepted by employees and supervisors as trustworthy? How can the employee feel sure that what he says will be regarded as confidential? And how can the interviewer overcome any reservations? This is an important problem and merits further consideration.

To begin with, it is probably necessary that a relationship of mutual confidence exist between employees and management before a program of this sort can succeed satisfactorily. In the present instance, the personnel counselor had an added advantage in that many of the employees and supervisors had already seen the earlier interviewing program work out in practice. Their experience with that program showed them that management's pledge of confidence had, in fact, been faithfully carried out. Consequently, when the personnel counseling program was started many employees immediately identified it with the old interviewing program and took it for granted that confidences would be respected.

The chief task in overcoming feelings of reticence and apprehension, of course, resides with the interviewer himself. In order to understand how this can be accomplished, it is necessary to understand the attitude and behavior required of a good interviewer. First, the interviewer must be sincerely interested in people and in their problems and he must be able to make this interest convincing to everyone he sees and meets. Secondly, by everything the interviewer says and does he must encourage in employees and supervisors the attitude he wishes them to hold toward him. He does this not only by being sincere and cordial but also by assiduously refraining from making any value judgments of what they tell him. The interviewer must free himself from making any judgments of right and wrong about what he sees or hears. He sees to it that his own sentiments are not acted upon by those of the speaker. The interviewee must feel free to say anything he wishes to the interviewer and this process is not encouraged if the interviewer registers approval or disapproval. By carefully refraining from making value judgments either of people or of the things they say or do, the interviewer thus, over a period of time, builds up for himself a certain type of social personality. He comes to be regarded by everyone in the situation for what he is, as a person to whom anyone can talk freely, and if he has done his job well he will be regarded in the same light as the patient regards his doctor or the client his lawyer.

The analogy of the doctor-patient relationship may be carried a little further because it is this kind of relationship which the interviewer is seeking to establish for himself with employees and supervisors. The doctor-patient relationship is only one of several socially recognized situations today in which people may talk and act differently than they would under the constraints of ordinary social conventions. The social acceptance of these relationships, however, evolved slowly over a long period of history. Even in the doctor-patient relationship a long process of social conditioning was necessary in order for it to obtain its present character. The social attitudes toward this relationship are now fairly well stereotyped, so much so in fact that a new doctor entering upon medical practice does not have to give this phase of his work much thought. Of course it is begging the question to say that the interviewer-employee relationship should be like the doctor-patient relationship. It can never be exactly like this relationship because the interviewer is not ordinarily associated with the major crises in life such as birth, sickness, and death. It is fair to say, however, that the interviewer-employee relationship is similar in character to the doctor-patient relationship, but unlike the latter there is as yet no socially recognized place for it in the industrial organization. As a consequence, the interviewer must undertake the task of creating for himself a professional role, and his success depends largely upon what he says and does.

What the Counselor Says and Does

The counselor does not exercise authority or give advice. What then can he actually accomplish? Is he a person who collects a great mass of material merely for his own information and, if so, what real "good" does he do? The answers to these questions are not so difficult as they may at first appear.

In order to make clear how the counselor acts in his face-to-face relations with employees, let us describe the case of an employee who is being interviewed. This imaginary employee will be called Mary Jones. Let us assume that Mary Jones has for some weeks past been displaying symptoms of discontent and unrest. Her efficiency has decreased somewhat, her attendance has become irregular, and she seems fretful and moody. This change in her behavior has come to the attention of her co-workers and her supervisor. The counselor herself has observed the change in her behavior and has on several occasions listened to Mary's friends and supervisor comment about it. So at the supervisor's request she has taken Mary to the interviewing room and the interview is already well under way.

As a result of her training and experience the counselor knows that the source of Mary's dissatisfaction may lie in any one of several areas. Throughout the interview she is constantly looking for "leads" in what Mary says which will indicate the most probable area in which the real trouble lies. It may well be, for example, that her dissatisfaction with her work is an expression of complications arising in her personal life outside the plant. In such an event the counselor would encourage her to talk freely in that area. By expressing herself freely about her personal life, Mary might by that very process come to a new understanding of what her real difficulty is. If not, subsequent interviews may be indicated and a more thorough exploration of her personal situation may be necessary. In problems of this kind, of course, no direct action could be taken inasmuch as the counselor never attempts to make an independent investigation of an individual's personal affairs outside the plant. The counselor's sole object is to lead the employee to a clear understanding of her problem such that she herself comes to realize what action to take and then assumes responsibility for taking it.

Let us assume, however, that in the case of Mary Jones the difficulty is not one of personal maladjustment. Let us assume that she is discontented wtih her work and would like to be transferred to some other kind of work. With a problem of this kind the counselor would attempt to get her to state as clearly as possible the reasons for her dissatisfaction with her present job. The counselor would be looking for echoes of strained relations with her co-workers or with her supervisors because difficulties in either of these areas might well account for Mary's dissatisfaction. Let us assume, however, that there seems to be no particular difficulty in these areas. Instead, the counselor's impression of Mary is that she is a capable, hard-working girl, anxious to improve her economic status. What then does the counselor do? She may do a number of things. In the first place, having made sure that Mary understands the reasons for her dissatisfaction with her present work and also knowing that Mary has a fairly specific understanding of what other kind of work she wants, she might ask her if she has ever discussed the problem with her supervisor. Mary replies that she has thought about discussing it with her supervisor but has never done so. The counselor asks her why. Mary answers that she really doesn't know why but guesses that he might misunderstand her. Now at this stage of the interview the counselor is focusing Mary's attention upon a possible source of remedying her problem. She is directing her attention toward the supervisor. After some discussion, Mary concludes that many of her fears are groundless and decides that she will see her supervisor.

The next day the counselor is in the department and is called over by the supervisor. He says he wants to talk to her about Mary Jones. Mary, he says, came to him yesterday and said she wanted a transfer to a different kind of work. He is perplexed as to why she is dissatisfied with her present job and what he should do about her request. The counselor at this stage may ask the supervisor a number of questions such as: Did Mary tell you why she is dissatisfied with her work? Do you see any possibilities for advancement within your own department which would obviate the necessity for a transfer? Do you think that Mary understands these possibilities? Questions of this kind, as will be readily seen, may give the supervisor a number of ideas. He may very likely say that he has always thought of Mary as a good worker and had planned to advance her to other work as rapidly as possible. Following this discussion with the counselor, he then calls Mary up to his desk and gives her a more adequate understanding of the situation. As a result of this process, she goes back to her work in better spirits. She is restored to her normal effectiveness and her efficiency may rise.

The case of Mary Jones has been cited primarily to illustrate the manner in which the counselor operates. It will be readily seen that the counselor accomplishes a great deal even though at no time does he give advice. He functions as a catalytic agent. He stimulates action of the kind described and in so doing tends to strengthen not only the relationship between supervisor and employee but in fact the whole network of relations in the group. The role of the counselor is thus that of carefully listening and observing, of making diagnoses, and then stimulating the most effective kind of action on the part of the various other agencies in the structure whose formal function it is to deal with the particular problem under consideration.

Major Problems to Which the Counseling Program is Addressed

The general utility of a program such as personnel counseling can best be understood by specifying more clearly the general human problems to which this activity is addressed. As has already been pointed out in the preceding chapter, three major processes which result in human problems of administration are: (1) adjustment of the individual to the industrial structure; (2) communication and control; and (3) changes in the social structure. How can the personnel administrator assist management in effectively meeting these problems? Can a personnel counseling program which has direct access to work situations and to successive levels in the supervisory structure be effectively directed toward these major problems? The discussion of these questions will not only serve to show the major purpose of the personnel counseling program but it will also show how this kind of nonauthoritative agency serves to control and to direct those human processes within the industrial structure which are not adequately controlled by the other agencies of management.

The manner in which the personnel counselor can address himself to the various problems arising in the individual's adjustment to the social structure is readily seen. The counselor stands outside of the network of relations in which the individual supervisor or worker spends his working days. He can thus look at this system of relations objectively, and he is in a good position to see the various problems arising in these relations and ways in which they may be remedied. Moreover, provided the interviewer has a satisfactory interview relationship with employees and supervisors, he can readily detect any symptoms of maladjustment and can arrive at a fairly sound approximation of the nature of the difficulty. The problem may be one of orientation. If so, the counselor is probably in the best possible position to assist. In industrial situations there are fairly frequent movements among the personnel of a given department, and supervisors are transferred or moved to other jobs from time to time. The counselor, however, has an intimate understanding of the situation in its entirety over a long period of time; he in effect becomes a kind of social historian. He can readily understand the background of many problems occurring in the present, and with this kind of knowledge he can easily assist either employees or supervisors in achieving an adequate orientation to the situation. He accomplishes this purpose, of course, through interviewing the individuals concerned. In the case of an employee who is failing through some kind of faulty orientation the counselor, through his understanding of the employee on the one hand and the situation on the other, directs the employee's thinking into those areas which he needs to take into account in order to achieve an adequate adjustment.

The same technique is applicable to all other problems of orientation and particularly to certain of these problems which occur at supervisory levels. A new supervisor in an organization, for example, must learn a great deal about the situation before he can function effectively. In this process the counselor can help the incoming supervisor accomplish a satisfactory orientation. Similar problems arise when the supervisor is promoted from one level to another. The person promoted must make some kind of adjustment. He must, for example, redefine his relations with his superior, with his co-workers, and with those people with whom he formerly associated as an equal. This process can be greatly speeded up through the aid of someone to whom the person promoted can talk freely.

The counselor can also help to control and direct the evaluation the individual makes of himself and of his situation. In so far as he can do this he is, of course, contributing directly to some of the major human problems of management. Tendencies toward obsessive thinking on the part of employee or supervisor can readily be detected and alleviated by the interviewer. This is particularly true when the tendency toward obsession seems to be induced by defective personal interrelations. Any person in an industrial organization who feels insecure tends to attribute a peculiar meaning or significance to many factors which he would otherwise never notice. Many cases have already been cited to illustrate this point. As a rule, there is no one in industrial organization generally whose particular function it is to assist him. The counselor, of course, is in an excellent position to direct his attention to this whole range of problems.

In so far as the counselor can improve the individual's adjustment to the structure, he also assists in the process of communication, for problems of defective evaluation and orientation lead directly to defective communication. In the same manner, the counseling program is directed to problems of control. The counselor is in a position to contact representatives from all other organizations in the company who have anything to do with the shop situation. If the counselor has an adequate understanding of the shop situation, he can in his interviews and discussions with these representatives from other organizations raise questions which will direct their attention toward certain aspects of the human situation which they might otherwise overlook — for example, questions concerned with the effects of too rapid change in the particular shop situation.

There are, in addition, two other ways in which a program of this kind may be of use. In the first place, the material obtained by the counselor provides, within the limits of the premises of the activity, an accurate source of information for management. Many problems which the counselor encounters at the work level, of course, cannot be transmitted. A general appraisal of the work situation, however, can sometimes be made without in any way violating the confidences of employees or supervisors. As a matter of fact, it is possible with a program of this kind to keep management accurately informed as to the general state of morale within the factory and as to the major factors which are affecting the attitudes of employees. In the second place, the information collected provides an excellent source of material for supervisory development and training. In this respect the personnel counseling program is similar to the interviewing program except that the material collected is much more descriptive of total situations and of the day-to-day problems confronted by the average supervisor.

CONCLUSION

In conclusion it should be emphasized that the foregoing description of the personnel counseling program is very brief and is intended only to illustrate one way of applying systematically and continuously the point of view and the techniques which were developed in the research. It should not be thought of as a complete statement of the counseling program, nor should the illustrations given be regarded either as typical or as covering the wide range of problems with which this program actually deals. It may also be well to say that for the investigators and management at Hawthorne, personnel counseling is still an experiment and is not regarded as a panacea for all employee relations problems. The program has been developed slowly over a long period of time and only after much experimentation and reflection. There is no evidence to suggest that it could be transplanted and be made to work effectively in some other plants where conditions are radically different — this for two reasons: In the first place, it can be seen that the successful organization of such a program requires the particular skills of diagnosis and interpretation that were developed by the research. These skills cannot be acquired in a short time. Without them personnel counseling would become a ritual rather than a method of learning. In the second place, the particular way in which the point of view developed by the research is being applied (i.e., in the form of personnel counseling) has been shaped to meet the needs of a particular situation. For that reason it works especially well in that situation. For the same reason it is doubtful if it could be applied equally successfully anywhere or everywhere in that specific form.

If, however, the investigators were asked to generalize their experience for personnel administration, they would have no hesitancy in saying this. Adequate personnel administration in any particular industrial plant should fulfill two conditions:

(1) Management should introduce in its organization an explicit skill of diagnosing human situations. The skill should be "explicit" because the implicit or intuitive skills in handling human problems which successful administrators or executives possess are not capable of being communicated and transmitted. They are the peculiar property of the person who exercises them; they leave when the executive leaves the organization. An "explicit" skill, on the other hand, is capable of being refined and taught and communicated to others.

(2) By means of this skill management should commit itself to the *continuous* process of studying human situations — both individual and group — and should run its human affairs in terms of what it is continually learning about its own organization.

INDEX

INDEX